North American Exploration

North American Exploration

VOLUME 2

A CONTINENT DEFINED

JOHN LOGAN ALLEN, EDITOR

UNIVERSITY OF NEBRASKA PRESS   LINCOLN AND LONDON

© 1997 by the University of Nebraska Press

All rights reserved

Manufactured in the United States of America

☻ The paper in this book meets the minimum
requirements of American National Standard
for Information Sciences—Permanence of
Paper for Printed Library Materials,
ANSI Z39.48-1984.

Library of Congress Cataloging-in-
Publication Data

North American exploration / John Logan
Allen, editor.

p.   cm.

Includes bibliographical references and index.

Contents: v. 1. A new world disclosed—

2. A continent defined—

3. A continent comprehended.

ISBN 0-8032-1015-9 (cloth : alk. paper).

ISBN 0-8032-1023-x (cloth : alk. paper).

ISBN 0-8032-1043-4 (cloth : alk. paper).

1. North America—Discovery and
exploration.   I. Allen, John Logan, 1941–

E45.N67 1997

96-33025

917.04—dc20 CIP

Contents

Illustrations

Maps

A Continent Defined

Introduction to Volume 2

JOHN L. ALLEN

The six chapters in this volume encompass the exploration of North America from the Spanish *entrada* of the sixteenth century to the British and Russian explorations of the Pacific coastal regions in the closing years of the eighteenth century. Like the chapters in the preceding volume, these contributions differ in tone and approach, as befits a work of collaborative scholarship. Yet, each of the chapters in volume 2 of *North American Exploration* deals with the second critical period of the exploration of the continent, the time when the various regions of North America were brought to the light of European science and the time when that science began to understand the continent in ways very different from those of the sixteenth century. The process of "discovery," or finding, gave way to the process of "exploration" and, as the traditions of Enlightenment science developed, to understanding. No longer was North America thought of as an Asian promontory; the Renaissance worldview had given way to an Enlightenment geographical understanding based on a detailed examination of both Atlantic and Pacific coastal regions and on considerable penetrations of the continental interior. And although there were, by the end of the eighteenth century, still vast regions of terrae incognitae in North America, the basic outlines of the continent itself had been defined.

The volume begins with "Spanish Penetrations to the North of New Spain" by Oakah L. Jones Jr., emeritus professor of history, Purdue University. In his comprehensive examination of the *entrada* and the exploration of the Borderlands, Jones notes that in the lands of northern New Spain and "La Florida" were two types of explorers: pathfinders and explorer-colonizers. The pathfinders explored and discovered the first native cultures and marked trails and geographical features across regions previously unexplored. The explorer-colonizers conducted explorations before or after establishing temporary or permanent settlements. Moving from the Caribbean Islands to the Florida and Carolina coasts and briefly to Chesapeake Bay, or from Mexico City into the kingdoms and provinces of northern New Spain—Pánuco, Sinaloa, Sonora, Pimeria Alta, the Californias, Nueva Vizcaya, New Mexico, Nuevo León, Coahuila, Texas, and Nuevo Santander—the pathfinders and explorer-colonizers thrust northward into what is now the United States. Their explorations encompassed vast areas, and with each succeeding expedition, knowledge of geographical features and native cultures expanded. Whether led by curiosity for the "northern mystery," tall tales, the search for rich and exotic civilizations, or a quest to find the mythical Straits of Anián, these Spanish explorers established the European presence in the United States.

As the Spanish were directing their attention to the northern frontiers of New Spain, the French were gaining a foothold along the northeastern margins of the continent. Two chapters, "Early French Exploration in the North American Interior" by Professor Conrad Heidenreich of York University and "French Exploration in North America, 1700–1800" by Professor W. J. Eccles of the University of Toronto, describe the nature of the extensive French exploratory endeavor from the first entry into the Gulf of Saint Lawrence to the furthest penetration of the continental interior by any Europeans in the eighteenth century. Heidenreich points out:

All French exploration had at its roots four general aims: (1) staking territorial claims against other European powers; (2) discovering major passages to the west, north, and south across the continent; (3) missionizing native groups; and (4) searching for exploitable natural resources, especially furs and minerals. These are the motives that drew the French into the interior when circumstances permitted. Curiously, few of these motives were present in any discernible form among the Dutch and the English who had settled the Atlantic coast. There was little English exploration except the hunting expeditions of settlers into the woods and valleys to the rear of their settlements. Except for an expedition by Harmen Meyndertsen van den Bogaert to the Mohawk country in 1634, much the same can be said of the Dutch. Both Dutch and English societies were primarily inward-looking, obsessed with local matters; the only important motives for action were the farm, the local community, and the dictates of an uncompromising religion.

The focus of Heidenreich's chapter is the seventeenth century, during which time the French thrust pierced the continent from the Saint Lawrence Valley to the Great Lakes and eventually across the drainage divide west to the Mississippi, south to the Gulf of Mexico and north to Hudson Bay. He notes, "Considering the few people involved, the distances covered, and the difficult physical obstacles faced, this was a magnificent achievement, made even more significant when compared with the absence of any similar exploration by the Dutch and the English inland from the Atlantic seaboard and the shores of Hudson Bay during the same period." Heidenreich not only provides an overview of the French explorations up to 1700 but also discusses French exploration as a scientific process, furnishing a structure and background for the main factors that influenced the progress of exploration over time.

In Eccles's chapter, French exploration of the eighteenth century is detailed; the author pays particular attention to the journeys of French travelers in the interior portions of the continent up through the end of the eighteenth century, including the French occupation of the Ohio and Mississippi Basins, the move up the Missouri, and the drive of the La Vérendryes toward the Rocky Mountain region. He also includes a discussion of the role of French exploration in the trans-Mississippi and other areas during the period of Spanish occupation of Louisiana Territory. A focal point of Eccles's chapter is the French attempt, during the four decades preceding the conquest of New France, to reach the Pacific Ocean overland by way of the mythical Mer de l'Ouest. He notes: "Another powerful incentive for French thrusts into the Far West was the lure of commercial profit: in the Northwest, from the trade for furs with the Indian nations; and in the Southwest, from the establishment of trade relations with the Spanish settlements in northern New Spain—to be more precise, between New Orleans and Santa Fe. Thus the map of the interior of North America gradually began to unfold and to be depicted by such eminent cartographers as Guillaume Delisle, Jacques-Nicolas Bellin, Zacharias Chatelain, and Nicolas de Fer." Eccles also draws our attention to the critical role played by Native American populations in the process of French exploration. He states: "It was . . . the Indian nations that called the tune to which the French had to dance. The French had to master the Indian languages—Algonquian, Iroquois, Sioux—in a multiplicity of dialects; they had to adhere rigorously to Indian protocol at meetings and master the Indian style of oratory, with its grandiloquent use of metaphors that put one governor-general of New France, the flamboyant Louis de Buade, comte de Frontenac, in mind of the Senate of Venice, which he had once addressed. The French also had to provide liberal 'presents' on all official occasions." Finally, Eccles provides a vibrant look at the life-style of the French voyageurs and coureurs de bois, who were the "shock troops" of French continental penetration during the eighteenth century.

In the next two chapters, Richard I. Ruggles, emeritus professor of geography at York University, and Professor Alan V. Briceland of Virginia Commonwealth University examine the activities of British explorers before the nineteenth century. Although, as Eccles and Heidenreich have noted, the British were less involved in far-flung exploratory endeavors than the French, this does not mean that their efforts to bring the darker regions of the continent to light were without reward. Ruggles notes how, farther north, at the same time that the French were moving toward the Mississippi Valley and the plains and Rockies, British explorers penetrated the interior of Canada from their bases in the Hudson Bay region, with this penetration culminating in Alexander Mackenzie's crossing of the Rocky Mountain cordillera, the first European traverse of the continent since the travels of Alvar Núñez Cabeza da Vaca more than 250 years earlier. Ruggles points out that much of this British exploration was carried out under the guise of the "Company of Adventurers," better known as the Hudson's Bay Company, and of the the North West Company—both fur companies bent on the consolidation of new hunting groups and client native populations and engaged in fierce competition with one another. Ruggles rightly concludes that much of British exploration before the nineteenth century was highly commercial in nature. He notes: "Commerce was the primary agency in the exploration and discovery of the northern part of America. Exploration was the necessary consequence of a burgeoning trade in furs, whereas geographical inquiry was a lesser inducement for coasting intricate and dangerous shorelines and venturing across the vast interior of the continent." Three purposes—trade profit, colonial advantage, and mineral riches—were at the forefront of British activity for the century and a quarter following the first British entry into the Hudson Bay region.

Briceland, in dealing with British exploration in what is now the United States east of the Mississippi and Missouri Rivers, also describes an exploration process that is commercial—although perhaps less explicitly so than the fur-trade-oriented exploration of the Canadian interior. He states, "Colonial Englishmen are generally considered to have been less adventurous explorers of the North American interior than their French and Spanish rivals." He adds that the prominent American historian John Bartlet Brebner "devoted only thirty-six pages of his four-hundred-page, 1933 study *The Explorers of North America, 1492–1806* to British exploration in what has become the United States. Names such as Soto, Coronado, Champlain, and LaSalle are well known, but with the exception of John Smith, the names of the important English explorers are virtually unknown. Because the great Appalachian chain, the mountains the Indians called the Endless Mountains, impeded the way west for all but one of the seventeenth-century English colonies, the English appear to have lagged behind their French and Spanish rivals in the speed with which they explored the interior." They even appeared to lag behind their commercial British counterparts farther north. Yet these colonial Englishmen undertook a number of remarkable, if little-known, journeys of discovery between 1607 and 1804. Briceland adds:

> By 1804, Anglo-Americans had viewed and mapped almost the entirety of North America east of the Mississippi River and, north of Saint Louis, even farther west. English exploration did not proceed at a steady pace but moved in fits and starts. Most of the eastern portion of the United States was successfully explored in the seventeenth century. By 1700, virtually all of the important routes of travel east of the Appalachians, generally river valleys, had been visited, mapped, and assessed by the colonials. In addition, most of the Deep South and the great river systems of what was viewed as the West—the Ohio, the Tennessee, and the Mississippi—had been visited by Englishmen, who returned to tell others what they had seen and how it might be reached. . . . Although there were exceptions, three major motivations evidently drove the process of English exploration. Virtually all exploration activity involved a search for animal skins, for marketable land, or for a passage to the Pacific and the wealth of the Orient. Occasionally the way into an unknown area might be pioneered by an interpreter-diplomat ordered into Indian territory or by a military expedition, but more often than not those in the lead were searching for furs, land, or a water passage to the western ocean.

In that sense, this period of exploration was little different from those that preceded or followed it.

In the final chapter of the volume, Professor James R. Gibson of York University takes a regional rather than a national approach and describes how Spanish, French, British, American, and Russian navigators explored the Pacific coastal area through the voyages of George Vancouver, Robert Gray, and other late-eighteenth-century explorers. The dominant themes of this essay are the search for a commercial route through the continent (from a western terminus) and the development of the northwestern trade, particularly in pelts (e.g., sea otter), which made the coastal region of economic as well as strategic importance. Gibson notes:

> On the world map of the middle of the eighteenth century, the Pacific coast of North America, with the exception of New Spain, was one of

the few shorelines that remained unknown to nonnative peoples. . . . Indeed, the entire North Pacific was so unknown that when Jonathan Swift published *Gulliver's Travels* in 1726, he confidently set the imaginary and dilapidated island empire of Laputa (including Balnibarbi, Glubbdubdrib, and Luggnagg) off the coast of Japan and made Brobdingnag, the mythical land of giants, a six-thousand-mile-long peninsula of California. This anonymity was simply the result of the relative locations of the imperial powers and the directions of their colonial expansion. Britain, Holland, Portugal, and Spain had expanded overseas from western Europe to the Atlantic margins of the Americas and Africa and to the Indian Ocean shores of Africa and Asia first, leaving the more forbidding North Pacific and Arctic coasts of Asia and North America for last. By the eighteenth century, only Britain and France, unlike Holland, Portugal, Russia, and Spain, lacked convenient springboards for Pacific exploration; all ports of call in South America were controlled by Portugal or Spain, the Cape Horn entrance (the Drake Passage) was difficult, and Holland and Spain controlled the western approaches of the East Indies and the Philippines. . . . While the maritime imperial powers of western Europe were penetrating the South Pacific for 'gold, God, and glory,' continental Russia was pushing overland from eastern Europe to the North Pacific in quest of 'soft gold' (sable fur), but the tsar's men had to consolidate their control of the vast Siberian wilderness, in addition to coping with unstable southern and western frontiers, before being free to cross the inclement northern reaches of what they called the 'Eastern Ocean.' Thus, it was not until the late 1700s that the leading imperial nations—Britain, France, Russia, and Spain [joined by the new nation of the United States]—finally met on the Northwest Coast and began to delineate and demarcate this terra incognita. . . . Thus was the stage set for the subsequent struggle between the United States and Great Britain for the territory and resources of the Pacific Slope.

This struggle will play a central role in the third and final volume of this work, the volume that discusses the exploration of North America in the nineteenth century.

9 / Spanish Penetrations
to the North of New Spain

OAKAH L. JONES JR.

By the mid–sixteenth century, one of the most brilliant periods of exploration in North America had concluded with the great *entradas* of Francisco Vásquez de Coronado and Hernando de Soto. From Juan Ponce de León's discovery of the Florida peninsula in 1513 through the last gasp of early exploration in the American Southeast following Soto's journey, Spanish explorers such as Lucas Vásquez de Ayllón had discovered much of the Atlantic coastline of North America from present-day South Carolina southward to the tip of the Florida peninsula. Alonso Alvarez de Pineda had explored the Gulf coast of La Florida and westward to the Mississippi River and beyond, along the Texas coast to Pánuco in northeastern New Spain. Soto and his successor Luis Moscoso had penetrated the interior of the continent, exploring much of the present southeastern United States, crossing overland to the Mississippi River, and penetrating westward into the interior of eastern Texas and Oklahoma. Alvar Núñez Cabeza de Vaca and his companions, on an epic trek, had moved across the coastline of Texas and penetrated the interior of northern New Spain between today's states of Tamaulipas and Sonora and had moved into the American Southwest. And Coronado had journeyed from northern Mexico across present-day Arizona and New Mexico into the western interior of the continent, coming to a stop in central Kansas and giving Europeans their first glimpse of the North American Great Plains.

These early explorers had searched for mythical kingdoms (albeit ones probably patterned after actual Native American towns): Cíbola and Quivira in the Southwest; Chicora, Coosa, and Cofitachequi in the Southeast. They had sought to identify regions, particularly in the Southeast, as "new Andalucias" or other American analogues of Spanish provinces. They had searched for precious metals and gems. And they had looked for the water passage across the continent to the Pacific, a passage that had become a prime objective of most European explorers since the continental character of North America had gradually been realized in the European mind. These great searches and their accompanying reports of geographical features, Native Americans, and flora and fauna, revealing as they were, were often vague and confusing on exact locations, distances, and directions. Although they served to acquaint others with this vast region, the explorers of the first half of the sixteenth century did not succeed in promoting the immediate, effective occupation of La Florida and the southeastern area of the present United States or of the vast region of the American Southwest from the Texas coast to Arizona and north to Kansas. During the last half of the sixteenth century, their efforts would finally bear fruit in the establishment of colonies—tenuous and widespread and thinly populated but colonies nevertheless—in La Florida and New Mexico. And in the seventeenth and eighteenth centuries, as both explorers and colonizers, the Spanish would continue to push northward and westward from New Spain into the vast hinterland of North America.

As was the case for explorers during the initial phase of Spanish exploration in North America, the motives for continued investigation of the continent included the search for mythical kingdoms and advanced native civilizations, the expansion of Spanish power and prestige, the quest for a water passage to the Pacific, the drive for economic gain and control of trade, the attempt to consolidate Spanish territorial control against the incursions of its major rivals France and England, curiosity and acquisitiveness and adventure, and finally, the missionary zeal to Christianize the native peoples of North America. The establishment of a solid colonial base in the Caribbean and New Spain provided explorers from the mid–sixteenth century on with the capacity to engage in their explorations, and this coincidence of capacity and motivation virtually ensured the continuation of Spanish exploration and colonization.

Like the first Spanish exploratory activities in North America, the explorations that followed the great *entradas* of the 1540s were, for the most part, privately financed, recruited, and equipped. Explorers were, nevertheless, provided permission and license by officials of the Crown or of the Catholic Church. Expeditions were generally small in size and carried limited amounts of provisions; the parties were expected to live off the land, meaning generally that food had to be obtained from Native American populations wherever possible. The level of geographical information provided to explorers before their journeys began was often limited to what their backers could provide or purchase from the booksellers and ateliers of Europe and from the few Spanish explorers who possessed maps of regions or accounts based on the journeys of their predecessors. Indeed, although a half-century of exploration had allowed the broad outlines of North American geography to appear on European maps, relatively little of the Spanish exploratory effort worked its way onto those maps. Even the most accomplished explorers, such as Coronado or Soto, paid little attention to mapmaking or the acquisition of geographical knowledge; the course of their travels was often set as much by Native American information as by their own decision-making processes. And given the competitive nature of much Spanish exploration, such geographical information that did come out of an exploration was jealously guarded—not only from Spain's European rivals but also from other Spanish explorers. The results of discoveries were recorded in Seville on the *padrón real* ("master chart"), but the publication of this chart was prohibited by Spanish officialdom.[1] Much of Spanish exploration was, therefore, a continued rediscovery of things already known to a previous generation of explorers. As historian David Weber has written: "That Baja California was a peninsula, that New Mexico existed, and other lesser details of geography uncovered during the initial phases of Spanish exploration, became lost from view. Discoveries were remade as Spaniards continued to search North America for a strait to Asia, wealthy civilizations, and other fabulous places long after the so-called age of exploration had ended."[2]

In both the American Southeast, known as "La Florida," and the regions north of New Spain or Mexico were two principal types of explorers: pathfinders and explorer-colonizers. Pathfinders were those who explored and discovered the first Native American cultures and marked trails and geographical features across regions previously unexplored. Usually they were not colonizers. Examples of this type of explorer included Ponce de León, Cabeza de Vaca, Alvarez de Pineda, Soto, Coronado, and Pánfilo de Narváez during the earliest period of Spanish exploration and Fray Agustín Rodríguez, Francisco Sánchez Chamuscado, Fray Francisco Silvestre Vélez de Escalante, and Antonio de Espejo from the mid–sixteenth century on. The second group, the explorer-colonizers, generally consisted of those who conducted explorations before or after establishing settlements (temporary or permanent). Examples of this type included Vásquez de Ayllón before the Soto *entrada* and Pedro Menéndez de Avilés, Juan de Oñate, Francisco de Ibarra, Francisco de Urdiñola, Tristán de Luna y Arellano, Eusebio Francisco Kino, Juan Bautista de Anza, Gaspar de Portolá, Alonso de León, the Marqués de San Miguel de Aguayo, and José de Escandón thereafter. In addition, some of these explorers can be classified under both headings, since they sometimes carried out reconnoitering expeditions over the region they subsequently pacified and colonized (e.g., Escandón and Anza). Whether pathfinder, explorer-colonizer, or both, Spanish explorers from the mid–sixteenth century to the early nineteenth century were responsible for some of the more significant additions to geographical knowledge made by any European group in North America.

Exploration and Colonization in La Florida

The explorations of Vásquez de Ayllón, Soto, and others during the first half of the sixteenth century had provided the Spanish with a reasonably solid (though often misunderstood) base of geographical knowledge of the American Southeast. In the early years of the 1550s, the publication of Francisco López de Gómara's *Historia general de las Indias* reawakened Spanish interest in the Southeast by repeating the legends of Chicora, the "new Andalucia" portrayed by Vásquez de Ayllón as lying along the American coast north of the Florida peninsula and promising a fruitful and abundant land just waiting for colonization.[3] The publication of the reports of the Soto expedition, in the form of the narrative of the "Gentleman of Elvas" in 1557, supported the notion that a fertile region similar to southern Spain existed north of the Florida peninsula and also gave highly favorable information on "Coosa," a rich province in the upper basin of the Tennessee River in present-day northwestern Georgia, and on the pearl-rich kingdom of "Cofitachequi," near present-day Camden, South Carolina. Other reports from the Soto expedition had also reached Spanish officials, if not the literate public; a letter from Soto veteran Gerónimo López to the king contained a glowing report on La Florida, "a big land, populated, and filled with many of the things of Spain, including vines, trees that give nuts like the chestnut, fields full of cattle [bison?], and forests of all sorts."[4] López also speculated on the possibility of a way to China through this land, and the widespread circulation in Europe of maps showing the mythical "Sea of Verrazzano" as a possible route to the Pacific from the Atlantic added to Spanish incentives to put behind them the failure of Soto's *entrada* at yielding immediate benefits and to begin the reinvestigation of the Southeast. A final imperative for Spanish action in the Southeast was French privateering in the Caribbean and the news that the French had established a colony on the Brazilian coast and might soon do the same in La Florida. In late 1557 the Spanish government "issued an order for the settlement of a port on

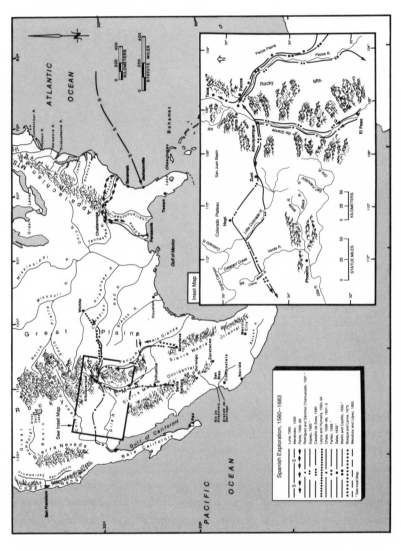

Map 9.1 Spanish Exploration, 1560–1683.

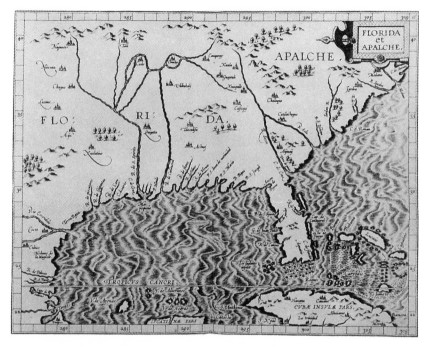

9.1 Map of "Florida and Apalche" in Cornelius Wytfliet, Descriptionis Ptolemaicae augmentum *(Louvain, 1597). This map is taken from the first atlas to be devoted entirely to the New World. Although cruder than other maps of the period, this map does show some geographical information that was obtained from the early Spanish explorations and that does not appear on other period maps. Courtesy John Carter Brown Library at Brown University.*

the northern coast of the Gulf of Mexico and the development of a string of settlements along a road from that port passing through Coosa to a settlement at the Point of Santa Elena [present-day Tybee Island, Georgia] on the Atlantic coast."[5]

The earliest exploratory attempt to comply with the edict from the Crown was unsuccessful, although a significant new feature was added to geographical knowledge. As early as 1544 a Franciscan missionary, Andrés de Olmos of Tampico, had envisioned the development of the Gulf coast from the Río Pánuco to the peninsula of Florida, beginning with a plan to settle Native Americans from La Florida in the nearby village of Chichimecas in New Spain. Adept at native languages and always interested in bringing the Catholic faith to Native Americans on distant frontiers, Olmos was the first recipient of the official edict of 1557 and was authorized to establish a mission settlement at Santa Elena on the Atlantic coastline and a second one at a site in La Florida to be chosen. This venture was entrusted to the responsibility of Luis de Velasco, the viceroy of New Spain, who soon realized that further examination of the coast from the Río de las Palmas to La Florida was necessary to determine an appropriate site for future settlement. He sent out two exploratory voyages in 1558–59, led by Guido de Labazares and Gonzalo Gayón, "to explore the ports and bays on the coast of Florida" before undertaking a colonizing effort. Between 3 September and 14 December 1558, Labazares, departing from Veracruz, explored along the coast of Texas and beyond to the east, missing the mouth of the Mississippi but discovering and entering Mobile Bay, "the largest and most commodious in all that coast," taking possession of it for Spain. The weather not being favorable for further exploration, Labazares failed to enter Pensacola Bay and returned to Veracruz. His brief but important voyage was succeeded by another one, led by Gayón, who sailed from San Juan de Ulúa to Havana and then counterclockwise around the Gulf to a port he called "Polonza" (Pensacola Bay) and to the coast of Apalache before returning to New Spain.[6]

Although neither of these voyages resulted in the temporary or permanent occupation of La Florida, the king's decision to occupy Santa Elena on the Georgia coast did lead to a major effort to settle the area originally seen by Vásquez de Ayllón in 1526. Furthermore, the discovery of Pensacola Bay aroused the interest of Velasco, an expansionist in his own right and a believer in the Soto report of the rich province of Coosa north of the Gulf. Although Velasco's primary concern was a Gulf coast settlement that could provide access to Coosa, he was also developing a strategic interest in an Atlantic coast settlement that could provide protection against French privateers.[7] Accordingly, he commissioned Tristán de Luna y Arellano, formerly a cavalry captain and second-in-command during the expedition of Coronado, to lead a venture that would achieve both of Velasco's objectives. With his appointment confirmed by the king, Luna was instructed to plant a settlement at Pensacola Bay or Ochuse, march overland to Santa Elena, found a second town there, and assume the duties of governor of this region.[8]

After extensive preparation, the expedition sailed from San Juan de Ulúa on 11 June 1559. It consisted of eleven vessels, including shallow-draft one-hundred-ton barks for coastal exploration, and a total of 1,500 people—500 soldiers (one-half of them cavalry) drawn from settlements at

Oaxaca, Zacatecas, and Puebla de los Angeles, along with 1,000 women, children, Indian allies, and blacks. With these ships and people went six Dominican priests and many of the followers of Soto. The force also took 240 horses, cattle for breeding, tools for farming and building, and provisions of hardtack, bacon, dried beef, cheese, oil, vinegar, and wine.[9] Thus the enterprise was intended not only to explore but to settle the land and to convert the Native Americans encountered there.

After a month at sea Luna landed first at Mobile Bay, the "Bahía de Filipina" of Labazares, before arriving at Pensacola on 15 August. Impressed with the bay variously known as "Ochuse" or "Polonza" and commonly called Santa María de Ochuse, Luna noted that it was "so secure that no wind could ever do any damage whatsoever."[10] Partly because of the excellence of this port, he selected and laid out a townsite for a traditional Spanish city to be named Santa María de Filipino, the first such Spanish settlement in the present United States. He sent out an expedition twelve days after arriving with the objective of exploring the river draining into Pensacola Bay; led by Soto veteran Alvaro Nieto, this expedition learned little (other than that the river was unnavigable). On 19 August, Luna's expectations as to the safety of the bay were proven false when a hurricane struck, destroying eight ships, in which many people drowned and most of the provisions were either lost or ruined. Luna then sent one of the remaining vessels back to New Spain with news of the disaster. Ill and delirious himself and upset with the unhealthiness of Ochuse, as Pensacola was now called, he decided to move back to Bahía de Filipina (Mobile Bay), and in about mid-February 1560 he did so, after having received supplies from Veracruz the preceding November. Ascending the Alabama River, he reached present Monroe County, Alabama, where he found native villages deserted and where he founded a settlement called Santa María de Nanipacana.[11]

Luna now decided to visit the Coosa region described by Soto's expedition, but his illness and the deterioration of his own mind prevented him from leading an expedition intended to found a new settlement there. Instead he sent out two hundred persons, commanded by Mateo del Sauz, in mid-April 1560. After a difficult march and much suffering, the expedition reached the Coosa vicinity and discovered that the rich province promised by the Soto reports was anything but abundant. The Spanish founded a town, but starvation, illness, and bickering during the sweltering summer led to its disintegration and abandonment. The survivors returned to Santa María de Ochuse. Ships from New Spain arrived there with provisions and reinforcements, including Captain Diego de Biedma, fifty recruits from

Campeche, and Fray Gregorio de Beteta, formerly of an expedition led by Fray Luis Cancer. With them came the viceroy's order to occupy Santa Elena as soon as possible to counter the reported threat of a French presence north of La Florida. Luna promptly dispatched two of his vessels with an expeditionary force headed by his nephew Martín de Hoz and accompanied by Captain Biedma and Fray Gregorio. This force departed on 10 August but went to Cuba, where it was struck by another hurricane, and the fleet returned to San Juan de Ulúa in New Spain, thereby aborting Luna's effort to settle Santa Elena and convert the native peoples there.[12]

Meanwhile, Luna was subjected to a mutiny in September when he tried to get his men to march overland to Santa Elena. By 30 January 1561, the viceroy decided to replace Luna with Angel de Villafañe, the commander of the San Juan de Ulúa garrison, charging him not only with responsibility for the Pensacola settlement but also with the immediate settlement of the Point of Santa Elena. With fifty men and provisions, Villafañe arrived at Ochuse in early March. He assumed the governorship of La Florida and Santa Elena (not yet established) on 9 April, and Luna sailed for Havana.[13]

The fifty-six-year-old Villafañe now determined to carry out the viceroy's orders to occupy Santa Elena. Leaving Captain Biedma and fifty men to garrison Ochuse, he sailed with over two hundred persons for Havana, where he chose one hundred of them for the voyage north to Santa Elena, releasing the rest of the original complement. When he left Havana, Villafañe's force had dwindled, because of desertions, to seventy-five soldiers and some servants and sailors. The expedition traversed the Bahama Channel and entered the "Río de Santa Elena" in 33° north latitude on 27 May 1561. Observing that Santa Elena was not a good harbor and that there was no land considered suitable for settlement, Villafañe sailed northward along the present-day North Carolina coast to the Cape Fear River (which he called the Jordan). Still finding no suitable harbor, he continued northward along the outer coast to the vicinity of Cape Hatteras, where a hurricane struck the fleet on 14 June, causing the loss of two ships and twenty-five men. With his force depleted and with no site located for settlement, Villafañe decided to return to Española first and then to Cuba.

One final exploration remained for the Luna-Villafañe enterprise: that of Antonio Velásquez, the factor of Villafañe's Florida expedition. In June 1561 Velásquez had sailed north from Havana to attempt a rendezvous with Villafañe somewhere along the Atlantic coast. A storm (probably a different one from the hurricane that ended Villafañe's coastal exploration) struck his caravel and drove it northward, well beyond Cape Hatteras and near the entrance to Chesapeake Bay (the "Bahía de Santa María" of the Spanish). Landing on the Virginia shore of the lower Chesapeake, Velásquez encountered friendly natives, two of whom decided to accompany the Spaniards, who by this time had decided to return to Spain rather than to Cuba. In September 1561, having successfully made the Atlantic crossing, Velásquez sent a report of his voyage to Madrid; he gave information on a land to the north of "Cabo de Trafalgar" (Cape Hatteras) "that held promise of being the new Andalucia that Ayllón had sought but not found" in his 1525–26 expedition.[14] How much this favorable report, when weighed against the failure of the Luna-Villafañe enterprise, factored into the Spanish decision to try again to establish an Atlantic coastal colony is not known.

The two-year expedition of Luna and Villafañe failed to establish settlements but did contribute to the advancement of geographical knowledge of the southeastern United States. The group discovered Mobile Bay, penetrated the interior of today's Alabama, reestablished contact with the Coosa Indians, and rediscovered the site of Pensacola Bay. It also developed more knowledge of the Atlantic coastal region, although, in the absence of any surviving maps or charts, it is uncertain whether the Spanish image of the geographical configuration of the coastal region was appreciably advanced from that portrayed on maps of the 1520s and 1530s. What was different was an appraisal of the land quality of the region below the 35th parallel, an appraisal that varied considerably from that of Vásquez de Ayllón and other early observers; rather than a "new Andalucia," the reports of the Luna and Villafañe expeditions concluded: "It seems to us that there is no land where settlement can be made nor a port suitable for it, nor native people who could be congregated nor joined to the Christian doctrine. . . . Nor in all that we have seen is found gold or silver or a good disposition of land for settlement."[15] In spite of this appraisal, the Spanish objective of tying the Gulf and the Atlantic coastal regions together and of settling Santa Elena persisted in the years that followed.[16]

The reports of French threats to settle the region along the coasts of present-day Georgia and Florida, as well as South Carolina, served as the impetus for Spain to occupy La Florida four years later. Holding longer to the geographical concept of the Sea of Verrazzano (an eastern extension of the Pacific into the North American continent, producing a narrow isthmus somewhere around the 40th parallel) than other European powers, the French were interested in establishing on the Atlantic coast a colony from which this sea and, therefore, a route to the Orient might be discovered. In addition to this economic incentive was a religious one; by the mid–sixteenth century, Protestantism had grown in France to a force causing severe religious and political tensions. Gaspard de Coligny, admiral of France, supported the cause of the French Huguenots (Protestants) by sponsoring the establishment of a Huguenot colony on the coast of Brazil on an island in Río de Janeiro harbor as early as 1555. Seven years later Jean Ribaut (or Ribault), an experienced French privateer sponsored by Coligny, sailed from Le Havre and set up the small colony of Charlesfort on Port Royal Sound (the "Santa Elena" of the Spaniards), but after Ribaut returned to France, internal conflict caused the abandonment of the settlement. René Laudonnière, who had been second in command to Ribaut, in 1564 led another party of Huguenots to America and established Fort Caroline on the Saint Johns River in La Florida. Weak leadership, some rebellious settlers, a frantic search for gold, neglect of farming and subsistence, and troubles with the Native American nations all contributed to the decline of the colony. Even the arrival of reinforcements led by Ribaut the following year did not help, since they were hindered by a severe storm. In 1565 the settlement was captured by the Spaniards, who executed the French captives. Retaliatory raids by both countries continued for some years thereafter until the project was abandoned completely by its French sponsors in 1572.[17]

This French thrust into La Florida led to the permanent Spanish settlement of the region by Pedro Menéndez de Avilés. An Asturian with considerable naval expertise and experience, Menéndez had become one of the captains-general of the Spanish Indies fleets by 1554 and had developed the idea of yearly fleets between the Americas and Spain. He proposed a master strategic plan for the occupation of key sites ranging from the Río Pánuco in New Spain across the Gulf of Mexico to La Florida and up the Atlantic coast as far as Chesapeake Bay. Having made four voyages to America himself, Menéndez proposed, as early as 31 August 1555 in a letter to the king, that a settlement be made along the Bahama Channel. Not only would such a fortress serve to protect Spanish ships returning to the home country, but ships damaged by storms could take refuge there and shipwrecked sailors would no longer be subjected to attack from hostile native peoples.[18] Although Lucas Vásquez de Ayllón, son of the former explorer, originally held a contract to found a settlement in the coastal region (possibly as far north as Chesapeake Bay), he defaulted on this agreement in February 1564.[19]

When the demand for a Spanish colony on the Atlantic coast became imperative in the face of the actual French threat and the possibility of an English one as well, Menéndez's proposal of 1555 was recalled, and in February 1565 he was asked to summarize for the king what was known about La Florida and the French colonial efforts there. Menéndez confirmed the official concerns over French and English activities so close to the Antilles and noted, in a letter to Philip II, that settlement in La Florida by Spain's enemies presented three dangers: such settlements could serve as a base for attacks on Spanish shipping; they could serve as a base for direct assault on Spanish possessions in the Caribbean; and they could serve as a base for the discovery of the arm of the sea that supposedly lay five hundred leagues north of Mexico and connected the Atlantic and the Pacific. French or English discovery of this arm of the sea, whether visualized as the Sea of Verrazzano or viewed as an early articulation of the Straits of Anián concept, could endanger Spanish trade with the Orient and could even threaten New Spain itself.[20] Menéndez enlarged on this geographical concept in writing, at the same time, to the father-general of the Jesuits, "La Florida was near New Spain, Tartary and China, and the Spice Islands, being either a continent joined to the first two or separated from them by an arm of the sea along which it would be possible to communicate between them and La Florida."[21] In response, King Philip II issued a contract on 15 March 1565 for Menéndez to undertake the exploration, settlement, and religious conversion of natives in La Florida as a buffer against the French and English threats. The Spanish government's concern over the incursion of its rivals into territory that it considered strategically important was demonstrated by the provision of direct financial assistance to Menéndez from the royal treasury; such a use of state funds to support exploration and colonization was rare indeed.

With a sizable force of fifteen hundred persons, Menéndez sailed from Cádiz on 29 June 1565, stopped at San Juan, Puerto Rico, and Santo Domingo, and anchored at an inlet on the Atlantic coast of La Florida near today's Cape Canaveral on 28 August. Proceeding northward, Menéndez landed and founded, on 8 September, the settlement of San Agustín (Saint Augustine), naming it in honor of that saint's day. One week later he sailed to search for the French at Fort Caroline. Unable to reach that fort by water, he returned to Saint Augustine and then led a force of about five hundred men overland for a surprise attack on the French fort, which he successfully captured. On that site he founded a second Spanish settlement named San Mateo, with three hundred Spaniards as a garrison force. In the meantime Ribaut's force had arrived from France and attempted to attack Saint Augustine from the sea, but a storm drove the Frenchmen onto the coast below that Spanish post. There a Spanish force attacked the French survivors, forcing the surrender of all but a few. The captives were massacred, their throats cut by the Spaniards at Matanzas, south of Saint Augustine.

The destruction of the French settlement gave the Spanish more than just an uncontested strip of territory along the Atlantic coast. It also yielded precious geographical information in the form of maps and books that Menéndez apparently utilized in letters he wrote to Philip II in October and December 1565. In these letters, Menéndez demonstrated far more detailed geographical knowledge than he had in his previous letter to the king, particularly about a supposed channel that cut through the Florida peninsula and that connected the Atlantic and the Gulf by way of the "Rio San Mateo," or Saint Johns River, and also about the Sea of Verrazzano and the Straits of Anián geographical notion. In his geographical conceptions, the key to the geography of North America—and thus to the economic and strategic utilization of the continent—was Bahía de Santa María, or Chesapeake Bay. North and west of the Chesapeake was a mountain range at the western foot of which lay a great arm of the sea that stretched toward Newfoundland and was navigable the entire distance. This arm of the sea stretching northeastward connected with another than ran northwest to the Pacific from around the 42nd parallel to approximately 48° north latitude. The western outlet of this arm of the sea was possibly within a hundred leagues of China. Menéndez linked this V-shaped strait with the "great waters" reported to the north by the chroniclers of the Coronado expedition by noting that the natives who lived along the strait subsisted on "the cows of New Spain [bison] that Francisco Vásquez Coronado found on those plains." These natives were also believed to trade the skins of the "cows" with Newfoundland traders, probably the French. In Menéndez's geographical thinking, all the French needed to do to control the continent was to sail southwest from Newfoundland to a point near the Chesapeake and establish bases from which to attack not only the Spanish colonies he intended to develop along the Atlantic coast but also, through the interior plains, the mines of New Spain itself. Making the Chesapeake region even more important, Menéndez continued, was the fact that it was—as Vásquez de Ayllón had posited four decades earlier—a new Andalucia with rich agricultural potential for the production of sugar, vines, cattle, hemp, wheat, and rice, with abundant naval stores and salt, with silk and pearls, and with "all sorts of fruits."[22] These geographical conceptions seemed to pose a strong argument for the Spanish exploration and settlement of the Chesapeake region, and for a time at least, Menéndez directed his thoughts to that objective.

In the meantime, consolidation of his gains along the coast was necessary; after the destruction of Fort Caroline, Menéndez explored the coast northward to Port Royal Sound (which he deemed the best in all of Florida) and, on what is now Parris Island, built Fort San Felipe. Nearby he established the colony of Santa Elena before returning to Havana for the winter of 1565–66.[23] At some point during the winter of 1566 Menéndez received information that somewhat tempered his enthusiasm for the Chesapeake Bay region. Members of a Spanish expedition from the Philippines to New Spain stayed in Havana that winter, and among them was the Augustine friar Andrés de Urdaneta, viewed as one of the primary Spanish authorities on the Pacific Ocean.[24] The expedition Urdaneta had accompanied had made its way eastward across the Pacific via a "great circle" route and, hence, had crossed the Pacific in northern latitudes. On the basis of what Urdaneta had learned on this voyage, part of which headed southward along the Pacific coast of North America, the friar informed Menéndez that the Straits of Anián formed a narrow entry into the Pacific well north of the 50th parallel of latitude. This representation of the Straits was to become the standard Spanish view of the Northwest Passage from the 1570s on; the Sea of Verrazzano concept, on which Menéndez had based his plans for the Chesapeake, diminished in popularity, and the beginning of its withering may have come out of Menéndez's conversations with Urdaneta in the winter of 1565–66.

In any event, Menéndez embarked from Havana on 10 February 1566, bound for the Gulf coast of La Florida, his enthusiasm for Chesapeake settlement considerably lessened. He landed first at Ponce de León Bay, where he unexpectedly encountered a Spaniard in a canoe. Hernando de Escalante Fontaneda had been a captive of the Calusa Indians for fifteen years, but Menéndez secured his release, and Escalante became an interpreter for Menéndez over the next two years. In search of other shipwrecked captives and perhaps of possible sites for settlement, Menéndez sailed northward to Tampa Bay before returning to Cuba. On a second voyage after June 1566, he shifted once again to the Atlantic coast of La Florida searching for a strait that crossed the peninsula and that might connect San Mateo with the southwestern coast of Florida. His exploration of the Saint Johns River, however, revealed that this route did not contain the desired strait. Next he sailed to Santa Elena again, naming it his capital in August 1566 and viewing it as his primary base for further exploration north and west. From Santa Elena he dispatched expeditions in both directions before departing for the Antilles.

The first of these expeditions was instructed to make discoveries of the interior between La Florida and New Spain, linking Santa Elena with Zacatecas, which was beginning to emerge as the center of the Mexican silver-mining region that would become so important for later developments in New Spain's northern frontier. Menéndez believed that the mountains to the northwest of his Santa Elena settlement (the Appalachians) were the same mountains as those in which Zacatecas lay (the Sierra Madre Oriental). Such a northeast-southwest mountain chain had been one of the geographical misconceptions rising out of the Soto explorations in the southern Appalachians. Menéndez, moreover, greatly underestimated the distance between the Florida coast and northern New Spain, fixing it as approximately eight hundred miles whereas the actual distance is about eighteen hundred miles. Hoping to find silver in the end of the mountain chain nearest Santa Elena, Menéndez viewed a link between the two silver regions as critical, particularly if that connection could be established well inland and away from the depredations of French and English pirates in the Caribbean and the Gulf of Mexico.[25] In addition to establishing a route between the Atlantic and northern Mexico via the interior, Menéndez instructed this expedition to pacify native populations and to search for precious metals and gems.

Chosen to lead this expedition, as well as a subsequent follow-up exploration, was Captain Juan Pardo.[26] The first Pardo expedition, with 125 soldiers, departed Santa Elena in early November 1566 and headed northwestward using the same route as had the Soto expedition a quarter-century earlier. The party reached a large river (the Savannah River?), which it followed upstream, probably as far as northwestern South Carolina, to the foot of the Blue Ridge Mountains, before returning to Santa Elena in 1567. With new orders from Menéndez, Pardo left Santa Elena again on 1 September 1567, following the same route northwestward toward the mountains but then turning south "toward Zacatecas and the San Martín mines," obviously ignorant of the great distance separating the southern Appalachians from the Mexican interior.[27] Before finally turning back, Pardo and his men pushed beyond the Coosa River, probably reaching the vicinity of present Gadsden, Alabama.[28] On both of his expeditions, Pardo—unlike Soto before him—planted small garrison settlements along the way. Although at least one of these settlements may have lasted until as late as 1584, nothing further was heard from the Spaniards left in these small outposts.[29] Nor, obviously, was Menéndez's objective of an overland route between Florida and northern Mexico achieved.

The second expedition dispatched in 1566 was equally unsuccessful. This endeavor was designed to settle the Chesapeake Bay region, viewed with such hope by Menéndez late in 1565 but probably less critical to his plans for the Spanish future in North America after his 1566 conversations with Urdaneta. The Chesapeake expedition, accompanied by Dominican missionaries, was beset by violent storms north of Florida. After becoming lost somewhere near Roanoke Island and not wanting to risk facing stormy weather on a return to Florida, Domingo Fernández, the expedition's pilot, turned east for Spain and made port at Cádiz in October. With this last enterprise a failure, Menéndez himself departed for Spain in May 1567, after seeking to establish peace with the indigenous peoples of La Florida. Although he never returned to La Florida, Menéndez maintained his financial and administrative interest in the region, and one year before his death in Spain on 17 September 1574, he sent out his last exploratory venture from Spain.[30] This expedition, commanded by his nephew Pedro Menéndez Márquez, reconnoitered the Atlantic coast from the Florida Keys to Chesapeake Bay but did not contribute anything of significance to Spanish geographical knowledge of the region.[31]

As an excellent example of the explorer-colonizer of North America, Menéndez accomplished much, though not all, of what he had set out to do. He had failed to find a strait that crossed northern Florida and that would provide Spain with a water route connecting the eastern and the western coasts of the peninsula, thereby facilitating trade, provisioning, administration, and defense of Spain's far-flung, isolated possessions. He had also failed to establish an overland route between Florida and northern New Spain and had not achieved a successful settlement of the Chesapeake Bay region. But within a period of less than two years of his departure from Spain in 1565, he had planted three settlements—San Agustín, San Mateo, and San Felipe—that outlasted their founder. Furthermore, he had explored both coasts of the Florida peninsula, from Tampa Bay on the Gulf coast to Santa Elena on the Atlantic coast. His careful explorations revealed that no strait across the peninsula existed near the Saint Johns River, and his expeditions contributed greatly to Spanish knowledge of the coastline of today's southeastern United States. He not only discovered navigational routes, studied and recorded coastal features, and linked the Florida settlements to a supply base at Havana but also found a passage via the Dry Tortugas as a shortcut for the fleets coming from New Spain to Havana. Menéndez also consolidated much preexisting geographical knowledge on not just the Southeast but the North American continent in general. By the end of his tenure in La Florida, Spanish geographical lore of the broader continental outline contained two major elements: the Straits of Anián, relatively narrow in width and entering the Pacific Ocean somewhere around the 50th parallel of latitude; and a range of mountains stretching from near the Atlantic coast just west of Chesapeake Bay toward the Sierra Madre Oriental of New Spain. Neither of these conceptualizations represented anything close to geographical accuracy, but they continued to dominate Spanish geographical thinking about the continent for more than a century. In terms of land quality, the Spanish image after Menéndez no longer contained the major element of "a new Andalucia"; rather, the prevailing view became one of a relatively poor and sandy coast needing much effort before it could support a sizable European population. All these accomplishments—in addition to establishing settlements in La Florida, eliminating the French threat, founding a regional government, and installing the Jesuits as the first religious in La Florida—gave birth to what historian Eugene Lyon has called "the enterprise of Florida."[32]

With the occupation of La Florida and Santa Elena, expeditions by *adelantados* in the southeastern part of the present-day United States declined in number and size to what were mostly reconnoitering ventures. Replacing early civil-military explorers were the first purely missionary ones. Lured by reports of an Indian whom Spaniards called "Don Luis de Velasco," after the viceroy of New Spain, the Jesuits established a short-lived mission on 10 September 1570 among the Powhatan Indians on the lower James River in Chesapeake Bay. All three missionaries there died in an attack by Native Americans on 9 February 1571, and a relief ship in the following summer could not find any survivors. Thereafter the mission remained abandoned, and Spain did not attempt to reoccupy the site, leaving it open for English settlement at Jamestown in 1607.[33]

After 1573, Franciscan missionaries began to replace the Jesuits in La Florida. They extended their religious activity into the Guale region (today's southeastern Georgia), especially after 1597. Although this thrust was primarily an occupational one resulting in the establishment of more than fifty missions in La Florida over the next century, missionaries were also explorers in the Southeast, just as they were in the expansion of New Spain northward into the Southwest and the Pacific coastal region. An example of this exploratory activity was the circuit of Fray Luis Jerónimo de Oré, the Franciscan commissary-general, in 1616. Traveling by foot and canoe, he journeyed through the entire Florida mission system. In the process he not only traveled over older routes but also discovered new ones as he visited each of the Timucua missions in La Florida and Guale.[34]

By 1627 the English and the Dutch were attempting to move into the northern Gulf coastal region of La Florida, so Spanish Governor Luis de Rojas y Borja dispatched two expeditions, both led by Pedro de Torres, to reconnoiter the Apalache region and the interior to the north. With twenty soldiers and sixty Indian allies, Torres on his first expedition marched overland to and from the Apalache area; on his second journey he penetrated the interior as far north as "Cofatachqui," where Soto had visited earlier. Governor Luis de Horruytiner supported the establishment of the first resident mission at Apalache in 1633 and sent the first ships to find a port nearby so that the missions could be supplied by sea instead of by the long and arduous overland route. This expedition succeeded in sounding the port at the mouth of the Saint Mark's River and in marking the channel, where the later settlement of San Marcos was located.[35] After the Timucua rebellion at midcentury, Spaniards occupied San Marcos de Apalache in 1676, although its fortifications were not completed until several years later.[36] Thus by the latter part of the seventeenth century, Spanish explorers, colonizers, and missionaries had planted military posts at San Agustín, San Mateo, and San Marcos (Santa Elena had been abandoned in 1587, and its settlers had moved to San Agustín),[37] as well as an extensive system of Franciscan missions in La Florida and Guale, while simultaneously surveying both coasts of La Florida and penetrating the southeastern interior of the North American continent.

In spite of all this activity, Spanish geographical knowledge of the continent was not appreciably more advanced than it had been a century earlier. In the Spanish image, the Straits of Anián still existed far to the north, and the Spanish still tended to view the Appalachian system as being more extensive than it actually was, particularly in an east-west direction. The paucity of extensive volumes on North America and of accessible Spanish maps of the region, however, limits our understanding of exactly what they did or did not know about the Southeast. As had been the case earlier in their colonial tenure in North America, the Spanish permitted little geographical information to leak out of the Archives of the Indies in Seville; Spanish explorers did not publish the accounts of their journeys, nor did Spanish cartographers produce anything like the great atlases or geographies being made in the ateliers of Italy, France, England, and the Netherlands.

Toward the end of the seventeenth century, the French once again caused Spain to expand in La Florida as well as in Texas. Responding to the plan of Diego de Peñalosa, the exiled former governor of New Mexico, who suggested conducting an expedition to the Río Grande and to northern New Spain's mines, René Robert Cavelier, sieur de La Salle, took advantage of the French king's interest in the project to propose his own plan to Louis XIV for the occupation of the mouth of the Mississippi River with a future goal of conquering the mines of Nueva Vizcaya in New Spain. The king accepted this proposal and granted La Salle four ships for the expedition to establish a colony at the mouth of the Mississippi. La Salle, who had already founded a fur-trading empire in the Great Lakes region and had descended the Mississippi to its mouth with Henri de Tonti in 1682, sailed from France on 1 August 1684 with three hundred men on the four ships provided him. After a delay in Santo Domingo, three of the ships continued into the Gulf of Mexico, missed the mouth of the Mississippi, landed at Matagorda Bay on the Texas coast in January 1585, and established their settlement of Fort Saint Louis inland on Garcitas Creek. One misfortune followed another, including the capture of some settlers by Karankawa Indians, the foundering of one of the ships, the loss of many of the provisions, the rise of internal dissension, and the prevalence of illness among the remaining colonists. By 1687, La Salle took some of his followers eastward to find the Mississippi, but conspirators murdered him in a camp near the Brazos River. Meanwhile hostile natives attacked the colony on Garcitas Creek and destroyed it, killing all but a few of its occupants.[38]

La Salle's colony and the later threat of French occupation of the Gulf coast and the Mississippi River brought a renewed burst of Spanish exploration, as well as increased interest in occupation of both the Gulf coast of La Florida and Texas.[39] Five expeditions led by Governor Alonso de León of Coahuila to locate La Salle's colony ultimately resulted in the initial occupation of eastern Texas by 1691. Likewise the French threat and the news that the English planned expeditions to the Gulf coast spurred new Spanish exploration and the occupation of Pensacola before the end of the 1690s. Pensacola Bay became the focus of Spanish interest during the regime of Viceroy Conde de Galve and his successors.

By order of King Charles II, the viceroy dispatched a fleet commanded by Martín de Zavala to take possession of "Panzacola Bay," the same location that had been explored by Luna in 1559. Accompanying the Zavala fleet was Don Juan Jordán de Reina, who had previously visited Pensacola Bay in 1686 while searching for La Salle's colony and who had named it "Panzacola"; he now officially took possession of Pensacola before proceeding to Havana. There he prepared an expedition of two small vessels, fifty men, and six cannons, which sailed from Havana on 6 November 1698, reaching Pensacola Bay (then known as La Bahía de Santa María de Galve) eleven days later.[40] Meanwhile Viceroy Conde de Galve had ordered the preparation of an occupying expedition from New Spain to consist of three ships, three hundred men organized into three companies, and provisions for the presidio to be established at Pensacola. After lengthy preparations, this fleet sailed on 15 October 1698 under the command of Andrés de Arriola and was accompanied by Jaime Franck, a professional engineer who was to construct a fort and prepare the defenses of Pensacola. The fleet reached there on 21 November, only four days after the arrival of Jordán de Reina's small force from Havana.[41]

Whereas the Spanish occupation of Pensacola in 1698 was not technically an exploration per se, it resulted from the knowledge gained during Luna's expedition and his residence at Ochuse in 1559–61, from the renewed fear of French occupation of the Gulf coast in the late seventeenth century, and from the earlier visit of Jordán de Reina there in 1686. With the establishment of a fortified post on Pensacola Bay (moved twice within the vicinity thereafter), the period of Spanish exploration and settlement in La Florida and the present southeastern United States came to an end. By 1698, Spanish pathfinders and explorer-colonizers had discovered much of what today comprises the coasts of Florida, Alabama, Mississippi, Georgia, and the Carolinas. They had also reported and mapped considerable portions of the interior of the present southeastern United States, even though relatively little of this geographical knowledge had become a part of the fund of general European geographical lore. Finally, their explorations had led to the permanent Spanish settlement of isolated posts reaching from Pensacola across the Florida peninsula to San Agustín and San Mateo.

Yet, as historian Robert Weddle has noted, "Exploration was a continuing concern of the various European powers until near the end of the colonial period."[42] In the Southeast thereafter, Spanish exploration was incidental to the consolidation of control, changes in territorial administration, and new threats presented by France, Great Britain, and finally the United States before the Adams-Onís Treaty of 1821, which ceded Florida to the United States. However, exploration of northern New Spain and the

American Southwest, an enterprise begun in the third decade of the sixteenth century, would remain a continuing major activity of Spaniards until Mexican independence in 1821.

Northern New Spain and the Southwest

The advance of the *frontera septentrional* ("northernmost frontier") of New Spain became a continuous goal of the Viceroyalty of New Spain (begun in 1535), with its resulting problems as well as its achievements. The northern frontier was a dynamic region of constantly opening new areas, discovered by both pathfinders and explorer-colonizers and faced with an almost continuous need to adapt to newly encountered Native American groups who understandably resisted the advance of Spaniards into their domains. The evidence of this continuous exploration, pacification, and settlement refutes historian John Francis Bannon's contention that "the year 1543 can be said to close the Age of the Conquistadores in North America" and that "far-ranging exploration was at an end."[43] Of course, Bannon was thinking only of the expeditions of Coronado, Soto-Moscoso, and Juan Rodríguez Cabrillo and Bartolomé Ferrelo, but he somewhat contradicted himself when he added, "The age of Spanish northward movement was about to open."[44]

As in La Florida and the southeastern part of the modern-day United States, various motives encouraged Spanish explorers and colonizers in the vast northern region. Of primary importance was the desire to find mineral deposits that offered wealth for both the discoverers and the king. Geographer D. W. Meinig observed, "The Spanish intensively probed that north in search of precious minerals, making a series of discoveries of rich silver deposits, and establishing a number of great mining camps."[45] Silver became the great incentive for Spanish exploration, along with serving as the basis of the economy in northern New Spain, and by the mid-1560s Mexico's mining frontier had pushed into the extreme southern part of what is now the state of Chihuahua.[46] Discoveries at Aviño, Topia, Santa Bárbara, Zacatecas, Guanajuato, and San Luis Potosí in the sixteenth century and at San José del Parral, Santa Eulalia, and Guarisamey thereafter made silver the principal quest of many explorers and settlers. They were joined soon by farmers, stock raisers, artisans, merchants, and day laborers, who not only established themselves on the frontier but also contributed to the growth of other economic pursuits.

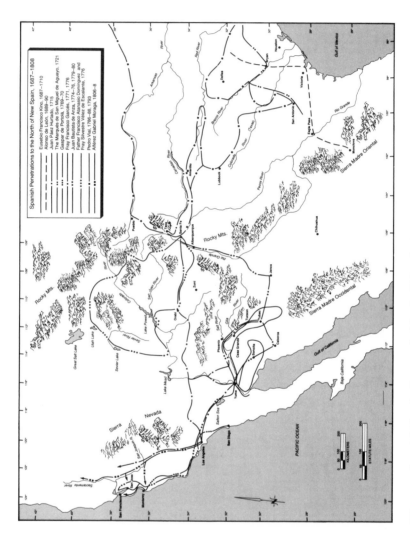

Map 9.2. Spanish Penetrations to the North of New Spain, 1687–1808.

Yet, not all Spaniards explored and colonized for the purpose of discovering silver. Simultaneously and independently, some also sought to establish the sovereignty of Spain over the indigenous peoples they encountered.[47] Exploration was additionally undertaken to discover possibilities for settlement and to search for basic geographical information.[48] Some explorers and conquistadores, such as Luis de Carbajal, sought new kingdoms to conquer for themselves and searched for Native Americans as slaves to supply the labor they needed for their economic enterprises. Many, especially in the sixteenth century, searched for mythical lands and kingdoms—the "Río de las mujeres," the Seven Cities of Cíbola, and Gran Quivira. Although this last motive diminished in later years, it never ended: Spaniards continued to seek new rumored domains, such as the "Kingdom of the Tejas," or pursued the long, fruitless quest for the Straits of Anián. Likewise, the missionary goals of spreading Christianity and westernizing the Native Americans were of major importance as motivations for exploration and for the establishment of missions almost everywhere in the north. Franciscans and Jesuits led the way into northern New Spain, as well as the present southwestern United States. They served not only as missionaries but as explorers of unknown lands. Father Eusebio Francisco Kino, for example, spent twenty-four years in the Pimería Alta of today's northern Sonora and southern Arizona and was both missionary to the Pima Indians and explorer of lands reaching to the Colorado River, to the Gulf of California, and along the Gila River.

The geographical knowledge of the northern frontier in the mid–sixteenth century was sketchy and sparse, in spite of the travels of Fray Marcos de Niza, the great *entrada* of Coronado, and the epic overland journey of Cabeza da Vaca. No map from the Coronado expedition survived; there is evidence that such a map once existed, for Coronado mentioned it in a letter to Viceroy Antonio de Mendoza. Apparently in reference to the route that Fray Marcos had taken, Coronado wrote Mendoza in August 1540, "Since I send Your Lordship a drawing of this route, I will say no more about it here."[49] In European maps of the 1540s through the end of the century, some Coronado place-names such as Quivira, Cíbola, and Tiguex appeared, but these were usually badly misplaced, located somewhere in the vague interior of an even more vague North American continent; yet, they were the only vestiges of the accumulation of geographical lore by Coronado. Apparently, the Spanish of the mid–sixteenth century still held to their concepts of a "great water"—the false Sea of Verrazzano or the Straits of Anián—north of Coronado's route. There were also faint intimations of a mountain range (the Rockies?) somewhere in the interior, but none of the Spaniards on New Spain's northern frontier could have given detailed information on the great water, on the mountains, or even on the Colorado River, discovered by Coronado's men. Like their image of the American Southeast, the Spanish conception of northern New Spain and the American Southwest was limited at best. Nor would this condition soon change appreciably in spite of the great period of exploration about to begin.

Northern New Spain

The Mixtón War of the early 1540s in Jalisco temporarily halted Spanish exploration and expansion to the north. The discovery of rich silver deposits at Zacatecas in 1546 renewed Spanish interest in exploration and settlement in northern New Spain thereafter. The focal point of this interest was the region north of Zacatecas, later named Nueva Vizcaya. This territory (presently the states of Durango and Chihuahua, along with northern Sinaloa and southern Sonora) had first been penetrated in 1531 by Nuño Beltrán de Guzmán, who crossed the Sierra Madre from west to east and reached perhaps the vicinity of the Río Nazas in Durango. Illness and lack of supplies apparently caused this expedition to turn back, but it was the first to reach the *meseta* ("tableland") of central Mexico and the first to make contact with the Tepehuan Indians. Two years later Captain José de Angulo, with fifty Spaniards and four hundred Native American allies, marched from Culiacán and crossed the sierra to the plains and valleys of Durango or Guadiana, discovering the Topia range in the process but failing to continue farther eastward toward the destination of Tampico because of hostile natives, cold weather, and lack of food supplies.[50]

With the production of silver at Zacatecas in the late 1540s and the ensuing base of population, the Spanish now had a fixed northern outpost for additional exploration, and the next expedition entered the present state of Durango from Zacatecas in 1552. Commissioned by the newly established Audiencia of Nueva Galicia to explore and pacify the Native Americans north of Zacatecas, Captain Ginés Vázquez de Mercado in 1552 reconnoitered the regions of San Martín, Aviño, and Sombrerete before camping, near the end of the year, in the Guadiana Valley, the site of the later city of Durango. He searched for a reported "rich hill of silver" described by Coronado on his return from the explorations of the Southwest in 1542, although Coronado neither crossed the Sierra Madre nor visited the Guadiana Valley on that expedition. Vázquez de Mercado thought he had discovered this fabled deposit and described his find, but it was not a source of silver, as he and others hoped. It was iron ore, one of the richest in all of Mexico; it was not worked until the latter half of the nineteenth century, long after Mexico achieved its independence from Spain. En route back to Zacatecas, Vázquez de Mercado was wounded in an encounter with Native Americans, and he died soon afterward.[51]

In 1554 seventeen-year-old Francisco de Ibarra led his first exploratory expedition from Zacatecas into what became Nueva Vizcaya, and for the next twenty years he became the principal explorer, colonizer, and silver entrepreneur of this vast area on both sides of the Sierra Madre. With a small body of soldiers and Native American allies and financed largely by his uncle Diego de Ibarra (one of the "Big Four" silver operators at Zacatecas), Ibarra explored northward to the valleys of the Río Nazas and the Río de San Juan in today's state of Durango, discovering the silver deposits reported earlier by Vázquez de Mercado at Aviño, San Martín, and Sombrerete. After this three-month expedition in 1554, Ibarra and others explored, colonized, and promoted the development of missionary ventures at Nombre de Dios and in the Guadiana Valley in addition to starting mining activity in southern Durango. In 1556, for example, an expedition from Zacatecas led by Juan de Tolosa and Luis Cortés, with about fifty Spaniards and a number of Native American allies, marched northward in search of mineral deposits. It largely retraced the route of Ibarra, grossly exaggerated the wealth and numbers of inhabitants of the region, and succeeded in antagonizing the Native Americans who had previously been friendly to Ibarra.[52]

Viceroy Velasco encouraged and supported Spanish expansion into Nueva Vizcaya, as he did for La Florida and the Philippine Islands.[53] He issued the commission to Francisco de Ibarra on 24 July 1562, appointing him governor and captain-general to explore, conquer, and settle the lands north of San Martín and Aviño. Ibarra was to accompany Fray Gerónimo de Mendoza, other Franciscan friars, and lay brother Lucas into the territory and assist them in converting the natives there in addition to founding a villa or chartered town at a site Ibarra was to select. Furthermore, he was instructed: "Make settlements where you deem best, according to the location, fertility of the soil, and quality of the site."[54]

Thus Ibarra now became an explorer-colonizer, having previously been a pathfinder. His expedition of 1562–63 was privately financed (again, largely by his uncle) and was organized in Zacatecas with 170 soldiers, 3 Franciscan missionaries, a number of Native American auxiliaries, and "some" black slaves. It marched to San Martín before Christmas 1562 and

left there on 24 January 1563, after a grand celebration marked by the playing of music and the firing of weapons. Ibarra and his force advanced to
Nombre de Dios and Aviño, then continued northwestward to the San
Juan Valley and Topia in the Sierra Madre in search of the reported fabu-
lously rich Kingdom of Copala. In April 1563 Ibarra sent Captain Alonso de
Pacheco with a small contingent to locate a site suitable for settlement in
the Guadiana Valley. Ibarra later joined Pacheco and on 8 July 1563, formally founded the villa of Durango (or Guadiana, as it was sometimes
called) as the capital of the Kingdom of Nueva Vizcaya. He then returned
to complete the conquest of the mountainous Topia district to the northwest before coming back to the Nombre de Dios region, where he founded
a second town on 7 November 1563.[55]

Ibarra's explorations and foundings of settlements did not cease with
these early activities. In the spring of 1564 he marched again to the mountains of Topia via the Río Nazas valley and Santa Bárbara in today's southern Chihuahua. Thereafter he blazed a new trail over the Sierra Madre to
the Río Fuerte area of Sinaloa, where he founded the town of San Juan de
Sinaloa in June. From there he moved southward and in January 1565 founded the community of San Sebastián de Chiametla, which became his principal residence near the mines of the region for the next ten years. Ibarra's
last major exploratory venture began in May 1565. With sixty soldiers and
some Native American auxiliaries, he set out from Sinaloa into what is today southern Sonora, crossing the lands of the Yaqui and Opata Indians.
Turning eastward, he crossed the Sierra Madre and entered the northern
part of the present-day state of Chihuahua. There he and his followers became the first Europeans to see and describe the extensive ruins of the ancient city of Paquimé, or Casas Grandes, before they returned to Sinaloa by
the end of June.[56]

Thus Francisco de Ibarra as pathfinder and explorer-colonizer opened a
huge region for Spanish settlement and future exploration on both sides of
the Sierra Madre. His expeditions contributed greatly to the geographical
knowledge of the Sierra Madre Occidental and of regions on both sides of
this mountain chain, such as those in Sinaloa, Sonora, Durango, and
southern Chihuahua, although little of this knowledge passed from the
Spanish to other Europeans. Soon others began to explore, discover silver
deposits, and plant settlements for both agricultural and mining pursuits
at Santa Bárbara, San Juan del Río, and Valle de San Bartolomé.[57] Still
others would follow in the seventeenth and eighteenth centuries, leading
to the discovery of new silver bonanzas at San José del Parral and Santa Eu-

lalia, to new relationships with native peoples, and to new geographical information that greatly expanded Spain's knowledge of the vast northern frontier. Franciscans established ten mission stations east of the mountains before 1590, and Jesuits such as Gonzalo de Tapia and Martín Pérez entered Sinaloa first in the following year.[58] Thus began the exploration and founding of missions that brought Spaniards into contact with the Yaqui, Mayo, Seri, Opata, and other Native American groups in the march northward in the territory between the Sierra Madre and the Gulf of California.

Sinaloa during the first third of the seventeenth century contained the three Spanish communities of San Miguel de Culiacán, San Juan de Sinaloa, and San Sebastián de Chiametla. Culiacán was administered by the Audiencia of Nueva Galicia while the other two villas were under the jurisdiction of the Kingdom of Nueva Vizcaya, with its capital at Durango. Although silver mining in the mountains of Chiametla had begun as early as the 1560s, by the turn of the century the town had declined greatly, and Sinaloa struggled to maintain its existence. In fact, its limited resources, poverty, scarcity of native populations, and few Spaniards, who lived in an isolated frontier region between the Sierra Madre and the Gulf of California, all became factors in the expansion farther northward in the seventeenth century.[59]

Thus began a century of exploration and expansion northward into what ultimately became three provinces: Sinaloa (from the Río Acaponeta to the Río Mayo); Ostimuri (from the Río Mayo to the Río Yaqui); and Sonora (north of the Río Yaqui to the Gila River in present-day Arizona). The continuous effort of Spanish explorers and miners to find silver deposits was a major motivating factor in this movement, as was the Jesuit advance to Christianize and westernize the various Native American nations. Likewise, *entradas* were made to find fertile lands suitable for agriculture (usually in the river valleys), pasturage for the region's leading economic enterprise of stock raising, and deposits of salt for use in the patio process of separating silver from its ore. Finally, the search for pearls in the Gulf of California and in the harbors of Sinaloa and Sonora also motivated Spanish exploration and expansion.[60]

In the vanguard of this northward movement were soldiers and Jesuit missionaries, both of whom served as explorer-colonizers in Sinaloa and Sonora. With the entrance of Fathers Gonzalo de Tapia and Martín Pérez into Sinaloa in 1591, the Jesuits began a century of exploration and establishment of mission stations that ultimately reached as far north as the vicinity of Pimería Alta in northern Sonora by 1687, when Father Kino began his twenty-four years of residence, missionary work, and exploration among the Pima Indians of present-day northern Sonora and southern Arizona.

Jesuit missions, new silver mines, and military presidios became the primary establishments of Sinaloa and Sonora throughout the seventeenth century and afterward. Connecting them was a coastal road, once called the "Cíbola route," running northward from the Río de las Cañas in the south to the limits of the mobile, advancing frontier in the north. This road, used by Fray Marcos, Coronado, and Ibarra, was in regular use throughout the century. In 1698 Marcos de Tapia Palacios, of the Audiencia of Nueva Galicia, and Jacinto de Fuensaldaña, governor of the province of Sinaloa, traveled over and described it en route from Guadalajara to the presidio of Sinaloa.[61] For contact with the rest of Nueva Vizcaya, explorers, beginning with Guzmán, Angulo, and Ibarra, opened three trails across the Sierra Madre: the first and oldest ran from Durango to Chiametla and to Sinaloa via Papasquiaro and Topia; the second headed in a more northerly direction from the mining district of San Juan through Ostimuri to San José del Parral in today's southern Chihuahua; and the third traveled from the Río Bavispe in northern Sonora to Janos, Casas Grandes, and Namiquipa in northern Chihuahua after 1650.[62]

Missionaries explored the vast area on both sides of the Sierra Madre and occupied it extensively. By 1637 the bishop of Durango (Guadiana) reported to the king that the Jesuit missions covered "one hundred leagues" (approximately 260 miles) north of Sinaloa to the Río Mayo, an area in which the missionaries raised more than one hundred thousand head of livestock. From this region they pushed on northward to the Río Yaqui and subsequently into the valley of Sonora to work among the Pima and Opata Indians. By 1645 one report indicated that they had thirty-five principal missions and numerous *visitas* (outlying villages without resident missionaries) in a continuous stretch of 600 miles.[63]

Accompanying the Jesuits were the prospectors for mining deposits in the northern region and the soldiers for the protection of both settlers and missionaries. Explorers, such as Pedro de Perea, seeking silver bonanzas, began in about 1650 to develop new mining districts in the valley of Sonora, as well as in those revitalized areas of San José de Copala and Nuestra Señora del Rosario in the Chiametla region of southern Sinaloa. In Sonora mining camps or districts (*reales*), discoveries of silver occurred from 1666 to 1683 at San Juan Bautista, San Miguel, San Ignacio de Ostimuri, and Nuestra Señora de la Concepción de los Frailes (near which miners settled the town of Alamos).[64] Aiding both the missionaries and the miners were the expeditions led by Diego Martínez de Hurdaide and Pedro de Perea, both captains of the presidio of Sinaloa, for exploration and for the pacification of the Native Americans. Martínez de Hurdaide, for example, from 1595 until his death in 1626, personally led many expeditions to the sierra of Chinipas and the Río Fuerte to search for mineral deposits, subjugate Native Americans, and establish settlements, such as the presidio of Montesclaros in 1610–12. In 1608 he made expeditions beyond the Río Fuerte to the Río Yaqui, subsequently establishing the first missions among the Yaquis and also, later, among the lower Pimas. On his last campaign in 1625, Hurdaide led an expedition to the mountainous region on the banks of the upper Río Fuerte to suppress a Native American uprising. His successor, Pedro de Perea, in 1640 began the exploration and settlement of the region north of the Río Yaqui (called Nueva Andalucia) and succeeded in establishing the northernmost Spanish posts in the interior of Sonora by 1650.[65]

On the northeastern frontier of New Spain, explorers and colonizers discovered and developed new regions as they penetrated northward over nearly two centuries. Although the Pánuco area had been explored and colonized before the end of the 1520s, no further steps had been taken in this region until after 1550, when settlement began near San Luis Potosí among the pacified Guachichiles Indians.[66] Exploration of the Saltillo-Parras district in modern-day Coahuila began in the period 1575–95, but this region remained a part of Nueva Vizcaya until 1786. The rest of Coahuila was not settled until the last quarter of the seventeenth century; its limits extended north of the Río Grande into today's Texas. This advance was prompted by the fear of the reported French incursions on New Spain's northern frontier, especially the expedition of La Salle. Both military and missionary motives led to the exploration and occupation of Monclova and other sites in Coahuila by 1689.[67]

Luis de Carvajal y de la Cueva became the original explorer and colonizer of Nuevo León after 1579, following his own explorations seven years earlier in an attempt to close the gap between San Agustín in La Florida and the Río Pánuco in northeastern New Spain. On this expedition he led 40 cavalry and 180 Native American auxiliaries on a ten-month march to open a road between the mines of Nueva Galicia and the Río Pánuco, but his journey took him northward, crossing the Río Grande. As a result, he developed a plan that he presented to the king and the Council of the Indies on 28 March 1579. In it he outlined his objective to link New Spain and La Florida, pointing out that the Gulf coast was entirely unprotected. He further explained that he intended to promote private interests to discover mines and take Native Americans captive for sale as slaves to finance the new kingdom he proposed.[68] The plan was as worthy as that of Menéndez, and it met with about as much success.

King Philip II issued Carvajal a royal license at the end of May 1579, for the discovery, pacification, and settlement of Nuevo Reyno de León, a region roughly defined as extending westward to the borders of Nueva Vizcaya and Nueva Galicia and northward from the Río Pánuco two hundred leagues (about 520 miles). In June 1580 Carvajal sailed from Sanlúcar in Spain, but difficulty in recruiting the two hundred men he had been authorized for the expedition delayed him until 1584. In that year he explored and settled his assigned domain, founding the communities of León (now Cerralvo) and San Luis (present-day Monterrey) temporarily. Thereafter his explorations in search of silver and slaves, along with his defiance of royal authorities and his alleged Jewish family heritage, not only led to constant unrest and hostility with the native populations but also to his arrest, trial by the Inquisition in Mexico City, and death in prison in 1590.[69] Permanent occupation of Nuevo León occurred in 1596 and afterward with families from León and Saltillo, led by Captain Diego de Montemayor, and new sites were located for settlement by Governor Martín de Zavala in the period 1625–37.[70]

José de Escandón ultimately explored and settled the region of northern New Spain between Texas and the Río Pánuco in the period 1747–55. To counter the French influence from Louisiana, halt Native American hostility, and promote the Christianization of natives, he received a contract in September 1746 authorizing him to explore and settle what became the province of Nuevo Santander (today's Tamaulipas), extending from the Río Pánuco to the southern limits of Texas at the Río Medina and Río Guadalupe. This license permitted Escandón to enter and establish settlements as an explorer-colonizer over a vast region, including territory both north and south of the Río Grande del Norte. With previous experience leading expeditions into the Sierra Gorda between the Río Pánuco and Querétaro, he personally led a reconnoitering expedition of one hundred men into his assigned province in 1747. This exploratory venture was intended primarily to locate suitable sites for future settlement where water was plentiful, land was fertile, and friendly Native Americans could be attracted to missionary work. Following the return of this expedition, Escandón began planning and recruiting processes for the settlement of Nuevo Santander, a task he personally led on a second expedition from Querétaro on 2 December 1748 with 755 soldiers, 2,515 colonists, wagons, livestock, and provisions. Over the next seven years he or his appointed followers established twenty-three communities, including Camargo, Reynosa, Revilla (now Guerrero), and Mier on the southern bank of the Río Grande and two ranching settlements, Dolores and Laredo, on the northern bank. Escandón contributed about one-half of the finances necessary for these explorations and colonizations, with the royal government supplying the remainder. His meticulous attention to detail, his careful planning, his selection of sites after reconnoitering the territory, and his personal leadership all distinguish Escandón as one of Spain's most successful explorer-colonizers in the entire Spanish colonial period.[71] His ventures not only established Spanish communities in present Tamaulipas and Texas but also explored both sides of the Río Grande del Norte, the southern Texas coastline, and the interior of today's northeastern Mexico.

Although Spanish exploration and settlement of the interior of northern New Spain evidently continued over more than two centuries, it should also be noted that Spanish seafaring explorations along the Pacific coast of North America began in the 1520s and continued thereafter, ending in about 1603. After a long period of neglecting this region, the Spanish resumed exploration in 1769 with the occupation of Alta California, and subsequently a burst of exploratory activity occurred on the northwestern coast until nearly the end of the eighteenth century.

These explorations are covered elsewhere in these volumes, yet we need to include a summary of them here because they related to the overall Spanish explorations northward and sometimes were tied into the land expeditions penetrating northern New Spain. Beginning in 1527, when Hernán Cortés sent Alvaro de Saavedra on an exploration of the Pacific from Zacatula on the western coast of New Spain, Spanish seafaring expeditions reached out first to Baja California and the coastlines of Sinaloa and Sonora and later to Alta California and the northwestern coast of North America as far as present-day British Columbia and Alaska. Cortés sent out two other maritime expeditions in the 1530s: one, under Hurtado de Mendoza, traveled to the Río Fuerte in Sinaloa; the other, under Fortún Jiménez, discovered Baja California. Francisco de Ulloa, with three ships, sailed northward in 1539, making discoveries in the Gulf of California and reaching the mouth of the Colorado River before exploring both coasts of Baja California and continuing up its Pacific side to the vicinity of Cabo del Engaño. The major voyage of Juan Rodriguez Cabrillo in 1542–43 explored the outer coast of Baja California, discovered San Diego Bay, Drake's Bay, and the

Santa Bárbara Channel, and subsequently, under Bartolomé Ferrelo after the death of Rodríguez Cabrillo, explored northward as far as the present-day Oregon coastline. Although Spanish explorers crossed the Pacific from east to west, no return route was discovered until 1565, when Fray Urdaneta did so and returned to the California coast from the Far East before continuing southward to New Spain, where he played the role, described earlier, in shifting Menéndez de Avilés's interest away from Chesapeake Bay. In 1595 the expedition of Sebastián Rodriguez Cermeño, returning from the Philippine Islands, was shipwrecked at Drake's Bay on the California coast, but he and his crew, in an improvised vessel, made their way southward along the coast to New Spain. Royal interest in the protection of this far-flung region after Cermeño's experience, the visit of Sir Francis Drake in 1579, and the visit of Thomas Cavendish seven years later, along with the necessity of protecting the Manila galleons and the reports of the false discovery of the Straits of Anián, all contributed to the dispatch of the exploratory venture of Sebastián Vizcaíno in 1602–3. Vizcaíno, with three ships, ran the coast of Baja California and Alta California, entering Magdalena and San Diego Bays, exploring Santa Catalina Island, and discovering Monterey Bay but missing San Francisco Bay, just as previous expeditions had done.[72]

Not until the latter half of the eighteenth century did Spain once again become interested in further explorations of the Pacific coast and the settlement of Alta California. A burst of exploratory activity occurred in response to a perceived foreign threat first from Russian expansion and later from British merchant and naval ventures into the region claimed by Spain. The occupation of Alta California by land and sea expeditions in 1769–70, led by explorer-colonizer Gaspar de Portolá and Fray Junípero Serra, resulted in the permanent founding of today's California. Supported by the irregular supply service from distant San Blas in Nayarit on the western coast of New Spain, this occupation necessitated land expeditions from Sonora and New Mexico in the decade that followed. Juan Bautista de Anza explored the land route from Tubac in Pimería Alta (present Arizona) in the period 1774–76, in the process discovering a route from Sonora to Alta California, crossing the Colorado River near today's Yuma, and reaching San Gabriel and Monterey before establishing the first settlement at San Francisco. In that same era Fray Francisco Garcés began a series of explorations from present Arizona westward in the hope of discovering a land route between the two provinces of Pimería Alta and Alta

California and beginning missionary work among the Native Americans of the lower Colorado River.

Maritime expeditions to the north of Alta California in the period 1774–95 not only were numerous but contributed greatly to Spain's scientific knowledge of flora and fauna, the coast and its geographical features, and the Native American inhabitants of a vast region reaching as far north as the southern shore of Alaska and the western coast of British Columbia. Juan Pérez in 1774 voyaged in the *Santiago* to 55° north latitude, discovering and exploring Nootka Sound on the western coast of Vancouver Island along the way. Bruno Heceta and Juan Francisco de la Bodega y Quadra, in two ships the next year, explored northward, with Heceta discovering both Trinidad Bay and the mouth of the Columbia River in 1776 and with Bodega finding Bodega Bay as he coasted northward as far as 58° north latitude. After Captain James Cook's visit to the northwestern coast in 1776, another Spanish expedition led by Ignacio Arteaga and Bodega sailed northward as far as 60° north latitude. Afterward the Crown suspended further explorations until the late 1780s when the threat of British merchant vessels engaged in the sea otter trade and British claims to sovereignty on the northwestern coast brought about a resumption of Spanish exploration and finally the establishment of Spain's northernmost post at Santa Cruz de Nootka (Nootka Sound).

Alejandro Malaspina's scientific voyage reached the northwestern coast in 1791 after the voyages of Esteban José Martínez to Nootka and Alaska in 1788–89, and Nootka was occupied in 1790. Manuel Quimper and Gonzalo López de Haro, under Malaspina's command, explored the Strait of Juan de Fuca in 1790 to determine "once and for all" whether a strait connecting with it led to the Atlantic—the mythic Straits of Anián were once again a goal of Spanish exploration.[73] Malaspina himself examined the northwestern coast and the coast of Alta California, visiting Yakutat Bay, Prince William Sound, Bucareli Sound, Nootka, and Monterey before departing for the Philippine Islands and returning to Cádiz via Australia, New Zealand, Peru, Chile, the Islas Malvinas (Falkland Islands), and Montevideo in Uruguay. Other Spanish explorers, such as Juan Francisco de la Bodega y Quadra, Jacinto Caamaño, Salvador Fidalgo, Dionisio Alcala Galiano, and Cayetano Valdés, in 1792 continued their explorations and discoveries around Vancouver Island, within the Strait of Juan de Fuca, and along the Alaskan coast. With the signing of the second Nootka Convention between Spain and Great Britain in 1793, the abandonment of Nootka by the

Spaniards in 1795, and the subsequent upheavals in Europe in the Napoleonic era, Spanish exploration of the northwestern coast came to an abrupt end.[74] However, this intensive Spanish exploratory activity contributed greatly to the advancement of knowledge concerning the region and its geographical features, its flora and fauna, and the Native Americans who inhabited it. Furthermore, exploration of the Pacific coast supported and extended Spain's efforts to penetrate the northern interior of New Spain and revealed that exploration by sea and by land continued to be a dynamic activity until the end of the eighteenth century, a fact also apparent in Spanish exploration of the present-day southwestern United States.

The exploratory activities of the Spanish on the northern frontiers of New Spain had resulted, by the late eighteenth century, in a relatively precise geographical conception of both the *frontera septentrional* and the Pacific coast, even though some maps continued to show California as an island late into the eighteenth century. Although the Straits of Anián were still a geographical fixture for the Spanish (as they were for the English and others until early in the nineteenth century) and although virtually no coherent information on the interior existed, the Spanish knew and understood well the northern New Spain lands that they had explored and settled by the opening of the nineteenth century. More accurate assessments of land quality had replaced the "new Andalucias" of the early and mid–sixteenth century, and although an occasional reference might have been made in the literature of New Spain to interior civilizations of vast riches, no one took those rumors terribly seriously by the late 1700s. Nevertheless, in spite of the relative accuracy of the Spanish view of the lands they had possessed, they guarded their geographical knowledge as jealously in the early 1800s as they had from the beginning. There were no Spanish equivalents of Richard Eden, Giovanni Battista Ramusio, Richard Hakluyt, Theodor de Bry, or other chroniclers of New World exploration, and for many Spaniards (those not possessing access to the official reports in the Archives of the Indies or in church documents), the land of northern New Spain was still a frontier of mystery. But as mysterious as it might have seemed, it was not as mysterious as the interior of what is now the southwestern United States. This land, explored first as early as 1540 and settled before the end of the sixteenth century in the upper Río Grande valley, was still—for those Spaniards outside the official circles and for others—a terra incognita. It remained so in spite of the magnificent efforts of explorers from Oñate to Escalante and Pedro Vial, most of whom contributed enormously to geographical information only to have it buried in the archives.

Indeed, it was not until the publication of Alexander von Humboldt's *Interior Provinces of New Spain* in the early 1800s that the rest of the world could appreciate the significant additions to geographical awareness made by hardy Spanish explorers in the plains, mountains, and deserts of the Southwest.

The Southwest

Although there have been many differing interpretations of what constitutes the Southwest, Spanish exploration and settlement there took place in Texas, New Mexico, Pimería Alta (today's southern Arizona below the Gila River and northern Sonora), and Alta California (present California). Both enterprises occurred over nearly three centuries and resulted in extensive official knowledge of the geography, the flora and fauna, and the Native Americans of the region. Furthermore, settlement eventually followed exploration, resulting in a population of more than forty thousand inhabitants, mostly in communities and their environs, by the end of the Spanish colonial era in 1821.

It should be remembered that the present southwestern United States was once the *frontera septentrional* of New Spain and that exploration extended even beyond that region. Explorers reached the Great Plains to the north and east, as well as the northwestern coast from present Oregon to southern Alaska. Their expeditions brought them into contact with new Native American nations and bands, as well as into encounters with the expansionist activities of France, Great Britain, and in the late eighteenth century, the United States.

The early exploration of the Southwest began with the voyage of Alvarez de Pineda in 1519 along the Texas coastline, Cabeza de Vaca's trek with his three companions across southern Texas in 1528–36, and Coronado's great journey as far as central Kansas in 1540–42, yet these explorations were only the beginning of Spanish activity in the Southwest. In fact, exploration continued, with occasional interruptions, until the end of the eighteenth century and the early years of the nineteenth. It took place chronologically first in New Mexico, then in Texas, and finally in Pimería Alta and Alta California.

Thirty-nine years passed between the end of Coronado's *entrada* and the renewal of exploration of New Mexico, exploration that resumed in a burst of activity between 1581 and 1605. Many reasons contributed to this delay and neglect. Among them were the dashed hopes resulting from Coronado's failure to find wealth or rich kingdoms. Yet, there were other reasons. The outbreak of the Mixtón War in Nueva Galicia, the discovery of a silver bonanza at Zacatecas, and the expansion of New Spain into Sinaloa, Sonora, Nueva Vizcaya, Nuevo León, and Coahuila all diverted Spanish attention and interest as well as resources, as did royal emphasis on imperial problems such as the English threat of Queen Elizabeth, struggles in Europe against rivals, and Spanish expansion in South and Central America. Still, the seeds had been planted. Franciscans never forgot the Native Americans discovered and described in the north, and civil officials knew of this huge region, a target of future settlement and colonization.

Between 1581 and 1598 five pathfinding and exploration-settlement expeditions entered New Mexico and the Great Plains, ultimately resulting in Spanish occupation of New Mexico by Oñate in 1598. The first two trips originated in northern Nueva Vizcaya (southern Chihuahua) near Santa Bárbara and Valle de San Bartolomé. The expedition of Fray Rodríguez and Captain Sánchez Chamuscado took place from 5 June 1581 to 15 April 1582 and was primarily a religious venture. Fray Rodríguez planned an expedition and obtained the viceroy's permission after he had heard a report at his station of Valle de San Bartolomé from a Native American who told him of a country in the north inhabited by large settlements of people who raised cotton for clothing and had a plentiful food supply. Three friars (Rodríguez, Francisco López, and Juan de Santa María), nine soldiers commanded by Sánchez Chamuscado, and some nineteen Native American servants set out from Santa Bárbara on 5 June 1581. Among the military personnel were Hernán Gallegos and Pedro de Bustamante, both of whom became the expedition's principal chroniclers. Ascending the Conchos River to its junction with the Río Grande del Norte at La Junta de los Ríos, the small force encountered the Patarabueyes Indians there before proceeding up the western bank of the Río Grande to the Pueblo Indian region of New Mexico, pioneering a new route in the process. After reaching the vicinity of today's Bernalillo, Fray Santa María set out alone on 7 September to report their discoveries in New Spain, but he was killed by Native Americans en route. Thereafter the remaining party explored the Río Grande valley as far north as the Queres villages, visited the plains east of the Manzano Mountains where it encountered and described bison, and visited Acoma and Zuñi before returning to a village called Puaray on the Río Grande. Leaving the two friars, at their request, to teach Christianity to the Pueblos, Captain Sánchez Chamuscado led the soldiers southward on the return trip to Santa Bárbara; they arrived, after the death of their commander, on 15 April 1582.[75]

The second expedition was a follow-up to that of Rodríguez and Sánchez Chamuscado. Commanded by Antonio de Espejo, a successful cattle rancher of the northern frontier who offered to lead a rescue mission for the friars left in New Mexico the previous year, this expedition had as its secondary motive the investigation of rumored mines to the west of Zuñi. Although a servant named Francisco who had remained with the friars arrived in Santa Bárbara and reported their deaths, there was still some doubt whether one of them might still be alive. Espejo—with fourteen or fifteen soldiers, Fray Bernaldino Beltrán of Durango, 115 horses and mules, some servants, and provisions—departed from Valle de San Bartolomé on 10 November 1582. Diego Pérez de Luxán, one of the soldiers, became the principal chronicler of this expedition, which followed the route of Fray Rodríguez and Captain Sánchez Chamuscado down the Río Conchos to the land of the Patarabueyes at La Junta de los Ríos. Encouraged by reports that the friars were still alive in New Mexico, Espejo and his followers proceeded up the Río Grande to the lands of the Sumas and Mansos near today's El Paso by early January 1583. Three weeks of marching northward brought them to abandoned Native American pueblos above present Elephant Butte, where Native American visitors informed Espejo that the friars had been killed. He decided to press on anyway. With a small detachment after 10 February, he visited the villages of Chilili and Quarai east of the Manzano Mountains and then rejoined his forces on the Río Grande. They marched to Puaray by 16 February, where they verified the deaths of the two friars.

Thereafter Espejo and his party advanced to the Queres pueblos and ascended the Jémez River to Zía Pueblo, where Espejo took formal possession for the king of Spain. On 28 February he set out westward, reaching Inscription Rock (El Morro) on 11 March after passing Laguna and Acoma. Three days later he arrived at the Zuñi villages. Leaving five soldiers and Fray Beltrán there, Espejo, nine other soldiers, and eighty Zuñis continued westward on 11 April, visiting the Hopi villages, where he was received courteously. With only four soldiers (the other five and the Zuñi allies remained at the Hopi towns), Espejo now explored westward in search of the rumored mines. This expedition crossed the Little Colorado River near present Winslow, Arizona, marched through Salt Creek Canyon and the Verde River valley, and reached outcrops of mostly copper with little silver near today's Jerome, Arizona. Returning to the Hopi towns and then to Zuñi, Espejo reunited his forces. At Zuñi, Fray Beltrán now became determined to return to New Spain. With five soldiers as an escort, he departed and reached Santa Bárbara safely. Espejo and the eight remaining soldiers marched to Puaray, which they reached after a fight with Querecho Indians (possibly Navajo-Apaches). After 27 June he explored the Tano pueblos of the Galisteo Basin, reached Pecos Pueblo, and started homeward on 15 July by a route east of the mountains following the "Río de las Vacas" ("River of the Cows," or Pecos River) southward, possibly crossing western Texas through the Big Bend country to La Junta de los Ríos. On 10 September 1583, after a ten-month absence, Espejo's force reached Valle de San Bartolomé, having pioneered a new route in eastern New Mexico and western Texas in addition to exploring both east and west of the Río Grande in central New Mexico and northern Arizona.[76] Espejo's highly favorable reports on the upper Río Grande were widely circulated in the northern provinces and included tales of a great lake in the interior, farther to the north than the expedition had traveled. Whether Espejo's accounts were available outside of New Spain and Spain is not certain, but on many late-sixteenth and early-seventeenth-century European maps of the region, this mythical lake became a prominent feature. Perhaps more important, a number of the most influential maps—including those accompanying various versions of Hakluyt's *Voyages*—also carried the words "Nuevo Mexico" across the lands that Espejo had explored.[77]

The archbishop of Mexico wrote of the lands explored by Espejo: "If what they tell me is true, they have indeed discovered . . . another new world."[78] On the strength of such opinion, the Crown authorized the viceroy of New Spain to explore, pacify, and colonize the potentially rich "new world." Before official exploration could take place, however, two unauthorized expeditions moved into New Mexico, western Texas, and the Great Plains. The first of these, in 1590–91, was an exploring-colonizing venture. Led by Gaspar Castaño de Sosa, the lieutenant governor of Nuevo León when Luis de Carvajal had been arrested by authorities in 1589, the expedition was intended as a colonizing enterprise from its start but without royal authorization and indeed in defiance of the viceroy's orders to prevent further slaving raids on the Native Americans of northern New Spain. Castaño and his 160 to 170 followers, along with cattle, corn, wheat, and at least ten carts, departed from Almadén (Monclova) on 27 July 1590. They reached the Río Grande del Norte on 9 September and entered the Pecos River valley seventeen days later, some fifteen to twenty miles below today's Sheffield, Texas. Following the Pecos northward, Castaño, with an advance party of twenty-one men and seventeen servants, reached Pecos Pueblo on 31 December, where they attacked the natives.

After killing many of them and seizing others to act as guides, Castaño then marched westward, possibly through Glorieta Pass to the Santa Fe and Río Grande region between 7 and 10 January 1591. He established his followers first at San Marcos Pueblo and later at Santo Domingo Pueblo, where he was arrested by Captain Juan de Morlete on 29 March. Morlete had been instructed by the viceroy to overtake Castaño and his followers, arrest them, and bring these unauthorized colonists back to New Spain for trial. He and his force of forty soldiers seem to have followed the Río Grande to Santo Domingo, but on the return route with his prisoners, Morlete evidently crossed the river near today's El Paso and then traversed northern Chihuahua by a more direct trail to Santa Bárbara.[79] Thus it appears that Morlete pioneered a new route from El Paso, probably passing by the later sites of Carrizal and Chihuahua directly to Santa Bárbara instead of using the familiar path along the Río Conchos and the Río Grande. Furthermore, this new route may have been the same one followed by Oñate in 1598 in his march north to occupy New Mexico.

The second unauthorized expedition occurred in 1593 as an offspring of a punitive campaign sent by Governor Diego Fernández de Velasco of Nueva Vizcaya to punish the Toboso Indians and other natives for robbing cattle ranches in this kingdom. Without sanction, its leader, Captain Francisco Leyva de Bonilla, decided to invade New Mexico. He established a base at San Ildefonso Pueblo, then marched eastward to the Great Plains, where another member of his party, António Gutiérrez de Humaña, murdered Leyva with a butcher's knife and took charge himself. Plains Indians attacked the expedition, killing Gutiérrez de Humaña and all the others except for five Native American allies, two of whom eventually reached a native *ranchería* ("campsite"). One of these, Jusephe (Joseph), survived a year of captivity (his companion was killed by Apaches) and finally escaped, making his way to New Mexico to relate his tale of the expedition's disaster to Oñate in 1598.[80]

The fifth and final expedition of the period 1581–98 was that of explorer-colonizer Juan de Oñate, an aristocrat of New Spain, born in Zacatecas and holder of the king's mandate to settle New Mexico in much the same way as Menéndez had been given permission to colonize La Florida—with the exception that Oñate's enterprise was to be conducted entirely at his own expense. Although his royally authorized colonizing enterprise of 1598 was not intended primarily for exploration, Oñate, after establishing the first settlement in New Mexico at the junction of the Río Grande and the Río Chama, was an explorer thereafter. His contract with the king makes it clear that exploration was an intended product of his colonial enterprise and that Oñate was to search for, among other things, a strait through North America. Underestimating the distance across the continent (as did virtually all the Spaniards in New Spain), Oñate believed that New Mexico could be supplied by sea, perhaps via the Straits of Anián, which he hoped to locate to the north. He had even requested (and been granted) the right "to bring two ships annually to the Pueblo country."[81] En route from Santa Bárbara and Valle de San Bartolomé with his 400 men (130 with families), 83 wagons and carts, and more than 7,000 head of livestock, he and his nephew Vicente de Zaldívar opened a trail directly from the Río Conchos to the Río Grande del Norte near the later town of El Paso del Norte (present Ciudad Juárez). Here he officially took possession of New Mexico on 30 April 1598, thereby ensuring that El Paso and its later settlements would remain a part of New Mexico instead of Texas for the entire Spanish colonial era.

After founding San Juan de los Caballeros in July as the first Spanish community in New Mexico, Oñate turned to explorations east and west of the Río Grande valley. In the next seven years at least six expeditions, led by Oñate himself or by the brothers Vicente and Juan de Zaldívar, reconnoitered the territory from the Gulf of California to the Great Plains. In 1599, for example, Vicente de Zaldívar and sixty men, guided by Jusephe, the fugitive from the Leyva expedition, journeyed through Pecos Pueblo and northeastward on the Great Plains to hunt bison. Oñate in the same year made his first exploration going southward initially to visit the pueblos of Jumanos Indians and to find salt beds east of the mountains. Thereafter he marched westward in search of the "South Sea" (the Pacific Ocean or the Gulf of California), where he hoped to find pearls. His expedition visited Acoma, Zuñi, and the Hopi mesas, from which Oñate sent Captain Marcos Farfán with eight soldiers to find the mines that Espejo had discovered and reported near Jerome, Arizona. They set out on 17 November 1599, found an old shaft with blue ore in a wide vein, established mining claims, and brought back samples of what was copper ore and shells worn by the natives, who said the shells came from the ocean thirty days' journey to the west. Neither this expedition nor the later one of Zaldívar succeeded in reaching the Gulf of California.[82]

In spite of this failure to reach the Pacific, the Spanish belief in the proximity of the ocean to the newly established New Mexican colony persisted, and the official idea that the continent of North America was narrow did not diminish in strength. A Florida governor wrote in 1600 of reviving

Menéndez's interest in a route from the Atlantic to Zacatecas and suggested following a route laid down by Juan Pardo three decades earlier, crossing the Blue Ridge and traveling west "until we come upon the people from New Mexico."[83] The viceroy of New Spain, at the same time, noted that the distance between New Mexico and the newly established (and since lost) English colony at Roanoke "though not actually known, is not thought to be too great."[84] Nor would Oñate's own explorations into the Great Plains dispel the notion of the proximity of Atlantic and Pacific.

From 23 June to 24 November 1601, Oñate explored nearly seven hundred miles of territory on the Great Plains, marching with more than seventy men (including two Franciscan friars and the guide Jusephe), seven hundred horses and mules, eight carts (quite probably the first wheeled vehicles on the Great Plains), and four artillery pieces, traveling from Pecos Pueblo to the Pecos, Gallinas, and Canadian Rivers, following the last one eastward before turning north to the Arkansas River. Evidently Oñate reached the vicinity of today's Kansas River on this journey, which also met peaceful receptions at Apache *rancherias*, reported sightings of many bison, and discovered the site of the Native American attack on the Gutiérrez de Humaña party. From about the same point reached by Coronado six decades earlier, Oñate turned back because of the exhaustion of his draft animals and the restiveness of his men; had he not turned back, he later wrote, he could have reached the Atlantic, "which cannot be very far away."[85]

Three years later, from 7 October 1604 to 25 April 1605, Oñate led his last exploratory venture, this time westward in search of the South Sea. With thirty soldiers, Fray Francisco de Escobar, and lay brother Juan de Buenaventura, Oñate visited Zuñi and the Hopi villages, continued westward to the Little Colorado River (where some mining was done), then took Bill Williams Fork to the Colorado River, subsequently passing the mouth of the Gila River and discovering the mouth of the Colorado River where it entered the Gulf of California. On this journey Oñate encountered many new Native American nations and bands, established the feasibility of an overland route from New Mexico to the Gulf of California, erroneously concluded that Baja California was an island, explored much of today's Arizona, and left his mark permanently on Inscription Rock (El Morro) in western New Mexico during his return journey from Zuñi to the Río Grande.[86]

Thus by the time of his removal as governor of New Mexico, Oñate had clearly established himself as both a pathfinder and an explorer-colonizer.

And yet, in spite of the achievements of his explorations, the geographical image of New Mexico (and the entire Southwest) still remained so fuzzy in the minds of Spanish officialdom that the viceroy himself would comment that he was uncertain whether "the seven cities of Cíbola, discovered by fray Marcos de Niza and which Francisco Vásquez de Coronado tells of having visited," were "a part of the same . . . now under Don Juan de Oñate."[87] The mythical Straits of Anián existed, and the official Spanish view of the continent was of a narrow landmass with less than a thousand miles separating the Atlantic from the Pacific. Coming out of the Oñate explorations was the first map ever to show any part of the interior of the North American continent based on firsthand observation; on the back of this crude map (which shows portions of the courses of the Arkansas River and some of its major tributaries) is a note that describes the location of Quivira (central Kansas) as being approximately five hundred miles from the "the coast of Florida in the Mexican gulf."[88]

Exploratory expeditions during the seventeenth century from New Mexico and La Junta de los Ríos penetrated eastward mostly as missionary ventures in search of the Jumanos Indians, who demonstrated a willingness to convert to Christianity while seeking protection from their enemies on the southern plains. As early as 1629–32, Father Juan de Salas, escorted by soldiers, reached the Jumanos on the Nueces River (not the present Nueces, but the Río Conchos of western Texas), and Fray Alonso de Benavides visited the saline pueblos east of the Manzano Mountains before 1630. Captains Hernando Martín and Diego del Castillo conducted an expedition from New Mexico in 1650 to the Río Conchos region; four years later Captain Diego de Guadalajara with thirty soldiers from Santa Fe reached the same place.[89] Later explorations from El Paso del Norte after its occupation in 1659 and from La Junta de los Ríos properly belong to the exploration of Texas.

During the eighteenth century, Spanish explorations continued both eastward and westward from the settled Río Grande valley of New Mexico. They were conducted for various reasons: to rescue captive Pueblo Indians, to survey unexplored territory, to locate reported foreign interlopers (mostly Frenchmen), to establish trading alliances and friendly relations with plains peoples, and to open new trade routes between New Mexico on the one hand and Texas, Saint Louis, Pimería Alta, and Alta California on the other. Sergeant Juan de Ulibarri's military expedition of 1706 to rescue captive Picurís Indians from Apaches on the Great Plains also explored a region northeast of New Mexico into present southeastern Colorado and western Kansas. The group reached a place called "Cuartelejo," from archaeological evidence apparently in today's Scott County, Kansas. Ten years later Juan Páez Hurtado, with 36 soldiers, 52 settlers, and 150 Pueblo Indian auxiliaries, conducted an expedition to the Great Plains and reached the vicinity of today's Amarillo, Texas.

Spain's deep concern with French intrusions onto the Great Plains and trade with the Native Americans there led to two other explorations eastward from New Mexico. The first of these, led by Governor Antonio Valverde y Cosio, occurred in 1719, departing from Taos Pueblo on 20 September and reconnoitering southeastern Colorado before its return. In the following year Pedro de Villasur, with 42 soldiers and 70 Pueblo Indian auxiliaries, conducted an expedition northeastward from Santa Fe and Taos in search of reported French traders. It reached the area of the present junction of the Platte and Loup Rivers in central Nebraska but ended in disaster when Villasur and forty-four others died in an attack by Pawnee and Oto Indians.[90] Although these explorations carried Spaniards far into the western interior of the continent and must have added significantly to local knowledge and awareness of the Great Plains environment, they left no formal geographical lore in the form of journals or maps. Thus, for all practical purposes, the Spanish image of the continent was little different after this period of penetration of the Great Plains region than it had been before. The same cannot be said for the following expeditions into the areas adjacent to New Mexico—the great pathfinding explorations of the late eighteenth century by Father Francisco Atanasio Domínguez, Fray Escalante, Captain Anza, and Pedro Vial.

Domínguez and Escalante were Franciscan missionary explorers who blazed a long trail through today's western New Mexico, southwestern Colorado, eastern Utah, and northern Arizona. The origins of their exploration form an intriguing tale. By the 1760s, the Spanish from New Mexico had finally penetrated into the southern reaches of the Rocky Mountains in search of gold and silver. These mineral searches reached as far north and west as the junction of the Uncompahgre and Gunnison Rivers, and by 1775 a considerable amount of geographical lore on the southern Rockies had accumulated in the various mission settlements of New Mexico. The Franciscan missionary at the Zuñi pueblo, Fray Escalante, was more curious than most and collected as much information as he could from the gold and silver prospectors, hoping eventually to penetrate the mountain regions to the north and west and convert the native peoples there. Among the tales that Escalante had heard were stories of bearded natives to the northwest;

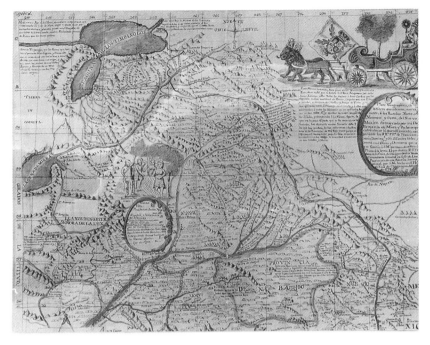

9.2 "Plano Géographico, de la tierra descubrierta, nuevamente, à los Rumbos Norte Noroeste y Oeste, del Nuevo Mexico" (Bernardo Miera y Pacheco, 1777). The Miera map is arguably one of the most important maps ever drawn of the American West, largely because it portrayed some real geographical features (the Utah lakes, for example) that did not appear on other maps for more than half a century and because it offered the initial cartographic verification of some mythical or apocryphal features (such as the Rio San Buenaventura). Speculation has it that Alexander von Humboldt relied heavily on this map in his great early-nineteenth-century map published in The Interior Provinces of New Spain. By permission of The British Library.

he concluded that they were survivors or descendants of survivors of Spanish ships wrecked on the California coast and concluded that he should go in search of them and, in the process, pioneer a new route from the New Mexican settlements to the new Spanish missions in California.

In the summer of 1776 Escalante and his companion Father Domínguez departed from the Río Grande valley of New Mexico to search for the "bearded Indians" and for a possible route from Santa Fe to Monterey, the newly established capital of Alta California. Accompanying them were eight men, including Bernardo Miera y Pacheco, a soldier-cartographer who would produce the greatest Spanish map of the western interior. This small party would end up as the first explorers of European extraction to enter the previously unknown lands of the Great Basin. Their trek took them north up the valley of the Río Grande and then northwest into southwestern Colorado, where they reported "ruins of large and ancient Indian settlements" (possibly Mesa Verde). From the headwater regions of the Gunnison River they traveled north into the upper Colorado River drainage and along the western side of the Rockies. This range of mountains, Miera noted, was "the backbone of North America, since the many rivers that are born of it empty into the two seas, the South Sea [Pacific] and the Gulf of Mexico." The expedition crossed the Green River in eastern Utah, which it named the Buenaventura River. From the Green, the party crossed to Utah Lake just south of the Great Salt Lake and then traveled southwest across the Utah Desert into northwestern Arizona until heading east and crossing the Colorado above the Grand Canyon at the site still known as "The Crossing of the Fathers." They traveled through the country of the Navajo ("all mesas and cliffs and is much lacking in water but they have sheep and goats and weave fine blankets")[91] and returned to Albuquerque in January 1777.

The travels of the Domínguez-Escalante party were recorded on a map drawn by Miera; although the map is a reasonably faithful reproduction of the territory covered by the expedition, particularly the complex drainage system of the central Rockies and adjacent regions, it also carried mythical material—such as the bearded Indians, with whom the fathers never came in contact. Most important for later generations were two geographical features: the "Laguna de los Timpanogos," a large lake north of Utah Lake that probably represented native informants' information about the Great Salt Lake and that verified the Spanish belief in a large interior lake, a belief current among the residents of northern New Spain since the mid–sixteenth century; and the Green River, called by the name that would haunt cartographers well into the next century—the "Rio San Buenaventura"—a stream that became synonymous with a water route to the Pacific Ocean from the central Rockies and that was still accepted by geographers as late as the travels of John C. Frémont in the 1840s. On a more positive note, Miera commented that the long-held Spanish belief in a Sea of Verrazzano or the Straits of Anián was probably a myth, since he and his Franciscan companions had traveled a great distance north without learning anything of such an arm of the Pacific. Miera's map was a landmark—not just for Spanish cartography but for North American cartography in general—and almost alone among the products of Spanish exploration, it came to the attention of the world community relatively soon, after it was used by Humboldt as the base map for his magnificent map of the American Southwest in *The Interior Provinces of New Spain*, published in 1815.[92] Although the missionaries did not reach their intended objective at Monterey and failed to establish an overland route between Santa Fe and Alta California, Escalante and Domínguez did explore an entirely new, vast region of the Great Basin and encountered many Native American nations and bands whom they hoped to convert to Christianity and westernize thereafter. Their expedition is one of the true epic treks in North American exploratory history.[93]

Three years after the return of the Domínguez-Escalante party, Governor Juan Bautista de Anza of New Mexico, with over six hundred Spaniards and Pueblo Indian allies, conducted a punitive expedition against raiding Comanches led by Cuerno Verde. While the intended purpose was not exploratory by nature, this expedition was the first to traverse the San Luis Valley of southern Colorado and northern New Mexico, visit the Pike's Peak region, and proceed southward from there along the eastern slope of the Rocky Mountains back to New Mexico. Thus it explored an extensive region that today comprises southeastern and south-central Colorado.[94] The Spanish, operating out of New Mexico, had now explored the eastern and western margins of the Colorado Rockies; although such exploration had doubtless added to an understanding in New Mexico of the mountainous region to the north, the significance of their endeavors for general geographical knowledge, and of their tendency to guard their geographical knowledge, is indicated by the fact that, at the time of the expedition of Meriwether Lewis and William Clark in 1804–6, Thomas Jefferson—more knowledgeable about the geography of the western interior than perhaps any other person—was not even aware of the existence of the central Rocky Mountains.

The final New Mexican expeditions were those of Pedro Vial, a Frenchman employed by Spain, who endeavored to locate routes and to open trade between Santa Fe on the one hand and San Antonio, Saint Louis, Natchitoches, and New Orleans on the other in the period from 1786 to 1806. His explorations over long trails across the Great Plains revealed the feasibility of trade between Spanish settlements. Likewise he blazed paths in 1792–93 that would later become the route of the Santa Fe Trail. Furthermore, he opened trade with many native nations, including the Comanches, Taovayas (Wichitas), Otos, and Pawnees. Alone or with small par-

9.3 *"Mapa geografico de una gran parte de la America Septentrionale . . ." (Manuel Agustín Mascaro, 1782). Mascaro's published map was the primary vehicle for the transmission of Spanish geographical lore to Europe and the world near the end of major Spanish exploration in North America. The results of the great explorations of the 1770s can clearly be seen on the map's interior portions. By permission of The British Library.*

ties, Vial traversed thousands of miles and was the first explorer and true pathfinder to show that Spanish communications and trade were possible from Santa Fe to Saint Louis, San Antonio, New Orleans, and Natchitoches.[95] Vial's estimation of distances, however, was still considerably foreshortened. In his diary he noted that had Indian troubles not turned him back, he could have reached the Mississippi from New Mexico in a twenty-five-day march; the actual distance is about twice that. Clearly, as late as Vial's journeys, the Spanish in New Mexico still held to the view that continental distances were much less than they actually are. Throughout the later period of the New Mexican colony, before independence in 1821, officials worried continually about an invasion from the British posts on Hudson Bay![96]

Vial's explorations of trade routes took him back and forth across New Mexico's neighboring province of Texas, a region that had been initially explored by Spaniards from three directions in the period 1519–43. Alvarez de Pineda explored the Texas coastline in 1519 as part of his maritime expedition from La Florida to the Río Pánuco. Cabeza de Vaca and his three companions trekked across southern Texas from Matagorda Bay to the Río Grande del Norte between 1528 and 1536. Moscoso and the remnants of the Soto expedition entered Texas from the east in 1542, reaching the vicinity of the Brazos River near today's Waco, Texas, before they returned to the Mississippi River. From the west in the summer of 1541, Coronado and his army penetrated the Texas Panhandle, discovering Palo Duro Canyon and traversing most of the rest of this region en route to and from Quivira. Finally, it should be noted that Caspar Castaño de Sosa's colonizing venture of 1590 crossed western Texas by following the Pecos River valley northward and that Oñate's exploration of the Great Plains in the fall of 1601 also penetrated the present state of Texas. Yet, further exploration of Texas awaited the seventeenth century, after many other northern frontiers of New Spain had been settled and consolidated. Missionary interests, first among the Jumano Indians of southwestern Texas and later among the Tejas tribes in eastern Texas, along with Spanish fears of French intrusion in the 1680s, became the principal motivating factors in the resumption of Spanish exploratory efforts, ultimately leading to the decision to colonize Texas, temporarily from 1690 to 1693 and permanently after 1716.

From La Junta de los Ríos (present Ojinaga, Chihuahua), Father Juan de Salas began to visit the lands of the Jumano Indians in 1629–32, reaching as far east and north as the Concho River of Texas (not to be confused with the Río Conchos in the state of Chihuahua). In 1683 two delegations of Jumanos visited Governor Antonio de Otermín at El Paso del Norte (present-day Ciudad Juárez), asking for missionaries and the opening of trade between them and Spanish settlements on the Río Grande. Juan Sabeata, a Jumano who had been baptized and now lived in the Native American villages at La Junta de los Ríos, asked for Spanish missionaries for his people on the plains and for their protection from the raids of Apaches near the "Nueces River" (the Concho River, not the present Nueces). On 15 December 1683, an expedition headed by Captain Juan Domínguez de Mendoza and Fray Nicolás López of La Junta de los Ríos set out first from Real de San Lorenzo, near El Paso del Norte, and later from the region of La Junta. Authorized by the governor of New Mexico (then residing at El Paso because of the Pueblo Revolt), this expedition was intended to examine the "Nueces River" country carefully, learn about the Jumanos and other native nations of the region, and bring back specimens of pearls reported to be found there. Fathers López and Juan Zavaleta were charged with the religious objectives of the expedition. Domínguez de Mendoza and López led the group across the Río Grande del Norte near La Junta de los Ríos and proceeded northward, passing probably close to today's Alpine and Fort Stockton in western Texas on 5 and 11 January 1684, respectively. Two days later the men reached the Salado River (the present Pecos River) and crossed it on 17 January, ultimately marching to the "Nueces" (Middle Concho River) on the thirty-first. Here, near today's San Angelo, Texas, they heard reports of friendly Native Americans in the "Kingdom of the Tejas" to the east and received messengers from there. Therefore, the expedition pushed on eastward some fifty miles, evidently arriving at a point on the Colorado River of Texas before deciding to return after having been attacked several times by Apaches. Back at La Junta de los Ríos by late May, this expedition had explored a vast new region of western Texas, taken possession for the king of Spain, and revealed much about the Native American inhabitants from the Río Grande del Norte eastward to the reported villages of the "Kingdom of the Tejas."[97]

Another exploratory expedition penetrating Texas did so from Coahuila between April and June 1675. It was authorized by the alcalde-mayor (the chief municipal officer) of Saltillo to cross the Río Grande del Norte in response to requests of Coahuiltecan Indians for missionaries. Fray Juan Larios, who had established a missionary station at Pueblo de Luna near Nuestra Señora de Guadalupe south of the Río Grande, accompanied by Fray San Buenaventura and an escort of ten soldiers led by Lieutenant Fernando del Bosque, was this expedition's principal leader. The party set out on 30 April 1675, crossed the Río Grande on 11 May near today's Eagle Pass, Texas, and continued to a point on the "Nueces River" (Middle Concho River) in present Edwards County, Texas. The Larios-Bosque expedition, though it failed to establish missions north of the Río Grande, was the first authenticated one to cross this river below the Pecos River and travel from there into today's Texas. On its return, having encountered many Coahuiltecan Indians who desired to receive missionaries, its coleader, Bosque, recommended that Spain establish three settlements of missionaries in Texas, all protected by a presidio of not less than seventy soldiers.[98] Yet colonization did not result, probably because the French threat from La Salle's establishment of Fort Saint Louis on Garcitas Creek in Texas caused Spanish authorities to shift their attention to another region, nearer the coastline of Texas.

La Salle's reported journey and presence somewhere on the Gulf coast of Texas caused a frenzy of activity by Spanish authorities, who dispatched four maritime expeditions between 1686 and 1688 from Veracruz and La Florida and five overland expeditions in the period 1686–91, first from Nuevo León and later from Coahuila. All had the same basic objective: to locate the French leader and his force, destroy any French settlement, and remove all Frenchmen as captives from the designated area belonging to Spain. While the seagoing expeditions found nothing but the wrecks of La Salle's ships, the land ones, led by Captain Alonso de León, gradually reached farther eastward until they found concrete evidence of the site of the French fort on Garcitas Creek. De León originally set out from Monterrey, Nuevo León, with fifty men in late 1685, but he reached only the southern bank of the Río Grande before returning along the Mexican coast and the Río de las Palmas in 1686. His second expedition began in the following year from Coahuila, where de León had become governor and captain of the presidio at Monclova. It crossed the Río Grande but turned back a short distance beyond. In 1688 his third venture again crossed the river and finally encountered one Frenchman, Juan Jarri, who had survived the destruction of the fort by Karankawa Indians and was now living among natives in southern Texas. De León brought Jarri (also called "Juanillo") back with him to Coahuila and then sent the Frenchman under escort to the viceroy in Mexico City.[99]

Ordered by the new viceroy, the Conde de Galve, to find and destroy La Salle's settlement, de León marched from Monclova on his fourth exploration on 23 March 1689. With him went forty men from the presidios of Nueva Vizcaya and an equal number of men from those of Nuevo León.

Guided by Juanillo and a native named Quems, they reached the Río Grande near the later site of the presidio of San Juan de Bautista on 1 April, crossed it, and continued eastward and northeastward to the Río Guadalupe, which they crossed near today's Victoria, Texas, on 15 April. With Father Damián Massanet, the two Native American guides, and twenty-five soldiers composing the advance party and de León following with the main body, on 22 April they found the remains of Fort Saint Louis on Garcitas Creek about five miles above its mouth. Father Massanet described the scene of devastation there, with houses sacked and burned, chests broken open, and three yet unburied bodies (including one woman) on an open field. The following day the expedition continued to Bahía del Espíritu Santo (Matagorda Bay), where they saw the wrecks of La Salle's vessels. Marching back to Fort Saint Louis on 25 April, they soon had two unexpected visitors. Juan de L'Archeveque and Santiago Grollette, two Frenchmen clad in antelope skins, reached de León's camp, and the cacique of the Tejas Indians also paid them a visit. On 3 May, de León's force headed back toward Coahuila, with the two Frenchmen accompanying it. The expedition crossed and named the Nueces River in recognition of the many pecan trees found there and arrived at Monclova ten days later. De León then sent the two French captives to the viceroy in Mexico City with news that eighteen other Frenchmen were reportedly living among the Tejas Indians.[100]

De León's fifth and final expedition was a follow-up to the fourth one. Instructed by the viceroy to inspect Matagorda Bay carefully, ascertain if any Frenchmen were still living in the region, burn the remains of the fort, and communicate with the Tejas Indians to find out if they were willing to receive ministers of the Holy Gospel, the governor of Coahuila again left Monclova between 26 and 28 March 1690. With him went ninety soldiers from Sombrerete, Zacatecas, Saltillo, and Nuevo León (twenty additional soldiers from Nueva Vizcaya had been authorized but had not yet arrived and would join de León later on the trail), as well as Father Massanet and four other priests, one lay brother, 150 loads of flour, 200 cattle, 400 horses, and 50 firelocks. They traveled over the same route de León had used in the previous year and reached the site of Fort Saint Louis on 25 May. After seeing no traces of Frenchmen there, they burned the fort, inspected Matagorda Bay, and departed from their camp on the Guadalupe River, heading for the villages of the Tejas Indians in eastern Texas. Joined by the soldiers from Nueva Vizcaya en route, the full party crossed the Colorado River of Texas, saw herds of bison, and encountered two French boys, Pedro Muni

(Pierre Meunier) and Pedro (Pierre) Talon, before entering the first village of Tejas Indians. On 26 May, de León and Father Massanet selected a site for the establishment of a mission on the Neches River, erecting the first Texas mission, dedicated to San Francisco, on 1 June. Leaving priests and three soldiers there, de León and Father Massanet led the rest of the expedition, including the two French boys, on its return to Monclova, arriving there in early July.[101]

This last expedition of de León led directly to the occupation of eastern Texas by Coahuila's new governor, Domingo de Terán, and the founding of three missions there in 1691. This venture also stopped along the banks of the Río San António, held the first Catholic Mass at the site, and noted the fertility of and the abundance of water in the region and the friendliness of nearby Coahuiltecan Indians. Although the eastern Texas missions were abandoned in 1693, the explorations of de León and Father Massanet planted the seeds that bore fruit with the reoccupation of Texas in 1716 and the settlement of San António de Béxar (present San Antonio, Texas) two years later. In the early 1720s the Marqués de San Miguel de Aguayo reinforced the Texas settlements and established a presidio at La Bahía, which was later moved twice and was ultimately located at its permanent site near today's Goliad, Texas.

In the century that followed, until Mexico's independence from Spain in 1821, exploration largely occurred from within the province of Texas instead of from other regions of northern New Spain, except for the expeditions of Vial. Three centers of population developed in the region: San António and San Fernando de Béxar, La Bahía, and eastern Texas (Los Adaes at first and Nacogdoches later). The growth of the cattle industry led to an interest in improving trade with Coahuila, Nuevo León, New Orleans, and New Mexico, thereby promoting Vial's explorations. Likewise the presence of large numbers of Spanish mustangs promoted the horse-catching ventures of Philip Nolan, who penetrated the boundaries of Texas legally at first and illegally later near the turn of the century, reaching the vicinity of the Brazos River near present Waco, Texas. Finally the objective of establishing friendly relations and trade with the natives led to explorations and settlements such as the missionary-presidio site at San Sabá in the period 1757–72 and resulted in the treaties arranged by Athanase de Mézières with the "Naciones del Norte" in northeastern Texas and along the Red River in the latter half of the eighteenth century. With this, exploration northward by Spain was nearly over; the contributions to general geographical knowledge had been minor, although the Texas rivers began to appear on a number of European maps as early as the mid–eighteenth century. To the west, however, a similar process had been going on—in Pimería Alta and Alta California—and these explorations did add appreciably to the fund of European and American geographical information on the Southwest.

Between the Altar River in Sonora and the Gila River in present Arizona lay the territory designated by Spaniards as Pimería Alta, or the upper land of the Pima Indians. It was not a separate province during the Spanish period but a part of the combined one of Sinaloa and Sonora. Jesuit missionary Father Kino began the exploration of Pimería Alta from 1687 until his death in 1711, establishing mission stations ranging south and north of the present international border between the United States and Mexico, with his headquarters at Nuestra Señora de Dolores. Although other Jesuits, as well as military officers, conducted explorations in Pimería Alta after Father Kino's death, the region became important to Spain after the Pima Revolt of 1751 and the occupation of Alta California (today's California) in 1769. In fact, it became important primarily as a land route between Sonora and Alta California, thus tying the two regions into a close relationship that promoted exploration.

Father Kino reached Pimería Alta and founded his first mission there after February 1687. Thus began twenty-four years of missionary activity, exploration, and writing. According to his own account, he made more than fifty expeditions. These journeys discovered new lands and Native Americans to the north and west. Several times he explored the Gila River, and twice he descended the Colorado River below the mouth of the Gila, once reaching the Gulf of California and crossing beyond it into Baja California. He discovered that the Sea or Gulf of California "ended completely," concluding that Sir Francis Drake had been wrong and that "California is not an island," as it had appeared intermittently on European maps since the mid–sixteenth century. Therefore he proved that a land route was possible between Sonora and Baja California. His map was the earliest to show the Gila and Colorado Rivers in their approximate true geographical context, along with much of southern Arizona, according to information derived from his explorations with Lieutenant Juan Mateo Manje in 1692 and again in 1693.

Father Kino penetrated today's Arizona first in 1691 and again in 1694. Reaching the valley of the Santa Cruz River on his first *entrada*, he became the second European and the first since Coronado to enter this region of Arizona. In 1694 he discovered the ruins of Casa Grande and reached the Gila River. Subsequently he established three missions within the present boundaries of Arizona: at San Xavier del Bac near today's Tucson and at Guevavi and Tumacácori, both between Tucson and Nogales. Father Kino's explorations revealed the geography of Pimería Alta, and his missions led to the establishment of friendly relations with the Pimas. Furthermore, on his expeditions he succeeded in creating friendly relations with the Cocomaricopa, Yuma, and other native nations near the junction of the Gila and Colorado Rivers. Without doubt, he exemplifies both the pathfinder and the explorer-colonizer in the overall development of Spanish exploration and penetration of interior North America.[102] Moreover, he left a series of maps—at least one of which was published in 1705 in the Jesuit *Missionary Letters*—which were eventually absorbed into general European cartography and increased exponentially the geographical understanding of the California region and the lower Colorado River basin.[103]

After the expulsion of the Jesuits from New Spain and other overseas kingdoms in 1767, and the occupation of Alta California two years later, Fray Francisco Garcés, a Franciscan, became the missionary at San Xavier del Bac. From there, in the decade of the 1770s, he became a major explorer of the Gila River valley to its junction with the Colorado River. Likewise, he extended his work to the Native Americans of the Yuma region until his death in the uprising of 1781 there. In 1771 he made his initial journey along the Gila River, reaching near its mouth at the Colorado River but missing the actual junction of the two rivers. His explorations continued west of the Colorado into the Imperial Valley of today's California. He and Father Juan Díaz accompanied Anza's reconnoitering expedition of 1774 to find a land route between Tubac in Pimería Alta to Alta California, and Fray Garcés joined Anza's colonizing expedition of 1775–76 to California.

Garcés remained among the Yumas on this latter expedition instead of proceeding with Anza all the way to Alta California. From here he explored extensively, visiting the Native Americans of the lower Colorado River region, descending that river to its mouth, and exploring lands near the head of the Gulf of California. Later in the same year of 1776 he conducted a major exploratory expedition north of the junction of the Gila and Colorado Rivers, ascending the latter before striking out westward to find another route to San Gabriel in Alta California via the Mojave River and Cajón Pass. From San Gabriel, near today's Los Angeles, he trekked northward, endeavoring to blaze a new trail through interior California to present Bakersfield and Tulare Lake, before turning eastward to the Colorado River. There, after crossing the river, he continued eastward to the pueblos of the Hopis of eastern Arizona, hoping to open communications with them and convert them to Christianity. Thus Garcés pioneered a new trail across northern Arizona, on a journey that traversed previously unexplored lands.

Three years later Garcés and another missionary were ordered by the viceroy to go to the junction of the Colorado and Gila Rivers to establish missions among the Yumas. With Father Juan Díaz and an escort of twelve soldiers, Garcés proceeded westward from the valley of the Santa Cruz River to the intended site, arriving in August 1779. For the next two years he labored against the difficulties of isolation, shortages of food, scarcity of provisions, and insufficient financial support, but he succeeded in founding two mission settlements with both military and civilian inhabitants combined in each community. On 17 July 1781, the Yumas rose in rebellion during the visit of Captain Fernando de Rivera y Moncada and forty families of colonists from Sonora en route to Alta California. Two days later the rebellious Native Americans killed Fray Garcés.[104] An accomplished cartographer, Garcés left a number of maps in the archives in Seville; unfortunately, none of them became available to European cartographers, and the results of his explorations were not fully understood until the nineteenth century.

The expeditions of Juan Bautista de Anza, presidial captain of Tubac, whom Fray Garcés accompanied, took place in the period 1774–76. The intent was first to explore and open a land route between Pimería Alta and the new Spanish settlements of Alta California, thereby reducing their dependence on the port of San Blas and on supply by sea from New Spain. Once the route had been explored, Anza on his second expedition was to lead colonists from Sinaloa and Sonora to populate and strengthen Spain's hold on Alta California. Anza set out on his exploratory expedition from Tubac on 8 January 1774, accompanied by Fathers Garcés and Díaz, twenty soldiers from the presidio of Tubac, an Alta California soldier, a Pima interpreter, and eight other Native Americans—thirty-three in all. With 35 packloads of provisions, 65 head of cattle, and 140 horses, the expedition traveled southwestward to the Pima missions of Altar and Caborca. Following trails earlier marked by Fathers Kino and Garcés, Anza continued westward to the junction of the Colorado and Gila Rivers, where he was warmly received by Chief Salvador Palma and the Yumas. Crossing the Colorado River, Anza and his small party proceeded westward, attempting to cross the sand dunes of the Colorado Desert but instead turning southwest to go around them. Crossing the Sierra Nevada, they reached San Gabriel on 22 March after a journey of seven hundred miles from

Tubac. From San Gabriel, Anza and part of his force moved northward to Monterey and returned to Pimería Alta, arriving back at Tubac on 26 May.[105]

Having explored a route to Alta California, Anza with his second expedition of 240 colonists, including 155 women and children, in 1775–76 marched to San Gabriel, using a shorter route along the Gila River valley to its junction with the Colorado River and then following the previously explored trail through southern California to its destination.[106] Along with Garcés, he had pioneered what would come to be known as "the Old Spanish Trail." The sketch maps produced by Anza were duplicated and embellished by Miera, and like Miera's map of the Domínguez-Escalante exploration, they became available to Humboldt in the early nineteenth century and formed an important part of the base data used by the German geographer in his 1811 master map of the Southwest, "Map of the Kingdom of New Spain," which remained the best cartographic representation of the region until American military explorers and boundary surveyors moved into the area after the Mexican War.

Among the Spanish penetrations into interior California by land exploration, few took place away from the coast between 1769 and 1800. One of them, a small force led by Sergeant José Francisco de Ortega, accidentally discovered San Francisco Bay on 1 November 1769 while en route from Monterey in search for Drake's Bay. Garcés, as related previously, had ascended the San Joaquín Valley to Tulare Lake in 1776, the same year in which José Joaquín Moraga crossed the San Joaquín River, but little systematic exploration of interior California occurred until the second administration of Governor José Joaquín de Arrillaga (1802–14). Father Juan Martín explored eastward into today's Kern County, reaching Tulare Lake in 1804, and in the following year Father Pedro de la Cueva of Mission San José ventured ten to fifteen miles to the east before being attacked by natives. Yet Governor Arrillaga was not deterred, and he promoted the search for possible mission sites in the interior as a solution to his problem of preventing the flight of mission Indians to unconverted tribes there.[107]

Four expeditions were made into the interior in 1806, the most important one headed by Alférez ("Sublieutenant") Gabriel Moraga, starting with twenty-five men and Father Pedro Muñoz from San Juan Bautista on 21 September. Penetrating the San Joaquín Valley and crossing its major river, the party discovered a slough, which they named "Mariposas" (Butterflies), found the Merced River, and passed over many other rivers as they marched first northward and later southward to the Kern River and Tejón Pass, finally reaching San Fernando, north of today's Los Angeles, on 3 November after two and one-half months of exploration. Moraga thereafter became California's greatest interior explorer, a true pathfinder, for the next decade and a half. In 1808 he journeyed northward to explore the river country as a possible site for the establishment of additional missions in northern California. Leaving Mission San José on 25 September with eleven men, he forded the San Joaquín River near today's Stockton, ascended the Calaveras River to its source in the Sierra Nevada, proceeded northward to the vicinity of today's American River, and camped on the banks of the Feather River. Crossing it, he marched westward to the upper Sacramento River before returning to San José on 23 October. In 1810 he headed expeditions to the Carquines Strait and today's Suisun region, primarily as a retaliatory campaign to punish Native Americans who had committed depredations on the Christian communities, and later in the same year he conducted several shorter interior explorations. From 1812 to 1814 Moraga made three overland journeys to the Russian settlements at Bodega Bay and Fort Ross, becoming acquainted with the terrain of present-day Marin and Sonoma Counties north of San Francisco. Expeditions to capture runaway mission Native Americans occurred after 1815, and Moraga (now a lieutenant) in 1819 headed one of them to capture fugitives and to punish Mojaves for an attack on San Buenaventura. Departing from San Gabriel on 22 November, he crossed Cajón Pass and marched across the Mojave Desert to the vicinity of the eastern boundary of California before returning on 14 December. This was his last known exploration or campaign, but his achievements as a pathfinder revealed much about interior California, its river valleys, its mountains, and its passes while providing information that would be useful in the expansion of California under Mexico in the years that followed.[108]

What Christopher Columbus initiated with the discovery of America in October 1492 was an age of exploration that in North America spanned three centuries of further exploration, conquest, and settlement led by Spanish soldiers, missionaries, civil authorities, and friendly Native American allies. The expeditions were undertaken for various motives: to search for mythical kingdoms, wealth, the Straits of Anián, slaves, and runaway Christian natives; to establish Catholic missions in which to convert Native Americans to Roman Catholicism and westernize them; to defend Spain's far-flung holdings from European rivals, such as the French, British, and Russians; to explore and reveal the geography and inhabitants of many *tierras desconocidas* ("unknown lands"); to provide economic gain for both individuals and the king; and to locate sites for future expansion and settlement. These ventures numbered in the hundreds when one considers all those made for exploration as well as the numerous punitive campaigns.

Gradually pathfinders opened a vast region of North America stretching from La Florida to Alta California and from Nueva Galicia and Nueva Vizcaya in the central part of New Spain to the present Southwest of the United States. They were supplemented by explorer-colonizers, who planted Spanish communities, settlers, and institutions permanently in the lands they explored in North America. Their pioneering efforts were accomplished with great human hardships, were often supported by relatively few men, and were tenuously financed at best. That they succeeded is evident. Their explorations and discoveries not only covered a vast area reaching from the Atlantic Ocean to the Pacific but contributed greatly to the expansion of the many facets of geographical knowledge of North America's interior and facilitated the permanent settlement of northern New Spain as well as the present-day southwestern and southeastern United States.

Pathfinders and explorer-colonizers replaced myths with realities but sometimes also created new myths concerning the geography of the continent. Perhaps their greatest significance was in the human aspect of their many explorations. The experience of each venture demonstrated the courage, fortitude, and leadership of explorers, both those who led and those who participated. Simultaneously, the explorers reported intensively and extensively on the Native Americans whom they met, thereby providing much information about native groups: organization, economies, societies, customs, traditions, and languages. Such information enabled Europeans to understand better the original inhabitants of the Americas and provides us with one of the most important historical sources on Native American cultures.

The Spanish penetration of the interior of North America in the two thrusts into La Florida and northern New Spain was a long, arduous, and successful experience. As historian John B. Brebner once observed, "The whole train of North American events runs in a continuous line from the work of Columbus."[109] Spanish explorers were the advance agents in the *encuentro de dos mundos*, or the "meeting of two worlds." In this role they not only sought material gain and many other goals but also furthered advancements in knowledge and brought two distinct peoples and cultures—European and Native American—into contact with each other to begin the creation of the concept of America.

10 / Early French Exploration in the North American Interior

CONRAD HEIDENREICH

During the seventeenth century, the French penetrated from the Saint Lawrence Valley to the Great Lakes and eventually across the drainage divide west to the Mississippi, south to the Gulf of Mexico, and north to Hudson Bay. Considering the few people involved, the distances covered, and the difficult physical obstacles faced, this was a magnificent achievement, made even more significant when compared with the absence of any similar exploration by the Dutch and the English inland from the Atlantic seaboard and the shores of Hudson Bay during the same period.

This chapter outlines the achievements of French seventeenth-century inland exploration. Prefacing the substantive section on the actual voyages of exploration is a brief discussion of French exploration as a scientific process and a discussion of the main factors that influenced the progress of exploration over time. These discussions furnish the structure as well as some of the necessary background for the more substantive portions of the chapter. Wherever possible, the discussion presented here has been based on primary documents and maps.

The Nature of Exploration

Most seventeenth-century French journeys of exploration and discovery for which the documentation has survived tended to begin by defining general or specific aims. This step was followed by gathering information from natives or coureurs de bois who were inclined to share knowledge. Finally, guides were hired, equipment was assembled, such as canoes and trade goods to pay for food and further information, and the journey was undertaken. On their return, many explorers presented verbal, written, and/or cartographic reports of what they had discovered. These precise steps were followed not because the people involved planned their work in such a systematic manner but because these steps were a rational way in which to proceed. The impetus for all exploratory ventures arose from occasionally specific and, in most cases, multiple motives. There was no such thing as aimless exploration. Aims were discussed, goals defined, and orders given in verbal form or, in the case of a major effort, in terms of a written commission. Whether or not the immediate aim of an expedition was narrowly defined—such as a military expedition into hostile lands or the establishment of trading and diplomatic relations with a remote native group—all French exploration had at its roots four general aims: (1) staking territorial claims against other European powers; (2) discovering major passages to the west, north, and south across the continent; (3) missionizing native groups; and (4) searching for exploitable natural resources, especially furs and minerals. These are the motives that drew the French into the interior when circumstances permitted. Curiously, few of these motives were present in any discernible form among the Dutch and the English who had settled the Atlantic coast. There was little English exploration except the hunting expeditions of settlers into the woods and valleys to the rear of their settlements. Except for an expedition by Harmen Meyndertsen van den Bogaert to the Mohawk country in 1634, much the same can be said of the Dutch. Both Dutch and English societies were primarily inward-looking, obsessed with local matters; the only important motives for action were the farm, the local community, and the dictates of an uncompromising religion.

Methods of exploration and the technology used by the French were developed early in the seventeenth century, largely by Samuel de Champlain and his contemporaries. Although Champlain may not have been the first to realize that inland exploration could be carried out only with native help, he was the one who pioneered the methods that would eventually carry the French to the foothills of the Rocky Mountains. Nothing could be farther from reality than the popular misconception of the intrepid explorer pushing into the wilderness to make discoveries. Although the interior was unknown and a wilderness to the Europeans, it was neither to the native inhabitants. Champlain realized very early that interior exploration was impossible without native cooperation. First, peaceful relations had to be negotiated with the local native population and then a secure base of operations established. All the sixteenth-century French expeditions foundered because they did not take these two steps before they ventured away from the security of their ships. Next, Champlain questioned natives about the geography of the rivers and lakes that were beyond the limits of French knowledge. Wherever possible, he would get several independent accounts and compare them. Not trusting the earlier method of developing translators and guides by kidnapping them, he began the important custom of exchanging French and native youths so that each might learn the language and customs of the other. This method, he and the native leaders agreed, would establish trust between the two sides and keep both well informed. All previous expeditions had foundered when it came to using European technology on inland exploration. Champlain was the first to trust himself and his men to travel in canoes with natives as guides and with native provisions. Whenever possible, travel was by rivers and lakes, rarely overland by foot and never by horse. Terrain conditions simply did not permit the latter two methods.

The nature of the data gathered was often dependent on the aims of a voyage and the interests and competence of the observer, all of which varied over time. At the most basic level, data were gathered on transportation routes (rivers and lakes), major vegetation species, fish, animal life, minerals, and locations of native groups. Some explorers observed distance, latitude, and compass directions. Beginning in the 1630s, Jesuit missionaries timed lunar eclipses in order to calculate longitude. A few explorers, especially in the first half of the seventeenth century when contact with native groups was still a relatively novel experience, made very detailed observations of native life, even compiling dictionaries of native languages.

Although almost a truism, it is nevertheless worth stating that an increase in geographical knowledge did not occur unless the explorer knew where he had been and could describe to others what he had found and how to repeat the journey. A description of findings in an organized and unambiguous manner is therefore a vital part of the exploratory process. Unquestionably, much information was transmitted in verbal form, since not all explorers were literate. Others kept diaries or wrote and published extraordinarily detailed accounts, often accompanied by maps. In fact, the matter of keeping records was considered of such importance that in 1670 the intendant of New France, Jean Talon, ordered all explorers to keep diaries and to report on their journeys when they returned. In 1686 the cartographer Jean-Baptiste-Louis Franquelin was appointed at Québec to interview returning explorers, with the view of keeping the maps of New France up-to-date. Maps were considered an essential method of documenting the entire process of exploration and discovery. Much information has undoubtedly been lost over time or was never properly recorded. However, some information, perhaps most of it, has survived, permitting one to piece together a fairly complete account of at least primary exploration.

Most explorers were simply content to describe what they saw. Only a few attempted to place their discoveries into a broader geographical context. This task was usually done by professional cartographers and cosmographers back in France. An exception was the Jesuit missionaries, some of whom tried to adapt discoveries to theoretical constructs of North American geography, whereas others theorized on native customs, behaviour, and origin. Although many individuals made qualitative assessments of what the New World had to offer, Champlain also attempted a quantitative assessment.

The discoveries that were reported and the hypotheses that were recorded about further discoveries to be made eventually led to more exploration. Beyond what was known, there was always another river and another lakes system to be explored; perhaps the route across the continent, which reason and rumor dictated, was there. There was always another group of natives to be contacted for trade and/or attempted conversion to Christianity, and there was always more territory to claim for the Catholic king against the Dutch and English who were clinging to the Atlantic coast.

Major Periods of French Exploration

Human endeavours never progress smoothly over time. They usually move through periods of vitality interspersed by periods of relative inactivity. French seventeenth-century exploration of the interior was no exception to this rule. Although the basic motives that drew the French to the interior changed little over time, except for occasional shifts in emphasis, the actual progress of exploration was largely determined by a number of broadly interrelated factors: relations with native groups or individuals; relations with the Dutch and English; and a number of internal concerns, principally the fur trade and missionary efforts. Since ecclesiastical and government powers were centralized and pervasive, policies formulated by these bodies strongly influenced the above factors.

Probably the most important factor that influenced seventeenth-century French exploration was the relationships established with native groups. The French obtained geographical information from natives, hired them as guides, traveled with natives, lived among them, and learned from them. Almost all would-be explorers knew that they would not get far without native help. To work with natives effectively, the French had to establish peace with those among whom they settled and had to forge diplomatic ties with others through existing native alliance systems. When necessary, alliance systems were extended to other, more remote groups. Such procedures took time and, in the case of some native groups, were not always successful over a prolonged period. In any case, the French-native alliance networks benefited not only exploration but also the fur trade, the mission field, and French territorial expansion. Since good native relations lay at the core of French success in North America, these networks were not left to chance. Both the government and the ecclesiastical authorities shaped policies and saw to it that they were carried out. Complicating the problem of forging good native relations, however, was the warfare that had been plaguing the Saint Lawrence–Great Lakes area since before European contact. Native alliances were for defence and war against mutual enemies. The partners within the alliance system traded with each other and on occasion exchanged people. The French, wanting to trade with various native groups and enlist native help in exploration, were obliged to join existing native alliance systems and eventually prove their worth by participating with their allies in warfare. Whenever there was serious warfare, or whenever good relations with a native group could not be established, French endeavours—be they missions, trade, or exploration—were disrupted.

Whereas good French relations with the native groups were fundamental to the course of exploration, relations with the European powers, especially the English, also affected it. Although neither the Dutch nor the English conducted any significant inland exploration, their presence affected French fur trade and native relations. Some French exploring and military expeditions were undertaken to forestall English commercial expansion and perceived territorial ambitions into areas the French considered to be in their commercial interest.

The fur trade and missions were two other endeavours that significantly affected exploration, as did government directives associated with these activities. Although exploration was never forbidden, occasionally circumstances did not actively encourage it. From 1633 to the late 1660s, Frenchmen, except missionaries and their associates, were forbidden to travel into the interior unless they had special permission. This was ordered by the government to encourage natives to bring their furs to the Saint Lawrence posts, to allow the missionaries a free hand in their work, and to keep Frenchmen on the Saint Lawrence farms, where they were needed. Although illegal travel and trade occurred, this obviously had to be kept quiet, since the penalties for getting caught were severe. Consequently, if new territories were probed by coureurs de bois, as these illegal traders were called, little information of their exploration would have come down to us. The explorers of this period were the missionaries, who by training and many also by inclination were eminently suited to the task.

In 1663 the administration of New France was reorganized. The colony became a royal province of France and was given, among other officials, an intendant who held the special task of developing its economy. The first intendant to take office in New France was Jean Talon. Forbidden by his minister, Jean-Baptiste Colbert, to build trading posts in the interior and have Frenchmen engage directly in the fur trade, Talon, encouraged by Governor Daniel de Rémy de Courcelle, sponsored exploring expeditions. The task of these men was to encourage established native customers to continue coming to the Saint Lawrence posts and to contact new native groups and encourage them as well. Other aims of these expeditions were to search for minerals and to stake French territorial claims against English encroachment. These efforts vastly expanded French knowledge, especially after 1668, when these policies were put into effect.

As time progressed, keeping Frenchmen out of the interior became increasingly difficult. In 1681 the stricture against traveling west of Montreal to trade was lifted in favour of a licensing system. The effect was an increase in the flood of traders to the interior, many without licenses; these traders accelerated exploration. As direct French involvement in the fur trade increased, the role of missionaries in exploration became ancillary. Notwithstanding their secondary role, the missionaries remained prime conveyors of information on the results of exploration.

These, then, were the broad factors that, in combination, were in large part responsible for changes in the process of exploration. Considering these changes, one can divide seventeenth-century French exploration into three major periods. The first period runs from 1600 to about 1650. The first of three phases of this period was dominated by the activities of Champlain and ended in 1613 with his unsuccessful journey up the Ottawa River. During this important phase in exploration, the French built their settlements and established good native relations to the extent that inland exploration became possible. The second phase ended in 1629 when the English took over Québec for the next four years. During this phase, the French pushed exploration to the eastern Great Lakes and began to live among the natives, especially the Hurons. During the third phase, after 1632, Jesuit missionaries extended and consolidated knowledge of the Saint Lawrence and eastern Great Lakes area through their own explorations and the descriptions they put together into journals and maps. The period came to an abrupt end in 1650 when the Iroquois wars terminated the French presence west of Montreal.

In 1654 a peace made with the western Iroquois groups for four years reopened the interior to the French. During this second period (1654–65), attention focused on three areas: the Iroquois country became better known through Jesuit missionaries; Lakes Michigan and Superior were penetrated by coureurs de bois and Jesuits; and the first probes were made up the rivers north of the Saint Lawrence toward Hudson Bay by traders and missionaries. This period was a prelude to the final one, which began in about 1665 with the administrative reorganization of New France, the defeat of the Iroquois, and the beginning of a government-sponsored exploration programme. Although the trend toward greater French activity in the interior is plainly visible before 1665, it is clear that Rémy de Courcelle's and Jean Talon's decision to encourage exploring expeditions in 1668, competition from the fledgling Hudson's Bay Company by 1670, and Jean-Baptiste Colbert's decision in 1681 to pardon the coureurs de bois and issue licenses to travel to the Great Lakes gave a tremendous impetus to exploration. During the last third of the century, the Great Lakes area became completely known, and expeditions crossed the Great Lakes divide both to Hudson Bay and to the Mississippi. This was a period of rapid French expansion during which furs poured into Montreal and, after 1684, wars raged with the Iroquois. By the mid-1690s the Iroquois were being defeated and a glut of beaver pelts had saturated the market. These two events prompted the French Crown to close most of the interior posts in 1696 and to order the return of the traders and soldiers to the colony, thus bringing to an end a century of exploration.

Period 1: 1600 to 1650

Pioneering Exploration on the Saint Lawrence River (1600–1613)
During the last quarter of the sixteenth century, official French interest in the New World was rekindled. In addition to the important fisheries and the beginning of a profitable fur trade on the Atlantic coast and the Gulf of

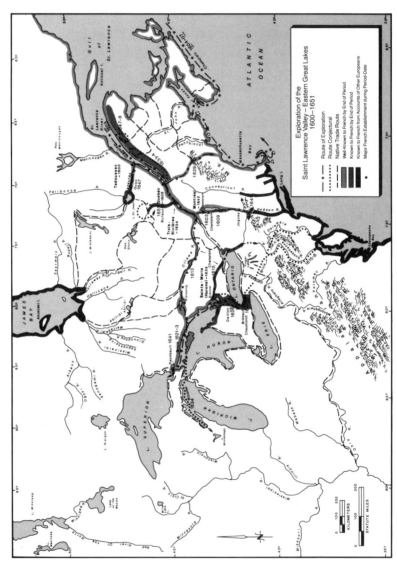

Map 10.1 Exploration of the Saint Lawrence Valley–Eastern Great Lakes, 1600–1651.

Saint Lawrence, a quickening interest in the area by the English convinced the French Crown that something had to be done to consolidate French claims. As everyone knew, the obvious way to do that was to establish colonies, to begin exploration, and to stake formal claims of possession. The problem, however, was that neither the Crown nor the merchants who traded in the area had the capital to undertake colonizing ventures. The only practical solution was for the Crown to grant a monopoly on trade on the condition that settlement and exploration be carried out. The first such monopoly was granted in 1577 but was not taken up by its recipient, the Marquis de La Roche de Mesgouez, until 1598. In the meantime another attempt was made to acquire a monopoly, this one by Jacques Noël and Chaton de La Jannaye. Noël was a nephew of Jacques Cartier and claimed that his uncle had never been properly paid for his services, while La Jannaye also claimed that he was owed money by the king. Persuaded by the claimants, Henri III granted a monopoly early in 1588, conditional on colonization and exploration. However, the merchants trading in the Gulf of Saint Lawrence and on the river, backed by the towns out of which they operated, objected so strongly in favour of free trade that the monopoly was rescinded before an expedition could be mounted.[1] The opposing views of the "free traders," who were interested in maximizing profits, and the "monopolists," who promised financial support for settlement and missionaries in return for exclusive trading rights, were a recurring theme in the economic development of New France.

Ten years after the aborted venture of Noël and La Jannaye, La Roche reappeared on the scene, ready to take up the monopoly that had been promised to him. King Henri IV, reminded that his predecessor, Henri III, had already made such a grant to La Roche, renewed it with the stipulation that La Roche take claim of the country, build a settlement, subdue the local inhabitants, and propagate the faith among them.[2] La Roche's choice of a location for his settlement was unfortunate: Sable Island, just over one hundred miles east of Canada's maritime coast in the Atlantic. In 1603, after five years of untold hardship, the last miserable remnant of eleven colonists out of an original sixty, was rescued from the island.

Scarcely had La Roche's monopoly been taken up when Pierre Chauvin de Tonnetuit, a former officer to Henri IV, also applied for a monopoly in the trade. On 22 November 1599, Chauvin was granted an exclusive monopoly on the condition that he "should colonise the country [Canada] and form a settlement there."[3] Immediate objections were heard from La Roche and the merchants. To appease La Roche, Chauvin was placed nominally under La Roche's command, his monopoly extending only along the Saint Lawrence near Tadoussac. The objections of the merchants were put aside. For his first voyage in 1600, Chauvin chose François Gravé Du Pont as his lieutenant. Both men had had considerable experience in Canadian waters. On arrival at the mouth of the Saguenay River, Chauvin chose Tadoussac as the site for his settlement and had a house built. Gravé, who had explored the Saint Lawrence River a few years earlier as far up as Trois-Rivières, advised against the site, preferring one "higher up the river."[4] Pierre du Gua de Monts, soon to play an important role in the early exploration of Canada, felt the same as Gravé. When the expedition departed, sixteen "colonists" were left behind in a house, twenty-five by eighteen feet, at Tadoussac. No effort had been made at exploration. Some of the men died during the winter; those who survived did so because they were taken in by local natives.

During the next two years all pretense of colonizing and exploration were dropped as Chauvin concentrated on the fur trade and fishing. This, coupled with the continuing clamour of the merchants for free trade, led Henri IV to reexamine Chauvin's monopoly. To press colonization and exploration and keep the merchants quiet, Chauvin formed a company in which he and any merchants who wanted to join would be partners and in which all costs, including a colony, were to be borne equally. This was not to the liking of the merchants, who wanted to reap profits with minimal expenses, and most of them quickly dropped out of the prospective deal. Soon after, early in 1603, Chauvin died, and Henri IV, bypassing La Roche, assigned the monopoly to another old comrade-in-arms, Aymar de Chaste. De Chaste, with a group of Rouen merchants, outfitted two ships for a voyage in 1603, commanded by Chauvin's experienced colleague Gravé. A passenger on one of the ships was Samuel de Champlain, who had been asked by de Chaste "to see the country and what the colonizers might accomplish there" and "give the King a faithful report thereon."[5] In other words, Champlain was asked to do a resource and settlement evaluation of the Saint Lawrence Valley. The results of this voyage were published by Champlain within a month of his return to France.[6]

The expedition departed from Honfleur on 15 March 1603 and arrived at Tadoussac on 24 May, a crossing of seventy days. Accompanying the expedition were two Montagnais Indians who had been taken to the court of Henri IV in 1602. As soon as the French landed at Tadoussac, an Indian council was called, presided over by the Montagnais chief Anadabijou. The returning Montagnais brought a message to their chief from the king of France that he "wished them well, and desired to people their country, and to make peace with their enemies (who are the Iroquois) or send forces to vanquish them."[7] The Montagnais, in accepting this message, probably regarded it as the conclusion of an alliance that covered the subject of trade, settlement, and aid in warfare. With the Montagnais was a group of Algonquins under their chief Tessouat (Besouat) and a party of Etchemins who had come to aid the Montagnais against the Iroquois. Champlain was to learn later that Tessouat's Algonquins were the Kichesipirinis from the Ottawa River near what is now Pembroke, Ontario; the Etchemins were probably the Maliseet-Passamaquoddy Indians from the Saint John and Sainte Croix Rivers. After this meeting, Champlain saw and described birchbark canoes for the first time. They impressed him as being light, faster than a rowboat, twenty to twenty-three feet long and up to four feet wide; they could be paddled by two people and hold up to one thousand pounds of baggage. A month later he would unequivocally state that they were the only means by which any exploration could be accomplished.

On 11 June, Champlain began his explorations by traveling about fifty miles up the Saguenay River and questioning the natives about its source. What he got was an excellent description of a route that can be identified as follows: up the Saguenay past the falls of Chicoutimi to Lac Saint-Jean, up the Chamouchouane, Mistassini, or Péribonca River to Lac Mistassini, and from there to "a sea that is salt."[8] Champlain reasoned that this sea was "some gulf of this our sea [the Atlantic], which overflows in the north into the midst of the continent"—a remarkable hypothesis in view of the fact that this "gulf," now called Hudson Bay, was not "discovered" until 1610. Distances were described by the Montagnais in terms of days of travel by canoe. Champlain converted these to leagues by reckoning 12 to 15 leagues a day (30 to 40 miles) over such a difficult route. The distance from Tadoussac to Lac Mistassini was given as ten days, which converts to 120 to 150 leagues. At 2.5 miles to the French land league (*lieue commune*), this distance would come to 300 to 400 miles, the actual distance being about 340 miles. As far as is known, Champlain was the first European to make such detailed notations on native geographical information.

On 18 June, Champlain set off from Tadoussac in a bark (a large open boat with at least one mast and sail) for the Lachine Rapids. Along the way he noted islands, shoals, vegetation, land quality, and the major rivers that discharged into the Saint Lawrence. At Trois-Rivières he commented favourably on the suitability of the site for a settlement and tried to sail and row up the Saint Maurice River. Having failed on the Saint Maurice, Champlain tried on 30 June to sail up the Richelieu River. As the current quick-ened, the French took to their rowboat but were not able to make much headway, nor could they drag or portage their boat through the dense for-est. Champlain did, however, get a good native description of the route up the Richelieu, across Lake Champlain, and down the Hudson River to "the coast of Florida," in all "some 100 or 140 leagues," or 250 to 350 miles (the actual distance across this route is closer to 400 miles). What probably mis-led Champlain was that over such a route the natives could cover much more than 12 to 15 leagues per day. Back on the Saint Lawrence the next day, Champlain tried a canoe for the first time, and on 3 July the party fi-nally reached the mighty Lachine Rapids. Here he came to a conclusion that would have a fundamental impact on his and all future French explo-ration of the interior:

> This current [Lachine Rapids] extends for three or four leagues, so
> that it is vain to imagine that any [European] boats could be conveyed
> past these rapids. But he who would pass them must provide himself
> with the canoes of the natives, which a man can easily carry; for to
> transport a boat is a thing that cannot be done in the short time neces-
> sary to enable one to return to France to winter. And besides the first
> rapid, there are ten more, for the most part difficult to pass; so that it
> would be a matter of great toil and labour to be able to see and do by
> boat what a man might propose, except at great cost and expense, be-
> sides the risk of labouring in vain. But with the canoes of the natives
> one may travel freely and quickly throughout the country, as well as
> up the little rivers as up the large ones. So that by directing one's
> course with the help of the natives and their canoes, a man may see
> all that is to be seen.[9]

Although this may not seem like a profound observation, in 1603 it was. No European explorer before Champlain had come to such a conclusion, and almost no seventeenth-century explorers except the French used canoes in their travels. The adoption of the canoe enabled them to leave their ships and coastal settlements, unlike the Dutch and the English, who virtually never used this mode of transportation.

While at the rapids, Champlain collected the first of three stories from different Algonquin informants of the geography of the upper Saint Law-rence and the Great Lakes.[10] In two of the three cases, his informants drew maps for him, the second one of which he seems to have incorporated into his large map of 1613. From the three stories, two of which mentioned salt-water in the westernmost lakes, Champlain concluded that the South Sea

(Pacific Ocean) was about four hundred leagues (one thousand miles) distant. He would send Jean Nicollet in 1634 to try to find this salt sea.

After returning to Tadoussac, Champlain surveyed the southern shore of the Saint Lawrence to Percé and the northern shore from the Manicouagan River back to Tadoussac. While at Percé, Champlain conversed with another member of the expedition, the merchant Jean Sarcel de Prévert, who was investigating and trading along the southern shore of the Gulf of Saint Lawrence. While opposite Prince Edward Island, the merchant had heard of copper deposits across the Isthmus of Chignecto and had sent some men with Micmac guides to investigate. In 1604 Champlain would locate the same deposits at Advocate Harbour on the Minas Channel. The ships left Tadoussac for France on 14 August. On 24 August the expedition departed from Gaspé and reached Le Havre at the mouth of the Seine River on 20 September.

In his three-month stay on the Saint Lawrence, Champlain accomplished a great deal. He surveyed the Saint Lawrence in a much better fashion than Jacques Cartier. He wrote the first observations of Montagnais life. He pioneered the use of native informants and in so doing accumulated a substantial body of geographical information. He was the first European to comment on the necessity of using native canoes and guides in the process of exploration. Lastly, he published an account of the expedition immediately after returning, in order to stimulate interest in a continuing effort.

After the expedition returned to France, its members learned that de Chaste had died and with him the monopoly that made further work possible. Fearing the worst, Champlain hurried to have an audience with the king: "I showed [him] the map of the country, with the very special account I drew up for him."[11] Neither the "special account" nor Champlain's map of 1603 seems to have survived. The latter was probably used as a base for the western portion of his "Carte Geographiqve," engraved in 1612.[12] King Henri IV seems to have been easily persuaded to grant a new monopoly, and on 31 October, 8 November, and 18 December 1603, Pierre du Gua de Monts received the necessary commissions and wide powers as vice-admiral and lieutenant-general over all the North American lands "from the 40th degree [of latitude] to the 46th, and as far inland as he is able to explore and colonise."[13] Although the commissions had as their northern limit 46°, they clearly included all of Acadia (the maritime coast north of Cape Cod) as well as the Saint Lawrence River and the Gulf. The monopoly was for the fur trade, not the fisheries, and was supposed to last for ten years. In

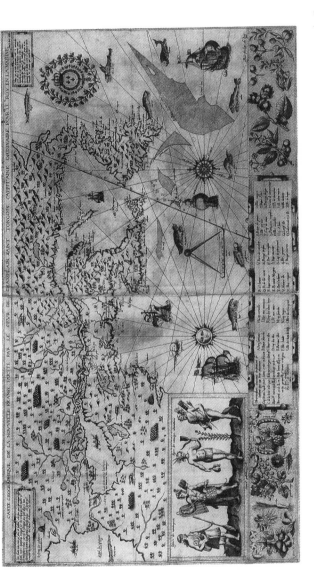

10.1 *Map of New France (Samuel Champlain, 1612), published in an early edition of Champlain's* Voyages *(Paris, 1613). Except for Newfoundland, this map is based entirely on surveys conducted by Champlain and on native accounts gathered by him between 1603 and 1609. The two large lakes on the western part of the map are Lakes Ontario and Erie. They were copied from one of three sketch maps drawn for Champlain by Algonquin informants in July 1603. The map has a peculiar orientation because Champlain constructed it for navigators who sailed with uncorrected French compasses. Courtesy of the Rare Book Collection, National Library of Canada.*

return, de Monts was required "to bring about the conversion to Christianity of the people inhabiting this country . . . to maintain, keep and preserve the said regions under our power and authority . . . to treat for and to make peace, alliance, and confederation, lasting friendship, correspondence and communication with said peoples . . . [to] especially people, cultivate, and settle the said lands . . . [to] make or cause to be made explorations and surveys" and to "cause to be built and constructed one or more forts, public places, towns (etc.)." It was an extremely detailed commission of which the above clauses were only the main requirements. Originally de Monts was required to take over one hundred settlers a year, but this number was considered to be unrealistically high and was reduced to sixty. Champlain, requested by de Monts to fulfill the obligations for exploring and surveying, again promised to make the king "a faithful report of all [he] saw and discovered."[14]

In de Monts, King Henri IV finally found someone who was enthusiastic about undertaking the task of colonizing and exploring—in addition to being capable, energetic, and high enough in authority to override the objections of the free traders and command the respect of the Crown. A number of merchants from the French cities of Rouen, Saint Malo, La Rochelle, and Saint Jean-de-Luz joined with de Monts. According to Champlain, de Monts decided to begin his colony in lands farther south than the Saint Lawrence, for "the little he had seen had taken away any desire of his to enter the great river Saint Lawrence, having on the voyage [in 1600] seen only a forbidding country. He desired to go further south in order to enjoy a softer and more agreeable climate."[15] With an eye on commerce as well as colonization, de Monts sent three vessels to trade at Tadoussac while his and another vessel, carrying 120 workmen, set out for Acadia. The venture that would finally plant a permanent French colony in North America left Le Havre on 7 March 1604.[16]

From 1604 until 1607, French exploration, largely by Champlain, was confined to the coast of Acadia from Cape Breton Island to the western reaches of Nantucket Sound. During those years the major bays and river mouths were explored and mapped. As he had done on the Saint Lawrence, Champlain collected a wealth of native geographical information. In addition, native trade contacts were made and tokens of friendship exchanged, especially with groups of the Abenaki, Etchemin, and Micmac Indians. Although de Monts's first choice for a settlement (Sainte-Croix on Dochet Island in the Sainte Croix River) was a terrible mistake, the location at Port Royal, in the Annapolis Valley of Nova Scotia, to which the settlement was moved in 1605, was more successful. Substantial buildings were erected, land was cleared, and farming was begun. De Monts, however, still held out hope for a permanent colony farther south and ordered in 1606 that such a search be made. Before Champlain's original surveys could be extended much beyond Cape Cod, news came in 1607 that de Monts's monopoly had been canceled. The free traders had won again. There was nothing to do but abandon Port Royal and return to France. Although other Frenchmen, notably one of de Monts's associates, Jean de Biencourt de Poutrincourt, reopened Port Royal, formal French attention now shifted permanently to the Saint Lawrence.

The experiences gained by Champlain and Gravé in the Saint Lawrence region and Acadia were now used to try to persuade de Monts not to give up. Champlain consulted with de Monts and convinced him that he should seek an audience with the king in order to request a monopoly that would return efforts to the Saint Lawrence Valley. His arguments, which were accepted by de Monts, were as follows: that the area above Québec had good agricultural prospects; that the Saint Lawrence area was better than Acadia for the fur trade; that the Saint Lawrence area had a greater potential for missionizing and trade because it had a higher density of native people than Acadia, especially if the interior agricultural groups could be contacted; that the French were already well known and liked by the natives of the Saint Lawrence; that a site for a post along the river offered excellent protection from foreign powers and competitors; and last, and perhaps most significant for further exploration, that the Saint Lawrence seemed to be the passage by which China could be reached.[17] Those were persuasive arguments, and on 7 January 1608, the king gave de Monts a one-year monopoly.[18] Although the commission mentioned nothing about a colony, it did stipulate a settlement in which Frenchmen could locate and trade freely. Champlain was placed in charge of building a fortified trading post, whereas Gravé was in charge of native relations and the trade.

The post at Québec was begun in 1608 and was ready for occupation by the time winter set in. As in Acadia, scurvy and dysentery attacked the men, and only eight of twenty-eight survived the winter.[19] In the spring of 1609 Champlain received orders from de Monts to begin exploration and then return to France in the fall with a report of what he had discovered. According to French historian Marc Lescarbot, it was Champlain who decided to go south into the Iroquois country rather than west toward the Great Lakes "on the ground that southern lands, from their mild climate, are always the more agreeable."[20] Champlain, on the other hand, stated that the decision to go south was reached through discussion with Gravé and that both men were acting on instructions from de Monts, whose interest in the lands south of the Saint Lawrence was well-known.[21]

Expediency was probably a major reason to proceed south. Champlain needed guides, and the Montagnais, "our allies," promised to act as guides in return for French participation on raids planned against the Iroquois. Henri IV had made assurances as early as 1602, to the Montagnais and their allies, that such aid would be forthcoming. These assurances were reiterated by Champlain in September 1608. It was therefore decided that Champlain would accompany the Montagnais. The expedition was joined by Hurons (Ochateguins) and Iroquet Algonquins, who had also come to make an alliance with the French. At the mouth of the Richelieu River some of the native allies went home, and at the Saint Louis Rapids below Chambly, Champlain had to decide whether to abandon his boats and proceed in canoes or to abandon the expedition. Although eager to explore, he did not want to risk his men going to war in vessels in which they had had no experience. After debating the matter, he sent all but two volunteers back to Québec and joined the sixty native warriors in their canoes. This act, on 12 July 1609, marked the beginning of French inland exploration. As they passed the Saint Louis Rapids Champlain remarked, "No Christians but ourselves had ever penetrated to this place."[22] The expedition moved south, along the western shore of Lake Champlain, and on the twenty-ninth spotted an Iroquois war party on a point near the southern end of the lake. After three musket shots, which killed two of their chiefs, the Iroquois fled. The French had proved themselves to their allies by actively participating in war, and in the process they had explored an important waterway. At the mouth of the Richelieu River, before the party broke up, Champlain was asked if he would go "to their [the Huron] country, and aid them continually like a brother"; he recalled, "I promised them I would."[23]

In the fall, Champlain returned to France, as he had been ordered. Immediately he reported to de Monts and then to the king that a new group of natives had been discovered (the Hurons) who would help him "to complete the exploration of the region of the great river St. Lawrence, on condition [the French] carried out the promise to assist them in their wars."[24] That year the clamour of free traders was so great that de Monts could not get a renewal of his monopoly. Knowing that they would probably run a deficit, de Monts and his partners nevertheless decided to continue the post at Québec and sponsor Champlain's explorations. Back at Québec in the spring of 1610, Champlain was hopeful that either he would explore "the Three Rivers [Saint Maurice] as far as a place where there is such a large sea [Hudson Bay], that they [the natives] have not seen the end of it" and would "then come back by way of the Saguenay to Tadoussac" or he would go with the Hurons to see "their country and the great lake, and some copper mines."[25] Both journeys had been promised to him the previous year but were postponed at the request of the natives. Instead, Champlain again joined them in an attack against the Iroquois, this time at the mouth of the Richelieu River.

Although Champlain thought it was unfair that he should undergo risks to explore and seek out new native groups only to have the free traders reap the benefits, he was obviously creating a special relationship between himself and the natives he was aiding in war. The other traders were regarded by the natives as "women, who wish to make war only upon [the Indians'] beavers," an observation that was reinforced in native eyes when some of the French traders stripped the dead Iroquois of their blood-soaked furs.[26] Again Champlain heard of far-off copper deposits and was given a copper sheet the natives had prepared by melting and hammering together nodules. Just before some of the native groups departed, Champlain, in consultation with Gravé, approached Iroquet, chief of the Onontchataronons, to see if he would take a French youth with him "to learn the language . . . to learn what their country was like, see the great lake, observe the rivers and what people lived in that region, while at the same time [the boy] might explore the mines and the rarest things among the tribes."[27] The youth, probably Étienne Brûlé, was eager to go, and after some hesitation Iroquet accepted him. Iroquet's group, Ottawa Valley Algonquins who often wintered in the Huron country, was a good choice. Brûlé had a chance to see a great deal and learn two languages. In return, Champlain accepted a Huron youth named Savignon. This very important exchange marked the beginning of the French *truchement* (interpreter) system, which became so important to all future French endeavours in the interior. When Champlain returned to Québec he received the news that Henri IV had been assassinated. This meant a trip to France to seek new political support for his ventures. As Champlain sailed home, Henry Hudson was making his way south along the eastern shore of the bay to the north, to eventually winter in James Bay.

The year 1611 did not bring Champlain any closer to further exploration. Friendships were renewed with each native group, presents were exchanged, and again he was promised that "next year" he would be guided either up the Saint Maurice or along the route to the west. Champlain gathered more geographical information, as well as sketch maps, from native informants. Both Champlain and the natives were delighted by the progress their respective youths had made. This time three youths were placed among the natives: Brûlé with the Hurons, Nicolas de Vignau with the Kichesipirinis on the Ottawa River, and a third boy, employed by a trader named Bouvier, with Iroquet's Algonquins.

Soon after Champlain arrived in France he was severely injured. The following year (1612), he and de Monts devoted their energies to placing their company on a more secure basis. In the late summer of that year, Vignau returned from New France with the electrifying news that he had been up the Ottawa River to Hudson Bay, where he had seen the remains of an English ship.[28] Armed with this news, his writings, and maps, Champlain now sought an influential patron who had enough power and influence at court and among the merchants to take decisive control of New France. Eventually he found such a person: Henri de Bourbon, prince de Condé, heir-presumptive to the throne. The prince de Condé was appointed viceroy of New France and Champlain his lieutenant, with a twelve-year monopoly on the trade along the Saint Lawrence River and with broad administrative powers. One of the tasks specifically spelled out was the search for "the easy route to the country of China and the East Indies."[29]

Back at the Lachine Rapids in May 1613, Champlain discovered that only a few natives had come to trade.[30] These complained that they had been poorly treated the previous summer by the traders, that they had been told that Champlain was dead, and that the French would no longer help them in their wars.[31] The result was disastrous to the year's trade and to Champlain's hope for explorations. Champlain knew how closely aid in war, trade, and exploration were linked. He therefore decided to contact the interior groups on his own and assure them of continuing French goodwill. The expedition, made up of Champlain, Vignau, an interpreter ("Thomas"), two other Frenchmen, and a native guide, departed for the Ottawa River on 26 May 1613. This French expedition into the interior was the first to be paddled by Frenchmen. They not only were exploring new country but also were learning how to paddle and portage canoes and to ignore the constant annoyance of the mosquitoes. On 3 June they hired a native guide, who was to paddle stern in one of the canoes, a task not yet mastered by the French. Finally, on the seventeenth, they reached Morrison Island at the middle of the Ottawa River near the present city of Pembroke, Ontario. Here was the encampment of Champlain's old Kichesipirini Algonquin ally Tessouat, whom he had first met at Tadoussac in 1603. It was with Tessouat's people that Vignau had spent the winter of 1611 to 1612. In a council, Champlain explained, through Thomas, that he cherished the French friendship with the Algonquins, that he wanted to aid them in their wars, and that he hoped to borrow canoes and guides to take him to the Nipissing bands in order to bring these Indians into the alliance. From the Nipissings, Champlain planned to travel to the "northern sea" that Vignau had seen. The Kichesipirinis tried to dissuade Champlain by pointing out that the route was difficult and that the Nipissings were unfriendly sorcerers and poor warriors. After Champlain dismissed these arguments, the Kichesipirinis turned on Vignau and discredited him as a liar who had never been to the northern sea. Fearing for his life, Vignau eventually confessed to Champlain that he had lied. Furious and disappointed, Champlain returned to the Saint Lawrence.

Some scholars have wondered who was lying, Vignau or the Kichesipirinis.[32] Tessouat was certainly not telling the truth about the dangers of the journey to the Nipissings and his relations with them, which were friendly. Vignau also certainly could not have seen a wrecked English ship in 1611, unless he was exaggerating the size and complement of the *Discovery's* longboat, in which Hudson and eight others had been set adrift. Most probably, Tessouat did not want Champlain to visit the Nipissings for fear that the Kichesipirinis would have to share the French trade. Vignau likely concocted a plausible story from native accounts about a route to the "northern sea," a story augmented by him when he returned to France in the fall of 1612 and heard news of Hudson's voyage.[33] Vignau's insistence that his story was true was probably prompted by his knowledge that the route he had described and mapped for Champlain actually existed; he may have lied when he maintained that he had been over that route.

The phase of exploration ending in about 1613 had seen some accomplishments. Alliances had been made with the Montagnais, Algonquin, and Huron Indians, without whom exploration was impossible. The native trade had developed slowly, but at this point in their relation with the French, at least the Algonquins and the Hurons desired French military aid more than French trade goods. Much native geographical information had been recorded, among which tales of routes to salt seas in the western and northern regions held out intriguing possibilities. A permanent base of operations had been established at Québec, and the French had learned to survive the North American winter. They were also beginning to learn how to use canoes and native guides. One of the major accomplishments was the small cadre of interpreters, at least one in the Huron language and two or three in Algonquian. For Champlain, the major disappointments were the lack of progress in exploration, the lack of missionaries among the natives, and the absence of any effort to establish an agricultural settlement at Québec.

Exploration of the Eastern Great Lakes (1615–1629)
During the year 1614 considerable effort was expended ironing out the administrative and commercial aspects of New France. In an agreement with the merchants who became part of the company under the prince de Condé's monopoly, Champlain was to be furnished with four men from each ship sent to trade in furs; he could use these men at Québec or as help in explorations. The merchants were also to bring out six families a year as settlers. With these concerns temporarily out of the way, Champlain now sought advice on what missionaries might be interested in coming to New France. On suggestion from the secretary to the king, Louis Houel, Champlain contacted the Récollets, a reformed Order of the Franciscans, and in the spring of 1615, three priests and a lay brother embarked for New France.[34] Their arrival at Tadoussac on 24 May 1615 marked the introduction of the Catholic Church to the Saint Lawrence colony.[35]

Immediately after his arrival at Québec, Champlain set out for the Lachine Rapids, where the annual trade between the French and the natives took place. Along the way he met the Récollet father Joseph Le Caron, who had already been at the rapids and was returning to Québec to pick up his vestments, which he needed for a mission to the Hurons. Although Champlain would have preferred that Le Caron spend one winter at Québec before attempting a journey to the Huron country, the priest was eager to go. Champlain and Gravé met with the Hurons, who were again requesting aid in their wars, this time adding that they needed French help because Iroquois raids made it difficult for them to travel to the Saint Lawrence. After consulting with Gravé, Champlain "came to the conclusion that it was necessary to assist them, both to engage them the more to love [the French] and also to provide the means of furthering [his] enterprises and explorations which apparently could only be carried out with their help, and also because this would be to them a kind of pathway and preparation for embracing Christianity."[36] While Champlain got his equipment ready at Québec, Le Caron and twelve men that Champlain had planned to take with him left the rapids with their Huron escort for the Huron country. Somewhat distressed at this because Le Caron's party was ill equipped and had only four or five men who knew how to use firearms, Champlain followed them with an interpreter, his servant, and ten natives. In eighteen days he reached Lake Nipissing, where he rested for two days among the Nipissings, who gave the men "a very kind reception," and on 1 August, the party reached the Huron country. The entire trip of 550 miles had been done in twenty-one days of paddling, averaging 26 miles per day, which is excellent time considering that they were traveling upstream most of the way, with many portages.

What impressions did the first Europeans who traveled this route have of the country they saw? All that has survived from Le Caron's party is a letter in which he detailed the tribulations of a first-time canoe paddler—great fatigue from paddling, portaging, and unfamiliar food.[37] Champlain, on the other hand, left a good geographical account including short notations on soil quality, vegetation, animals, and native life. Commenting on the rock and pine-covered surface of the Canadian Shield, he called it a "frightful and abandoned region" where he "did not see in the whole length of it ten acres of arable land, but only rocks and a country somewhat hilly."[38] When he came to Georgian Bay, called Lake Attigouautan by the Hurons, he renamed it "la Mer douce" (the Freshwater Sea).[39] Champlain almost certainly knew that this sea was not going to be saltwater, because Brûlé had seen it in 1610–11. In contrast to the unprepossessing nature of the rocky shores of Georgian Bay, the Huron country was, according to Champlain, "very fine, mostly cleared, with many hills and several streams, which make it an agreeable district."[40] Along the way from the Lachine Rapids to la Mer douce, Champlain questioned natives about the river routes that led to the Saguenay and James Bay. When he got to the mouth of the French River, an Ottawa chief drew for him a map—"with charcoal on a piece of tree bark"—of the Georgian Bay–Lake Huron area. Most of this information probably survived on the map that Champlain had engraved in 1616 but that, unfortunately, was never published.[41]

Champlain spent all of August exploring the country of the Hurons and their villages. On 1 September he and ten men set off with an army of five hundred Hurons to make war on the Iroquois. Brûlé joined twelve Hurons who were sent by their chiefs to contact the Susquehannocks, who were also enemies of the Iroquois. The Susquehannocks were apparently interested in concluding an alliance with the French and had promised to aid the Hurons with five hundred men.[42] Champlain's expedition followed the Trent River system from Lake Simcoe to Lake Ontario and crossed the eastern end of the lake in the lee of the Duck Islands to the vicinity of Henderson Bay. Here they started overland and eventually crossed the Oswego

River near Lake Oneida. Some four leagues farther (nine to twelve miles), the party attacked a major village situated beside a "pond."[43] The target was likely an Onondaga village somewhere between Lakes Oneida and Onondaga. After attacking the village and laying siege to it for six days, the army withdrew to the Huron country the way they had come. Although Champlain had wanted to return to Québec along the Saint Lawrence, the Hurons would not take him because they considered the route too dangerous. Champlain spent the winter exploring the Huron country and visited the neighbouring Petun and Ottawa Indians. As a result of this visit, in 1619 he published the first brief ethnography of the Hurons.[44]

The route that Brûlé followed to the Susquehannocks is not clear. The traditional route favoured by historians has Brûlé and his party crossing the Niagara River and making their way to the main Susquehannock village on the lower Susquehanna River.[45] Champlain, on the other hand, basing his words on the observations of Brûlé, placed the Susquehannocks "only three short days' journey" from the village he attacked.[46] This would situate the Susquehannocks on the North Branch of the river, an area they had supposedly abandoned late in the sixteenth century.[47] From the Susquehannock village, Brûlé explored "the river to the sea," usually taken to mean the Susquehanna River, although on his map of 1632 Champlain seems to imply that this was the Delaware River. On his way home from the Susquehannocks in 1616, Brûlé was captured by the Senecas, who released him after a few days when he promised to make the Senecas "friends with the French and their enemies, and to make them swear friendship for one another."[48] Champlain finally saw his interpreter again in July 1618.

The voyage to the Hurons in 1615–16 was the last voyage of exploration made by Champlain. He had been to the "sweetwater sea," he had proven French goodwill to the Hurons, and very important, he had put the fur trade on a secure basis by bringing the Hurons into the alliance. To Champlain and the natives, an alliance and aid in war were preconditions to trade, and together these eventually led to exploration.[49] In 1617 he was apparently ready for another trip, but the natives did not show up.[50] By 1618 the company was in trouble again, and Champlain increasingly had to spend time and energy trying to promote New France at the court. To do so, he emphasized the future of the colony as a place for settlement with a diversified economy. Although over time Champlain increasingly became an administrator concerned with placing the colony on a secure basis, he never lost his zeal for exploration. In a number of memoranda and subsequent meetings with merchants, the Paris Chamber of Commerce, and the court, Champlain continued to push exploration as a necessity for the colony.[51] He was convinced that further work would quickly lead to the "north and south seas" and that these "would be the means of reaching easily to the Kingdom of China and the East Indies, whence great riches could be drawn."[52] In fact, Champlain tried to convince the Paris Chamber of Commerce that China was only six months' journey from the Saint Lawrence. Exploration, however, had to be financed, and as Champlain pointed out on a number of occasions, neither the merchants nor anyone else supported it financially, and those who undertook it ran personal risks and were not adequately rewarded.[53] In other words, Champlain, who had been wounded three times leading his native allies into combat, who had forged alliances and thereby promoted the fur trade, who had made significant geographical discoveries, eventually became wearied by the lack of financial support and by the fact that others were benefiting from his work. With increased administrative responsibilities and a population of less than sixty in the colony, Champlain felt that he was not in a position to carry on the work himself. In 1622 he wrote, "My task will be to prepare the way for those who, after me, shall engage in this enterprise [exploration]."[54] In the years after 1616 he assiduously interviewed people coming from the interior, hoping to learn any new geographical information.

During the years of the 1620s, exploration did not cease altogether. Every year, trader's agents were sent among various native groups "to keep them on good terms with [the French] and to induce them to come to trade."[55] Some agents went to the Huron country, occasionally accompanied by priests; others went to the Algonquins. We hear of some even among the Petun and the Neutral Indians.[56] All of these agents were fluent in at least one native language. Their specific task, for which they were well paid, was to seek out native groups and families and bring them to particular traders at the annual trade at the Lachine Rapids. The agents were not traders themselves and must not be confused with the later coureurs de bois. They were young men, beginning with Brûlé in 1610, whom Champlain, followed by other traders, had placed among the natives to learn the native language and customs. Only a few names have been preserved: Brûlé, La Vallée, and Grenolle, all Huron interpreters, and Nicolas Marsolet and Jean Nicollet, who were respectively Montagnais and Algonquin interpreters. These men traveled widely, and some may have made significant discoveries. The problem is that none recorded their ventures, and the fragments recorded by others lead only to endless speculation. It is certain

MER DU NORT GLACIALLE

10.2 Map of New France (Samuel Champlain, 1632). This summary map of Champlain's explorations was published in a later edition of his Voyages (Paris, 1632). It may be taken to represent the full extent of geographical knowledge contributed by the entire series of explorations by Champlain. Lakes Ontario, Erie, and a portion of Huron are visible. Particularly interesting is the "Mer du Nort Glacialle" just to the west of Hudson Bay. Courtesy of the John Carter Brown Library at Brown University.

that Brûlé and Grenolle had been at least as far as Sault Sainte Marie before 1623. They had probably seen Lake Superior and had possibly picked up some copper along the southern shore.[57] Whatever geographical information they passed on was either confusing or misinterpreted by Champlain.[58] Brûlé, Grenolle, and La Vallée had all been to the Neutral country between the Grand River, the western end of Lake Ontario, and the Niagara River in what is now southern Ontario.[59] Brûlé's enthusiasm about the country of the Neutral Indians was infectious enough for the Récollets to attempt a mission there. This trip was undertaken by Father Joseph La Roche Daillon between October 1626 and the summer of 1627. It resulted in the first brief description of the Neutral area and its inhabitants.[60]

The last exploration before the conquest of New France by the English in 1629 was an expedition sent by Champlain on 16 May of that year to explore the route from Québec over the Chaudière and Kennebec Rivers to the Abenakis on the Atlantic coast. The man sent on this mission returned on 15 July 1629 with a full geographical report.[61] The immediate object of the journey had been to contact the Abenakis with the request that they trade corn to the colony at Québec, which was being starved into submission by an English blockade of the Saint Lawrence. Unfortunately for the French, Abenaki help did not come soon enough. Five days after the man returned, Champlain felt obliged to capitulate to Lewis Kirke and Thomas Kirke. Although the colony was seized two months after peace had been declared between England and France, it took until July 1632 for the French to get the colony back. Interestingly, Champlain furnished the French ambassador to England with "a map of the country [New France] to show to the English the explorations [the French] had made and the possession [the French] had taken."[62] This map and other "memoranda" were used as justification for French claims to much of what is now eastern Canada. The map and memoranda submitted by Champlain are likely incorporated in his map and writings of 1632. These show that the French had a solid grasp of the geography of eastern Canada to the Huron country. Stretching west was a huge body of water combining Lakes Michigan and Superior, holding out hope for a passage to the Orient.

During this phase of exploration, most of what is now southern Ontario was penetrated by the French. Good reports of what was seen were written by Champlain and the Recollet friar Gabriel Sagard. Unfortunately, the *truchements*, who traveled extensively and freely among the Algonquian- and Iroquoian-speaking groups allied to the French, left nothing, or as in the case of Jean Nicollet, their writings may have been lost. That they passed on some interesting bits of information orally can be gleaned from Champlain and Sagard, both of whom mention conversations with the likes of Brûlé and Grenolle. Some of these men probably knew far more than the few fragments of information that have survived but chose not to share their discoveries. The *truchements* were in a powerful and lucrative position. As Father Paul Le Jeune put it in 1632, "He who knew their language well would be all powerful among them [the natives], however little eloquence he might have."[63] They knew native languages, canoe routes, and locations. To share this information could have meant competition and was therefore not to their advantage. Probably mainly for this reason, the Recollets had problems getting the *truchements* to teach them the native languages.[64]

Jesuit Exploration from Huronia (1632–1650)
In 1626 Cardinal Richelieu became "Superintendent General of Navigation and Commerce of France," with absolute control over all French shipping, commerce, and its colonies. Determined to create strong colonies for France, he organized in 1627 the Compagnie de la Nouvelle-France, also known as the Company of the 100 Associates. The company charter, a long and complex document that touched every facet of colonial life, gave the new company a fifteen-year monopoly on all commerce except the fisheries; it required that colonists be taken to New France, and it excluded all religions except the Catholic Church.[65] Although Richelieu favoured the Capuchins as spiritual advisers to the colony, he was persuaded to hand the task to the Jesuits, at the same time banning the Récollets. All of these decisions had a profound influence on future exploration. However, the capture of the new company's four supply ships by the English in 1628 and the English occupation of Québec in 1629 put a temporary halt to further French plans.

Québec was reoccupied by the French on 5 July 1632. Their first task was to rebuild the settlement, which had been burned by the English, while the three Jesuits who had arrived began studying the native languages. The superior of the order at Québec was Father Paul Le Jeune, an unusually gifted and able person interested in, among other things, geography and astronomy. On 22 May 1633, Champlain returned, bringing with him four more Jesuits. Almost immediately they met with various native groups, renewed old friendships, and requested that the Indians take missionaries to live with them. At this time Champlain reiterated his earlier promise to have a settlement erected at Trois-Rivières, where he hoped natives would settle and intermarry with the French: "We shall be one people."[66] In a meeting specifically with the Hurons, Champlain showed himself particularly eager that they take missionaries with them.[67] The matter of Huron-French intermarriage was reiterated as late as 1637.[68] In 1634, Jesuit plans, probably in consultation with Champlain, were sharpened. Missions were to be opened among the major native groups beginning with the populous and centrally located Hurons. Jesuit residences were to be established at Québec and Trois-Rivières, and natives were to be encouraged to settle near them for instruction in everything from agriculture to Catholicism.[69] These plans were similar to those first announced by Champlain in 1621 to 1622. At that time he had hoped that these native communities would provide him with a secure source of guides for exploration.[70]

In the summer of 1634 three priests, accompanied by four hired men, settled in the Huron country to begin a mission. With one exception—the journey of Jean Nicollet—the Jesuits became the sole explorers in the Great Lakes basin for the next twenty years. This happened because the trader's agents and the *truchements* who had roamed the interior became redundant as the 1630s progressed. Monopoly control over the trade by the Compagnie de la Nouvelle-France eliminated the competing traders, for whom the *truchements* had worked as agents. Simultaneously, the Hurons increasingly took an interest in the fur trade and eventually in the carrying trade to the Saint Lawrence. These two factors combined to make the *truchements* unnecessary in the interior but still necessary at the posts on the Saint Lawrence. Added to this was the fact that the Jesuits saw no place in their missionary plans for anyone not closely associated with them, especially as they became increasingly competent in the native languages. Through arrangements with the company, the Jesuits gained complete control of the French presence in the interior and were therefore in the position to bar any potentially disruptive influences—such as some of the *truchements* had been in the 1620s. Although the priests were of course primarily missionaries, they also became explorers over time, as they developed new missionary fields or, because of their linguistic qualifications, took on diplomatic missions. For this, the Jesuits were eminently suited. They were interested in and curious about their surroundings, they were literate, and they were trained in the natural sciences and in the making of systematic observations. Champlain must have realized all this when, in a gesture that was as symbolic as it was rational, he left in his will "to Father Charles Lalemant" his "compass and copper astrolabe with the proportional dividers."[71] Champlain's most valuable scientific instruments, which he had with him on all his explorations, were therefore given on his death, Christmas Day 1635, to a Jesuit, Father Lalemant.

During the first year that Father Le Jeune was in the colony, he tried to establish the difference in time, and therefore in longitudinal distance, between Québec and France. Champlain had used two methods, dead reckoning over the courses his ships had sailed and compass variation, a method later discredited.[72] Using these, he had arrived at a longitudinal distance between Québec and Paris of about 78.5°, the true distance being 73.5°.[73] Le Jeune also used two methods. The first involved the calculation of the angle between Québec, the geographic pole, and Dieppe (longitudinal difference) by spherical trigonometry.[74] His answer of 91°38', or 6 hours and 6 minutes of time, was incorrect by 19° because the great circle distance between Québec and Dieppe that he used in his calculations was only a rough estimate. What is so extraordinary is that a priest, sitting in a log structure in the wilds of North America, knew that the only way in which such calculations could be made correctly was by means of the spherical haversine formula, and he actually completed correctly the necessary calculations. Le Jeune's second method was by an eclipse of the moon.[75] He evidently tried to time the eclipse at Québec and took the time when it was predicted in France out of an almanac. The difference in time ("about six hours"), converted to degrees, gave him the longitudinal difference. Since the results from the two methods tended to support each other, Le Jeune concluded that Québec was roughly 6 hours or 90° of longitude from France. The accuracy of Le Jeune's answers is less important than the fact that he had the theoretical skills to derive accurate answers. To derive them, he needed accurate data. Between 1632 and 1694, the Jesuits recorded ten lunar and seven solar eclipses, some with astonishingly accurate results.[76] Le Jeune seems to have made his observations and calculations simply because he was interested. In 1642, however, the Jesuits were asked by "certain persons . . . for some remarks on the Eclipses . . . in this country."[77] Who these "certain persons" were is not known, but the year in which the request was made coincided with the arrival at Québec of Father Francesco Bressani, a Jesuit who was trained in astronomy and mathematics and whose subsequent observations of eclipses were among the best made in seventeenth-century North America.

On 18 October 1633, Father Le Jeune departed Québec with a hunting group composed of a Montagnais extended family that was beginning its winter round on the southern shore of the Saint Lawrence.[78] By the time he returned to Québec on 9 April in the following year, the party had covered approximately three hundred miles. Although this was not meant to be a journey of exploration (Le Jeune joined the Montagnais to learn their customs and language), this trip remains to this day the best description ever written of Montagnais winter activities, and it added significantly to French understanding of the rugged country inland from the southern shore of the Saint Lawrence.

The last act of exploration performed by Champlain was to send Jean Nicollet on his celebrated trip to the Winnebagos in the summer of 1634.[79] Little is certain about this journey except that it took place. Champlain was probably the initiator because Nicollet would never have undertaken such a trip without the governor's orders. His primary task was to arrange a peace between the Hurons and the Winnebagos, the latter often called Puants, from *eau puante* ("stinking water"). The Algonquins called them Ouinipigou (Winnebago) while the Hurons called them Aoueatsiouaenhronon. In each case the root of these words means both "stinking water" and "salt water."[80] Judging from their name, the French therefore suspected that the Winnebagos lived beside a salt sea. Because such a sea was expected near the country of the Puants, Nicollet was to explore this possibility. For this reason Nicollet took along "a grand robe of China damask, all strewn with flowers and birds of many colours"—just in case he encountered the Chinese.[81] If we assume that the year 1634 is correct, he left the Huron country with seven Hurons no earlier than mid-August and must have returned to the Huron country before winter set in.[82] In 1635 he was back at Trois-Rivières.

Although the mission to conclude a peace was said to have been successful, news came in June 1636 that the Winnebagos had broken "the treaty of peace" and made war on some of the Lake Huron Ojibwa groups.[83] Scholarly opinion is divided on where Nicollet had gone. According to traditional opinion, he traveled along the shore of Lake Huron through the Straits of Mackinac to the bottom of Green Bay, where the Winnebagos lived.[84] More recently a case has been made that Nicollet traveled from Lake Huron to Lake Superior and visited the Winnebagos on Lake Nipigon.[85] If it was the Winnebagos that were visited by Nicollet, then the latter hypothesis is most improbable because there is no ethnohistorical or archaeological evidence that the Winnebagos ever inhabited the northern shore of Lake Superior.[86] Moreover, the Jesuits wrote that the Winnebagos lived "about three hundred leagues Westward" of the Hurons, not northward as would have been the case had they lived on Lake Nipigon.[87] Did the Jesuits learn from Nicollet's journey anything that might give one a clue as to where he went? In 1640 they described Lake Huron as follows: "This sea is nothing but a large Lake which, becoming narrower in the West, or the West Northwest forms another smaller Lake which then begins to enlarge into another great Lake or second fresh-water sea."[88] Nowhere in this or any other passage is there mention of two lakes (Michigan and Superior) that enter Lake Huron. In fact the French did not know that there were two lakes until 1646 at the earliest.[89] The next passage makes it clearer that the "second fresh-water sea" was Lake Superior. After mentioning the Ojibwa bands of the northern shore of Lake Huron, the writer of the passage, Father Le Jeune, mentions the Baouichtigouians (Saulteurs), "that is to say, the nation of the Sault, for in fact, there is a Rapid, which rushes at this point into the fresh water sea [Lake Huron]. Beyond this rapid [Sault Sainte Marie] we find the little lake."[90]

Both of these passages mention a smaller lake. The first passage says that it *enlarges* into the second freshwater sea, whereas the second passage says that this little lake is beyond Sault Sainte Marie. This little lake can be none other than Whitefish Bay, which is indeed beyond the Sault and enlarges into Lake Superior. The father continued with his description as follows: "Passing this smaller lake [Whitefish Bay], we enter the second freshwater sea, upon the shores of which are the Maroumine [Menominees]; and still farther, upon the same banks, dwell the Ouinipigou [Winnebagos]. . . . In the neighborhood of this nation are the Naduesiu [Dakota Sioux], the Assinipour [Assiniboines], the Eriniouai [Illinois], the Rasaouakoueton [a group of the Ottawas], and the Pouutouatami [Potawatomis]."[91]

Le Jeune completed this thought a few pages later: "It is highly probable one can descend through the second great lake [Superior] of the Hurons and through the peoples that we have named. . . . Sieur Nicolet, who has advanced farthest into these so distant countries, has assured me that, if he had moved three days' journey further upon a great river which issues from this lake, he would have found the sea. . . . Nevertheless, as we do not know whither this great lake tends, or this fresh-water sea, it would be a bold undertaking to go and explore those countries."[92] Again, the only interpretation possible is that the second great lake is Lake Superior and that the river Nicollet meant was the Saint Marys River, which is the only river that issues from that lake.

What is consistent in all of these passages is the physical geography being described. What we do not know is how much of this geography, except the native names, came directly from Nicollet. What is also consistent is that we do not have even a hint of the existence of Lake Michigan until

1646. If Nicollet knew of Lakes Michigan and Superior, he did not pass on this information. What is not consistent is the placing of the native groups in relation to the geography mentioned. The Menominees and the Winnebagos both lived on Green Bay at the time the passage was written. The Dakotas lived at the headwaters of the Mississippi but could have roamed as far east as the southwestern end of Lake Superior. The Assiniboines were west of Lake of the Woods and the Illinois on the Illinois River. The Potawatomis and the Nassauakueton Ottawas were located between the Straits of Mackinac and the Sault.

The evidence discussed above can lead to alternate guesses as to where Nicollet went. He could have gone to the entrance of Lake Superior and perhaps some distance along the southern shore of the lake, where he met the Winnebagos, who then carried his belongings overland for two days to get to their villages.[93] There is no reason why the Menominees and the Winnebagos could not have roamed as far north as the southern shore of Lake Superior. Alternatively, since Lake Superior, the Saint Marys River, and Sault Sainte Marie had been known since Brûlé's days and since no one knew that two large lakes emptied into Lake Huron, Nicollet and the Jesuits may have assumed that he had traveled into Lake Superior when in fact he had traveled into Lake Michigan. The forgotten people in all this are Nicollet's seven Huron guides, who must have known where they were going. It is hard to believe that they would have taken any route to the Winnebagos except the most direct one, which is the Lake Michigan route. If this was the case, then all of Nicollet's information on Lake Michigan was transferred to Lake Superior, the only large lake "West or West Northwest" of Lake Huron that the Jesuits knew anything about. Of these alternatives, the latter seems the more plausible. These circumstances raise the question of whether Nicollet contributed anything useful to the history of exploration and discovery when his contemporaries and successors were, and still are, confused about where he had been. What Nicollet did lay to rest was the notion that China was some manageable distance west of the Hurons. But this of course did not stop speculation that it was simply a bit farther away.

Throughout the 1630s, the Jesuits perfected their knowledge of native languages and, in spite of the disruptive effects of various epidemic diseases that ravaged the native populations, became established in the Huron villages. In 1639 they began the construction of Sainte-Marie among the Hurons, a fortified mission in the centre of the Huron country. In 1640 the mission was sufficiently completed with a staff of thirty men, of whom fifteen were priests, that new missions could be undertaken. The first of these was to the Neutrals in the Niagara Peninsula of Ontario. This mission was entrusted to Fathers Jean de Brébeuf and Pierre-Joseph-Marie Chaumonot. They departed from Huronia with two laymen on 2 November 1640, not returning until 19 March the following year.[94] Although many Frenchmen, including Father La Roche Daillon, had been to the Neutrals before them, Brébeuf and Chaumonot returned with much more complete knowledge of the country. From their description, of which only a summary by Father Jérôme Lalemant has survived, we can be fairly certain that the fathers got as far as the Onguiaahra (Niagara) River and probably crossed it to the Neutral villages on the eastern side. Although the falls of Niagara are not mentioned in Lalemant's abbreviation, they are in a geography of 1648, written by a Jesuit priest to clarify the location of missions.[95] Since we know of no Europeans who visited the area between 1641 and 1648, we can assume that this mention of a "waterfall of a dreadful height" comes from the journey of Brébeuf and Chaumonot. Brébeuf may have continued eastward from the Neutral country and visited the Senecas. He was accused by the Hurons of having done so, but in the absence of corroboration from French sources, the evidence is not conclusive.[96] On their return from the Neutrals, the priests and their companions spent two days crossing a large frozen lake, probably Lake Simcoe.[97]

In 1640 the Jesuits also attempted to open a mission among the Nipissings. This was not accomplished until the following year, by Fathers Claude Pijart and Charles Raymbaut. On their return from Lake Nipissing they witnessed a large gathering of Great Lakes natives near the present Parry Sound and were invited by the Saulteurs to visit them in their country.[98] Father Raymbaut returned to the Huron mission and, together with Father Isaac Jogues, embarked for Sault Sainte Marie at the end of September. After paddling for seventeen days, they reached the Sault. Here they learned more about the geography of Lake Superior, including a good description of how to get to the Sioux inland from the western end of the lake. The opening of this mission would eventually lead to the discovery of Lake Michigan in about 1646.

The Iroquois country had interested the French ever since Champlain. It was reported to be a bountiful country with a milder climate than the Saint Lawrence Valley. The first Frenchmen said to have been there was Jean Nicollet, who had been sent by Champlain in 1624 to help arrange a peace between the Mohawks and the Montagnais.[99] How much geographical information he brought back is uncertain because Champlain made no mention of the trip.[100] On 11 December 1634, the Dutch surgeon Harmen Meyndertsen van den Bogaert, with two companions, made a journey through the Mohawk country as far as the main Oneida village near the present Munnsville, southeast of Lake Oneida. Their object was to investigate the rumour that "French Indians" were among the Iroquois trading for furs. They returned to Fort Orange on 21 January 1635 with an excellent description of the Mohawk and Oneida villages.[101] The Oneidas seem to have told van den Bogaert that the French had been among them in August 1634, but there is no French confirmation for such a trip. What is likely is that the Iroquois had traded briefly on the Saint Lawrence and that "French Indians" had been in Iroquois villages during the summer of 1634, when the two sides were trying to arrange a peace.[102] The French, at any rate, continued to pick up information on the Iroquois country through captives and returning Montagnais war parties. In 1637, for example, a Montagnais chief even drew a map of the Mohawk country for Governor Pierre Montmagny.

On 5 June 1641, two Frenchmen—François Marguerie de La Haye and Thomas Godefroy—returned from the Mohawks, where they had been prisoners since the previous autumn.[103] Their description of the route through Lake Champlain to the Mohawk River was probably used on a map drafted late in 1641 by the surveyor Jean Bourdon.[104] More complete information on the geography of the country between the Saint Lawrence and Mohawk Rivers came from the journeys of Father Isaac Jogues. The father undertook his first trip to the Mohawks as a captive from 9 June 1642 to November 1643.[105] A summary of his observations was written in a geographical account, *Novum Belgium*, in 1646.[106] Similarly, the capture of Father Bressani in April 1644 and his release to the Dutch in August of the same year added to the earlier accounts.[107] Father Jogues set out for the Mohawks again on 16 May 1646, this time as an ambassador from the governor to try to conclude a peace with them. He was accompanied by the surveyor Bourdon.[108] The party returned on 27 June, having made "a tolerably accurate map of these regions."[109] On 24 September 1646, Father Jogues went again to the Mohawks, hoping to continue the mission he thought he had begun earlier in the year.[110] On 18 October 1646, he and his companion were killed by the Mohawks at the village of Ossernenon.[111]

Just as the route to the Mohawks and the Dutch became better known in the 1640s, so did the route to the Abenakis and the English. One of Champlain's men had first explored the latter route in 1629 by proceeding up the Chaudiere River, portaging across the divide, and traveling down the Kennebec to the coast. On 24 June 1640, an Englishman appeared on the Saint

Lawrence, having passed over this route with twenty Abenakis.[112] He wanted to explore a route over the Saguenay system to Hudson Bay. After entertaining him, the French shipped him home from Tadoussac and noted, "This poor man would have lost fifty lives, if he had as many, before reaching this North sea by the way he described." With Father Gabriel Druillettes's diplomatic mission to the Abenakis and to English settlements in 1646 over the difficult Chaudiere-Kennebec route, this system of "Rivers iron-bound with rocks" became the standard French overland route to the Atlantic coast.[113]

As the Jesuits became more familiar with the Montagnais bands who visited and received religious instruction at Trois-Rivières and Tadoussac, they felt compelled to make an effort to stay with their flock, even on the Indians' winter rounds. In the winter of 1643–44 Father Druillettes followed a Montagnais hunting party near Tadoussac and again in 1649–50.[114] In neither case has an adequate description survived of where they went. In the winter of 1647–48 Father Druillettes went with a hunting party "to the land of Shades . . . and frightful mountains and forests, where the Sun never looks upon the earth, except by stealth."[115] From 8 October until 30 April, this party had hunted through the Notre Dame Mountains in the watershed of the Matane River. Similarly, on 27 March 1651, when the ice was still on the lakes and rivers, Father Jacques Buteux and four Frenchmen began to follow a band of Christian Attikameks up the Saint Maurice River. One of those who accompanied him was Thomas Godefroy, who, along with François Marguerie, had brought the first geographical account of the Iroquois country to the French in 1641. The party did not reach Trois-Rivières again until 18 June. During that time, Father Buteux was priest to the Montagnais with whom he was traveling. It was the first time any Europeans had ascended the difficult Saint Maurice River, probably reaching the central part of the watershed. The following year Father Buteux attempted the same journey but was caught and slain by the Iroquois. A far better description of exploration has survived from Father Jean de Quen's journey to Lac Saint-Jean in 1647.[116] The purpose of his trip was to visit some Christian converts among the Kakouchakhi (Port-Epic) Montagnais who were ill. He departed from Tadoussac on 11 July, in one canoe guided by two Montagnais. The party paddled up the Saguenay River to the falls of Chicoutimi. Many other Europeans had been this far, but from here the party struck south and then west along the Chicoutimi River and after many portages reached Lac Saint-Jean. Partway along the southern shore they found the natives they were seeking. These natives were astonished at the undertaking and greeted "the first Frenchman who . . . ever set foot in their land." De Quen founded a mission near the mouth of the Métabet-chouane River. In later years he repeated the journey many times.

With the opening of a mission to the Nipissings and the Algonquin bands of Georgian Bay in 1641, the French became more familiar with the northern parts of Lake Huron. Following the initial ventures of Fathers Pijart, Raymbaut, and Jogues, the missions were continued by Fathers Pijart and René Ménard in 1643, by Pijart with Father Leonard Garneau in 1644–45, and by Pijart with Fathers Joseph-Antoine Poncet and Ménard to 1649.[117] Following where these missionaries and their helpers went is not possible, but in the process of their missionary work, probably in 1645, they or their servants produced conclusive evidence of the existence of two lakes beyond Lake Huron. The actual letters announcing the discovery have not survived except through a letter by Mother Marie de l'Incarnation (Guyart) to her son.[118] This letter, dated 10 September 1646, relates chronologically some of the main events at Québec. Following a mention of the departure of Father Druillettes to the Abenakis (29 August), she stated that letters had arrived from the Huron country. The arrival of these letters coincided with the return of Médard Chouart Des Groseilliers from Huronia on 29 August, where he had been working for the Jesuits.[119] The important part of the letter is as follows: "The letters we have received from the Huron mission have informed us that a new country has been discovered and its entrance found. It is the nation of the gens de mer, called in the native tongue Ouinpegouek ikimouek.[120] . . . it is even intended to risk going upon a great sea that is beyond that of the Hurons, and by which it is claimed that the road to China will be found. By means of this sea, the water of which is fresh, it is hoped that even more countries will be found, on its shores and in the lands beyond."[121]

The entrance to the "new country" can be none other than the Straits of Mackinac, and the "great sea" must be Lake Michigan. This observation is confirmed by Father Paul Ragueneau's regional geography of the Great Lakes, a work written in April 1648.[122] He begins by describing Lake Huronas "a Lake whose circuit is nearly four hundred leagues, which we call the fresh-water Sea. It has a certain rise and fall of tide, and at the extremity farthest from us communicates with two other Lakes which are still larger."[123] This is the first unequivocal mention of both Lake Superior and Lake Michigan. Further in his geography, Father Ragueneau is more explicit. After mentioning the Saint Marys River and the great rapids at the Sault, he gives Lake Superior its modern name for the first time and proceeds to mention Lake Michigan and the peninsula between them: "This superior Lake extends toward the Northwest,—that is between the West and the North. A Peninsula, or a rather narrow strip of land, separates that superior Lake from a third Lake, which we call the Lake of the Puans, which also flows into our fresh-water sea [Lake Huron] by a mouth [Straits of Mackinac] on the other side of the Peninsula, about ten leagues farther West than the Sault. This third Lake extends between the West and Southwest—that is to say, between the South and the West, but more toward the West—and is almost equal in size to our fresh-water sea."[124]

The evidence seems to point to the conclusion that before 1648, probably in 1645, the French had discovered the Straits of Mackinac or had at least come to the realization that there were two lakes beyond Lake Huron. Is the fact that Des Groseilliers arrived at Québec at the same time as the letters with the news of Lake Michigan significant? In 1645–46 and perhaps earlier, Des Groseilliers was in the employ of the Jesuits in the Huron country. He may have been one of the Frenchmen who accompanied the fathers on the Algonquin mission in the northern parts of Lake Huron, or he may have traveled and made native contacts for them. In later years Pierre Esprit Radisson, Des Groseilliers's brother-in-law and companion after 1659, recalled, "My brother [in law] made several journeys when the Fathers lived about the Lake of the Hurons, which was upon the border of the sea."[125] These "several journeys" could have taken place only before Des Groseilliers's return to Québec in the summer of 1646. It may be that the "discovery" of the two upper lakes was made in 1645 through the Jesuit mission on Lake Huron and that Des Groseilliers was one of the Frenchmen involved in it.

Through the 1640s, Iroquois pressure on the French and their native allies increased. Except for a brief peace with the Mohawks from 1645 to late in 1646, the decade was one of unrelenting raids and counterraids. In 1648 the Iroquois, armed with Dutch muskets, began to launch more devastating raids into the Huron country. A year later the Huron mission was destroyed, and in 1650 the French withdrew from the interior to the Saint Lawrence settlements. With a permanent population of not more than one thousand people pitted against an Iroquois army of potentially two thousand men and with their fur trade, their missions, and their allied native groups destroyed, the French confined themselves to the vicinity of their forts on the Saint Lawrence, expecting the final onslaught at any moment.

The accomplishments of French exploration to 1650 are neatly described in two sets of related documents: Father Paul Ragueneau's geography of

1648; and Nicholas Sanson's maps "Amerique Septentrionale," engraved in 1650, and "Le Canada, ou Nouvelle France," engraved in 1656. There is little doubt that when Father Ragueneau was writing his geography he consulted the base maps later used by Sanson.[126] These documents show an enormous increase in geographical knowledge since 1629. The existence of all the Great Lakes was known. Frenchmen had seen parts of all these lakes with the possible exception of Lake Erie. Whatever macro-geography of these lakes could not be obtained by direct observation was supplemented from native accounts and maps. The Lake Champlain corridor to the Mohawks was explored and mapped. The rugged lands on either side of the Saint Lawrence, as well as the Tadoussac and Lac Saint-Jean area, were penetrated and better understood. Eclipse data, calculations of latitude, and innumerable observations of distance and compass direction led to a vastly improved understanding of the space relations between the main geographical features of New France. Finally, an incomparably better understanding was derived of the distribution and ethnography of the native population of northeastern North America. In the Great Lakes area alone, the French maintained contact with at least thirty named native groups and knew of many more. Many Frenchmen could speak one or more of the native languages, and traveling and living with the natives no longer posed great problems. As had been the case with Champlain's first journey from the Saint Lawrence, native guides and companions were present on every journey undertaken by a Frenchman; without them, travel to the interior was still impossible. Although a route to China had not yet been found, persistent rumours of a salt sea to the west held out hope for the future.

Period 2: 1654 to 1665

With the defeat of the Ottawa Valley Algonquin groups and of the Huron, Petun, Nipissing, and Neutral Indians, the Algonquin bands of Lake Huron and the Michigan Peninsula fled westward, most of them to the southern shore of Lake Superior and to Green Bay. On the Saint Lawrence, Fort Richelieu was abandoned in June 1647, and at Montreal and Trois-Rivières, the Iroquois were "continually laying ambuscades, and holding [the] French so closely that no one ventured upon a ramble, to even the least distance, without manifest danger of losing his life."[127] By the early 1650s Montreal was down to fifty inhabitants, men were fleeing from Trois-

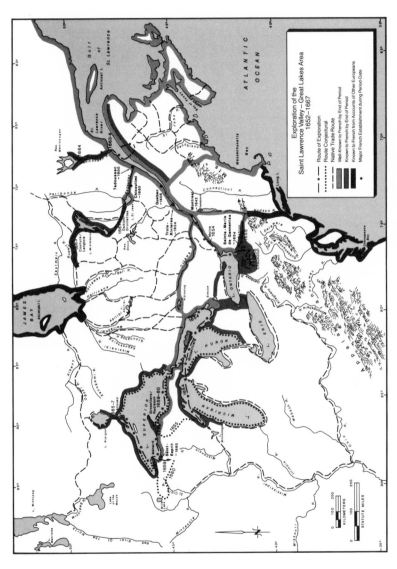

Map 10.2 Exploration of the Saint Lawrence Valley–Great Lakes Area, 1652–1667.

Rivières, and the fur trade was in ruins.[128] There was even serious debate about whether the colonly should be evacuated and whether the men "should have to go back to France."[129] Then, when the general outlook was bleakest, sixty Onondagas arrived at Montreal on 26 June 1653 with the request that the French consider a peace.[130] This abrupt change in affairs was greeted as a sign of divine intervention, a miracle, especially since the peace proposals came from the Iroquois.[131] Negotiations were completed in September, including all the Iroquois except the Mohawks.

The reasons the Iroquois wanted peace are complex and not completely known. The Onondagas and the other western Iroquois clearly wanted to develop a trade, war, and peace policy that was independent of the one that the Mohawks had foisted on them since the beginning of European contact. And the Iroquois tribes, especially the Mohawks and the Onondagas, clearly wanted the remnant Huron population of three hundred to five hundred people, near Québec, to join them. The Onondagas realized that whichever Iroquois tribe had the best relations with the French, especially the Jesuits, would have an edge in negotiations. Finally, the western Iroquois needed a peace in the east in order to concentrate their war efforts against the Erie Indians to the west of them. To gain a diplomatic edge over the other Iroquois, the Onondagas shrewdly insisted on getting from the French the one thing that the French wanted to give them: "the building of a French Settlement within their territory, and for the formation there, in the course of time, of a fine colony."[132] The peace not only opened the Iroquois country west of the Mohawk to exploration but also lifted the Iroquois blockade of the Ottawa River route to the west.

The person chosen by Governor Jean de Lauson to undertake the journey to the Onondagas in order to finalize the peace and examine the possibilities for a French settlement was Father Simon Le Moine. His journal account, covering the period from his departure at Québec on 2 July 1654 to his return on 11 September, is a classic journey of exploration.[133] He was the first European to report on the upper Saint Lawrence between Montreal and Lake Ontario and the first after Champlain to visit the Onondagas. This visit led to a second one, lasting from 19 September 1655 to 30 March 1656, by Fathers Claude Dablon and Pierre-Joseph-Marie Chaumonot.[134] In 1656, after a considerable amount of debate, the decision was made to "build a new Sainte-Marie" among the Onondagas.[135] Eventually fifty Frenchmen went to build the mission of Sainte Marie de Gannentaa on the eastern shore of Lake Onondaga.[136] From this base the priests visited the Cayuga, Oneida, and Seneca Indians, their visits resulting in good geographical and ethnographical descriptions, especially of the Onondagas and their country. What impressed the Jesuits was the mild climate, the excellent soils, the many types of fruit trees, and the abundance of salt-water springs between the Seneca and the Oneida areas. The Lake Onondaga country, where the site for a settlement was chosen by their Iroquois hosts, was described as "one of the most commodious and most agreeable dwelling places in the world, without excepting even the levee of the River Loire."[137]

During the winter of 1657 to 1658, the French at Sainte Marie began to feel increasingly uneasy about their situation. Fearing an attack that they would not be able to withstand, the fifty-three occupants of the new mission abandoned it on 21 March 1658 and made a harrowing dash through ice and storms to Montreal, where they arrived on 23 April.[138] The Iroquois mission was temporarily abandoned, but it had led to the first thorough investigation of the lands south of Lake Ontario by Europeans.

As news of the impending peace spread through the colony in the summer and fall of 1653, both the French and visiting natives from west of Lake Huron entertained the hope that the fur trade would be reopened. The natives promised to bring two thousand compatriots in 1654, with "the Beaver-skins which they have been amassing for the past three years," whereas the Frenchmen planned "to go on a trading expedition, to find the Nations that are scattered here and there."[139] Fearing a general exodus of the able-bodied male population toward the west at a time when peace was still insecure, Governor Lauson issued an edict on 28 April 1654 in which he forbade "all persons of no matter what station . . . to go and trade without a permit."[140] This was the beginning of the so-called permit *(congé)* system, which sought, among many other things, to regulate the number of Frenchmen who could leave the colony for the interior. To travel west, a person had to seek an audience with the governor or his designate to apply for permission.

In June 1654, to the great joy of everyone, 120 Tionontati (Petun) and Ottawa traders arrived at Montreal from Green Bay, laden with furs.[141] These traders also brought the news that it was only a nine-day journey from where they lived to "the sea separating America from China."[142] According to Mother Marie de l'Incarnation, they also spoke of "a very spacious river beyond their country that leads into a great sea that is held to be the China Sea."[143] This news and the possibility of revitalizing the fur trade led Governor Lauson, in consultation with the Jesuits, to allow two Frenchmen (Des Groseilliers and an unknown companion) to return with the natives' canoe brigade to their country.[144] Unfortunately only a few references by the Jesuits and a confused version of the trip by Pierre Esprit Radisson,[145] who concocted the account from conversations with Des Groseilliers, have survived.[146]

Des Groseilliers departed on 6 August 1654 and returned toward the end of August 1656. Where he and his companion went is speculative. If Radisson's account can be trusted, the pair headed up the Ottawa River and by way of the Mattawa River, Lake Nipissing, and the French River to Georgian Bay.[147] The party then split, with Des Groseilliers heading south. Although the passage describing this trip is vague, Des Groseilliers and his Huron-Ottawa guides apparently passed the Penetanguishene Peninsula, where they saw the deserted villages of the Hurons, and then went on to circumnavigate Lake Huron through the Straits of Mackinac to Rock Island at the head of Green Bay.[148] It was now the hunting season, probably October, which meant that they had spent the latter part of August and September on Lake Huron. From Rock Island they traveled to the bottom of Green Bay just before winter set in. Here they visited all the native groups around the bay as far inland as Lake Winnebago. Most of these natives were refugees from the Iroquois wars. They also heard of other groups including the Dakota, Illinois, and Cree Indians.[149]

Des Groseiliers's subsequent movements are more obscure. In the spring of 1655 he seems to have traveled out of Green Bay and south along the western shore of Lake Michigan, "the most delightsomest lake of the world."[150] Having been south "about the great sea," he "came back by the north" (on the eastern shore) and in October arrived at "the strait of the two Lakes of the Stinkings [Lake Michigan] and the Upper Lake [Superior]."[151] Des Groseilliers, it seems, had circumnavigated Lake Michigan to the Straits of Mackinac or the Sault. His native companions now wanted to return to Green Bay, but he wanted to visit the Saulteur and Cree Indians. By this time Des Groseilliers knew that the Ottawas and the Saulteurs were in touch with the Crees, "from whence they have the beavers that they bring to the French."[152] For the fur trade again to become viable, he needed to make contact with them. Although we are not told how Des Groseilliers got to the Saulteurs or where they lived, this is not too difficult to determine. Later references make it clear that the Saulteurs and Ottawas had fled from Lake Huron along the southern shore of Lake Superior to Keweenaw Bay, the Ontanagon River, and Chequamegon Bay. At these locations, definitely the latter two, they met the Crees, who often wintered on the southern shore of the lake. Thus Des Groseilliers probably continued by way of Sault Sainte Marie along the southern shore of Lake Superior until he met the Saulteurs. Among them were a number of Frenchmen and the Crees whom he wanted to meet. Since it was now very late in the season, he decided to winter with them.[153] Early in the spring, the French and 150 native men, women, and children began a trek on snowshoes overland to a river where they made canoes. After eight days they arrived among the Potawatomi and Matouenock Indians. Here they obtained corn and then, after an unspecified period, returned to "the first landing isle," where they "were well received again."[154]

This appears to be a description of an overland trip to the headwaters of the Menomonee or Escanaba River and down one of those rivers to Rock Island, at the mouth of Green Bay, where Des Groseilliers had first landed in 1654 and had been made to feel so welcome. The Potawatomis whom he met along the way lived at several locations around Green Bay at that time. According to the chronicler Nicolas Perrot, the Mantouechs (Matouenoks) lived forty leagues north of Green Bay toward Lake Superior.[155] Since the Crees were at war with the Dakotas, the wintering party was likely at Ontonagon, not Chequamegon, which bordered the Dakota hunting range. In 1659, when Des Groseilliers, this time accompanied by Radisson, met an encampment of Crees just west of the Keweenaw Peninsula near Ontonagon, "they were transported with joy" that the two men had come back and had kept "the promise to come and see them again."[156] At any rate, Des Groseilliers spent the remaining spring and early summer trying to persuade the various native groups to undertake the journey to the Saint Lawrence. Rumours that the Iroquois were still at war delayed the trip, and Des Groseilliers feared he would have to remain in the interior for a third year. Finally persuaded, 250 Huron, Ottawa, Algonquin, and Saulteur Indians, in fifty canoes, got under way and reached the Saint Lawrence in late August, to a tumultuous welcome.[157] Des Groseilliers not only had brought fifty thousand to seventy-five thousand pounds of fur but also had made contact with a large number of people and seen new lands.

The prospect of a harvest of furs and souls prompted the formation of two French groups hoping to join the 250 natives on their journey home. These included "thirty young Frenchmen . . . to bring back furs" and two priests, Fathers Druillettes and Garreau, a brother, and three lay servants, "well versed in the Huron and Algonquin tongues . . . to carry Jesus Christ to a country abounding equally in crosses, in darkness, and in death."[158] The two parties did not get far. News of Mohawk raiders on the Ottawa River caused the thirty traders to return. The priests were ambushed, and although they eventually got back to Montreal, Father Garreau was mortally wounded and soon died. This effort temporarily ended any thoughts of further exploration and missionary work.

Unable to go west, Father Druillettes compiled information about the two areas that were of major interest. From Montagnais at Tadoussac, Attikameks at Trois-Rivières, and various Algonquin groups to the west he obtained details on the canoe routes that led north to James Bay. The Jesuits had heard that the northern Crees had a large population willing to receive missionaries. The problem for the Jesuits was how to get there. From Des Groseilliers, Father Druillettes heard about the multitudes around the southern shore of Lake Superior, Green Bay, and areas to the west and south. This news seemed to be confirmed by natives who also mentioned huge populations, "all more populous than were the Hurons of old, who numbered thirty or thirty-five thousand souls within the limits of seventeen leagues."[159]

Father Druillettes's final report was sent to France as a letter, accompanied by a map. Both the letter and portions of the map have survived, although in a somewhat altered form.[160] The first route he described was the Saguenay, Lac Saint-Jean, and Chamouchouane River route to Lac Mistassini and, via the Rupert River, to James Bay. The entire distance, according to native reports, could be covered in roughly twenty days. The second route was up the Saint Maurice River to Lac Goeland and down the Nottaway River to the bay. From Lac Goeland one could also travel east to the Chamouchouane and the Saguenay system. This distance could supposedly be covered in an overly optimistic fourteen days. The third route ran from Lake Nipissing up the Sturgeon River and down the Abitibi River to James Bay, a journey of fifteen days. The fourth route was up the Wanapitei or Spanish River to the Abitibi or Mattagami River and down to the bay. The fifth route went from Lake Superior three days up the Nipigon River to Lake Nipigon and in four more days down the Ogoki and Albany Rivers to James Bay. From Lake Nipigon another river led west, probably the Ogoki and English Rivers system to Lake Winnipeg. Besides the five routes leading north, Father Druillettes also recorded a way of bypassing the lower Ottawa River, which was often blockaded by Mohawk raiders. This route led from Lake Huron through Lakes Nipissing, Temagami, and Témiscamingue to the headwaters of the Ottawa River and from there to the Saint Maurice River and down to Trois-Rivières. The only route not mentioned, but known from native reports since the explorations of Vignau and Champlain in 1613, was the Ottawa River–Lake Témiscamingue–

Lake Abitibi–Abitibi River route. The map "Tabula Novae Franciae," engraved in 1660 and based in part on Father Druillettes's map, shows that the natives also used the upper Ottawa River to get to the Bell River and from there to the Nottaway River and James Bay. Thirty years after Father Druillettes had compiled this information, the Saguenay, the Ottawa River–Lake Témiscamingue, and the Nipigon-Albany routes had all been explored and mapped by the French.

The collapse of the Onondaga mission and with it the peace negotiated with the western Iroquois threw the colony into a dual crisis that affected the future of both the missions and trade. With the destruction of Sainte Marie among the Hurons in 1649, and the new Sainte Marie de Gannentaa in 1658, two very costly mission experiments had ended. This latest blow came at about the same time that the Sulpicians were beginning to question the hitherto unchallenged supremacy of the Jesuits in ecclesiastical and secular affairs. The Jesuits and their supporters had to think about two questions: What was their role in the colony and among the natives? Was a large central mission, expensive to build and operate and vulnerable to attack, the optimal way to effect native conversions? Retrenchment without giving up the missionary field was obvious. Not only were the Jesuits unwilling to give up the prospect of interior missions, there was no other group with the experience to take them over. The solution that was eventually adopted was to attach a priest, accompanied by servants with trade goods, to a well-disposed native group that would take them along and permit them to live in the native camps and villages. The priest would attend to spiritual affairs while the servants would use the trade goods to compensate their hosts, as well as to trade and thus defray the cost of the journey. This rethinking of the methods by which the missions were to be operated was put into effect in 1660.

Mohawk raids on the lower Ottawa River had been an ongoing problem for native traders traveling to Montreal, but canoes managed to get through with minor skirmishes. Des Groseilliers had brought fifty canoes in 1656, and in 1657 at least thirty, perhaps as many as sixty, canoes arrived.[161] With the French retreat from Onondaga in the spring of 1658, any travel on the Ottawa River became extremely hazardous. In 1658 nine canoes from the west arrived and, in 1659, only six canoes.[162] What fur the colony received came from the Attikameks and others to the north of Trois-Rivières and Tadoussac. The western region had become a problem again, one that desperately needed a solution. At the root of both the missionary and the trading dilemmas were, of course, the poor relations with the Iroquois. Their hostility curtailed any effort west of Montreal and put life within the colony in constant danger. Although diplomacy continued after the collapse of the peace in 1658, the French increasingly felt that only a military solution would end the Iroquois problem. Since the colony did not have the necessary manpower to take on the Iroquois, its members eventually petitioned the home government for troops.

While the Jesuits were rethinking their obligations and the colony was barricading itself against renewed Iroquois attacks, hoping for the arrival of an army from France, Des Groseilliers with his brother-in-law Pierre Esprit Radisson offered the new governor, Pierre de Voyer d'Argenson, a proposal to revitalize the dying fur trade. The two were willing to risk their lives "for the good of the country" by traveling to the interior in order to bring back the native traders and their furs. It was to be the successful 1654–56 voyage all over again.[163] The governor, however, refused to give his permission unless the two explorers agreed to take two of his men along and give him 50 percent of the profits when they returned.[164] Rankled by what they considered to be an unreasonable request, Des Groseilliers and Radisson went to the Jesuits in the hope that they would intercede. However, due to the "shame put upon them" as a result of the debacle of the Onondaga mission, the Jesuits had temporarily lost the influence to help.[165] On 1 August six canoes of Mississauga and Saulteur Indians arrived from the interior with the request that after completing their trade, some Frenchmen return with them as an escort.[166] Both the governor and the Jesuits offered to provide men and asked the natives to wait until a party could be assembled. The Mississaugas were, however, anxious to go and were easily persuaded by Des Groseilliers and Radisson to take them instead.[167] Without permission (in fact, against express orders), the pair departed under cover of darkness early in August 1659 on another major trip of exploration. Their hope was that when they returned, they would not be punished, since "the offense was pardonable because it was to everyone's interest."[168]

The party of Mississaugas, Saulteurs, a couple of Hurons, and the two Frenchmen headed straight for Lake Superior, exactly where Des Groseilliers wanted to go. After a portage across the base of the Keweenaw Peninsula, the party met some Crees, who were happy to see Des Groseilliers and his trade goods back among them. Late in the season the group beached at the bottom of Chequamegon Bay. While the natives departed to find their village, the two explorers built a "fort," cached their merchandise, and had a carefree time hunting and fishing. When Radisson wrote about these events ten years later, he recalled the exuberance the two felt at living in a bountiful environment with people who helped them and never put demands on them: "We were Caesars, [there] being nobody to contradict us."[169]

Two weeks after they had arrived at Chequamegon, the natives returned and escorted the two Frenchmen on a four-day walk south to their village. This village stood beside a small lake "eight leagues in circuit," probably Lac Court Oreilles in what is now Wisconsin. As soon as they arrived, they participated in the Feast of the Dead, an important ritual in which the dead of relatives, friends, neighbours, and allies are buried in a common grave. Radisson correctly interpreted it as "a renewing of friendship." When winter arrived, the village population broke into hunting groups "to seek our living in the woods." This was a period of travel, hunger, and death, with the Indians reduced to boiling and eating leather. Radisson estimated that over five hundred people died of starvation. In early spring, as the hunting groups were reuniting, two Dakota Sioux arrived among them. The visit eventually developed into a full conference with the Dakotas at the Saulteur village. At this time the two Frenchmen promoted a peace between the Dakotas and their traditional Cree enemies. They also promised trade relations between the French and the Dakotas. By midspring Des Groseilliers and Radisson were in the Dakota village in order to finalize the new relations. This village stood some twelve days by foot from Lake Superior, perhaps in the Mille Lacs area of Minnesota, where the eastern Sioux (Dakotas) were located at that time. They may have resided as far as the edge of the prairie, since Radisson mentioned that the Sioux had little wood to burn or utilize.[170] After a sojourn of six weeks, the pair returned with their native companions to Lake Superior, and after another five weeks, they reached Chequamegon. Here Radisson had an accident and for eight days suffered severely from frostbite and exposure.

In the late spring, when "crumbs of ice" were still on Lake Superior, the two explorers left Chequamegon to visit the Crees on the northern side of the lake. From this point on, Radisson's journal is most vague.[171] Some scholars have suggested that the pair traveled to James Bay and back with the Crees, but this is impossible. Since the ice in Lake Superior breaks up in early April, this would not have given them sufficient time to paddle to James Bay, travel "from isle to isle," return to Chequamegon, and be back on the Saint Lawrence by 19 August. Radisson was probably recounting geographical material obtained from the Crees, just as he recounted Sioux stories of a huge lake to the north of them (Lake Winnipeg?) and an enormous river on which one could navigate for more than forty days (the Mississippi?).[172] These stories may have been interpreted as yet more evidence that the Pacific was not too distant.

Sometime in July, Radisson and Des Groseilliers got a large fur brigade together and set off for the Saint Lawrence. After spotting a canoe of Iroquois, the Cree contingent turned back. On the lower Ottawa, at the Long Sault, the group paddled past the remains of an early May battle between the Iroquois and Dollard Des Ormeaux and his sixteen companions.[173] Finally, they arrived on 19 August 1660 at Montreal, with sixty canoes and three hundred natives, carrying furs worth two hundred thousand livres.[174] As soon as they arrived, they were arrested for disobeying the governor's orders. Des Groseilliers was briefly imprisoned, and the two were fined and taxed about 40 percent of their furs.[175] The argument that they had done the colony a service was substantially ignored. Embittered, the two explorers decided to take their complaints to Paris. Eventually both men wound up in the service of England and, with their information on the Crees and the fur resources of the lands south of James Bay, were instrumental in founding the Hudson's Bay Company.

As soon as Radisson and Des Groseilliers returned, they were questioned by the Jesuits about the geography and the native groups to the west. A few weeks earlier, Father Druillettes had interviewed a Nipissing traveler, Michel Awatanik, about the geography of his journeys.[176] These accounts confirmed much of the information that Father Druillettes had gathered in 1656. The journey of Awatanik is worth mentioning because it was one of the few cases of native exploration that is in the documentary record. Awatanik left Green Bay with his family in June 1658. He apparently wanted to find a route to the Saint Lawrence that bypassed the Mohawk blockade of the Ottawa River. The summer and the following winter were spent visiting various refugee Algonquin bands near Sault Sainte Marie and along the shores of Lake Superior. In the spring of 1659 he traveled "by short stages . . . about a hundred leagues" and arrived at James Bay. Awatanik, who had received religious instruction and been baptised, probably took the Nipigon-Ogoki-Albany route in order to visit a refugee Christian Nipissing community on Lake Nipigon.[177] On James Bay he seems to have coasted among the islands, including Akimiski, and visited other refugee Algonquin communities. Among these and the resident Crees, he spent the winter of 1659–60. Of the two routes to the Saint Lawrence—the Nottaway–Saint Maurice and the Rupert-Mistassini-Chamouchouane—

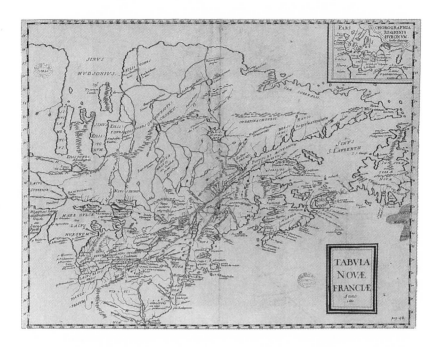

10.3 "Tabula Novae Franciae, Anno 1660," from François Du Creux, Historiae Canadensis (Paris, 1664). The geography of the Great Lakes and the inset of the Huron country are based on information gathered by the Jesuits before 1650. The northern rivers system was compiled by Father Gabriel Druillettes late in 1656, from interviews with Médard Chouart Des Groseilliers and various natives. This is the most interesting and informative midcentury printed map of New France. Courtesy of the National Archives of Canada, NMC 6341.

Awatanik chose the latter in order to avoid potential Iroquois raiders. Father Druillettes finally met Awatanik near Tadoussac.

Using information from Radisson, Des Groseilliers, Awatanik, and others, as well as the map "Amerique Septentrionale" (1650) by Nicholas Sanson, Father Druillettes put together a concept about the geography of North America; his model lasted well into the eighteenth century and was to have a profound impact on further exploration in the seventeenth century. It is the earliest, most complete rationalization for a "Sea of the West." The centre of this model was Lake Superior and Green Bay, along the shores of which were many peoples, most of them refugees from the Iroquois wars, and among whom were some Christians. Food and fur resources were bountiful, some of the native groups practiced agriculture, and there were large deposits of lead, pure copper, "turquoise" (probably Lake Superior amethyst), and gold. This central lakes system was connected to the east by a lakes and river route that led to the Atlantic. Near the western end of Lake Superior was another river, "beautiful, large, wide, deep, and worthy of comparison . . . with our great river St. Lawrence."[178] This river led south "about 300 leagues . . . to the bay of St. Esprit, which lies on the thirtieth degree of latitude, in the Gulf of Mexico."[179]

The river in the report can be none other than the Mississippi. According to Sanson's map, the bay of Saint Esprit is at the mouth of a large river coming from the north, probably the Mississippi. According to both Sanson's map and Father Druillettes's model, to the southwest of Lake Superior, two hundred leagues away, was another lake that emptied into the Vermilion Sea. The Vermilion Sea on Sanson's map is the Gulf of California, the lake (Taosy) is possibly the Great Salt Lake, and the River de Norte by which this lake empties into the Vermilion Sea is the Colorado. North of Lake Superior was Hudson Bay. The two were connected by several river routes. Access to Hudson Bay from the Atlantic was by Hudson Strait. Farther west, Hudson Bay joined Button Bay, which itself was open to the southwest, a passage begging to be explored because, so the model went, it led to the Western Sea. "These two Seas, then, of the South and of the North, being known, there remains only that of the West, which joins them, to make only one from the three."[180] News from a people at latitude 47° and longitude 273° (the Sioux) "assured us that ten day's [sic] journey Westward lies the Sea, which can be no other than the one we are looking for,—it is this knowledge that makes us believe that the whole of North America . . . [is] surrounded by the Sea on the East [Atlantic], South [Gulf of Mexico], West [Pacific] and North [Hudson Bay] . . . and that it only remains now to push on some degrees farther, to enter nothing less than the Japan Sea [Pacific]."[181] A year later, Father Paul Le Jeune wrote, "We have long known that we have the North Sea [Hudson Bay] behind us . . . ; that this sea is contiguous with that of China, to which it only remains to find an entrance; and that in those regions lies that famous bay [James Bay], seventy leagues wide by two hundred and sixty long, which was first discovered by Husson [Hudson]."[182] The French therefore believed that the Atlantic joined—through Hudson Strait and Hudson Bay—a passage to the Western Sea. This sea could also be reached from Lake Superior. The question that was posed was not whether the sea existed but how far away it was. The strategy to be adopted for future exploration was therefore clear:

first, to establish a mission at the hub of the radiating river and lakes system, the thickly populated Green Bay–Lake Superior area, and from there search for the river that led to the Western Sea, as well as the river that led to the Southern Sea (the Gulf of Mexico); second, to search for the route to Hudson Bay, establish a mission among the populous Crees, and then search for the northwestern passage that led to the Western Sea.

The return of Des Groseilliers and Radisson with all their news and three hundred friendly natives was an opportunity that could not be missed to begin the western missions. Fathers René Ménard and Charles Albanel were assigned to the task, accompanied by the servant Jean Guerin and six traders, among them Adrien Jolliet, who later spent considerable time exploring the Lake Superior area. They departed on 27 August from Trois-Rivières.[183] At Montreal, Father Albanel was refused further passage by the natives, but the rest continued. The party moved into winter quarters at Keweenaw Bay on 15 October. After a hard winter during which they almost starved, they crossed the Keweenaw Peninsula and made their way westward along the southern shore of Lake Superior. Judging from a map dating to the late 1670s, Father Ménard got as far west as Chequamegon.[184] From there, in early August, he and the armorer Claude David headed inland to the Huron-Algonquin-Saulteur village visited earlier by Des Groseilliers and Radisson. Along the way Father Ménard got lost and died. The map indicates the site of his death, *"icy mourut le P. Meynard,"* south of a little lake in the headwaters of what appears to be the Chippewa River in northern Wisconsin. Jean Guerin died the following year, in September. Nothing is known about the traders except that they arrived back at Montreal on 25 July 1663 in thirty-five canoes with 105 natives. Not only had the Jesuits lost two men, but the trade that was to defray the cost of the venture fell eight thousand livres short of breaking even. Since the natives who brought the Frenchmen back wanted to return quickly, a new expedition had to wait for the following year.

After Father Ménard had left on his way west, the Jesuits had begun contemplating a journey to the north. During the winter of 1660–61, the Nipissing trader Awatanik "entertained us with a full account" of the people to the north and the annual "fair" that they had there. This was an opportunity not only to open a new mission but also to determine if the "passage to the Sea of Japan is to be found there."[185] The men chosen for this journey were Fathers Claude Dablon and Druillettes. They were accompanied by three traders: Denis Guyon, François Pelletier, and Guillaume Couture. Atawanik and his family were the guides.[186] The expedition started from Tadoussac on 1 June 1661, heading up the Saguenay River. On Lac Saint-Jean they learned that the Cree guides they were to meet had been slain for killing and eating some of their own people in acts of winter hunger and madness.[187] A few days later the two daughters of Awatanik, their guide, died as a result of convulsive seizures, making the grief-stricken father incapable of acting as a guide.[188] On 19 June they entered the Chamouchouane River and six days later, after an interminable series of portages, reached its junction with the Chigoubiche River. Here they followed the Chigoubiche to its source and, after more difficult portages, reached Lac Chamouchouane, the Normandin River, and finally Lac Nicabau. It had been a very difficult route, including sixty-four portages and carryovers. Now raging forest fires and fear of marauding Iroquois prevented the party from going on. At Lac Nicabau (longitude 74°5' west of Greenwich) the Jesuits took their latitude at 49°20' and calculated their longitude at 305°10' east of the prime meridian of Ferro (Nicabau is 304°14' east of Ferro). These two observations have an error of only 2' of latitude and 56' of longitude, astonishingly accurate considering the conditions under which the measurements were made and the instruments that were available for use. From these observations they correctly concluded that they had reached "a place midway . . . between the two Seas, that of the North and that of Tadoussac."[189]

The failure of natives to arrive from Lake Superior and the presence of Iroquois raiders on the Saint Lawrence prevented any exploration in 1662. In the following year Governor Pierre Dubois Davaugour requested Guillaume Couture to head an expedition that would complete the work begun by Fathers Dablon and Druillettes. Couture, who had been on the 1661 journey, chose Pierre Duquet and Jean Langlois to accompany him. The expedition left Québec in mid-May in the company of forty-four canoes of natives. Following the Saguenay-Chamouchouane route, they reached Lac Mistassini on 26 June. In spite of severe weather conditions, they crossed the lake to the entrance of a river "that empties into the Northern Sea."[190] The river could be none other than the Rupert. Here the natives refused to go farther, and the trio had to head back.

The Jesuit mission to Tadousac and the surrounding area had been established for many years. In the winter of 1663–64 Father Claude Nouvel and the trader Charles Amiot traveled with a Montagnais hunting group.[191] The party left Ile Saint Barnabé on 7 December, slowly hunting up the Rimouski drainage system and across the divide to Rivière des Trois Pistoles, finally arriving at Ile aux Basques on 25 April. They then crossed the Saint

Lawrence to the northern shore, where they met a group of Papinachois. Hearing that they were returning to their homeland, Father Nouvel and Amiot decided to join them. The group left the mouth of the Rivières des Escoumins on 3 May and traveled eastward from one river mouth to the next until they reached the Rivière aux Outardes. On 2 June they proceeded up the river for one day. The next day was spent portaging across the five-kilometer neck of land between the Rivière aux Outardes and the Manicouagan. Proceeding up the river, the party reached Lac Manicouagan on 9 June. While preaching among the local Papinachois, the missionaries met other peoples from farther to the north. As far as is known, this was the first expedition up any of the rivers east of Tadoussac.

In 1663 the Lake Superior natives had come to trade and returned Father Ménard's companions. A year later, on 5 July 1664, 220 men arrived, including eighty Crees who wanted a Jesuit to return with them. Although Father Claude Allouez hastily came from Trois Rivières to Montreal, he was too late to accompany them.[192] On 3 August 1665, 400 Ottawas arrived at Trois Rivières accompanied by an unknown Frenchman who had spent the previous year with them.[193] This time Father Allouez was ready, and on 8 August, he left with them for the *pays d'en haut* (the interior west of Montreal). Six Frenchmen accompanied him, but in different canoes. Once out of sight of Montreal, the natives balked at taking a nonworking passenger who, they thought, killed children through the rites of baptism.[194] Eventually Father Allouez found passage with a friendlier group and started wielding a paddle. On 2 September they cleared the Sault and entered Lake Superior. By the end of the month they arrived at Chequamegon, where there were now two large villages, one composed mainly of fugitive Huron-Petuns and the other of Algonquian speakers, primarily Ottawas. It was a superb centre for Father Allouez's new mission of Saint Esprit.

Over the next year Father Allouez had visits from virtually every native group in the area, ranging from the Illinois in the south to the Sioux in the west and the Crees in the north. He also heard of "the great river named Messipi" which was just beyond the Sioux, who lived "in a country of prairies, rich in all kinds of game." The natives also told him that farther west, "toward the setting Sun," the earth was "cut off, and nothing is to be seen but a great Lake whose waters are ill-smelling, for so they designate the Sea." According to the Crees, their rivers flowed into Hudson Bay, where they had seen Europeans.[195]

On 6 May 1667, Father Allouez set off with two natives in a canoe for the northern shore of Lake Superior.[196] Fishing along the way and collecting copper on Isle Royale, the party reached the mouth of the Nipigon River on the twenty-fifth. Here they rested for two days waiting for the ice on Lake Nipigon to break. After paddling on Lake Nipigon for six days, during which time they were also looking for an "outlet" to the lake, they finally came to their objective, a camp of fugitive Nipissings among whom were twenty Christians from the days of the Nipissing mission of the 1640s. Father Allouez spent two weeks with them, until about 18 June, and on 3 August, he was back at Québec (a trip of forty-six days). We know nothing of his return journey. Did he first return to Chequamegon, or did he just continue east along the northern shore of Lake Superior and become the first European to circumnavigate the lake? The distance from the Nipigon River east to Montreal is about 900 miles, whereas the journey by way of Chequamegon and the southern shore of Lake Superior is 1,250 miles. In the former case he would have had to travel at 20 miles per day and in the latter case 27 miles per day. In 1665 the distance between Sault Sainte Marie and Montreal (590 miles) was covered in twenty days going downstream and twenty-five days upstream; from Sault Sainte Marie to Chequamegon (380 miles) was twenty-nine days (1665), and from Chequamegon to the Nipigon River (280 miles) was nineteen days (1667), for a total distance of 1,250 miles in sixty-eight to seventy-three days. Admittedly, the natives were fishing as they were paddling on the two Lake Superior legs of the journey, but it hardly seems possible that this distance could have been covered in forty-six days even if he had hurried. In view of these calculations and of the knowledge the Jesuits had about the northern shore of Lake Superior when next they wrote about it in 1669, it seems probable that Father Allouez was not only the first European to see Lake Nipigon but also the first to travel the entire northern and eastern shores of Lake Superior.

Period 3: 1665 to 1700

In 1663 the administration of New France was totally reorganized. No longer a colony administered by the Compagnie de la Nouvelle-France, it became a royal province of France. Like all the other provinces, it was now governed directly by the Crown through the minister of finance, Jean-Baptiste Colbert.[197] Colbert's long-term plan was to develop France's colonies as suppliers of raw materials to the home country. To do that, they had to be physically secure and have a large degree of economic self-sufficiency. Among the many administrative changes made by Colbert was to

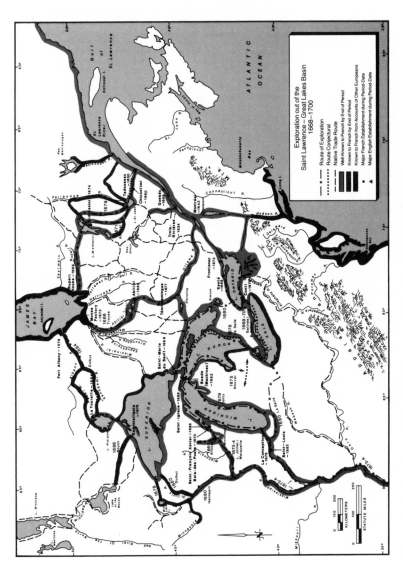

Map 10.3 Exploration out of the St. Lawrence–Great Lakes Basin, 1668–1700.

give the new province an intendant who was to be in charge of justice, administration, finance, and economic affairs. Colbert realized, however, that his administrative changes and economic plans would not get very far unless the Iroquois problem was solved. Deputations had been received from Canada for a number of years with urgent pleas to send troops. Accordingly, in 1665, a new governor, Daniel de Rémy de Courcelle, an intendant, Jean Talon, and a lieutenant general, Alexandre de Prouville de Tracy at the head of twelve hundred seasoned troops with veteran officers, were sent to Canada.

Tracy's orders regarding the Iroquois were unambiguous: "Exterminate them in their own country."[198] When the troops arrived in the summer of 1665, they were put to work immediately in the construction of forts up the Richelieu Valley to act as bases for military operations. Alarmed by these developments, the Onondagas and Oneidas arrived to negotiate a peace. The French, however, were determined to destroy at least the Mohawks. Hoping to catch the enemy unaware, Governor Courcelle marched six hundred men in January 1666 toward the Mohawk villages. Although he accomplished little, the Mohawks were sufficiently impressed to initiate peace negotiations. While these were going on, some Frenchmen were killed by Mohawk warriors. This ended what little trust the French had in Iroquois diplomacy, and in September 1666, Tracy and Courcelle led their army of twelve hundred men, accompanied by one hundred Hurons and Algonquins, into the Mohawk country. Although few Mohawks were killed, their villages and food supplies were totally destroyed and their lands claimed for France by right of conquest. This ended, for some time, the Iroquois threat and reopened the interior just as had the peace of 1654.

Whereas Tracy's orders focused on the military security of New France, those given to Intendant Talon involved the economic growth and security of the colony. In Talon's orders was little that pertained to exploration. In fact, Colbert expressly ordered Talon not to get involved in territories beyond those that could be settled, with one notable exception: Talon was strongly encouraged to find and exploit mineral deposits, especially copper deposits, "which have been proved by explorations that have been made, to be very abundant."[199] For the first few years of his administration, Talon was extremely busy with the Saint Lawrence colony and left the interior to the Jesuits.

In October 1668, a month before Talon was to return to France, he took the opportunity to promote two new enterprises that sent Frenchmen other than Jesuits into the interior. The first of these involved the Sulpi-

cians at Montreal, who had been requested several times by the Cayuga Indians in the Bay of Quinte area on the northern shore of Lake Ontario to
open a mission in their village of Kenté.[200] Talon and Governor Courcelle
were delighted to support this request. Two priests were sent, Abbés
Claude Trouvé and François de Selignac (Fénelon). These were the first Europeans after Champlain on the northern shore of the lake. By November
1670, Abbé Trouvé had traversed the entire northern shore to the Seneca
village of Tinaouataoua, which was a few miles northwest of the present
city of Hamilton, Ontario.[201]

Talon's second enterprise involved the copper deposits he had been ordered to find and exploit. When Father Allouez had returned to the colony
from Lake Superior in 1667, he had brought a large piece of copper to
Talon.[202] This evidence, added to the many stories of the abundant deposits of copper, induced Talon sometime in 1668 to hire the traders Jean
Peré and Adrien Jolliet, for one thousand livres and four hundred livres respectively, to find the copper deposits and an easy route by which the ore
could be transported to the Saint Lawrence.[203] The two departed in the
spring of 1669 in four canoes loaded with trade goods, evidently with the
intention of trading while they were looking for the copper mine.[204] When
the pair got to Lake Superior, they found some Iroquois prisoners among
the Ottawas, one of whom was willing to show them "a new route here-
tofore unknown to the French," one that would lead them to Lake Ontario.[205] The two now decided to split, with Peré continuing in the Superior
country while Jolliet, guided by the Iroquois, paddled south to Lake Ontario. Early in September the latter group reached Lake Erie and two days
west of Long Point hid its canoe and walked overland, reaching the Seneca
village of Tinaouataoua on 23 September. Here Jolliet met Sulpician Fathers
René de Bréhant de Galinée and François Dollier de Casson, traveling in
the opposite direction. Jolliet, guided by the Iroquois, had in fact found the
route that Talon hoped would be there. A year later Fathers Dollier and
Galinée were to confirm this discovery. Peré, in the meantime, seems to
have done very little to find the copper mine. In 1669 the Jesuits reviewed
native stories about the occurrence of copper and added that they hoped
new discoveries would be made in 1670.[206]

In 1669 both the Jesuits and the Sulpicians broadened their operations.
While the Jesuits were active toward the northwest, the Sulpicians hoped
to explore and to open missions toward the southwest. When Father Allouez had returned briefly to the Saint Lawrence in 1667, after an absence of
two years, he found the colony physically secure and plans under way to

expand the missions, including a renewal of those to the Iroquois. As had been tried on Father Ménard's and Allouez's earlier missions, committed laypeople were to accompany the fathers in order to procure food and to erect lodgings and a chapel.[207] In 1668 Father Jacques Marquette joined Father Allouez, followed in 1669 by Father Claude Dablon, who opened a mission at Sault Sainte Marie. For some years, Father Allouez had wanted to visit the Green Bay area in order to see firsthand what the possibilities were for establishing a mission. His opportunity came in November 1669, when he left the Sault with two companions at the request of the Potawatomis to investigate complaints about French traders who were mistreating them.[208] The interior trade was illegal to Frenchmen, but ever since the Jesuits had started taking lay helpers on their trips and especially after the Iroquois defeat, coureurs de bois, as these illegal traders were called, came in increasingly larger numbers to the interior native villages. Whether they did much exploring at this time is not known. Father Allouez encountered two Frenchmen near Michilimackinac and eight more in a village at the bottom of Green Bay. From December 1669 to April 1670 he visited all the villages around Green Bay. On 16 April he headed up the Fox River, through Lake Winnebago, and up the Wolf River to the main Outagami (Fox) village. Although Frenchmen had preceded him, Father Allouez was the first European to leave a description and a map of the route. On his return from the Fox village, Father Allouez went up the Fox River west of Lake Winnebago. Here he heard that the Mississippi was only six days away. On 20 May he set out for Sault Sainte Marie and then returned to Green Bay in the fall with Father Dablon.

While Father Allouez was contemplating his journey to Green Bay and while Peré and Jolliet were supposed to be looking for copper, the Sulpicians were hoping to open a missionary field toward the southwest. Early in 1669, Abbé Queylus, head of the Sulpicians at Montreal, had heard from a Shawnee captive among the Ottawas that there was an easy route through Lake Ontario to his homeland in the Ohio Valley and that he could conduct the Sulpicians there.[209] Abbé Queylus discussed the matter with Father Dollier, and the two went to Governor Courcelle for permission to organize an expedition to the Shawnees on the Ohio River, a journey that Dollier was supposed to lead. Courcelle received them enthusiastically but suggested that they join forces with the twenty-six-year-old adventurer René-Robert Cavelier de La Salle, who was also planning a western journey. Abbé Queylus, who had little confidence in La Salle, now suggested to Father Dollier that he take Father Galinée with him, since the latter had the knowledge to make maps and could lead them out of the wilderness in case La Salle deserted them. According to Galinée, La Salle wanted to find the Ohio River, which he believed flowed west and at the end of which, after seven or eight months' travel, was the sea to China.

The expedition left Montreal on 6 July 1669, in seven canoes with twenty-one men, guided by two canoes of Senecas. Although La Salle claimed to speak Iroquois, the Sulpicians decided to hire their own interpreter, a Dutchman who spoke Iroquois but unfortunately little French. When the Frenchmen got to the Seneca village, they discovered not only that La Salle could not speak Iroquois but also that the Senecas were at war with the Shawnees of the Ohio Valley. The Senecas would not supply guides or allow the French to ransom a Shawnee prisoner. Increasingly nervous among their Seneca hosts, the French decided to join some friendlier Senecas who were going to Lake Ontario and who promised to show them an alternate and easier route to the Ohio. On the way to the western end of Lake Ontario, the expedition passed through unexplored territory. As the group crossed the strong currents emanating from the mouth of the Niagara River, they could hear the falls but did not have time to visit them. Father Galinée stated that Abbé Trouvé had told him he could hear the falls on a clear day at Kenté, some two hundred miles up the lake. From Burlington Bay at the western end of Lake Ontario, the expedition made its way to Tinaouataoua, where it met Adrien Jolliet.

In the meantime La Salle had become ill and wanted to turn back. It is clear from Galinée's account that he did not believe that La Salle's illness was genuine. La Salle, with the change in plans, the lateness of the season, and his own inexperience, probably felt that it was not "healthy" to continue the journey. In any case, Abbé Queylus's fears were realized; La Salle deserted the Sulpicians and returned to Montreal. Fathers Dollier and Galinée also began to have second thoughts about the Ohio. After speaking to Jolliet, they decided to look for the Potawatomis, who spoke an Algonquian language that the missionaries thought they could understand better than Shawnee. Jolliet had also told them that the Potawatomis lived close to a river that could take them to the Shawnees if they wanted to go there at a later date. The helpful Jolliet then supplied them with a sketch map of how to get to their destination and the location of a canoe he had hidden on Lake Erie.

On 1 October the expedition left Tinaouataoua for the headwaters of the Grand River. Here the Dutch interpreter and two native guides—the original Shawnee and another one who had been a captive at Tinaouataoua—

were sent ahead to find Jolliet's canoe. None of the three were ever seen again. The rest of the expedition, all Frenchmen, stumbled down the rapids of the Grand River, which was then in the season of low water. Eight days later they reached the shore of Lake Erie, which they followed for another three days to the mouth of the Black Creek near modern Nanticoke. Here they decided to winter. Although a search party found Jolliet's canoe two days west of Long Point, there was no sign of the interpreter or the guides. Due to a mild winter and a bountiful environment, the party had plenty of food. On 23 March 1670, on the shore of Lake Erie, the explorers took formal possession of the country, and three days later they continued their journey west. On the first day one of their canoes with its baggage was blown away in a strong wind. Part of the group now had to walk along the shore. After crossing Long Point and beating their way through swamps and thickets along the shore, the men finally came to Jolliet's canoe on 10 April. A few days later, after a particularly long and fatiguing day, the party camped at Rondeau Point. Because the men were tired, only the canoes were taken to high ground. During the night a storm caused the water level to rise, and by the morning all their baggage had been swept away. This disaster meant that their plans had to be abandoned. It is probable that neither the canoe nor the baggage would have been lost if they had had native guides. After consulting with each other, they decided not to return by the way they had come, thinking that it would be easier and safer to paddle to the Jesuit mission at Sault Sainte Marie and there join a native canoe brigade that might be heading to Montreal. Now moving more rapidly, they entered the Detroit River and passed through Lake Saint Clair, commenting that it was freshwater, not saltwater as noted on Sanson's (1656) map. Continuing north, along the eastern shore of Lake Huron, they reached the Sault on 25 May. Three days later they headed for Montreal, where they arrived on 18 June.

Although Fathers Dollier and Galinée were very disappointed by their lack of success in opening a mission, it is clear that Intendant Talon thought their journey was significant. In September 1670 he commissioned Simon-François Daumont de Saint-Lusson to travel northwest to Lake Superior in order to look for copper and to take formal possession of the country. At about the same time, La Salle was requested to explore the southwestern route that he had begun unsuccessfully the previous year and that the Sulpicians had been forced to abandon. In a letter to the king on 10 October 1670, Talon announced that with these two "persons of resolution," he was launching an exploration programme that included orders "to keep journals in all instances and reply, on their return, to the written instructions I have given them; in all cases they are to take possession, display the King's arms and draw up reports of the proceedings to serve as titles."[210] In the same document Talon sent a copy of Galinée's map and an abstract of discoveries. A month later Talon wrote to Colbert that he had news that two English vessels were trading on James Bay guided by Des Groseilliers and that he intended to dispatch someone overland to explore a route and contact the Crees to persuade them to travel south to trade with the French.[211] He also mentioned that he was getting disappointingly vague reports from Peré about the copper mine the trader was supposed to be looking for.[212] In a reply to Talon, Colbert, ever the promoter of economic enterprises, wrote, "To discover the South Sea passage [by La Salle], is very good; but the principal thing you ought to apply yourself, in discoveries of this nature, is to look for the copper mine."[213]

Daumont left Montreal in October 1670 and wintered on Lake Huron, where he traded for furs. On 14 June 1671, at Sault Sainte Marie in a most impressive ceremony, he took formal possession of the upper Great Lakes for the king of France.[214] As far as is known, he did not look for copper. In fact the Jesuits wrote that summer, "At present we have no very definite knowledge on the subject [of copper], because no thorough surveys have been made." They added, however, "There are parent mines which have not yet been discovered."[215] A year later Father Dablon reported that Peré had discovered a copper mine at Lake Superior and that a party was sent to make a thorough investigation.[216] As for La Salle, there is no evidence that he undertook any explorations until after 1678.[217]

With Daumont supposedly making discoveries to the northwest and La Salle in the southeast, Talon now turned his attention to a route to Hudson Bay. His aims in commissioning such a voyage were several, all of them prompted by the news of the English activities. Once the route was found, the explorers were to look around the bay for a safe harbour where ships could winter and a fort be built. This fort was to serve as a base from which to supply vessels to "discover a channel between the North and South Seas," presumably between Hudson Bay and the Pacific.[218] The explorers were also to claim the land around the bay for France and to persuade the Crees to trade with the French. The men chosen by Talon were Paul De Saint-Simon and Sébastien Provencher, whereas the Jesuits, who had long been interested in such a venture, supplied their veteran missionary to the Montagnais, Father Charles Albanel. It was Father Albanel's special task to establish a mission. The expedition departed from Tadoussac on 22 August

1671 after having obtained three very reluctant guides.[219] By 7 September, they were at the western end of Lac Saint-Jean and decided to send one of their party back to Québec to get safe-conduct passes from the bishop, the governor, and the intendant in case the English created problems. When the passes arrived on 31 October, it was too late in the season to continue, so the decision was made to winter at Lac Saint-Jean.

On 1 June 1672, the party proceeded up the Chamouchouane River, but instead of continuing west toward Lac Nicabau as the earlier explorers had done, they took the Rivière Nestaocano, portaged to the Metawishish, and reached the eastern lobe of Lac Mistassini (now Lac Albanel) on the eighteenth. From there they descended by way of the Rupert River to James Bay, where they arrived at the deserted English trading post on the twenty-eighth. Their stay on the bay was very brief. An attempt was made to travel to the annual meeting place of the Crees at Pointe Goyeau, but strong winds forced a retreat. Father Albanel preached to the Crees, and on 5 July, the party began its return. The king's standard was raised in a ceremony of formal possession on 9 July at Lake Némiscau and again on the nineteenth south of Lac Mistassini. On the twenty-third the men reached Lac Saint-Jean, and on 1 August, they had returned to Tadoussac. Father Albanel repeated this trip in 1674, but on reaching the mouth of the Rupert River, he was arrested by the English as a spy and deported to England. He did not return to Canada until 1676. Louis Jolliet, with his brother Zacharie and seven other men, made the journey in 1679 but explored different rivers from the ones taken by Father Albanel. Jolliet went up the Mistassini River and across to Lac à L'Eau Froide and then down the Témiscamie to Lac Mistassini. On his return from James Bay, after crossing Lac Mistassini, he followed up the Témiscamie and portaged across to Rivière Péribonca, following it downstream to Lac Saint-Jean.[220] Between 1672 and 1679, the French had finally explored three of the principal rivers to Lac Mistassini, as well as the main route from there to James Bay.

On 4 June 1672, Colbert sent Talon a letter that made western exploration an important aspect of official policy. Following his prime directive, which was to promote population growth, he noted: "There is nothing more important for that country and his Majesty's service than the discovery of the passage to the South Sea [the Pacific]. His Majesty wishes you to offer a large reward to those who shall make that discovery."[221] Talon's response was almost immediate. Since La Salle had accomplished nothing to date, Talon looked elsewhere and fixed on Louis Jolliet to head an expedition. According to Father Dablon, Jolliet was an excellent choice: he was young (about twenty-seven years old) and an experienced traveler; he had been born in the country (Québec); he had tact, prudence, and courage; and he spoke Algonquian. Father Dablon chose as Jolliet's companion Father Jacques Marquette, who had wanted to undertake such an expedition ever since he had come to the Ottawa mission in 1668. Father Marquette was also a relatively young man (thirty-five years old) with experience in the upper Great Lakes. Besides his tremendous desire to undertake the journey and his knowledge of the native groups of the area, Marquette was also an enormously gifted linguist who had attained fluency in six native languages since his arrival in Canada in 1666. Their task was to find the great river the natives had mentioned so often and to ascertain into which of the seas it emptied.[222]

This proposal was endorsed by the newly arrived governor-general, Louis de Buade, comte de Frontenac, just before Talon returned to France in November 1672. As usual, the encouragement for such an enterprise by the government did not mean a financial commitment. Like Daumont, Jolliet was issued a licence to trade in furs in order to raise the money to defray his costs. For this purpose he formed a company (*société*) with his younger brother Zacharie and five others. Shortly thereafter they departed the Saint Lawrence colony and arrived at the mission of Saint Ignace on the Straits of Mackinac on 6 December. Here Jolliet made preparations with Father Marquette for the journey, as well as traded with his partners in the surrounding area. In true fashion, he noted, "We obtained all the information that we could from the natives who had frequented those regions; and we even traced out from their reports a Map of the whole of that new country; on it we indicated the rivers which we were to navigate, the names of the peoples and of the places through which we were to pass, the Course of the great River, and the direction we were to follow when we reached it."[223] For provisions they took corn and smoked meat, and on 17 May 1673, the two departed with five other men in two canoes from Michilimackinac.

Their first stop was among the Menominees, who attempted to dissuade them from undertaking the trip. Along the way, they were told, were warlike people; the great river was dangerous, and the heat in the lands to which they were traveling was excessive. After traveling up the Fox River through Lake Winnebago to the great Mascouten village on the upper Fox River, the Frenchmen were told more or less the same thing. They were now at the limit of previous French exploration. The inhabitants of the village were astonished at the sight of seven Frenchmen, without guides and in only two canoes, daring such an extraordinary and hazardous expedition. The party was traveling, uncharacteristically, without native guides. But guides were needed to get through the tributaries and swamps of the upper Fox River and across the portage to the Wisconsin River. Two Miami guides were hired, and after they took the party across the twenty-seven-hundred-pace portage, they returned home. On 17 June Father Marquette noted that the party safely and joyfully entered the Mississippi.

Paddling south, they did not see any sign of human beings until 25 June, when, following a path from the western bank of the river, they came to three Illinois villages on the northern side of the Des Moines River. Here they stayed for five days. Again the Indians attempted to convince them that the journey was too dangerous for them to proceed. When the expedition reached the mouth of the Missouri River, there was little doubt left that the Mississippi discharged into the Gulf. As to the Missouri, the statements given by natives regarding its course led Father Marquette and Jolliet to speculate that by means of it, one could reach the Vermilion (California) Sea. From the standpoint of later exploration, this was a speculation of enormous importance. Proceeding south, the expedition passed the Ohio River and eventually reached the village of the Akamseas opposite the mouth of the Arkansas River. Here they learned, through an interpreter they had picked up earlier, that they were only a ten days' journey from what they were certain was the Gulf of Mexico. A calculation of their latitude gave them 33°40′, which Father Marquette figured was only two or three days' journey to the Gulf, which he placed at 32° latitude. Although his latitude for the Arkansas was nearly correct, his information on the northern limits of the Gulf was underestimated by about two degrees. In fact, a ten days' trip to the Gulf was more nearly correct than two or three days. After questioning the natives at Akamsea, Father Marquette and Jolliet decided not to go on. Their decision was based largely on the fear that French interests would be compromised if they fell into Spanish hands. From what the natives said, they were certain that the Spanish were present along the northern shore of the Gulf of Mexico.

On 16 July the expedition turned around and departed from the Akamsea village. In order to "greatly shorten [their] road," they proceeded up the Illinois River. At the Illinois village of Kaskaskia near the present Starved Rock, Illinois, they paused briefly. Both the river and the village impressed Jolliet and Father Marquette to the extent that when the villagers asked them to return, they promised to do so. After crossing the Chicago portage, they paddled up the western shore of Lake Michigan and reached the Jesuit mission at Green Bay by the end of September.

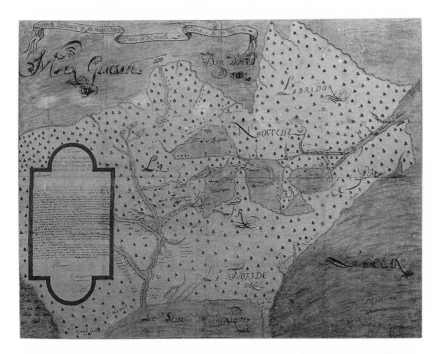

10.4 "Nouvelle decouverte de plusieres nations dans la Nouvelle France en l'annee 1673 et 1674" (Louis Jolliet, 1675). Although cartographically primitive when compared with many other French maps, the Jolliet map depicts what was probably the most universal French image of the interior of North America in the years immediately following his explorations. The Mississippi system is clearly visible and both the upper Mississippi, via close connections to the "Mer Glaciale," and the Mississippi's western tributaries (hidden by the legend), via the Gulf of California (far southwestern corner of the map), would seem to provide water routes across the continent from Atlantic to Pacific. Courtesy of the John Carter Brown Library at Brown University.

The success of the expedition and its possible consequences were recognized by those immediately involved.[224] To the Jesuits, the newly discovered lands had enormous potential for a mission, especially that vast area along the Mississippi from the Des Moines River to the Arkansas and along the Illinois River, which was occupied by the Algonquian-speaking Illinois Indians, who appeared to be friendly, populous, semisedentary, and eager to have a missionary. To Jolliet, the Illinois River valley had excellent potential for a new colony. The area was easy to reach, the climate was mild, and all the natural resources were plentiful. Concerning the route that had been discovered, one would simply have to dig a canal through "half a league of prairie" at the Chicago portage and one would be able to go by ship from Niagara to the Gulf of Mexico. As for the route to the Vermilion Sea, the obvious solution lay up the Missouri River. In the meantime, however, Colbert, who was never enthusiastic about exploration, wrote to Frontenac on 17 May 1674 that he did not approve "distant discoveries" where no Frenchmen could settle, unless it was an area of economic importance that was being threatened by other European powers or it was a route that led to one of the southern seas and was more southerly than the Saint Lawrence. He also did not approve of Frenchmen trading in the interior. Instead he wanted the natives to continue to bring their furs to Montreal. Finally, although he did not want to restrict Jesuit activities, he felt that they would serve a more useful function in the Saint Lawrence colony.[225] Frontenac's reply to Colbert on 14 November was a confused rendering of the expedition, accompanied by a map by Jolliet.[226] If Frontenac had any enthusiasm for furthering these discoveries, he was careful not to mention it. The governor even accused the Jesuits of being in the interior only "to get beavers," and for the time being, that is where matters rested.

The Jesuits, however, decided to pursue the discoveries of 1673, by opening a mission to the Kaskaskias as Father Marquette had promised. Although still exhausted and ill from the Mississippi voyage, Father Marquette went to the Illinois Indians in October 1674.[227] After wintering on the Chicago portage, he reached Kaskaskia early in April. Far too ill to continue his mission, Father Marquette decided to return to Saint Ignace at Michilimackinac. He died on the eastern shore of Lake Michigan, probably at the mouth of the Pere Marquette River. Interestingly, on his return to Kaskaskia, Father Marquette reported a number of coureurs de bois trading with the Illinois. It seems that some Frenchmen had grasped the economic potential of the area.

Unrelated to the major thrust of late-seventeenth-century French exploration out of the Great Lakes basin was the first known expedition into the lower Michigan Peninsula. Late in 1675, Father Henry Nouvel, superior of the Ottawa mission, was asked by a band of Amikwas for a missionary to accompany them to their winter hunting grounds.[228] Father Nouvel decided to go himself and, armed with a map prepared from Amikwa descriptions and accompanied by two Frenchmen, departed Saint Ignace on 8 November. After hugging the western shore of Lake Huron, they paddled into Saginaw Bay and, on 1 December, entered the Saginaw River.

On 7 December they reached their winter quarters, which appear to have been somewhere near the headwaters of either the Flint or Shiawassee River. From this base they traveled to hunting camps throughout the Saginaw drainage system.

French exploration after 1675 was dominated by two rival groups, each identified with particular people and their associates. The Lake Superior–Green Bay–Michilimackinac area had become the trading domain of the coureurs de bois. Of these, Daniel Greysolon Dulhut was the most prominent; with associates such as Jean Peré, he actively engaged in extending trading through exploration. As illegal traders, they did not receive backing through official channels but from the merchants of Montreal, who outfitted them and received their furs. To the south, the lower Great Lakes were dominated by the Iroquois, and the recently discovered Illinois Valley was as yet little touched by French trade. This entire area quickly came under the control of La Salle and his men, aided and under the protection of Governor Frontenac.

Exploration through the southern Great Lakes to the Ohio, Illinois, and Mississippi Rivers was highly dependent on control of Lakes Ontario and Erie. Both Intendant Talon and Governor Courcelle had wanted to establish a fort on Lake Ontario as a base for further explorations, as well as a place from which to trade with and threaten, if necessary, the Iroquois. Notwithstanding Colbert's refusal to permit the construction of such a fort, Governor Frontenac had Fort Frontenac built at the mouth of the Cataraqui River (Kingston, Ontario) in the summer of 1673. This action incensed the merchants of Montreal, who began to fear competition from the governor in the fur trade. This fear led them to increase their efforts in the upper Great Lakes. To a skeptical Colbert, Frontenac justified his actions as a military necessity. Frontenac knew that as governor, he could never get away with operating an illegal fur trade himself; he therefore cast about for someone to do it for him. The logical person was his protégé La Salle, who had acted as commandant of the fort during the winter of 1673–74. With Frontenac's unqualified support, La Salle left for France to petition the king to be granted the fort and its surroundings as a seigneury subject to similar obligations as those of other seigneuries. In the petition he also requested letters of nobility as reward for the "voyages and discoveries which he [had] made at his own expense during the seven years he spent in the country." On 13 May 1675, all of La Salle's requests were granted.[229] He was not given a fur trade monopoly or permission to engage in exploration, however. He was obliged to maintain and garrison the fort and bring settlers to the seigneury. On his return, La Salle threw himself wholeheartedly into the fur trade, ignoring almost completely the obligations of his grant.

While La Salle and Frontenac were consolidating their grip on the fur trade around Lake Ontario and while the Montreal merchants, through the coureurs de bois, traded in the upper Great Lakes, Louis Jolliet was petitioning the court to be permitted to found a settlement in the Illinois country. In essence he was asking for a seigneury similar to that granted to La Salle. This request was refused by Colbert on 28 April 1677 on the grounds that settlements should be confined to the Saint Lawrence colony.[230] In November 1677 La Salle traveled to France to petition for permission to explore toward the west, to locate the mouth of the Mississippi, and to build forts along the way.[231] Through the connivance of Frontenac and powerful lobbyists as well as bribery of some of Colbert's civil servants, La Salle was granted, on 12 May 1678, what had been refused to Jolliet. Although the king had nothing "more at heart than the Discovery of that Country, where there is a prospect of finding a way to penetrate as far as Mexico," and permitted La Salle to erect forts and engage in the "fur trade of Cibola," he absolutely forbade any trade with the natives in the upper Great Lakes and with others who brought "their beaver and other skins to Montreal."[232] According to contemporary maps, such as Sanson's of 1650, Cíbola was the southwestern interior of North America, north of New Spain. Various writers have interpreted this wording to mean that La Salle had been given a trade in bison skins to defray the cost of his explorations.

On 15 September 1678, La Salle was back at Québec with thirty workmen and a large shipment of equipment including rigging for a vessel he wanted to build on Lake Erie.[233] With La Salle were two newcomers who were to have a significant impact on exploration: his able lieutenant, Henry de Tonti, and his chaplain, the Recollet father Louis Hennepin. La Salle's plans were strikingly similar to the suggestions made by Father Dablon in 1674 after the Jolliet-Marquette explorations.[234] With Fort Frontenac secure on Lake Ontario, he wanted to add at least two more forts at major transshipment points, one at Niagara and the other on the upper Illinois River. He already had two ships on Lake Ontario and was now planning to build two more, one to sail Lakes Erie, Huron, and Michigan and the other to travel the Illinois and Mississippi Rivers to the Gulf of Mexico. It was a bold plan to open the southwestern interior of North America to commercial exploitation, not to the exploration and settlement he had promised the king.

Almost immediately after arriving at Québec, La Salle sent a party to

Niagara, where the men built, under Tonti's direction and eventually with Seneca permission, a trading post (Fort Conti) at the mouth of the Niagara River. While the post was under way, a bark (the *Griffon*) of about forty-five tons was built at the exit of Lake Erie above the falls.[235] On 7 August, with the *Griffon* completed, the group set sail and reached Michilimackinac twenty days later. Here the expedition split. Tonti was sent to Sault Sainte Marie to apprehend some deserters who had made off with quantities of La Salle's trade goods.[236] Following that he was to reunite with the others at the southern end of Lake Michigan. After trading at Michilimackinac in contravention of his orders, La Salle sailed to Green Bay, where he did the same. With its hold full of fur, the *Griffon* was now sent back to Niagara while La Salle set off on 19 September with fourteen men in four canoes for his rendezvous with Tonti.[237] Instead of stopping at the Chicago portage, probably because he did not know it was there, La Salle went on to the mouth of the Saint Joseph River, where he arrived on 1 November. Not seeing any sign of Tonti, he proceeded to build a small post (Fort Miami) and set out buoys for the *Griffon*. Twenty days later Tonti arrived, having paddled down the eastern shore of Lake Michigan. Others had preceded him, but it appears to be from this trip that the first detailed maps of the coast were made.[238]

In spite of the lateness of the season and any knowledge of the whereabouts of the *Griffon*, La Salle decided to abandon Fort Miami and proceed to the Illinois River. On 3 December thirty-three men in eight canoes went up the Saint Joseph River looking for a portage that would take them to the headwaters of the Illinois. After searching in vain for a couple of days, they were shown the portage to the Kankakee River by their native hunter. By the end of the month they reached the Kaskaskia village where Father Marquette had begun a mission. From there they went down the river to the southern end of Lake Peoria, where La Salle began the construction of Fort Crèvecoeur on 15 January 1680. With the fort under way, the desertion of six more men, and still no news of the *Griffon*, La Salle ordered the construction of a second bark and laid plans for two expeditions. Michel Accault and Antoine Auguel were to take a canoeload of trade goods and head north up the Mississippi, to be met later in the year at the mouth of the Wisconsin by La Salle's men with more trade goods. They were probably ordered to built a post at the confluence of the two rivers. Father Hennepin decided to join this party. Fearing that the worst had happened to the *Griffon* and needing supplies as well as rigging for the new bark, La Salle decided to return to Fort Frontenac with four men and his native hunter. He left Tonti in charge of Fort Crèvecoeur with the remaining nineteen Frenchmen. On 29 February, Hennepin and his two companions departed down the Illinois, followed by La Salle on 2 March, heading in the opposite direction. Disasters befell each of the three parties.

Shortly after La Salle departed, he met two of his men coming from Michilimackinac.[239] These he sent on to Tonti with instructions to build a new fort on top of a rocky eminence upstream from Fort Crèvecoeur.[240] While Tonti was away examining the new site, fourteen of the remaining crew sacked the fort, stole the trade goods, and deserted. Tonti was left with seven men, including two priests. Immediately he sent two men after La Salle to tell him what had happened. With the fort in ruins, Tonti retreated to the Illinois village of Kaskaskia, near which he was supposed to have built the new fort. On 2 September, Kaskaskia was attacked by the Iroquois. Eventually Tonti and his men were released, and they decided to go to Michilimackinac. Along the way one of the priests was killed. Near Green Bay, a very ill Tonti spent the winter in a Potawatomi village and finally reached Michilimackinac on 15 June 1681.

While Tonti was having his problems, La Salle was on one of the most arduous journeys ever undertaken in seventeenth-century North America.[241] The party had left Fort Crèvecoeur in a canoe but had to proceed on foot from somewhere along the Kankakee River due to icy conditions. On 24 March they stumbled into Fort Miami. Rather than wait for the ice to leave Lake Michigan, La Salle decided to head overland to Lake Erie. The exact route they took is not known. Since they walked most of the way and eventually reached the Detroit River, they likely headed due east from near the mouth of the Saint Joseph River. This was the first time that Europeans had crossed the lower Michigan Peninsula. When they reached the Detroit River, La Salle sent two of his men to Michilimackinac to ascertain the fate of the *Griffon*. With his remaining two Frenchmen and the native hunter, he continued on foot along the northern shore of Lake Erie. About 150 miles from Niagara, they were too ill to proceed on foot and built a canoe, in which they reached Fort Conti, the Niagara post, on 21 April. They had covered some 750 miles in fifty-one days, mostly on foot, during the worst season for traveling. At Niagara, La Salle learned that the ship bringing his supplies from France had been wrecked. He now hurried to Fort Frontenac and went on to Montreal to raise credit for the supplies he needed. Back at Fort Frontenac in July, he heard the news that Fort Crèvecoeur had been destroyed and that some of the thieves and deserters were on their way through Lake Ontario to Albany, having also destroyed Fort Miami, stolen

La Salle's furs at Michilimackinac, and pillaged Fort Conti. La Salle and nine men went out in an armed bark and by the beginning of August had captured three canoes with twenty men. On 10 August, after placing the deserters under arrest at Fort Frontenac, La Salle departed for Michilimackinac with twenty-five men. At the mouth of the Humber River, where Toronto is now located, he split his party. Thirteen men with the heavy baggage went by the longer but easier route through Lake Erie, while he, with the remaining men, went up the Humber, across Lake Simcoe, down the Severn River, and along the shore of Georgian Bay, reaching Sault Sainte Marie on 16 September.[242] He then proceeded to Michilimackinac looking for Tonti, who was at that time fleeing from the Iroquois up the Illinois River. At Michilimackinac he met with the rest of his party, and while they followed, he dashed ahead with eleven men down the eastern shore of Lake Michigan to what was left of Fort Miami. Here he left five men to rebuild the post, while he, with the other six, went on to the Illinois country. On 1 December he saw Kaskaskia, which had been destroyed by the Iroquois. Mutilated corpses were everywhere. Fearing for Tonti, he went on to the ruined Fort Crèvecoeur and finally to the junction of the Illinois and the Mississippi. Retracing his steps, La Salle reached Fort Miami at the end of January 1681. Here he remained, trying to unite the Miami and the Illinois against the Iroquois. When the ice was out of Lake Michigan, he headed for Michilimackinac, where he finally met Tonti at about the end of June.

The party composed of Accault, Auguel, and Hennepin also ran into problems. After equipping themselves with native maps, they left Fort Crèvecoeur on 29 February and reached the Mississippi on about 7 March, where ice conditions stopped them until 12 March.[243] Proceeding up the Mississippi, they reached the southern end of Lake Pepin on 12 April, where they were captured by an Issati (Santee Dakota) war party that was on its way to raid the Miami and Illinois Indians. The three Frenchmen now began a nineteen-day journey to the Santee village: up the Mississippi, past the falls of Saint Anthony (named by Hennepin), and finally five days up the Rum River to Mille Lacs. Here Hennepin met four natives from the Far West, who assured him that "there was no such thing as the Streights of Anian [the Northwest Passage]; and that in their whole Journey they had neither met with, nor passed any Great Lake; by which Phrase they always mean the Sea, nor any Arm of it."[244] There were large rivers running north to south but no seas to the west or northwest. After three months in the Santee Village, Father Hennepin and Auguel, now re-

10.5 "A Map of a Large Country Newly Discovered in the Northern America Situated between New Mexico and the Frozen Sea" (Louis Hennepin, 1697). Hennepin's
map, published almost two decades after his travels, reflects the high degree of accuracy of French knowledge of the Great Lakes and Ohio River drainage areas by the
closing decades of the seventeenth century. Courtesy The Newberry Library.

garded by the Santees as guests, were taken on a bison hunt. Rather than
heading west, the Santees were persuaded to go south to the junction of
the Wisconsin, where Father Hennepin told them they would meet La
Salle's men with trade goods. By mid-July they had reached the Wisconsin.
Not finding anyone there, they began their return north. At the Buffalo
River they met some Santees who made them go south again. Some days
later they heard that five Europeans had arrived among the Dakotas, and
on 28 July, just north of the Wisconsin River, they met Daniel Greysolon
Dulhut and two of his men. The entire group now returned to the Santee
village at Mille Lacs, picking up Dulhut's other two men at the mouth of the

10.6 A buffalo (along with a possum and a pelican) from Louis Hennepin's Nouvelle découverte d'un très grand pays *(Paris, 1697). This is the first major rendering of a buffalo* (bison bison) *since the woodcuts and engravings at the time of the early Spanish entry into the Great Plains. Like the Spanish views, Hennepin's buffalo resembles a European bovine more than it does the major herbivore of interior North America. Courtesy The Newberry Library.*

Sainte Croix River. They remained at the village from 14 August until the end of September. Armed with a map from one of the Santee headmen, the eight Frenchmen descended the Mississippi and eventually reached Green Bay by way of the Wisconsin and Fox Rivers.

The meeting between La Salle's men and traders such as Dulhut was timely but hardly fortuitous. Ever since Frontenac and La Salle had begun their fur trade in the lower Great Lakes, and especially after the voyage of the *Griffon*, the coureurs de bois, aided by the Montreal merchants, had accelerated their trade in the upper Great Lakes. In 1681 Intendant Jacques Duchesneau, who had started complaining about the illegal fur trade to his superiors Colbert and the Marquis de Seignelay when he had arrived at Québec in 1675, made an exaggerated estimate that there were at least five hundred men every year west of the Great Lakes in an arc from the Illinois and Miami Indians to the south to the Sioux and Assiniboines to the northwest.[245] As far as the Crown was concerned, these men were outlaws who traded without permission. They intercepted native traders who would otherwise have gone to Montreal, where furs were traded and taxed. On occasion these men even traded with the English. Although Dulhut always claimed that he was not a coureur de bois, his was a frequent name not only in Duchesneau's dispatches but also in those of La Salle, who was equally vociferous in denouncing his rival.[246]

Dulhut had already been to the Santees before he met Father Hennepin and the others.[247] In September 1678 he had traveled to the upper Great Lakes determined to explore the lands of the Sioux and Assiniboines and to make peace between them. Such a peace would have been a tremendous boon to the fur trade. After wintering near Sault Sainte Marie, he set off for the western end of Lake Superior. Here he met the Santees and accompanied them to their village. On 2 July 1679, he raised the French coat-of-arms in the Santee village and eventually also in the villages of neighbouring Dakotas, the Sisseton and Wahpeton Indians. On 15 September he met with the Assiniboines and Dakotas and made peace between them. While he was among the Santees, he sent three men to explore westward. How long they were gone or where they went is not known. When they returned to Dulhut, they had with them some salt, which had been given to them by men from a Dakota war party. This salt allegedly came from a "great lake whose water is not good to drink."[248] This lake, they were told, was twenty days from whatever location the two Frenchmen had managed to reach. Although some scholars have speculated that this may have been a report on the Great Salt Lake in what is now Utah, it does not seem possible, in view of the distances involved (about one thousand miles in a direct line from the Mille Lacs) and the number of intervening native groups, that the Dakotas could have been raiding that far before they had horses.

Dulhut planned to investigate this report and "to penetrate then to the sea of the west-northwest coast, which is believed to be the Vermilion Sea." In June, Dulhut, his four men, and an interpreter went from the western end of Lake Superior up the Bois Brulé River, portaged half a league to upper Saint Croix Lake, and from there descended the Sainte Croix River to the Mississippi.[249] Here he learned of the predicament of La Salle's men and decided to break off his western journey in order to rescue them. In March 1681, after guiding La Salle's men to Green Bay, Dulhut left for Montreal, hoping to clear himself of charges that he was a coureur de bois. Unfortunately he left for France before he could learn that on 2 May 1681 the king had issued both an edict pardoning the coureurs de bois and an ordinance establishing a system of licenses *(congés)* to regulate the fur trade.[250] Dulhut, Accault, Auguel, and Father Hennepin had shown how to get to the Dakota country. The edict and ordinance of 2 May 1681 now opened the entire interior to a legalized fur trade, which meant the construction of posts and an increase in the number of Frenchmen traveling to the interior. In twenty years, from the days of Radisson, Groseilliers, and the traders with Father Ménard, the number traveling to the *pays d'en haut* had grown to several hundred men. The Great Lakes were now known in all their detail.

While Dulhut was on his way to France, La Salle left Montreal to engage in his last exploratory project from Canada. His aim this time was to find the mouth of the Mississippi River. On 19 December he was back at Fort Miami with Tonti and a party of twenty-three Frenchmen.[251] From there they went by canoe to the Chicago portage, rediscovered by Tonti in September 1680. By now everything was frozen, so they had to drag their canoes and equipment until they found open water on the Illinois 60 leagues (150 miles) below Kaskaskia. On 6 February they reached the Mississippi and five days later the mouth of the Ohio, the river La Salle had wanted to explore when he had first come to Canada. On about 25 February they reached the site of the present city of Memphis. Here they stayed for nine days waiting for some men who had become lost in the forest. During that time they built a small post, which they named Fort Prud'homme after one of the men. During their stay they heard of the Chickasaws to the east, who would later become such a problem to the French settlers at the junction of the Missouri. On 5 March they continued south. Seven days later the expedition arrived near the mouth of the Arkansas River, the farthest point reached by Jolliet and Father Marquette. Finding the natives friendly, La Salle stayed until 22 March. While there he erected the king's arms and claimed the land for France.

South of the Arkansas, the river was more heavily populated, and the farther south they went, the more hostile the natives became. On 27 March they passed the mouth of the Red River, and on 7 April, they reached the Gulf of Mexico. Here they explored a few of the channels of the delta and on 9 April, in an impressive ceremony, took possession of the country in the name of the king. (Almost exactly four years later, Tonti was at the same spot and removed the standard erected by La Salle to higher ground. At that time Tonti was searching for La Salle's ill-fated expedition to the

Texas coast.) On 10 April, short on rations, the expedition turned around. Along the way they were greeted by hostility until they got to the Taensas Indians near the Arkansas River. At Fort Prud'homme La Salle fell ill, and the party split. Tonti reached Michilimackinac in mid-July and La Salle in September. From Michilimackinac La Salle wrote dispatches to Frontenac at Québec explaining what he had discovered.[252] Unknown to him, Frontenac had been replaced as governor by Joseph-Antoine Le Febvre de La Barre. La Barre, as it turned out, was allied with the merchants of Montreal and proceeded to try to undermine La Salle's position at the court. Following the receipt of La Salle's report, he wrote the king that in his opinion, La Salle's discovery of the mouth of the Mississippi was inconsequential and that La Salle's report was "accompanied by a great deal of falsehood."[253] In the return letter written 5 August 1683, Louis XIV replied to La Barre, "[La Salle's] discovery is very useless, and such enterprises must be prevented hereafter, as they tend only to debauch the inhabitants by the hope of gain, and to diminish the revenue from the Beaver."[254] This letter and one written to Intendant Duchesneau on 10 May 1683, opposing further exploration, effectively ended, for the time being, officially sanctioned journeys into new lands.[255]

Out of favour with the colonial authorities, La Salle returned to France late in 1683, in order to rebuild his reputation and to promote a plan to establish a colony among the Taensas of the lower Mississippi. At the court he met Abbé Claude Bernou, who had for some years been promoting a scheme to establish a French colony near the mouth of the Rio Grande to serve as a base for conquering the silver mines of adjacent New Biscay, a province of New Spain. The two men combined forces and, by the spring of 1684, had convinced Jean-Baptiste Colbert Seignelay, now minister of the marine, and Louis XIV of the efficacy of their plans. La Salle's powers of persuasion were such that by the summer of 1684, he was sailing for the Gulf of Mexico in four ships accompanied by 320 persons. By late December he was near the Mississippi delta but, because of mistaken observations made by himself in 1682, believed the Mississippi to be much farther west, near the mouth of the Rio Grande. Accordingly he headed westward. Near Matagorda Bay on the Texas coast the expedition anchored and began to search for an outlet of the Mississippi. In spite of several weeks of futile searching, La Salle decided to disembark on 14 February 1685. In the process the largest of his ships, the 170-ton *Aimable*, was wrecked, and a fight developed with local natives who were trying to help themselves to the cargo.

In March, La Salle's naval escort, the *Joly* commanded by Pierre Beaujeu, returned to France. It now became imperative that a fort be built, and by May, Fort Saint-Louis was under way. The site was not well chosen, and the heat, humidity, hard work, poor leadership, and poor rations were taking their toll. La Salle's colony was dying before it could get started. In October the explorer set off along the coast in the hope of finding a branch of the Mississippi while the *Belle*, a bark of 60 tons, joined the search offshore. La Salle returned in March 1686, having found nothing, and departed again at the end of April to renew his search. A few days later, news came that the *Belle* had been wrecked. La Salle marched off northeast of Fort Saint-Louis and crossed a number of rivers, only to return ill and exhausted in October without having achieved anything of note. On 12 January 1687, he began his final search for the Mississippi, hoping eventually to reach the Illinois country and help for his colony. La Salle was accompanied by seventeen men, leaving twenty-five people behind, including seven women; these twenty-five were all that was left of the nearly two hundred who had begun the colony. On 19 March, La Salle was assassinated by Pierre Duhaut, one of his companions. Seven men who were not implicated in the murder continued their journey, led by Henri Joutel, and reached the Illinois country in September. A little over a year later, in December 1688, Fort Saint-Louis was destroyed by Karankawa Indians. A few survivors were later taken from the Indians by the Spanish who had been searching for La Salle's colony. Thus ended what some have dubbed an ill-conceived venture made even more uncertain because it was led by a headstrong person who, although he had great personal courage, lacked leadership abilities, was prone to making hasty decisions, and cared too little for the feelings and limited abilities of others.

In 1682 Daniel Greysolon Dulhut had returned to Canada. Although he was cleared of wrongdoing, he was unable to obtain a trading and exploration concession similar to the one La Salle had obtained. Back in Canada, he found favour with the new governor, from whom he obtained a license to trade in the Northwest. When he arrived there in the summer of 1683, he found among the various native groups great disaffection toward the French and increasingly closer relations between them and the English on James Bay. To accomplish anything, Dulhut had to bring the various groups back to the French and persuade them, especially the Crees and Assiniboines, not to trade with the English. In view of the outbreak of renewed hostilities with the Iroquois, uniting the Great Lakes natives to the French cause was especially important. To this end, Dulhut and others traveled widely in the Great Lakes area.[256]

In 1684 Dulhut was ready to tackle the English on James Bay. Sometime early in the year he sent his brother Claude Greysolon de La Tourette to Lake Nipigon to build a post in order to intercept and trade with any natives going to the English fort at the mouth of the Albany River. In June 1684, with the post built, Dulhut met with natives on their way to James Bay and sent along with them three Frenchmen: Jean Peré, Jacques La Croix, and Des Moulins.[257] Their main objective was to make their way to the mouth of the Nelson River with letters to Jean-Baptiste Chouart, the son of Médard Chouart Des Groseilliers. Dulhut hoped that Chouart would desert the Hudson's Bay Company and rejoin the French. The fact that there were routes from Lake Superior to James Bay had long been known from native accounts, yet no Frenchmen had traveled them. In mid-July the three arrived at Fort Albany, stating that they were going to the Nelson River to pick up eight Frenchmen. They also wanted to purchase provisions.[258] Since Dulhut's interception of native furs had caused the company considerable damage (according to company accounts, at least ten thousand skins per year) and since the English considered the three to be spies, they were arrested. Peré was eventually deported to England and made his way back to Canada in 1686. The other two escaped from Charlton Island in James Bay and joined some natives who were going to Michilimackinac.[259]

The route these three had taken to James Bay has usually been described as the Ogoki-Albany system, partly because La Tourette's fort was near the mouth of the Ogoki and partly because this is the easiest canoe route. The only evidence for the actual route taken are the maps of the period, especially those of Jean-Baptiste-Louis Franquelin, who was the cartographer in charge at Québec with keeping French maps up-to-date. The year Peré returned to Canada, Franquelin drew a map that is the first record of both the route taken by Peré and that used by the expedition of Pierre de Troyes, discussed below.[260] From this map it is evident that the route taken by Peré went from the eastern shore of Lake Nipigon up the Onaman River to Onaman Lake. From there he portaged and paddled through streams and little lakes to the headwaters of the Kenogami River, which eventually flows into the Albany. A year later, Dulhut's men built Fort des Français at the junction of the Kenogami and Albany Rivers. This was the place that all the native canoes coming from the northern shore of Lake Superior had to pass in order to get to Fort Albany. Once a route was discovered and its commercial potential realized, the French moved rapidly to exploit it. With the building of this post, the Ogoki-Albany route likely came into use.

In 1685 the incompetent Governor La Barre was recalled and replaced by Jacques-René Brisay de Denonville. The new governor was faced with a number of problems, among them new hostilities from the Iroquois and increasing competition from the English on James Bay. Three months after his arrival at Québec, he wrote to his minister that he planned to expel the English from Hudson Bay.[261] From the French point of view, Hudson Bay was French territory. His was a daring plan: to send an overland expedition to James Bay and capture the three English posts. His choice as commander was a captain in the regular troops, Pierre de Troyes, who had just arrived with him in Canada.[262] The expedition was to be financed by the Compagnie du Nord, which had a strong interest in the northern trade. Under his command, de Troyes had thirty soldiers of the Troupes de la marine and seventy Canadian militia who were familiar with canoes and fighting under Canadian conditions. As a choice for a route to James Bay they decided on the most direct one, leading from Montreal up the Ottawa River through Lake Témiscamingue and eventually north to Lake Abitibi and then down the as-yet-unexplored Abitibi River to Moose Factory on James Bay. The expedition left Montreal on 20 March 1686 in thirty-five canoes. Battling bad weather and terrible ice conditions on the Ottawa River, they reached the junction of the Mattawa and Ottawa on 12 May. On 2 June they arrived at Lake Abitibi. At the southern end of the lake they built a fort and, by means of detailed models, planned their upcoming assault on the English posts. On the sixth they departed from the fort, and they entered the Abitibi River in the late afternoon of the seventh. They were now in unknown territory. The 225 miles of the difficult Abitibi River, with nineteen portages and many rapids, were accomplished in twelve days. Considering the number of men involved, the time of the year, the difficulties of the route, and the fact that only one man was lost, this was a remarkable feat. It is no wonder that, when Moose Factory was attacked at dawn on 20 June, the occupants were caught entirely by surprise. Rupert House was taken on 3 July, and after a brief siege, Fort Albany fell on the twenty-sixth. James Bay was now in French hands, and the last of the three major routes to the bay had been explored and mapped.

It is fitting that the last significant journey of exploration to emanate from Canada in the seventeenth century was the one that laid the foundations for the important journeys by members of the La Vérendrye family in the eighteenth century. The journal of the seventeenth-century voyage was paraphrased in a letter written by Intendant Michel Bégon on 12 November 1716, who outlined a programme for western expansion and for renewal of the fur trade. According to the letter, this journey took place in about 1688 and was undertaken by Jacques de Noyon, probably under orders of Dulhut.[263] Noyon started up the Kaministiquia River to Dog Lake. From there he went up the Dog River to a small lake on the height of land, probably Muskeg Lake, and made his way by a swamp and little stream to Lac des Milles Lacs. From that lake he entered a small stream (probably the Seine River) and, traveling downstream for two days, came to a waterfall (Sturgeon Falls). Shortly after that he entered Rainy Lake. At the western end of the lake, on the banks of the Rainy River, he built a post and wintered. While he was there, the Assiniboines told him wonderful stories of bearded white men on horses, fortified towns, ships, and a city with stone walls, stories they had probably heard about the Spaniards. They also told him that if he followed the Rainy River, he would get to Lac aux Isles, or Lac Assiniboines (Lake of the Woods), at the western end of which was a river that emptied into the Western Sea. Noyon was in no position to pursue these stories, and so he returned to Lake Superior in the spring of 1689. His journey, however, was an important precursor in the renewal of the search for the Western Sea, a search this time begun by Zacharie Robutel de La Noüe in 1717 and continued by La Vérendrye after 1728.

With the English substantially eliminated from James Bay, La Tourette, Dulhut, Pierre Le Sueur, Perrot, and other traders were having such success procuring furs that they were creating a glut of beaver pelts on the market. At the same time the expensive Iroquois wars were winding down, with the French and their native allies as victors. These two events, as well as Jesuit complaints that the traders in the interior were undermining their missionary effort, persuaded the king to retrench French activities. In May 1696 he ordered an end to the system of licenses, banned the trade in beaver, and ordered all posts closed except for Fort Frontenac and Fort Saint-Louis des Illinois on the southern frontier near the English. All traders, soldiers, and coureurs de bois were supposed to return from the interior. Although not all men did return to the Saint Lawrence, this reversal of policy effectively prevented further exploration from Canada until the fur trade picked up again in 1716.

A Summary of One-Hundred Years of French Explorations

The extent of geographical knowledge gained by the French during the seventeenth century is exemplified by Guillaume Delisle's map "Carte du

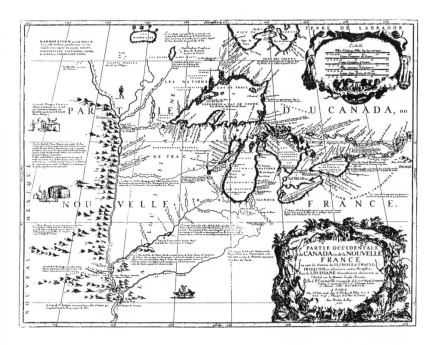

10.7 "Partie Occidentale du Canada ou de la Nouvelle France," by Vincenzo M. Coronelli, published in Coronelli, Atlante veneto (Venice, 1690). This map, from Coronelli's great atlas, is a curious mixture of accurate geographical information and fictitious geography. The numerous legends on the map contain extensive ethnographic data on the native peoples with whom the French explorers had come into contact in the latter half of the 1600s. Courtesy of the National Archives of Canada, NMC 6411.

Canada," engraved in 1703.[264] This shows that the French had a clear grasp of the Saint Lawrence Valley and the Great Lakes and a good knowledge of the space relations between Hudson Bay and the Great Lakes as well as of three connecting routes: the Saguenay-Mistassini-Rupert route, the Ottawa-Abitibi route, and the Nipigon-Albany route, shown incorrectly on this map as connecting to the Moose River. The Mississippi River had been explored and its headwaters sketched in from native accounts. The Iroquois country south of Lake Ontario was well-known and mapped in great detail. Areas outside direct French knowledge were the interior north of the Saint Lawrence and east of the Saguenay, the area northwest of Lake Superior, and the Wabash-Ohio Valley. There were reasons for these gaps

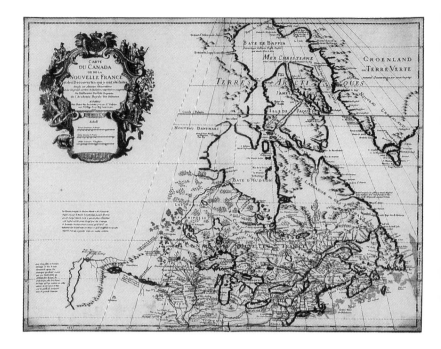

10.8 "Carte du Canada ou de la Nouvelle France" (Claude and Guillaume Delisle, 1703). This Delisle map is the most complete representation of the extent of French knowledge of northern North America at the end of the seventeenth century. It was based on material in the archives of various French ministries responsible for North American affairs. Like other cartographers, the Delisles incorporated Lahontan's fictitious geography on the western portion of their map. Courtesy of the National Archives of Canada, NMC 10648.

in knowledge. The northern interior of Québec is extremely rugged and was thinly populated. After the routes to James Bay were discovered and posts and missions erected on the periphery of the area, the French had no reason to want to travel into it. The area northwest of Lake Superior seems, on the surface, to have been a logical area for early penetration because later experience showed that it held the only practical route to the west. This fact was not known in the seventeenth century, however, and until the Mississippi had been explored along with some of its tributaries, French attention was diverted southwest, not northwest. In addition, the Northwest was the scene of frequent conflict between the Sioux to the south and the Crees and Assiniboines to the north. Rather than set up posts between these opposing groups, the French preferred to contact each native group separately. Operating between them was far too dangerous unless a firm peace could be arranged. As for the third area, the French had heard of the Ohio River by the mid-1640s, as a possible route to the west. By the time they were on sufficiently friendly terms with the Iroquois who controlled access to the Ohio, however, the valley was no longer of prime interest to them. The valley did not produce valuable furs in adequate quantities, its inhabitants had been dispersed by the Iroquois, and alternate routes had been discovered to the Mississippi. Exactly when the French explored the Wabash-Ohio system is not known. It may have been just before 1700, when traders moved to the Wabash in order to contact the Miamis who were getting reestablished there.

The motives that originally pushed the French into the interior and continued to do so throughout the seventeenth century were the fur trade, the missions to the more populous native groups, and the hopes of finding an easy route to the Pacific Ocean. Most often these motives were mentioned together as reasons for undertaking voyages of exploration. The French court was only occasionally interested in exploration. On those occasions, it hoped to find a western passage, discover minerals, and meet the dangers of English competition in the fur trade. Exploration in support of an expanding fur trade contributed enormously to geographical discovery but was never really sanctioned by the court. As far as the Crown was concerned, the fur trade was supposed to be operated by the natives bringing their furs to the Saint Lawrence posts. Frenchmen were to stay in the colony, farm the land, and defend it if necessary. All the senior French ministers noted, with some chagrin, that journeys of exploration usually degenerated into fur-trading ventures. Although this observation was somewhat unfair, one must note that the passage to the Western Sea, a passage that was always promised, was never found. The rivers never seemed to flow in the hoped-for direction, and most often, furs had to be traded to defray the cost of exploration because the niggardly Crown would never contribute anything. In some respects, missionaries were ideal explorers. They were good observers, literate, and interested in geography. Their prime objective was, however, the conversion to Christianity of native people, and once they were established in a community, that objective was achieved. Nevertheless, except for explorations after 1670, when the fur trade rapidly accelerated in the interior, missionaries either did, or participated in, much of the exploratory work.

Along with the rapid growth in knowledge about the North American interior came the remarkable adaptation by the French to North American environmental and human conditions. At the beginning, two enormous hurdles had to be overcome: good relations had to be established with resident native groups; and the French had to learn how to survive a winter without losing half their men. To these two skills they had to add three more: how to travel over water in the summer; how to travel over snow and ice in the winter; and how to live off the land. The fur trade and the French willingness to take the side of their trading partners in the war against the Iroquois helped establish good native relations. French attitudes toward natives in general were also a moderating influence. Generally speaking, the French considered natives to be human beings with whom they could communicate, from whom they could learn, and with whom they could live. For those French who knew the natives well, there were no major physical or mental differences between the two groups. Although all natives had some cultural values the French abhorred, the French hoped that these would disappear over time, especially once Christianity was accepted. As Champlain observed early on, exploration could be carried on only with native help. That was true, but he might have added that the French had to be adaptable and willing to learn from the natives who were willing to help them. This the French did, and by the 1670s they were traveling in the interior in summer or winter, in safety and with some degree of self-assurance. Native guides were almost always present, but dependence on them lessened over time as French travel skills and linguistic abilities developed.

Seventeenth-century French exploration in North America owed its success in large part to the remarkable interplay between the French and the native cultures they encountered. In some ways this success was all the more remarkable considering the tiny population base from which the French operated. In 1608 Québec had a permanent population of only twenty-eight. The entire colony had sixty-eight hundred people when Dollier and Galinée began their push west in 1669 and only double that number at the end of the century. For such a colony to exist, let alone engage in extensive exploration, people of all cultures had to cooperate with a great deal of diplomacy and understanding. Obviously, animosities surfaced on occasion, but the lessons in human relations learned in the seventeenth century would ultimately lead the French to the Rocky Mountains and would set the pattern for English explorations after the defeat of New France in 1760.

11 / French Exploration in North America, 1700–1800

W. J. ECCLES

During the eighteenth century, the French thrust their exploration of North America far to the west of the Mississippi, up the Missouri beyond the Platte, and along the Saskatchewan to the foothills of the Rocky Mountains. They also established themselves, briefly, on Hudson and James Bays. All the principal rivers north of the Great Lakes, as well as all the tributaries of the Mississippi, became known to them. For the four decades preceding the conquest of New France they strove, without success, to reach the Pacific Ocean overland by way of the mythical "Mer de l'Ouest." Another powerful incentive for French thrusts into the Far West was the lure of commercial profit: in the Northwest, from the trade for furs with the Indian nations; and in the Southwest, from the establishment of trade relations with the Spanish settlements in northern New Spain—to be more precise, between New Orleans and Santa Fe. Thus the map of the interior of North America gradually began to unfold and to be depicted by such eminent cartographers as Guillaume Delisle, Jacques-Nicolas Bellin, Zacharias Chatelain, and Nicolas de Fer.

Most of the information used by these cartographers to draw their maps, which today delight with their artistry and impress with their remarkable accuracy, was supplied by the royal officials at Quebec, who, in turn, obtained it from officers stationed at the western posts, from fur traders, and from missionaries. Nor was it only the land that was being explored. These men who voyaged in the Far West, some of them residing there for years on end, also explored the culture, the mores, the cosmology, and the religious beliefs of the Indians with whom they interacted. Of necessity, they had to adjust to, and indeed adopt, the Indians' way of life. The outlook, the way of life, of the Indians who encountered the French also underwent a profound change. For both parties, this was a form of exploration, a mental glimpse of strange new worlds. Although France claimed title to all these lands by right of "prior discovery," the French did

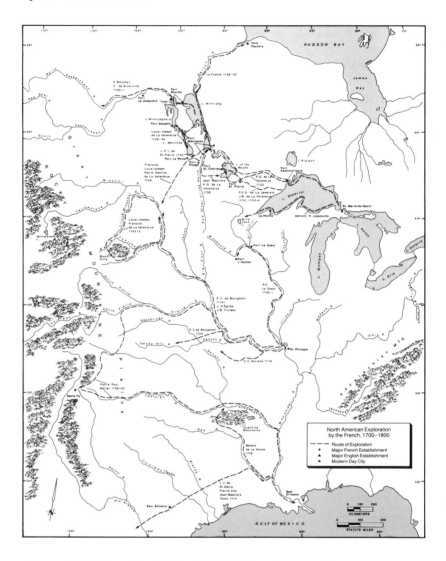

Map 11.1 North American Exploration by the French, 1700–1800.

not dare apprise the Indian nations that the title to their country had been claimed by the monarch of a country thousands of miles away, at the far side of a vast ocean. The lands around the Great Lakes basin, in the Mississippi Valley, and across the northern plains remained Indian territory. There the writ of the king of France did not run very far.[1]

It was, therefore, the Indian nations that called the tune to which the

French had to dance. The French had to master the Indian languages—Algonquian, Iroquois, Sioux—in a multiplicity of dialects; they had to adhere rigorously to Indian protocol at meetings and master the Indian style of oratory, with its grandiloquent use of metaphors that put one governor-general of New France, the flamboyant Louis de Buade, comte de Frontenac, in mind of the Senate of Venice, which he had once addressed.[2] The French also had to provide liberal "presents" on all official occasions. The French word *présents* in this context was really a euphemism for "tribute," since the French could not bring themselves to admit that they were obliged to pay anything to the Indians. Yet the tribute had to be paid to ensure that the Indian nations would allow the French to travel through their lands and establish trading posts on Indian land for their mutual convenience. The Indians could not possibly conceive of the French having the effrontery to claim possession of their lands, and the French were careful never to mention such a notion to them—just to the British, who also laid claim to a third of the continent, of which they had seen only the shoreline, by virtue of a royal patent issued in 1609. Were any Frenchman to have told the Indian nations that their lands had, in some mysterious fashion, become French territory, the consequences would probably have been fatal. In fact, French claims to sovereignty in the Indian country extended no farther than the range of a musket from the palisades of their forts, and sometimes not even that far. This hidden factor would impede French exploration of the Far West until the conquest of Canada, the end of the French regime in North America, and would frustrate the ardent desire of the French Crown to have one of its subjects be the first European to reach the Pacific by an overland route.

In the seventeenth century the French had had to reconcile themselves to the fact that the political framework of the Indian nations was pure anarchism. Combined action—major undertakings such as moving a village to a new site, waging war, or making peace—could be carried out only by consensus, for all Indians were free; no one, no group, could compel an Indian to do anything that he chose not to do. This eventually was to be their undoing as the European invaders continually encroached on their lands. Early on, during the Franco-Iroquois wars, the French also had to master the Indian style of warfare: the ambush, the swift savage attack, then a swifter retreat to avoid being taken captive in a counterattack and subjected to the long, drawn-out torture ceremony. For the Indian, it was far better to die fighting than suffer that fate.

In their travels the Canadians adopted the Indians' mode of dress, birchbark canoes, snowshoes, and toboggans. The legendary voyageurs who, in the eighteenth century, made the long journeys into the interior of the continent were barely distinguishable from the Indians. They were men with powerful physiques, no fat on their frames, accustomed to paddling in a canoe from sunrise to sunset, carrying two- and three-hundred-pound loads on their backs over the portages, using a tumpline stretched over their foreheads, straining their neck muscles. They wore their hair in a pigtail, frequently sheathed in an eelskin, and their faces, arms, and thighs were as bronzed as an Indian's. In the early spring they signed on at Montreal for a voyage to Detroit, Michilimackinac, Kaministiquia, La Poste du Sud, La Poste du Nord, La Baie, and eventually, la Mer de l'Ouest. In late August they returned to Montreal in time for the harvest, their canoes loaded with a year's catch of furs. For their summer's toil they were paid 300 to 450 livres, as much as a skilled artisan earned in a year. (As an educated guess, the eighteenth-century Canadian livre had the buying power of twelve 1990 U.S. dollars.)

The trade goods intended for the western posts had to be transported by cart from the warehouses of the Montreal merchants to Lachine, some fifteen miles from the town, where the turbulent rapids barred the route. There, above the rapids, the thirty-six-foot *canots de maître* were loaded. The voyageurs then doffed their breeches and stripped down to a loose blouse, *mitasses* (leggings) that wrapped around their calves, a *braguet* (breechclout), and deerskin moccasins.[3] This was the Indians' mode of dress, adopted because of its practicality. Breeches would quickly have become sopping wet as water dripped from paddles or sloshed over the canoe's gunnels in choppy water. Squatting all day in wet clothing would have invited rheumatism and pneumonia, whereas water ran off bare thighs rubbed with bear grease and *mitasses* could be wrung out and dry ones donned when the canoe brigade halted each hour for a few minutes' rest and a smoke while the storyteller among them spun a tale. Once ashore for the night, the men put on breeches to keep the mosquitoes and blackflies at bay. In the canoes, along with the trade goods were textiles and items of clothing in bales, hardware in chests, and eau-de-vie comprising spirits such as cognac, armagnac, marc, calvados, and wine in small kegs. There were also supplies for the post commandants, who were not to be denied the amenities to which they were accustomed at home. They were provided with ample supplies of such items as wine, eau-de-vie, vinegar, olive oil, molasses, butter, salt, pepper, spices, soap, candles, and writing paper.[4]

The voyageurs had to make do with humbler fare. Their rations were meagre; valuable space could not be wasted, and the less there was to carry over the portages the better. They were allowed two *pots* (four quarts) of eau-de-vie for their own consumption to aid the digestion. Since their basic rations consisted of cornmeal, boiled with bear grease, and dried venison or salt pork, a tot of brandy would have been welcome. In addition to food, they had, every one of them, to take with them a serviceable musket and had to present it for inspection on their return on pain of three months in prison if caught without it.[5] They did, however, provide for their own amusement; one voyageur is on record as having obtained some goods, including six violin strings, for his own use during his ensuing voyage.

The canoes went west in a convoy under the command of an officer in the colonial regulars, the Troupes franches de la Marine. It was not safe for one or two canoes to venture alone into the Indian country; the pillaging of canoes was all too likely, and resistance could mean a swift death.[6] Each canoe carried a sheet of birchbark to patch a damaged hull, a few lengths of wattap—a thin, long, flexible white pine root used to sew on patches, which were then sealed with spruce gum—a large sponge, and a square of canvas used as a sail in a following wind.[7]

Some voyageurs opted to serve at a western post for three years, with a renewable contract. These were the *hivernants*, the winterers. Some of them remained in the West most of their lives, took Indian girls as wives, and returned to the Canadian settlements only occasionally. They were the progenitors of the métis nation.[8] At the posts their duties were to venture out to the remote Indian villages to barter for furs. They had to master the languages of the tribes they sought to bring into the French commercial empire, be astute diplomats, never give offence, adhere rigorously to Indian protocol in all their dealings, be generous with "presents" (for there was nothing the Indians detested more than parsimony), but at times let it be known that they could, if need be, summon the power of the French Crown and hence would tolerate no nonsense. Sometimes this veiled threat worked; often it did not. The French Crown was remote, and the French were very thin on the ground compared with the many hundreds of warriors the Indians could muster. Thus these French traders had to discover at the outset which tribes were regarded as friendly by the tribe presently being dealt with and which were seen as hostile, for it could be fatal to establish relations with a tribe at war with the one then being approached. More than a few Canadians lost their lives for making that mistake.[9]

The French had encountered this problem early in the seventeenth century and were to encounter it time and time again in the eighteenth: progress farther into the interior became blocked because a nation would not allow an ancient and current foe to acquire firearms and iron weapons from the intruding Frenchmen. For far too long, scholars have maintained that these nations, beginning with the Hurons in the 1640s, refused to allow the French to make contact with more distant nations because they wanted to retain an imagined middleman's position in the fur trade, whereby they obtained furs from more remote tribes in exchange for European goods and then traded the furs to the Europeans at a handsome profit. This economic determinist concept views the Indians as being motivated by European socioeconomic values, as capitalist entrepreneurs in moccasins, seeking to buy cheap and sell dear.[10] Such a concept was quite alien to the Indians' way of life, to their social values. Moreover, had profit been their motive, what could they have done with it?

What is made plain in the tangential evidence produced by the French commandants at the western posts—officers such as Paul Marin de La Malgue at La Baie-des-Puants (Green Bay), Pierre Gaultier de Varennes de La Vérendrye at la Mer de l'Ouest, and the French explorers in the Southwest, Bénard de La Harpe, the brothers Pierre and Paul Mallet, and Etienne Veniard, sieur de Bourgmont—is that the opposition to French exploration of the West stemmed not from the Indians' desire to obtain or retain a middleman's position in trade but from their desire to prevent the French from supplying their foes with arms and ammunition. In February 1700 Pierre Le Moyne, sieur d'Iberville, wrote to the minister of marine from Louisiana to inform him that Henri de Tonti and the other French with the Illinois Indians did not believe that Pierre-Charles Le Sueur could go in safety to the Sioux, among whom he intended to establish a trading post, without being pillaged en route by the Illinois, who were determined to prevent the French from supplying arms to their ancient foe. The Illinois had, Iberville noted, already pillaged eleven Canadians and seized three thousand livres weight of beaver pelts.[11] In fact, the Poste des Sioux was established and reestablished several times and always had to be abandoned whenever the Sioux became vexed.[12]

Thus it was that the French had to inch their way slowly into the interior, establishing good relations with first one nation and then with another farther on that was not an enemy of the first nation and then only after obtaining the latter's consent. It became a major factor in French policy that the commandants at the western posts were to strive to maintain peace among the various nations.[13] Sometimes these officers were treated with disdain by their Indian allies when they refused to join in a campaign to seek revenge for the slaying of some of their own men.[14] Among these peoples, war was the normal state of affairs, as it was among the European states, and it had been for as long as men could remember, for only in battle could warriors prove their claim to courage and valour and hence acquire a reputation and an enviable status in their society.

These Canadian fur traders who lived among the nations of the Northwest became almost as much Indian as French and took Indian girls as wives, sometimes on a temporary basis and sometimes permanently; the temporary practice came to be referred to as "savouring the wine of the country." These marriage alliances were regarded favourably by the Indians, since they strengthened the bonds between the two races, but they were frowned on by the royal officials and the clergy, who maintained that the offspring of these marriages combined the worst features of both races.[15] Yet without this close relationship, the French could not have voyaged as they did among nations that did not trust them, that feared them to a point, but that had no love for them.[16]

Nor were the French the only explorers. The Indians also explored the strange world and way of life of the French, whom they regarded with some disdain. To them the French appeared to be physically stunted, with repulsive hair on their faces and bodies. Worse still, the inability of most of the Frenchmen to speak any language of the Indians was a clear indication that they were mentally retarded. Their salted food was inedible, and many of their customs were utterly barbaric. Moreover, the Indians had to teach them how to survive in the wilderness, how to make canoes, snowshoes, and proper clothing, how to lure big game within sure range of an arrow or musket ball. Yet the Frenchmen held a certain fascination, which was to prove fatal for the Indians. Their ironware and firearms had advantages over the Indians' own tools, utensils, and weapons; their tobacco was fragrant, and their eau-de-vie set a man up wonderfully, transporting him to the spirit world in short order.[17] Most of all, since there were so few of them in the Indian country, how could they possibly constitute a serious threat? The Indian nations therefore frequently sent delegations to Canada to discuss vexing problems, issues, and alliances and to discuss exactly what the French were about; one surmises that they went in much the same frame of mind as that of present-day American tourists venturing into the Province of Quebec.

While at Montreal or Quebec conferring with the local governor or the governor-general, they expected to be feted royally and to participate in a generous exchange of "presents" according to Indian custom. At all these meetings, Indian protocol had to be followed, religiously; hence the speech-making could last for days. No matter how long an Indian orator spoke, he had to be heard out in attentive silence; an interruption would have been regarded as an intolerable insult. The French became very adept at these ceremonies, larding their own speeches with metaphors to emulate the oratory of the Indians. These occasions were a considerable charge on the colony's budget, but it had to be borne. When an Indian delegation established its camp near Montreal and ran short of meat, a Canadian's cow, pig, sheep, or dog was killed for the pot. Early complaints by the French on this score received a curt answer: the French were allowed to hunt game in the Indians' country; therefore, they should extend the same courtesy to the Indians.

Paul Marin de La Malgue, commandant at La Baie-des-Puants (Green Bay), stated that his attempts to prevent an outbreak of warfare among the nations in his region had cost him over ten thousand livres for "presents" to calm things down.[18] On one occasion he wrote to his brother-in-law, Claude Deschambeau, at Montreal warning the latter that he had promised some of the Indians of his district, who were about to send a delegation to confer with the governor-general, that while the Indians were there, Deschambeau would be pleased to put on a magic lantern show for them. He was sure that they would be suitably impressed.[19]

Quite a number of delegations from nations allied with the French were sent on trips to France, all expenses paid, to be regaled and shown the splendours of Versailles and Paris. One can well imagine the tales they had to tell when those who survived returned to their wilderness villages, accoutred at council meetings in the dress of French courtiers.[20] More than likely the tales did not all redound to the credit of France and the French. The squalor of Paris, the stench of Versailles—it could be smelled thirty miles to the east when there was a brisk western wind—would likely not have been to the liking of the men of the forest, lakes, and prairies. In all probability the Indians' innate superiority complex would have been strengthened. Still, they must have become aware of a wider world and had their horizons lifted, just as had the many hundreds of Canadians who voyaged to the Indian country, who lived among its peoples for months and years, and who became a people very different from their French antecedents, who never ventured farther than a day's walk from their native villages and were never out of sound of the bells of their parish churches. All of this was exploration, exploration of *mentalités*.

Exploration at the Beginning of the Eighteenth Century

In the year 1700, how far did the knowledge the French possessed of the geography and topography of North America extend? Today we can seek the answer only from contemporary documents, maps, and to some extent, archaeological evidence. The documents and maps tell us that the French had some knowledge of the shape of things to the west as far as Lake Winnipeg and to the north well beyond the Hudson Bay–Saint Lawrence River watershed. They also had preconceived notions, derived from information passed on to them by the Indians, of what lay beyond Lake Winnipeg. By the end of the seventeenth century, Canadian coureurs de bois had voyaged west well beyond Lac des Assiniboines, which would have been either Lake of the Woods or Lake Winnipeg, more likely the former.[21] Thus they would have gone beyond the Canadian Shield, out of the boreal forest dense with spruce, fir, tamarack, jack pine, poplar, aspen, and birch, with its millions of lakes amid the muskeg, and out onto the prairies, flat as a billiard table for hundreds of miles in every direction. To the north lay the gently rolling, wooded parkland, then the tundra. The transition from the topography of the Shield to that of the prairies was sudden and startling; one moment the voyager was surrounded by densely timbered, jumbled rocky ridges, the rivers a steady succession of rapids and cascades, and then, abruptly, one emerged onto the flat, green plain, covered with dense, waist-high grass where herds of millions of buffalo grazed, along with numerous elk. Above was the dazzling blue sky that seemed to stretch forever. Once at Lake Winnipeg, the voyager had a choice: the Nelson River led northeastward to Hudson Bay; and the Saskatchewan beckoned, upriver, all the way to the Rocky Mountains.

More than river routes was needed to travel in that country. One needed a means of transport—which for the French was an enlarged version of the Indians' birchbark canoe—and adequate food supplies. The canoes used from Montreal to Kaministiquia, at the western end of Lake Superior, were the *canots de maître*: thirty-six feet long, carrying a crew of eight to ten and a six-thousand-pound cargo. Beyond Lake Superior, the small *canots du nord* had to be used: twenty-five feet long, with a crew of five or six men and a cargo of some three thousand pounds.[22] Fortunately the supply of white birch trees was adequate, and the great buffalo herds, along with elk, deer, moose, bear, ducks, geese, fish, wild rice, and corn, provided more than enough food most of the time. Unfortunately this game supply could make itself scarce, suddenly vanishing at inconvenient times and reducing the voyageurs to the verge of, and sometimes beyond, starvation.

Then suddenly, in the year 1700 on the eve of the War of the Spanish Succession, King Louis XIV made the momentous decision that would shape the course of North American history to the end of the century. He decreed that the English colonies must not be allowed to expand beyond the crest of the Allegheny mountain range.[23] He and his ministers had a vague idea where those particular mountains were and how far they extended. Beginnings were then made on the establishment of a new colony in the lower Mississippi Valley, predictably named Louisiana.[24] Another incipient colony, named Detroit, a dependency of Canada, was established on the Saint Clair River between Lakes Erie and Huron. Louisiana was intended to block any advance that the English of the Carolinas might try to make to the Mississippi and beyond to threaten New Spain. A grandson of Louis XIV was very soon to sit on the Spanish throne, hence France had to protect Spain's American colonies.[25] Detroit was intended to give France command of the Great Lakes and block that route to the Far West to the English colonials. France thus gained control of the two great waterways leading into the interior of the continent. The only other entry, Hudson Bay, was navigable only a few weeks in the summer, and the Hudson's Bay Company held only one post on James Bay, vulnerable to attacks from Canada. The French held the main post, Fort Bourbon, which controlled the mouths of the Nelson and Hayes Rivers. Although those two rivers gave access for canoes to the interior, they flowed through difficult terrain where game was scarce, "the starving country."[26] For the Crees of the prairies it was a risky race to get to the bay posts and back before getting trapped by the ice. French imperial policy now required that military outposts be established throughout the West. From this point on, the economics of the fur trade were subordinated to penning the English colonials between the Appalachian mountain range and the Atlantic. That was to remain French policy in North America until 1783. In 1696, faced with a glut of beaver pelts that had bankrupted the trade, the French government had sought to bar the Canadians from voyaging west in search of furs. Now, suddenly, the ban was lifted. In response the Canadians flooded into the Far West, both to the north and to the south.[27] In 1713, when the Treaty of Utrecht ended the War of the Spanish Succession, Louis XIV made territorial concessions in America to avoid having to make them elsewhere. Significantly, he made them in the East rather than in the West. He ceded Newfoundland to Great Britain, but that concession was far more apparent than real.[28] He also ceded part of Acadia and Fort Bourbon in Hudson Bay to the British. Thus French dominion in the West was retained, but only to the extent that the Indian nations sanctioned it. Indian country it remained; the Indians were de facto sovereign, and the French had to toe their line.

In 1714 the company with the sole right to market beaver pelts in France discovered that the huge glut of fur in its warehouses had been ruined by insects and vermin. Suddenly demand exceeded supply. The Canadian fur traders responded by thrusting farther west and north; new canoe routes were established, previously unknown tribes were drawn into the French economic orbit, and vast new regions were explored. Yet these voyageurs and traders were not interested in exploration for exploration's sake. Only when the fur supply of a region became depleted would they press on. The farther they went, the greater became the costs of transportation and the risks to life and limb.

In 1715 Louis XIV died and was succeeded by his five-year-old grandson. A regency, headed by Philippe, duc d'Orléans, Louis XIV's nephew, was to rule until the young king came of age. Under this regime, France entered a period of peace and prosperity; some would claim this was the most civilized era in modern history.[29] During these years and for the rest of the century, French intellectuals were keenly interested in all branches of science. The Duc d'Orléans was in the vanguard, and the advancement of knowledge became government policy. In all the major cities and towns, members of scientific societies met to discuss the more recent discoveries, experiments, and concepts. Intellectuals with means at their disposal established their own laboratories, where they conducted strange experiments. Voltaire, for example, wasted considerable time and energy striving to measure the weight of fire. His mistress, the Marquise de Châtelet, had her own laboratory. Frederick the Great of Prussia named her Madame Venus-Newton. Yet much that was truly worthwhile emerged.[30] The French made great advances in astronomy, geography, and particularly, cartography.

The Early Search for Routes to the West

The regent and the Conseil de Marine were eager to have the mystery of North America west of Lake Superior and the Mississippi unraveled. The strange concept of a vast inland sea stretching from the Pacific inland into present-day Saskatchewan and South Dakota was accepted by all at the time; no one disputed its existence.[31] In his 1717 map, Guillaume Delisle, "Geographer Royal," depicted this sea to the north of California and New Mexico. The farther west the French advanced in their search for this Mer de l'Ouest, the farther it receded, always remaining just another ten to fifteen days' journey away. This odd notion may, to some degree, have been based on the seventeenth- and eighteenth-century French desire for symmetry in all things. Three large bays, inland seas, were known to exist: Hudson Bay to the northeast; the Gulf of Mexico to the southeast; and the Gulf of California to the southwest. Surely, then, a fourth such vast inlet had to exist in the northwestern segment of the continent.

During this period the French had no true concept of the vast extent of the continent. The knowledge of the royal officials at Quebec, knowledge passed on to the Conseil de Marine, was based on the vague reports of illiterate voyageurs whose personal experience had been expanded by the information they gleaned from the Crees and the Sioux. Those Indian descriptions, filtered through the language barrier, and their crude maps, sometimes merely drawn in the sand at a beach or on a piece of birchbark with a charred stick, fed the conceptions and misconceptions of the geography of North America in the minds of the French. Such conceptions conditioned what lay ahead for French explorers in western America. Unfortunately, the regency was neither willing nor able to foot the bill for the exploration it so ardently desired. Given the appalling state of French government finances after a quarter century of war, this was not surprising. Thus other means were found, although these proved to be self-defeating.[32]

Yet another powerful motive for French exploration was the new policy of excluding the Anglo-Americans from the trans-Appalachian region. Thus from 1700 on, the French fur traders and detachments of the colonial regular troops began to voyage up the Mississippi and its tributaries from Louisiana and down from Canada by way of the Great Lakes to the Illinois country, establishing fur trade posts with military garrisons. To the southwest these posts served to establish what eventually became a clandestine trade with the Spanish settlements to the north of Mexico, the areas that would later become Texas and New Mexico.

In March 1714 Captain Claude-Charles Dutisné led twelve Canadian militiamen to the Wabash River. They expected to be met there by two other detachments of Canadian militia, one coming from Quebec and the other, commanded by Pierre Dugué de Boisbriand, from the French posts in the Illinois country. Their orders were to establish a fort to prevent English traders from the Carolinas from making contact with the Miami and Natchez nations. When the Illinois and Quebec detachments failed to show up, Dutisné set off with his men southward, through the Illinois country to the French base at Ile Dauphine in Mobile Bay. En route they discovered some promising silver deposits in the Osage country.[33] On this and subsequent voyages, Dutisné established good relations with the various Indian tribes. This was the key to any attempt by Europeans to discover the true extent of the continent. Frequently, he and other Canadian officers were prevented by a tribe from proceeding farther to a more distant nation for fear that the French would provide a hostile, or potentially hostile, tribe with arms. Despite this, during the first two decades of the eighteenth century, the French established themselves securely in the Mississippi Valley, with settlements in the country of the Illinois at Kaskaskia and Cahokia and among the Natchez on the Red River at Natchitoches (today pronounced "Nakatesh"). The latter post was well within the region to which Spain had laid claim, without, of course, any regard for the territorial rights of the peoples who had occupied the country for millennia; being pagans, in Spanish eyes, these peoples had no rights to anything other than that extended to them by the bountiful mercy of His Most Catholic Majesty, upon their having embraced the true faith, that of Rome.

Thus, sidling east to west, crabwise, the French explored the major tributaries of the Mississippi. The French had several motives for these dangerous voyages into the unknown interior. One was the desire to acquire wealth by means of the trade in furs, hides, and hopefully, silver deposits; another was the need to provide the posts with supplies; but more enticing was the prospect of clandestine trade with New Spain, trade that was free of duties and taxes. Another motive was the imperial policy of France to deny access to the west to the English colonials. Officers in the Canadian regular troops, the Troupes franches de la Marine, who wanted to advance their careers had to carry out the orders emanating from Versailles, regardless of consequences. For these reasons, the French voyaged far into the southwestern and northwestern regions of the continent. Some years later the cartographers in France dutifully strove, with remarkable success, to interpret the information provided by these explorers and put it all on maps.

All of this occurred when tension between France and Spain was growing, eventually ending in war. In Louisiana the French had begun establishing commercial and military alliances with the Indian nations in regions to which Spain had long since laid claim and had established a few scattered mission-post settlements. A Canadian officer, Louis Juchereau de Saint-Denis, in 1714 spent several months among the Natchez Indians. A settlement, centred at Fort Rosalie, was subsequently established at the site of present-day Natchez. That the French had to tread very warily was made all too plain when, in 1729, a stupid commandant sought to sequester a large section of the Indians' cultivated land. The response by the Natchez was swift: the entire settlement was destroyed, the garrison and settlers massacred.[34]

Saint-Denis had previously, between 1700 and 1701, explored the territory between the Red and the Ouachita Rivers. He then was given the command of Fort-du-Mississippi, some fifty miles from the mouth of the river, a post he held until the fort was abandoned in 1707. He also voyaged up the river as far as present-day Ohio and made a number of exploring and trading trips in present-day Texas, then part of New Spain. The French in Louisiana were able to provide European goods to the Spanish settlements at much lower prices than could the Spanish merchants at Mexico City, some fifteen hundred miles distant from Santa Fe. French costs of transportation, largely along the rivers, were far lower; moreover, most of the goods going to Mexico City from Spain were of French origin.[35]

In 1713 Antoine de La Mothe Cadillac, governor of Louisiana, appointed Saint-Denis to be the leader of an expedition to try to find an overland route to the northern Spanish missionary outposts and mining settlements. Saint-Denis had traveled through much of the territory previously; he had a command of the principal Indian languages and was well versed in their strict protocol. Moreover, he was an exceptionally skilled diplomat and possessed considerable charm. With him he took as guides the brothers Pierre and Jean-Baptiste Talon, who, as youths, had accompanied René-Robert Cavelier de La Salle's expedition to discover by sea the mouth of the Mississippi and there to establish a colony. That ill-fated effort self-destructed at Matagorda Bay. The Talon brothers were then taken in by the local Indians, were subsequently ransomed from them by the Spaniards, and many years later, after amazing adventures, had returned to Louisiana.[36] Saint-Denis and his men, guided by the Talon brothers, proceeded up the Red River and established a post on an island, naming it Saint-Jean-Baptiste-des-Natchitoches, amid beautiful, rolling, well-wooded country.

The following year Saint-Denis set off for the Spanish posts on the Rio Grande. When he reached the country of the Teja tribe, he sent all but three of his men back to Mobile. Eventually he and his remaining men arrived at San Juan Bautista (present-day Piedras Negras, Mexico). The commandant, Captain Dominigo Ramòn, was taken aback at the sudden appearance of these foreigners from out of nowhere, but since France and Spain were not then at war, he received them courteously. Yet he felt obliged to place them under open arrest until he obtained instructions from the viceroy as to how they should be treated. This took several months, but Saint-Denis put his leisure time to good use: he wooed and won the hand of Captain Ramòn's granddaughter, Doña Emanuela.

In early spring 1715 a squad of cavalry arrived to escort Saint-Denis and one of his men, Médard Jalot, to Mexico City. During his lengthy interrogation there by the Spanish authorities, Saint-Denis made much of his attempt en route to Santa Fe to locate a Spanish missionary, Fray Francisco Hidalgo, who in 1711 had appealed to the French to help him reestablish his mission among the Masinai Indians. Saint-Denis succeeded in ingratiating himself with the Spaniards. They quickly came to realize that he knew the country to the north far better than they did; moreover he had established good relations with the Indian nations, something that the Spaniards had not been able to do. Thus the viceroy accepted his offer to guide an expedition to establish Spanish control of the territory to the northeast, present-day Texas.

The expedition, with Saint-Denis as second-in-command, paused long enough at San Juan Bautista to allow him to marry Doña Emanuela. It then proceeded to the northeast, establishing four mission posts among the Indian nations. This gave the Spaniards some semblance of suzerainty over the region to within a few miles of Natchitoches, thereby blocking any further French encroachment into New Spain from that direction. An uneasy, undefined border came into existence between New France and New Spain, along with a flourishing French contraband trade.

In 1716 Saint-Denis was in Mobile, where he organized a smuggling expedition and set off for the Rio Grande. This time he pushed his luck too far. At San Bautista, Captain Ramòn felt compelled to place him under arrest and impound his goods. Once again he was sent to Mexico City, this time to spend several months in jail. Eventually he was released and told never to show his face in Spanish territory again. By 1719 he was back at his Louisiana plantation with his Spanish wife. After the 1719–21 Franco-Spanish war he was appointed commandant at Natchitoches, where his duties included keeping an eye on the Spanish at Los Adayes, established as the capital of Texas, just fifteen miles west of Natchitoches. In 1744, plagued by financial difficulties, he decided to move to New Spain with his family, but he died in June of that year before he was able to put his affairs in order. He

was an extraordinary man, having earned the respect of the French, the Indian nations, and the Spaniards, who feared his influence over those fear-
some peoples.[37]

Another noted explorer of the Southwest was Bénard de La Harpe, who
in 1719 voyaged up the Red River valley and then rode overland to the Canadian River near its junction with the Arkansas. He was accompanied by
a competent surveyor, the Sieur de Rivage, who carefully mapped the
course of these tributaries of the Mississippi. They managed to outflank
the Spanish posts and opened up a thriving trade with the Comanches and
Apaches, supplying them with arms and ammunition, greatly to the dismay of the Spanish officials.[38] It was in this fashion that the French drew
many of the tribes of the Southwest into their imperial orbit; yet it was also
this thriving trade that hindered exploration. Why voyage farther west to
seek what one had already found?

Despite the determination of the Spanish authorities to exclude the
French from their territory, they could not do it. The Spaniards did not
dominate the Southwest; the Indian nations did, and early in the eighteenth century they were well supplied with horses. Moreover the French
had established far better relations with these tribes than had the Spanish.
The French not only had the decided advantage of cheaper goods but also
had no hesitation in trading muskets, something that the Spaniards were
loath to do. The French nevertheless persisted in their attempts to establish
a steady trade with the Spaniards at Taos and Santa Fe. In addition, there
was always that perpetual will-o'-the-wisp, the hope of discovering an
overland route to the Pacific.

It was to the north, on the Missouri River and eventually the Saskatchewan, that the French made their greatest effort to discover the true
extent of the continent. Here too, the Indian nations proved to be the major
obstacle. The French could go nowhere without their consent and, usually,
their guidance. In 1719 the commandant at Kaskaskia in the Illinois country, Pierre Dugué de Boisbriand, dispatched Captain Dutisné up the Missouri to discover its source. Dutisné made his way as far as the Osage River
and up it for some two hundred miles. Then he and his men encountered
the Panis (Pawnees), who prohibited them from traveling farther. The Indians could not allow Dutisné to establish commercial relations with their
ancient enemies the Comanches, for trade always entailed military support.[39]

The extent of the Indians' resistance to the European invasion of their
country was made plain when the Spaniards learned of the French en-

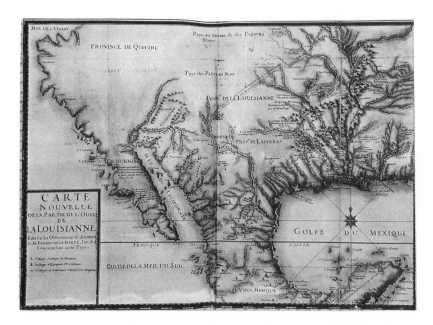

11.1 "Carte Nouvelle de la Partie de L'Ouest de la Louisianne" (Bénard de La Harpe, [1720]). Of the surviving maps of the French period, the La Harpe map is one of the few that was drawn directly from field sketches by the explorer himself. Although other French maps of the early eighteenth century were more accurate, the La Harpe map shows the developing French image of the interior, including the "Mer de l'Ouest" (Sea of the West), which would become such a focal point of continued French western exploration. Courtesy of the Library of Congress.

croachment into the region to which they claimed to hold title. In 1720 Lieutenant Don Pedro de Villasur with a small detachment, forty-five Spaniards and sixty Indians, was dispatched northwest from Santa Fe to block any further French intrusions westward. At the junction of the North and South Platte Rivers, the detachment was attacked by the Panis. All but thirteen of the Spaniards were slaughtered.[40]

The most colourful and intrepid of all the French explorers of the Southwest was Etienne de Véniard de Bourgmont, an adventurer with a checkered career. He voyaged farther up the Missouri than any European before him. More than that, he compiled detailed reports on the topography, geography, and ethnography of the region, information that enabled the cartographer Guillaume Delisle to prepare his magnificent map of Louisiana and the Mississippi with its tributaries.

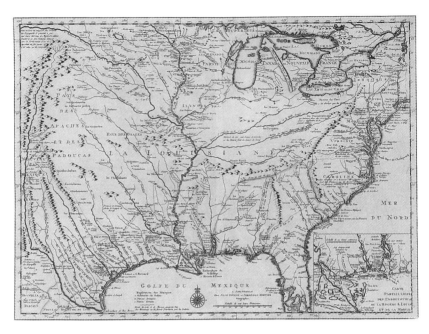

11.2 "Carte de la Louisiane et du Cours du Mississipi" (Claude and Guillaume De-lisle, 1717). This map, like its companion "Carte du Canada . . ." (1703), was care-fully researched by the father-and-son team of Claude and Guillaume Delisle. Much copied and occasionally augmented, this was the most important map of the Missis-sippi Valley until the end of the century. Unlike most other early maps, it shows the routes of some explorers: Soto-Moscoso in 1539–43; La Salle in 1687; Tonti in 1702; and Saint-Denis in 1714–16. For the Mississippi River, the Delisles used maps pre-pared by Le Sueur in 1702 and, for the lower Missouri Valley, the explorations of Bourgmont in 1714. The map reproduced here is a faithful reengraving by the firm of Covens and Mortier in about 1730. Courtesy of the National Archives of Canada, NMC 118122.

In 1695, Bourgmont appears to have been deported to Canada, likely by his parents to prevent him from bringing disgrace on the family at home. This was a common practice, preferable to having a libertine son incarcer-ated in the Bastille by *lettre de cachet*. In Canada he served as a cadet in the Troupes franches de la Marine. He must have impressed his superiors, for in 1705 he received the much coveted "expectancy" of an ensign's commis-sion. A commission in that corps was not easily acquired; it could not be bought but had to be well earned. Every officer had to serve in the enlisted ranks as a cadet, usually beginning at the age of fifteen; then, after some ten years of active service, he could hope to receive his commission when a vacancy occurred.[41] In 1702 Bourgmont had taken part in an expedition down the Ohio led by Louis Juchereau de Saint-Denis. Four years later he was placed in temporary command at Detroit. Having to serve under the corrupt La Mothe Cadillac could not have been agreeable. This may account for Bourgmont's desertion in 1706. The ensuing six years he spent among various Indian tribes, leading the life of a renegade coureur de bois. During this time he became enamoured of a Missouri Indian girl, took her as his wife according to Indian custom, and had a son by her. This gave him considerable influence in the councils of her nation. It also caused him to be denounced by the missionaries at Kaskaskia. They did not have a good word to say about him; according to them, he was utterly debauched and leading the most dissolute of lives.

Be that as it may, in 1712 Bourgmont made his way to Mobile and offered his services to the French officials at that outpost of the friable French empire. He proposed to appease the nations along the Missouri and bring them to accept an alliance with the French. In France, despite the ongoing War of the Spanish Succession, the Conseil de Marine maintained its interest in North America. France and Spain were then closely allied in the European war, hence the notion that a profitable trade could be established with the remote mining towns of northern Mexico. The French also hoped to discover along the Missouri silver deposits as rich as those being exploited by the Spaniards to the south. Mission posts could win the natives to the Gallican branch of the Roman Church, and there was always the hope that a route would be found to the Pacific by way of the yet to be discovered Mer de l'Ouest. Finally, as the commissaire ordonnateur at Mobile, Marc-Antoine Hubert, cynically put it in a dispatch to the Conseil de Marine, once the French were securely established along the Missouri, the French could then, with the aid of the Indian nations, at any time drive the Spaniards out of what would later become New Mexico, Texas, and California. These were the motives for the French advance in the Southwest: commerce, industry, religion, science, imperialism—a heady mixture.

Thus Bourgmont was sent off to the Missouri River in March 1714. For the ensuing four years he explored it as far as the Cheyenne River in present-day South Dakota. He established good relations with the tribes he encountered and worked on his two reports, the one mapping the course of the river and the other, entitled "Exacte description de la Louisiane," giving the location of the Indian nations along the course of the Missouri and its principal tributaries: the Missouris, Otos, Panis, Panimakes, Iowas, Makasblancas, Padoucas, and Arikaras.[42] These were the nations that controlled the country between Louisiana and Mexico. Bourgmont, having ascertained that the mines being worked by the Spaniards could not be far distant and that the possibility of establishing a profitable commercial connection appeared promising, slowly made his way back to Mobile.

By the time Bourgmont arrived at Mobile, France and Spain were at war. After serving in that military imbroglio, he sailed for France, taking his young Missouri son with him. The Conseil de Marine had come to regard him as the only man capable of arranging a peace settlement between the nations now incorporated in a loose alliance with the French and those nations' ancient foes, the Padoucas (Comanches). It was the age-old story, repeated over and over again in North America in that epoch: "Friends of my enemies are my enemies." Bourgmont was commissioned a captain, the highest rank in the Troupes franches de la Marine, appointed commandant of the Missouri country, and made a member of the highly coveted Ordre militaire de Saint-Louis.[43]

In January 1722 the Compagnie des Indes, responsible for the administration and development of Louisiana, commissioned Bourgmont to establish the long-projected fort on the upper Missouri. This was intended to serve as a secure base from which to bring the Comanches to terms, to establish commercial relations with the Spanish settlements to the south, and to pursue the search for a viable route to the western ocean. Once all that had been accomplished, according to the itinerary of the officials comfortably ensconced at Versailles—who assumed that two years would suffice—then Bourgmont was required to bring a delegation of Indian notables from the region to France to impress them with the might and grandeur of the king and his subjects. As an inducement for Bourgmont, the distinct possibility of the granting of a title of nobility was dangled.

Bourgmont thus duly did as he was bid. He returned to Louisiana, and after many delays, his party set off and reached the villages of the Missouri Indians in November 1722. During the ensuing winter he and his men built Fort d'Orléans some 200 miles upstream of the Mississippi. Bourgmont's account of what then ensued deserves to be reviewed, for it gives a vivid picture of what the French encountered in their attempts to push ever farther into the Southwest. On 25 June 1724, an advance party commanded by Ensign Saint-Ange, consisting of one sergeant, one corporal, eleven soldiers, and two engagés (hired hands), set off upriver for the Comanche country, the nation that was barring French access to the Spanish settlements in present-day New Mexico. A week later Bourgmont followed with the main party, which consisted of two cadets, two soldiers, one drummer, one engagé, a valet, and one hundred Missouri warriors led by their eight war chiefs and the grand chief of the nation. With them were also sixty-four Osage warriors led by four of their war chiefs.

In mid-July, disease, in the form of a virulent fever, struck the party. Bourgmont had purchased some Comanche slaves, whom he intended to return to their own people as a goodwill gesture, but on 11 July two of them succumbed to the disease. Bourgmont also had two bouts with the fever; he had himself bled and purged according to current European medical practice and somehow survived. Fourteen of the Indians in the party were stricken, and another Comanche slave died. At this the Osages fled, likely spreading the disease far and wide.

A party of Canzés (Kansas) then paid a courtesy call and made it clear that the "presents" Bourgmont offered were quite inadequate. They expected at least twice as much. He must somehow have managed to assuage them, for they subsequently presented the daughter of their chief to him, a girl of some thirteen to fourteen years old, to take as his wife. Bourgmont discreetly stated that he had to decline, politely, since he already had a wife. After due deliberation, the Kansas proposed that the girl be wedded to Bourgmont's son but that, since he was only ten years old, they should keep the girl for him until he was old enough to marry, which would then cement the incipient Franco-Kansas alliance in the Indian fashion.

With that issue settled, Bourgmont sent the sick and, significantly, the slaves and furs so far garnered in trade back to Fort d'Orléans in twenty-three pirogues. By that time, July 1724, Bourgmont was again desperately ill, suffering from *mal de reines*, lumbago so severe that he could not sit astride a horse; yet he remained in command. He dispatched a Canadian engagé, Gaillard, with two Comanche slaves, both of them clad and equipped in the best Indian style, along with letters for the Spanish authorities, a passport written in Spanish, and a letter written in Latin for any Spanish missionary who might be encountered. Gaillard was instructed to inform the Comanches that the purpose of the French in coming to their country was to arrange a peace settlement between them and the nations with whom they were constantly at war. Bourgmont estimated that they were then ten days' journey from the Comanche villages. He was so enfeebled that he was being carried on a stretcher and finally had to give up. He had himself transported back to Fort d'Orléans to recuperate from his ailment.

Meanwhile, on 25 August, Gaillard's advance party, accompanied by two

Osage warriors, reached the Comanche villages, where, the report states, they received a warm welcome. That is credible, since they posed no possible threat. More to the point, they had brought two Comanches back from captivity, and Gaillard showed them how the impressive French muskets worked. No doubt he promised them a steady supply of those arms if they agreed to an alliance with the French. Accompanied by a delegation of Comanches, Gaillard then proceeded to a Kansas village, but at first sight of the dreaded Comanches, the Kansas, fearing an attack, panicked and fled.

Word of this was sent to Bourgmont, who immediately dispatched Ensign Saint-Ange with three soldiers to the Kansas village to sort things out. He himself set out once again on 20 September. Gaillard, accompanied by three Comanche chiefs and three warriors, rejoined Bourgmont at his camp near the Kansas village. Bourgmont received them in style: he held a parade and gave a grand salute of musketry, the drummer no doubt beating away, after which came the ceremony of the "presents." Three days later, on 5 October, at a large assembly of the French, the Kansas Indians, and delegates from the Otos, Comanches, Missouris, and Ayoois (Iowas), Bourgmont made his speech proposing a general peace between all the nations, including the Panis, Panimakas, Osages, and the distant Illinois. The Comanches tentatively agreed to this, provided the French saw to it that there would be no treachery.

The following day Bourgmont, with his son assisting, distributed generous "presents" to all the tribesmen. That was followed by a day of speeches. On 8 October the French departed for the Comanche villages, arriving there ten days later. They found themselves at a village of 140 cabins, 800 warriors, over 1,500 women, and some 2,000 infants. The imbalance of the sexes reflected the heavy casualties suffered in the perpetual tribal wars; to redress the balance, the men had to provide for up to four wives each. On 19 October an assembly was held with a day of speeches and the customary "presents." Bourgmont requested that the Comanches not bar the French from going to the Spanish settlements but instead serve as guides. He pleaded that the peace agreement recently concluded be honoured, and then he bestowed the "presents" that he had brought from the king of the French; these included muskets, ball and powder, cooking pots, axes, knives, awls, blankets, and trinkets for the children.

The chief of the Comanches responded by promising to keep the peace; he added that if the French should ever need the aid of two thousand warriors, they need only to ask him. This was clearly a none-too-subtle indication that it was the Comanches, not the French and their wavering allies, who were the dominant force in that part of the world. The chief also assured Bourgmont that his people would not prevent the French from visiting the Spaniards who were twelve days' march distant. He remarked that the Spaniards were not as generous as the French had now shown themselves to be; the Spaniards traded one horse for three buffalo hides but never muskets and only a few knives and axes. The Comanches expressed their gratitude for the return of two of their enslaved people and gave Bourgmont seven horses as a gesture of thanks. He, in reply, assured the Comanches that the tribes allied with the French would hand over their Comanche slaves in exchange for horses. This exchange indicates the limit of the diffusion of horses among the plains Indians at that point in time, 1724.

Throughout these ceremonies the Comanches were much taken with Bourgmont's son. They held a feast for their guests, extending their hospitality to providing them with some of their young women. In traditional Indian fashion, that sealed the treaty between the French and the Comanches. Although the precarious state of Bourgmont's health did not allow him to continue to Santa Fe as he had intended, he had accomplished a good deal—a treaty with the Comanches that might well open the way to Mexico. He had also explored a vast territory. That, under the circumstances, was no mean feat.

Bourgmont and his men then made their way back to the Missouri, where boats of buffalo hides stretched on wooden frames, akin to Celtic coracles, were made for some of them; the rest proceeded on horseback. By 5 November, they had reassembled at Fort d'Orléans. Bourgmont then began writing his account of their epic five-month journey for submission to the Conseil de Marine. This Relation was signed and certified as a true account by Ensign Saint-Ange *fils*, the sieur Renaudière, Ingénieur pour les Mines, Sergeant Dubois, and nine of the men, only two of whom made their mark with a cross, doubtless after having had the Relation read to them in the requisite manner.[44]

What Bourgmont neglected to mention in his Relation was that the nations that had agreed to the general peace had also consented to send a delegation to France. For the members it was to be a voyage of exploration in foreign and exotic parts. When the delegates arrived at New Orleans, the cheese-paring bureaucrats, in typical fashion, reduced the Indian delegation to four, plus the slave of the Missouri delegate, the daughter of a chief. After maritime disasters in no way unusual in those waters—the first ship they boarded at New Orleans sank before it was out of the roadstead—

they eventually landed in France and arrived in Paris in September 1725. If they then claimed possession of the country by right of "prior discovery," it is not mentioned in the extant French documents.

The directors of the Compagnie des Indes gave the delegation a warm welcome. They and a few idly curious members of the court then had to endure lengthy speeches, with Bourgmont interpreting, before the exchange of "presents" according to Indian custom: silk breeches and surcoats for the men, layered dresses for the Missouri lady—which must have bewildered her—and, in return, fine furs, doeskin blouses for the men, and short doeskin shift dresses for the ladies, all embroidered with strange materials in intriguing designs. The ladies of the court perhaps sighed when they considered how much more comfortable the Indian women's mode of dress—resembling a latter-day miniskirt—was compared with what court fashion required them to wear.

On 22 November the Duc de Bourbon, member of the Regency Council, presented the Indian delegates to the royal court at Fontainebleau; two days later they were presented to the fifteen-year-old monarch. Then followed the inevitable, interminable, incomprehensible speeches that must have tried the young king's patience: from the Indians' flowery speeches, replete with metaphors, to the French speeches, which Bourgmont must have had a hard time making acceptable, all were full of promises, all of them very insincere. When it came to arrogance, Louis XV, no doubt quite unaware, surely had met his match. During their two-month stay, the Indian delegates were taken on a stag hunt with the king, were given tours of Paris, and were shown the fountains at Versailles and Marly. They, in turn, gave one of their religious dances, which must have bemused the courtiers; at any event, it does not appear to have had any noticeable effect on the French ballet.

The Indian delegates were apparently not overly intimidated by all that they saw and heard during their venture into darkest Europe. When they returned to their own country, within the year the French had to abandon Fort d'Orléans. Subsequently it was used as a base by itinerant Canadian fur traders who had no interest whatsoever in exploration or French imperial policy; the fort merely allowed them to tap a rich source of furs. For these fur traders, as much Indian as French, the history remains to be written.

Bourgmont remained in France, and according to the scanty accounts that have survived, he there married a rich widow and was ennobled for his services.[45] Some explorers have fared better, many far worse. As for the

Indian explorers of France, who knows? At least the ghastly future in store for their descendants was not revealed to them as the despoliation of their country continued relentlessly, with the explorers in the vanguard.

Fourteen years elapsed before the French, in 1739, again made a serious attempt to establish a trade route to the Spanish settlements in Mexico despite the strict but ineffectual prohibitions of the government at Madrid. The brothers Pierre and Paul Mallet and seven associates, with the sanction of the royal officials at New Orleans, set off from Fort de Chartres in the Illinois country. They hoped to find that the Missouri River would eventually lead to the Spanish settlements in the Southwest. Along the way they encountered some Arikaris who managed to convey to them that the Missouri would not take them where they wanted to go. They then turned back, crossed overland to the Platte, and followed its southern branch to the Sangre de Cristo range of the Rocky Mountains. They had acquired an Indian slave who had once been enslaved by the Spaniards; on being promised his freedom, he agreed to guide them to the Spanish settlements. Turning south, with the forbidding, abrupt wall of the Rockies on their right, they made their way to the Spanish mission at Picuries (near Taos, New Mexico), and on 22 July 1739, they arrived at Santa Fe.

The Spanish officials were somewhat taken aback at the sudden appearance of these Frenchmen. Yet they were contravening no Spanish laws, since they had lost most of their merchandise when their packhorses were swept away while fording a river. They were, nonetheless, detained until a decision could be obtained from the viceroy at Mexico City, some fifteen hundred miles away. It was therefore nine months before a courier arrived with the answer; meanwhile the laws of hospitality prevailed, and two of the Canadians married local señoritas. When those two were informed that the viceroy had decreed that the French intruders had to leave Spanish territory forthwith and not return without first obtaining official permission, they opted to enter the service of Spain in order to remain with their wives. The others in the party declined the viceroy's urgent invitation to enter the Spanish service and explore the country to the west of the mountains; here, it was reported, just a mere three months' journey away, were cities, by the ocean, inhabited by people who were clad in silk. The mythical cities of Cíbola—always they were just a few months, or weeks, farther west.

On 1 May 1740, the Mallets and five of their compatriots set out to explore the upper reaches of the Pecos Valley, hoping to find a river flowing eastward to the Mississippi. After two weeks of vain searching, two members of the party became discouraged and turned back, choosing to return to the Illinois country by the way they had come. The Mallets and the other three Canadians continued alongside a stream that they had been following on horseback for the previous four days. They eventually encountered Indians whose language was known to some of them and were thus able to obtain fresh mounts. By mid-June the stream they were following became deeper and broader, so, in a fashion typical of the Canadians of that era, with only knives for tools they cobbled together two elm-bark canoes. Turning their horses loose, they embarked in their frail craft and were swept down to the Arkansas River, then on to the Mississippi and New Orleans, arriving there in March 1741.[46] Appropriately enough, the rivulet-stream-river that they had followed through present-day New Mexico, Texas, Oklahoma, and Arkansas to Louisiana is still named the Canadian River.

It had been an epic journey. For five men to have attempted to travel through the lands of so many nations, numbering thousands of warriors, most of them armed and mounted as well as, or better than, the Canadians—and not all of these tribesmen well disposed toward foreign intruders—that alone was remarkable; the fact that they lived to tell the tale was even more so. The feat says much for their skills as linguists and diplomats. Although a tribe might welcome French traders bringing firearms and ammunition, rarely would such a tribe allow them to proceed farther in case they provided arms to a hostile tribe along the way.

Eventually the Mallets settled down to farm and trade with the Indians near the Arkansas post. Then, in 1750, the commandant at Fort Boulaye on the Arkansas, Louis-Xavier Martin de Lino de Chalmette, decided to try once again to establish trade relations with Santa Fe. He took Pierre Mallet with him to New Orleans and put the proposal to the governor, Pierre de Rigaud de Vaudreuil, who gave it his official blessing along with letters of introduction to the Spanish commandant. Some New Orleans merchants also provided letters of credit, promising to supply Santa Fe with merchandise at relatively low prices.

Pierre Mallet then set off by canoe with three companions. They certainly made a leisurely journey. It took them about two months to reach Natchitoches, where they stayed for some weeks before pushing on to the Spanish outpost at Caddoacho (near Texarkana on the present-day Texas-Arkansas border). That part of the journey took them some three months, during which time the Comanches pillaged most of their goods. Yet they persisted and pressed on to Pecos, arriving there in November 1750 and receiving a very frosty welcome. They were placed under arrest, sent to Santa Fe, and from there moved to El Paso, where Governor Tomas Velez auctioned off what few goods remained to them and used the proceeds to send them, under armed escort, first to Chihuahua and then to Mexico City. There the viceroy had them interrogated and then shipped off to Spain to be dealt with by the Casa de Contratación. With that they vanished. Knowledge of their ultimate fate is likely entombed somewhere in the archives at Simancas.[47] It is unlikely that they ever saw Louisiana again. They had explored much of New Spain, but a Spanish jail had not been on their itinerary.

Despite the viceroy of Mexico's reiteration of the ban on clandestine commerce with New France, such trade proved to be profitable for all concerned, particularly for the Spanish officials at Los Adayes, established to prevent it; hence a thriving trade was eventually established between Louisiana and Santa Fe. The French no longer had any need to thrust westward toward that city. The French also supplied the Indian nations of the Southwest with goods at prices that the Spaniards could not match and thus drew them into the imperial orbit of France. The Louisiana traders became as influential in the region between the Missouri and the Rocky Mountains as their Canadian counterparts were in the far Northwest.[48]

The Fur Trade and the Search for the Western Ocean

Whereas the French in the Southwest had concentrated their efforts on establishing commercial links with New Spain, the French in the Northwest strove to bring the continent's true extent and shape to light. One person who contributed a good deal to the direction this search would take cannot, strictly speaking, be termed an explorer, since he voyaged only where others had gone before; he was a Jesuit priest, Father Pierre-François-Xavier de Charlevoix. After serving as a prefect for some years at the Collége Louis-le-Grand in Paris, where Voltaire was one of the students under his charge, and being ordained a deacon in 1705, he was sent to Canada to teach grammar at the Collége de Québec. He was fairly young, twenty-three, and he found himself living among elderly fellow Jesuits who had served as missionaries for many years among the nations of the Great Lakes basin and north beyond the Hudson Bay watershed. After retirement from the mission field, they had returned to the Collége de Québec to assume light teaching duties. From them Charlevoix garnered a wealth of information about the *pays d'en haut* (the region west of Detroit—to the Canadians of that era, the term had an almost mystical aura, akin to "Camelot" in the America of the 1960s, a land where all things were possible). In 1709 Charlevoix was ordered back to France to begin his four years of theological studies. That completed, in 1713 he was ordained a priest and once again assigned teaching duties at the Collége Louis-le-Grand. While he was there, the Regency Council assigned him the task of recommending where the border of Acadia should be drawn after its cession to Great Britain by the Treaty of Utrecht.

Before Charlevoix had completed that tricky task he was given another assignment: to investigate the tales that had been circulating for years in both France and New France of the Mer de l'Ouest—a vast inland sea, the Mediterranean of North America, that gave access to the Pacific Ocean and hence to the fabulous riches of Cathay. The commercial possibilities of a route that would obviate the voyage around the southern tip of South America, where the most dangerous waters in the world for ships of sail were to be encountered, were still as tantalizing as they had been to Samuel de Champlain in 1617.[49]

The regent and the Conseil de Marine, in their wisdom, decided that it would be best to send a Jesuit, rather than a military expedition, into the West to seek the coveted route to the Pacific. A military expedition would be expensive and likely to arouse suspicion in the minds of some members of the British government, not to mention their American colonists, who regarded the French in Canada as minions of Satan. Were they, however, to learn of a solitary Jesuit traveling in the Far West, they would likely assume that he was merely on a tour of inspection of the western missions. Thus on 1 July 1720, the thirty-eight-year-old Jesuit embarked on a naval flute, *Le Chameau*. He did not enjoy the sea voyage, arriving at Quebec on 23 September, to his way of thinking, barely alive. The following March, winter far from over, he set off from Quebec in a horse-drawn sleigh, or *cariole*, for Montreal. It was the beginning of a long journey. Early in May, once the Saint Lawrence was free of ice, his little expedition—two canoes and eight voyageurs, with Captain Jacques Hertel de Cournoyer as guide, commandant, and companion—left for the *pays d'en haut*.

Rather than take the customary Ottawa River route to Lake Huron, they went up the Saint Lawrence, with its succession of tumultuous rapids, to Fort Frontenac at the eastern end of Lake Ontario. From there they journeyed to Niagara, then Detroit, and on 28 June 1721, Charlevoix arrived at

Michilimackinac, the main base of the western fur trade. All the way Charlevoix had made careful observations, compass in hand, on the shorelines
of the lakes, estimating distances from one point to another and constantly
checking latitudes. This information was later put to good use by the chief
engineer at the Dépot des cartes et plans de la Marine, Jacques-Nicolas Bellin, whose consequent maps remain to this day a superb example of the
cartographer's craft.[50]

At Michilimackinac, Charlevoix met Jean-Paul Legardeur de Saint-
Pierre and Jacques Testard de Montigny, veteran officers with years of
service at the western posts. With Montigny, Charlevoix continued his
voyage to Fort Saint-François at La Baie-des-Puants (Green Bay), where
Montigny was to take over the command. He there sought information
from the woodland Sioux concerning a great river that was reputed to flow
westward into the southern sea. Learning little that made sense, he returned to Michilimackinac, where he met Zacharie Robutel de La Noue,
the commandant at Kaministiquia, the post at the western end of Lake Superior, and Father Joseph-Jacques Marest S.J., who played an active political role among the nations of the region, including the Sioux. That nation
was a thorn in the side of the French throughout their regime and vice
versa; for that simple reason, French traded weapons to, and were allied
with, the ancient foes of the Sioux. In the eighteenth century, several attempts were made to establish a mission and trading post among the Sioux
at the headwaters of the Mississippi; they all ended in failure.[51]

Charlevoix intended to spend the winter in lower Louisiana to gather as
much information as he could concerning the best river route to the western ocean. On 29 July 1721, he set off with a veteran officer, Robert Groston
de Saint-Ange, as his guide. They proceeded by way of Lake Michigan and
the Saint Joseph, Kanakee, and Illinois Rivers to the Mississippi. Their
progress was retarded when Charlevoix became ill, and thus they did not
reach Natchez until December and New Orleans until 10 January 1722.
Once there, the weary Charlevoix was stricken with jaundice. That forced
him to abandon his plan to return to Quebec the way he had come. In
March 1722 he embarked on a naval flute bound for Canada. It never got
there. After many misadventures he ended up in Plymouth, England,
aboard a wretched merchantman, where he had to spend three weeks
waiting for the ship's clearance to France. He eventually landed at Le
Havre on Boxing Day; two days later the ship sank at its mooring. On 20
January he presented the lengthy report on his travels to the Comte de

Toulouse, an illegitimate son of Louis XIV and member of the Regency Council. Shortly thereafter he presented the report to the minister responsible for colonial affairs, the Comte de Morville.

Charlevoix had spent two and a half years in Canada, the *pays d'en haut*, Louisiana, and Saint Domingue (Haiti). He had acquired a great deal of information, yet the conclusions in his report proved to be erroneous. He concluded that the Mer de l'Ouest lay somewhere between 40° and 50° latitude and that the Missouri River was the best route to follow because, at its headwaters and over the height of land, rivers would surely be found that flowed to the inland sea. He proposed that a mission be established among the woodland Sioux to bring them into an alliance with the French and so put an end to their barring the way to the Far West. He even offered to serve there himself, although he did not have a word of Sioux at his command. His offer was not taken seriously, and none of the overburdened missionaries serving in the West could be spared from their arduous duties for the dubious prospect of attempting, once again, to establish a mission among a powerful nation that was markedly hostile to the French. Thus the proposal came to nought.[52]

The French government, first that of the regent and then that of King Louis XV after he attained his majority, pursued the aim of having the French be the first to cross the continent overland to the Pacific and thus establish before the entire world the land's true extent. Keen though the regent, the king, and the Conseil de Marine were to see this accomplished, they were not prepared to foot the bill. Given the chronic state of French government finances, particularly after a quarter century of war, the money was not to be found. It was therefore the Canadian fur trade that was made the shaky financial vehicle for the exploration of North America. The scheme now proposed was that the Crown would establish a chain of posts in the Far West, at an estimated cost of forty-seven thousand lives.[53] These posts would be used to establish trade connections among nations with whom the French had never had direct relations, some of whom had obtained French, or English, goods indirectly from other tribes. The Crown expected that once in place, the posts would be maintained by the Canadian fur traders, who would be licensed to exploit the trade in the various districts. This proposition proved to be very attractive to the Canadian fur trade establishment. Unfortunately, trade proved to be anything but the handmaiden of exploration; in fact, it proved just the reverse. As an exasperated minister of marine commented, somewhat unfairly, "It is not the Sea of the West that they seek, but the Sea of Beaver."[54]

Fortunately, at that point in time, the Canadian fur trade had revived. Although beaver pelts then accounted for less than half the value of the furs exported from Quebec, beaver was a staple, always in some demand by European hatmakers. Thus when it was discovered that the twenty years' accumulated glut of beaver pelts in French warehouses had been destroyed by insects, rodents, and rot, the demand for the fur suddenly soared and along with it that for luxury furs such as martin, fox, and ermine. The Canadian fur traders were willing and eager to meet the demand.

The mechanics of the trade then employed were complex, and changes were made from time to time to cope with shifting circumstances in both Canada and Europe. As before, beaver pelts and moose hides had to be sold to the Compagnie de l'Occident, John Law's creation, which held the sole right to market those particular products in France. In return the company had to pay the Canadians fixed prices, regardless of the quantity offered. All other furs were sold at auction in France.

From this point on, the Canadian fur trade became an instrument of French imperial policy.[55] At Forts Frontenac and Niagara the trade was controlled by servants of the Crown and was closely regulated by the commandants, to ensure that the prices offered to the Indians for their furs were generous enough to deter them from going across the lake to traders in New York. They had to be kept away from the English at all costs, even if it meant that the Crown had to subsidize the trade from time to time. At Detroit and Michilimackinac, the commandants were empowered to issue licenses *(congés)* to traders at fixed rates, usually five hundred livres, the proceeds of which were intended to defray the costs of maintaining the posts. Farther west the *pays d'en haut* was divided into districts: La Poste du Sud, the area south of Detroit; La Baie, comprising Green Bay and the headwaters of the Mississippi; and eventually La Mer de l'Ouest, which came to include everything west of Lac de Pluie (Rainy Lake). The commandants of these districts played an active and profitable role in the fur trade, but they had to pay most of the costs of maintaining their respective posts. The profits they garnered, although considerable, were nowhere near as great as some in Canada tried to make out.[56]

The post commandants' responsibilities were to strive to maintain peace among the fractious tribes in their respective territories, to ensure that the Indians were kept well away from the Anglo-American packhorse peddlers, and to chase any of the latter who ventured into French claimed territory back from where they had come, in strict conformity with the French interpretation of the terms of the Treaty of Utrecht. In addition the commandants at La Baie, at Kaministiquia, and later at La Mer de l'Ouest were required to have their men explore the rivers in their territories to the sources in the hope that at least one would be found to flow out of, or into, the Mer de l'Ouest—hence the name given to this westernmost district. On these requirements the official instructions for the post commandants were very specific.[57]

That the Regency Council was serious in its desire to have the continent explored to the far western limits was made clear in 1717 by the appointment of Lieutenant Zacharie Robutel de La Noue to command an expedition to establish posts at Kaministiquia, Lake of the Woods, and Lac des Assiniboines (spelled "Assinibouels" by the French). Once that had been accomplished, La Noue was to send some of his men in search of the inland sea, the Mer de l'Ouest, then believed to be merely some fifteen days' journey beyond Lake of the Woods. Unfortunately, at the time, war was once again raging between the Sioux, the Crees, and the Assiniboines. It proved impossible to venture into that war zone.[58] At least that was La Noue's account when he returned to Montreal in 1721, and it certainly deserves credence. In the face of that failure and Father Charlevoix's recommendation that the western ocean would be best approached from a base on the upper Mississippi, a mission and trading post was established at Lac Pepin in the country of the woodland Sioux, but like all the previous attempts there, it soon had to be abandoned. The Sioux would not tolerate it once they discovered that the French were trading arms to their foes—the Crees, the Assiniboines, and the Illinois.[59]

The man who turned things around and opened up the route to the Far West was the acting commandant of La Poste du Nord, Pierre Gaultier de Varennes de La Vérendrye. In 1727 this forty-two-year-old Canadian seigneur returned to Canada, having sought fame and fortune in France with the Régiment de Bretagne in the War of the Spanish Succession, surviving musketball wounds and sabre slashes at Malplaquet but finally realizing at war's end that there was no future for him in France. Back home in New France, to help scrape a living on his seigneury, he regained his old ensign's commission in the Troupes franches de la Marine; he also took a wife, whose dowry did little to spare them from a life of genteel penury. He improved his circumstances to a modest degree when his brother agreed to share the command of La Poste du Nord, along with its perquisites. While at the Nipigon post near the northern shore of Lake Superior, La Vérendrye questioned the Crees and Assiniboines about the lands farther west, having them draw maps of the region on a sheet of birchbark. From this information he formed in his mind a concept of the geography of this unknown country. The Mer de l'Ouest, he quickly came to realize, was much farther away than had previously been imagined. There were, it appeared, vast lakes beyond Lake of the Woods, which previously had been thought to be the Mer de l'Ouest, but that inland sea now surely lay much farther to the west.

The Indians spoke of a great river, the "River of the West," beyond these intermediary lakes, but whether it flowed into these lakes from the west or out of them to Hudson Bay remained a mystery. In modern parlance, was this River of the West the Saskatchewan or the Nelson? La Vérendrye concluded that only by the establishment of a post on these western lakes could the answer be found. Here, clearly, his major difficulty was his inability to speak Cree and his dependence on others to interpret for him.

On his return to Canada from the *pays d'en haut*, La Vérendrye presented his conjectures and the information he had so far garnered to support them to the governor-general, the marquis Charles de Beauharnois de La Boische, and to Intendant Gilles Hocquart. They accepted his vague but intriguing concept of what lay beyond the lakes already known to the French. They were easily convinced that his proposal to press on to the Mer de l'Ouest by way of the lakes known to exist northwest of Lake Superior—none of which, it now appeared, were the inland sea—and then on to the River of the West deserved the support of the Crown. Nor was it lost on all concerned that the proposed posts in that region would enable the Canadians to forestall the flow of furs to the Hudson's Bay Company posts.

The governor-general and the intendant decided that in the spring of 1731 La Vérendrye should return to the western region to establish a post on Lac des Assiniboines, later to be named Lake Winnipeg, but the Crown would provide only a meagre two thousand livres for Indian "presents." La Vérendrye himself was therefore required to raise the capital needed. He would be granted a three-year monopoly on the trade in the region, and out of the resulting profits, he had to mount an expedition to press on to the Mer de l'Ouest. In the customary fashion of the fur trade community, he organized a *société* ("company") comprising himself, his eldest son Jean-Baptiste, his brother-in-law François-Christophe Dufrost de La Jemerais, and a group of Montreal merchants who invested some forty-three thousand livres in the venture for the first year's expenses.

On 8 June 1731, La Vérendrye set out from Montreal with his sons Jean-Baptiste and Pierre, La Jemerais, and fifty-odd voyageurs. They arrived at

Kaministiquia on 26 August, whereupon most of the engagés refused to go any farther. They claimed that the route ahead was, from all accounts, extremely difficult, nothing but one portage after another, with whitewater all the way. What was far worse, the Indian nations of the region were reputed to be hostile. La Vérendrye managed to prevail on the bolder among them to press on with Jean-Baptiste and La Jemerais while he stayed at Kaministiquia. The advance party reached Rainy Lake in the autumn and built Fort Saint-Pierre, the first of the eight posts that La Vérendrye would eventually have built in the district that came to be named La Mer de l'Ouest. The following spring they advanced to Lake of the Woods, escorted there by a party of Crees and Assiniboines. There they built Fort Saint-Charles, which La Vérendrye used as his main base during the ensuing years.

He, his sons, and La Jemerais were still confident that the Mer de l'Ouest could not be too far off. When this surmise was conveyed to the minister of marine, the official decided that there was no need for the Crown to invest further funds in an enterprise whose purpose would so soon be accomplished. The minister, Jean-Frédéric Phelypeaux de Maurepas, was also disenchanted by the slow progress that had been made so far. He could not imagine that traveling in that part of the world posed problems that were not encountered when traveling from Paris to Bordeaux. He became convinced that the sole concern of the commandants at the western posts was the profits they derived from the trade with the Indians. To a degree he was right, for it was those profits and those profits alone that sustained the French effort to discover the geographical extent of North America.

Had the minister torn himself away from Versailles and ventured to New France to see things firsthand by voyaging to the *pays d'en haut*, he would have discovered that the annual canoe brigades, skirting the northern shore of Lake Superior, could be held up for days by high winds. Some voyageurs, impatient, put out and had their canoes swamped by the surf. If somehow they survived, the société that had hired them held them responsible for the loss of goods.[60] All too often such impatience cost men their lives. At every portage there was a crude wooden cross to mark where voyageurs had chosen to run the rapids rather than portage and had failed. In calmer weather, on the lakes and rivers, the breeze blew away the clouds of mosquitoes, blackflies, and deerflies that made life miserable ashore at the edge of the forest. Only a smoky fire, a pipe of pungent Canadian tobacco, and bear grease on exposed skin helped to keep the insects at bay. In the wilderness there was always the risk of sudden illness or injury; nothing could be done if an appendix ruptured or a careless ax stroke sliced a leg open. Tripping over a root while toting two ninety-pound packs over a portage could cripple a man, and an encounter with a hostile Indian band who resented the foreigners' presence and coveted their goods could prove fatal.[61]

Once the voyageurs reached Kaministiquia, the real misery began. The rivers and lakes between there and Lake Winnipeg formed a maze where men could search for days for the portage trail to the next lake or river; once found, the narrow Indian trail could be blocked by windfall trees requiring hours of ax work to clear a way through, only to find that the trail led nowhere. This route northwest was a steady climb to the height of land separating the rivers flowing into Lake Superior from those going to Hudson Bay—a climb of some nine hundred feet above Lake Superior requiring over sixty portages to Lake Winnipeg. Since that lake was shallow and the surrounding land was flat as a billiard table, the water could be whipped into high and choppy waves in minutes by the winds sweeping for hundreds of miles across the prairies. A sudden gust could swamp a canoe in seconds. Over the years things improved as better tracks were discovered and as constant usage made the portage trails wider and smoother, but the endurance of the first Canadians who ventured into that land must have been tried to the limit.[62] It was not an easy way to make a living, but it must have had its compensations for these men. It was a challenge; many if not all of them rose to it and gloried in it. They proudly boasted that they were *les hommes du nord* ("the men of the north").

La Vérendrye and his lieutenants, in their dealings with the Crees and Assiniboines, gathered information about a nation that lived in houses similar to those of the French, a people with light-coloured hair who spoke a language that sounded much like French. All manner of strange accounts had circulated in Canada for some time about such peoples in the Far West. A Jesuit who arrived in the colony in 1734 wrote that the voyageurs talked of people some 1,100 leagues (2,750 English miles) from Quebec who had white skins and beards, were subjects of a king, lived in French-style houses, and raised horses and other domestic cattle. Father Nau surmised that they were Tartars, or refugees who had fled Japan; at any rate, he thought they should offer a fertile field for evangelism. He then added a note of caution: one had to be skeptical of such tales, since nowhere else in the world did a people tell lies as habitually as did the Canadians.[63]

In 1735 La Jemerais decided to go in search of these people. They turned out to be the Mandans. At the time, La Jemerais had no idea that they lived close by the Missouri, some 750 miles from Lake of the Woods. Nor did he or his brother-in-law realize that to go in that direction would lead them away from the true "River of the West," the Saskatchewan. During these years La Vérendrye had to devote himself to cementing a firm trade relationship with the Crees, Assiniboines, and Monsonis, on whose lands his posts were located. Unfortunately, this alliance earned him and his men the bitter enmity of those nations' foes, the Sioux and the Ojibwas. This enmity would cost him dearly. In 1734 he reluctantly allowed his son Jean-Baptiste to accompany a Cree-Assiniboine war party in a campaign against the Sioux of the prairies. He also supplied them with arms and ammunition. Once on the move, the war chiefs revealed that their true objective was to strike at the Sioux of the river. They fell on the Sioux, inflicting heavy casualties. Having helped to spill Sioux blood, the French had to take the consequences.

Meanwhile La Vérendrye had to return to Montreal to make new financial arrangements. The existing deal had proven to be inadequate; costs had exceeded returns year after year, and appeals to the minister of marine for aid constantly fell on deaf ears.[64] In his absence his men established Fort Maurepas near the mouth of the Red River. When he returned to Fort Saint-Charles, La Vérendrye was greeted with the sad news that La Jemerais had succumbed to a malady of some sort. His men had struggled to get him back to Fort Saint-Charles, but he died en route. Worse was to come.

The following year, 1736, his son Jean-Baptiste, Father Jean-Pierre Aulneau S.J., and nineteen of his men were caught on an island in Lake of the Woods by a Sioux war party. Thirsting for revenge against the French for their support of the Crees and Assiniboines two years earlier, the Sioux massacred the entire party, leaving the arrow-pierced, mutilated bodies for the crows and wolves. This, La Vérendrye maintained, made it impossible for his men to venture farther west, with their lives already being at risk where they then were.[65] Five or six companies of Troupes franches de la Marine could have resolved that problem in short order, but the governor-general could not authorize such an expensive undertaking without the minister's prior approval, and the comte de Maurepas would never have entertained the notion.

In 1737 La Vérendrye and his men mapped the Manitoba lakes and garnered more information about the River of the West. What was encouraging was the production of some two hundred thousand livres weight of furs and a large number of slaves, mostly Sioux, prisoners taken by the

Crees and Assiniboines. A healthy young Indian slave brought up to four hundred livres at auction in Montreal.[66] La Vérendrye was to boast of the number of such slaves he shipped out of the West over the years.[67] The following year he established Fort La Reine at the site of present-day Portage la Prairie, and then, with his sons Louis-Joseph and François, twenty-six Canadians, and twenty-five Assiniboines, he set out for the Mandans and eventually reached their main village in present-day North Dakota. He believed that he was then within a few leagues of the fabled River of the West, but he made no attempt to push on. Instead he sent his son Louis-Joseph, who reached the Missouri near where it veers sharply out of the southwest. For lack of a guide, Louis-Joseph did not venture as far as the Great Bend of the Missouri. Had he done so and followed it far enough, he would have realized that the Missouri could not be a viable route to the western ocean. Yet one can hardly criticize him on that score; traveling that far would have required a journey of some weeks into unknown country inhabited by nations all too likely to be hostile. Without a strong Indian escort that had good relations with those peoples, such an expedition would have been a risky proposition. Still, two years later the Mallet brothers did make the journey.

As it was, the information acquired led La Vérendrye to suspect that the river Louis-Joseph had reached would not lead to the Mer de l'Ouest, but before he could be sure enough to begin searching in other directions for the River of the West, he needed more certain information. Since the river they had stumbled on, the Missouri, appeared not to flow in the desired direction, where it finally ended up was of no import.

During these years La Vérendrye was commuting back and forth between his western posts and Montreal as he sought to resolve his everpressing supply and financial problems, seemingly caused mainly by his untrustworthy Montreal business associates, who pursued only their own interests and left him in the lurch time and time again. He was, in truth, no better an entrepreneur than he was an explorer, but at least he did try. He knew that he could never hope to bequeath wealth to his sons. What was of far greater importance to him, as to his Canadian peers, was to pass on a name, a reputation that would live far longer than mere money would last; in short, he sought *la gloire*. Thus, despite the chaos of his financial affairs and his failing health, in June 1741, at age fifty-six, he set out on what was to be his final voyage in search of the Mer de l'Ouest.

Once he reached Fort La Reine, his most urgent task was to restrain the nations around his posts from renewing their war with the Sioux. He also had to decide which route to take to accomplish his mission, the Missouri or the Riviére Blanche (the Saskatchewan). He chose the Missouri. He sent some local Indian guides with his sons Louis-Joseph and François, as well as two Canadians who had wintered with the Mandans, to the Mandan villages. From there they proceeded west-southwest across the plains in search of the Gens de Chevaux (horsemen, probably Cheyennes), who, it was hoped, would guide them on to the inland sea. They proceeded, on foot, from one Indian village to another, obliged to go in whichever direction their Indian guides chose, for reasons best known to themselves.

When they eventually reached the Gens de Chevaux, all was desolation. The Indians' villages had been attacked by the Gens du Serpent (a generic Indian term for an enemy tribe, likely the Kiowas); the men and old women had been slaughtered, the young women and children taken as slaves. The La Vérendryes gained some information about mountains, beyond which lay the sea. Although a major campaign of reprisal against the Gens du Serpent was clearly brewing, the Canadians and their guides decided to carry on. By 1 January 1743, the mountains were in sight.

Which mountains these were—the Black Hills of South Dakota or the Big Horn range of the Rocky Mountain cordillera—is by no means clear. The account given by Louis-Joseph La Vérendrye is not very informative; he tersely stated: "For the most part they are well wooded with timber of every kind and appear very high. I was greatly mortified not to be able to climb the mountains as I had wished."[68] That does not seem to be an accurate description of the Big Horn range, which rises precipitously to over thirteen thousand feet; nor would one, on regarding that forbidding sheer rock wall, be likely to contemplate scaling it as though an afternoon's outing would suffice for the task. The Black Hills, on the other hand, rising to over seven thousand feet (the highest mountains east of the Rockies, higher than the Blue Ridge Mountains of Virginia and the Carolinas), would certainly have seemed very high to La Vérendrye, who had never seen any mountains that high in his life and who had spent months and years on the plains. All that, combined with the fact that they traveled at a slow pace in a meandering fashion, inclines one to think that the La Vérendryes got no farther than the Black Hills and never saw the Rockies.[69]

By the time they arrived in sight of the mountains, the war party had grown to several thousand—two thousand warriors and a horde of women and children, as entire villages joined the party en route. There were Minitaris, Beaux Hommes (Crows?), Gens de la Belle Fourche (Cheyennes?), Gens de l'Arc (Pawnee-Arikaras?), and likely others. Such a group, bent on vengeance, had to proceed slowly, since the men had to hunt for food along the way. They eventually reached the villages of the Gens du Serpent, which they found abandoned. The La Vérendryes' Indian allies immediately panicked, fearing that the enemy had left to attack their villages, defenceless with themselves absent. They swiftly departed. That brought the French expedition to a halt. To Louis-Joseph and François, pressing on beyond the mountains without their Indian escort seemed hopeless, so they turned back. Traveling east-southeast, they reached the Missouri on 19 March 1743. Ironically, they had marched through the Mer de l'Ouest, as depicted by Guillaume Delisle on his 1717 map, without getting their feet wet.[70]

Along the way they buried a lead plaque, brought from Quebec and engraved with the king's arms, and erected a stone cairn over it to symbolize their having taken possession of the land for France. When the Indians inquired what they were doing, they prevaricated. Rather than explain that the Indians had just lost possession of their country by some mystical means, the La Vérendryes told them that the plaque and cairn were there merely to mark the occasion of the visit.[71] On 2 July 1743, La Vérendrye's sons arrived back at Fort La Reine. It had been a great adventure, but little more. The western ocean was as far away as ever. At least one thing was now clear: voyaging to the southwest was not the way to go to reach the Sea of the West. The French therefore turned to the Saskatchewan.

Meanwhile Pierre La Vérendrye had been busy consolidating the family's hold of the country around the Manitoba lakes. Fort Dauphin at Lake Winnipegosis, Fort Bourbon northwest of Lake Winnipeg, and Fort Paskoya on the Saskatchewan were established. Those posts, at long last, opened up the best route across the continent to the Rocky Mountains and beyond. The Comte de Maurepas, however, remained convinced that the La Vérendryes were not really concerned with western exploration but only with the profits derived from their trade in furs and slaves. The minister's displeasure was made known to La Vérendrye by the governor-general, and La Vérendrye felt compelled to resign his post as commandant of La Mer de l'Ouest before he was dismissed in disgrace; but two years later, in 1746, he was reappointed to the command. He craved and now pleaded for just one more chance to have the glory of being the first Frenchman to reach the western ocean. It was denied him. He died in December 1749, at age sixty-four. He left his sons a paltry estate, valued at a mere four thousand livres, barely enough to support one Canadian noble family for a year.[72]

In the Northwest, as the French slowly advanced up the Saskatchewan, they encountered the same problem as had their fellow countrymen in the Southwest: the suspicion and hostility of warring tribes. The Crees and Assiniboines were warring with the forest and plains Sioux and, farther west, with the Blackfoot. These tribes were liable to turn on the French without warning, at any time, if they came to suspect the latter of trading arms to their foes. Another problem was that the French in the West, both to the north and the south, were so few. By the mid–eighteenth century, fewer than 1,000 Canadians, including a handful of women, were at the Great Lakes posts and La Mer de l'Ouest. In 1754, when French expansion in the West had reached its farthest limits and the hostilities in the Ohio Valley sparked the Seven Years' War, the troops garrisoning the posts from Fort Frontenac on Lake Ontario to Pascoyac on the Saskatchewan numbered a mere 261 officers and men.[73] In addition there were the men of the fur trade and a few missionaries. The fur traders included the voyageurs, not more than 500, who spent the summer months voyaging between Montreal and the western posts; when a campaign had to be waged in the West, they were pressed into service. There were also the *hivernants*, who remained in the West for years at a time, and the storekeepers and clerks, who staffed the posts year-round for their respective *sociétés*. The total number of these men of the trade was unlikely to have exceeded 600 at any one time in the eighteenth century. As for the legendary coureurs de bois, their numbers can only be guessed at—most likely they were fewer than 200. Renegades all, the role they played in extending French influence in the West was, to say the least, equivocal, for they had been assimilated by the Indians and had cut themselves off from Canadian society.

For the France of Louis XIV, the regency, and Louis XV, this was imperialism on the cheap. Yet this handful of Frenchmen, Canadians by birth or adoption, laid claim to the lion's share of the continent for over half a century. It was this circumstance, the parsimony of the French government, that stalled the advance of the French across North America. The officers commanding the posts at La Baie and la Mer de l'Ouest were commanded to send detachments of men up the Missouri and Saskatchewan Rivers to their sources, then across the imagined height of land to seek the rivers that flowed into the western ocean.[74] But the officers received no help from the Crown for this search.

The 1753–54 journal and relative correspondence of Lieutenant Paul Marin de La Malgue clearly indicated that while he was in command at La Baie, his main concerns were to keep the tribes in his district at peace and to prevent them from establishing trade relations with the Anglo-American traders who were trickling over the Appalachians from Pennsylvania, Virginia, and the Carolinas with packhorse trains. Yet the execution of his orders depended on his *société*'s ability to garner enough furs to cover the post's costs and return a reasonable profit on the partners' investment. Marin also had to fend off assaults on some of his men, whom he had sent to discover the source of the Mississippi. These assaults were launched not by hostile Indians but by Louis-Joseph Gaultier de La Vérendrye, commandant at Chagouamigon on the southern shore of Lake Superior. La Vérendrye stripped Marin's men of their goods and threatened to ship to Montreal in chains any more of them who were caught trading in what he claimed was his territory. Only the intervention of the governor-general brought him to reason.[75] Given such preoccupations, Marin likely lacked both the resources and the inclination to engage in exploration for exploration's sake.

The final attempt by the French to reach the western ocean was made by Jacques Legardeur de Saint-Pierre, a veteran officer of the Troupes franches de la Marine with many years of service in the West. He had served at Fort Beauharnois in the Sioux country in the 1730s and in the savage campaigns against the Fox and Chicasaws. He had commanded at Fort Miami, in present-day Indiana, and in 1747 he was appointed commandant at Michilimackinac. He had also seen much service during the War of the Austrian Succession. Along the way he had mastered the Cree language. With that background and record, it is not surprising that Governor-General Jacques-Pierre de Taffanel, marquis de La Jonquiére, passed over the La Vérendryes and chose Saint-Pierre to make yet one more attempt to reach the Mer de l'Ouest—to do what La Vérendrye and his sons had conspicuously failed to do. By this time, however, the French were becoming increasingly skeptical of the very existence of the inland sea.[76]

On 5 June, Saint-Pierre left Montreal with nine canoes, seven men in each. He was permitted to take as much merchandise, arms, and ammunition as he felt would be needed, including eau-de-vie. He was also placed in command of that year's canoe convoy.[77] Included with the engagés and the soldiers for the posts' garrisons was a Jesuit missionary, whom Saint-Pierre came to regard as an encumbrance; he not only could not speak Cree and hence had no hope of instructing these Indians in the Christian faith but also had neglected to bring the scientific instruments required to fix latitudes and make accurate maps. That purpose, rather than evangelism, was likely the reason he had been sent with the expedition. When Saint-

Pierre discovered these shortcomings after arriving at Michilimackinac, the main base of the western fur trade, he unceremoniously shipped the priest back to Montreal. At Michilimackinac, Saint-Pierre had to spend several weeks organizing the logistics of the expedition: additional engagés had to be hired, food supplies obtained, arrangements made with local merchants for supplies to be sent on to the posts before the winter freeze, and an adequate supply of "presents" obtained for the Indians who would likely be encountered en route.

By early autumn the expedition was at Fort La Reine. Saint-Pierre noted in his journal that the route was extremely difficult, with thirty-eight portages to Lac de Pluie (Rainy Lake), varying from four leagues to a quarter-league (the French league was approximately two and one-half English miles). He found the local Crees well enough disposed but extremely demanding and impertinent. Being first and foremost a soldier, he attributed this to their not having been treated with sufficient firmness previously. He noted that no matter how much they received as "presents," they were never satisfied; given half a chance, they would empty the storehouses of the king. His previous postings had been among the Indians of the Great Lakes, who had endured the French presence for more than half a century, two generations, and hence had grown wary and knew how far the French could be pushed. The Crees west of Lake Superior did not stand in awe of the French, for they could always deal with the English at Hudson Bay, as could also the Assiniboines. Saint-Pierre was soon to learn that it was the Indians, not he and his few men, who held the whip hand. Thus when he strove to make them end their wars with the Sakis, Puants, Sioux, and Renards, it was to no avail. The Crees and Assiniboines had warred with those tribes for longer than anyone could remember. Much blood had been spilled; the spirits of their slain warriors could not rest easy in the spirit world were they not to be avenged. They saw no reason whatsoever why they should do the bidding of a French officer with a mere handful of men; their affairs were none of his business.

Apart from that, Saint-Pierre's most immediate and pressing problem was the food supply. The posts at Lake of the Woods and at the mouth of the Winnipeg River, he discovered to his dismay, were not as well stocked as he had been given to believe. He therefore had to divide his men into three parties. He sent his ensign, Joseph Boucher de Niverville, to winter with one party at Fort Pascoyac on the Saskatchewan. There they staved off starvation by netting fish under the ice. Another group wintered with the Indians and likely fared better. Saint-Pierre and the remainder of his men stayed at Fort La Reine. The main problem facing them, apart from the shortage of food, was the cold. In that part of North America, present-day Manitoba, the temperature can go down to minus 40° Celsius, remaining there for weeks on end. As the men emerged from their draughty cabins at daybreak to saw the firewood that spelled the difference between life and frozen death, they would have seen not one sun peer over the eastern horizon but three, five, and occasionally seven, all in a horizontal line. These were what were named, decades later, "sun dogs"—an optical illusion caused by the refraction of the sun's ray on ice crystals at extremely low temperatures. The spectacular beauty of the phenomenon was likely lost on Saint-Pierre and his men.

When spring finally came, they were too enfeebled to continue the search for the Mer de l'Ouest. Moreover the Crees and Assiniboines were again at war, not only with the Sioux but also with the Blackfoot, the Brochets, and the Gros Ventres. The route to the Far West by way of the Saskatchewan was thus closed to the French. Saint-Pierre drew the obvious conclusion that there could be no hope of discovering where the Saskatchewan would lead them until the Indian wars were terminated. He also concluded that the route La Vérendrye had taken, by way of the Missouri, would lead only to the Spanish settlements, so the Saskatchewan it had to be.

During the ensuing winter Saint-Pierre devoted his efforts to ending the Indian wars. He purchased prisoners taken by the Crees and Assiniboines and instead of shipping them to Montreal for sale as slaves, as La Vérendrye had been wont to do, he sent them back to their own people as a peace gesture. That and a lavish distribution of "presents" gave him reason to hope that a general peace settlement could be arranged. He also promised the tribes farther west that he would establish a post 300 leagues (750 miles) up the Saskatchewan. He sent ten men off in two canoes, and according to his journal, they made their way upriver to the Montagnes des Roches. Since there are no mountains of any sort along the Saskatchewan until the Rocky Mountains are reached, that is where the post must have been established. Saint-Pierre named it Fort La Jonquière. While they were there the Canadians garnered what he enigmatically referred to as *un amas considerable*; presumably that phrase meant a sizable quantity of either food supplies, cached for future consumption, or furs. Ensign Niverville had planned to follow the advance party in a month's time, but in the interval he was stricken with a serious malady and incapacitated; his men held out little hope of his survival. Meanwhile Saint-Pierre had to go to Kaministiquia to supervise the transport of the year's supplies, shipped from Montreal by his partners in the Société de la Mer de l'Ouest. By 7 October 1751, he was back at Fort La Reine making preparations to join Niverville as arranged.

Then suddenly his plans were shattered. Two of Niverville's Canadians with four Indians arrived to tell of the ensign's continued illness and of a treacherous attack by the Assiniboines on the "Ihatche-8-lini" (the symbol "8" was used by the French to denote a "oua" sound coming from deep in an Indian's chest rather than from the mouth or throat); these latter Indians, it had been hoped, would guide the French as far as the "Kinirege-8-ilini." A large party of Assiniboines had arrived at Fort La Jonquière, where they found forty to forty-five tepees of Ihatche-8-lini. Seeing themselves as far superior in the number of their warriors, they could not resist the temptation to score an easy victory over their ancient foe, and they attacked without warning. As usual, only the young women and the children were spared, to be swept away as slaves. This the Assiniboines did despite their having assured Saint-Pierre, after being loaded down with "presents," that they would keep the peace. They made the rules, however; those that the French sought to impose counted for little or nothing.

Much here has to be read between the lines of the only piece of evidence extant, the rough draft of Saint-Pierre's journal. Who were the "Ihatche-8-lini," or the Yhatchéillini (Saint-Pierre spells the word in a variety of ways), and the "Kinirege-8-ilini"? Obviously the Ihatche-8-lini and the Assiniboines had been enemies for a long time; in that region, they must have been the Blackfoot, known today as the Bloods, the Piegans, and the Blackfoot proper. Their hunting territory then extended no farther east than the junction of the Battle and North Saskatchewan Rivers, well to the west of the forks of the latter river. Who were the "Kinirege-8-ilini"? A latter-day guess is that the name merely means "pike eaters."[78]

Saint-Pierre wrote that never in his thirty-six years among the Indians had he encountered anything so perfidious. He was forced to abandon Fort La Jonquière and with it all hope of finding a way through the mountain barrier to the western ocean by the Saskatchewan river route. The Blackfoot would now slaughter on sight any Frenchmen they encountered. He therefore began seeking other rivers that would lead to the West rather than to New Spain or Hudson Bay. The Indians he questioned declared that they knew of no such river—except for one old man, who stated that not too long ago a post had been established not far from where his people went to trade for goods similar to those that came to them from

Canada. He explained that the traders were not English but were not as white-skinned as the French. The way to them, he stated, lay west-north-west, toward the midsummer setting sun. Saint-Pierre sent the man off, with two Crees, bearing a letter to the commandant of this mysterious trading post. He hoped to receive a reply the following year. There is no mention in the Canadian dispatches to the ministry of marine of a reply having been received.

What were the French to make of such accounts? Did they know that the Russians had established posts on the Pacific coast? Most likely, they did not. Perhaps the Indian in question had encountered Spaniards trading on the coast of present-day British Columbia. Who knows? Or perhaps that crafty old Indian, knowing what the French wanted to hear, offered it to them and then made off with a canoeload of "presents," chuckling to himself along the way.

While Saint-Pierre was at Fort La Reine, with only five marines of the garrison—the rest of them and the engagés having been sent off to hunt—two hundred Assiniboines suddenly burst into the fort and dispersed among the buildings. Saint-Pierre berated them, in Cree, for their insolence. One of them answered, in Cree, that they had merely come to have a smoke, meaning that this was just a social visit. Then a marine dashed to Saint-Pierre and told him that some of the warriors had broken into the guardroom and were seizing the muskets. One of the intruders warned Saint-Pierre's Assiniboine interpreter that they intended to kill all the French and pillage the fort; the French were no longer welcome in their country, and this was their way of putting an end to the French presence.

When told that, Saint-Pierre seized a brand from the fireplace, strode off to the powder magazine, knocked the top off a keg of gunpowder, and then strode back into the midst of the startled Assiniboines, with the open keg under his arm and the burning brand poised over it. He told them in Cree, and they needed no interpreter, that he saw what they were about to do but that before they could do it, he would take them all with him to the Spirit World. At that they panicked, turned, and fled, almost knocking the palisade gate off its hinges. Yet the Assiniboines had the last word, for the time being. The following spring, while Saint-Pierre and his men were at Kaministiquia, the Assiniboines burned Fort La Reine to the ground. Such were the problems the French commandants in the West had to face in their quest for the western sea.

The efforts of Saint-Pierre, and of Marin at La Baie, to end the renewed war of the Sioux with the Crees and Assiniboines came to nought. Saint-

Pierre finally gave up and categorically stated that there was no hope of reaching the western ocean overland as long as the Indian nations were at war. For this state of affairs he, illogically but in keeping with the French frame of mind, held the English at Hudson Bay responsible. On that score the Canadians were paranoid: the English were to blame for everything; they were plotting under every bed. To resolve the problem the soldier's way, Saint-Pierre proposed that the English be driven out of Hudson Bay. He declared himself willing and eager to lead an expedition to accomplish that end.[79]

On 9 August 1753, Saint-Pierre was relieved of his command at La Mer de l'Ouest by Sieur Louis Luc de La Corne and was posted to the Ohio country. The French were about to invade the Ohio Valley in force to fend off the fur traders and land speculators of Pennsylvania and Virginia who coveted the territory and were backed by a powerful hawkish faction at Westminster. Upon the death of Marin, commandant of the French expeditionary force, Saint-Pierre succeeded to the command and there received and saw off the future first president of the United States of America.[80] The following year he was recalled to Montreal to serve as commandant of the Indian allies of the French in the campaign to block the Anglo-American invasion of Canada by way of Lake Champlain. He was killed in the battle at Lac Saint-Sacrement (Lake George). So ended the career of an intrepid, valiant soldier who had done much to unravel the mystery of the Far West.

Interestingly, his journal contains no mention of the inland sea that they all had been seeking. Apparently he had come to realize that any such sea had to be beyond the great mountain barrier, since it was not to be found on the prairies. What is one to make of this rough draft of Saint-Pierre's journal? It is the only evidence we have of what the French were doing in the West at that time, apart from his commission as commandant at La Mer de l'Ouest, a document that spelled out what he was required to do, namely, discover a route to the inland sea and from there to the Pacific; the *congés* for his canoes and *engagés* are revealing, as are his contracts with his Montreal fur trade associates. Are we to reject his journal as a fabrication, as did the Anglo-Canadian historians A. S. Morton and J. B. Brebner, or should we accept it at face value?[81] Did the French establish a post within sight of the Rocky Mountains, or was their westernmost post somewhere well to the east of the fork of the North and the South Saskatchewan? According to one author, the site of Fort La Jonquière was near the present-day town of Nipawan, Saskatchewan, at 104° longitude.[82] Yet a post there would have served no useful purpose and would merely have forestalled the post at Pascoyac. Saint-Pierre stated, unequivocally, that his men established a post at the Montagnes des Roches, and the only mountains in western Canada are the Rocky Mountains. From the western edge of the Canadian Shield to those mountains, along the Saskatchewan River, the land is flat or gently rolling parkland. Moreover, the men clearly were well within the country of the Blackfoot, whose hunting grounds extended nowhere near as far east as the forks of the Saskatchewan.

Moreover, what motive could Saint-Pierre have had to give a false version of events? He admitted that he had failed in his quest for the Mer de l'Ouest and gave convincing reasons why. What has come down to us is a preliminary draft of the journal, or report, that he, like all other post commandants, was required to keep for the scrutiny of the governor-general, much as ships' captains were required to keep a log. Had the governor-general suspected for one moment that Saint-Pierre's journal was not a true account, he would merely have had to interrogate, under oath, Ensign Niverville, Saint-Pierre's second-in-command, and the marines and engagés who had served under them. To have been caught in a deception would have irrevocably ruined Saint-Pierre's career; only a fool would have risked that, and Saint-Pierre was nobody's fool. Since he was subsequently appointed to senior commands in the Canadian forces, the governor-general and the intendant had obviously not lost confidence in him. Thus, all things considered, one has to accept that the French likely did establish an outpost, Fort La Jonquière, in the shadow of the Rocky Mountains, if only for a few months. Where exactly was its location? No one knows; an educated guess suggests the present-day site of the town named Rocky Mountain House in western Alberta, where those mountains are clearly in forbidding sight.

During the war years, 1754–60, the Canadian forces roved through and came to know well the country between the Allegheny Mountains and the Mississippi while their war parties, based at Fort Duquesne at the forks of the Ohio, ravaged the frontier settlements of Pennsylvania, Virginia, and the Carolinas. Before that, Canadian fur traders had voyaged down the rivers leading to James Bay. In the regions sufficiently well populated by nomadic Indian hunting bands, they established trading posts, which greatly reduced the flow of furs to the Hudson's Bay Company.[83] For the employees of that company, "asleep on the shores of the frozen sea," the interior of the continent was terra incognita. What little knowledge they had was derived from a renegade coureur de bois, Joseph La France, who

CARTE
DRESSÉE PAR M. GUILLAUME DEL'ISLE
Au commencement de ce Siecle, pour servir à ses
Conjectures sur l'Existence de la Mer de l'Ouest
Publiée par M.ʳ Joseph Nicolas Del'Isle Novemb.1752

55
50 Aïsinipoils CANADA 50
Sioux Lac
Pointe du Supérieur Nipiffiniiens
S.Esprit
45 MER DE L'OUEST Ontaonacs 45
C.Blanc Aonia Hurons
C.Mendocin Neu-
Quivira Panis tres
40 Riv.ᵉ de l'Ouest Ilinois 40
Cibola
Nouveau Virginie
35 Mexique 35
Choumans Caroline
MER 30
30
DU
SUD 25
25 MEXIQUE
4.ᵉ Carte

11.3 "Carte Dressée par M. Guillaume Del'Isle" (1752). Although Guillaume Delisle, like many of his contemporaries, was fascinated by stories and theories about a
vast sea in the western part of the continent (the Mer de l'Ouest), he was circum-
spect regarding what he published. After his death in 1726, his half-brother Joseph
Nicolas Delisle and his son-in-law Philippe Buache began to publish maps and reports that mixed reality, theory, and outrageous wishful thinking. As "Carte
Dressée par M. Guillaume Del'Isle" shows, the authors often credited their illus-
trious predecessor with the concepts displayed on their maps in order to gain credibility for a geography that few people at midcentury believed. Courtesy of the National Archives of Canada, NMC 38506.

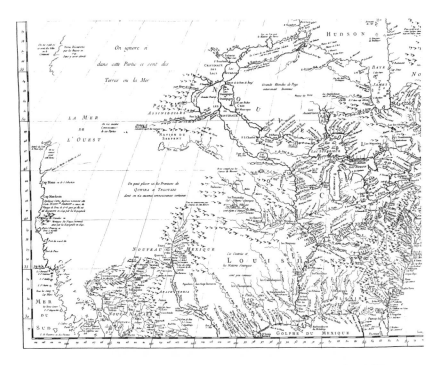

11.4 "Carte de L'Amerique Septentrionale" (detail), Jacques-Nicolas Bellin, 1755. The southwestern quarter of Bellin's large map is shown here. This is the most authoritative summary of French geographical knowledge of North Aemrica published before the end of the French régime. As chief cartographer for the French Ministry of the Marine, Bellin had access to all the latest information, including Louis Bonnecamp's survey of the Ohio River (1749) and a map produced by members of the La Vérendrye expeditions in 1740. Bellin also used information from British explorations to Hudson Bay, published in 1748. Courtesy of the National Archives of Canada, NMC 21057.

had made his way during the summer months of the years 1739–42 from Sault Sainte-Marie to York Factory. The reliability of the information he actually provided is in serious doubt.[84]

The defeat of the Marquis de Montcalm's ill-led army and the subsequent surrender of Quebec to the British army in September 1759 foretold the demise of French power in North America. The following year, on 8 September, the French army—the Troupes de Terre, the Troupes franches de la Marine, and the Canadian militia—abandoned by their Indian allies, had to capitulate to the truculent Major General Jeffery Amherst, commander in chief of the British armies poised at the gates of Montreal. Three years later, by the terms of the Treaty of Paris, France ceded Canada, with ill-defined limits, to Great Britain. At the same time, France was obliged to cede Louisiana, west of the Mississippi, to Spain. That put an end to French exploration of North America; that is, it put an end to exploration directed by the French to further French national aims.

Until the end of the century, and well beyond, men such as Peter Pond of Connecticut, Alexander Henry from New Jersey, the Frobishers from Yorkshire, and Simon McTavish and James McGill from Scotland, guided by Canadian voyageurs and interpreters, proceeded to pick the bones of the Canadian fur trade's carcass—like the carpetbaggers of the post–Civil War United States. In the process, they voyaged farther and farther into the Northwest. Most notable among them was Alexander MacKenzie, who, in 1789, with four Canadian voyageurs, made his way down to the Arctic Ocean along the river that today bears his name. Four years later, with eight voyageurs to guide him, he accomplished what the French had attempted, with a remarkable lack of success, for decades: he breached the Rocky Mountain barrier. On 21 July 1793, he and his men reached the shore of the Pacific Ocean. They were the first Europeans—one Scot and four *Canadiens*—to cross the continent overland to the Pacific Ocean.[85] Yet that feat was accomplished by virtue of the experience garnered by the Canadian voyageurs during the preceding century. They surely deserve some of the credit for the achievement. Without them, the voyage could not even have been contemplated.

In the Southwest, the territory of Louisiana, exploration by the French, per se, ceased. If the French in Spanish Louisiana did engage in exploration of the Far West, they did so under Spanish, not French, auspices. The officers of the Troupes franches de la Marine, most of them Canadians, adjusted easily to Spanish rule, accepting commissions in the Spanish army and, some of them, appointments to the Cabildo.[86] These French no longer had any incentive for western exploration, no need to strive for the trade route to Santa Fe, since that route was now wide open for them. Farther north, when the French at the Illinois settlements discovered that all the territory east of the Mississippi had been ceded to Great Britain, which meant in effect to the rapacious Anglo-Americans, most of them moved across the river to where a New Orleans company, Maxent Laclède et Compagnie, had established a trading post near the mouth of the Missouri. Being under Spanish rule seemed likely to be more tolerable than being at the mercy of the old, implacable foe, the British. This new settlement rapidly expanded, was named Saint-Louis-des-Illinois, and soon became the main base for the fur trade along the Missouri.[87]

One of the main tasks of the Spanish officials now became to find a way to keep the Canadian fur traders, hirelings of British merchants at Montreal, out of the northern regions of Louisiana. It was believed that they had begun to stir up trouble among the Indian nations. To put an end to that behaviour, the Spanish had to find the true source of the Missouri and then establish a chain of garrisoned posts upriver to gain the allegiance of the Indian nations; that was clearly essential, for with the support of the plains Indians, the Spanish could drive away the British operating out of Canada. The chief instrument of this policy was to be the Saint-Louis fur-trading community. Thus the expatriate Canadians of the Illinois country now moved up the Missouri and its tributaries to the headwaters at the foot of the Rocky Mountains.

In 1793–94 the "Company of Explorers of the Upper Missouri" came into being, a company that concerned itself only with exploration for furs. Jean-Baptiste Truteau was dispatched with eight men to establish trade relations with the Mandans. Predictably, the Teton Sioux barred the route. In any event another Canadian, Jacques d'Eglise, had preceded Truteau to the Mandans, and two other Canadians, Ménard and Réné Jusséaume, had been trading with the Mandans and Gros Ventres for years.[88] Most likely there were scores more like them, men whose names have gone unrecorded. Meanwhile, somewhat ironically, to the north, Canadian employees of the North West Company competed for the trade of the Missouri River basin.

By this time, in the Far West, French had become the lingua franca.[89] Among the Indian nations, "Français" became a generic word for Europeans—French, Spanish, English, or American. The names of the trading posts, some eventually to become towns and cities, were French, as were the names of rivers and lakes and mountain ranges. Even the terms applied to many of the West's indigenous nations—Teton Sioux, Nez Percé, Bois Brule Sioux, and others—were derived from the French. All attest to the prior presence and predominance of the Canadians.

In the eighteenth century the French had four main aims in their thrust into the Far West: to discover new supplies of furs; to find new tribes to proselytize the faith of the Church of Rome, a motive that was considerably diminished as the century wore on; to penetrate and dominate the Spanish commercial empire by land; and to be the first to discover the inland sea that would lead to the Pacific. While in pursuit of those aims,

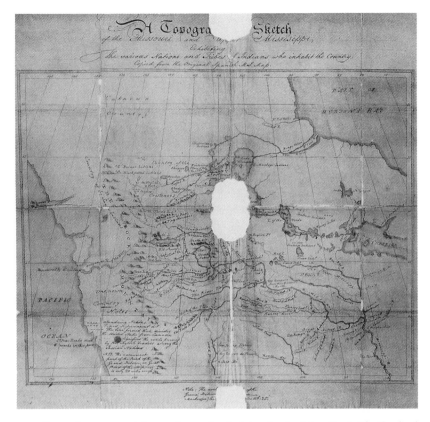

11.5 *Copy of a manuscript map drawn by Antoine Soulard (c. 1800). The Soulard map is arguably the final French map of the western interior. Although the Library of Congress gives its date as "circa 1800," it was more likely produced around 1795, with perhaps several copies being made between 1795 and 1798. The map shows the French conception of the Missouri basin and farther west at the turn of the century and was based on the late-eighteenth-century Saint Louis fur trade up the Missouri River to the Mandan villages. Courtesy of the Yale Collection of Western Americana, Beinecke Rare Book and Manuscript Library.*

among other things, the French filled in the map of North America from the Atlantic to the Rocky Mountains, from Hudson Bay to the Gulf of Mexico, bequeathing French names to rivers and lakes, future towns and cities, along the length and breadth of the continent to mark their passing.

Why, then, it must be asked, did the French fail in their attempts to find an overland route to the Pacific? The answer is not hard to find. The French were too few in number, and the Indians were too powerful, too suspicious, too proud, and too independent; they were then sovereign nations, lords of their domains. They distrusted, not without cause, the motives and intentions of all Europeans. They always stated, "This far, perhaps; but no farther." Another major factor was the failure of the French Crown to provide adequate support. To proceed with impunity through the Indian country and establish the necessary garrisoned posts for a supply line over three thousand miles long would have required a sizable military expedition, at least as large as that required for the Chickasaw campaign of 1739—in which the Canadian contingent had numbered some five hundred men.[90] The cooperation of the Crees and Blackfoot, implacable enemies, to find one of the very few passes through the Canadian Rockies would have been imperative. This route could have been found but would have been very expensive, costing perhaps as much as the royal court squandered in a fortnight. The government of the day balked, and hence the French drive to reach the western ocean fell short. Then came the War of the Conquest, and suddenly New France was no more.

Why, then, did a Scottish fur trader, Alexander Mackenzie, and two American army officers, Meriwether Lewis and William Clark, succeed where the French, with their far greater experience and finesse in dealing with the Indian nations, had failed? In the years immediately after the conquest of Canada, the Montreal fur traders expanded the fur trade far into the Northwest, seeking new sources of supply for the seemingly insatiable European market. The manpower of the trade—the voyageurs, clerks, interpreters—remained Canadian (French), but the owners and directors of the new companies, successors to the old Canadian sociétés, were now tough and ruthless Scotsmen, Yankees, and Yorkshiremen. Despite the efforts of the British authorities at Quebec, these traders, totally without scruples, used liquor in the trade to a degree unknown previously. The North West Company traders plied the Indians with a delightful but deadly concoction called "high wine," made of a mixture of brandy, dark rum, sweet sherry, tawny port, cloves, nutmeg, and cinnamon, with water added according to circumstances. The Far West was flooded with the wine. The Indian nations became totally debauched. Once addicted, the Indians would do virtually anything to get more, including trap the animals to extinction. They refused to trade meat supplies at the trading posts for anything but liquor.[91]

The brutal trading methods of the "Nor'Westers" eventually aroused the hostility of the western Indian nations. They decided to drive the traders out of their country, and they struck the posts on the Assiniboine in 1781. Then, in the autumn of that year, a terrible smallpox epidemic swept through the West. It had been brought from the south by the Saulteux and the Sioux, who had attacked smallpox-smitten American invaders of their lands. Wearing the clothing of the slain Americans, they contracted the disease and unwittingly spread it far and wide, all through the Northwest. Entire tribes were wiped out.[92] After that, the Indian nations—reduced in numbers to a mere fraction of their former strength, besotted with liquor, and totally demoralized—could no longer offer any resistance to the advancing Europeans. The Far West was now wide open to traders, explorers, and, eventually, settlers. And that is how the West, to the Pacific, was finally won. Liquor and microbes succeeded where the best efforts of the French had failed.

12 / British Exploration of Rupert's Land

RICHARD I. RUGGLES

Commerce was the primary agency in the exploration and discovery of the northern part of America. Exploration was the necessary consequence of a burgeoning trade in furs, whereas geographical inquiry was a lesser inducement for coasting intricate and dangerous shorelines and venturing across the vast interior of the continent. The impetus of the pioneer trading expedition of the ship *Nonsuch* into Hudson Bay in 1668 was not discovery, which was a relatively unimportant motive; rather, the goals were to gauge the potential of the trade in furs with the Cree Indians in the Bottom of the Bay,[1] to assess the feasibility of this large region as a colony, and to advance the quest for valuable minerals. These three purposes—trade profit, colonial advantage, and mineral riches—were at the forefront of British activity for the following century and a quarter, stemming from this trial British trading venture.

Whereas geographical curiosity played a muted role in the exploration history of the northern and western regions of the continent, geographical strategy was pivotal. Trading enterprises found it vital to unravel the interconnections of rivers and lakes and their outflow to seas, to measure directions and distances between significant nodes along the emerging paths of trade, to surmount mountainous barricades, to map out the interdigitations of tundra, forest, parkbelt, and grassland, and to become cognizant of the territories of the peoples of the region.

Based on such knowledge, groups expanded their facilities, jockeying for trade advantage in reference to the geographical pattern of their rivals' trade economies. The backers of the first English expeditions were enticed to invest in a venture that was to be intruded into an existing system; their strategy was the eventual circumvention of the geographical pattern of the French fur trade concentrated in the Saint Lawrence–Great Lakes basin. This would allow the merchants to carry their goods directly into the heart of the continent. To pursue this stratagem successfully required that the new syndicate assert right of control over territories stretching beyond the coasts of Hudson and James Bays and therefore over this land's products, which were exchanged in a lucrative trade with its native inhabitants.

The strategy in common use over several centuries was for investors interested in the exploitation of a region to form a joint stock company and to persuade their sovereign to grant it a royal charter with a document that would ensure monopoly right of trade, along with many other perquisites in that region, considered by the company as a colonial fiefdom. This was the procedure followed by the London stockholders of the newly created "Governor and Company of Adventurers of England Trading into Hudson's Bay"—that is, the Hudson's Bay Company (HBC). Wisely choosing as its first governor Prince Rupert, count Palatine of the Rhine, governor of the Mines Royal, and cousin of the monarch, the company presented a petition to King Charles II pleading that he grant it a royal charter to the area into which its stockholders had made their first successful foray.

Rupert's Land and the Royal Charter of the Hudson's Bay Company

On 2 May 1670, the company's charter was signed, and its stockholders were affirmed as the "true and absolute Lords and Proprietors" of an area of unconceived size and extent. They were allowed "the sole Trade and Commerce" of this vast region—that is, they were granted a monopoly of trade in the area. Also, they posssessed the rights to "Fishing of all sorts of Fish, Whales, Sturgeons, and all other Royal Fishes" and to "other considerable Commodities." Their sovereign also confirmed their control over "all Mines Royal, as well discovered as not discovered, of Gold, Silver, Gems and precious Stones, to be found or discovered within the Territories." This land was to be "reckoned and reputed as one of our . . . Colonies in America, called Rupert's Land."[2] As lords and proprietors, the company could make laws, judge civil and criminal cases, and impose penalties. It could erect forts, appoint commanders, use armed force, and request assistance from all officers and subjects of the monarch.

Thus, the company was empowered to establish a trading system in Rupert's Land, an area envisaged to encompass, in a rudimentary fashion, the "Seas, Streights, Bays, Rivers, Lakes, Creeks and Sounds . . . that lie within the entrance of the Streights commonly called Hudson's Streights, together with all the Lands, Countries and Territories, upon the Coasts

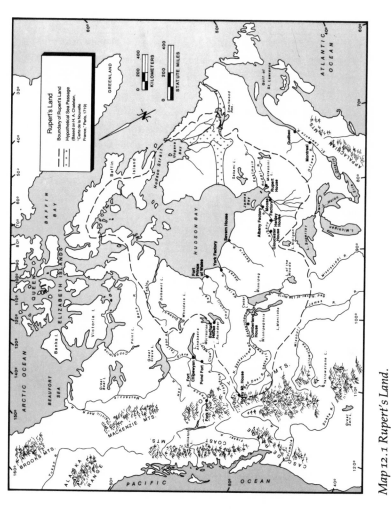

Map 12.1 Rupert's Land.

and Confines of the . . . aforesaid, which are not now actually possessed by . . . any other Christian Prince or State." The king and the company had thereby arrogated to themselves, unknowingly, title to an enormous estate extending to the sources of all rivers discharging into Hudson and James Bays and Hudson Strait. They also had disqualified any French claims to the northward extension of New France and to any charter rights granted by His Christian Majesty of France in this same northern and western region. Moreover, the imprecise nature of the charter's territorial delimitation made it possible for the "Adventurers" to claim monopoly of trade over any strait that might be found to originate within Rupert's Land, even one leading west eventually to the Pacific Ocean and to the Orient. As the king in his charter stated (albeit overstressing the eventual importance of such a purpose), the 1668 venture of the *Nonsuch* was intended to find a passage into the south sea, since such a discovery would be of "great Advantage to Us and Our Kingdom." There was thereby interwoven into the evolving fabric of commercial transcontinentalism, represented by the Hudson's Bay Company through its charter, a continuing thread of that older and larger geographical strategy, the search for a shorter, more economical, and hopefully safer water passage around the north of, or across the northern part of, the American continent, from the harbours of western Europe to the Pacific and to the riches and markets of the Orient. Moreover, the prospect of a Northwest Passage from the eastern region embraced the complementary expectation that a western opening to the strait lay somewhere along the northern Pacific littoral. The quest was embellished by reports of the putative findings of such conjectural entrances by various seamen—for example, Juan de Fuca, Martin d'Aigular, and Bartholomew de Fonte—and was sustained by the potential success of some future explorer.

The Geography of Competing Trade Strategies: From Hudson Bay and the St. Lawrence to the Pacific

Immediately after the signing of its charter, the new company began the tenancy of its domain and initiated its trading system, which eventually expanded to the outermost western boundaries of Rupert's Land and beyond. For many decades, until 1763, the company's trade structure— based on factory entrepôts at the bay shore, to which its Indian customers brought their furs and which were connected by ship lanes to London—

was in a continuous contest with the organization set up by French groups. The French were centred at Montreal and Québec and were supplied through the Saint Lawrence Gulf and the Saint Lawrence River. The initial end run of British-native trade, carried long distances from the far-flung reaches of bay-flowing rivers and out from the Manitoba lakes and the Saskatchewan country, was later slowly countered by the flanking action of French traders. They built posts at Rainy Lake and Lake of the Woods and passed directly to the heart of Rupert's Land. The French commandant Pierre Gaultier de Varennes de La Vérendrye and his associates opened fur-trading posts in the midst of Indian tribes, on the Red and Assiniboine Rivers, at the Manitoba lakes, and up to the forks of the Saskatchewan River. Also, coureurs de bois passed over the northern watersheds of the Great Lakes and the Saint Lawrence River and pressed on into bay-oriented river basins.

With the northward extension of British North America after 1759–63, a fur trade vacuum was left by the retreat of French merchants and traders from Canada. It was filled gradually by British merchants based especially in Montreal and fur traders operating out of Michilimackinac and eventually out of Grand Portage near the western end of Lake Superior. "Independents," later designated "Pedlars," then "Canadians," and finally "partners" and "employees" of the North West Company, exerted growing stress in the established system of operation of the Hudson's Bay Company—so much so that the company was eventually forced to copy its competitors, sending out its own servants to peddle goods and setting up shop inland at advantageous locations. Cumberland House, the first HBC post in the interior, opened in 1774 just off the lower Saskatchewan River. Thereafter, the routes from the bay and from Montreal contended for main-line advantage. These tracks converged at Cumberland House.

By 1776, Canadian traders outreached those from the Hudson's Bay Company; they moved faster and farther by passing north from Cumberland House across the portage from the Saskatchewan basin into the upper Churchill River system. They had crossed from the Churchill into the Athabasca-Mackenzie basin by 1778, thereby extending through and beyond Rupert's Land into an immense northwestern region of rich fur resources. HBC men followed in 1790. Although the HBC had also put some effort into searching for a Pacific passage entrance from the northwestern coast of Hudson Bay, and had supported private trials to some degree for the same purposes, it lagged behind its rivals' attempts to discover a riverine crossing of the continent from the Athabasca country to the Pacific

Ocean. This goal was achieved in 1793 by Alexander Mackenzie, a partner in the North West Company, after a disappointing diversion down the present-day Mackenzie River to the Arctic Ocean in 1789. Although his exploratory success had great geographical significance, its ultimate purpose was that of trade, and it had little commercial consequence at this time.

The Montreal trading partners had maintained hopes of simplifying their very lengthy transport links through the discovery of an easier riverine approach to the fur resources of the northwestern region of the continent from a Pacific coast entrance. Mackenzie's track up the Peace, down the Fraser, and over to Dean Channel was certainly not it. And the possibility of finding a navigable sea channel across the continent had also been refuted by this time, at first through the evidence gained by Samuel Hearne's transect from Churchill across the Barren Grounds to the mouth of the Coppermine River at the Arctic coast. Finally, George Vancouver and his colleagues produced detailed coastal charts of the northwestern Pacific coast and could vouchsafe no entrance to a sea passage along its entire length.

The most useful river connection between the interior and the ocean was not revealed for some years after Mackenzie's crossing. This was the Columbia River and its tributaries, especially the Kootenay, Okanagan, and Pend Oreille Rivers. Mackenzie had assumed that he was on the Columbia when he struck west from the south-flowing river to the Pacific shore. Also, Simon Fraser, believing that he was descending the Columbia, reached the Strait of Georgia in 1808 only to become aware that he had been mistaken; he had traveled a different river (the Fraser), a useless route for trade. Meanwhile, David Thompson, a former HBC apprentice who had become disappointed at not being given greater exploratory and mapping tasks and who had switched to the North West Company, was supported by the partners in crossing the Rocky Mountains in 1807 to pioneer their trade in the upper and middle Columbia basin. In 1811 he became the first European to travel along the lower course of the Columbia River to its mouth, only to find the American Fur Company there in a trading post. Again, the Montreal-based company had beaten the Hudson's Bay Company traders in breaching the boundaries of Rupert's Land, this time over the continental divide and into the transmontane West.

HBC men did not duplicate this action until 1810, when Joseph Howse spent a season in the Flathead region of the upper Columbia basin. But the company did not follow up this venture until 1821, when it took over the assets, the employees, and the trading organization of the North West

Company by uniting with it into a much-enlarged and more powerful enterprise. This joint company fell heir to the Columbia River trade route to and from the interior of British Columbia, to the former posts, and to the trade entrepôts at Fort William and Michilimackinac, in effect to the long track through the Great Lakes to the terminus at Montreal. Although the Hudson's Bay Company had lost some of the lesser trade skirmishes with the vigorous partners of the North West Company, it had survived more efficiently over the long haul. The Hudson Bay and the Saint Lawrence tracks were finally integrated under one aegis, as were the two trading organizations.

Such a union had been proposed for different reasons and publicized by several persons in the late eighteenth and early nineteenth centuries. However, the idea had not been accepted by either company or by the British government. Alexander Dalrymple, a proponent of British trade leadership and a staunch believer in the existence of a transcontinental Northwest Passage and its use as the logical British trade route to the Pacific, urged on his peers his hypothesis that there should be an amalgam of the major British trading companies into one great monopoly. The Hudson's Bay Company, the North West Company, and the East India Company together could thereby command the trade of British America and the Orient. And Alexander Mackenzie, after his Pacific expedition, proposed that the two British-American enterprises be linked together, thus utilising the best features of both trading systems—including supplying the new trading organization through Hudson Bay ports and using the shorter supply lines of the former Adventurers of England to the northwestern interior and to the Pacific coast.

Coastal and Lower River Exploration of the Bay and the Initiation of Inland Wintering Journeys, 1668–1754

For over three decades after Captains Luke Fox and Thomas James had coasted most of the western shores of Hudson and James Bays in 1631–32, European mariners remained outside of this great embayment.[3] What, then, did the expedition members of the ship *Nonsuch* or their London financial supporters in 1668 know of this vast sheet of water or expect of its peripheral lands? The answer is "very little"; what was known was garnered from a few journals, books, and maps, which provided snippets of descriptions of harbours visited and segments of coastlines viewed from

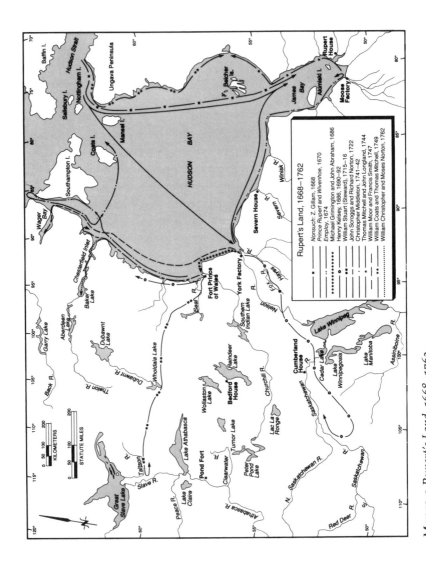

Map 12.2 *Rupert's Land, 1668–1762.*

passing ships. Terra incognita lay inland just beyond the shore, of varying and largely unknown dimensions. The great peninsula of Quebec could be most reasonably appraised since some astronomical observations had been taken by travelers on the eastern shore of the bay, on the northern shore at Hudson Strait, on the Labrador coast, and on the Saint Lawrence Gulf and the Saint Lawrence River. A little less certain was the distance separating the Bottom of the Bay from the shores of the Great Lakes; and to the west was an immense void, whose width was completely unknown and which was therefore geographically enticing. Certainly, the internal pattern of waterways over this whole northern part of the continent was a conundrum. Two years later, in 1670, when the HBC Adventurers became suzerain over the charter territory, no one—king, prince, or commoner— had any ideas as to the area's boundaries and dimensions. These were gradually revealed as the officers and servants of the new company, and others, began to explore, map, and describe the interior geography of this political and commercial region.

The company was accused, on several occasions during the first half-century and more of operations, of neglecting its obligation to take part in "discovery" or, more specifically, of not being more seriously engaged in the search for an entrance to the imagined strait. This complaint had the added imputation that the governor and the committee were not taking on the responsibility given to them by the charter of quickly and fully occupy-ing the lands assigned to them and thereby were not upholding national trade interests as much as they should or could and as assiduously as other groups would, given the same opportunity. But the governor and the com-mittee of the company had already decided on general trading procedures by the time of the first major HBC expedition in 1670, when its two ships— the *Wivenhoe* and the *Prince Rupert*—entered Hudson Bay, one sailing southeast down the Eastmain to Rupert River in James Bay and the second crossing southwest to the mouth of the Nelson River. There, the land was claimed in the name of the sovereign and for the company.

The rudimentary trading strategy was to investigate the major river es-tuaries on the southern and western shores of the bay and to establish sev-eral main entrepôts or factories there. The news of the company's arrival would be broadcast inland, mainly through local natives, who would be in-formed that useful, good-quality trade goods awaited groups who would come down to the bay in the open seasons over longer distances. The com-pany did not intend either to trade from its ships standing at various an-chorages or to open fur-trading posts inland in Rupert's Land. The correspondence does clearly reveal that the committee encouraged some of its young men to travel inland to winter with returning Indians and to prevail on them to come back down to the factories the following season. However, even if such a passive trading system had not been favoured, and if active inland exploration and post construction had been stressed, this would have been essentially an impossible task at this time, since control over Rupert's Land was being contested by the French. French penetration came first by a trading concern that journeyed to the Hayes River mouth and then by a military force traveling overland from Québec City to the Moose estuary. This force captured Moose Fort, then Rupert House and Albany Factory. On several occasions during the ensuing years, French naval forces swept into the bay. The company had all it could do to maintain even a vestige of control over the shores of the bay from 1682 to 1713.[4] Through the years the Hudson's Bay Company would establish five forts— Rupert, Moose, Albany, Severn, and York—but it would be able to keep command over only one during the time of troubles, either Albany or York. Finally, in 1714, a British expedition arrived at York to retrieve it from a small French force and to reestablish company hegemony over Rupert's Land.

During the time of contesting with the French for control over Rupert's Land, up to 1714, only one servant of the company had answered the call to winter inland, a journey that had been preceded by a training trip north up the Hudson Bay western coast, and one employee had traveled a few miles up the Nottaway River at the Bottom of the Bay. The objects of most exploration were to search river mouths for good ship anchorages and inspect onshore sites for trading posts or simply to make an hydrographic examination of the shores of the mainland and offshore islands. Otherwise the men kept close to the forts or were busy with the exigencies of conflict. Nevertheless, significant contributions to geographical knowledge were made during this initial period of company activities in the Hudson Bay region, from 1670 to 1754.

In 1670 the expedition on the ship the *Wivenhoe* had found no natives and had been blown by gales away from the Nelson River mouth, where the party had expected to erect a post and to winter; the decision was then made to abandon this task and instead to join the *Prince Rupert* at the mouth of the Rupert River at Charles Fort (later Rupert House). With the expedition were Medard Chouart, self-styled Sieur Des Groseilliers, and his wife's half brother, Pierre Esprit Radisson—both of them disillusioned former coureurs de bois of New France now in the employ of the British.

These two men had been instrumental in engaging the attention of Prince Rupert and of financial backers in their tentative scheme to outflank the French fur traders in the New World and had been on the trial expedition of the *Nonsuch* in 1668. Both were to play an important part in the early period of exploration. In the spring of 1671 Radisson and a small party were away from Charles Fort for two months at Moose River, their journey being the first and longest exploratory trip by members of the new company. Later that year another trading party also made its way to the Moose River mouth. On the way back to Britain after 1 July 1671, smaller boats were often sent out from the ships to explore parts of the Eastmain coast and also Charlton Island. The company did not send out any ships in the summer of 1671 but did so the following years. In 1673 a post was constructed on an island in the mouth of the Moose River, and one of the ships, with Groseilliers on board, sailed north of Nelson River to try for a second time to establish a post there. Again, there was no success. In the summer of 1674 Thomas Gorst, a crew member, can be claimed to have been the first company employee to travel inland, although his journey was only a few miles to the foot of the lower falls in the Nottaway River. During that same summer, Gorst accompanied Groseilliers to Moose Fort from Rupert House, while a party on the ship *Employ* sailed north along the western shore of James Bay. The latter stopped in at Albany River, rounded Cape Henrietta Maria, looked in at the Severn River, and planned to open a post at the mouth of the Nelson River. On this third occasion, difficult ice conditions in the bay prevented this attempt. This was the journey most fully rendered in map form during the early years, for one of the crew, Thomas Moore, was the likely author of the chart of the western side of James Bay from Moose River to Cape Henrietta Maria.[5]

As noted earlier, the normal annual cycle was for trade to be conducted at the several factories over the year with local Indians and in summers with natives arriving from inland. One or more ships would arrive in the late summer from Britain, and the returns were sent back. On occasion a ship would remain over the winter for use on the bay, but normally only a skeleton body of men stayed behind at the forts. By 1681, Rupert, Moose, and Albany had become operative trading posts, and a depot on Charlton Island served the James Bay area. In 1682 the situation began to change drastically. In the first place, two disparate trading companies came to the mouths of the Nelson and Hayes Rivers to compete with the Hudson's Bay Company, which had finally sent out a party to open York Fort. One party was from Boston and was led by the son of Zachariah Gillam, who had been the captain of the *Nonsuch* in 1668 and who was at this time captain of the *Prince Rupert* and was with the HBC house-building party. The second group was La Compagnie du Nord from New France, directed to the Hayes River by Radisson and Groseilliers, who had left the British company's employment in 1674 over disagreements as to the operation of the trade in Rupert's Land. The French group managed to capture both of the rival British parties and to disperse the men either south to the company factories or to Québec City. In 1684 the tables were turned when two company ships came to the Nelson-Hayes estuary and, with Radisson (now re-employed by the HBC) on board, took over the French Fort Bourbon with its accumulated furs and finally built York Factory on the banks of the Hayes River.

In 1686 the Bottom of the Bay was attacked by a French force under Chevalier de Troyes in a spectacular river-borne invasion from the Saint Lawrence and over Ottawa River, Lake Timiskaming, Lake Abitibi, Abitibi River, and Moose River interconnections. In a short time Moose Factory, Rupert House, and Albany Factory were taken, before the raiders retreated upriver, back to New France.

During these years, only two expeditions were sent out from the established factories in the bay to explore and to search for new factory locations. The committee members had assured the local governor, "Great discoveries may in time bee made by our small Vessels cruizing up and downe."[6] The Severn River, visited several times, had a post erected on its lower course in 1685. In 1686 Michael Grimington and John Abraham sailed the *Hayes* sloop from York north to the Churchill River, found it a "faire River," picked out a suitable post site, and returned to their home post.

In 1689, war was declared between Britain and France. One result of the hostilities was the prevention of the arrival in Hudson Bay of a ship under the command of Captain John Ford, who had been ordered by the company to undertake a search of the coast north of the Churchill River. Unfortunately, the French captured his vessel before it cleared the British Isles.[7] His instructions were to seek a larger river, called by some the Dering, take possesssion of the land there, build a cabin in which to winter, and then try to move inland up the river for the purpose of discovery. The name "Dering" was not applied to any river in particular. It may have been the Seal or Thlewiaza River or even Chesterfield Inlet and Baker Lake with the Kazan River tributary to them. In the spring of that same year two ships were dispatched from York Fort to the Churchill River with house-building equipment, trade goods, and a work crew to construct a post on the site recommended by Grimington and Abraham in 1686. With this expedition was Henry Kelsey, nineteen years old and soon to become one of the greatest explorers of Rupert's Land.

In the summer of 1686 Kelsey was sent north from Churchill with a young Indian companion to contact Indian groups and to encourage them to come to the new factory to trade. Kelsey may have volunteered for this task as a source of adventure; in light of his forthcoming pioneer journey to the interior plains from York Fort, this summer's trip served as an effective training exercise. Kelsey and his Indian companion were carried north about 60 miles up the coast in the *Hopewell* by Captain James Young but were prevented from proceeding farther because of sea ice conditions.[8] After being set ashore, they traveled northward for about 150 miles, remaining close to the coast. The terminus of their travels was probably somewhere near Eskimo Point. Five days before they stopped their traverse, they crossed a large river, likely the Thlewiaza River, about three miles from the sea, and north of it they killed what was likely a musk-ox, although Kelsey called it a buffalo. He may have been the first European to see and describe this beast. They did not come across any people in their travels, but Kelsey was persuaded to turn back by his companion's fear that they would encounter Inuit. Apparently they retraced their tracks and went on past the ship drop-off point to Churchill post, arriving there on 26 July. They had failed in their purpose of persuading Indians to come to trade at the new fort, since they had met none. Even if they had succeeded, it would have been to no avail, since the new fort caught fire in early August, and the full party returned to Nelson Fort. The Churchill site was abandoned until 1717. Apparently, the company did not think that Kelsey had reached Dering River, and thus this name was not deemed to apply either to the Seal River, to the Thlewiaza, or to other intermediate streams.

So far, the company had not elicited a response from its governors in the bay to find men to send inland. Besides Radisson and Groseilliers, who had years of experience in traveling in New France and were accustomed to handling canoes and living rough and with Indians, the company had only one lightly seasoned field man to call on. The purpose of such journeys would not be to gain geographical expertise but to "gett an Acquaintance and Comerce with the Indians"[9] and "by all faire psuasion & kinde usage to Invite them to come downe & trade only at our Factories."[10]

By 1690, only Henry Kelsey had accumulated some travel knowledge, gained on the company's only long-distance overland trek the previous year. On 12 June 1690, he was sent off from Nelson Fort with a band of Assiniboine Indians who were on their way back to the plains. Much is still in-distinct about his activites and his routes over the two years until his return to the bay in the summer of 1692. This is due particularly to the fact that Kel-sey left a journal, partly written in poetic form, that did not come into authoritative possession for many years; he provided only a few compass directions, and his description of the countryside was vague. The general roster of events is that he reached a location that he named Deering's Point, from which he moved inland to the plains and to which he returned in the summers of 1690, 1691, and 1692. There have been several suggestions as to the exact position of Deering's Point, but one characteristic that has been definitely acknowledged is that it was a collecting locale, a place of "re-sortance" for Indians. Two logical locations are at the western end of Cedar Lake near the entrance of the Saskatchewan River and at the large bend of this river, named Pasquia (Basquia), where the present settlement of The Pas is sited.

In the late summer and autumn of 1690, Kelsey went farther into the in-terior from Deering's Point to meet Indian groups and to persuade them all to remain at peace and to go down to the bay to trade in the spring. The route taken was probably similar to that followed the next year, for he de-scribes the country in language similar to that used later. Furthermore, he mentioned in 1692 that he met an Indian group to whom he had given a promise to return. In July 1691, after receiving needed supplies and trade goods from York Factory at Deering's Point, he started off again with the major purpose of contacting the Naywatame Poets.[11] He accompanied a small group of Assiniboines. After eight days they caught up with a larger band of these Indians, who had left the point ahead of them. During the first four days en route they had used canoes, traveling along wooded streams and through shallow ponds and marshes with high grass, but had then cached them and had struck off across wooded country, generally fol-lowing a river course, called by the natives the Waskashreeseebee. After leaving the river valley, Kelsey noted that fir woods began to give way to poplar and birch groves with fields covered with heath or barren ground, which occurred increasingly. This would mean that the party was leaving the boreal forest and entering the parkbelt. By his estimation, after some forty miles of this pleasant land, he noticed that the area was more barren, until on 20 August they had reached the outermost edge of the forest. He had also seen large herds of buffalo for the first time, quite probably the first such siting for a European since Francisco Vázquez de Coronado's ex-pedition of 1540–42.

After crossing forty-six miles of "barren ground," that is, of short-grass prairie, with here and there a small pond, they reached a higher land with poplar-birch cover and an abundance of small ponds, the haunts of an excellent supply of beaver. By 7 September, they had arrived at another grassland plain to the west of the higher ground. As the party went out onto the grasslands they joined other groups of Assiniboine Indians, an enlarging throng determined to go to war against their enemies, the Blackfoot Indians. While feasting and pipe-smoking with them, the young traveler urged his hosts to continue hunting and not to engage in conflict. He warned them that the York Factory governor would refuse to trade with them if they became bellicose. On hearing that a small group of Naywatame Poets (Blackfoot) was camped some distance to the north, Kelsey went with a small advance party, including an interpreter, and cautiously entered enemy territory, until they made contact. Each party agreed that neither would attack the other. The Blackfoot chief also consented to go to Deering's Point the next spring to begin trade with the company. This did not occur, however, partly because some Cree Indians later attacked and killed some Blackfoot natives but mainly because such an action was far outside the cultural experience and the territory of these people. They were grassland natives, who neither built nor used canoes. Such a journey into the forests, muskeg, and marshlands of the lower Saskatchewan River valley would be far beyond their experience, and they would be passing through extensive areas under their enemies' control. Kelsey spent the remainder of the autumn and winter out in the plains before returning to Deering's Point and eventually to York Factory.

A possible general course of Kelsey's journey from his campsite at the Saskatchewan River was to the southwest. The Waskashreeseebee was likely the Red Deer River. They reached the parkbelt-grassland edge, perhaps near Humboldt, Saskatchewan, and to the west of the Quill Lakes, which Kelsey does not mention. After crossing the slough-scattered, barren plain, they reached the hill lands, probably those that lie south of Watrous and that stretch northwest to form the Allan Hills. While some of the group hunted and trapped in the higher lands and the remainder moved ponderously onward, Kelsey formed his advance party and proceeded northwest out onto the grassland plain, past the end of the Allan Hills. This level land stretches parallel to and to the east of the South Saskatchewan River. His meeting place with the Blackfoot group was likely east or northeast of Saskatoon.

Kelsey's accomplishments, like those of many other explorers, were not acknowledged until long after his death. In fact, it was not until 1749, at the Parliamentary investigation into the company's trade monopoly, that notice was drawn to his venture, and it was not until well into the twentieth century that his place in Canadian geographical exploration became apparent. He was the first European to view the interior plains of Canada and the vegetative succession in Canada. Moreover, he was the first European to travel to and to live intimately with Indians in the western and northern regions of Canada, to depend so fully on Indian knowledge and culture, and to use the Indians as a vital aid in exploration. He followed normal Indian tracks along waterways and through the lands and met Indian groups at their collecting points. He trapped beaver and hunted buffalo with them. For a lightly educated young man, he showed considerable ability in understanding their life and customs and in writing pioneer descriptions of interior tribal culture. His journey was not recorded on a company map after his return to York Fort or later. The company did have the benefit of his experience gained in his journeys, however, since he became a senior official at several factories on the bay shore later.

After 1714, when Albany and York Factories were once more back in operation and the company could turn its attention to the burned or dilapidated posts at other southern river mouths, York Fort became the most active centre of operations. Through its Indian trading contacts, York Fort was much more in a frontier location than was Albany. York had the advantage at this time of freedom from French competition in its catchment area, although it had had no contact or trade with the Indian groups that lived north of the Nelson-Saskatchewan-Churchill basins. This was a region of vast and vague extent, to which York Fort was the closest post. The strategic, and strong, location of the Cree Indians (who had become middlemen in the exchange of furs) in the Nelson-Saskatchewan-Churchill area had forced the Athapaskan Indians from the northern Churchill basin into more distant northwestern territory. The factory was also the logical starting point in the inauguration of trade with Inuit hunters along the northwestern coast of Hudson Bay. Kelsey's travels into this vicinity had had no useful trade result, since he had not met any of these people.

This most important post was placed under the command of two vigorous and experienced men, James Knight as governor and Henry Kelsey as his deputy. They not only had to rebuild the post but also had to regain the confidence of Indians inland in the Nelson-Saskatchewan–Manitoba lakes area, Indians who had been affected by the wartime loss of the factory for several years, on several occasions. As an extension of company policy,

Knight and Kelsey were resolved to persuade the Crees to reduce hostilities with the Northern Indians so that these people could pass unharmed to York Factory to trade. They began to hear more about these natives, not only from the Crees but also from several Northern (Chipewyan) women who had been captured as slaves by the Crees. They also heard interesting reports of rivers leading to a great sea and determined to send an emissary, William Stuart (Stewart), to the region in which it might be located. Stuart's main purposes were to effect a truce between the two antipathetic groups and to bring Northern Indians to the bay to trade. But he was also to bring back geographical information to aid the factors in developing their concepts of the far interior area.

Although Stuart was chosen as the emissary, in fact the most critical member of the party was a Chipewyan woman who spoke Cree. Her task was to guide the group to her home region and to act as interpreter and intermediary with her people. Similar to Kelsey on his journey, Stuart was to act as a peace negotiator, although he was traveling with Cree Indians who were not particularly concerned about whether peace was the outcome of the mission. Also like Kelsey, Stuart wrote a meagre journal of his mission. He described enough to indicate that their course took them out of the boreal forest and into the sparsely wooded Barren Grounds. His entire trip took from 27 June 1715 to 7 May 1716, about a year, and except for the short summer of 1715, which was spent traveling north to the Churchill River and beyond to the Seal River, it was almost completely a winter trek over ice, snow, and frozen tundra and forest.

Stuart very likely overestimated his distances. He calculated that he had reached about one thousand miles northwest of the factory, to about 67° north latitude. Neither figure could have been true. A direct course of that distance would have brought them to the vicinity of the lower Coppermine River, as would the latitude measurement. If one plots his courses, the end point of his journey would lie somewhere south of Great Bear Lake, between it and Great Slave Lake. This would have been a most unusual location for the terminus of the trip. The object was to speak with some of the Chipewyans, and these natives did not live in this area but instead in the Athabasca Lake–Slave River country. He would not likely have been guided to the territories of the Dogrib and Yellowknife Indians. His distance estimations, in relation to the time taken to make his return circuit, were much too generous. When one compares the journey of sixty days, including those on which they lay by, with the later trip of Hearne in 1771 over an approximately similar route, the discrepancy becomes noticeable.

Hearne traversed the region with a small group, led by a noted traveler and trading captain who could move his band as swiftly as any other over this country. From Churchill, for example, in somewhat over two months, they had reached Wholdia Lake, northeast of Lake Athabasca. Stuart, on the other hand, was accompanied by a considerable number of Crees, and even if traveling as quickly as possible, they had to search for food and would have been slowed down by the mass movement. Stuart also described their course as leading from timbered country into the "Barren Desarts" and then into treed land again, the trees growing larger to west-northwest. This latter area, he noted, was an excellent hunting ground for deer (caribou) and moose, as well as fine beaver country. The land east of the Slave River is within the boreal forest, and it does increase in density of vegetation from east to west. In 1772, on his return course to the bay, Hearne commented on the good hunting for wood caribou, moose, and buffalo in this wooded area.

The Stuart expedition started off with about a dozen Cree Indians but quickly increased in numbers to possibly 150 in all, a size most unlike an inoffensive party of goodwill. Fortunately, while on the march, they split into smaller bands, since it was impossible to keep such a large population in provisions. Since the bands moved broadly along the same general course, but some days apart, and since Stuart's group was not in the lead, he could not keep control over their actions. Tragically, when they were well to the west, reaching the wooded area, Stuart was horrified to come across the remains of a Chipewyan camp, with nine bodies of persons who had been shot by one of the Cree groups. His group broke into general pandemonium, with the Indians crying out that they should flee back east before the avenging Chipewyans could overtake them. Accompanied by Stuart's urging, the Chipewyan woman was able to calm the group and arranged for them to wait for ten days while she went to talk with her people. When the time was nearly up, she returned with a party of 160 Northern Indians, from a camp nearly 600 strong. A long and successful parley took place, and the two groups promised to preserve peace. The Chipewyans also agreed to trap, to engage in trade, and to allow ten young Chipewyan men to accompany Stuart back to York to learn Cree, in order later to act as interpreters and guides.

The large group, when it left York Factory in 1715, had crossed the Churchill River apparently just upstream from the estuary, had kept a more northerly bearing to Seal River, and then had struck generally northwest across the Barren Grounds, well away from the tree line. Their course likely lay across Nueltin, Snowbird, and Wholdia Lakes, into the Thoa and eventually the Taltson River valley. It is not clear whether they reached the Slave River. Their return journey took roughly the same course back to the factory. This was the second useful European view of the far inland country, on this occasion cutting northwest rather than southwest out from the boreal forest, through the thinning woods of the forest tundra, and out into the open lands of the tundra before plunging back into the northern forest again. Geographically, the results were only indirectly usable. Stuart was unversed in geographical observation or mapmaking. However, the company factors were undoubtedly able to gain a reasonable amount of oral information from him.

The expected benefits to York Fort trade did not take place at this time, however. Peace did not prevail. Crees continued to raid against the Northern Indians along their whole arc of control, nor would they accept any Northern Indians to live among them. Indeed, so unfriendly were the local Crees to the ten young Chipewyans that Governor Knight, afraid for their safety, outfitted them, gave them presents, offered them instructions regarding the trade, and sent them on their way home; unfortunately, when they had reached the Churchill River area, they were all killed by Inuit. The company then decided that York was too far south to be the proper post for the development of the Northern Indian trade. Stuart was sent with a building crew back to the Churchill site in June 1717, and Knight came north in July. With him was another Chipewyan Indian slave woman as an interpreter, a Chipewyan youth, and Richard Norton, a young company apprentice. Before the fort was completed, these three were sent off on a further attempt to initiate the trade with the Northern Indians. The hope was that they could reach the new factory in reasonable safety both from the Crees to the south and the Inuit to the north, on a track largely across the Barren Grounds. There is little documentary information on this party's course, or its duration inland, but Norton apparently spent until the spring of 1719 on this mission, in the same general area as his predecessor. The venture was successful in that, along with Stuart's contact, Northern Indians did begin to trek southeast, usually each summer to conduct trade at Churchill Fort, officially named Prince of Wales in 1719.

In addition to establishing interior Indian trade, the factors at Churchill hoped to develop trade with Inuit groups living up the coast to the north, especially to gain benefits from the white whale fishery. James Knight in particular had woven together mentions of copper and gold, and other metals, into the supposition that these were located near the passage past or across the north of the continent; he thus expected to find workable deposits and thereby gain wealth of unforseeable value. Therefore, he also hoped to find the entrance to the strait or passage at the coast of northern Hudson Bay. Between the summers of 1719 and 1722, four groups were sent north from Churchill, one each summer, to seek out whale oil and whalebone from the Inuit, to look for copper mines, and to make what discoveries they could. Few Inuit were met, and only meagre trade resulted; no metals were found and no significant discoveries made. The last and most far-reaching of the trips in this period, by John Scroggs and Richard Norton, stopped at the mouth of Chesterfield Inlet in 1722 but went no farther up it. They likely called at Daley Bay and turned back at Cape Fullerton, at the entrance to Roes Welcome Sound. They had the further task of trying to find out the fate of Knight's expedition. He had retired from HBC employment in 1718 and raised a two-ship venture from London in 1719. Part of the financial support came from the company. By 1721 nothing had been heard from either ship. Scroggs and Norton found traces of the expedition on Marble Island, when returning to Churchill from Cape Fullerton.

By the time of his retirement, Knight had gained a broad conception of the continent, one that was, in the large, reasonably accurate; but he held several major misconceptions. The most significant was the idea that seventeen rivers lay beyond Churchill to the north, an idea that Knight had gained from the young Indians who had returned with Stuart. He received reports of a river valley famous for its copper sources and of some river near which yellow metal was obtainable and which was on the western coast of the continent. He had fitted these into his river framework and had concluded that the last four rivers at least were on the western coast. Knight believed that he had disentangled the intricacies of the north of the continent and would be able to solve the Northwest Passage mystery. He was not successful and hardly had started before tragedy overcame his venture. Evidence gathered later indicates that after a discouraging search the first summer, he and his men had put up for the winter of 1719–20 on Marble Island. Gradually overcome by scurvy, some died, and the remainder, too weak to sail in the following summer, died or were killed by Inuit. Most of the useful personal material and that from the ships was scavenged. After this, no further attempts were made by the company or private organizations to search for the strait until the mid-1730s.

For well over a decade the situation may be said to have been routine and uneventful, with greatest emphasis placed on the renovation and enlargement of the main factories. Starting in 1731, the company began to come under increased pressure from the French as La Vérendrye and his party entered Rupert's Land through Lake of the Woods and began to conduct trade with Indians in the Manitoba lakes area and the Nelson-Saskatchewan region. Also that year, Arthur Dobbs, a gentleman of wide interests in administration, commerce, science, and surveying, began a research project examining available exploratory materials; he became convinced that there was a strait, somewhere north of Cape Eskimo on the northwestern coast of Hudson Bay, that would lead through the land and on to the Pacific Ocean. A complicated agreement was reached between him and the Hudson's Bay Company for a discovery expedition. Due to numerous delays, two ships captained by James Napper and Robert Crow came from London in 1736, wintered at Churchill, and went north only to Whale Cove, 62°10′ north. They engaged in a small amount of trade with Inuit there, discovered nothing new, and retreated south. The company lost interest in further extensive and costly searches for the passage but did send a ship under Francis Smith, for six summers, to trade at Whale Cove or other points. Exploration was not involved.

Dobbs was infuriated with the company for its apparent lack of interest in his program. Having supporters within the higher circles of British government, by 1741 he had gained the backing of the Admiralty, which put two ships at his disposal, and he hired two experienced ship captains away from the company. Christopher Middleton, in charge of the expedition, and William Moor, after wintering at Churchill in 1741–42, set off northward in June 1742; they entered the bight behind Marble Island, previously unexplored, and named it Rankin Inlet. They sailed past Chesterfield Inlet without stopping, entered Roes Welcome Sound, and reached their hoped-for strait. They later named this body of water Wager Bay; after examining its shores, they found it to be an extended arm of the sea. They then pressed north and discovered Repulse Bay and the entrance to Frozen Strait.

Middleton returned to Britain and wrote Dobbs a report that eliminated Rankin, Wager, and Repulse Bays as possible entrances to a passage; he was attacked by Dobbs as being untruthful in his conclusions. Dobbs became increasingly a pamphleteer, hostile to the trade monopoly of the Hudson's Bay Company and accusing it of inactivity in exploration and discovery. He was able to mobilize pressure groups so well that the Admiralty later inquired into his charges against Middleton. A second, quite spectacular victory was the posting by Parliament of a £20,000 reward to be given to the first British subject to discover the Northwest Passage. And, more practically, he was able to float a company for a final expedition to search for the fateful strait.

Rankin Inlet was the designated candidate for this entrance, but both Wager and Chesterfield Inlets were to be essayed also. Two ships were wintered at York Factory in 1746–47, and the following summer Captains William Moor and Francis Smith, also a former company captain, went north. They searched Rankin Inlet and eliminated it from consideration, as they did Wager Bay. Chesterfield was given a cursory examination, only far enough from the entrance to satisfy them that freshwater was pouring out from it. Dobbs seized on this incomplete analysis, castigated the captains, and asserted that Chesterfield Inlet must certainly be the strait leading to the western ocean. Dobbs had included two historians, Henry Ellis and Theodore Drage, who duly produced publications admonishing the HBC for its lack of support for exploration and who declared the region as being very amenable for settlement.[12] They also decried the trade monopoly of the company, supporting Dobbs. In 1748 Dobbs and his supporters petitioned the Crown for incorporation as a company to be granted exclusive rights to the lands they had discovered or should discover adjoining Hudson Bay and Hudson Strait. Despite an adverse decision by the Crown, they were able to create such public pressure that a Select Committee of Parliament received evidence in 1749 from both sides. The final vote of the House on the committee report supported the rights of the HBC in its charter territory.

After the unsettling experience of the investigation, the company carefully examined the evidence presented from all sources and became more active up the coast. The instructions given to their captains, and the purposes noted for the various trips, contained the phrase "voyages of discovery and trade" but did not state that the passage entrance was of central interest. Captain James Walker was assigned this task each summer from 1750 to 1754. Little trade resulted, and in fact in 1753 near Marble Island his ship was attacked by a large crowd of Inuit. Exploration was fitful and unsuccessful also. A new element was introduced in 1752 when the Churchill factor instructed Walker to search for the entrance to a large river, Kiskstack-ewen, which was said to run from a bay into the interior for a long distance along which were many natives who could augment the trade. Walker was replaced as northern ship captain after having neglected to try searches farther north than Whale Cove in 1754.

On the opposite shore of the bay, the Eastmain, more detailed investigation of the coast, river mouths, and embayments was undertaken in the 1740s. Here also some interest had been generated in possible interior water features. Indians had reported three large lakes east of the coast at about 60° north, where the fur trade could be expanded with both Indians and Inuits. More enticing still were the map outlines of a strait at about this latitude breaking the bay coast and leading perhaps to a Labrador fiord or to Ungave Bay. Either terminus of such a strait could ease the dangerous passage for company ships using Hudson Strait.

Thomas Mitchell and John Longland, shipmasters, were dispatched in 1744 from Moose Fort, north along the Eastmain, but reached only 57° north. Mitchell made detailed hydrographic sketches of two of the main estuaries, the Fort George and Great Whale Rivers, and the expedition also searched, for the first time, the almost landlocked Richmond Gulf (Lac Guillaume Delisle), called by them by the Indian designation "Wenipegg." The governor and the committee scolded Mitchell and ordered another trip for 1748, which did not take place. Rather, in 1749 Captains William Coats and Mitchell were sent from London in command of two vessels with detailed exploratory and surveying instructions, as well as requirements to find a satisfactory new post site up the coast. In addition to trying to locate the mouth to the potential strait leading eastward, they were to make detailed geographical and hydrographic observations, collect natural materials, and draw coastal charts. Turning south from Hudson Strait, they carried out many of their instructions, though the passageway proved to be a chimera of geographical imagination. They chose a site for a trading post in Richmond Gulf. The prefabricated parts of the building, prepared at Albany Fort, were transported by Mitchell and John Yarrow in the summer of 1750 to the gulf, where it was assembled, and normal trading operations were initiated.

Although by the 1740s, three company servants had made transects for hundreds of miles inland to the vicinities of the South Saskatchewan and Slave Rivers, most employees had not traveled many miles from the seacoast and had mainly hunted, fished, and collected firewood. The company pressed the chief factors to have the lower courses of their rivers and their estuaries examined, measured, and mapped. In 1740 George Howy, the Moose Factory sloopmaster, provided details of the lower forty miles of the Moose River and prepared two adjacent charts, above and below the fort. Joseph Robson undertook similar activities in the lower courses of the Hayes and Nelson Rivers from 1744 to 1746. As a stonemason, with some experience in surveying, Robson also prepared several hydrographic charts of the estuaries for the use of company captains. The York factor, James Isham, after recommending that a new post be built at Severn River and receiving approval, sent Christopher Atkinson and Richard Ford there in 1754 to measure and map its lower twelve miles and to choose an appropriate trading house site. Isham himself, with several other servants, measured up the Hayes and Nelson Rivers some miles and provided the details to London. But it was not until February 1754 that Isham chose Anthony Henday for a more extensive task. Henday was to be the first of a new group of servants wintering inland and traveling to the Saskatchewan country to meet Indian bands to exhort them to maintain intertribal peace, to trap, and to come down to the bay to trade. In a form of apprenticeship, he was sent off with three Indian companions, dragging a measuring wheel, up the Hayes River on the ice to the Foxe tributary some 100 miles, then along this interconnection to the Nelson River and back down this stream about 140 miles to the fort. He was burdened with a plethora of field instructions that would have been too much for even an experienced traveler. But the exercise did provide useful local data to the company and prepared Henday for his momentous journey west to within sight of the Rocky Mountains.

Inland Wintering on the Plains, 1754–1774

James Isham, chief factor at York Factory, was undoubtedly the most respected of the company officers in Rupert's Land, and his advice typifies that offered by those opposed to building houses inland. He supported peaceful penetration of the country by traveling upriver and kindliness and peacemaking by inland-wintering servants. While the French held Canada, the best defence, he affirmed, was to support extensive inland journeys to keep the peace, to draw Indians to the bay, and to try to jockey them past the French traders. He also tried to counter various notions in Britain as to the amenable quality for settlement of the interior west of the bay.

From 1754 until 1774, when the company made a historic policy change, wintering was in force. York Factory was the centre of operations, although William Tomison made two journeys to the plains from Severn House, Joseph Hansom was sent from Churchill to the Saskatchewan regions, and Samuel Hearne trekked northwest into the Barren Grounds

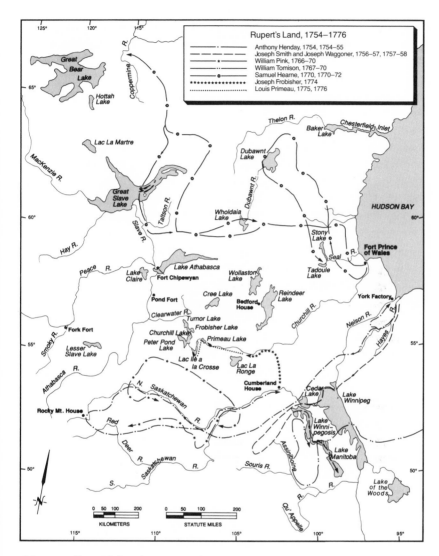

Map 12.3 Rupert's Land, 1754–1776.

from Churchill. "Expedition" is too pretentious a term to apply to these so-journs; like the trips of Kelsey, Stewart, and Norton, these journeys consisted of the accompaniment of an Indian band by one, two, or three servants, and the post journal references to their departures and returns could not be less cryptic and unemotional. Besides Hearne, who traveled to the Coppermine River, some nineteen servants took part in wintering on the plains over these two decades. From 1754 to 1763, for example, six men were involved in ten separate journeys, and in the following decade, thirteen individuals were traveling with Indian bands. Of all these persons who reached the Saskatchewan plains, only a few—such as Matthew Cocking, Henday, and Tomison—have become part of the saga of western Canadian exploration. The others are familiar to specialists but unknown to the layman. Henday, who made the inaugural trip, kept a reasonably full and accurate daily journal, expanding the knowledge of the plains well to the west of Kelsey's locus of activity more than sixty years earlier. Apparently he was the first European to sight the wall of the Rocky Mountain front in Canadian territory.

Putting any precise bounds to their travels is difficult. Very likely, the winterers wandered on the northern grasslands and in the parkbelt between the Manitoba lakes and the South Saskatchewan and beyond this river up to the foothills of the Rocky Mountains and into the North Saskatchewan River country. The drier southern prairies were not approached by company employees during this period. Competition from the French dwindled as they lost control of New France after 1763. This pattern did not change until the vacuum left by the coureurs de bois was gradually filled by Pedlars operating out of Montreal and Québec in new British Canada. Competition from the Pedlars threatened to spread farther afield into the Nelson-Churchill regions.

There is far less disagreement on the route followed by Henday than there is on that of Kelsey, although there are some variations in interpretation. Henday provided numerous directions as well as mileages, discussed much more of the environment through which he was passing, and made a sketch.[13] He left York Fort on 26 June 1754, followed the Hayes-Foxe river system to Cross Lake, followed the Moose Lake–Summerberry River connection to the Saskatchewan River, and in twenty-two miles of paddling reached Pasquia. After several days of rest the Indian party, with Henday, traveled north of the Pasquia Hills, following the Carrot River, until it left the river valley, passing across level land with good woods and crossing creeks of sweet water. He went out of the parkbelt, likely somewhere near Humboldt, and into the grasslands or, as he described the area, level land with short grass, dry woods, and nothing but salt lakes (sloughs). The group had met a number of Assiniboines, whom Henday tried to induce to travel to the bay. Their unanswerable reply was that this would be somewhat silly, since they were conveniently supplied by French posts on the

Saskatchewan River. On reaching the high, forested banks of the Wape-sekcopet (South Saskatchewan) River, Henday and his guides crossed it and angled northwest to another large river, the Sechonby (North Saskatchewan), somewhere along its great southern bend. From there to the northern bend of the Red Deer River, their course seemed to follow somewhat of an arc, first moving along the northern slopes of the Eagle Hills, then crossing the southern tributaries of the Battle River, and continuing southwest over rolling plains, with pleasant valleys and hillocks ridged with tree bluffs. During these last several days Henday's party made its first contact with the Blackfoot Indians, a small group of whom were ahead of their main camp, which they said lay west of the Red Deer River crossing, near its northern bend.

On 14 October they reached this camp of over two hundred tents and lay by for three days feasting, trading, and negotiating for the Indians' inclusion in the company's trade. Henday and his entourage then moved southwest, decreasing in size as various groups left to hunt and trap. The weather was still pleasant, with gentle frosts at night and with a few snow flurries—an Indian summer to perfection. Having crossed the Red Deer River again, the travelers were about to enter a more forested landscape. Henday spent the late autumn wandering in the country to the north, into the Clearwater River valley. There, he had reached his westernmost penetration on the plains, at about 115° west longitude. For some time he had glimpsed the Rocky Mountain peaks glistening in the sun, the crestline being about forty miles to the west and southwest. The winter was spent between the Clearwater River valley and the North Saskatchewan River, which they reached in early March 1755, at about 114° west. There they established a camp, where large congeries of Indians collected, built canoes, and equipped themselves for the downriver voyage to York after the ice breakup. By 19 April, the canoes and crews were ready for embarkation. Near the junction of the Battle River with the North Saskatchewan, they traded with some one hundred tents of Blackfoot Indians, and near present Prince Albert, they traded with about seventy tents of the same tribe. After a journey that lasted one week short of a year, Henday, then a seasoned traveler, reached York Factory.

Henday had not completely fulfilled the original instructions given to him on the eve of departure. In the first place, his route to and from Pasquia had not touched on the Little Sea (Lake Winnipeg) of the French traders. He had been asked to determine whether this was a large lake or whether it was an open sea, as its name implied. As requested, he did, however, suggest a location for an inland post that would not be too far from Hudson Bay (but that would be a useful place to trade) to save inland Indians from the last long haul to York Fort. He suggested Moose Lake, north of Cedar Lake, between Cross Lake and the Saskatchewan River, a location that was already an Indian meeting place. Nothing further was done about this at the time.

Joseph Smith and Joseph Waggoner provided the answer to the query concerning the Little Sea in their 1756–57 travels. They were the first company men to pioneer a more southerly road from York to the interior, a route that became a main track on later occasions. This followed the Hayes River through Knee and Oxford Lakes and then the Echimamish River into the eastern channel of the Nelson River and Little Playgreen Lake. Moreover, these two men were the first HBC men to enter Lake Winnipeg and cross into Cedar Lake and Lake Winnipegosis. For the late autumn and winter months, they passed west across the Swan River, over the western slopes of Duck Mountain, across the Assiniboine River, and through the denuded and snow-laden parkbelt landscape west of this river. The return began at Swan River, where they camped with a band of Indians heading for the bay, for two months making canoes, packing, and preparing food. They noted in their journal that they had to range for twenty miles to find enough birchbark, since local supplies had been exhausted. Their return course lay over Mossy Portage, the first time that company servants took this route, to Cedar Lake, then along the northern shore of Lake Winnipeg to Playgreen Lake and the string of rivers and lakes used on their way inland. They suggested to their factor that Playgreen Lake would provide a useful future house site; it was a collection point, it had excellent fishing for sturgeon, and its shores supported a considerable volume of suitable timber.

Within a week of arriving at the factory, they were off again with their Indian companions to the same general area. On this occasion, however, they explored south along the length of Lake Winnipegosis, across Meadow Portage into Lake Manitoba, and far enough south on this lake to reach the grasslands, their "Barren Ground," on the southwestern shores of this lake. Not all wintering servants were considered to be successful traders or welcome employees. Isham cited one, George Potts, as not being "a fitt person to Entertain amongst Englaish Men, having 3 bad properties. Drinking, pilfering, Swearing."[14] Moreover, he had not brought one beaver in trade goods back with him from inland in June 1761! From 1766–67 to

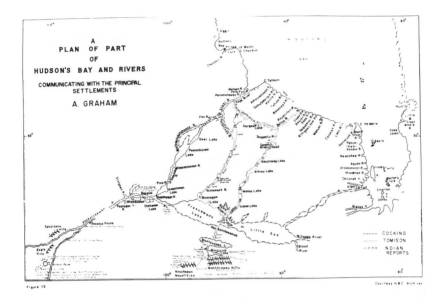

12.1 *"A Plan of Part of Hudson's Bay and Rivers" (A. Graham, 1770). This map shows the near western area from the Hudson–James Bay shore to the Manitoba lakes and along the Nelson-Hayes and Saskatchewan Rivers to just west of the forks of the latter river. Two original maps by Andrew Graham, of 1768 and 1770, have been combined in this transcription by Richard Ruggles from the originals in the Hudson's Bay Company Archives, Provincial Archives of Manitoba* G.2/15.

1769–70, six men were sent inland from York Fort each year. In the first year Louis Primeau (Primo) pioneered the fur trade in the Beaver River valley, a tributary of the Churchill system, and the others fanned out up the Saskatchewan River, into the northern Red Deer River area, in the country south of the Saskatchewan River. In 1767–68 Primeau, again in the North Saskatchewan River area, gave the unsettling report of meeting a Pedlar, Francois Le Blanc (Saswe), from Montreal, on the Saskatchewan River. This was the first time that a member of the new wave of traders from British Canada had been seen so far to the west of the Manitoba lakes. Similar reports of Pedlars to the Severn Fort factor precipitated two expeditions in 1767–68 and 1769–70.

William Tomison went inland from Severn Fort. In the first year Indians revealed that Pedlars operated at least five cabins, three on the Assiniboine and two on the Red River. Tomison left Severn House on 16 June 1767, followed the Severn River to cross either the Berens or Pigeon River, and went down to Lake Winnipeg. Apparently he traveled south with his Indian guides to the entrance of the Winnipeg River and met Francois Le Blanc there with twenty-four coureurs de bois in six well-laden canoes. This Pedlar went on to the Saskatchewan River near Nipawin, where he was seen by Primeau. Tomison spent the winter moving around the lower end of the lake, urging the local Assiniboines and Crees to promise to carry their furs to company posts at Hudson Bay. He was not too successful in his pleas, for the new Canadian traders were serving the Indians well from their adjacent posts.

The following autumn and winter, Tomison was sent away again. On this occasion, after reaching Lake Winnipeg, he and his Indian guides crossed it to use the Dauphin River connection to Lake Manitoba, paddled northwest in this water body to Meadow Portage, and then, with the onset of freezing weather and snow, left their canoes and wandered west on snowshoes through parkbelt country, dragging sleds, hunting buffalo, trapping game, and meeting other Indians. He reached the Assiniboine River, having crossed over the Riding Mountain upland. For the following three winter months he roamed up this valley with his Indian hosts. The party, ultimately exceeding several hundred tents, hunted, feasted, drummed, and danced. Eventually they arrived at their canoe-building camp on the southern shore of Dauphin Lake, from which the flotilla was launched on 18 May. Most of the Indians stayed behind at a Pedlar cabin on the Mossy River and traded some of their furs there. Even Tomison's closest companions had traded some of their furs there, and only with some difficulty was he able to draw them away to accompany him. Having heard at this Canadian house a rumour that Severn Fort had been abandoned, he returned to York Factory instead. By the midsummer of 1770, rival traders had been augmented considerably in the interior, and they increased their pressure, especially on the York trade, over the following three years. The Canadian independent fur traders James Finlay and Joseph Frobisher of Montreal had arrived on the Saskatchewan River in 1773, and Frobisher had induced Louis Primeau to abandon the Hudson's Bay Company and join him at a house constructed at Cumberland Lake, a strategic location for Indian movement between the Saskatchewan and Churchill Rivers.

The Pedlars also interfered somewhat with the flow of furs to Churchill. Therefore, in the summer of 1773, Joseph Hansom, a young servant at this factory, was sent inland to the Saskatchewan Valley to judge the possible effects on Churchill. Hansom was guided by Indians from Fort Prince of Wales to Southern Indian Lake, Churchill River, and southwest through Kississing and Athapapuskow Lakes to Cumberland Lake and the Saskatchewan River. After wintering at Cumberland and gathering a band of Indians to go with him to sell their furs at Churchill, he was very disappointed to find that Joseph Frobisher had transferred northward, built another cabin directly across the route to the Churchill River, and was highly proficient in taking many of the best furs of his Indian companions. Hansom thus learned, very directly, of the extent and consequences of the competitor's trade. In the 1774 trading season the Pedlars had passed north from the Saskatchewan into the Churchill system for the first time.

The Revival of Exploration along the Hudson Bay Coast, 1753–1772

In testimony to the parliamentary committee, the Hudson's Bay Company claimed that it had supported a number of searches of the coast beyond the Churchill River, that it had lost a considerable sum of money in aiding Knight's company to mount an exploring expedition, and that it had given early backing to Dobbs's program. The HBC stated that if a passage did exist, it must be sought farther to the north than either Knight had expected or than Dobbs's two main expeditions had proved it not to be. To ensure that all unexplored openings would be scrutinized, and particularly that the one major break in the coastline, at about 64° north latitude, which Captains Moor and Smith had entered but rejected as a sea passage, would be thoroughly examined, the company renewed its exploring and trading voyages out of Churchill. The company wanted to find out if the reported Kisk-stack-ewen River was in fact the incompletely searched opening and, once and for all, if this was the long-sought passage.

James Walker, who had proved to be unsatisfactory as an explorer, was replaced as the shipmaster by John Bean for three seasons starting in 1755. He was joined for the first trial by Moses Norton. Trade was a common thread of all voyages, but coastal searching was always given as an equal purpose, with the River Kisk-stack-ewen as the goal. On the first trip, Bean was thorough in his examination of the coast for some distance north of 64° latitude, but he did not try south of this position. Naturally, he was unsuccessful in his quest, since the entrance to Chesterfield Inlet was in the un-

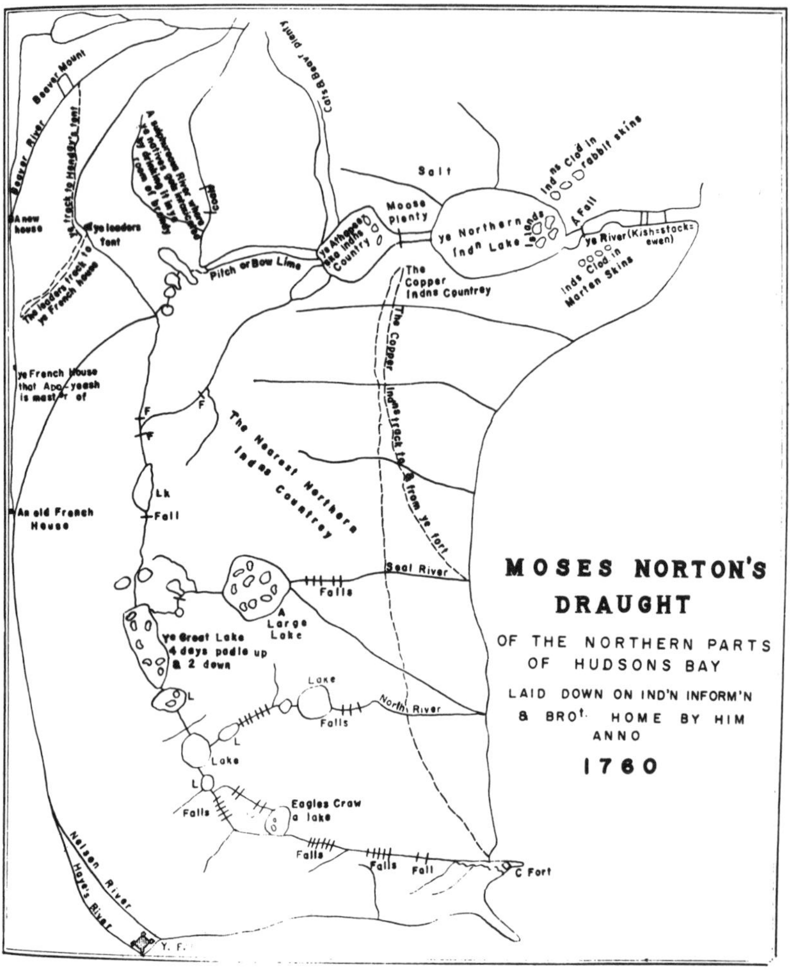
MOSES NORTON'S
DRAUGHT
OF THE NORTHERN PARTS
OF HUDSONS BAY
LAID DOWN ON IND'N INFORM'N
& BROt. HOME BY HIM
ANNO
1760
Beaver Mount
Beaver River
A new house
ye leaders tent
The leaders track to ye French house
Pitch or Bow Lime
Salt
Moose Plenty
ye Northern Indn Lake
Islands
A Fall
ye River (Kish=stack=ewen)
The Copper Indns Countrey
Indns Clod in Marten Skins
ye French House that Apo-yeash is mast'r of
An old French House
Lk
Fall
The Nearest Northern Indns Countrey
The Copper Indns track to & from ye fort
Seal River
Falls
A Large Lake
ye Great Lake 4 days padle up & 2 down
Lake
North River
Falls
L
Lake
Eagles Craw a lake
Falls
Fall
C Fort
Nelson River
Haye's River
Y. F.

12.2 "Moses Norton's Draught of the Northern Parts of Hudsons Bay" (Moses Norton, 1760). This map shows the Canadian north from York and Churchill Factories along with the Hudson Bay and Arctic shores, with the Nelson-Saskatchewan and Churchill River systems, to Lake Athabaska and Great Slave Lake. Direction and scale on the map are inconsistent. The map was prepared by Moses Norton from Indian information and was drawn on animal skin. Richard Ruggles produced this transcription from the original in the Hudson's Bay Company Archives, Provincial Archives of Manitoba G.2/8.

explored section. On the second trial he again started too far north and became convinced that there was no inlet. Finally, in 1757 he did not even look for the embayment but instead carried on trade at Whale Cove and went as far north as Marble Island. He had managed thereby to miss the inlet in all three voyages. A change of sloopmaster resulted, but the northern voyages again became trade-oriented for several years.

Finally, in 1761, the committee offered Moses Norton, who was then second-in-command at Churchill, the equivalent of a year's salary as a reward for the discovery of the long-sought Kisk-stack-ewen River. His first action was to send William Christopher in the sloop *Churchill* in the summer of 1761 to look north of Marble Island and up to the southern position of the region that had been examined by Bean. There, in this interstice, he not only located the "grand River" but also sailed up it about 100 miles. This may not have been a much longer distance than that of Moor and Smith's entry, but the voyage accurately pinpointed this major feature and opened the door to the final assault by Christopher and Norton the following summer. By 5 August 1762, approximately 161 miles from the entrance, the explorers were "in Bad hopes here being no tide and ye River But 1 mile over."[15] Their expectations were completely dashed after they had entered a freshwater lake, which they named Baker Lake, had sailed in the ship's cutter around its shores, and had even gone some 5 or 6 miles up a small rivulet at the western end of the lake until it shallowed to two feet. After this rebuff, the party returned to the ship and to Churchill. By this time, the possibility that a strait to the western sea had its entrance in Hudson Bay had been negated as far north as Repulse Bay. For another decade, summer voyages took place from Churchill, but they were associated with the Inuit trade or with a new whaling enterprise. Neither type of venture produced much profit for the company, and whaling ended in 1772.

Inland Wintering on the Barren Grounds, 1769–1772

Moses Norton, the child of an Indian mother and Richard Norton, had become well-versed in the geography of the northern and western interior behind Churchill Factory because of his antecedents and his contacts with Northern Indians resorting there to trade. Of particular importance were two Chipewyans, Matonabbee and Idotlyazee, who provided a sketch map and other information for the preparation of a map by Norton.[16] Although the maps subverted primary compass directions and ignored the protuberance of Boothia Peninsula, they provided skeletal details of a vast region northwest to the Coppermine River and Great Slave Lake and west and southwest to Athabasca Lake and the Athabasca River and to the upper Churchill system. The factory was basically dependent on the trade from this region. Its factor was also hopeful of increasing the flow of Indian customers from this area and was affected by the recurrent ambition to find metal deposits, as well as by a general desire to become better acquainted with the factory's hinterland that lay behind the renewal of inland wintering. Although Samuel Hearne was the successful aspirant after this goal, the first man inland was John Potts, who left the fort on 10 July 1765. He was back five days later, apparently ill and unable to proceed.

Hearne was a young sailor attached as mate to Churchill sloops. On 1767 and 1769 whaling and trading voyages to Marble Island, he had gained some training in the use of navigational instruments and became accustomed to the exigencies of travel. The general goals of the inland-wintering project have been outlined. More specific tasks were to determine the course of the Coppermine River to see whether it was navigable, to note the character of its mouth to find out if it in fact entered Hudson Bay, and to observe the location of woods in relation to the river and the soils of the area. Hearne was also to reconnoitre other rivers as possible sites for settlement. If he could not find the Coppermine River, he was to pass across the upper reaches of Wager Bay and Chesterfield Inlet and assess their suitability for post sites. And finally, he was to ascertain whether there was a strait at lower latitudes leading west from Hudson Bay. This was a full package of instructions indeed! Hearne tried three times to carry out his mandate. After the waterways had frozen and the spongy and watery muskeg had hardened in early November 1769, his party of some local Cree and Chipewyan Indians started off, into the Seal River valley and northwest about two hundred miles in all. They had difficulties locating food in the Barren Grounds, their Cree guide deserted them, and they were forced to return to Churchill, reaching there on 11 December 1769. In late February 1770 a second attempt began, on this occasion with dogs, sleds, and only five Indian companions and guides. They reached much farther than previously: northwest across the Seal River, north across the Thlewiaza and Kazan Rivers to Yathked Lake, west to Dubawnt Lake, and beyond on the Barren Grounds. It was midsummer, too late to travel on to the Coppermine. A few weeks later, in any case, Hearne shattered his astrolabe, and since he was determined to take accurate astronomical observations, he decided to return to the factory, arriving there on 25 November 1770, to get another instrument.

Fortunately, on the way home he met the experienced Chipewyan leader Matonabbee, who agreed to conduct him to the Coppermine River via "the shortest and best way."[17] With nineteen Indians on 7 December 1770, and meeting up with the full northern party some distance on, Matonabbee led Hearne to Nueltin Lake, to Wholdaia Lake, and on northwest to Artillery Lake. On the way they encountered other groups of Northern Indians engaged in hunting game, particularly caribou. One group had been organized into a war party with the objective of an Inuit camp known to be located near the mouth of the Coppermine River. Their track lay past Aylmer Lake, Contwoyto Lake, and on to a point on the Coppermine River about twenty miles above its mouth. The war party, with a very reluctant Hearne, who was unable to prevent them from attempting a savage attack, fell on the small Inuit party at the lower rapids. Hearne named these Bloody Falls, in memory of this atrocity. Immediately afterward, they passed downstream to the river mouth. The return trip included a visit to part of the Coppermine Hills, where native copper deposits were said to be located. Far from appearing to be a rich source worthy of further attention, here Hearne found only a small lump of the metal. Back again at Contwoyto Lake, they joined several groups, including the women and children left behind in their rapid trek to the scene of the massacre. Moving south across the Barren Grounds they entered the forests between Lac de Gras and McKay Lake, north of Great Slave Lake. The expedition crossed the eastern curved arm of this lake on the ice, moving from island to island to the southern shore. Traveling southwest to the Slave River, they followed it upstream for about thirty miles. Turning east, they eventually passed most of the same large lakes as they had on their outward journey, although their course was slightly to the north. Churchill Factory was reached on 30 June 1772.

Hearne had met his most important objectives. He had reached the Coppermine River, saw that its mouth was in the Arctic Ocean and not in Hudson Bay, mapped its lower course, and noted that it was not navigable. He could report that timber of building size lay far away to the south and that there was no local soil of any quality. The metal deposits seemingly were of little value. Because of the successful conclusion of the goal of reaching the Coppermine River, he need not, and did not, search the western ends of Wager and Chesterfield Inlets. And finally, since he had cut across the continent from Churchill at a northwest angle to the Arctic coast (its first sighting by a European), he could cancel the expectation that a sea passage to the Pacific transected the bay at these lower latitudes.

British Traders from Hudson Bay and Canada on the Plains

With the relinquishment of French sovereignty over New France in 1763, a new fur trade system, already in gestation, replaced that of the coureurs de bois, voyageurs, and merchants of Montreal and Québec oriented to France. The effective end of French trade had occurred in 1759. Even so, a few stray traders remained in the country. There was also a knowledgeable cadre of businessmen and former fur-trade employees in Montreal and Québec, where the English and Scottish merchants were settling in. The new British administration in 1764 proclaimed direct control over the western fur trade, prohibiting white traders from going west of Michilimackinac, which was to be the outermost centre of exchange. However, commanders at this post did not adhere strictly to regulations and licensed several French and English Canadians to extend their business into the Lake Superior region. Naturally also, the eastern merchants pressured the administration to change its regulations. They wanted to be financiers and suppliers for an enlarged commerce. In 1765, for example, Alexander Henry the Elder was given the monopoly of trade of the Lake Superior area. In 1761 Indians even reported to the HBC factor at Moose Fort that "English" traders were appearing in the upper reaches of some of the James Bay rivers. In the summer of 1764 the Moose factor heard that nearly one hundred persons in fifteen canoes, led by an Englishman, were coming up to the "back" of the settlements at the Bottom of the Bay and were using former French guides and voyageurs.[18] None of these reports could be verified. Yet many experienced guides, interpreters, and voyageurs were being hired by the Montreal and Québec merchants.

The increase in Pedlar trading in the 1760s had increased the number of inland HBC servants being sent to the interior but had not led to a change in the established policy. However, several of the factory senior officials had even earlier requested that some of the winterers watch out for good sites for the potential building of posts, mainly at nodes where Indians collected in the course of their annual movements. In 1754 Henday had suggested Moose Lake; Smith and Waggoner had been taken by the opportunities at

Playgreen Lake. Pasquia and the Grand Falls near the mouth of the Saskatchewan River at Lake Winnipeg were other recommendations.

The first definite meetings of company servants and Pedlars occurred in 1767. Tomison saw Francois Le Blanc at the southern end of Lake Winnipeg and was informed about other French Pedlars on the Assiniboine and Red Rivers. In that same year Le Blanc was also seen by Primeau on the Saskatchewan River. Also by 1767, an English trader had built on Cedar Lake, and the next year, one had erected a house on the Saskatchewan. Finally, as noted previously, the company was faced with the further indignity of having the Pedlars move ahead of it into the Churchill basin, north of Cumberland House Lake in 1774.

These developments by the early 1770s, combined with a detailed report made by Cocking of the situation in the Nelson-Saskatchewan region in 1772,[19] led to the inescapable conclusion that the company had to alter its trade strategy or face even more serious consequences. Cocking had stated that the wintering system was no longer successful, that it would be necessary to build a house in the Saskatchewan River region, that a fleet of freight canoes should be built, and that a shuttle system for ferrying trade goods and returns to this post should be organized. Hearne, who had been chosen by the York factor to lead the house-building expedition and who had accepted the task, had suggested that probably more than one fort should be erected up the Saskatchewan.[20] He concluded that although the Hudson's Bay Company had the advantage of a transport route that was much shorter that the Pedlars' haulage distance, the company had more problems getting proper canoes built by the Indians. However, faced with large quantities of quality company goods that were cheaper than the goods of the Pedlars, Indians would likely prefer HBC goods. The Pedlars' generous supply of brandy and rum weighed heavily in the balance, unfortunately.

Hearne chose to build on Cumberland House Lake rather than on any other site (especially Pasquia) because he judged that a greater concourse of Indians would be met there. The location was also within easy access to the parkbelt and grasslands to the south and west and to the forest Indians to the north. Completed in the autumn and winter of 1774, this post had already decreased in value, since the Pedlars had outflanked it with two cabins upriver and one at Portage du Traite on the Churchill; Hearne's post was also bracketed by Pedlar posts at Pasquia and Cedar Lake. Nevertheless, the two British opponents were preparing for a new phase and form of competition, one buttressed by far-ranging exploration.

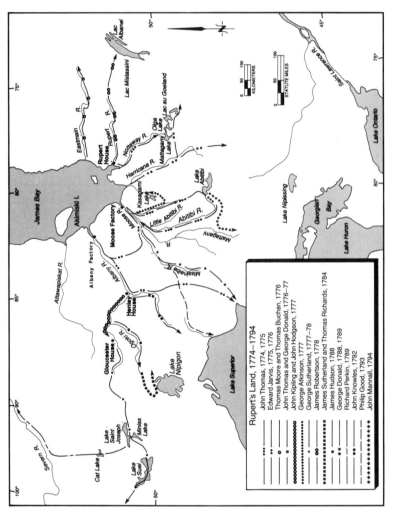

Rupert's Land, 1774–1794

• • •	John Thomas, 1774, 1775
───	Edward Jarvis, 1775, 1776
───	Thomas Moore and Thomas Buchan, 1776
─○─○─	John Thomas and George Donald, 1776–77
○○○○	John Kipling and John Hodgson, 1777
* *	George Atkinson, 1777
○ ○	George Sutherland, 1777–78
▪▪▪▪▪	James Robertson, 1778
▪ ▪ ▪	James Sutherland and Thomas Richards, 1784
▪ ▪	James Hudson, 1788
* *	George Donald, 1788, 1789
▪ ▪	Richard Perkin, 1789
─ ─ ─	John Knowles, 1792
─ · ─ ·	Philip Good, 1793
✲✲✲✲✲	John Mannall, 1794

Map 12.4 Rupert's Land, 1774–1794.

Inland from the Bottom
of the Bay and the Eastmain, 1774–1778

By 1774, much more was known about the lakes and rivers and the harsh, rocky uplands of the Rupert's Land watershed north of the Great Lakes and the Saint Lawrence River basin than about the country just behind the southern factories on the James Bay shores. Several exceptions should be noted. Lake Mistassini and the Rupert River had been viewed by French travelers in 1663 and 1672 but not by company servants. Abitibi Lake and the Abitibi River, and the lower Moose River, were invaded by French forces in 1686, who then returned to Québec. No company man had gone very far up the Moose River. Only the Albany River to the Kenogami tributary had become a regular pathway for a few traders going to Henley House.[21] But this waterway had not even been measured and mapped by 1774.

The measurement, detailed examination, and mapping of the lower Albany River, particularly the rapids, waterfalls, and portages, was completed in three seasons beginning in the spring of 1774. Henley House was enlarged in 1775 to act as the centre of inland operations, to enable the exploration of the upper river and its tributaries, and to open trading posts. Part of the plan proposed for inland expansion was to build wooden freight boats to carry supplies as far upriver as possible, hopefully to Henley and perhaps to some future forts. Unfortunately, the Albany was found to be navigable for such vessels only thirteen miles past Henley. Two large lakes became the goals of much exploration of the Albany, Mepiskawaucau and St. Ann's, both of whose locations were unknown but were apparently toward Lake Superior. The young surgeon at Albany, Edward Jarvis, agreed to try to find the first of these large lakes, but there were no Indians who would act as guides, partly because of the Indian unrest inland. To gain travel experience, he agreed to a shorter journey, for which two natives were found to accompany him. From 3 October to 19 December 1775, they journeyed up the Albany River to the Chepy sepy (Cheepay River), a south-bank tributary that lies about two-thirds of the way to Henley and flows from a group of small lakes halfway to the Missinaibi River. From these lakes the party pushed across to this river, walked down its northern bank to the main Moose River, and followed this to Moose Fort and on to Albany Factory. The trip took longer than expected, and the Albany factor had expressed some apprehension that an accident had occurred. He was later able to report "the pleasure of Mr Jarvis's Company" though "half starved, & greatly fatigued with his Journey."[22]

During that same period, reports arrived at both Henley and Albany that a Pedlar house had been opened on a lake "Meshippicoot," south of them, and also that several French-Canadian cabins were busy in the southern area. Jarvis and John Martin were dispatched in late May 1776 to investigate the Meshippicoot report. Guided by two Albany Indians, they traveled up the Kenogami or South Branch of the Albany, then up the Kabinakagami and through interconnecting lakes and rivers, which carried them to their goal. There were two French Pedlar houses on the shore, but none operated by an English trader. Moreover, they found that the lake was "no more than a small Bay of Lake Superior"; in fact it was Michipicoten Bay of that lake.[23] After visiting for several days, they followed the same path back to Albany, arriving there in early July. Again, the party had found little in the way of provisions on the way home and were exhausted, so much so that Jarvis declared this to be his last exploratory journey and begged off from such further excursions.

The official letters from the company committee for the 1777 season, which had arrived on the previous ship, had presented general orders to proceed with inland movement in the Albany, Moose, and Rupert River basins and to build houses at appropriate sites. This would require "Active and Diligent Men & one . . . who knows the use of an Instrument to determine Latitudes and Longitudes by which We may be furnished with intelligible Plans of the Country."[24] As a result of Jarvis's expedition across to Lake Superior, the company decided that this somewhat distant locale could best be served from Moose Factory. Therefore, the Albany Factory's efforts were to be put into the upper Albany, with the first house inland to be in this area. John Kipling and John Hodgson, surveyor and mapmaker, offered and were chosen to lead the building party. Indian guides and hunters were arranged, and the men headed off in early June 1777. Their final choice of site for Gloucester House was on the northern side of Upashewa (Washi) Lake. This was over two hundred miles above Henley but slightly downriver from two lakes that had been their stated destination. This original goal was Lakes Makokobitan and Eabamet, which John Martin and John Hodgson had perhaps reached in 1776 when they were away from Henley for over three weeks, though their destination was not given. As the new post was being built, a young servant was sent on from the new buildings upstream to reconnoitre the two lakes and to hold a possible site in reserve there if the Upashewa locale did not work out. Also, in the late

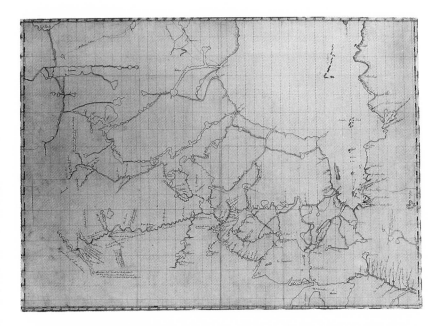

*12.3 "A Map of Hudsons Bay and interior Westerly particularly above Albany"
(J. Hodgson, 1791). This manuscript map extends from Hudson and James Bays and
Lake Superior west and north to the Red and Assiniboine Rivers, the Saskatchewan
and Churchill Rivers to Lake Athabasca and Great Slave Lake. The map is likely by
Edward Jarvis and Donald McKay. Courtesy of the Hudson's Bay Company Ar-
chives, Provincial Archives of Manitoba, G.1/13.*

summer, the Albany factor sent his young personal servant, George Sutherland, to Gloucester "to discover the Country & penetrate into the track of
the Canadians."[25] He was the first European known to have used the route
from Gloucester House past Lake St. Joseph to Lac Seul and from there
north to Red Lake. Whether he used the Pigeon or the Bloodvein River, he
finally reached Lake Winnipeg and then returned, by 27 June 1778, to Albany Fort, with definite news of considerable Canadian activity in the
Manitoba lakes and western Albany basin. He was "a perfect Skeleton."[26]
The company decided that the Winnipeg vicinity should not be served
from Albany because of its greater closeness to the Severn and York tracks
and the difficulty of obtaining local provisions.

In the summer of 1775 John Thomas attempted to explore the Nottaway
River inland from the seacoast, to find a useful way to reach the large inte-

rior lakes—Matagami, Waswanipi, and Abitibi. Pedlars were active there and to the south, and the company thought that several posts in this region could act as a buffer for Moose Factory and Rupert House trade. Lake Matagami was within three days' travel of Thomas, who was the first servant to ascend the river. But there were too many rapids and falls to portage, and the fact that the Indians did not regularly follow its course convinced him that he should advise the company against using the Nottaway River. This was incidental to the main efforts up the Moose and Abitibi Rivers. In 1774 Thomas had reached Abitibi Lake by ascending the French River, a tributary of the lower Moose, to the Turgeon River, and he then portaged some distance into the Abitibi watershed. He finally returned from the lake down the Abitibi River. The French River was again followed in the autumn of 1777, on this occasion by George Atkinson with companions, at first by paddling in canoes while the water was open and then, after building sleds, by hauling these on the river and finally overland to the northeast to Mesackame (Kesagami) Lake. Although they had difficulty finding suitable logs, a house was erected there.

The course of development of the Moose River branches was related more to its western tributary, the Missinaibi, than to its more easterly one. This river was the main thoroughfare for the Indians traveling between James and Michipicoten Bays. To try to counter Pedlar influence from Lake Superior, John Thomas was named master at Michipicoten and was ordered to open a house there. To aid in this operation, he dispatched a building party, headed by Thomas Atkinson; with George Donald as surveyor and mapmaker, its task was to build an intermediate post near the "great fall" at Wapiscogamy on the Missinaibi River. They started off on 16 October 1776, got to the site on 11 December, and began to put up the buildings. In the spring Thomas started for Lake Superior and took Donald with him to prepare a sketch map of the route. Although they reached that lake, having got lost between the upper Missinaibi and Michipicoten Bay, Thomas decided that this last forty or so miles was just too difficult to use regularly. Better would be a site on Missinaibi Lake, situated at this river's source. After an initial trial, their partly built cabin was abandoned because of Indian hostility, and all effort was now concentrated at Wapiscogamy House.

From 1776 to 1778, there was minor activity behind the Eastmain. Thomas Moore and George Atkinson were involved in obtaining knowledge of the Rupert and Slude Rivers. The main focus of interest was Lake Mistassini. In 1776 Moore traveled twenty-five miles up the Slude River, leaving Thomas Buchan to proceed farther. A journey lasting several weeks saw Buchan back at Eastmain House, reporting his inability to find the lake. James Robertson tried the Rupert River in 1778 and reached Lake Mistassini. He was sent back again to build a temporary cabin and to trade near the lake.

Into the Upper Churchill River Basin, 1774–1778

From 1774 to 1778, Cumberland House carried on company trade without any supporting posts inland. The house became the base for annual wintering journeys to intercept Indians and to sojourn in the same haunts as in earlier years. Samuel Hearne believed that one of the company's weakest points was its transport methods. He was also convinced that servants needed to be trained to manage canoes, that higher pay was needed for inland work, and that a new form of light wooden boat should be designed that could carry heavy loads but that could still be hauled relatively easily across cleared portages. The company should not try to match the Canadians post for post but should build at strategic points, two being needed first. One of these should be upriver on the North Saskatchewan, with the second to the northwest of Cumberland, to deal with the middle and upper Churchill trade. In 1778 Robert Longmoore was chosen to establish the first of the recommended posts, that on the North Saskatchewan. The building party passed the forks of the great rivers and reached the cluster of Canadian cabins, the so-called Middle Settlement, which was about halfway to the main southern bend of the river. Since it was October and the ice was beginning to form, and since they were unsure of the supply of building wood ahead, they stayed where they were, finished a structure, named it Hudson House, and settled in for the winter.

The number of Canadian houses had increased, with the westernmost houses about three hundred miles above Cumberland. Fort du Traite had been opened at Frog Portage by the Frobisher brothers in 1774 to waylay Indians passing on the way to the bay. The Canadians built upriver houses to gather in regional furs. Various independent traders had found it profitable to coalesce into groups, supplied by specific Montreal or Québec merchants. They would travel inland from Michilimackinac and, after 1776, from a new depot at Grand Portage. There smaller canoes would take over the goods, which could be managed along the lesser waterways of the Northwest. Once in Lake Winnipeg, or on the Saskatchewan, the partners would disperse to various winter quarters. For example, 6 traders led a group, with 124 men in 30 canoes, to Cumberland House Lake in 1775; 4 of the traders with some crew went north and built at Amisk Lake, 1 went south to Dauphin Lake, and 1 went on up the Saskatchewan River. In 1775 Louis Primeau ascended the Churchill and erected a cabin at Primeau Lake, a part of the Churchill River chain just below Lac Ile à la Crosse. In the summer of 1776 Primeau and Thomas Frobisher traveled on to La Crosse, and after examining the shores, they chose a site on its north-western side. These last two years of upriver progression had brought Europeans for the first time along the intricate length of the middle and upper Churchill River, a corridor from which later travelers would branch north and northwest into vast fur forests beyond the border of Rupert's Land.

Inland from the Bottom
of the Bay and the Eastmain, 1779–1794

The expanded network of inland trading posts in the midst of the customers of the HBC emphasized the need for a careful survey of the major riverways linking these posts to the bay factories and, from this survey, the provision of an accurate latitude and longitude graticule onto which the network could be plotted. In 1778 Philip Turnor, a trained surveyor, was hired as the first "Inland Surveyor" and was dispatched to York Factory. For a five-year period, he investigated and mapped these river systems, beginning with the Nelson-Hayes-Saskatchewan as far as Hudson House, the Albany to Gloucester House, the Moose past Wapiscogamy House, and on over the divide to Lake Superior and the Abitibi to Lake Abitibi and back through Masackame Lake to Moose Fort. On most of these journeys and others, he followed established routes and did not go far afield from them; but he was a careful observer of these routeways. He performed other tasks in exploration, surveying, mapmaking, and trading over the years, including acting as a teacher of practical astronomy and sketch-mapping to several young company servants who appeared to have an aptitude for exploration, surveying, and mapping. Peter Fidler and David Thompson in particular were associated with him on the Saskatchewan, and George Donald and John Hodgson at the Bottom of the Bay.

Canadian activity behind James Bay spurred the Albany and Moose factors to try to continue probing the upper river basins. George Sutherland, in 1779, went off with a new employee, a former Canadian trader traveling southwest of Gloucester House. How far or into which area they traveled is not known, but the hunting and the fishing were so poor that they were reduced to eating their own clothing and any animal to be found, including mice. They were so starved, weak, and crippled that Sutherland had to be carried on a litter down to Albany. Regrettably, for some years after this the factors found it difficult to enthuse company servants for inland service. Moreover, the factories did not attract many Indians from long distances who were willing to act as guides into their own regions.

Turnor and his small crews were the only active travelers until the summer of 1784. Two projects were planned for this season. Albany decided to have a route explored between Gloucester House and the sought-after Lake St. Ann's, and a new house was to be built up the Albany some distance above Gloucester. Only the first was successful. As a preliminary outing in late May and early June, James Sutherland and Thomas Richards, with several Indians, made a rapid two-week trip to Lake Pashkokogan, which lay about 170 miles above the post at Gloucester House. There they made notes on a possible house site. A month later they were off from Gloucester to search for Lake St. Ann's, reaching their destination only by following their guides' directions. They struck southwest from the Albany River, across the Ogoki River and on to the northeastern shore of the large lake. It was Lake Nipigon, which had previously been called by several names other than St. Ann's by the French and by cartographers. Sutherland advised against building a post at Nipigon or servicing this region from Gloucester. For various reasons, the new house project was not started that summer but was begun in 1786. Instead of building at Pashkokogan, the group leader, John Best, chose to build Osnaburgh House at Lake St. Joseph, farther up the Albany. To extend the range of this new post, James Sutherland was chosen to further the company's knowledge past St. Joseph Lake and especially to go into the Monotogga country, which lay southwest toward Rainy Lake. An Indian who knew this more distant area refused to accompany him because of reports of smallpox raging inland. Sutherland reached only Lac Seul.

The Albany factor was able to get several servants to take on the task of reaching Lake Nipigon via the Ogoki River, but the attempts were not immediately successful. A writer at the fort, James Hudson, almost reached his goal in 1788, but his guide refused to go on the last stage from Ogoki River to the lake. Another incomplete trial was made by Richard Perkin, a gunmaker at Albany, who was away for a month in the late spring of 1790, traveling from Henley House up the Ogoki River. In spite of his claim that the lake he had reached was Nipigon, evidence indicates that it was actually Lake Ogoki. The following summer John McKay, a former Canadian trader, completed the search by using one of the western tributaries of the Kenogami, which is the southern branch of the Albany River. He came back to Gloucester House.

To the west and northwest of Osnaburgh House, Canadian traders had penetrated into the lakes and rivers of the upper Severn River basin and into those flowing west into Lake Winnipeg. The HBC decided that several posts should be opened in this large region as both feeders and as shields for Osnaburgh. Cat Lake was chosen first in 1788, and John Best opened a cabin there. The following year, Richard Perkin was sent to reconnoitre the country from Cat Lake northeast to the Severn River and down this to Severn House. Two other posts were built by the end of 1790, one at Red Lake and the other at Lac Seul on the site examined by James Sutherland several years earlier.

John Knowles finally realized the aspirations of the Albany officers to identify and bring Lake Mepiskawaucau into the company orbit, but this was only on his second try in 1792. The first attempt was in 1791, one made confusing by his journal and his sketch map, decried by his superiors as "a heap of absurdities and nonsense."[27] The mysterious Lake Mepiskawaucau was probably Long Lake, not far east of Nipigon, and was reached by the Pagwachuan tributary of the Kenogami.

Despite an attempt to get to Lake Abitibi to open a house, Philip Turnor, who had just been transferred into a trading position, wintered at the Frederick House River junction with the Abitibi River. He decided to go to Frederick House Lake to put up a trading post in the spring of 1785. Abitibi Lake did not receive its own house until 1794; in the meantime, Frederick House was the centre of activities, including the support of several exploratory journeys. In 1787 Turnor went to Abitibi Lake and south to Lake Temiskaming to assess Canadian competition. The Harricanaw River was explored by George Donald from its headwaters to its mouth in 1788, and he also ranged along the upper Nottaway and through the watery tangle from Lake Mattagami through Lake Waswanipi in 1789. Another active traveler was John Mannall, a young writer assigned to Frederick House. His first trip from there was a short one to Abitibi Lake, where he stayed the winter in 1788–89. In 1794 Mannall made two investigative tours for the Moose factor in the spring, surveying the rivers and lakes in the Mattagami River–Lake Kenogamissi district and searching for a house site there so that later a post could be built to counter Canadian traders. Immediately after, he returned to Abitibi Lake and struck east up the Sarre River to look for a possible post site. Mannall recommended against a post there, suggesting that it be built at Abitibi Lake. He was later sent back to Lake Kenogamissi to head a construction party at the lake that he had explored.

Only one long exploratory trip was made from the upper Moose River during this time. In 1791 old Wapiscogamy House (Brunswick House)[28] was closed and its operations transferred up the Missinaibi River some distance to New Brunswick House. Since another cabin was considered essential even farther south to counter the Canadians, Philip Good, who was trained to take latitude and longitude observations and to make sketch maps, was sent out from New Brunswick House in June 1793. His course lay southwest across to the Kabinakagami River and Lake Kabinakagami, to the lower course of the Pic River, and on to Lake Superior. A cabin, tried out on the Kabinakagami River, was soon deserted for want of customers. Instead a cabin was opened on Missinaibi Lake, where an earlier temporary cabin had been constructed and then abandoned.

Canadian Traders Enter the Athabasca Country, 1778–1788

Peter Pond, born in New England, was an experienced fur trader in 1778 when, backed by the Montreal fur merchants, the Frobisher and McGill brothers, and Simon McTavish, he was outfitted with four canoes, supplies, trade goods, and sixteen canoemen to carry the Canadian trade beyond Ile à la Crosse into the Athabasca fur country. Pond pioneered the route over Methy Portage, that is, through Churchill and Peter Pond Lakes, up the La Loche River to Lac La Loche, and then up and over the rocky ridge of the water divide, from which he could see a thirty-mile sweep of the Clearwater River valley. The first Europeans to cross into the Arctic-flowing Mackenzie system, Pond and his party canoed down the Clearwater River to the Athabasca, turned north, and built a cabin on the river about forty miles above its mouth in Lake Athabasca.

At this time a major geographical enigma existed in the northwestern region of the continent: the area west from the Coppermine River mouth to the Bering Sea. The general position of the Pacific coastline into the Aleutians had been roughly established by Russian and Spanish navigators. But the disposition of land and water in the vast void inland from the Pacific and Arctic Oceans and the Bering Sea was known only to its indigenes. First, the expansion of the fur trade into the Athabasca region was based on the search for virgin fur country, but associated with this practical desire was a concomitant aspiration, that of finding a passage across to the Pacific coast. This latter purpose was unlikely to have loomed very large in the thoughts of these pioneer traders. However, in 1776 Alexander Henry the Elder and Joseph Frobisher had canoed down the Churchill River from La Crosse to Frog Portage with a number of Northern Indians who described their concepts of the geography of this immense area. These descriptions were sufficiently vivid to spur Henry to develop thoughts of an overland trade route from Montreal to the Pacific; he detailed his ideas in a memorandum sent to Sir Joseph Banks, president of the Royal Society in 1781, for this gentleman's "Perusal and Amusement."[29] The essence of his plan was that the trade venture should proceed by the normal route to Ile à la Crosse and from there to the Orrabuscow (Athabasca) carrying place (Methy Portage). Over this portage, according to Indians, there was a large river that ran westward, down which one could proceed to the sea, "which cant be any very Great Distance."[30] This river mouth could not be too far from the strait separating North America from Asia. A ship should be built and a convenient harbour be found for the trade. A return trip should follow the same route but should digress to Hudson Bay, for British manufactures could be sent there to fetch large profits in a valuable new commerce. He did not explain the role of the Hudson's Bay Company or its monopoly of trade in Rupert's Land, but it is interesting to note that he was likely the earliest proponent of a joint HBC-Canadian venture.

Canadian traders were without direct competition from the HBC beyond Methy Portage for twelve years after Pond's entry. In the spring of 1779 he brought out half of an excellent load of furs and had to leave the other half for conveyance in 1780.[31] In 1779 a series of small trade partnerships and several individual merchants joined together into an early phase of the North West Company, in which Pond was a minor partner. He was not back at his post, the Old Establishment (Old Pond Fort), until 1783–84. Other Canadian traders moved into the Athabasca area in the meantime. Pond was an unusual man; he was a self-taught geographer and mapmaker with an obsession for speculation about the configuration of the land and water patterns that lay beyond his post. He found it of great interest and value to question Indians about their home areas and about information they had gained from their contacts with other tribes. Yet, his life centred on meeting Indians and competing with his fellow traders. During the 1783–84 season he undertook some exploration. He partly explored

Lake Athabasca but apparently did not go beyond it onto the Slave River. Undoubtedly he had received indeterminate information on the great lakes that lay north of Athabasca, and he had met several Indians who had been with Hearne's party to the mouth of the Coppermine. Moreover, he had likely talked with Alexander Henry in 1779–80 and 1781 and would thus have had a rough idea of this somewhat similar-minded trader's geographical ideas. During the 1784–85 winter, while at his Athabasca post and later in New England and Washington, Pond drew his first map of the West and Northwest, which he presented to the American Congress, along with a memorial, which was basically a personal geography of the western side of the continent. Pond may have wanted to arouse greater interest and activity in the western and northwestern regions of the continent. If so, he failed. The map indicates that he knew of the great wall of the cordillera stretching north and west and of the connection of Athabasca to Slave Lake, and he postulated an unnamed river flowing north from this lake into the Sea of the North West (the Arctic Ocean).

In the spring of 1785 Pond traveled north to Montreal, contacted the leading North West Company partners there, and with the Frobisher brothers, prepared a memorial indicating interest in further exploration and discovery in the Northwest. Pond also draughted a new version of his map, which he presented, with his memorial, to the lieutenant governor of Québec to try to engage British government interest. This officer was enthusiastic about the possibilities and wrote to the Colonial Office, recommending action. As in Washington, Pond's attempt failed in London. His map indicates that Pond's geographical concepts had not changed since the previous year, though they were slightly enlarged. He showed a river flowing north from Slave Lake, now through a third large lake, Red Knife, and out into the "supposed . . . Ice Sea." Significantly, along the northern coast of the Pacific Ocean, just north of the end of the wall of mountains, lay the lower end and mouth of Cook's River.[32] Also, the River of Peace was depicted flowing from the southwest into the southern shore of Slave Lake.

Pond was heavily engaged, again for the North West Company, in Athabasca country on his return there in the 1786 open season, and he was in competition with another small Canadian group. Both sent working crews north from their posts on the Athabasca River to Great Slave Lake to erect adjacent cabins near the delta of the Slave River and to contact Indians in the region. In 1787 the small groups merged into the North West Company, and Pond himself went north to explore Great Slave Lake. How far he went

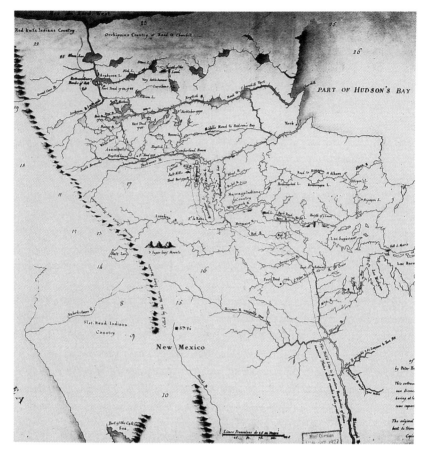

12.4 Copy of a map presented to the U.S. Congress by Peter Pond (1785). Although Pond's map contains much speculative geography, he apparently knew of the Rocky Mountains and of a great river (the Mackenzie?) flowing northwestward into the Arctic Ocean. Courtesy of the Library of Congress.

on the lake is not known, but his geographical configuration of the lake and its drainage changed significantly, and for the better.

Pond—energetic, a good organizer, and especially able in arranging food supplies and transport—was a driving manager of the fur trade. But his personality weighed against him. He was somewhat of a recluse, was brusque, and was considered eccentric and even violent. On two occasions, one just the previous winter, he had been closely associated with the tragic deaths of two competing traders. As a result, although cleared of direct guilt, suspicion remained. Circumstances had combined by the summer of 1787 to force his withdrawal from Athabasca and from active trade. His colleagues in the North West Company decided that he should be replaced by a younger partner, one who had been in charge of the Churchill River district for two years. This man was to move to Pond's fort on the Athabasca River to spend the 1787–88 trading season with Pond, learning about the management of the district. This season of contact was a far greater learning experience than Alexander Mackenzie had expected and was one that altered the whole later course of his life.

Mackenzie Learns about the Northwest from Pond

During this season of intimate contact with Peter Pond, Mackenzie was transmuted from a fur trader into an explorer and geographical visionary. He had not had a lengthy experience in the trade: he had worked in the Montreal office of fur merchants from the age of fifteen to twenty and had outfitted to trade at Detroit and then Grand Portage for only one year before being assigned for two seasons the responsibility for the trade in the Churchill region at Ile à la Crosse for the merchants Gregory & McLeod. When his superiors were absorbed into the new North West Company, he was sent on to Athabasca in the autumn of 1787 as submanager and, at the age of twenty-four, as heir apparent to Pond. It was obvious to the company that he was of a determined nature, was self-confident to the point of arrogance, was intense and strong-minded, and had shown high powers of organization. His further career proved that he had rugged physical strength and high stamina, was sturdy, and drove himself and his men to his stated goal. He was also willing to glean information from Pond and regional native contacts and found himself absorbed by the geographical orientation of Pond and by the latter's goal of reaching the Pacific coast and establishing a suitable transcontinental trade route.

Mackenzie learned much from Pond, even though later Mackenzie did not credit him with his tutorial services. Pond was a quarter-century veteran. He had been able to conduct trade over long distances, had organized the Athabasca department for almost a decade, and was the first European to travel over Methy Portage, to enter the Mackenzie River system, and to visit Lake Athabasca and the lower Peace River. He also had by this time envisaged a well-integrated geography of the Northwest and had produced two maps delineating his spatial ideas of this vast area. In contrast,

12.5 Copy of a map drawn by Peter Pond and dated "Athabaska July 1787." This later map is indicative of Pond's increasingly sophisticated view of the Canadian interior. It also provides the essential blueprint for the route that Mackenzie would follow to the Pacific a few years later. The map reproduced here is a copy of Pond's original, which is in the Hudson's Bay Company Archives. Courtesy of the National Archives of Canada, NMC 11618.

Mackenzie had little geographic and no cartographic expertise. However, he had energy, some education, a willingness to learn, and enormous confidence in himself. Mackenzie must have assimilated Pond's configurations from his two previous maps and from a new map of the North and West across to the Pacific and beyond to Russian Kamchatka, completed in 1787.[33]

By the time of Pond's departure for good from the western interior, in the summer of 1788, he and Mackenzie must have come to an agreement that Mackenzie would strike out for the Pacific Ocean and would follow a course of action based largely on Pond's conceptions. The 1787 map delineated the fateful changes in Pond's geographical suppositions. Athabasca and Great Slave Lake, connected by the Slave River, were both much closer to their actual shapes although much enlarged. No longer did Great Slave Lake drain north to a large body of water that "ebbs and flows," that is, to the northern ocean. Instead, a broad river flowed slightly southwest from the western end of Great Slave Lake for some miles, dropping over a great waterfall; it was open-ended, that is, it showed no direct connection with other drainages. But it did point directly as an arrow to the open end of the lower course of Cook's River, which led to the northern Pacific coast. There could hardly be a more direct inference that this was a unitary but disconnected waterway than the relationship of the two terminal sections. Above the void in the river, Pond placed a caption noting the "vast quantity" of driftwood along the coasts of the northern Pacific shore, flotsam "no doubt carried thither by the Araubaska [Athabasca], Peace & Mountain Rivers," all of which he indicated as flowing eventually into the great westward-flowing river draining the interior. Pond's map did not postulate a Northwest Passage crossing the continent in temperate latitudes. A chain of lakes and rivers traversed the land to the east-northeast of Great Slave Lake, Hearne's "route to the North Sea." If there was a passage, it had to be farther north of the northwestern coast of Hudson Bay and out across the northern sea to the Bering Strait. Mackenzie was, similarly, not concerned with or expecting to come across a historic transcontinental strait.[34] His goal was to follow the great river from Great Slave Lake to the Pacific mouth. According to Pond, the distance from the lake to the Pacific was less than 20° of longitude, and the axis of the river bore southwest by about 4° of latitude from its source to its mouth. This was established in Mackenzie's plan of action. Actually, Pond's estimated longitude position of the river exit was 20° (about 700 miles) too far west of its actual location. There is no indication that Mackenzie was overwhelmed by the expected length of his future journey.

The Journey to the Frozen Ocean
along the River of Disappointment, 1789

Mackenzie left on his frustrating voyage on 3 June 1789 and arrived back 102 days later. Before his departure he had arranged to have his cousin

Roderick Mackenzie, also a trader, join him in the open season in 1788 as assistant in Athabasca. He sent his cousin on to Lake Athabasca to open Fort Chipewyan, a new post on the lakeshore just east of the Athabasca River delta. The regional headquarters of the North West Company was moved here, and it was from this post that the expedition departed later. Moreover, in 1788 he sent Laurent Leroux, who had been trading south of Great Slave Lake, to its northern shore to trade with Chipewyan and Slave Indians and to inform them of Mackenzie's expected arrival in the early summer of 1789. They promised that they would meet him there before the expedition's entry into the "grand river" that would later bear the explorer's name. In addition to the leader, the group included four French-Canadian voyageurs, two with wives; a young German; a Chipewyan Indian, English Chief, as the main guide; and other natives. The Indians acted as provisioners, the women mended garments and made mocassins, and the party, whenever possible, obtained fish and game from the Indians they met en route.

Over three weeks after leaving Fort Chipewyan, on 29 June, Mackenzie located the main exit of the grand river and began its descent. For about four days the group followed its broad channel heading slightly northwest, a disappointment to some degree since he had hoped it would wend to the southwest. Moreover, no high waterfall was encountered, and he had expected to get to such a major natural feature before about 235 miles had been passed. On the fourth day Mackenzie received a greater shock: he had the first view of the ramparts of the present-day Mackenzie Mountains, which impeded the river's course and caused it to make an abrupt change of direction, not to the southwest but almost directly north. For many miles the river channel was shut in by the Mackenzie and Franklin ranges. On 10 July, having encountered a party of Loucheux Indians the previous day who stated that the group would soon meet Inuit peoples and in ten or eleven days would reach the sea, Mackenzie obtained a latitude reading of 67°47' north. He must have been increasingly suspicious as to the outlet of the river, since they had been pressing northwest daily. He and Pond had hoped to reach the western sea near 60° north. Nor was there any break leading west through the wall of the cordillera. In fact, after only three nights they had traversed the deltaic marshlands and reached one of several islands out in what Mackenzie called a lake. The open water beyond the island was frozen over.

Apparently, he had not even then realized that he had issued out some distance into the sea. The water was quite muddy and was fresh rather than saline. The Loucheux guide had always used the word "lake" to refer to this body of water, and the party had seen the two previous large delta fans (the Athabasca and Slave Rivers) embouching into large lakes. In addition it had been three—not ten or eleven—nights to the water. In spite of chasing whales in the open water areas, in spite of catching a type of fish unknown to Mackenzie but known to English Chief as also native to Hudson Bay, and in spite of having their campsite inundated by rising water (tides) on two successive nights, the explorer did not indicate in his later report for these days that they had reached the sea. Nevertheless, the party started on 16 July for the river channel, beginning their return voyage. Only then did Mackenzie admit that he had reached the sea, the northern ocean, and that his expectation of having gained the western ocean must be rejected. His application of the name "River of Disappointment" to the grand river that now bears his own name reflects his disenchantment and frustration.

During the journey both down and up the river, Mackenzie had become aware of the various Indian bands inhabiting the region; his force had met and conversed with some of them, had obtained local provender from some of them, had seen some of them even if they had remained out of contact, had noticed that the party was being observed at times by some, and had been chased by others. Mackenzie had questioned the natives whenever possible. Much of the geographical detail in the information he obtained was apocryphal. Many of the long-distance descriptions had passed through the sieve of verbal transfer from one tribe to another. Some was of value in extending Mackenzie's ideas on northwestern geography. Indeed, one Indian's report and map sketch on the region west of the Mackenzie Mountains induced the explorer to invite him to lead the explorer on a side journey west over the mountains to seek the ocean, or "Whiteman's Lake." The native declined to do so, to the relief of the rest of the party. A Dogrib Indian spoke of a river, larger than the Mackenzie, that lay on the other side of the mountains and that flowed into the sea (likely the Yukon River); here there was a kind of beaver with almost red skin (seal), and "large canoes" frequented the ocean. Drawing a map in the sand, one Indian displayed a very long point of land projecting west. This was Alaska, according to Mackenzie, near the extremity of which was a white man's fort. There was a river flowing to the sea on whose lower course west of the mountains people were living. The settlement was considered to be Unalaska and the river, Cook's River. Although all Indians spoke of massive mountain areas to the west, they also referred to these heights as being the source of rivers flowing to the ocean. Mackenzie was increasingly alerted to the need to seek suitable rivers to use to cross the mountains and lead to the ocean. In mid-August he made a cursory examination of the lower Liard River, which did not appear to be a potential route west. After fifty-five days on the river journey, thirty-one of them struggling upstream, the expedition crossed Great Slave Lake, went up the Slave River, passed the mouth of the Peace River, and reached Fort Chipewyan.

Mackenzie ended this historic enterprise on a negative note, disappointed that his prime purpose had not been fulfilled. He had not provided the North West Company with a suitable supply route to the Pacific Ocean. There was no easy route to the sea from Great Slave Lake, and a northern sea passage was frozen over even through the middle of summer. Although his findings were negative, he had corroborated the evidence, given nearly two decades earlier through Hearne's journey to the Arctic coast, that there was no overland strait at temperate latitudes. If there was a practicable continental crossing, it would have to be sought via a trans-mountain river route. Mackenzie decided to try the Peace River.

The Peace River Journey to the Western Ocean, 1792–1793

Mackenzie was apparently contemplating his next trial even on the way upstream on the grand river. It took two years before he became involved personally, but in the meantime he put preparatory activities in effect. He was at work in Athabasca during the following two trading years, with the greatest expansion being up the Peace River. He wanted to advance his jumping-off point as far up the river as possible. In 1790 Alexander McLeod was sent up the Peace to build a post, which he established at the mouth of the Whitemud tributary. This was some distance beyond the first cabin erected by Charles Boyer in 1788, at the mouth of Boyer River. Later in the summer of 1792, in order to get ready for the beginning of the expedition, McLeod ordered a small party to go upriver to the confluence of the Smoky and the Peace and there construct Fork Fort. Mackenzie went out to Lake Superior each summer with the returns. En route in June 1790, he met the Athabasca-bound Hudson's Bay party led by Philip Turnor from Cumberland House. This must have been humiliating for the very proud Mackenzie. They talked about his journey to the Arctic, and it became obvious that Mackenzie's lack of surveying experience and his paucity of instrumentation had resulted in few useful observations. In his journal Turnor noted of

Mackenzie: "[He] does not seem acquainted with observation which makes one think that he is not well convinced where he has been."[35]

This embarrassment could have been partly responsible for Mackenzie's decision to undergo some training in astronomical observation, to become familiar with basic instruments, and to buy a set of these when he returned to Britain for the 1791–92 season. His purchases were not state-of-the-art equipment. For example, his sextant was an obsolete model, and his compass was not graduated in degrees. His chronometer was not accurate, running quite slowly before the commencement of his trip. He also broke his thermometer. Nevertheless, although his longitude results had the greater errors, he had become relatively proficient in determining geographical coordinates.[36] To aid him, he had the Fort Chipewyan longitude and latitude results that Turnor and Peter Fidler had worked out. He also had Cook's readings for various Pacific coast locations, so that he worked out intermediate positions quite well. While in the East and in Britain, he took the opportunity to read the most up-to-date material on the region, and he was well aware of geographical literature, maps, memoirs on trade strategy, and private and government plans for exploratory journeys through the area.

The most active participant in planning for a viable route to the Pacific during these years was Alexander Dalrymple, cartographer of the East India Company, fellow of the Royal Society, and good friend of Samuel Wegg, governor of the Hudson's Bay Company. He was a staunch believer in the existence of a cross-continental passage and a proponent of imperial trade across the Pacific with China. The two great chartered companies, he proposed, should combine into one British enterprise. Since York and Churchill Factories on Hudson Bay were situated farther west than Grand Portage, these should be used as the major Atlantic-side ports, and a new harbour should be discovered and a port established on the Pacific coast. He was convinced that Great Slave Lake was connected by a great river to the Pacific coast, which itself lay much farther east than Cook had indicated, because the true coast was screened by an array of islands of varying size.

In 1789 Dalrymple laid out his proposal in his *Plan for Promoting the Fur-Trade and Securing It to This Country by Uniting the Operations of the East-India and Hudson's-Bay Companys*. He also published a map, "Lands about the North Pole," with an accompanying memoir. He had been given permission by Wegg to use company journals for this purpose. Dalrymple, with Captain George Dixon, had been able to command the attention and support of the Hudson's Bay Company and the British government. The proposal involved the following. Captain Charles Duncan of the Royal Navy, accompanied by Dixon, was to be put in command of a ship expedition under HBC instructions. They were to coast in the company brig *Beaver* south of Chesterfield Inlet to try to find an inlet that would lead easily to Yathked Lake by a connecting waterway. If this failed, they were to search north of Chesterfield for an entrance to a passage across to the northern ocean and from there to the Pacific. If this was not successful, they were to go up Chesterfield Inlet as far as possible, and if no water route was found, Captain Dixon was to load the boat on sleds and pass over the icy and snowy surface to Yathked Lake and from there to Slave Lake and by river to the Pacific. The HBC had no illusions that such an expedition would be possible or successful, but it wanted to deflect criticism that it did not support exploration.

The expedition was delayed in 1790 and was tried out in 1791. No passage was found, nor an easy inlet to lead by river connections to Yathked, and of course no route from the end of Baker Lake and the Chesterfield Inlet was discovered. News of Mackenzie's failure to follow a river to the Pacific reached England and brought an end to Dalrymple's schemes. In 1790 also, further British government action was reflected in two other ventures. One was a land expedition under Captain John Frederick Holland, to be integrated with a sea venture under Captain George Vancouver. Holland arrived in Québec in the autumn of 1790 to find that the plan for him to follow the great river from Great Slave Lake to Cook's River had already been negated. He returned to Britain instead. Vancouver's expedition had to be delayed until 1791 because of controversy between England and Spain. HBC support for Northwest Passage discovery died out until well into the next century, when the search became a major prerogative of the Royal Navy, entering into the Arctic archipelago.

On the heels of these failures, Mackenzie's second attempt to reach the Pacific began in the autumn of 1792, after his return to Athabasca. By 1 November, he had reached Fork Fort on the Peace River. During the winter he oversaw the trade, prepared for the spring departure, queried Indians coming from the region, and may have drawn a map of the northwestern area.[37] Apparently he expected to reach a large "Lake of the Plains," from which he hoped to take his canoe onto a Pacific-flowing river. Reality was quite different, and what lay ahead was to be a very arduous and dangerous venture. The single freight canoe with ten occupants and baggage set off upstream on 9 May 1793. In seventy-four days they traveled some twelve hundred miles to the side of a long ocean inlet. Over three-quarters of the distance was journeyed by canoe and the rest on foot, heavily laden. At the junction of the Finlay and Parsnip Rivers he accepted Indian advice to turn south up the Parsnip. With considerable difficulty they scrambled across the river divide onto a small tributary system of the Fraser River. Passing around the great northern bend of the Fraser, they turned south, paddling past the Nechako, the West Road (Blackwater), and the Quesnel Rivers.

The Fraser was becoming increasingly restricted between the high valley walls, and the Indians living along its banks were growing more menacing. Learning from his two interpreters that local natives had warned them that the river flowed a very long way south and that it was impassable in several places, Mackenzie decided to follow their advice to go back upstream and to head west on foot on a trail through the West Road opening. He had learned when he had entered the Fraser that the Indian name for it was Tacoutche Tesse, and he had become convinced that it was the upper stretches of the Columbia River, discovered by Captain Robert Gray of Boston and explored—in its lower reaches—by members of Captain George Vancouver's Royal Navy expedition. Along the trail from the Fraser, they followed a mix of small lakes and rivers, crossed from the West Road to the Dean River, and traveled on to the Bella Coola River. Mackenzie was escorted in canoes downriver to the intricate sea inlet system and across to the Dean Channel, still far from the open ocean. Because of a hostile reception awaiting him and his men, they ended their journey forward after seventy-five days. The return to Fort Fork followed essentially the same path and ended, after thirty-three days of travel, on 24 August. Mackenzie had missed meeting the Vancouver expedition, which had been surveying its way up the coast and had been charting the Dean Channel just a few weeks previously. Unfortunately, a landmark in exploration of the continent thus did not take place, since the European leading the first transcontinental crossing did not intersect with the naval surveyors of the western continental coast.

Mackenzie stayed at Fort Chipewyan over the winter and then left the North for good in the spring of 1794. The fact that he had not gained the open ocean or reached the coast at the Cook's River mouth prompted little chagrin. The explorer did not indicate his disappointment over not finding an easy route to the ocean either to his partners or to the public in his writings. He insisted that his route was practicable for future coast-to-coast trade. The North West Company did not agree with him. To his partners,

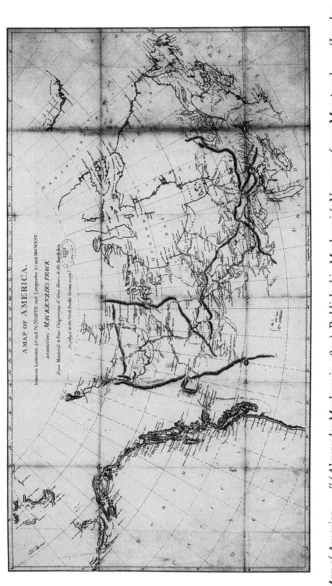

12.6 "A Map of America . . ." (Alexander Mackenzie, 1801). Published in Mackenzie's Voyages from Montreal . . . (London, 1801). This map is one of the most influential of the early nineteenth century. In particular, Mackenzie's confusion of the Fraser and the upper Columbia Rivers would cause Thomas Jefferson to assume a connection between the upper Missouri and the Columbia Rivers, thus setting in motion the explorations of Lewis and Clark. The map was drafted for Mackenzie's book by the great English cartographic house of Aaron Arrowsmith. Collection of John L. Allen.

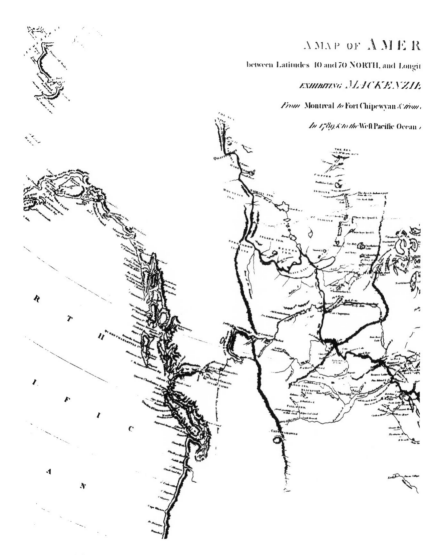

12.7 Detail from Mackenzie's "Map of America. . . ." This detail of Arrowsmith's Mackenzie map shows in perspective the routes followed by the Scot explorer down the Mackenzie River to the Arctic Ocean and up the Peace River and across the continental divide to the Pacific Ocean.

the expedition was a failure, for the road found was too long, circuitous, and dangerous. Company traders could no longer hope that the Athabasca country would be the nexus of an economical pathway for trade expansion to the Pacific coast. Another track would have to be found.

The Search for a Trade Route
from the Great Divide to the Pacific

The North West Company had beaten the Hudson's Bay Company traders into the Athabasca-Mackenzie fur regions, across the mountains to the Pacific, and finally, into the transmontane districts of the Fraser and Columbia Rivers. Nevertheless, it had an increasingly lengthy communication network to contend with. Mackenzie withdrew from field activities and entered the managerial ranks of his company. Simultaneously, he began to embroider on and to promote trade proposals, parts of which had been suggested earlier by Henry and Dalrymple. He proposed a trade consortium of all the companies, uniting together in one common interest. The Hudson's Bay Company should open its Hudson Bay factories for more cheaply delivered goods and trade returns, cooperating with the vibrant North West Company partners to provide furs, from the Pacific coast, for the East India Company market in China. Ships would ply this ocean to two ports, one north at Cook's River inlet and one at the southernmost limit of British claims, near the 42nd parallel. Neither of the monopoly companies was interested in this proposal, however, nor did his fellow partners support the plan. They focused their attention on making their supply route west more efficient. They built portage roads past the Ottawa River rapids and built several small vessels to ply the upper Great Lakes. Also, they hired David Thompson to survey and map the plains riverways and later to search for alternate roads to the Pacific Ocean.

The Hudson's Bay Company in 1791–92 had sent Philip Turnor, Peter Fidler, and Malcolm Ross to open trade past Methy Portage. Making a circuit of Lake Athabasa, they were the first to undertake this survey. They also made many latitude and longitude observations from Great Slave Lake down the Churchill River. But the company did not go back to face competition until a decade after this venture. It continued to try to find a road to Athabasca other than the one over Methy Portage. In the summer of 1793 Pond investigated the Seal River track from Churchill across to the middle Churchill River. That same season, David Thompson, who had been pre-

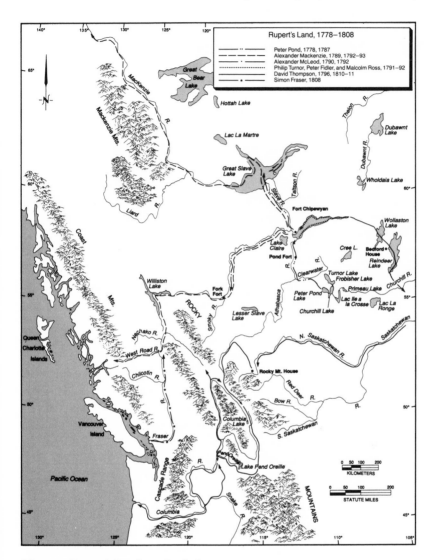

Map 12.5 Rupert's Land, 1778–1808.

vented from going on the Turnor expedition because of a broken leg, began a search for this alternate route. He went inland from the Grass River, across into the Burntwood River valley, and from there to the Churchill River. After canoeing up the river to the mouth of the Reindeer tributary, he apparently stopped there; his 1794 map of the Nelson-Churchill system does not include this feature, which according to the local Indians was the opening used by them to go to the north and west. Thompson was eager to carry on during the following season but was not supported as zealously as he wished by his superiors. Rather, he was ordered to increase the trade in the middle Churchill area. After continuously pressing for exploratory action, Thompson made his own decision to try the Reindeer River route. In June 1796, he left the junction with two Chipewyan guides, followed this tributary to Reindeer Lake, coasted halfway up its western side, and headed across to Wollaston Lake. After finding the Fond du Lac River on the northwestern shore, he passed down it through Hatchet and Black Lakes to the Fond du Lac end of Lake Athabasca. During the following autumn and winter, he and Malcolm Ross worked out of the new fort, Bedford House, which they had built at the western side of Reindeer Lake on the crossing to Wollaston. Thompson had become increasingly dissatisfied with the company's support for his desired role as an explorer and surveyor, and he had not sent his superiors any map sketches since 1795. For this, he had been strongly rebuked. He abruptly resigned at Reindeer Lake in 1797, made his way to the North West Company facilities, offered himself for this group's service, and was accepted for employment.

The Hudson's Bay Company did not decide to try to move across the Rocky Mountains to contest with its rivals for transmontane trade until 1809. It abandoned any attempt to use the Athabasca and Peace Rivers for this purpose. That summer, a trader for the HBC, Joseph Howse, was ordered to search for a reasonable way over the continental divide. He found a pass, later named for him, although he did not follow it through on this occasion. Again the North West Company had beaten the Hudson's Bay Company over this pass, which had first been used by David Thompson some years earlier. Also, the North West Company had crossed over the mountains in 1805, for the first time since Mackenzie's adventures, and had opened McLeod Post in the upper Parsnip Valley. Simon Fraser, John Stuart, and James McDougall, in the following year, had explored the upper Fraser tributaries, the Stuart and Nechako Rivers, and had begun to consolidate the trade in what Fraser called New Caledonia. Having rejected Mackenzie's path to Dean Channel, or an attempt up the Nechako River and across to the sea, Simon Fraser was deputed to work his way to the south down the Fraser River in 1808 to ascertain whether this was indeed the Columbia River and whether it would be at all usable as a trade route. After a hair-raising journey, through hostile Indian territory, Fraser reached the Strait of Georgia and was forced to give negative responses to both questions: the soon-to-be-named Fraser River was not the Columbia and had to be eliminated as a company route to the ocean because of its inherently unnavigable and precipitous drop from its source to the Pacific. The attention of the North West Company then turned to David Thomson and the upper Columbia River.

Thompson began his searches for a mountain crossing point in 1800, working out of Rocky Mountain House on the North Saskatchewan. He essayed the sources of the Bow, Red Deer, and North Saskatchewan Rivers but was unsuccessful until 1807 when he discovered Howse Pass from the last river and reached the upper Columbia, just above present Golden. He built Kootenae House upriver in the widening of Windermere Lake. By 1810, Thompson had led his companions down the Kootenay River to Pend Oreille Lake and the Pend Oreille River and had built cabins at the lake and on the Clark Fork River. That same year, Howse had accomplished his first foray over the mountains, through Howse Pass, leading a Hudson's Bay Company party south to the Flathead River and Flathead River Lake, where a wintering cabin was constructed. He returned to the Saskatchewan in the spring of 1811. Howse did not bring the company trade back into the Columbia system, however, because Indian warfare across the mountains made the use of his pass dangerous. Thompson also refused to use this pass and looked for one farther north, away from the danger to the south. He found an easier and more useful crossing over Athabasca Pass at the head of the Athabasca River. From there he crossed to the Columbia River at Boat Encampment, and up this river to pass over into the upper Kootenay River. During that same open season, in 1811, Thompson explored the Columbia River through its full middle and lower course to its mouth. Again, the North West Company had beaten the Hudson's Bay Company to the Pacific, on this occasion discovering the most usable water route to the western ocean from the Canadian interior.

The long contest between the fur enterprises supplied through Hudson Bay and the Saint Lawrence culminated initially in the victory of the fur traders who crossed the portage from the upper Great Lakes to the waterways of the interior plains. The French, and then the Canadians from Montreal, pressed into the charter territory of the Adventurers of England. Then, in the form of the North West Company, the Canadians outflanked the Hudson's Bay Company and passed beyond its watershed limits into the northwestern region of the continent. In search of a viable water route to the western ocean, its trader-explorers opened three unsatisfactory doors—the Mackenzie River, the pathway to Dean Channel, and the frightening canyon of the Fraser River—before discovering the cordilleran passage of the Columbia River to its Pacific Ocean outlet. All of these ventures provided magnificent chapters in North American exploration. Nevertheless, even with these battles won, the "Nor'Westers" finally lost the war to the more conservative forces of the Hudson's Bay Company, which was consolidating its trade within the charter confines of Rupert's Land. For a short time the HBC ventured into Athabasca and for a briefer sojourn into the region of the upper Columbia. The company explored, surveyed, and mapped the larger part of its trade domain. And in the process, the HBC's office, its supply and transport organization, its increasing network of trading houses and company officers and servants, and its shorter, basic supply lines to and within a more compact market area helped the company prevail over its opposition. By 1821, the Hudson's Bay Company had absorbed the North West Company and had inherited the Athabasca-Mackenzie fur regions, New Caledonia, and the Columbia River trade route to the Pacific Ocean.

13 / British Exploration of the United States Interior

ALAN V. BRICELAND

Colonial Englishmen are generally considered to have been less adventurous explorers of the North American interior than their French and Spanish rivals. Historian John Bartlet Brebner devoted only thirty-six pages of his four-hundred-page, 1933 study *The Explorers of North America, 1492–1806* to British exploration in what has become the United States. Names such as Soto, Coronado, Champlain, and La Salle are well known, but with the exception of John Smith, the names of the important English explorers are virtually unknown.

Because the great Appalachian chain, the mountains the Indians called the Endless Mountains, impeded the way west for all but one of the seventeenth-century English colonies, the English appear to have lagged behind their rivals in the speed with which they explored the interior. Nonetheless, between 1607 and 1804, colonial Englishmen undertook a number of remarkable journeys of discovery. Within a week of the landing of the first colonists at Jamestown, the process of exploration was set in motion. Steadily over the next two centuries, the English expanded their knowledge of their New World. By the end of 1607, they understood little more than what could be seen from a boat in Virginia's James River. By 1804, Anglo-Americans had viewed and mapped almost the entirety of North America east of the Mississippi River and, north of Saint Louis, even farther west.

English exploration did not proceed at a steady pace but moved in fits and starts. Most of the eastern portion of the United States was successfully explored in the seventeenth century. By 1700, virtually all of the important routes of travel east of the Appalachians, generally river valleys, had been visited, mapped, and assessed by the colonials. In addition, most of the Deep South and the great river systems of what was viewed as the West—the Ohio, the Tennessee, and the Mississippi—had been visited by

Englishmen, who returned to tell others what they had seen and how it might be reached. Although colonial explorers often claimed the territory they discovered in the name of the English Crown, their activities were seldom directly sponsored by the Crown or by its representatives in America. Expeditions of discovery generally required the approval of colonial authorities because of possible conflicts with the natives or European rivals; but the burdensome tasks of planning, organizing, and paying for exploration were almost always borne by private entrepreneurs. In the absence of governmental support, explorers went where the lure of profit drew them.

Although there were exceptions, three major motivations evidently drove the process of English exploration. Virtually all exploration activity involved a search for animal skins, for marketable land, or for a passage to the Pacific and the wealth of the Orient. Occasionally the way into an unknown area might be pioneered by an interpreter-diplomat ordered into Indian territory or by a military expedition, but more often than not those in the lead were searching for furs, land, or a water passage to the western ocean.

Certain individuals, such as John Lederer, John Peter Salley, and David Thompson, explored for the sheer joy and adventure of it; but for most, exploration was a tedious, dangerous, arduous, and even life-threatening way to feed and clothe oneself. It was work for the strong and the healthy. Most discoverers walked great distances carrying heavy loads, survived extremes of temperature, often went without food and sleep, and yet constantly had to keep their wits about them. Many who explored were hired employees, but many more were self-employed. For the most part, they probably did not think of themselves as explorers. Some were looking for a way to gain wealth, others simply for a way to survive. Few gave any thought to having a place in the history books.

Because England established a series of highly independent colonies, English exploration took on a regional character. The process advanced in different regions at different times. Initially, when Jamestown, Virginia, was the only English settlement, exploratory activity radiated out from that point. The planting of colonists at Plymouth and Boston led almost immediately to the exploration of New England. By the mid–seventeenth century, the settlement farthest to the southwest, Fort Henry, today's Petersburg, Virginia, became the center for explorations into the southern piedmont and mountains. After the English had settled Charleston and captured Albany in the early 1660s, those towns became the centers for the southern and northern pelt trading that propelled Englishmen toward the

Mississippi and the Great Lakes. In the eighteenth century, traders operating in the Ohio Valley looked to Philadelphia. The British capture of Québec in 1759 led to a rapid expansion of British knowledge of the former French possessions of Canada, Indiana, Illinois, and the upper Midwest.

The term "English exploration" as used in this chapter denotes activity that advanced the knowledge of interested persons in the English colonies about areas previously unfamiliar to them. The term "English" is misleading if applied to the explorers themselves. The ethnic heritage of the actual explorers was as likely to be German, Dutch, Irish, or Welsh as English. Colonial minorities appear to have migrated disproportionately into frontier areas, where they easily became caught up in dangerous wilderness ventures. Even the term "exploration" is misleading if construed in its popular connotation of going "where no man has gone before." Almost everywhere English explorers went, they followed well-beaten paths that thousands of Native Americans had been using for centuries. The English were advancing through well-populated territory. They almost never traveled into areas that were new to them without being led by native guides. On those occasions when they outdistanced the knowledge of their guides, they sought and gained assistance from local natives. Rarely did the English leave the beaten, single-file native highways and strike out indiscriminately cross-country. The English advanced into North America largely by moving from one native village to another.

A surprising number of those who ventured into the wilderness were accomplished, literate men who kept journals or left some record describing their routes and observations. Many more, however, were rough, poor, and illiterate. They left no journals. If someone else took note of their accomplishments in a business ledger or governmental report, their names might be known, but little of what they did survived them. Because the explorer, by virtue of his geographical isolation, also tended to be isolated from the written record, any history of seventeenth- and eighteenth-century exploration is of necessity incomplete. The names of a majority of those whose exploits should be chronicled in the story of English exploration have undoubtedly been lost to memory. Some of the best-documented explorations were among the earliest. When someone like John Smith or Edward Bland or John Lederer reasonably believed that he was the first European to see portions of this New World, he naturally wanted to relate the tale to others. Certainly, among the best tellers of such tales was the English adventurer John Smith, who sailed to Virginia with Captain Christopher Newport.

Exploring the Chesapeake

Christopher Newport's *Instructions* from his Virginia Company employers required him to employ almost half of the initial group of Virginia settlers in exploring the western reaches of the river on which the colonists settled. The company established Jamestown not so much as a settlement but as a base camp to allow an extended exploration of the interior. The company directed that half of Newport's explorers were to dig for minerals in the hope of discovering gold or gemstones while the other half were to penetrate the interior in search of a passage to the South Sea or the Pacific.[1] In the seventeenth century, the hunt for the South Sea would motivate much of English exploration in the New World.

Newport, clearly understanding the company's intent, began his explorations of the James River within a week of establishing his base at Jamestown in 1607. The settlement's weakness convinced Newport that he should take only twenty-four of the little more than one hundred men available to him. In part because of this shortage of manpower, Newport ordered that Captain John Smith, an experienced traveler in foreign lands, be released from confinement (he had been arrested for insubordination) in order to accompany the expedition.

The area being "explored" by the English was, of course, already populated by several thousand natives. While sailing up the James River in a shallop, Newport wisely asked for directions from several Indians in a canoe. When one native drew a sketch of the river, its falls, and two native kingdoms beyond the falls, the expedition's task was greatly simplified. Most intriguing of all was the native's depiction of the distant Quirauk Mountains, beyond which, recorded the expedition member and chronicler Gabriel Archer, "is that which we expected," an apparent reference to the sought-for South Sea. On the fourth day the shallop reached the shallows at what is today Richmond. Describing the falls, John Smith observed, "We were intercepted with great craggy stones in the midst of the river, where the water falleth so rudely, and with such a violence, as not any boat can possibly passe."[2]

Newport was determined to proceed on foot. He was, however, finally dissuaded by the vociferous arguments of Pawatah, the king of the local village, who stated that the Monacans, whose territory Newport would be entering, would attack the party. This would not be the last time that natives would use the hostility of their neighbors as an argument to prevent the passage of explorers beyond their territories. Before returning down-

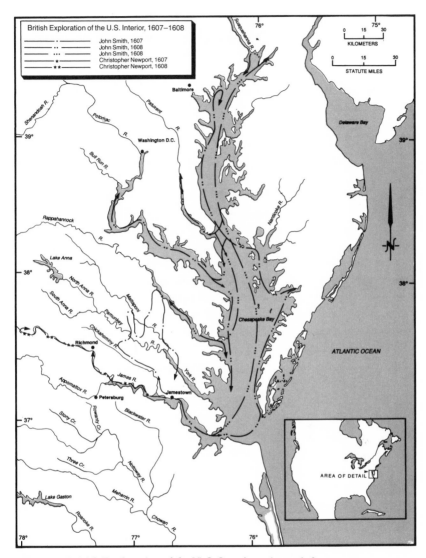

Map 13.1 British Exploration of the U.S. Interior, 1607–1608.

river, Newport ordered the construction of a large cross on a small islet at the foot of the falls. This practice of marking the landscape to symbolize English possession would be continued by later English explorers.

Newport returned to Jamestown on 27 May without having found either precious metals or the South Sea. Nonetheless, he had obtained two pieces of misinformation that would exert an enduring influence on seventeenth-century English exploration. Newport had seen numerous copper ornaments adorning the natives and believed the copper to have been mined in the interior, observations that kept alive the Virginia Company's quest for mines and minerals. Additionally, from his interviews with the natives, Newport had concluded that the Quirauk Mountains were only a few days' march to the west—and that they divided the continent in half. Beyond the mountains the rivers flowed into the South Sea. Newport's analysis would become the standard seventeenth-century Virginian view of the geography of North America. Here too, he breathed life into the Virginia Company's dream of becoming the conduit of trade to the Orient.[3]

With Newport's departure for England, the responsibility for exploring the rest of Virginia's rivers passed into the capable hands of twenty-seven-year-old John Smith. In December 1607 Smith was placed in charge of the colonists' small, shallow-draft barge and ordered to lead an expedition of eight men. His objective was to determine whether the Chickahominy River, a swampy river that flowed into the James eight miles above Jamestown, had a lake as its source. The Virginia Company's *Instructions* to its Virginia employees operated from the premise that "the passage to the other sea" would be "more easy" if a river could be located that issued from a lake. Such a lake, the company reasoned, might also be the source of a westward-flowing river.[4]

Other motives also inspired this venture. A majority of the governmental council at Jamestown despised Smith and had berated him for his timidity during a mission to gather food along the lower Chickahominy. By forcing Smith into an extended exploration, several of the colony's leaders secretly hoped that he might never return. Smith, who knew he was being ordered to perform a futile task, later justified this expedition as being necessary "to encourage our adventurers [investors] in England."[5] After rowing up the Chickahominy for seventeen miles, the little party reached Apokant, the westernmost native village on the river. Beyond Apokant, the river, already quite narrow, was no wider than a stream. Still, Smith pressed forward, although another ten miles convinced him that a canoe would be needed if the sought-for (but probably nonexistent) lake was to be reached. Returning to Apokant, Smith left six of his men with the barge and, with two companions and two Indian guides in a dugout canoe, paddled some twenty-two miles into flat swampy country a few miles northeast of the site of modern Richmond.

Toward midafternoon, Smith went ashore to reconnoiter, leaving his companions to prepare a meal. Finding the English party ashore and divided, some two hundred Pamunkey Indians, who had been tracking Smith's progress, captured Smith and killed his companions. As a prisoner under escort, Smith would become the first Englishman to traverse a significant portion of the extensive system of paths that connected the native villages of the Powhatan empire. Smith's captors led their prize to the nearby village of Rassawek, in what is today eastern Hanover County or western New Kent County, where the king of the Pamunkeys, Opechancanough, was then in residence. After a day or two at Rassawek, Smith was taken to a village some fifteen miles farther north, only to be returned to Rassawek a short while later. On or about 22 December, Smith was paddled across the Pamunkey River to the main Pamunkey village at what is today West Point, Virginia. Word had reached Opechancanough that the Tappahannocks, who lived twenty-five miles farther north on the Rappahannock River, sought revenge against an English captain who had earlier murdered their king. Smith was escorted cross-country in the late December cold to confront the Tappahannocks. When it turned out that Smith was not the captain they sought, he was returned to the vicinity of West Point to face three days of ritual and ceremony conducted by Opechancanough's priests.

Finally, when all was in readiness, the prisoner was conducted to Emperor Powhatan's residence at Werowocomoco on the northern shore of the York River. In a dramatic interrogation, conducted before a packed house of chiefmen and their ornamented women, Powhatan demanded an explanation for the English colonists' evident intent to settle in and explore his dominions. In a deliberately misleading reply, Smith sought to calm Powhatan's fears by asserting that the English had been driven into the bay by adverse weather. His and Newport's explorations of the James were intended primarily to discover a way to the salt sea that lay beyond the mountains, he declared, and secondarily to revenge themselves on the Monacans for the death of one of their men. Smith promised the imminent return of the great English warrior Newport and strongly hinted that Newport would exact revenge if any harm came to his loyal subordinate.[6]

Powhatan likely concluded that he must let the prisoner live, but he sought to transform Smith into an instrument of native diplomacy. Thus the stage was set for the famous scene in which Pocahontas, the chief's daughter, intervened during Smith's staged execution. By showing clemency, Powhatan hoped to transform Smith into a loyal subordinate. Thus, Smith not only was spared but was made a *werowance* (minor chief) by Powhatan and was given a tribal territory to command on the lower York River.

Twelve of Powhatan's trusted warriors paddled Smith across the York River to a point near present-day Williamsburg, and he reached James-town on 2 January 1608. He had spent the better part of a month being dragged around the countryside as a captive. The initial forty miles ex-plored in barge and canoe had been easy. The last approximately one hun-dred miles had largely been traversed on foot, under constant threat of death, in the dead of winter. Here again Smith's experiences with the na-tives were a portent of those of many later English explorers. Some natives were invaluable as guides or providers of information, but others posed the gravest danger that English explorers would face.

Five months after returning from captivity, Smith set forth once again, with a crew of fourteen in "an open Barge," to explore the great bay stretch-ing off to the north. The men crossed the mouth of the Chesapeake to the eastern shore. Beginning at Cape Charles, they explored many creek mouths and inlets in search of settlement sites with protected harbors. Running desperately short of drinking water, they pushed well up Mary-land's Pocomoke River looking for a source of that precious commodity. When they returned to the bay, a spring storm dismasted and swamped the barge, and for two days the explorers huddled on the beach of a small uninhabited island. The weather eventually moderated, enabling them to make repairs and to explore the half-mile-wide mouth of the Nanticoke River. Here, their initial approach to the shore was repulsed by a shower of arrows. However, a chance meeting with four native fishermen led to a rapprochement, after which "two or three thousand men women and chil-dren came clustering about [them], every one presenting . . . something."[7]

Sailing northward from the Nanticoke, Smith's expedition sighted "great high cliffs" on the western shore of the bay. Half a dozen miles north of the mouth of the Patuxent River, the Chesapeake Bay narrows to a width of only five miles. The 140-foot-high cliffs seemed to Smith and his men to offer release from the tedious flatness and aridity of the eastern shore. Crossing to the western shore, the barge and its crew continued northward along the densely forested shores of modern Calvert and Anne Arundel Counties. For seventy miles they observed fertile wooded valleys, "much frequented with Wolves, Beares, Deere and other wild beasts" but appar-ently devoid of human habitation. In all that distance, they discovered that only one harbor, the Patapsco of modern Baltimore, was suitable for large ships.[8]

They journeyed for two eventful weeks of exploration, but fatigue, spoiled bread, and an outbreak of illness among the crew forced Smith to turn back after reaching Pooles Island, a dozen miles north of the mouth of the Patapsco. Southbound, the barge paralleled the western shore the entire way. Just south of the "great high cliffs," the explorers came to the mouth of the Potomac. Smith was so intrigued by the size of this great river flowing from the west that he took "paines, to know the name of that seven mile broad river." The party followed the "Patowomek" (as they discovered it to be) to its falls above modern-day Washington, D.C., where they "found mighty Rocks, growing in some places above the grownd [sic] as high as the shrubby trees." Since some of the rocks were coated with a yellowish metallic deposit, the men set to collecting samples of earth liberally sprinkled with "yellow spangles" and questioned the king of the nearby Potomac Indians about the metal. He offered guides to lead Smith to a mine the natives had dug. Although the dangers of traveling on shore were, as Smith had discovered the previous December, much greater than those of coasting along the shoreline, the lure of gold was too great to be left undiscovered. Smith and his six men placed their Potomac guides in chains, entered Aquia Creek, and marched seven or eight miles inland into western Stafford County, Virginia. The mine proved to be "a great hole [dug] with shells and hatchets." The material it disgorged was traded to other tribes "to paint there [sic] bodyes . . . which makes them looke like Blackmores dusted over with silver." More samples were dug, but Smith admitted, "All we got proved of no value."[9]

Exploring the mouth of the Rappahannock, Smith ran the barge onto a sandbar. While waiting for the tide to free the vessel, Smith undertook to spear fish with his sword. Unfortunately, he speared a stingray and almost died from its poison sting. Recovering sufficiently, he guided the barge back into the James River, arriving at Jamestown on 21 July 1608. Three days later, resupplied and with most of the same crew, Smith set forth on a second exploration of the Chesapeake. He had been forced to turn back from the northern reaches of the bay just five weeks earlier at a place where the bay was still nine miles broad and ten fathoms deep. He believed, as did the Virginia Company, that the Pacific Ocean lay not far beyond the Virginia mountains. His first exploration had shown that the major rivers of the bay's western shore all led to falls, impeding access to the mountains. The northern unexplored reaches of the bay, broad and deep, still beckoned as the easy, profitable, and potentially history-altering route to the Pacific and the Orient beyond.

Coasting within sight of the western shore, the barge made good time. Smith reached the mouth of the Patapsco in just four days. Only a day or

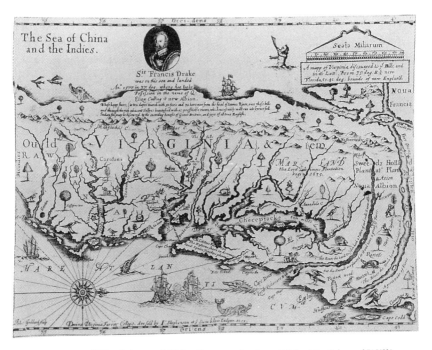

13.1 "A mapp of Virginia . . ." (John Farrar, 1650), published in Edward Williams, Virgo triumphans; or, Virginia Richly and Truly Valued (London, 1651). Farrar's map shows that, for some Englishmen at least, the conception of a narrow continent (or at least a narrowing of the landmass somewhere near Chesapeake Bay) still prevailed at least forty years after initial colonization. Courtesy of the Rare Books and Manuscripts Division, The New York Public Library, Astor, Lenox and Tilden Foundations.

two beyond where they had previously turned back, the explorers reached the head of the bay. They found that it was fed by the large Susquehanna River and three smaller rivers—the Northeast, the Elk, and the Sassafras. In crossing the head of the bay, the men, half of whom were again sick, "encountered 7 or 8 canoes-full of Massawomekes" (or Iroquois) returning from an attack against the natives of the eastern shore. Leaving the Massawomekes, the barge entered the Sassafras River. At modern Georgetown, Maryland, the village of the Tockwoughs, Smith noted the ownership of brass and iron tools, something unknown among the Powhatan tribes of the southern bay. The Tockwoughs explained that they had obtained these implements from the Susquehannocks, a "mightie people" who lived two days' journey to the north on the bay's "chiefe Spring." Smith immediately set the barge on a course for the Susquehanna River. Could it be, he must have asked himself, that the Susquehannocks were trading with the Spanish on the continent's western coast?[10]

The dream of a water route through the continent in the territory of the Virginia Company was dashed once more when, only a short distance beyond the river's entrance, rocks and shallows everywhere blocked the water routes to the west. The falls of the Susquehanna, the one thing that John Smith did not want to discover in July 1608, would ironically thereafter bear his name. An emissary was dispatched to the Susquehannocks to request a meeting, and a party of Susquehannock chiefs appeared three or four days later. After questioning the five leaders concerning the geography, tribes, and trade patterns of the interior, Smith concluded that the "Massawomek, and other people . . . inhabit upon a great water beyond the mountines." He learned enough, however, to realize that the "great lake, or the river," from which the Indians received their iron implements was a part of Canada and that it was from the French that the Susquehannocks obtained "their hatchets and Commodities by trade."[11]

Disappointed by the rivers at the head of Chesapeake Bay, the explorers turned south again to investigate the only two rivers thus far left unexplored, the Patuxent and the Rappahannock. Smith recorded that the nations along the Patuxent were "more civill than any" others he had encountered, but the river narrowed rapidly above Nottingham, Maryland; again he turned the barge around. The party received an altogether different reception some thirty miles up the Rappahannock. Smith had to deploy the Massawomeke and Susquehannock shields he had purchased at the head of the bay to deflect the shower of arrows that several hundred Rappahannocks launched against the occupants of the barge. Nonetheless, the barge was sailed and rowed to the location of modern-day Fredericksburg, where Smith disembarked his men to investigate the falls, search for herbs and minerals, and satisfy himself that there was no nearby lake from which rivers might flow both east and west. These activities were cut short when an attack by the Manahoac Indians drove the explorers into a hasty retreat.[12]

Only one area of the bay remained unexplored—the southern shore near modern Norfolk. Smith had no great expectations regarding this region but felt that it was "fit to know all our neighbours neare home." The barge sailed some eight miles up the steadily narrowing Nansemond River only to be ambushed from the shore. The English were able to seize the attackers' canoes, however, which they threatened to destroy, thus forcing a capitulation. The day ended with the natives loading the barge with corn as tribute for the victors. On 7 September, after a voyage of six and one-half weeks, Smith and his crew returned to Jamestown.[13]

In the meantime Captain Newport had carried word home to the Virginia Company that Smith, during his December captivity, had been told that there was a route to the South Sea through Chesapeake Bay. Just before exploring the bay, Smith himself had sent to London a rough sketch of the region showing the bay leading invitingly off to the northwest. The directors of the Virginia Company, facing impending financial disaster unless some dramatic discovery could be made in Virginia, dispatched Newport back to the colony with seventy new settlers. Newport carried strict instructions not to return to England until he had discovered gold, located a survivor of Raleigh's lost colony, or established the feasibility of a route to the South Sea. To assist in the last mission, the company had built a special barge that could be disassembled into five pieces for portage around rapids and falls.

After discussions with Smith, Newport realized that the only hope of achieving any of the company's three goals lay beyond the falls of the James River. Newport therefore took charge of 120 of the colony's 200 or so men and sailed for the falls. The barge was unloaded, but the pieces proved too heavy and unwieldy to be carried to the deeper water above the rapids. Smith, left behind by Newport, caustically dismissed the company's portable barge: "If he [Newport] had burned her to ashes, one might have carried her in a bag: but as she is, five hundred cannot, to a navigable place above the falls." Leaving the barge in pieces, Newport marched his small army some forty miles westward along the northern shore of the James. He found several likely places to locate mines and visited two Manakin Indian towns; nevertheless, to all intents he and his men returned to Jamestown empty-handed. The barge, left to the elements at the falls, remained behind as mute testimony to the shattered dreams of the earliest English explorers of the North American interior.[14] Both Smith and Newport would soon return to England, Smith carrying the message that the colony must stop its quest for quick riches in favor of self-sufficiency. His year of exploration had given him—and, through his writings, the English nation—a more realistic view of the New World, both its limitations and its possibilities.

During the first half of the seventeenth century, English settlement spread gradually up the rivers and across the peninsulas of Virginia's thoroughly explored tidewater region. Devastating Indian attacks in 1622 and 1644 slowed the process and made Virginians wary of the savage-inhabited, heavily forested wilderness beyond the fall line. The coastal plain south of the James River and the piedmont west of the fall line remained sparsely settled by the Indians and almost entirely unexplored by the English. Virginia's Indian trade was confined to nearby villages and to occasional visitors from more distant tribes.

Virginians Seek the South Sea

The earliest Virginia-based exploration of the interior was not undertaken until the late summer of 1650. Edward Bland, who was a member of a prominent London merchant family and who had just arrived in Virginia, shared the leadership of this expedition with Abraham Wood. Wood had spent most of his life on the Virginia frontier and was the military commander of Virginia's southwestern settlement, Fort Henry. It was Royal Governor Sir William Berkeley, however, who encouraged and authorized the 1650 exploration toward Carolina. As governor, Berkeley had been officially charged with stimulating exploration, expanding trade, and providing for the colony's defense. He was specifically charged to grant commissions "for discovery of the same Country [Virginia], and the Ports Bounds Limitts and Extents thereof."[15] Only once before, in 1641, had a group of Virginians petitioned "to undertake the discovery of a new river or unknowne land" beyond Fort Henry. Although they were granted permission to undertake the exploration, there is no evidence that an attempt was actually made.[16]

Bland and Wood were both prominent and well-placed businessmen. Bland had connections in England; Wood's contacts were Berkeley and the local natives. The Bland-Wood party took no trade goods when it set off from Fort Henry in the late summer of 1650. Taking with them only four packhorses with "Provision[s]" for seven men, the group was intent on exploring, not simply on expanding the Indian trade. Furthermore, the expedition offered military commander Wood an opportunity to learn the locations and dispositions of native villages that would be the objectives of militia retaliation should the natives precipitate another great uprising.

Bland appeared to have an additional motivation. The Bland family had lost a large quantity of goods wrongly confiscated by parliamentary authorities in the early days of the English Civil War. Parliament, always short of money, acknowledged but refused to rectify the mistake. The Puritan regime was also, in 1650, preparing to confiscate the property of Henry Frederick Howard, Lord Maltravers. Maltravers's property included a Virginia grant, the county of Norfolk, which extended along the coast from present Norfolk, Virginia, to New Bern, North Carolina, and inland fifty-five miles. John Bland and Co., the Bland family business, apparently had designs on this property. If the Blands could claim to have explored the region and to have opened it to settlement, parliamentary authorities might well be persuaded to grant Maltravers's Virginia grant to them in lieu of monetary claims. Thus Edward Bland, age thirty-five, set forth on 27 August 1650 to explore "New Brittaine," described as "being 120 Mile Southwest, between 35. and 37. degrees."[17]

Seven men ventured out from Wood's base of operation at Fort Henry on the Appomattox River. Six were Englishmen—the two leaders, two gentlemen, and two indentured servants. The key individual, however, was Pyancha, an Appomattox Indian who was already thoroughly acquainted with the region to be "explored" by the English. Pyancha's knowledge of southern Virginia, his coolness in a crisis, and his loyalty to Wood would prove critical to the safe return of his English companions.

Interestingly, the little party set off to the southeast rather than proceeding directly on their southerly mission. Evidently, they intended to visit a Nottoway Indian town near present-day Homeville, Virginia. As the party approached the Nottoway town, Pyancha was given a white flag and placed at the head of the party. Fearing that their sudden appearance might frighten the villagers, the men raised a shout. As it turned out, with most of the village's warriors away hunting, the hallooing of the English so frightened the Nottoway women and children that they fled to the surrounding woods. After this inauspicious beginning, the villagers were coaxed from hiding and showed the intruders "what curtesie they could." The Nottoways and other tribes subsequently sent runners to alert villages in the path of the English advance. This was the only time the natives would be caught unprepared by the explorers. Chounterounte, the Nottoway king, was initially determined to prevent further penetration by the Englishmen. He reasoned with them, attempted to exert his authority over them, and even uttered dire warnings "that the Nations we were to go through would, make us away by treachery." Unable to dissuade the outsiders and having no weapons to match their firearms, Chounterounte in the end had to settle for the inclusion of his brother, Oyocher, as a member of the explorers' party. The Nottoways' apprehensive reaction to the Englishmen indicated that the Iroquoian peoples of southeastern Virginia, living only a dozen miles beyond the Blackwater Swamp that marked the English boundary, were unaccustomed to English visits.[18]

After leaving the Nottoways, the explorers followed the Meherrin River to the west until they reached a fording place on the fall line at the site of modern Emporia, Virginia. Here they spent a day in the village of the Maherineck Indians, for whom they put on a demonstration of the power and accuracy of their muskets. After a day's rest, the adventurers, on the fifth day, set forth to the southeast, waded the Meherrin River, passed through a narrow gateway in the swamps of Fountaine Creek, and crossed into present-day Northampton County, North Carolina. They were headed into an area known today as Occaneechee Neck, bounded on the west and the south by the Roanoke River.

In writing about the expedition, Bland failed to clarify either the explorers' mission or their intended destination. Bland, however, had informed Chounterounte that his party's destination was the domain of the Tuscaroras, and a native runner had been dispatched to inform the Tuscaroras of the English party's interest in gaining information about two Europeans said by other Indians to be living in Tuscarora territory. Tuscarora territory lay south of the Roanoke River beyond Occaneechee Neck.

Whether the river proved too deep to ford or whether Bland and Wood had second thoughts about putting a major river at their backs Bland does not tell us, but apparently after reaching the river, the party turned westward along the northern bank to a point some four miles south of modern Weldon, North Carolina. When the natives suggested that they camp "upon the side of a great Swampp," Bland and Wood, sensing "nothing but danger" in the mood of the local natives, "removed to take . . . advantage for safety and retreate." Pyancha counseled Wood that the local tribe, the Hocomawanacks, were "very treacherous" and that they seemed angered by the sudden appearance of the English.[19]

On the morning of the day appointed for meeting with representatives of the Tuscaroras, as the party broke camp to investigate the nearby falls of the Roanoke and the two large islands that lay just below the falls, their Appomattox and Nottoway guides confronted them with evidence of imminent danger. The guides were convinced that a native conspiracy was afoot to prevent the party from returning to Fort Henry. Although scheduled to meet with Tuscarora emissaries near the falls that evening, the Englishmen—after visiting the falls, as they had told the local Indians they would do—headed northeast cross-country, taking pains to disguise their precipitous departure. Their immediate goal was to reach the main north-south path that led to safety. Although darkness forced them to camp near the present Virginia–North Carolina border, by noon of the following day they had reached the Meherrin village at Emporia. The town's leaders and most of its warriors were conspicuously absent. The inhabitants who remained gave indications to Bland "that they were angry at us."[20]

Alerted by Pyancha that "some plots might be acted against us, if we returned the way that we came," Bland and Wood headed north. Taking the shortest route to Fort Henry, they proceeded along the red clay hills that mark the eastern edge of the Virginia piedmont. Hilly terrain and heavy rains limited their progress on the eighth day to only twenty miles. The next morning they found themselves facing a flood-swollen Stony Creek. Afraid that delay might allow the array of native pursuers to overtake them, the explorers and their horses braved the rushing water. At dusk on the ninth day, after a journey of 120 miles, the expedition reached Fort Henry and safety.[21]

Although initial exploration of an area is often assumed to pave the way for others to follow, in this case, rather than opening the interior to further exploration, the Bland-Wood expedition discouraged similar attempts for almost two decades. From the explorers' accounts, Governor Berkeley and his councilors apparently concluded that only a large, well-armed force of men could travel safely in Indian territory. The expense of such a force, coupled with the governor's desire to maintain peace on the frontier, meant that twenty years would pass before another serious assault on the interior would be mounted.

In the half-century following Newport's and Smith's 1608 efforts to explore the tributaries of the Chesapeake in search of a passage to the Pacific Ocean, Virginians' interest in western exploration declined. Then, in a sudden burst of activity, a half-dozen expeditions were organized for the "purpose of discovering a passage to the further side of the Mountains."[22] Between 1669 and 1674, Governor Berkeley and his trusted supporter Abraham Wood provided the impetus for the first organized English attempts not only to discover a passage through the Appalachian Mountains but to accomplish "the discovery of the South Sea."[23] In this burst of discovery, the Virginia piedmont was explored along the Roanoke, James, South Anna, and Rappahannock Rivers. The central piedmont of North Carolina was opened to English trade, and the Appalachian Mountains were crossed not once but twice.

In the spring of 1669 Governor Berkeley, operating under the belief that the Pacific Ocean lay only two weeks' march west of Jamestown, organized a sortie into the piedmont by two hundred frontier militiamen; his objective was "to find out the East India Sea." At the last moment the project was canceled by a period of "unusual and continued Raynes."[24]

In truth, Berkeley had been thinking about (and postponing) this project for years. The obstacle that paralyzed him was not the great chain of mountains that the Indians described and that he believed ran through the middle of the continent; instead, the real impediment to western exploration was the knowledge that the Spanish already occupied the continent's western coast opposite Virginia. An English intrusion into Spanish territory might cost the governor his job, just as it had previously cost Sir Walter Raleigh his life. At a minimum, such an intrusion would alert the Spanish to the danger that Virginia posed to their possessions and would invite armed raids against the defenseless Virginia frontier. The possibility that an English exploring party might come under attack meant, according to Berkeley, that explorers could be allowed to go only "with such a strength that shal secure . . . [them] against al opposition whether of the Spaniards or Indians."[25]

In 1670 Berkeley authorized three attempts to locate a passage through the mountains. John Lederer, who undertook these missions for the governor, was a twenty-six-year-old native of Hamburg, Germany, who had recently arrived in Virginia. In March 1670 Lederer and three Indian guides traveled for two days from the head of the York River to the vicinity of Swift Run Gap on the Blue Ridge. After encountering "mountains higher than that [he] stood upon" (probably the Blue Ridge), Lederer turned back. Lederer's third exploration, undertaken in August 1670, was similar to the first. Departing from the falls of the Rappahannock with ten Englishmen and five Indians, Lederer reached the crest of the Blue Ridge, only to be again confronted by "another Mountain . . . of a prodigious height." Discouraged by the mountainous obstacle, the party retraced its steps eastward.[26]

Lederer's second trip, his most important and extensive exploration, began as a part of a militia expedition modeled on Berkeley's aborted 1669 plans. Major William Harris, accompanied by Lederer, volunteered to lead twenty-one Henrico County militiamen in an exploration of the approaches to the mountains west of the James River. Lederer carried a special commission from the governor authorizing him to proceed alone into the mountains themselves. Berkeley or Wood had evidently cautioned Lederer as to the dangers involved, for on his return he explained why he had not penetrated more deeply: "I though[t] it not safe to venture my self amongst the Spaniards, lest taking me for a Spy, they would either make me away, or condemn me to a perpetual Slavery in their Mines."[27]

Major Harris's company set out in May 1670 from the southern side of the James River at what is today Richmond. So fearful were they of becoming lost in the wilderness that they passed up the Indian paths and cut a new path along a straight compass course. This laborious process slowed their progress to five miles a day. The militiamen convinced themselves that the rolling piedmont hills of Cumberland and Buckingham Counties were the "mountaines" they sought. Thus, when Major Harris and his men arrived, on the twelfth day, at a wide northward-flowing river, they declared their mission accomplished and turned back to the comforting flatness of tidewater. In truth, they had reached the James some twenty miles northeast of modern Lynchburg at the point where today U.S. Route 60 crosses from Appomattox into Nelson County. They were still twenty miles east of the Blue Ridge.

When Major Harris ordered the return, Lederer produced his commission from the governor and received from Harris a horse, a gun, and several weeks of provisions—together with the loan of a Susquehanna Indian to serve as guide and interpreter. Why Berkeley had entrusted Lederer, a newcomer and a German, with a special commission is not known. Lederer was obviously a willing volunteer, but the governor's choice may have been influenced by diplomatic considerations; he preferred for a German to risk falling into Spanish hands than for an Englishman to do so.

Lederer and Jackzetavon, his guide, turned south "to avoid the Mountains." Five days and forty miles later they chanced on the village of the Saponi Indians located on the high bluff above the hairpin bend in the Staunton River west of current-day Charlotte Court House, Virginia. Since a lone European and an Indian posed no threat to them, the Saponis warmly welcomed them and after a day or two even urged that Lederer tie himself to the village through marriage. After several days, Lederer set forth paralleling the Staunton to the southeast. His destination was the island home of the Occaneechee Indians (where the Staunton and Dan Rivers join to form the Roanoke at Clarksville, Virginia).[28]

Because these islands constituted the major ford on the upper Roanoke River, the Occaneechees were regularly visited by other tribes and had, consequently, taken pains to fortify themselves. The day after Lederer arrived, six Rickohackan diplomats were invited to a celebration in their honor, only to be "barbarously murthered" at "the height of their mirth and dancing," by their hosts. The Occaneechees' treacherous ways made such an impression on the young German that he noted, "The very next day, without takeing my leave of them I slunk away with my Indian Companion."[29]

From this point, Lederer's route is a matter of some controversy. He claimed to have journeyed at least 114 miles in a generally southwest direction, to have visited six native villages, to have spent three days in a large marsh choked with reeds, to have stood on the shore of a lake so large that the southern shore could barely be discerned, and finally to have spent two weeks in "a barren Sandy desert, where . . . [he] suffered miserably for want of water." Because of the seeming incompatibility of these topographical features with the terrain of North Carolina, several early-twentieth-century scholars disparaged Lederer's veracity.[30]

Lederer's account was rehabilitated by the historian Douglas Rights in 1931. Rights traced Lederer along the Occaneechee or Trading Path, running diagonally across North Carolina from Hillsboro to Charlotte. Lederer's terminus, said Rights, was a Catawba village located just below the North Carolina–South Carolina border at what is today Fort Mill, South Carolina.[31] A comparison of Lederer's account with topographical maps suggests, however, that Lederer overstated his mileage by almost half and that his direction was more south than southwest. Apparently Lederer journeyed southeast to the vicinity of Henderson, North Carolina, where he visited the Oenocks. He then traveled down the corridor used today by U.S. 15 and I-85, visiting the Shackory Indians at Oxford, the Watarees at Creedmore, and the Saras at Durham. Just beyond the Sara encampment, Lederer entered "a continued Marish over-grown with Reeds." Until recently, just southwest of Durham was a twenty-five-mile-long, half-mile-wide swampy marsh that drained south into the Haw River. (What was once swampy New Hope Creek is now the bottom of B. Everett Jordan Lake.)[32]

Lederer forded the Haw and proceeded a few miles south to where the Haw and the Deep Rivers join (near Moncure, North Carolina) to form the Cape Fear River. Here, in 1670, was Ushery Lake. Today there is a floodplain seven miles long and two miles wide at this point. Informed by the local natives "that two days journey and a half from hence to the Southwest, a powerful Nation of Bearded men were seated," which he took "to be the Spaniards," Lederer thought it wise to begin his return to Virginia.

Seeking to avoid the troublesome marsh, Lederer headed east instead of north. After three days he entered "a barren Sandy desert," or deserted region, where the intense July heat had dried both springs and streams.[33]

Lederer had, in crossing the Neuse River just southeast of Raleigh, North Carolina, left the piedmont and entered the sandy Carolina coastal plain. After two weeks of erratic advance from one watering place to another, he emerged in mid-July at a Tuscarora Indian town near Rocky Mount, North Carolina. The natives directed him to a Roanoke River ford near Weldon. From Weldon, Lederer followed the same paths that twenty years earlier had brought Edward Bland and Abraham Wood to safety. On 18 July 1670, Lederer arrived at Fort Henry, completing a remarkable sixty-day journey of close to four hundred miles.

Much of what Lederer related on his return was so incredible that he would soon after be hounded from the colony by the "Affronts and Reproaches" of frontiersmen such as Major Harris, who labeled him a braggart and a liar.[34] Nonetheless, it was Lederer who dispelled much of the English terror of the interior. By returning safely after two months, he demonstrated that large, expensive, well-armed expeditions were not required for survival among the natives. He had shown that the organizing and financing of small exploring parties was within the means of strategically placed and wealthy individuals. Shortly after Lederer appeared at Fort Henry, Wood dispatched representatives to the Saponis to determine if they knew about a passage through the mountains. The natives responded that they could guide the English to another tribe who could show the Europeans the desired route.

A little more than a year after Lederer's return, Wood dispatched three trusted assistants—Thomas Batts, Robert Fallam, and Thomas Wood—to accomplish the undertaking begun by Governor Berkeley in 1669, "the discovery of the South Sea." They were not required to view the sea itself. The discovery of "the ebbing and flowing of the [tidal] Waters on the other side of the Mountains" would be sufficient proof and would reduce the risk of being captured in Spanish territory.[35]

Batts, Fallam, Wood, and Penecute, an Appomattox Indian guide, rode out of Fort Henry on 1 September 1671. They headed south along the same fall-line path that Lederer had followed during his return the year before. After a long day's ride, they camped near the Meherrin River northwest of Emporia, Virginia. The next day they turned west, using the Meherrin and the Nottoway Rivers as boundaries to keep them from going astray. The Saponis' town, eighty-five miles west, was reached in two days.[36]

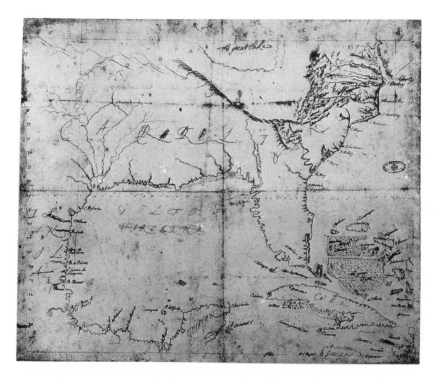

13.2 "Map of Carolana" (John Locke, 1671). The Locke map shows the English geographical image of the interior at the time of the Batts and Fallam exploration. The Appalachians are shown paralleling the coast, and northwest of them lies "the great lake" which may be a representation either of a huge inland sea or of the eastward extension of the Pacific known on earlier maps as "the Sea of Verrazzano." Public Record Office, London, MPI 11 (extracted from PRO 30/24/48).

Near modern-day Charlotte Court House, they crossed the Staunton River and were joined by additional Appomattox and Saponi guides. They stopped at the island village of the Hanathaskies on Long Island in the Staunton River to leave Wood, who had fallen ill. On 7 September, near Rocky Mount, Virginia, they first sighted the Blue Ridge. The easiest means of passage would have required a detour northward to modern Roanoke, but the explorers had instructed their guides to take the most direct route passable for horses. Their Saponi guides thus led them across the Blue Ridge at Adney Gap, fourteen miles south of Roanoke. Camping on the evening of 8 September at the foot of the western side of the Blue Ridge, they were the first Englishmen to have entered the Virginia mountains.

Still heading west, the party climbed the five-hundred-foot ridge that forms the eastern continental divide. After reaching its crest midway between modern Blacksburg and Christiansburg, they began a gradual descent into the valley of the New River. They came on the New River and the village of the Totero or Tutelo Indians, "circled about with Mountains" at present-day Radford.[37]

For two days they visited amicably with the Toteros, hired a guide, and arranged to leave their horses at the town. They began the mountainous leg of their journey by paralleling the New River into the heart of the Appalachians. On the evening of the expedition's twelfth day, they camped at present-day Narrows on the Virginia–West Virginia border, with the three-thousand-foot East River Mountain (the highest ridge in this section of the Appalachians) towering over them. The hardest and most dangerous part of the entire month-long journey was the twelve-hundred-foot climb up the steep mountain face. On reaching the crest, the climbers "set down very weary" to marvel at the "very high mountains lying to the north and south as far as [they] could discern." Beyond the crest, a brief descent brought them into the gently rising East River Valley, which led to present-day Bluefield, West Virginia.[38]

Near modern Princeton, West Virginia, the explorers, gazing westward from a mountaintop clearing, debated whether the South Sea could be seen in the distance. They "saw lying south west a curious prospect of hills like waves raised by a gentle breeze of wind rising one upon another." Fallam wrote, "Mr Batts supposed he saw sayles, but I rather think them to be white clifts." They continued westward, following ridges and the sides of hills and gradually descending the western slopes of the mountains. They had encountered no one since leaving the Toteros. To complicate matters, their food ran out on 15 September, and their Totero guide abandoned them. Fortunately, their Appomattox guides remained. Penecute knew nothing of this territory, but he was a good woodsman. The pace of the expedition slowed markedly as time was devoted to the search for food. After two days of subsisting on a diet of haws (the fruit of the hawthorn) and berries, the Appomattox returned to camp with some "good grapes" and "two turkies."[39]

For much of their journey across southern West Virginia, the explorers paralleled the Guyandotte River. When at modern-day Gilbert, West Virginia, where the Guyandotte turned northward, they continued west along Horsepen Creek to a deserted Indian town at what is now Matewan,

West Virglnia. Here on the Tug Fork, the river that divides West Virginia from Kentucky, the explorers conducted a short ceremony to lay claim to the territory on behalf of Charles II. With marking irons they set about carving initials into four large trees. The first tree was engraved with a symbol for the king; Governor Berkeley's initials were engraved on the second; Abraham Wood's were cut into the third tree. Last, the explorers carved their own initials, including a "P" for Penecute, on the fourth tree.

Their final act was to hack their way through a field of tall "weeds and small prickly Locusts and Thistles [grown] to a very great height that it was almost impossible to Pass." They intended to observe firsthand the ebb or flood of the tide and thereby to verify the distant presence of the South Sea. Discovering wet ground above water level, Fallam concluded that the tide was ebbing. To test this observation, they "set up a Stick by the water side" and convinced themselves that the river was indeed "very slowly" dropping. They would later acknowledge that they had not remained long enough to achieve certainty. Their hasty departure was precipitated by their guides, who feared the appearance of the local Moneton Indians. Fallam noted, "Our Indians kept such a hallowing that we darst not stay any longer."[40]

Modern knowledge of the extent of North America makes the measuring for a tide in a West Virginia river appear ridiculous, but given Batts's and Fallam's knowledge and experience, they had good cause to expect to find evidence for the close proximity of the western ocean. They knew that the effect of the Atlantic tide could be noted on the James and Appomattox Rivers as much as eighty miles inland. Beginning their journey from 100 feet above sea level, Batts and Fallam had traveled west for 185 miles, climbed a mountain almost 3,000 feet high, and then descended the western slope of the Appalachians for another 75 miles. They had arrived at a river very much like the Appomattox in appearance, at a place that they believed to be on a level with Fort Henry but that was in fact 500 feet above sea level. Since they thought that the Appalachians formed the backbone of the continent, they had every reason to expect this river to be a western tidal river.

Shortly after setting off to return by way of the same route that brought them, they once again strained their eyes westward and saw "a fog arise and a glimmering light as from water." They interpreted this as disclosing the presence of "a great Bay," which of necessity must be attached to a great ocean. The explorers returned to the Toteros' village, discovered that William Byrd I had been exploring in that area since they had passed, retrieved their horses, and set out for Hanathaskie. Thomas Wood had died at Hanathaskie, but the others arrived safely at Fort Henry on 1 October 1671.[41]

Batts and Fallam had become the first Englishmen to cross the Appalachians and to view streams and rivers that feed the Ohio and Mississippi Rivers. The waters of the New, Bluestone, Guyandotte, and Tug Fork all flow into the Ohio. In 1650 Bland had never been more than 60 miles from his starting place. Lederer was, at the farthest point of his travels, 175 miles from where he had begun. When Batts and Fallam stood beside the Tug Fork, they were 260 miles west of the frontier settlements of Virginia.

The activities of Lederer and of Batts and Fallam, in dissecting the piedmont from the Rappahannock to the Roanoke, had demonstrated that no significant groups of natives lived north of the Roanoke River valley. Only Lederer's journey into Carolina offered hope of either an expanded Indian trade or a passage through the mountains. Within three years of Lederer's visit, Virginia traders were trading with Carolina natives in the Oxford-Durham corridor.[42]

Lederer had been informed by various natives that there were two routes through the mountains. Batts and Fallam had exposed the defects in the northernmost of these passages. By 1673, Abraham Wood, who had spent sixty-six pounds sterling to finance Batts and Fallam, was ready to commit double that amount to an exploration of the more southerly passage. Wood's agent in this venture would be James Needham, an Englishman who had spent three years in South Carolina before coming to Virginia in 1673. Needham would be accompanied by Gabriel Arthur, an illiterate youth who was very likely indentured as a servant to Wood. Not surprisingly, the task Wood set for Needham and Arthur was the discovery of "the south or west sea."[43]

On 10 April 1673, Needham, Arthur, and eight Appomattox Indians set out from Fort Henry with "accomidation for three moneths," but no trade goods. Theirs was a mission of discovery, not commerce. Their first destination was Occaneechee Island, where they forded the Roanoke River. They followed Lederer's route as far as Sara (now Durham, North Carolina), but instead of turning south as he had, they proceeded west, becoming the first Englishmen to use the Traders Ford on the Yadkin River at modern Salisbury, North Carolina. After a visit to the Yadkin Indian town near the ford, they journeyed west to the native town of Sitteree, located on the Catawba River near current-day Morganton, North Carolina.[44]

The Sitteree Indians were, however, unwilling "that any should discover beyond them." The explorers returned to Fort Henry, where Needham and Wood prepared a bribe of trade goods to open the way. Providing four horses to carry the bribe, Wood sent his men out again on 17 May. Near Sitteree the English party encountered forty Tomahitan Indians who explained that they lived beyond the mountains and were on their way to visit their friends, the Occaneechees. The Tomahitans had stolen European goods from Spanish missions in the Florida panhandle and were exploring the possibilities of receiving similar manufactured goods by way of Virginia. Needham supplied eleven of the Tomahitans with a letter of introduction to Abraham Wood and offered himself and Arthur as hostages to be held at Occaneechee by the main party as a guarantee for the safety of those who would travel through to Fort Henry. After the return of this delegation, Needham, Arthur, and the Tomahitans set their course back toward Sitteree.

Four days of steady climbing after passing Sitteree brought them to the crest of the Blue Ridge, twelve miles east of Asheville. A half-day's descent from the 2,500-foot Ridge Crest, North Carolina, carried them to the French Broad River at Asheville. In the eleven days it took to travel the 185 miles of rugged terrain between the Blue Ridge and the Tomahitans' town, Needham and Arthur crossed five northwestward-flowing rivers, and "for severall days on their right hand as they travell[ed] still toward the sun setting," they witnessed over the mountains "a fogg or smoke like a cloud." Their path through the southern Appalachians was that followed today by U.S. routes 19–23, 19A, and 19–129 from Asheville through Canton, Waynesville, Sylva, Bryson City, Topton, and Murphy. Although the mountaintops in this region can be 5,000 feet above sea level, the path the explorers traveled followed the region's valleys at altitudes ranging from 2,100 to 2,600 feet. The five northwestward-flowing rivers they crossed were the French Broad, the Pigeon, the Tuckasegee, the Little Tennessee, and the Hiwassee. Beyond Bryson City the Great Smoky Mountains, with their characteristic "fogg or smoke like a cloud," were visible on the party's right.[45]

The explorers encountered no natives until they had passed beyond the mountainous southwestern region of North Carolina, which is today associated with the Cherokees. They found an abundance of game, but no natives and no beaten paths to follow. The Tomahitans' town was located in the northwestern corner of Georgia on the southern side of the Coosa River at modern Rome.

The two Englishmen and their one surviving horse were objects of great curiosity to the Tomahitan people. Anticipating this, the town's king had ordered the construction of an elevated platform so that the populace might "stand and gaze at them and not offend them by theire throng." Within a few days of the party's arrival, Needham began preparing for his return journey. Arthur, however, was to remain with the Tomahitans "to learne the language" and to serve as a sign of Needham's intention to return.[46]

After almost a month on the trail, Needham again reached Fort Henry. From Needham, Wood learned the dramatic news that the Tomahitans lived on a river that was said to be navigable to saltwater. Elated by the prospect that a route passable for horses had been discovered through the mountains to a navigable western river, Wood immediately announced the discovery to the Virginia Assembly. To his great disappointment, however, "not soe much as one word in answer or any encouragement or assistance [was] given" him by that body.[47]

Ten days after reaching Fort Henry, Needham and the twelve Tomahitans who had accompanied him were outbound once again. Accompanying them were several Occaneechees whom Wood had hired to serve as bearers. Their leader, Indian John, was also to serve as Needham's bodyguard. While crossing the Haw River, Needham sharply scolded one of the bearers who had "lett his pack slip into the water." Indian John was greatly offended, and his continual "wailing and threating" eventually forced Needham to attempt to reassert his authority. Needham threw a hatchet at John's feet and declared, "John are you minded to kill me." John let the hatchet lay but grabbed the loaded musket used "to kill meat for them to eat" and shot Needham dead.[48]

Up to this point, fate had not dealt kindly with Virginia's western explorers. Smith had left the colony under a cloud. Bland had died shortly after his adventure. Lederer had been ridiculed and run out of the colony. Thomas Wood had died in the wilderness, and now Needham had been murdered there. Only Abraham Wood, Batts, and Fallam had survived to resume ordinary lives.

As a consequence of Needham's death, Gabriel Arthur took over the exploration. Between the fall of 1673 and the spring of 1674 Arthur visited or viewed portions of every state east of the Mississippi and south of the Ohio and the Potomac Rivers, with one exception (Florida). As a result, he became the most widely traveled Englishman in seventeenth-century North America.

It had not taken Arthur long to figure out the Tomahitans' life-style. "The course of theire liveing," he would later tell Wood, was "to forage, robb and spoyle other nations." Needham's death forced Arthur into becoming a participant in Tomahitan foraging, robbing, and spoiling. When the news of Needham's murder reached the Tomahitans' town, several warriors seized Arthur. They tied him to a stake with "heaps of combustible canes a bout him to burne him." Only the timely return and intervention of the king saved Arthur's life. Since Arthur's safety could be guaranteed only by the presence of the king, and since the king was responsible for leading the tribe's war parties, Arthur was forced to travel with him on raids against distant enemies.[49]

The first of Arthur's enforced travels was undertaken in October 1673. Its destination was a cluster of Franciscan missions established by the Spanish to convert the natives of the Gulf coast. Arthur, given a "gun, tomahauke, and target," joined a war party of fifty on an eight-day, 240-mile march to the Apalachicola River where southern Georgia meets western Florida. After lying in wait by the side of a path for almost a week, the Tomahitans waylaid a lone "Spanniard in a gentille habitt, acoutered with gunn, sword and pistoll." Satisfied with this small cache of bounty, they returned home.[50]

The second of Arthur's journeys, undertaken in December 1673, was a raid against an Indian village just six miles from a little English trading post at Port Royal, South Carolina. The war party crossed northern Georgia on foot. On reaching the Savannah River, they constructed bark canoes for the 140-mile trip downriver. In a dawn attack, they slaughtered their enemies. During the Tomahitans' hasty retreat, Arthur might easily have slipped away to Port Royal, but his loyalty to Wood kept him with the Tomahitans. From Rome, Georgia, to Port Royal, South Carolina, is a 600-mile round-trip.

In the spring of 1674 Arthur, dressed, painted, and equipped as a Tomahitan warrior, set off to the north with sixty Tomahitans along what would later be called the Warriors' Path. This trek through eastern Tennessee and southeastern Kentucky brought them first to the "great towne" of the Moneton Indians on the Big Sandy River near its juncture with the Ohio. After a friendly visit with their allies the Monetons, the Tomahitans marched three days to the southwest to attack a village of another "great nation." Here, however, the attack was repulsed, and Arthur was taken prisoner. His captors—probably Shawnees—noticed that he was somehow different; they "scowered his skin with water and ashes, and when they perceived his skin to be white they made very much of him."[51]

Noting that his captors owned no iron implements, Arthur used sign language to inform them that pelts could be exchanged for knives and hatchets "a mongst the white people toward the sun riseing." The Shawnees then "carried him to a path [the Warriors' Path] that carried to the Tomahittans" and set him free. Apparently, the path was easily distinguished because Arthur successfully negotiated the three hundred miles back to the Tomahitans' town. Arthur's final journey with the Tomahitans was a 325-mile canoe trip along the Coosa and Alabama Rivers "to kill hoggs, beaver and sturgion." After five days and nights of continued travel, they came to a great saltwater bay so large that "they could not see land." The English had reached the Gulf coast at Mobile Bay, although they did not yet know it.[52]

In mid-May 1674 the king of the Tomahitans determined to accompany Arthur to Fort Henry, in part to explain that his people had not been involved in Needham's death. The king, eighteen Tomahitan bearers, Arthur, and a boy of mixed Spanish-Indian parentage reached Sara at present-day Durham without incident. Here, unfortunately, they were ambushed by four Occaneechees stationed there by Indian John to prevent Arthur's return. Through a long, terrifying night, Arthur and the Spanish-Indian boy hid together in the woods. When the Occaneechees finally departed, the Tomahitans were nowhere to be found.

Arthur had traveled this section of path four times the previous summer. Nevertheless, the path led toward, not away from, danger. Only at Occaneechee Island, on Indian John's homeground, could Arthur cross the Roanoke River. Under cover of darkness, he and the boy waded onto the island, crossed to the northern shore, and walked through the night before seeking a hidden resting place. Arthur, who had last seen Fort Henry on 17 May 1673, returned there on 18 June 1674. During his year with the Tomahitans he had crossed major portions of Virginia, North Carolina, Georgia, South Carolina, Tennessee, Kentucky, and Alabama. He had viewed, and may have entered, portions of Florida and West Virginia. He had traveled some twenty-five hundred miles on foot and another eight hundred miles by canoe.[53]

Arthur had unintentionally explored much of the South. Wood questioned him extensively. The account that Wood heard opened his eyes to the realities of the spaciousness of North America and the ruggedness of its mountain barrier. Wood apparently concluded that Arthur's salt bay was an extension of the Caribbean. The South Sea was therefore beyond reach, and so also was all hope of a large and steady trade with the transmontane Indians. With Arthur's return, Wood ended his exploring efforts. Virginia's brief age of exploration, 1650–74, was over. The age of the explorer gave way to the age of the trader, the pack trains, and the Occaneechee Path.

Approaches to the West from the Southern Colonies

Beginning in the late 1670s, William Byrd I and other Virginia entrepreneurs developed a regular trade with the natives of the South Carolina interior. In the last quarter of the seventeenth century, however, the locus of exploration shifted from Petersburg, Virginia, to Charleston, South Carolina. Charleston's proximity to major concentrations of native peoples, its port facilities, and its nearness to the Savannah River, which traders could use to transport trade goods, were important to its success in challenging the Virginia trade. But the presence of Henry Woodward was particularly critical to the speed with which the Charleston traders fanned out across the South.

King Charles II granted the Province of Carolina (extending from Virginia to Florida) to eight favored proprietors in 1663. That same year, Captain William Hilton undertook an exploration of the Carolina coast, in the process giving his name to Hilton Head Island. The following year the first English settlement south of Albemarle Sound was planted near the mouth of the Cape Fear River. Associated with this settlement was Henry Woodward, a young medical studies dropout turned ship's surgeon. Over the next twenty years Woodward became the most intrepid explorer of the Carolina-Georgia interior.

Woodward accompanied proprietary official Robert Sandford on a July 1666 reconnaissance of the Carolina coast. Whether in Virginia, Carolina, or New England, the initial acts of exploration by settlers were investigations of the coast. Woodward, clearly an adventurous type, volunteered to reside in a native village on the shores of Port Royal Sound "for the mutuall learning their language" and ways.[54]

Woodward had expected to remain with the natives for ten months. But before Sandford could return, a party of Spaniards patrolling the coast in canoes captured Woodward and carried him off to Saint Augustine, Florida. Because of his medical knowledge Woodward was soon accepted as the town's physician. Nonetheless, when English buccaneer Robert Searles sacked Saint Augustine in 1668, Woodward seized the opportunity and made his escape. Without money to pay for a passage to England, he enlisted on as privateer, only to be shipwrecked by an August 1669 hurricane on the West Indian island of Nevis. Four months later, by chance, a small fleet bound for Carolina put in at Nevis to refit. Woodward volunteered his services to the expedition's governor, Joseph West, and returned to the Carolina coast to assist in establishing a new settlement (initially named Charles Town) near the mouth of the Ashley River.

Because of his knowledge of the natives' language and customs, Woodward, unlike most other early Carolina settlers, was drawn to the interior. During the summer of 1670 the thirty-one-year-old Woodward, with the governor's support, undertook a series of reconnaissances along the Ashley and Cooper Rivers. The most extensive of these explorations was an eight-day, hundred-mile journey along the Cooper, Santee, and Wateree Rivers to an area twenty miles east of modern-day Columbia. Here he visited Chufytachyqj, the seat of an emperor who could allegedly command a thousand bowmen. The town was, according to Woodward, located in "a Country soe delitious, pleasant and fruitful, that were it cultivated doubtless it would prove a second Paradize."[55]

Interestingly, John Lederer was at Ushery, just 150 miles to the north of Woodward's position, probably at the very time Woodward was on the Wateree. Lederer turned back to Virginia out of fear of the Spanish after the natives at Ushery told him that bearded men were established two and a half days' journey south and west of his position. The only European likely to have been anywhere near Lederer was an Englishman, Woodward, who would dramatically expand Carolina's horizons in the same way and at the same time that Lederer was expanding Virginia's horizons.

Unlike Lederer, who had no official powers except those of observation, Woodward had some authority to bargain with the natives on behalf of Carolina authorities. On his return, he reported having "contracted a league with the Empr. and all those Petty Cassekas [caciques or kings] betwixt us and them." As a consequence of Woodward's exploration, that fall the emperor supplied the struggling colony with much-needed provisions.[56]

In the summer of 1671 Woodward was again on the move. He appeared briefly in Virginia on a secretive errand for Sir John Yeamans. William P. Cumming and the other authors of *The Exploration of North America, 1630–*

1776 believe that Woodward "retraced his way up the Santee and Wateree to the Esaugh [Catawba] tribe below present Charlotte, North Carolina, and from there following the [Occaneechee] path to General Wood's Fort Henry traversed the previous year by John Lederer."[57] If Woodward did reach Virginia by land and not by water, then Woodward was the first European to make an overland journey between Virginia and South Carolina. Therefore he, not Lederer, pioneered the discovery of the great trading path. Yet Woodward left no account of what should have been his most notable and remarkable adventure, a strange omission especially in light of the accounts that he provided of other, less spectacular travels.

Woodward was principally employed by the Charleston settlement "in the management of the trade and treaty of the Indians," but secretly he was in the pay of Carolina Proprietor Antony Ashley Cooper, the earl of Shaftesbury. Among his secret tasks, Woodward was to inform Shaftesbury by a clandestine code should he discover any sources of gold or silver. When no avenues to easy wealth were found during 1670 and 1671, Shaftesbury directed Woodward's talents toward "a trade with the Indians for Furs and other Comodities," leaving it to Woodward to determine with whom this trade should be opened. Shaftsbury's agent did not simply plunge off into the wilderness in a blind search for trading partners. Knowing better, he waited patiently for the natives to make the first move.[58]

In October 1674 ten members of an interior tribe, the Westos, arrived at Shaftesbury's Saint Giles plantation near the head of Ashley River. Although the Westos were feared as cannibals by the coastal nations, Woodward raced upriver to meet with them. He did not know a word of their language; yet he interpreted by their signs that they desired that he accompany them. Seizing the moment, Woodward set out, with only an hour's preparation, into a cold October drizzle. He had little notion of where he was headed, and his safety depended on the prospect that he would be of more use to the Westos alive than dead.

For a short time the expedition paralleled the Ashley to the northwest but then turned west, entering "a large tracke of Pines." After rafting across the Edisto River, the men traversed modern Colleton, Bamberg, Barnwell, and Aiken Counties. Eight days and 125 miles later they reached the Savannah River near Beach Island, South Carolina. The Westo "cheife," alerted by runners that an Englishman accompanied his warriors, waited on the Georgia shore. Woodward was paddled across the Savannah River by two men in a canoe to a sandy point opposite a hundred-foot-high chalky cliff, where he was "courteously entertained" by the chief. When the rain had let up sufficiently, the entire party paddled some three miles upriver to Hickauhaugua, the Westos' principal town. Hickau-haugua was located near present-day Augusta, Georgia, on a narrow point of land surrounded on three sides by the river.[59]

Woodward was the first European most of the Westos had ever seen. Consequently, his arrival at Hickauhaugua created a stir, similar to that aroused the previous year by Needham and Arthur's arrival among the Tomahitans. Woodward entered the town through "a concourse of some hundred of Indians, drest up in their anticke fighting garbe." The chief's dwelling, to which he was escorted, became so thronged by curious natives that many young people climbed on "top of the house to satisfy their curiosity." Ceremonies and feasting completed the day, with the Westos inundating their guest with "sufficient of their food to satisfy at least half a dozen of their owne appetites."[60]

Woodward spent ten days at the palisaded Westo village. Despite the language barrier, he learned a good deal from his hosts about the region's geography and the locations of other tribal groups. He discovered as well that the Westos were "well provided with arms, amunition, tradeing cloath and other trade," which they gained by carrying "drest deare skins furrs and young Indian Slaves" northward to exchange with Virginia-based traders. Nonetheless, when Woodward returned to Charles Town after twenty-seven days in the interior, he had secured a promise that the Westos would appear "in March wth deare skins, furrs and younge slaves" not in Virginia but at Shaftesbury's Ashley River plantation. Evidently, the 130-mile trek to Charles Town was shorter and easier for the Westos than the journey they had been making to their Virginia trading contacts. The trade with Virginia, barely established, was about to be challenged by a new breed of Charleston traders.[61]

For half a dozen years, the Carolina proprietors and their agent Woodward prospered from this new trading monopoly with the Westos and, through them, with other peoples of the interior. In retaliation, independent Charleston traders instigated what became known as the Westo War of 1680 in an effort to break the proprietors' monopoly and to open the way for their own exploitation of the interior. For a while, Woodward's star was in eclipse. He was forced to make a 1682 voyage to England to defend some of his actions before the proprietors. When he returned to Carolina, however, he carried a personal commission from the proprietors authorizing him to explore "the Inlands of our Province of Carolina . . . and what they do containe and also a passage over the Apalatean Mountains found out."[62]

As Woodward interpreted this commission, the propietors' central objective was not the exploration of terrain per se but the establishment of lucrative new trade contacts. Thus, in the summer of 1685 he set out from Augusta, Georgia, with half a dozen or so followers for a trek across the fall-line hills section of central Georgia. Their destination was the Chattahoochee River near modern Columbus. Here, on the boundary between Georgia and Alabama, were Coweta and Kasihta, the principal towns of the powerful Lower Creek Indians.

News of the English encroachment into territory previously the domain of the Spanish trader and missionary quickly reached Lieutenant Antonio Matheos at Fort Apalache in western Florida. Matheos, with 250 Indian allies, marched north into Creek country to arrest these Englishmen, who were building a small stockade for their trade goods. Warned of Matheos's approach, Woodward and his men fled the immediate locale, but not before Woodward had prepared a defiant message dated 2 September 1685. "I am very sorry," Woodward sarcastically wrote to Matheos, "that I came with so small a following that I cannot await your arrival. . . . I trust in God that I shall meet you gentlemen later when I have a larger following." The Spanish had to content themselves with punishing the natives and destroying Woodward's half-finished blockhouse. After Matheos had departed, Woodward emerged from hiding and resumed his trading. In December, when Matheos reappeared, Woodward again found sanctuary in the forests. This time, however, Matheos found something more tangible than a letter to carry home with him. He confiscated five hundred deerskins and twenty-three beaver skins from Woodward's rebuilt blockhouse before burning it and departing.[63]

Woodward remained on the Chattahoochee until spring when, having fallen ill, he was carried by native bearers in a litter back to Charleston. He died shortly thereafter. Although others would follow Woodward's path and would soon pass beyond the Chattahoochee, it was Woodward who had almost single-handedly pioneered the way west from Charleston into the heart of the Deep South.

By the early 1690s Charleston traders were familiar with Choctaw Territory in northern Alabama. They were also trading with natives on the Alabama and Tombigbee Rivers as far southwest as modern Mobile. In January 1704 former South Carolina Governor James Moore led a military expedition of fifty whites and one thousand Indians against Spanish forts and missions near modern-day Tallahassee, returning to South Carolina with fourteen hundred captives and the Carolinians' first knowledge of Florida's gulf coast.

The first Englishmen known to have entered the Appalachian Mountains from South Carolina were Surveyor General Maurice Mathews and planter-trader James Moore. In 1690 they explored a portion of Cherokee territory "out of curiosity to see what sort of Country we might have . . . and [to] make new and further discovery of Indian trade." Native opposition, however, prevented their crossing through the mountains. The first Englishman to reach and cross the Mississippi River was Carolina trader Thomas Welch. Welch and Anthony Dodsworth opened relations with the Chickasaws in northeastern Mississippi. Soon afterward, in 1698, Welch crossed the great river to establish relations with members of the Quapaw tribe who were living near the mouth of the Arkansas River.[64]

Not all the exploring in the American South moved from east to west or was confined to the Mississippi River basin. In the 1690s several renegade French coureurs de bois made their way east from the Mississippi and Ohio Valleys. In 1692 Martin Chartier passed from the Ohio River into Maryland. A few years later Jean Couture paddled the Tennessee River upstream into Cherokee territory and then followed Indian paths on into South Carolina. Couture, who had commanded a French post in Arkansas before falling out with his superiors, was persuaded by South Carolina Governor Joseph Blake in 1699 to lead a party of English traders back to the Mississippi by way of the Tennessee and Ohio Rivers. This expedition took along presents of ammunition and trade goods for the natives and a document claiming the Mississippi River for England. The South Carolinians who accompanied Couture hoped to establish a sufficient volume of trade with the Indians of the central Mississippi Valley to prevent the French from uniting Canada with Louisiana. They would fail to accomplish this goal, but by February 1700, when Couture and his Carolinians reached the mouth of the Arkansas after a journey of almost one thousand miles, at least some Englishmen had obtained a realistic picture of the terrain, the rivers, and the peoples of the southern interior of North America. From the time Christopher Newport and John Smith sailed west to the falls of the James until Thomas Welch stood on the western bank of the Mississippi in Arkansas, ninety-one years had elapsed. What had begun as a summer's adventure in search of the western ocean had stretched to a century-long enterprise; and although they did not know it, the English were less than halfway to their original goal.

The Penetration of New England

Carolina was not the only region in which the fur trade provided the spur to exploration. The pattern in New England was similar to that in Carolina, although the process in the former was begun a half-century earlier. In both cases, exploration began with scouting ventures up and down the coast. Next, the most inviting rivers were examined. Last, bold individuals began to move across the country; invariably, movement away from the rivers entailed the use of native guides.

As in the South, geographical features in New England dictated the pace and direction of exploration. Because of major physical and geopolitical barriers to westward exploration, the thrust of expansion and discovery in the Northeast was from south to north. The Allegheny Mountain barrier not only blocked the explorers' way west but also oriented the flow of the region's major rivers from north to south. New England's rugged hills and dense forests channeled those who would explore the interior into these northward-tending river valleys. The only feasible passage leading west through the Allegheny Mountains, the Mohawk River valley, was effectively blocked by the five powerful Iroquois nations that occupied and jealously guarded the region of central New York south of Lake Ontario. The Dutch at Fort Orange (today's Albany) presented a further obstacle because they zealously guarded access to the Iroquois.

The Plymouth Pilgrims of 1620 cherished few illusions about gold mines and passages to the South Sea, dreams that had so dominated the thoughts and activities of the first Virginia settlers. The Pilgrims quickly discovered that furs obtained from the Indians were their most valuable trading commodity. The Pilgrims conducted explorations to expand commercial contacts with the natives, a process that began in September 1621. A small party of Pilgrims exploring the nearby coast landed at the Charlestown section of present-day Boston, some forty-five miles from Plymouth. Guided by Squanto, they marched half a dozen miles inland toward what is today Medford, where they exchanged goods with several native women. Not long after that simple but profitable transaction, Plymouth's small coasting vessels were searching for natives as far away as the Maine coast. In 1625 Edward Winslow explored the lower portions of the Kennebec River. Several years later Plymouth traders established a trading post at modern Augusta, Maine; by 1630, they were operating in Penobscot Bay. The Plymouth traders were also drawn to New England's southern shore. Their

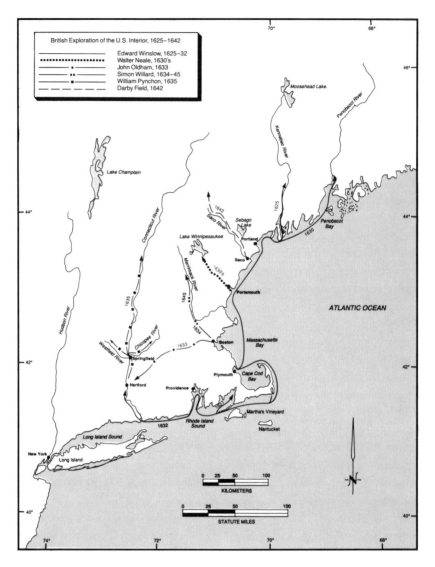

Map 13.2 British Exploration of the U.S. Interior, 1625–1642.

trading posts were operating in Buzzard's Bay after 1627 and in Rhode Island's Narragansett Bay by 1632.[65]

The Dutch trader-explorer Adrian Block had preceded the Pilgrims into the Connecticut River. In 1614, Block ascended the Connecticut almost as far as the Massachusetts boundary. In much the same way that the Westos would later seek out Henry Woodward, in 1631 the Mohegan Indians of the Connecticut River valley sent their chief, Waghinnacut, to both Plymouth and the new Massachusetts Bay settlement at Boston. Waghinnacut asked that English traders establish themselves in his territory. The Pilgrims dispatched Winslow to explore the possibility in 1632. Winslow explored the river as far north as present-day Hartford. The following year the Plymouth trader William Holmes, after running the guns of a small Dutch outpost near Hartford, established a trading station on a point in the river near the modern town of Windsor. In 1633 the Boston trader John Oldham completed the first overland passage from the bay colony to the Connecticut River. Oldham was assisted in this ninety-mile journey by several natives he met on the way. The Indian paths he followed later became known as the Connecticut Path. Oldham built his trading post at what is today Wethersfield.

The upper Connecticut River and the interior of Massachusetts were soon the domain of William Pynchon, a well-to-do, college-educated merchant who had arrived with the first contingent of Massachusetts Bay settlers in 1630. While living near Boston, he began a trade that made him aware of the wealth that might be reaped in a more advantageous location. In 1635 Pynchon, two associates, and an Indian interpreter used a small boat to explore the Connecticut River above Hartford in search of a location for a new trading post. The place they chose became Springfield, Massachusetts. The fur traders Pynchon hired and supplied fanned out from his position to explore the interior of much of New England.

The rapid depletion of beaver and other fur animals in the coastal areas forced traders all along the New England coast to do as Pynchon had done. The situation described by John Winter on Maine's Saco River in 1634 was typical of many traders in the 1630s. "The planters heare aboutes," declared Winter, "if they will have any bever must go 40 or 50 myles Into the Country with their packes on their backes."[66]

The role of explorer-trader played by Pynchon in the Connecticut River valley was reenacted by Simon Willard in the Merrimack Valley of Massachusetts and New Hampshire. In 1634, Willard obtained permission to locate at what would become Concord, Massachusetts. This site, seventeen miles west of Boston, was well beyond the frontier line. But more important for Willard's purposes, the Concord River on which he settled provided direct access to the Merrimack River and thereby to trade with the New Hampshire interior. By 1645, Willard and his associates had explored the Merrimack as far north as modern Concord, New Hampshire.

Like Pynchon and Willard, most New England traders were lured northward by the rivers and the coast; a few, however, became envious of the even greater profits being reaped by the Dutch to the west. The first significant attempt at western exploration was made in the early 1630s by Walter Neale of the Laconia Company. This company had been organized by Sir Ferdinando Gorges and others in an attempt to gain access to Lake Champlain and from there to the continental interior. The Piscataqua River, which has its mouth at modern Portsmouth, New Hampshire, was selected as the most likely route. Neale made several trips along the Piscataqua into southeastern New Hampshire but never came within two hundred miles of his objective.[67]

A second attempt to follow a Maine river to the west was made a decade later by Darby Field, an Irishman and a resident of the Portsmouth, New Hampshire, area. Field and two Indian guides paddled and portaged some seventy miles up the Saco River in southern Maine and began to ascend the White Mountains of New Hampshire a dozen or so miles south of Mount Washington. Several local natives offered to guide them into the mountains. Field passed the tree line and continued his climb for another twelve miles in "a continual ascent upon rocks." The local guides "accompanied him within 8 miles of the top, but durst go no further, telling him that no Indian ever dared to go higher, and that he would die if he went." From the mountaintop, Field imagined that he could see "the gulf of Canada" to the northeast, the coast of Maine to the southeast, and "the great lake which Canada river comes out of" to the west. Field's 1642 journey to the White Mountains took eighteen days.[68] He had penetrated about seventy-five miles inland from the coast. After the efforts of Neale and Field had become common knowledge, New Englanders put aside their dreams of Lake Champlain—just as John Smith and Abraham Wood had put aside their dreams of the South Sea.

During the summer of 1652, Massachusetts Bay authorities dispatched John Sherman and Jonathan Ince to explore for what was then a novel purpose—the clarification of boundaries. Massachusetts authorities interpreted their royal charter as establishing the colony's northern boundary at the source of the Merrimack River, and Sherman and Ince were dispatched to find that source. They followed the Merrimack to Lake Winnipesaukee, twenty-five miles north of Concord, New Hampshire, and some thirty miles southwest of the point that Field had reached ten years earlier. On the basis of Sherman and Ince's findings, Massachusetts annexed Maine that same year.[69]

By 1650, although most of the New England interior was as yet unseen by Europeans, the terrain of New England was pretty well understood and its major river systems had been explored. Even the most enterprising traders realized that the way to the fabled furs of Albany did not lie through further exploration of New England. The New England era of exploration slowed around midcentury; however, a new era was about to be opened with the English conquest of Albany.

Albany Traders Penetrate the Midwest

The Dutch had established Fort Orange, now Albany, where the Mohawk River flows from the west into the Hudson River. Each spring the Iroquois deposited at Fort Orange a wealth of pelts and in exchange carried away weapons, tools, cloth, and other European manufactures. Thus, unlike the New England and southern practice, in which the English trader took his goods to the native trading partners, the Dutch practice allowed traders to prosper by encouraging the natives to come to them. Because of this, New Netherland was not a hotbed of exploration. On only a few rare occasions did the Dutch need to enter Iroquois territory. When they did, they generally went as governmental emissaries, not as traders and explorers.

The earliest of these rare occurrences took place in 1616. It involved a two-man party, crossing from the Mohawk Valley to Lake Otsego at modern Cooperstown, New York. Although the men did not know it, they had discovered the headwaters of the Susquehanna River. The best-documented early Dutch journey occurred almost two decades later; three Dutch messengers, including Harmen Meyendertsz van den Bogaert, visited the Oneidas in December 1634, after a trek of about one hundred miles.[70] There were certainly other such ventures, but they were limited to travel to and from the principal towns of the Iroquois, who actively discouraged outsiders in their midst. In addition, the major Albany traders, whose livelihood depended on the Iroquois, guarded their own monopoly by preventing independent traders or settlers from traveling very far west of Albany.

No English colony was positioned sufficiently close to the Iroquois to offer competition for the Dutch. Nonetheless, the lure of the Iroquois fur trade produced at least two attempts to find a new route into their territory. The first was the Laconia Company's effort in New Hampshire during the early 1630s. The other occurred in 1644–45 when several Massachusetts merchants formed a company with the intent of circumventing Albany by way of the then-unexplored upper Delaware River. Captain William Aspinwell, one of the investors in the project, commanded a small expedition dispatched to the Delaware. The project came to naught when Aspinwell found his way blocked by a Dutch fortification. Aspinwell contented himself with exploring and trading on Delaware Bay before returning to Massachusetts Bay the following spring.[71]

After the English took control of the area they renamed New York in 1664, they continued to rely on the established Dutch traders and their Iroquois connections—with the furs now going to England instead of Holland. Of the earliest representatives of the English regime in New York, two were known to have penetrated the interior; these "Christians" (a term that probably denoted Dutch traders) traveled almost two hundred miles through the heart of Iroquois country to deliver a message from Governor Edmund Andros to the Senecas in 1677. Several other messenger parties, one led by Wentworth Greenhalgh, were also sent from Albany that year to other Iroquois towns.[72]

In 1683 Thomas Dongan became New York's governor. This imperial-minded Irishman was determined to press England's and New York's claims to the Great Lakes region beyond the Iroquois homeland. Dongan soon discovered that for more than a decade, French coureurs de bois had been selling furs purchased north of Lake Ontario at Albany. If strangers could accomplish this feat, Dongan reasoned, why not New Yorkers? Beginning in Dongan's first year as governor, New York authorities approved the hiring of renegade Frenchmen to show selected Albany traders the way to the west.

After obtaining Iroquois permission for English subjects to venture through their territory, Dongan authorized Johannes Roseboom of Albany to initiate the first English-sponsored exploration of the Great Lakes. In the fall of 1685, Roseboom's little flotilla of ten merchandise-filled canoes, guided by the French deserter Abel Merrion, followed the Mohawk River and native trails to Lake Ontario. They paralleled the southern shore of the lake west to the Niagara River, where they portaged south to Lake Erie. After a journey of three months and eight hundred miles, Roseboom and his men reached Michilimackinac, Michigan, at the head of Lake Huron. Informing the natives of their willingness to trade, the party then settled in to wait out the winter. The following spring they conducted a highly successful trading season and headed home. Assisted by Seneca warriors they met on Lake Erie, Roseboom and his explorers eluded French pursuit and made their return to Albany in the late spring of 1686.[73]

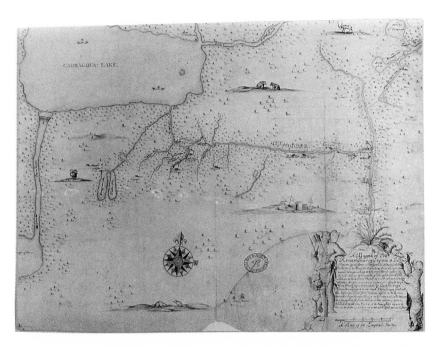

13.3 "A Mappe of Coll. Romer his Journey to the 5 Indian Nations going from New York to Albany" (Wolfgang Romer, 1700). The extent of English knowledge of the Hudson-Mohawk Valleys is shown on this map, as is fairly accurate information on Lake Ontario ("Cadragqua Lake") and its relationship to Lake Erie to the south. The map even shows a great falls (Niagara), just before the entry into Lake Ontario of the connecting river from Lake Erie. Courtesy of the Public Record Office, London, CO 700 New York 13A.

News that the English were deep in the interior of New France was a matter of consequence even three thousand miles away in London and Paris. Quebec's Governor, the Marquis de Denonville, raised a shrill cry of alarm. "Missilimakinak is theirs," he warned his superiors. "They have taken its latitude, have been to trade there with our Outawa and Huron Indians, who received them cordially on account of the bargains they gave." For his part, Governor Dongan informed his superiors that the Ottawa Indians, from whom his men had obtained "a good many beavers," were "about three months journey to the west and N.W. of Albany."[74]

The Albany trading community made immediate preparations to exploit the newly discovered route west. A much larger expedition was planned for the next year's trading season, but only a portion of it could be made ready for a fall departure. The plan therefore was to send out twenty-nine traders with twenty canoes under Roseboom's command that fall. They were to winter with the colony's Seneca allies on the shores of Lake Erie. From there, they could reach Lake Huron in time for the spring 1687 trading season.

A second party of traders, under the direction of Major Patrick Mac-Gregory, left Albany in April 1687 intending to rendezvous with Roseboom near Michilimackinac. Unfortunately for the English traders, Governor Denonville had ordered his military forces in the west to concentrate at Niagara for a summer campaign against the Iroquois. Since those traveling a lake by canoe generally stayed within sight of shore, Roseboom's flotilla, northbound on Lake Huron, ran straight into the arms of a stronger southbound French and Indian flotilla. A similar fate befell MacGregory and his thirty men on Lake Erie. The French escorted their sixty or so prisoners to Niagara and then to Quebec. After being imprisoned for four months and receiving a sharp warning to stay out of French territory, the captive explorers were returned to Albany.

The financial loss incurred in 1687, the increased risk of capture as the French established posts at Niagara, Detroit, and elsewhere along the route Roseboom had taken, and the outbreak of King William's War in 1689 effectively thwarted the English explorers' and traders' efforts to break through the mountain barrier by way of the Mohawk Valley and the Great Lakes. Occasionally an individual would claim, as did John Mashe, to have traveled to the westernmost of the Great Lakes, but after 1689 such assertions were very rare.[75]

Shortly after the closing off of the Ottawa trade, a new opportunity presented itself to the Albany trading community in an area that was then almost as isolated from the French as from the English. In August 1692 a delegation of one hundred Shawnees from northern Kentucky crossed from Pennsylvania into southern New York and made their way to Albany. The Shawnees, like the Tomahitans, Mohegans, Westos, and others before them, had come in the hope of showing English traders the way to their Kentucky homelands. With normal trade disrupted by the war with France, the Albany traders had the resources to make a major commitment to this new but risky undertaking.

The man chosen to head this expedition was Arnout Viele, an Albany Dutchman who for more than a decade had traveled extensively in Iroquois country as an interpreter-diplomat for the colony. Viele, who had lived "a long time with the Indians and frequently converse[d] with them," had been with Roseboom on Lake Huron but had lost his position as interpreter because he had supported an unsuccessful rebellion against the local authorities in 1689.[76]

Only scant information has been pieced together about this first known European exploration of the Ohio River valley. Viele, eleven companions, most of the Shawnee delegation, and a few loyal Delaware guides left Albany in early autumn 1692. They traveled south, crossing portions of present-day New Jersey and eastern Pennsylvania. They apparently followed the West Branch of the Susquehanna River into the mountains, reached some tributary of the Allegheny River, and floated down it to the Ohio River. Viele's "Christians" spent over a year exploring the Ohio and its tributaries. Evidently they spent most of 1693 in northern Kentucky with their Shawnee hosts, but Viele seems to have made contact with nations located as far west as the Wabash River border between modern-day Indiana and Illinois. If Viele and his explorers were indeed as far west as the Wabash, they had journeyed almost nine hundred miles south and west of Albany.

In February 1694 Gerrit Luykasse, two of Viele's Dutch traders, and two Shawnees reappeared at Albany on a mission "to fech powder for Arnout [Viele] and his Company." That August, Viele and his companions appeared out of the Pennsylvania wilderness—accompanied by hundreds of Shawnees who intended to relocate on the upper Delaware River and by the diplomats of "seven Nations of Indians" seeking either trade with the English or peace with the Iroquois.[77]

The two-year length of Viele's trip, the great distance involved, and the immense difficulties of crossing the Alleghenies with heavy packs precluded a second Ohio venture. Almost a quarter-century would pass before the English returned to the Ohio Valley in significant numbers. Nonetheless, Viele's 1693 Ohio exploration established him as one of the great seventeenth-century "English" explorers of North America. Viele's travels to Lake Huron and the Ohio River matched Gabriel Arthur's thirty-three hundred miles of wilderness travel. Both had crossed the Appalachians. Arthur had traveled farther on foot, but Viele had spent a much greater portion of his life living beyond the English frontier.

By the beginning of the eighteenth century the English had probed west of the Appalachian mountain barrier at three points—by way of the Mohawk, along the Susquehanna, and around the southern end of the mountains. In the Great Lakes and on the lower Mississippi, the French had been strong enough to maintain dominion over their Saint Lawrence, Huron, Erie, Maumee, Wabash, and Mississippi communications-and-supply lifeline. But between the Appalachians and the Wabash lay a kind of no-man's land. The upper Ohio River valley had largely eluded the notice of both French and English.

Pennsylvanians and Virginians Contend for the Ohio

In the eighteenth century, while English traders and governmental emissaries ventured into southern areas left unexplored in the late seventeenth century, the thrust of English exploration shifted northward. From Pennsylvania and Virginia, explorers in the guise of fur traders pushed into the no-man's land of the Ohio River valley via the West Branch of the Susquehanna and the upper Potomac River. Pennsylvania-based fur traders led the way.

Because of the extreme isolation of the Ohio frontier, few documents record when and how traders advanced from one area to another. Several clues suggest that the Albany "Dutch" had built several storehouses on the upper Ohio as early as 1725. Pennsylvania-based James Le Tort was trading in Ohio by 1727 and was reportedly preparing a 1728 expedition to the Miamis who lived south of Lake Michigan.[78]

In the second quarter-century, English traders vied with French traders throughout the Ohio and Wabash Valleys. Paul Chrisler Phillips, a leading authority on the fur trade, has stated that by 1748, "the advance of British colonial traders had jeopardized French fur trade on the Ohio and Wabash, and was dangerously close to cutting communications between Canada and Louisiana." One historian has estimated, "By the middle of the eighteenth century there were three hundred traders in the Ohio country." By 1748, the French commander of the Illinois region reported that Englishmen were even inciting the Indians along the Mississippi River.[79]

The first Virginians to enter the region came not for furs but for land and adventure. In 1742, five Virginians journeyed to the Ohio via a new and unexplored route. Their leader was John Howard, a carpenter. Their chronicler was John Peter Salley, a German farmer who lived near Natural Bridge in Virginia's Shenandoah Valley. Howard had obtained from the governor and the Council of Virginia a commission, as Salley later recalled, to "travel

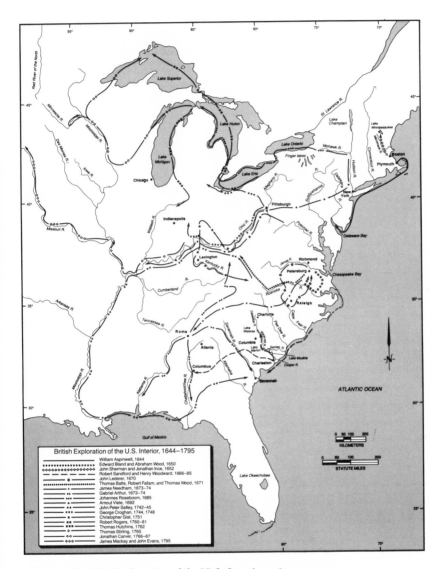

Map 13.3 British Exploration of the U.S. Interior, 1644–1795.

to the westward of this colony as far as the river Mississippi in order to make Discovery of the Country." Of all the seventeenth- and eighteenth-century English explorations, that of Howard and Salley most appears to have the character of a lark (as well as, possibly, Governor Alexander Spotswood's 1716 "Knights of the Golden Horseshoe" excursion). Salley

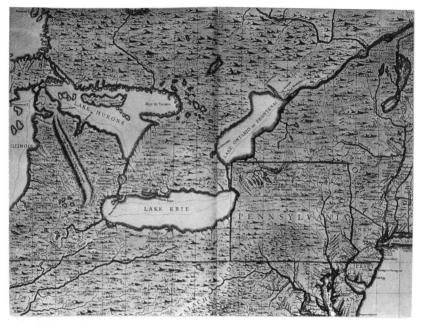

13.4 "Map of the Northern Colonies" (Henry Popple, 1733), map no. 6 from Popple's British Empire in America (London, 1733). This map illustrates the rapid growth in English knowledge of the interior in a period of a little more than half a century, as seen when this map is compared with the crude and largely speculative geography of Locke's map of 1671 (figure 13.2). Courtesy The Newberry Library.

and his companions had no goals in mind, except to share in a reward of ten thousand acres of western land. They were essentially five adventurers in search of adventure.[80]

Near Radford, Virginia, the explorers killed several buffalo and used the hides to construct a boat large enough for themselves and their supplies. Launching it on the New River, they floated some sixty miles westward into the heart of the West Virginia Appalachians. Near Beckley, West Virginia, they abandoned the river because of dangerous rapids and "a great many Falls." They traveled southwest on foot for two days, not knowing where they were or where they were going. Eventually, they came to a river, which they named the Coal River.[81]

Building a new "Barge," they floated the Coal to the Kanawha, the Kanawha to the Ohio, and the Ohio to the Mississippi. In early June 1742 they began a leisurely descent of the Mississippi. For a month they encountered no one. Then, near where Thomas Welch had traded at the mouth of the Arkansas River forty-four years earlier, the five Virginians were surprised and taken prisoner by a party of Frenchmen. Assuming the Virginians to be spies, the French authorities at New Orleans imprisoned them. After almost two years of close confinement, Howard and Salley organized separate attempts to escape. Howard was quickly recaptured, but Salley and another member of the party, assisted by a French inmate who knew the territory, constructed another hide boat, which they paddled across Lake Pontchartrain with paddles made from a bull's shoulder blade.

The fugitives fled east to the Gulf coast, took refuge with the Choctaws for two months, and then canoed along the Alabama shore. They went ashore east of Pensacola Bay and walked overland to the Creeks in central Georgia. From there they were sent along the long-used trading paths to Charleston. After a three-year absence, Salley, given up for dead by his family, reached his Virginia home. In all, Salley had traveled over two thousand miles. He and his companions were the first to explore central West Virginia; the rest of their route was, however, already well-traveled.[82]

Although a number of British traders had fanned out from western Pennsylvania into the old Northwest by the mid–eighteenth century, the most influential, and very likely the most widely traveled, was Irish-born George Croghan. Croghan was also Pennsylvania's interpreter and ambassador to the Indians of Ohio. In the late 1750s he was made a deputy to Sir William Johnson, superintendent of the Northern Department of Indian Affairs. Because of these varied roles, Croghan often spearheaded the British advance into territory previously known only to the French and Indians.

Because of Lake Erie's proximity to Detroit, English traders in Ohio avoided its southern shore in favor of the Ohio River. Croghan, however, made his way to the lake. In 1744 he opened trade with the Senecas at present-day Cleveland, Ohio, and with the Wyandots and Twightwees farther west at Sandusky. Threatened with retaliation for trading with the British, in 1748 the Sandusky tribes determined to put a greater distance between themselves and the French. The Twightwees, or Miamis, under their Franco-phobe Chief "Old Briton," resettled at Pickawillany on the upper portion of Ohio's Great Miami River near modern-day Piqua. Of necessity, Croghan shifted his trading activities from Lake Erie to Pickawillany and southwestern Ohio. The English presence at Pickawillany now threatened the French portage between the Maumee and the Wabash only seventy miles away and, therefore, communications between Quebec and

New Orleans. Four years later, a band of pro-French Indians would destroy Pickawillany, but at midcentury the British flag flew deep in the French interior, symbolizing the British claim to the Ohio Valley—a claim that, interestingly enough, was based in part on the 1671 exploration of Batts and Fallam.[83]

During the winter of 1750–51, Croghan and another Pennsylvania interpreter, Andrew Montaur, were dispatched with a message inviting the Ohio natives to attend a conference with Pennsylvania authorities at Logstown. Ironically, the two interpreters, representatives of Pennsylvania's fur trading interests, were joined at present-day Marietta, Ohio, by a land surveyor from Virginia. Christopher Gist had been sent to reconnoiter the region for the Ohio Company, a group of Virginia land speculators. The Maryland-born Gist, forty-four years old, had been lured from his frontier North Carolina home to identify prime agricultural tracts in what is today Ohio and Kentucky, but he wisely hid this fact from Croghan and Montaur.

Departing from Cumberland, Maryland, in October 1750, Gist traveled a trail (later known as Braddock's Road) that had been cut by Thomas Cresap for the Ohio Company and that connected the eastward-flowing Potomac with the westward-flowing Monongahela. On reaching the Monongahela, Gist floated downriver until by accident he came on Croghan, whose party he joined in January 1751. The interpreters and the surveyor traveled overland through southern Ohio to the mouth of the Scioto at modern Portsmouth. They then followed the Scioto north to the Lower Shawnee Town at present-day Chillicothe, where Croghan had one of his wilderness storehouses. From Chillicothe they rode ninety miles northwest across west-central Ohio to Pickawillany.

Gist left Croghan at Pickawillany, returned to the Ohio by way of the Little Miami River, crossed to the Kentucky side of the Ohio, and continued west until he reached the Licking River opposite modern Cincinnati. Here, he detected signs of a large hunting party, which he suspected of being "French Indians." Rather than risk capture, he turned southeast across Kentucky and made his way back to Virginia.[84]

A year earlier, another group of Virginia land speculators, led by Dr. Thomas Walker, a Fredericksburg surgeon, had discovered the Cumberland Gap. The Gap would be made famous as an avenue to the west by the Kentucky "Long Hunters" in the late 1760s. Using the Cumberland Gap, John Finley as early as 1767 and Daniel Boone in 1769 explored the interior portions of Kentucky.

The path that General James Wolfe discovered from the Saint Lawrence

River to the Plains of Abraham and the gates of Quebec led directly to the British occupation of a vast empire already well-known to the French and Indians but virtually unknown to all but a handful of British citizens. The expedition that would establish British control over France's western posts and simultaneously introduce Englishmen to a vast acreage from which they had previously been barred was assembled in the fall of 1760 at Presque Isle, modern-day Erie, Pennsylvania. Its commander was Major Robert Rogers of Rogers' Rangers, but second only to Rogers in importance was George Croghan. That fall the British took possession of Detroit, Fort Miamis at modern Fort Wayne, Indiana, and Fort Ouiatenon on the Wabash below today's Lafayette, Indiana. The following year, Rogers's men established the British presence at Michilimackinac, at Sault Sainte Marie, and at other smaller outposts on Lake Superior. In 1761, British forces also explored Lake Michigan, raising the Union Jack over Fort Saint Joseph at its southern end and Fort La Baye in Green Bay.

One of the earliest British accounts of this region is a journal kept by Ensign Thomas Hutchins, a British army engineer deputized by Croghan to map the newly acquired area. Hutchins traveled the water route to Fort Saint Joseph (present-day Niles, Michigan), then struck inland across central Indiana. He would later prepare one of the first British maps of the area between the Ohio River and the Great Lakes, a map based largely on this journey.[85]

Soon after the British had established their claim to the west, they were virtually driven out of their newly won empire by the native uprising known as Pontiac's Rebellion. By mid-June 1763 only Forts Detroit, Niagara, and Pitt remained in British hands. Two years later Croghan was again called on to lead a delegation to Illinois in an attempt to pacify Pontiac, the great Ottawa leader, and the last rebellious holdouts, the Illinois tribes. Croghan's small force failed to reach Illinois. Near the mouth of the Wabash, Croghan and his company were attacked and taken prisoner by a band of Kickapoos. Croghan's captors took their prisoners to Ouiatenon, where they were pressured by other natives to free the British. Soon after, Pontiac and the chiefs of four Illinois nations appeared at Ouiatenon. Croghan was thus able to gain their assent to allowing a peaceful British occupation of the French posts in Illinois.[86]

In the fall of 1765, the British sent a small detachment of soldiers, under Captain Thomas Stirling, to take possession of Fort Kaskaskia on the eastern bank of the Mississippi some sixty-five miles south of modern Saint Louis, Missouri, and with it, symbolically at least, the Illinois country. In

December 1765 Major Robert Farmer and his Thirty-fourth Regiment, having departed from Mobile, Alabama, arrived in Illinois after an eight-month ascent of the Mississippi.[87]

In June 1766 Croghan set off for Illinois a second time. Commanding a fleet of over a dozen craft, Croghan had been directed to deliver presents to the Illinois natives and provisions to the British garrison. Accompanying Croghan were Captain Harry Gordon and Ensign Thomas Hutchins, assigned to produce an accurate map of the course of the Ohio. In mid-August, after a journey of almost eight hundred miles, the diplomat and the cartographers landed at Fort Chartres on the Mississippi, forty miles above Kaskaskia.

Exploration between the Great Lakes and the Great Mountains

While Croghan, Gordon, and Hutchins mapped the Ohio and the British side of the Mississippi between British Illinois and Spanish Missouri, Major Rogers was initiating plans to send explorers across Wisconsin and to the west of the upper Mississippi in Minnesota. In recognition of his wartime service, Rogers had been given command of Fort Michilimackinac, a position he assumed in the summer of 1766.

Earlier that year Rogers had been in Massachusetts, where he had been introduced to a fifty-six-year-old, unemployed, ex-militia captain named Jonathan Carver. Carver, who had taught himself the rudiments of surveying and mapmaking, sought and gained employment under Rogers, as did another ex-soldier from Massachusetts, Captain James Tute.[88] Rogers had grandiose plans for himself and his Michilimackinac post, plans that brought Carver and Tute west. He not only hoped to steal the fur trade away from Spanish and French fur traders operating out of New Orleans by way of Saint Louis but also had revived the two-century-old British dream of finding a water route to the Pacific.

On a recent visit to Britain, Rogers had presented a plan to the Board of Trade; he proposed that the government finance a three-year expedition to search for the elusive Northwest Passage. Rogers's optimism arose out of another of those geographical myths that had so captivated the thinking of men like John Smith and Abraham Wood. He was convinced that once the source of the Mississippi River was located, only a short portage would be required "from thence to the River called by the Indians Ouragon, which flows into a Bay that projects . . . from the Pacific Ocean." Rogers, prone to overextend himself financially, had his sights set on winning a $20,000 Northwest Passage prize established by the British government in 1744. Rogers had promised Carver and Tute eight shillings a day to lay the groundwork for this project. They were to explore and map the upper Mississippi and beyond, in anticipation of future approval of the extended exploration by the Board of Trade.

Reaching Michilimackinac, Rogers teamed Carver with William Bruce, one of the first British traders to enter Wisconsin, and sent them to map the route (including the locations and sizes of Indian towns) from Wisconsin's Green Bay to the falls of Saint Anthony at present-day Minneapolis, Minnesota. Tute was teamed with the man said to have more influence with the Indians than any other in the region, James Stanley Goddard. Goddard and Tute followed Carver and Bruce into the Wisconsin wilderness but failed to catch up to them. With the coming of the snows, Tute and Goddard wintered on the Iowa side of the Mississippi near Prairie du Chien, Wisconsin. Carver and Bruce had by then already reached the falls, 125 miles farther north. From there they set off to the southwest to explore the Minnesota River. How far they advanced along the Minnesota is a matter of controversy. The most reasonable estimate is that they wintered near Swan Lake in present-day Nicollet County in south-central Minnesota.[89]

With the spring thaw, Carver led a party of Dakota Indians downriver to Prairie du Chien, where he joined Tute and Goddard. Here, in an attempt to earn native loyalty to the British trading post at Michilimackinac, the explorers gave away most of the trade goods, five hundred pounds worth, which Rogers had intended for the tribes that they would meet on their way to the headwaters of the Mississippi.

Believing that without further orders, they had no authority to proceed beyond the falls of Saint Anthony, the explorers headed off to the northeast along Wisconsin's Chippewa and Namekagon Rivers to Grand Portage on Lake Superior at the northeastern tip of Minnesota. The explorers were still eager to proceed along well-established French trading trails into modern-day Saskatchewan, but they had exhausted their supplies. They communicated their predicament, via the lake, to Rogers.

By the time Rogers received their message, he had made a number of enemies in his new post, and his superiors were questioning the large amounts already expended on unauthorized explorations. In short, Rogers could give Carver no more assistance. In August 1767 the exploring party piloted its canoes down the lake to Michilimackinac. Four months later Rogers was placed under arrest by orders of General Thomas Gage. Carver, who had never been paid for his efforts, returned to his native New England in the summer of 1768, intending to make money from the experience by writing a book about his adventures. From Green Bay to Grand Portage, Carver had traveled over one thousand miles through the farthest reaches of the Northwest. He was among the first British citizens to explore west of the Mississippi River.[90]

The western bank of the Mississippi had been confirmed as Spanish territory by the Treaty of Paris in 1763. In the years that followed that treaty, a few British traders may have crossed the river to try their luck, but in general the British had reached the western limits of the territory, from Illinois to the Gulf of Mexico, that was theirs to explore. North and farther west of Illinois, however, was another of those no-man's lands that occasionally existed between rival European powers. It was into this region that Rogers had probed, but the geography favored access from the south and from the north more than from the east. In the last decade of the eighteenth century, the struggle for empire focused along the Missouri River. The precursors who prepared the way for the 1804 ascent of the Missouri River by Meriwether Lewis and William Clark are not well-known; however, without their probings, Lewis and Clark may not have succeeded in reaching the Pacific.

In the late eighteenth century, those who thought themselves knowledgeable about the as-yet-unexplored West assumed that the Missouri River offered the best opportunity for discovering the long-sought water passage to the Pacific. As early as 1674, French officials had postulated that along the western reaches of the Missouri "one will perhaps arrive at some lake which discharges toward the west." A little later the narratives of Father Louis Hennepin suggested that the Missouri sprang "from a Mountain about twelve days' Journey from its Mouth" and that beyond the mountain "some great River" ran to the Pacific. In the eighteenth century the apocryphal account of Louis Armand de Lom d'Arce, baronde Lahontan, further popularized the idea of a "Long River," a tributary to the Mississippi, along which lived nations of Native Americans whose levels of civilization and wealth rivaled those of the Europeans. Thus, when the Spanish and then later the Americans acquired title to the lower Missouri, the orthodox belief was that the Missouri offered the most practicable route for the next great assault on the Pacific.[91]

British explorations undertaken by Robert Rogers and Alexander Mackenzie added two refinements to the geographical conception of the conti-

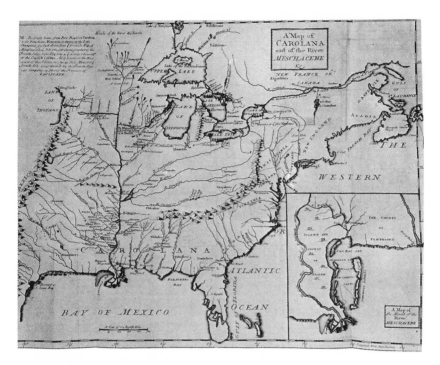

13.5 "A Map of Carolana and of the River Meschacebe" (Daniel Coxe, 1722), published in Coxe, A Description of the English Province of Carolana (London,
1722). The Coxe map shows the importance of French geographical thought in English conceptions of the interior. It also illustrates the persistence of the apocryphal
journey of Baron Lahontan, whose Lake Thoyago and Mozemleek peoples are shown
in the northwestern section of the map. For all that it is derivative and contains
much speculative geography, Coxe's map was a major part of early American images
of the western half of the Mississippi basin. Courtesy The Newberry Library.

nental divide. In the 1760s, Rogers proposed an expedition to find a pyra-
midal height of land on which, he believed, originated the great rivers of
the continent including the Mississippi and the "Ouragan." The discovery
of this continental high point would allow easy access in all directions. In
1793 Alexander Mackenzie of Britain's North West Company entered the
Canadian Rockies by way of the Peace River. Near its source he discovered
"a beaten path leading over a low ridge of land." This path of only a few
hundred yards had directed him to a westward-flowing stream. He had
crossed the continental divide by means of a low ridge and a short portage.

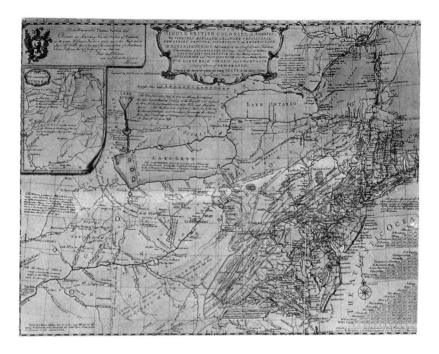

13.6 "A general Map of the Middle British Colonies, in America" (Lewis Evans, 1755). In sharp contrast to the Coxe map and its inventive geography, Evans's map was highly refined, indicating the growth in geographical knowledge over the course of only about a quarter-century. Evans's map was one of the most important of the later eighteenth century and was used in numerous legal situations, including treaty negotiations ending both the French and Indian (Seven Years) War and the American Revolution. Evans was the first cartographer to show clearly the configuration of the Ridge and Valley country of eastern Pennsylvania. By permission of The British Library.

The publication of Mackenzie's journals established in British minds the idea that at other places, such as at the source of the Missouri, only a very short portage would be required to pass from eastward- to westward-flowing rivers.[92]

The occupation of the eastern side of the Mississippi by the unpredictable citizens of the newly independent United States, coupled with the encroachments of British fur traders from Canada into what the Spanish considered their territory, stimulated Spanish fur traders based in Saint Louis to "ascertain the discovery of the Pacific Sea" by way of the Missouri.

Ironically, the two men who would undertake this project were a Scotsman and a Welshman.[93] In 1795 their trading-exploring party set out from Saint Louis, sponsored by the Spanish Compania de descubridores del Misuri ("Company of the Explorers of the Missouri"). Their mission was "to open a commerce with those distant and Unknown Nations in the upper parts of the Missouri and to discover all the unknown parts of his Catholic Majesty's Dominions through the continent as far as the Pacific Ocean." In addition, the men were to construct forts where necessary to prevent the continuing encroachment on the fur trade by the Canadians. The leader of this expedition was James Mackay, a Scotsman turned Spanish subject. Mackay had already traded at the Mandan villages on the upper Missouri in 1787, traveling to them from the north under the auspices of the Canadian North West Company; but around 1793 he moved into Spanish territory and changed his allegiance. Mackay's assistant was John Evans, a young Welsh adventurer who had recently come to America on a strange mission.[94]

A Welsh legend, which seems to have had its origin after the discovery of the New World, related that Madoc, a son of Owain, king of Gwynedd, had discovered a new land as early as 1170 while sailing far to the west. Madoc, so the legend said, returned to Wales, recruited settlers, and sailed away, never to be heard of again. When, in the seventeenth century, a Welsh minister claimed to have been captured in Virginia by a tribe of Indians who understood the Welsh language, the legend asserting a Welsh discovery of the New World was expanded to include the information that Madoc had taken with him a Welsh Bible that was still preserved by "Welsh" Indians. In the late eighteenth century, certain Welsh nationalists kept alive the belief that a tribe of "white" Indians, the descendants of Madoc's settlers, lived deep in the American interior.[95]

The legend of Madoc was a favorite theme of a Welsh poet and literary forger, Iolo Morganwg, who was in 1791 living in London. Influenced by Morganwg's stories and forged evidence, the Welsh community in London began a drive for funds to send Morganwg to America in search of the "white" Indians. When at the last moment Morganwg declined to make the journey, a relatively unknown young Welshman named John Evans was sent on the search instead. Evans might have had second thoughts if he had known that Owain never had a son named Madoc, that there were no Welsh Bibles until four hundred years after Owain's death, and that Morganwg regularly fabricated "historical" documents, but not knowing the truth brought Evans to Saint Louis and to the attention of James Mackay.[96]

Despite the romanticism of his initial motivation, Evans proved to be an intrepid explorer and outstanding cartographer. Evans's maps, edited by Mackay, would later provide major assistance to the Lewis and Clark expedition.[97] In late August 1795 Mackay and Evans, accompanied by thirty-two men, set forth from Saint Louis in four large boats filled with trade goods. In mid-October they rested and reprovisioned with the Oto Indians, just south of present-day Omaha, Nebraska. By November, the company had moved upriver, reached the Omaha Indians, and started construction of a fort on the western bank, near modern Sioux City, Iowa. Mackay held conferences with Chief Blackbird and his principal advisers, preaching to them about "the bad conduct that they had observed towards the [Spanish] traders" who had preceded Mackay and the advantages that would come from trading with the Missouri Company. Mackay thereby gained the support of the powerful Chief Blackbird.[98]

With winter setting in, Mackay devoted his time to replenishing his food and trade supplies and to completing the first fort built in present-day Nebraska. He named it Fort Charles in honor of Charles IV of Spain. While waiting for provisions and more trade goods from Saint Louis, Mackay sent out a party headed by Evans to investigate rumors of trouble among several tribes up the Missouri. Evans got as far as the White River of South Dakota before his party had to make a hasty retreat to Fort Charles because of Sioux hostility.

Worried over the intrusion of Canadian traders on the upper Missouri, Mackay again ordered Evans and a small party toward the Mandans. On 28 January 1796, he wrote a long list of instructions that delineated Evans's objectives. Mackay's concern over the Canadians was not that they would capture the fur trade but that they would take control of the upper Missouri River, the area he believed contained a passage to the Pacific Ocean. Evans was instructed to mark his route to the Pacific by "notching some trees or by some piles of stones engraved and cut," being sure "to place in large letters Charles IV of Spain" along with the day, month, and year "in order to serve as unquestionable proof of the journey." Evans was also cautioned to ascertain, but steer clear of, possible Russian settlements along the coast.[99] These latter instructions recall similar precautions urged on Lederer and on Batts and Fallam over 120 years before, when the British had feared that their exploration of the Appalachians would carry them into territory claimed by Spain.

Evans and his party traveled three hundred miles up the Missouri to the White River, only to be repulsed again by the Sioux. Despite the danger,

Evans was sent out yet once more in May 1796, armed with the power to confiscate the property of trespassing Canadian traders. Exploring the rivers and riverbanks as well as drawing remarkably accurate maps on this journey up the Missouri, Evans finally arrived at the Mandan villages (near present-day Bismarck, North Dakota) in September 1796 after a journey of over seven hundred miles from Fort Charles.[100]

Evans presented medals, flags, and presents to the Mandans in the name of Charles IV and received from them promises of allegiance to the Spanish monarch. He hoisted the Spanish flag above a small fort built by Canadian traders and renamed it Fort Mackay. In October, several of these traders returned to the villages, outnumbering Evans and his company. Evans survived two assassination attempts instigated by the Canadian traders and forced them from Mandan territory. His party remained with the Mandans during the winter of 1796–97.[101]

Evans lived six months among the Mandans, gathering as much information as he could about what lay westward beyond the villages. The Mandans differed from most other Plains Indians in that they were agricultural, had permanent log houses built within fortified log palisades, and were friendly to the point of promiscuity.[102] The myths about Welsh Indians had always pointed to the Mandans. Obviously, since Evans made no mention of this in his reports, he also realized that these were not the illusory Welshmen who were said to have preceded Columbus to the New World. In early May 1797, weakened by illness and hunger and realizing that the Pacific was far beyond his reach, Evans descended the Missouri only to find Fort Charles deserted. Mackay, who had been exploring what is now the state of Nebraska, had run out of goods and departed for Saint Louis.[103]

The importance of the Mackay and Evans expedition is summarized in Mackay's assertion that he had accomplished his mission "to pave the way for the discovery & Commerce of that vast Country on both sides of the Missouri & across the Continent to the Pacific ocean . . . as much as could be expected from the resources & support" that had been given him. Furthermore he claimed, "I also took a chart of the Missouri from its mouth to the wanutaries nation, which following the windings of the river is a little short of 1800 miles."[104] Mackay exaggerated his own mapmaking efforts, but without the seven Evans-Mackay maps supplied by Thomas Jefferson, Lewis and Clark may not have triumphed in their crossing of the continent.

Seven months after Evans had departed from the upper Missouri,

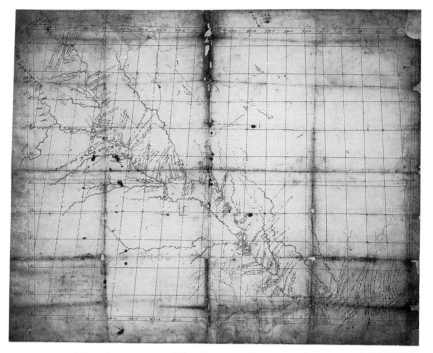

13.7 Map of the Missouri River (John Evans and James Mackay, c. 1797). Although the maps of the Evans and Mackay exploration are not striking in either their sweep or their detail, they were historically important as the first truly accurate maps of the Missouri River below the Mandan villages. This map was an important part of the geographical information available to Lewis and Clark before their 1804–6 expedition. Courtesy of the Library of Congress.

David Thompson, another young Welsh explorer and cartographer, reached the Mandan villages. He, however, had no interest in Welsh Indians. After leaving the employ of the Hudson Bay Company, Thompson had immediately joined the Canadian North West Company in May 1797 because he was offered more scope to pursue his life-long preoccupations with astronomy, cartography, surveying, and exploration. Indeed, his first assignment from the North West Company was to make a survey of the Canadian border regions with the United States and Spain. Although the survey would benefit the lucrative fur trade of the company, Thompson did not have to deal in trade. In ten months he traveled over four thousand miles, mapping the route from Lake Superior to Lake Winnipeg as well as much of Manitoba and Saskatchewan, an accomplishment that Victor

Hopwood, an authority on Thompson, calls "one of the world's great feats of surveying."[105]

In December 1797 Thompson, accompanied by a group of traders, crossed the wintry plains to the Mandan villages on the upper Missouri. Each day Thompson faithfully recorded temperatures, latitudes, and longitudes. Interestingly, Thompson's guide and interpreter for the journey to the Mandans was Rene Jussaume, who had instigated the assassination attempts on Evans only a few months earlier.[106]

Despite the dangers of traveling in winter, in February 1798 Thompson, who had returned to Canada, set off to the southeast in search of the source of the Mississippi River. In late April 1798 Thompson determined the source of the Mississippi to be Turtle Lake in north-central Minnesota. Later surveyors, however, have designated Lake Itasca, a few miles to the south of Turtle Lake, to be the headwaters of the Mississippi.[107]

Thompson's contributions have been largely overshadowed by those of Alexander Mackenzie. Nonetheless, Thompson was a careful and methodical explorer who included topography, geology, animal life, vivid descriptions of native life, daily meteorologic notes, maps, and latitudes and longitudes in his journals. His work was the basis of virtually every important map of the region published in the first half of the nineteenth century. In his twenty-eight years of exploration, he traveled over fifty-five thousand miles by foot, horse, boat, and dog sled, mapping much of the unknown territory of the Canadian interior. He would later explore beyond the Rocky Mountains and travel to the mouth of the Columbia River. Unlike John Smith in the seventeenth century or George Croghan in the eighteenth century, Thompson epitomized a new breed of explorer: one who utilized all the tools of science and cartography available to him.[108]

Mackay, Evans, and Thompson had explored significant portions of Nebraska, South Dakota, North Dakota, and northern Minnesota. With the knowledge they had gained and recorded, the newly independent United States was finally positioned for a successful drive to complete the two-hundred-year-old goal of reaching the Pacific.

14 / The Exploration of the Pacific Coast

JAMES R. GIBSON

On the world map of the middle of the eighteenth century, the Pacific coast of North America, with the exception of New Spain, was one of the few shorelines that remained unknown to nonnative peoples; the only longer uncharted coasts were those of the Arctic and Antarctic. Indeed, the entire North Pacific was so unknown that when Jonathan Swift published *Gulliver's Travels* in 1726, he confidently set the imaginary and dilapidated island empire of Laputa (including Balnibarbi, Glubbdubdrib, and Luggnagg) off the coast of Japan and made Brobdingnag, the mythical land of giants, a six-thousand-mile-long peninsula of California. This anonymity was simply the result of the relative locations of the imperial powers and the directions of their colonial expansion. Britain, Holland, Portugal, and Spain had expanded overseas from western Europe to the Atlantic margins of the Americas and Africa and to the Indian Ocean shores of Africa and Asia first, leaving the more forbidding North Pacific and Arctic coasts of Asia and North America for last. By the eighteenth century, only Britain and France, unlike Holland, Portugal, Russia, and Spain, lacked convenient springboards for Pacific exploration; all ports of call in South America were controlled by Portugal or Spain, the Cape Horn entrance (the Drake Passage) was difficult, and Holland and Spain controlled the western approaches of the East Indies and the Philippines.

The chief technical obstacle was an accurate method of determining longitude. The water clocks and even the later pendulum clocks were useless on a rolling ship; timekeeping with a half-hour sandglass was unsatisfactory because of premature upturning by a lazy watch; checking the log against the sun at midday was not always permitted by the weather; and dead reckoning (the measuring of courses and distances run) was also inaccurate, especially in the huge expanse of the Pacific. In the absence of trustworthy data, rough indications of the proximity of land were used: floating debris such as branches and seaweed; bird flights; changing water color; the scent of vegetation. To make matters worse, ships were often heavy, slow, crowded, and dirty; their keels had to be protected with copper sheeting or nails against shipworms; the storage and preservation of food and water were problematical, so that putrid water, rotten food, and dying livestock were not uncommon, at least until the canning process was discovered at the beginning of the nineteenth century; and both vermin, such as rats, cockroaches, maggots, and lice, and disease, including scurvy (until the beginning of the nineteenth century) and dysentery, took a heavy toll. Not until the late 1700s were navigational instruments such as the sextant (1731) and the chronometer (1735), and methods such as lunar distances, perfected for and made widely available to mariners. After the 1770s, chronometers, lunar observations, and immersions of Jupiter's satellites were in general use, although chronometric measurements seldom tallied with astronomical observations.[1]

While the maritime imperial powers of western Europe were penetrating the South Pacific for "gold, God, and glory," continental Russia was pushing overland from eastern Europe to the North Pacific in quest of "soft gold" (sable fur), but the tsar's men had to consolidate their control of the vast Siberian wilderness, in addition to coping with unstable southern and western frontiers, before being free to cross the inclement northern reaches of what they called the "Eastern Ocean." Thus, it was not until the late 1700s that the leading imperial nations—Britain, France, Russia, and Spain—finally met on the Northwest Coast and began to delineate and demarcate this terra incognita.

First came the Russians. Their arrival was simply an extension of their rapid eastward advance across Siberia from one river basin to the next in search of furs; the far North Pacific offered the Bering Sea instead of a river basin but also a handy Aleutian land bridge, as well as fur seals and sea otters, whose fur was to prove even more valuable than that of sables. Not uncharacteristically for the inexperienced Russians, a foreign mercenary, Vitus Bering, led the way in 1741 with the first Russian landfall on the North American mainland. He was quickly followed by a series of private fur-trading voyages, punctuated sporadically by state expeditions, along the Aleutians and the Gulf of Alaska coast, but the overextended, undermanned, and undersupplied Russians barely penetrated either into the continental interior or down the Northwest Coast, with the exception of the temporary (1812–41) and uneconomical venture around Fort Ross on the California coast.

The Russian advent was enough to alarm the exposed northern outposts of New Spain, and in the middle 1770s the jittery Spaniards launched a series of probes up the coast to locate and assess the Russian threat. But the Spaniards were already overextended in the Californias, and their expeditions accomplished little in the way of discovery, exploration, settlement, exploitation, or conversion; indeed, they barely made contact with their Russian quarry. Beginning in 1778 with Captain James Cook's last voyage, the British, no more experienced than the Spaniards but perhaps more determined and certainly better equipped, were much more successful. Although they failed to find a Northwest Passage (simply because a practicable one did not exist), they did discover both the coastal source of, and the Canton market for, sea otters, and from the middle 1780s until the end of the century the British dominated the maritime fur trade. Meanwhile, one of their number, Captain George Vancouver, in the first half of the 1790s made that traffic much more secure by carefully charting the coast for the first time and officially accepting the Spanish pullback at Nootka Sound, as well as inclining the Hawaiian Islands depot toward Britain. Nevertheless, by the turn of the century the British coasters had largely been displaced by the "Bostonians," New England shipmasters who were unfettered by the exclusive privileges of trading monopolies in the Pacific. They were led by Captain Robert Gray in 1787–91 in the *Columbia Rediviva*, the namesake of the river that he merely rediscovered but did enter and ascend while accomplishing the first American circumnavigation, fifteen years before the lagging Russians. Thus was the stage set for the subsequent struggle between the United States and Great Britain for the territory and resources of the Pacific Slope.

Russian Exploration

Although all of northern Asia and the North Pacific separated the Russians from the Pacific coast of North America, they nevertheless beat their imperial rivals to the scene. They faced fewer obstacles, with weaker native resistance and less foreign opposition, and fewer distractions, since their interest was primarily furs. Siberia's dense network of boatable rivers and fairly flat terrain, the closeness of the two continents at Bering Strait, and the handiness of the Aleutian causeway mitigated the enormous distances for the landlubberly Muscovites.

This is not to say that their advance was smooth sailing or, more aptly, clear coasting. It was spearheaded by Semyon Dezhnyov, a Yakutsk service-

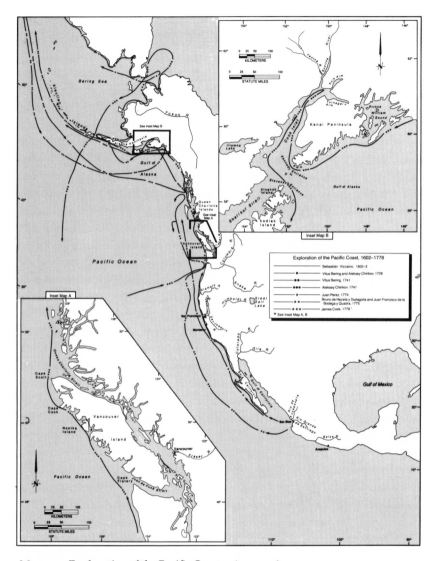

Map 14.1 Exploration of the Pacific Coast, 1602–1778.

man, who in the summer of 1648, only six years after the founding of Montreal, left Sredne-Kolymsk, the main Kolyma River outpost, at the head of four groups of eighty-eight other men in seven *kochas* (light but sturdy shallow-draft, flat-bottomed, curved-sided, single-masted vessels especially suited to plying icy waters) to seek a sea route to the Pogycha (Anadyr)

River and its reputed wealth of dark, long-haired sables, walrus ivory, and silver. The Russians were mostly *promyshlenniks*—freelance and versatile enterprisers, usually fur trappers and traders. In this year of exceptionally favorable ice conditions, their flotilla hugged the ice-free Arctic shoreline, but four *kochas* and their crews were lost, and the remaining three rounded the "great rocky headland"—probably referring to the Chukchi Peninsula, not Cape Dezhnev (East Cape). They threaded Bering Strait, thereby unwittingly demonstrating that Asia and North America were not joined, and reached the mouth of the Anadyr, where the twenty-five survivors wintered. (Several of them, incidentally, subsequently trekked overland to Kamchatka, married natives, and stayed.) Dezhnev's report on his successful exploit was buried in the Yakutsk archive, however, and was not retrieved until 1736 by academician Gerhard Müller, a diligent member of Bering's second expedition. In the meantime, the feat became common knowledge in Siberia but caused little stir because the land route from the Kolyma to the Anadyr proved much more practicable; besides, Chukotka (the far northeast of the Asian continent) was quintessentially remote and savage. Only later, when the question of a northeastern passage to the Orient was posed, did Dezhnyov's remarkable voyage attract wider interest.[2]

The question of a Northeast Passage did not lie behind Russia's first exploring venture toward the North American coast. This was the First Kamchatka Expedition (1725–29), ordered by Peter the Great at the end of his life in order to, in his own words, "find glory for the state through art and science," that is, undertake scientific exploration and discovery.[3] The Peace of Nystad of 1721 between Russia and Sweden had allowed the tsar to give more attention to less crucial matters than national survival, including the promotion of the sciences, as part of his attempt to modernize his country along western European lines—hence the opening of the Academy of Sciences in 1725 and the dispatch of the First Kamchatka Expedition in the same year. Its purpose was not to determine whether Asia and North America were connected, because the tsar already knew they were not, nor was it intended to discover a northeastern passage, because he also knew that such an Arctic route for sailing ships was not feasible; rather, the expedition was to explore the Pacific bounds of northeastern Siberia to determine their orientation and extent. The instructions of Peter's widow and successor, Catherine I, commanded Captain Vitus Bering, a Dane by birth but a veteran of the fledgling Russian navy, to build one or two ships in Kamchatka and sail northward near some supposed land in the Bering Sea—such as that shown on the 1725 atlas of Johann Komann—and "discover where it is joined to America," going as far as the first European settlement.[4] This first expedition of Bering's, comprising up to seventy-five men, did not sail until two and one-half years after leaving the new imperial capital of St. Petersburg, reflecting the problematical logistics that were also to plague the second expedition. Finally, on 14 July 1728, Bering sailed from Nizhne-Kamchatsk at the mouth of the Kamchatka River in the *St. Gabriel* with enough supplies for forty men for one year.

Hugging the Asiatic coastline, he reached as far north as 67° off Point Hope a month later before turning back "because the land does not extend farther to the north, and there is nothing beyond Chukotka or the eastern extremity."[5] In fact, Bering saw little, if anything, of the *bolshaya zemlya* ("big land," i.e., the American mainland) on account of fog, although he did sight Saint Lawrence Island. The following summer he again set sail, making a short and fruitless voyage off the eastern coast of Kamchatka, even missing the Commander Islands, so he rounded Cape Lopatka, the peninsula's southern point, and sailed to Okhotsk, Siberia's chief Pacific port.

The meager results of Bering's first voyage disappointed St. Petersburg, which decided to send him on a second, and bigger and better, expedition. But before this could be mounted, two Russians became the first Europeans to see the northwestern coast of North America. In the summer of 1732 Ivan Fyodorov and Mikhail Gvozdev left the mouth of the Kamchatka River in the *St. Gabriel*, Bering's old ship, with thirty-nine crewmen under orders to sail to the mouth of the Anadyr River to supply and reinforce the Russian contingent there against the rebellious Chukchis and then sail eastward to "examine and count the islands there [the 'big land'], and gather tribute from the inhabitants."[6] From the Chukchi Peninsula they sailed to the Diomede Islands, landing on one of them, and then on to the coast of the Seward Peninsula, where they did not go ashore, owing to "the head wind and the shallow sea." They coasted southward, sighting King Island, and returned across the Bering Sea to Kamchatka because of "the lateness of the season and the stormy weather."[7] Their voyage went unheralded, however, because of friction between the two leaders, the death of Fyodorov in 1733, the likelihood that they did not even realize that the "big land" was part of the North American continent, and the delay in reporting the voyage to St. Petersburg, where it did not become known before 1738.

Meanwhile, preparations were under way for Bering's second voyage, the Second Kamchatka Expedition (1733–42), also called the American Expedition. This was but one of nine components of the grandiose Great Northern Expedition, whose purpose, as Admiral Nikolay Golovin informed Empress Anna, was "to search for new lands, sail toward America and the Japanese islands and survey the coastline of Siberia." Golovin stated, "The description of these shores and the search for new lands and islands . . . will be very beneficial for the glory of Your Imperial Majesty as well as for the expansion of various regions and of the Empire itself." He added, "Further, this will add to the knowledge of navigation in those parts, [and] great Imperial benefit may result from searching for America."[8] The expedition was mounted because the Admiralty was not convinced that Bering's first voyage had demonstrated that there was no land between Kamchatka and America and also because not enough was known about the sea route along the northern coast of Siberia or about "the islands near Japan and a route to the east."[9] The real purpose of Bering's second voyage was to extend Russian sovereignty to northwestern North America with a view to enlarging the lucrative fur trade, but the aim of both his first and his second ventures was officially and publicly masked as an attempt to determine whether Asia and America were joined.[10]

The Second Kamchatka Expedition was an enormous undertaking, the largest exploring expedition the world had yet seen. It comprised up to one thousand men, including several prominent scientists in various disciplines, men such as Johann Gmelin, Stepan Krasheninnikov, Gerhard Müller, and Georg Wilhelm Steller, plus support workers, mainly transporters, who totaled another two thousand men.[11] Hundreds of tons of supplies and equipment, ranging from flour to anchors, had to be hauled thousands of miles by riverboat, packhorse, wagon, dogsled, and even reindeer across sometimes rugged, sometimes marshy, and often uninhabited Siberia to the Pacific coast, the worst stretch being the mountainous water divide between the Lena River basin at Yakutsk and the Pacific at Okhotsk.[12] St. Petersburg had assumed that Bering would be ready for sea by 1737 at a cost of 10–12,000 rubles, but by then he was no farther than Yakutsk and up to 300,000 rubles had already been spent. The first of the expedition's Pacific cruises took place in the summer of 1738, when Martin Spanberg launched the first of his three voyages to Japan, but Bering did not put to sea until 1740, seven years after leaving St. Petersburg.[13]

Bering and his second-in-command, Aleksey Chirikov, were to build two packet boats in Kamchatka and "proceed east as winds will permit, even as far as 67° north latitude" and to "search for the American coast or islands with great diligence and effort."[14] Originally Bering intended to

14.1 "Summary Map of the Bering-Chirikov Voyages of 1741," from A. Y. Yefimov, ed., Atlas geograficheskikh otkryty . . . *(Moscow, 1964). This summary map illustrates the relative sophistication of Russian knowledge of the Pacific coastal region nearly a half-century before British, Spanish, French, and American maps were produced with such accuracy. Russian geographical lore, however, did not work its way into western cartography. Courtesy of the Babbidge Library, The University of Connecticut.*

winter on the American coast, but this plan was thwarted by the ship-wrecking of some provisions at Okhotsk and the sidetracking of others at Bolsheretsk on Kamchatka's western coast. He therefore decided to undertake two separate expeditions, especially since his departure from the new port of Petropavlovsk (founded by Bering in 1740 on spacious and sheltered Avacha Bay on the peninsula's southeastern coast and named after his two ships) was delayed a month by drunkenness and preoccupation with a native rebellion on the part of Pyotr Kolesov, the commandant of Kamchatka.[15] Bering in the *St. Peter* (seventy-eight men) and Chirikov in the *St. Paul* (seventy-six men) finally left Petropavlovsk in mid-June 1741 and sailed southeastward. They soon became separated in windy, foggy weather, and each vessel headed eastward, missing the Aleutian Islands and crossing the Gulf of Alaska. The *St. Paul* was the first to sight the American mainland on 26 July at the southern end of the Alaskan panhandle in 55° north (the next day the *St. Peter* sighted the northern end in 58° north). Chirikov found the coast to be "irregular and mountainous," but he was unable to do much by way of exploring the land or contacting the natives because, off Lisianski Strait, he lost both of his longboats with thirteen men when they went ashore and failed to return, possibly swamped and drowned by strong riptides or killed by Tlingits.[16]

The crew also could no longer fetch water: "On July 27 we [the *St. Paul's* officers] took counsel as to whether we could go on, because we no longer had a small boat on our ship either to send ashore on reconnaissance or to take fresh water . . . and had only 45 [actually thirty-eight, on inspection] barrels of water left."[17] So, having cruised some 4,000 verstas (2,650 miles) of the American coast, Chirikov decided to return to Kamchatka. En route some of the Kodiak, Shumagin, and Aleutian Islands were sighted, and some Aleuts were contacted. By 27 September only six casks of water remained, and the daily need was five cups per man; two men had died of that age-old bane of long voyages, scurvy, and sixteen others, including the captain, were "very sick" with the disease, while the rest were barely fit for duty. [18] The return voyage was slowed by "contrary winds from [the] northwest and southwest almost continuously," and when the *St. Paul* finally reached Petropavlovsk on 10 October, only two casks of water (both boiled from seawater) were left, and seven men, including the astronomy professor Delisle de La Croyère, had died of scurvy. Twice on the return voyage Chirikov himself had nearly succumbed to the disease, and in fact he died in 1748 of an ailment caught on the expedition.[19]

Meanwhile, Captain Commander Bering in the *St. Peter* had made two landfalls in America, the first on Saint Elias [Kayak] Island, before deciding to head home on 10 August because of the lateness of the season, violent storms, heavy fogs, uncharted shoals, fear of the wind shifting from easterly to westerly, and sickness (five men were unfit for duty and sixteen others were suffering from scurvy).[20] The naturalist Steller, who wanted to stay longer and closely study the American mainland, accused the ship's officers of arrogance, ignorance, and timidity, remarking in disgust, "We have come only to take American water to Asia."[21] On the homeward voyage, water was procured on one of the Shumagin Islands (named after a crewman who died there). Some of the Aleutians were sighted, and violent weather was encountered; in late September–early October they were reversed by "an indescribable gale from the west," which lasted for three weeks and which was the worst that the mate, seventy-year-old Andreas Hesselberg, had experienced in fifty years at sea.[22]

By 4 November, only six barrels of water were left, and only eight men could do any duty. On 5 November Bering decided to land on present-day Bering Island, one of the Commander Islands (both named after the leader of the expedition), rather than try to make Petropavlovsk; they had "little fresh water" and scurvy had killed twelve men and disabled thirty-two others, including Bering himself, leaving only ten able to do some duty.[23] "We could not go on because we had no able-bodied men, our rigging was rotten, and our provisions and water were gone," reported one of the officers.[24] On Bering Island they found freshwater but only driftwood instead of trees, so tents had to be made from the weatherbeaten sails. The officers recommended that the *St. Peter* be beached so that it would not be blown adrift, but the men were too weak to do so, and on 28 November the ship was blown ashore and wrecked. Seventeen more men died of scurvy after landing, including Bering himself, who was succeeded in command by Sven Waxell. During the winter the survivors suffered from shortages of food and fuel, blizzards, two earthquakes, and marauding blue foxes, and they became addicted to gambling, mostly for sea otter pelts. They ate chiefly sea otters at first, then fur seals, and finally sea cows (manatees); the last afforded the best fare, and the men did not really start to recover until after they began eating the sea cows, some of which weighed up to eight thousand pounds and provided enough food for more than two weeks (indeed, this huge, tasty sea mammal was to prove so popular with subsequent Russian seafarers that by 1768, the Steller's sea cow was extinct). In the summer of 1742 the hooker *St. Peter* was built from the wreckage of the original, and in the autumn the forty-six survivors sailed in it to Petropavlovsk. This little vessel was still in service as late as 1752 as a transport between Okhotsk and Kamchatka.[25]

Thus ended the Second Kamchatka Expedition ten years after its launching. Because of its meager firsthand results and great cost in lives, however, it was not to be emulated by St. Petersburg for another half-century, not until the Russians were alarmed by Cook's third voyage. The American coast had been discovered but not explored, although the supposed islands and lands of Yezo (or Esso), Staten (or States), Company, and Juan da Gama in the far North Pacific—touted by French geographers like Guillaume Delisle and Philippe Buache—had been found to be as mythical as the fabled southern continent was to prove in the far South Pacific. (The revised geography was incorporated in the Russian *Academy Atlas* of 1745 and on Gerhard F. Müller's map of 1754–58.) And the bill was high: at least 1,500,000 and perhaps more than 2,000,000 rubles were spent on the expedition.[26] Moreover, although the expedition had strengthened Russian control of the Kamchatka Peninsula and the Okhotsk seaboard by augmenting old and establishing new settlements, such as Petropavlovsk, it had also underscored the difficulties of the Yakutsk-Okhotsk route and the desirability of finding a better one; nearly half of the expedition's ten years were spent on the transport of supplies over this leg of the tenuous Russian lifeline of empire. Fortunately for the Russians, they were not seriously challenged in the Okhotsk and Bering Seas and the Gulf of Alaska by imperial rivals, and when a challenge did come, it came late and lame on the more expendable Northwest Coast.

Chirikov was one of the few who persisted. In 1747 in a report to the Admiralty he recommended (in vain) that the state sponsor further voyages to the Aleutians and the American coast in order to explore, build forts, hunt fur bearers, and subjugate natives.[27] Some Russians believed that it would be cheaper and faster to send exploring expeditions to the North Pacific via the Amur River, thereby avoiding the horrendous Yakutsk-Okhotsk link. So beginning in 1753 the Russians attempted to continue the work of the Second Kamchatka Expedition by constructing vessels on the upper reaches of the Amur and sending them downstream to the Pacific, but this project was aborted when Peking in 1757 refused to allow the Russians to navigate the river through Chinese territory (Russia had relinquished most of the Amur basin by treaty in 1689 and would not regain it until the 1850s).

Finally, two state expeditions were mounted in the 1760s, but they encountered familiar obstacles and accomplished very little. In 1766 Lieutenant Ivan Sindt, who had accompanied Bering, made an unsuccessful voyage to the American coast opposite the Chukchi Peninsula. After having taken two years to reach the eastern coast of Kamchatka from Okhotsk, he then got only as far as Bering Strait on account of stormy weather, making 65° before returning. He claimed to have discovered eleven islands in place of Saint Lawrence Island, and these mythical "Sindt Islands" remained on Russian maps as late as 1793. The Krenitsyn-Levashov expedition of 1764–

71 was so secret that for some time it was not even reported to the Senate. It was officially termed the "Expedition to Inventory the Forests along the Kama and Belaya Rivers," but its instructions ordered it "solely to make a dead reckoning and description" of the Aleutian Islands; its real purpose was to make a "thorough description and location on the map" of the islands discovered by *promyshlenniks*, particularly Kodiak Island with a view to proving its insularity. The expedition left St. Petersburg in the summer of 1764, but the last of it did not reach Okhotsk until the autumn of 1765, and the four ships did not leave that port until a year later. Three days out they were separated, and subsequently all were blown ashore on Kamchatka; the two ships of the commanders were lost, including one with thirty of its complement of forty-three men, so only two ships sailed from Kamchatka on their mission in 1768. They visited several of the Aleutians and the Alaskan mainland, but the three-year voyage continued to be marred by mishaps and deaths, including that of Stepan Glotov, one of the most knowledgeable and successful *promyshlenniks*. During the winter of 1768–69, P. K. Krenitsyn lost sixty of his seventy men to scurvy. In the spring the survivors rendezvoused and returned to Kamchatka; in the summer of 1770 they again put to sea in two ships, but Krenitsyn drowned, and M. D. Levashov returned to Okhotsk, not reaching St. Petersburg until the autumn of 1771, more than seven years after leaving the capital. The expedition did prove that Unimak was an island and not an extension of the Alaska Peninsula, and it made an accurate instrumental determination of the latitude of the Aleutian chain, especially Unalaska Island (which was to be the possible site of the first permanent Russian settlement in North America in the middle 1770s). However, the venture remains so little known that the basic source of information on it is still an article published in 1852 in a government journal.[28]

Although Bering's two Kamchatka expeditions did not encourage the state sponsor, they did stimulate the private sector. While wintering on Bering Island in 1741–42, the *St. Peter*'s survivors saw "many herds of sea otters," and during their stay they amassed more than 700 pelts.[29] They returned to Kamchatka in 1742 with 600–900 skins; Chirikov had returned the previous year with 900.[30] The Russians soon discovered that these skins were highly prized by the Chinese; one skin brought 80–100 rubles (in goods) at Kyakhta on the Russian-Mongolian frontier, compared with 20 rubles in Kamchatka, 30 at Yakutsk, and 40 at Irkutsk.[31] This bonanza triggered a fur rush from Kamchatka southward along the Kurile Islands and especially eastward over the Aleutian causeway; the waters between the peninsula and the Commander Islands became known as the Otter Sea.

The very first private voyage, that of the *St. Peter* of 1743–44 to the Commanders, included two survivors of the Second Kamchatka Expedition. From 1743 through 1797, forty-two Russian private shareholding companies made nearly 100 voyages along the Aleutians and gained nearly 187,000 furs, mostly sea otter and fur seal, worth about 7,900,000 rubles.[32] This advance comprised three stages: 1743–54, when twenty-two voyages were made, mainly to the Commander Islands and the Near Aleutians; 1756–80, when forty-nine voyages were made, chiefly to the remaining Aleutian Islands, the Alaska Peninsula, and Kodiak Island; and 1781–97, when twenty-one voyages were made, mostly to the Pribilof Islands and the Gulf of Alaska coast. These stages followed the declining number and receding range of what the Russians called the "sea beaver" (*Enhydra lutris*), the most valuable fur bearer; thanks to the creature's low reproductivity, and Russian avidity, it had largely disappeared from the coast of Kamchatka by 1750 and from the shores of the Kuriles and Aleutians by 1780.

The Russian government encouraged and even assisted these private ventures because they enlarged the empire's territory, increased its population, and enriched its treasury by means of a 10 percent tax on the fur hunters and fur tribute on the new native subjects. The exaction of the fur tribute (*yasak*) and its enforcement by hostage taking (*yasyr*) were Tatar-inspired measures that had been perfected in Siberia. Thus on the Northwest Coast the Russians, unlike other Euro-American traffickers, did not trade with the Indians for furs; rather, they enserfed Aleut and Kodiak marksmen, who then hunted sea otters from kayaks in return for paltry rations. Consequently, the Russians got very few pelts from the Northwest Coast Indians, who demanded trade goods, and their catch was limited primarily to sea furs. Nevertheless, the Russians beat their Spanish rivals to the coast by more than three decades (and the British by almost four), giving them a considerable headstart in the sea otter trade. When the British finally arrived in 1778, they were told by a *promyshlennik* that there were four hundred Russians and as many Kamchadals in Russian America, including sixty to seventy Russians at the main settlement of Captain's Harbor on Unalaska Island.[33]

The Russian argonauts gradually discovered and explored the islands and coasts of the Bering Sea and the Gulf of Alaska, albeit little of the interior, since they were preoccupied with the maritime, not the continental, fur trade in North America. A few "drafts" (*chertyozhi*: maps without astronomically determined points) were compiled and have survived. Maps of the Aleutians were drawn by Mikhail Nevochikov in 1751, Pyotr Shishkin and Savvin Ponomaryov in 1762, Vasily Shilov in 1767, Afanasy Ocheredin in 1775, and Potap Zaikov in 1779, for example; Zaikov based his map on his voyage of 1772–79 with sixty-nine men in the *St. Vladimir* from Okhotsk to Kodiak Island and back. He lost twelve men but got 9,633 pelts (including 3,838 sea otter skins), 3,457 tails, and 333 pounds of walrus teeth.[34] However, the results of Russian explorations and discoveries, both state and private, in the North Pacific were not publicized. For whatever reason— the pervasiveness of state control, the underdevelopment of private publishing, the political and cultural estrangement of Russia from the West, Russia's siege mentality and xenophobia, the misguided belief that secretiveness would discourage the inquisitive—Russia's geographical accomplishments, in the form of instructions, logbooks, journals, maps, reports, and letters, were either not revealed or not published until long after the event. Consequently, like the Spanish achievements on the Northwest Coast, they were not appreciated and recognized abroad. For instance, the materials of the Second Kamchatka Expedition were classified, and only some of them were published, much later; they were not fully incorporated into the *Russian Atlas* of 1745, and S. P. Krasheninnikov's classic *Opisanie zemli Kamchatki* [Description of the Land of Kamchatka] was not published until 1755.

Not until 1754 were the expedition's results finally and fully shown, on the "New Map of Discoveries Made by Russian Ships on the Unknown Coasts of North America and Neighboring Lands . . ." compiled by the Geographical Department of the Academy of Sciences. This dispelled the myth of the existence of Juan da Gama Land, Company Land, Staten Land, and Yezo Land. The map was updated in 1773 ("Map Showing Discoveries in the Northern Part of America and Nearby Places Made by Russian Navigators during Various Voyages"), but it did not incorporate all the results of Russian voyages. Not surprisingly in view of such secrecy, Russian accomplishments were sometimes misrepresented, as in La Croyère's 1752 "Map of New Discoveries to the North of the Southern Ocean, in Siberia and Kamchatka, and to the West of New France."

Some Soviet scholars have asserted that Russian discoveries were deliberately misrepresented or falsified in the West in order to weaken Russian claims in the North Pacific sphere of international rivalry. Perhaps they are right. Certainly some Russian materials were stolen or smuggled, sometimes with the help of colleagues or bribes, and published in western Europe much later, often by savants who had served in Russia or visited there. Included in this latter category were such works as S. Muller's (G. F. Müller's) *Voyages from Asia to America, for Completing the Discoveries of the North West Coast of America* (London, 1761), Georg Wilhelm Steller's *Beschreibung von dem Lande Kamtschatka* (Frankfurt and Leipzig, 1774), and William Coxe's *Account of the Russian Discoveries between Asia and America* . . . (London, 1780).[35] Russian secrecy was such that Empress Catherine II (the Great) ordered that Coxe's book be translated into Russian "for her own perusal," even though the original sources were in the Admiralty's archives in Saint Petersburg under her very nose.[36] By way of substantiation the Russians did at least establish some settlements on the shores that they discovered and explored, for example, Captain's Harbor (c. 1774) on Unalaska Island, Three Saints Harbor (1784) on Kodiak Island, and New Archangel, or Sitka (1799), on Baranof Island in the Alexander Archipelago. In addition, metal plaques bearing the inscription "Land in Russian Possession" were buried here and there, but they could not be easily retrieved because the details of their location were sometimes mislaid or forgotten (similarly, the wooden crosses erected by the Spanish were usually soon dismantled by Indians for their nails or were eventually rotted or felled by the elements).

The Russian monopoly on the geography and peltry of the Bering Sea and Gulf of Alaska was finally broken by Cook's third (and last) voyage of 1776–80. He visited Unalaska twice in 1778 and Petropavlovsk twice in 1779, as well as Prince William Sound and Cook Inlet en route, gleaning information on Russian activities and disclosing information on his own. On Unalaska the British met Peter Natrubin, or Reuben, who claimed to have been a cabin boy on Bering's ship and to have been with him at his death (in fact, he was a henchman of the notorious Ivan Solovyov, who had bloodily suppressed the Aleuts of the Fox Islands); they also met Gerasim Izmailov, a veteran—and boastfully talkative, if suspicious—trader and mariner, who said he had sailed with Lieutenant Sindt in 1766. In Kamchatka they were introduced to Vasily Shmalev, who with his brother Timofey was one of the most experienced and knowledgeable Russian officials on the Pacific. For their part the Russians became well aware that Cook's expedition had accurately delineated the Northwest Coast and uncovered the potential of the sea otter trade; they certainly did not have to wait until the publication of Cook's account in 1784 to learn where he had gone and what he had found because in May 1779 at Petropavlovsk, the English astronomer traded "a Map of all our Discoveries on the Coast of America" for a Russian map of Kamchatka and its vicinity.[37] Alarmed by what they regarded as Cook's incursion into Russian waters, as well as by that of Jean François de Galaup, comte de La Pérouse (1785–88), who also visited Petropavlovsk (where Jean de Lesseps, later the sole survivor of the La Pérouse expedition, disembarked), the Russians reinforced their numbers and defenses in Kamchatka and mounted one abortive and one successful expedition to the far North Pacific.

To protect their North Pacific interests, the Russians decided in 1786 to construct a new port on the Okhotsk Sea (Okhotsk having proved an unsatisfactory harbor) and to dispatch four warships (five were actually readied by 1787) from the Baltic under Captain G. I. Mulovsky; however, the outbreak of war with Turkey (1787–91) and the prospect of war with Sweden (1788–90) interfered, and in 1788 the expedition was canceled and the squadron sent to the Mediterranean. In the meantime, a large-scale expedition was launched from Siberia under Captain Joseph Billings, an English veteran of Cook's last voyage. One of his lieutenants was Robert Hall, also an Englishman; another was Christian Bering, Vitus Bering's grandson; and yet another was Gavriil Sarychev, a Russian who is given credit— especially by Soviet scholars—for much of the venture's achievements. The expedition was suggested by William Coxe to complete the geographical knowledge of both sides of the far North Pacific, and it was submitted to Empress Catherine II by the naturalist and explorer Peter Pallas, one of many German scientists in Russian employ; the empress sent a decree to the Admiralty authorizing this "Northeastern Expedition" a month after the announcement in French newspapers in July 1785 of La Pérouse's voyage.[38]

The organization and political purpose of this expedition were, as usual, a matter of strict secrecy. Catherine's decree of 8 August referred to a "geographical and astronomical expedition to the northeastern part of Russia," and the instructions comprised twenty-five articles. According to these instructions, the expedition was undertaken "for discoveries on the easternmost shores and seas of Her Empire, for the accurate determination of the longitude and latitude of the mouth of the Kolyma River, for the fixing of the position of the shores of the great Chukchi Peninsula as far as East Cape, for the positioning on the map of the islands in the Eastern Ocean as far as the shores of America, and generally for better knowledge . . . of the seas lying between the mainland of Siberia and the opposite shores of America," and particularly "for a survey of the entire chain of numerous [Aleutian] islands stretching as far as America," including "the compilation of an accurate map of these islands."[39] In fact, the expedition was intended not only to clarify the conflicting information on the configuration of the Asiatic and American coasts of the Bering Sea but also to regulate relations with the Chukchis and to show the Russian flag in a frontier region—in other words, to fulfil both scientific and political purposes.[40]

The 141 participants were divided into several groups to explore the Okhotsk seaboard, Kamchatka, Chukotka, the Bering Sea, and the Aleutian Islands. Of the expedition's two ships, the *Glory of Russia* and the *Good Intent*, the latter was wrecked on a bar while leaving Okhotsk, so Hall built a replacement, the *Black Eagle*, at Nizhne-Kamchatsk. The position of the islands of the Bering Sea and the Gulf of Alaska were successfully determined; in particular, Sarychev accurately established the coordinates of the Aleutians and described in detail their physical and human geography.[41] The Russians found clear evidence of the extent of encroachment by their Spanish and British rivals by 1790. On Kodiak Island the expedition was told by Yevstrat Delarov, the manager of the Kodiak operations of the private Golikov-Shelikhov Company, that "the Spaniards were in the habit of visiting the [Russian] settlements yearly, and that the Russians obtained some provisions, and a considerable quantity of sea-otter skins from them, in exchange for hardware, beads, and linens."[42] The natives of Prince William Sound were heard to use the English words "no" and "plenty" and the Spanish "amigo"; they told Sarychev that every year two-masted and three-masted ships visited them and that this year (1790) two had also gone to Cook Inlet.[43] The expedition's members compiled a voluminous body of written materials, amounting to fifty-seven maps and plans and forty-two journals, very few of which were published (Sarychev's *Atlas* did not appear until 1804).[44]

Meanwhile, Russian *promyshlenniks* were continuing to push eastward, albeit now, in view of the longer and costlier voyages, in the form of fewer and larger companies. In the mid-1780s the Golikov-Shelikhov Company explored and occupied Kodiak Island and the adjacent coast of Alaska, including what the company called Kenai (Cook) Inlet and Chugach (Prince William) Sound. The company, with state assistance, sent three galliots with 192 men from Okhotsk in 1783.[45] G. I. Shelikhov, who had some influence in St. Petersburg, received substantial government support because he found "evidence that the English [were] moving . . . along the coast of America in the North Pacific, and that they anticipate[d] considerable profits."[46] Already by 1787 Shelikhov was warning the Siberian authorities that British fur traders were cruising and bartering "in our waters along the northeast [*sic*, northwestern] coast of America," with the first ship in 1785 getting eight hundred sea otter skins, followed by five coasters in 1786.[47] By then, however, the Russians were too late to forestall the British maritime fur traders. The Russians were already overextended, and Empress Catherine II likely had this in mind when she remarked in 1788: "A lot of expansion in the Pacific Ocean will not bring concrete benefits. To trade is one thing, to take possession is another."[48] Her Northwest Coast frontiersmen simply lacked the resources to keep their British rivals at bay or to push even farther (at least until 1799, when New Archangel was founded), so that when the first British fur-trading vessels arrived on the coast, they were unopposed from Prince William Sound southward to San Francisco Bay. The Russians told Captain Vancouver in 1794 that they numbered about 400, including 263 for the Lebedev-Lastochkin Company and the rest for the Golikov-Shelikhov Company.[49] They had several clumsy galliots and no warships. Even New Archangel was captured by the Tlingits in 1802 (and Slavorossiya on Yakutat Bay in 1805) and was retaken in 1804 only with the help of Russia's very first round-the-world expedition. By then Vancouver had already charted the Pacific coast, and the maritime fur trade had already peaked.

Spanish Exploration

His Catholic Majesty was the first imperial rival to be alarmed by the tsar's outreach across the North Pacific.[50] Spain claimed all of the Pacific drainage of North America, and it regarded the Pacific coast north of the viceroyalty of New Spain, that is, north of the Sea of Cortez (Gulf of California) and Baja California, as an imperial reserve for future exploitation.[51] Pope Alexander VI's bull of 1493 had divided the globe into a Spanish West and a Portuguese East, and the Treaty of Tordesillas of 1494 had drawn the dividing meridian 370 leagues (1 league equals 3 miles) west of the Cape Verde Islands. Also, the Laws of the Indies theoretically closed the "South Sea" (Pacific Ocean) to foreign shipping under pain of treatment as common pirates.[52] Spain feared for the safety of the richly laden Manila galleons, which every year from 1565 to 1815 sailed westward from Acapulco between 9° and 14° north with silver ingots and, more dangerously, eastward from Manila between 32° and 37° north with Oriental luxuries—and which somehow, apparently, never went off course and thus missed sighting the Hawaiian Islands.[53] Francis Drake's 1579 raiding along the western coast of the Americas (with a landfall somewhere near the Golden Gate) fore-shadowed depredations by the Dutch in the 1600s and by the British in the 1700s, including the capture of not only Spain's "China ships" but even Manila itself in 1762, whereas the ending of the Seven Years War in 1763 freed Britain for even more activity in the "Spanish lake." Meanwhile, the remoteness that had kept the Northwest Coast unknown and unchallenged for so long had, of course, been breached by the Russians. Spain had neglected "its" Northwest Coast because it had more than enough colonies and subjects to manage; moreover, the seventeenth century was a defensive rather than an offensive period for the motherland, which was beset by economic depressions, military defeats in Europe, epidemic diseases, and imperial rivals overseas.[54] Furthermore, despite the proximity of Mexico, Spain's position on the coast was weak, owing to the shortage of both people and shipping in New Galicia and Baja California; indeed, the very vulnerability of the *frontera del norte* made Spain all the more sensitive to foreign encroachment.[55]

This sensitivity was heightened by the supposed existence of transcontinental waterways across North America. These alleged straits were described in the apocryphal accounts of imaginary voyages by Lorenzo Ferrer Maldonado, Juan de Fuca, and Bartolomew de Fonte.[56] Maldonado claimed to have sailed from the Pacific to the Atlantic in 1588 via a passage that he called the Estrecho de Anian and that he said lay in 60° north. Fuca, a Greek pilot in the Spanish navy, in 1596 told one Michael Lok in Venice that in 1592 he had found a broad inlet he called the Entrée de Juan de Fuca between 47° and 48° north (coincidentally in the very latitude of today's Strait of Juan de Fuca) and had sailed through it for twenty days and reached the North Sea (his story was published in 1625 by Samuel Purchas in his *Pilgrimes*). In 1708 a letter by Admiral de Fonte was published in London in the *Monthly Miscellany; or, Memoirs for the Curious* in which he purported to have voyaged to the Northwest Coast and in 53° north discovered a passage (Rio de los Reyes) to the North Atlantic, as well as the archipelago of Saint Lazarus. The straits of Fuca and de Fonte were given publicity and credibility in 1752, when they appeared on a map published in Paris by the French geographer Joseph Nicolas Delisle. They helped to give rise to the legend of the Mer de l'Ouest, which was supposed to exist in the northwestern quadrant of North America with an outlet—the River of the West—to the Pacific between 44° and 45° north. They also lent credence to the existence of a Northwest Passage, which, would, of course, afford a much shorter route from Europe to the Pacific and the Orient than either Cape Horn or the Cape of Good Hope.

In 1745 the British Parliament passed an act offering a reward of £20,000 to any British subject (outside the Royal Navy) who discovered and navigated a strait from Hudson Bay to the South Sea. Within four years the Hudson's Bay Company had finished exploring the western coast of that bay and found no channel to the Pacific. Meanwhile, another putative strait had been added to the list by the voyage of Sebastián Vizcaíno, who during an eleven-month exploration of the Pacific coast in 1602–3 led three ships from Acapulco to Cape Mendocino (where he lost forty-two men) and discovered the harbors of Monterey and San Diego, which he believed could serve as havens for returning Manila galleons.[57] One of his pilots, Martín de Aguilar, reported finding a "swiftflowing river" (the Rogue?) around 43° north (the Rio de Santa Inez, or Entrée de Martín de Aguilar).[58] Most Spanish statesmen were skeptical of these various claims but also prudent enough to investigate them whenever circumstances permitted because should any of the waterways materialize, the North Pacific would no longer be a Spanish preserve, and the Spanish Main on the South Sea would be vulnerable to outflanking by imperial rivals.

That outflanking, however, was achieved not by the British or the French across North America but by the Russians across northern Eurasia. As early as 1761, and again more fully in 1764, Spanish envoys to St. Petersburg warned Madrid of Russian penetration of the far North Pacific and possible encroachment on the Northwest Coast.[59] Spain saw this Russian advance as a threat to the weakly occupied northwestern frontier of Mexico but moved slowly to meet the challenge, waiting until 1768 before ordering the authorities of New Spain to take any action. At the beginning of that year the Marqués de Croix, New Spain's viceroy, was instructed by Spain's minister of state, the Marqués de Grimaldi, to take measures for the protection of California (extending along the Pacific coast from Cabo San Lucas, the southern tip of the Baja peninsula, to Cape Blanco in 43° or even beyond) against Russian expansion from the north. The viceroy forwarded this order to Visitador-General José de Gálvez, who rated it a "weighty matter" and replied that he was taking "such measures" as he deemed "fitting for reaching that place by land or sea" in order to offset the repeated attempts by the Russians "to open communication with North America." Three years later, recalling this order, Gálvez wrote, "His Majesty [had] ordered me to take the necessary steps for safeguarding that peninsula from the repeated probings of the Russians, who arrive from the Tartar [Bering] Sea to reconnoiter the coast of northern California."[60]

This was the real motive behind the founding of the naval base at San Blas in 1767 and the opening of Alta (or Upper or New) California in 1769, although the pretext was the need for additional ports for the Manila galleons.[61] San Blas was to play a crucial role as the sole lifeline of the Californias, given the infeasibility of the overland route through the Sonora Desert; it served as the springboard for supplies sent to the missions and presidios (garrisons), for orders and news, and for fresh soldiers and padres.[62] From 1767 through 1791 eighteen supply ships, ranging from thirty-ton schooners to two-hundred-ton frigates, most of them built at San Blas, plied the California route, stopping most frequently at Loreto, San Diego, and Monterey.[63] At the same time, however, the Spanish tenure of the Pacific coast was weakened by the flaws of San Blas: its pestilential climate, its exposure to winds, its proneness to silting, and its distance from the Mexican ecumene.[64] Acapulco was a better port but lacked the shipbuilding timber (cedar) of San Blas. When Spain withdrew from the Northwest Coast at the end of the century, and Alta California became more self-sufficient (particularly in agriculture), San Blas declined.

The royal order of 1768 led directly to the "Sacred Expedition" from San Blas and Baja California for the occupation of Alta California before it could be penetrated by the Russians. King Carlos III, "being informed of the repeated attempts of a foreign nation upon the northern coasts of California, with designs by no means friendly to the monarchy and its interests," had ordered his Mexican viceroy to "take effective measures to guard that part of his dominions from all invasion and insult."[65] The Baja peninsula was exposed, numbering fewer than four hundred Spaniards (soldiers, missionaries, and miners) and a "very limited" number of Indians, who were scattered and nonagricultural; the only link with the mainland was the San Blas packet boat.[66] In January 1768 Visitador-General Gálvez and Viceroy de Croix drafted a plan for the occupation of Alta California as a bulwark for New Spain, since one of the primary concerns of Gálvez's visitadorship was the security of the northwestern frontier.[67] This stated the purpose of such an occupation: "Many dangers can be averted which now threaten us, by way of the South Sea, from certain foreign powers who now have an opportunity and the most eager desire to establish a colony at the harbor of Monterrey, or at some other of the many harbors which have already been discovered on the western coasts of this New World." They had in mind, in particular, "the continual attempts by which France & England [had] striven, for some two centuries, to find a passage from the North [Atlantic] to the South Sea, especially by [way of] their colonies in this North America [possibly via the River of the West, which, the Spaniards felt, might be the Colorado], and of the exertions that the Russians [were] making, through the Sea of Tartary, to penetrate into our very Indies." They added, "The Russians have been gaining an intimate knowledge of the navigation of the Sea of Tartary; and . . . they are, according to very credible and well-grounded statements, carrying on the fur trade on a continent or perhaps an island which, it is estimated, lies at the distance of only eight hundred leagues from the western coast of the Californias, which run as far as Capes Mendocino and Blanco."[68]

On 16 May at San Blas, Gálvez convened a council, which obtained "definite knowledge of the attempts [by] the Russians . . . to facilitate their communication with this America."[69] Here it was resolved to establish presidios and missions at both San Diego and Monterey and "to observe from there the designs of that nation and to frustrate them as far as possible," securing "to our august sovereign by this means the possession of that country against the pretensions of foreign interlopers."[70] Gálvez decided to outfit a land as well as a sea expedition because of the unreliability of navigation from San Blas. The land expedition comprised forty Spanish soldiers and thirty Indian volunteers under the command of Gaspar de Portolá, governor of Baja California.[71] It left Mission Santa Maria, Baja's northernmost, in March 1769 in two groups, which grew in size en route. The first land party—under Captain Fernando de Rivera y Moncada with fifty-one or fifty-two Indians, twenty-five "leather jackets" (soldiers), three muleteers, Father Juan Crespi, and 180–89 mules and horses—took two months to reach San Diego on 14 May; en route the men suffered from hunger and rough terrain, and only thirteen of the Indians made San Diego, five dying and the rest fleeing.[72] On 29 June the second land party, which included Father Junípero Serra, who was to become the leading Franciscan missionary of Alta California, arrived with Portolá, who brought 163 mules loaded with provisions.[73]

Meanwhile, the sea expedition of the packet boats *San Carlos*, with Captain Vicente Vila, and *El Principe* (or *San Antonio*), with Captain Juan Pérez, sailed from San Blas via La Paz with ninety men altogether. They were delayed by strong contrary winds, the prevailing northwesterlies. It took the *San Carlos* 110 days to reach San Diego, where the ship arrived on 29 April with everyone on board suffering from scurvy and most of them bedridden (only four could still walk, and two had died); even the *San Antonio* took 59 days, arriving on 11 April with half of its crew scorbutic (two had died of the disease).[74] The supply vessel *San Joseph* was lost at sea. When the first land party reached San Diego on 14 May, it found the sailors and soldiers of the two ships "filling a hospital on shore, recovering from the disease of loanda or scurvy"; so far, twenty-one sailors and two soldiers had died, and "nearly all" of the survivors were "very sick," with only six to eight sailors and three to eight soldiers able to work.[75] From San Diego the land expedition departed for Monterey on 14 June but missed the latter and went as far as San Francisco Bay, where it found "a very noble and very large harbor," "very good" land, abundant timber and water, and numerous, peaceable Indians—all the prerequisites for a mission.[76] For want of supplies, Monterey was not occupied, and on the return journey, which took twenty-five weeks, up to ten Indian villages with perhaps ten thousand residents altogether were found along the Santa Barbara Channel.[77] Monterey was finally occupied in the spring of 1770 by a joint land-and-sea expedition; on this occasion, incidentally, the Spaniards noted that the Santa Barbara Indians used cloaks and capes made of sea otter skins.[78]

The delay in the occupation of Alta California was symptomatic of the logistical difficulties that were to hamper Spanish operations on the Northwest Coast until the end of the century. Chief among them, perhaps, was "Fleurieu's Whirlpool," the general clockwise circulation of winds and currents in the northeastern quadrant of the North Pacific. As a result, ships sailing northward along the American coast were hindered by adverse winds and currents. Hence, for example, the transport *San Antonio* took three months in early 1770 to reach San Diego from San Blas, and this time was not unusual.[79] The problem and the Spanish solution were described by Miguel Costansó, an engineer who kept a diary of the 1769 land expedition to establish San Diego and Monterey: "The navigation of the outer coast of California presents an unavoidable difficulty on account of the prevalence of north and northwest winds, which, with little interruption, continue throughout the year, and are directly contrary to the voyage [northward], as the coast bears northwest to southeast. This makes it necessary for all vessels to keep away from the coast and gain sea room until they encounter more variable and favorable winds, with which, making as far north as they require, They can stand in to windward of the port for which they are bound."[80] Captain Vancouver was well aware that the practice of Spanish vessels was, in his own words, "to stand a great distance into the ocean, until they reach far to the northward of the parallel of the port whither they are bound, and then steer for the land," but he found that this maneuver was unnecessary because easterly and southeasterly winds blew most of the day and were frequently stronger than the sea (that is, landward) breezes; during the daytime, ships could turn to windward with the steady, moderate sea breezes.[81]

Once Alta California had been secured, however tenuously, the Russian establishments to the north could be reconnoitered. In the absence of Russian publicity, their intentions and attainments could only be conjectured, so observations by voyagers were necessary to verify the speculation. In February 1773 the Spanish emissary to Russia, the Conde de Lacy, informed Madrid that Russian traders had established themselves on the Northwest Coast, and in April, Minister of the Indies Julián Arriaga warned Viceroy Antonio Bucareli y Ursua of the Russian threat and ordered him to ascertain the extent of the advance and checkmate it.[82] Arriaga included in his 11 April dispatch to Bucareli a copy of the Conde de Lacy's 7 February report, which contained a chronology of Russian activities in the North Pacific from 1740 to 1765.[83] No voyage could be made until 1774, however, owing to the shortage of ships, navigators, and artillery on New Spain's Pacific coast. On 24 August 1773, Madrid ordered the dispatch of six naval officers to New Spain, but they did not arrive in time for the 1774 voyage. Meanwhile, in the early autumn of 1773 Bucareli supported a land expedition by Captain Juan de Anza from Sonora to Alta California because it "may forward the desire of his Majesty that efforts be made to investigate the new explorations of the Russians."[84] The Spaniards also intended to test the feasibility of the overland route to the Californias, since the sea links from San Blas and across the Sea of Cortez were being overtaxed (the Sonora Desert, however, proved too formidable).

Finally, in early 1774 the first Spanish voyage was launched to the Northwest Coast since that of Vizcaíno. It was made in the 225-ton frigate *Santiago*, or *La Nueva Galicia* (completed at San Blas in October 1773), under the command of Ensign Juan Pérez, a Mallorcan veteran of the Manila galleon run and an experienced pilot of San Blas. As was customary in Spanish expeditions, Pérez was issued a very detailed set of instructions to cover every major eventuality, and Viceroy Bucareli's instructions on this occasion were intended to regulate all future voyages from San Blas to the Northwest Coast. They stressed four essentials: the necessity of keeping complete and accurate logs; the proper way of approaching the coast in order to make a landfall around 60° north; a set of regulations for governing relations with the coastal natives; and directions for dealing with foreign vessels or establishments.[85] Pérez was ordered to take eighty-six men, with provisions for twelve months, and sail to 60° north; there he was to make a landfall and then follow the coast southward to Monterey, noting all places suitable for settlement and taking formal possession of them in the name of the king by erecting a wooden cross and burying a testament in a bottle at the base of the cross. He was given a detailed model for this ceremony, for the Spaniards adhered to the doctrine that sovereignty over *terra nullius* was acquired by the execution of a symbolic act of taking possession. He was also ordered to avoid contact with foreign settlements and vessels, to establish friendly relations with the Indians and to study them, to investigate the natural resources of the coast, and to keep an exact logbook.[86]

The *Santiago* left San Blas on 24 January with a crew of eighty-six, a small party of missionaries, artisans, and settlers for Alta California, and enough stores for a year. The vessel stopped for twenty-five days at San Diego to repair a sprung joint and to cut new masts and stayed for twenty-six days at Monterey to deliver supplies, disembark passengers, and enlist two padres. The departure from Monterey was delayed by calms until 17 June, and for the next month progress was retarded by contrary winds, bitter cold, heavy rain, and thick fog (meaning that celestial observations, crude as they were, could seldom be made); two and a half weeks after leaving Monterey, the ship was still in the same latitude as that port. By mid-July the *Santiago*'s water supply was alarmingly low, so Pérez was forced to try to make land instead of continuing to 60°. He reached the Queen Charlotte Islands, but adverse winds and currents and dense fogs prevented landing and watering; indeed, he encountered so much overcast and fog on this trip that he did not have his first clear view of a sunset until the evening of 4 August, two months after setting sail.[87]

He was met in ceremonious and friendly fashion by some Haidas, who were eager to trade, wanting mostly iron in exchange for Chilkat robes.[88] Since his ship was too large and unwieldy for inshore reconnaissance, since he lacked a backup vessel, and since the coast was unknown, Pérez was unwilling to risk making any landfalls and staking any claims. He reached 55° before turning back. Beset by a strong southerly current and thick fog, the ship put in to the outer harbor (San Lorenzo roadstead) of Nootka Sound (Santa Cruz de Nutka), where it was nearly blown ashore by a sudden change in wind direction. Again contrary winds prevented landing and taking possession, and again the Indians (Nootkas) were eager to trade, offering mostly furs for Monterey shells and iron knives.[89]

During the nine-week voyage from Nootka Sound to Monterey the *Santiago* was pounded by heavy seas and plagued by scurvy (*mal de loanda*, so named after the capital of Portuguese Angola). On this leg nearly two-thirds of the crew were immobilized by the disease; by 19 August, more than twenty men were unfit for duty, and by the twenty-first, six days from Monterey, one of the missionaries wrote, "The greater part of the crew are incapacitated from scurvy, with which nearly all are afflicted, some very seriously."[90] The ship returned to San Blas in October. The venture was not a success. Pérez did not reach 60° north, make any landfalls, lay formal claim to any territory, contact any Russians, convert any natives, or conduct much reconnaissance. His voyage demonstrated the difficulties and weaknesses of large-ship and single-ship expeditions, as well as the vagaries of coastal weather and the dangers of scurvy (the Spaniards did not use anti-scorbutics successfully until the voyage of Esteban José Martinez in 1789).[91] The great eagerness of the Haidas and Nootkas for trade and the high quality of their trade goods (furs) told the Spaniards that there was considerable potential for commercial relations between the coastal Indians and European mariners and that therefore the situation should be closely monitored; unlike Cook, however, they failed to recognize the real value of sea otter skins, perhaps because they did not yet know that these were prized by Chinese customers.[92]

The failure of Pérez necessitated another voyage. Besides, in the eyes of both Madrid and Mexico City, Alta California was still very vulnerable; the Spaniards were not numerous, the Indians were hostile and resistant to conversion, the church and the military clashed, agricultural output was inadequate, supply from Mexico was protracted and hazardous, and production was insufficient to justify state expenditure. The second voyage involved two ships, Pérez's flagship, the *Santiago*, and the thirty-six-foot schooner *Sonora*, or *Felicidad*, in order to enhance security and facilitate the reconnaissance of shallower and narrower inshore channels. They were commanded by two of the six naval officers who had just arrived in New Spain, the Basque Bruno de Hezeta y Dudagoitia (on the *Santiago*) and Juan Francisco de la Bodega y Quadra (on the *Sonora*). The six officers were accompanied by two pilots, who also joined the voyage, Esteban Martínez and Francisco Mourelle; Pérez also took part. The *Santiago* carried ninety men and enough supplies for one year and the *Sonora* twenty-nine men. Hezeta was under orders to reach 65° north and then explore and chart the coast southward and make formal claims.

The two ships left San Blas on 16 March 1774 accompanied by the California supply ship *San Carlos*, bound for Monterey. No sooner had the flotilla set sail than the captain of the *San Carlos*, Miguel Manrique, became deranged and had to be returned to San Blas in a launch and replaced. The voyage north was prolonged by contrary winds and currents, calms, a sprung bowsprit and a sprung topmast, and the slowness of the schooner, which had to be taken in tow by the frigate; not until 13 May did the *Santiago* get its first following wind since leaving port.[93] It took nearly four months to reach the coast of the Olympic Peninsula and four and a half months to make 49°, the expedition's northernmost point. Too much water was used; only two weeks into the voyage 9 of 103 quarter-casks were empty, and livestock were dying for want of water and fodder.[94] And already by 11 May two men had scurvy.[95]

On 10 June both ships put in to Trinidad Bay, where water, wood, and ballast were obtained, the schooner was careened, formal possession was taken, and two men deserted. Here were found seven springs, plenty of timber (including redwood), fertile soil, a sheltered harbor—with, however, a rocky bottom—and Indians who grew and pipe-smoked tobacco and "appeared to be keen at a bargain," especially prizing iron.[96] Leaving Trinidad Bay, the voyagers found that the northwesterly wind was still "the king of these seas."[97] The farther north they went, the rougher the ocean and the more frequent the fog and overcast, so that observations often could not be taken. On 9 July the *Sonora* nearly foundered in a squall; indeed, the schooner proved so unseaworthy that its crewmen feigned illness or injury in order to be allowed to transfer to the frigate, and service on the former was used as a means of punishment.[98] On 13 July strong winds drove both vessels upon the coast at Point Grenville (Washington State), farther south than had been planned. By then the entire crew of the *Santiago* had been sick for two days.[99]

Formal possession was taken of Grenville Bay (Rada de Bucareli). Here Bodega became the first European to learn the costly lesson that the well-developed sense of territoriality and sovereignty of the Northwest Coast Indians, their bellicosity, and their avidity for trade goods could easily trigger violence—a razor's edge, that was subsequently to be honed by the cupidity and ruthlessness of maritime fur traders.[100] On 14 July a wooding and watering party of seven men from the schooner (half its complement) was ambushed and killed by some three hundred Indians; they smashed the party's longboat and salvaged all of its iron ("Iron is what the Indians most prize, because iron articles are what they always ask for first when bartering"). In retaliation, the *Sonora*'s remaining crewmen killed six or seven of nine Indians in an approaching canoe.[101] By now the season was well advanced, the winds were still contrary, and more and more crewmen were being disabled by scurvy. So far nine crewmen had died, and by 19 July twenty-nine were on the *Santiago*'s sick list.[102] On that day the officers of the two ships held a council and decided to continue northward for several days in the hope that both the adverse winds and the scorbutic sailors would improve. The winds did become favorable, but the number of sick increased daily, with fourteen by the twenty-second and sixteen by the twenty-third; the officers unsuccessfully petitioned the commandant to return to Monterey.[103] On 31 July the schooner deliberately lost sight of the flagship, and on that day and on 2 August the officers again advised Hezeta to return, but he persisted in steering north; by then twenty-eight of the *Santiago*'s ninety-four men (many of them unseasoned hands) were flat on their backs, and ten others showed signs of scurvy.[104] On 10 August the Sierra de Santa Clara (Vancouver Island Mountains) were sighted, and on the eleventh Hezeta's officers again begged him to turn back. He finally agreed. They had reached 49°30' north instead of the intended 65°.

On 17 August Hezeta discovered the Bahia de Asunción (later called the Entrada de Ezeta) between Cabo de San Roque (Cape Disappointment) and Cabo Frondoso (Point Adams)—"the mouth of some great river or some passage to another sea," that is, the Columbia River.[105] The Spaniards concluded that this had to be "some great river," but they were unable to enter it and drop anchor because they did not have enough able-bodied men.[106] Thus it remained for Captain Robert Gray to become the first Euro-American to enter—albeit not ascend—the Columbia River. When the frigate reached Monterey on 29 August, fifty men were sick (including thirty-six with scurvy) and twelve men had died; the thirty-six sick with scurvy were transferred to the infirmary at Monterey, where Hezeta stayed for two months awaiting the *Sonora*.[107]

Meanwhile, Bodega and Mourelle in the *Sonora*, despite a shortage of food and water and the lateness of the season, had resolved on 5 August to continue northward: "If we did otherwise, his majesty must have incurred the expence of a fresh expedition."[108] The schooner caught a southwesterly wind and reached 58° north, sighting Mount Edgecumbe (San Jacinto), landing at Sea Lion Bay and Bucareli Bay (Sound) to take ritual possession, and contacting Indians but not finding de Fonte's strait.[109] Excessive cold, continuous rain, and illness and fatigue finally forced them to turn back, since by the end of August only two men could be mustered for each watch, one to man the wheel and one to handle the sails; moreover, the ship sailed "indifferently."[110] The *Sonora* reached Monterey on 8 October, after discovering and surveying Bodega Bay en route, with the entire crew suffering from scurvy, and they had to spend three weeks recovering at Monterey.[111] The *Santiago* and the *Sonora* returned together to San Blas on 20 November, with Juan Pérez dying at sea of typhus two days after leaving Monterey. In their eight-month absence, the packet boat *San Carlos* under Juan de Ayala had surveyed San Francisco Bay.

Bodega had found that the coast trended northwestward, although his calculations were exaggerated above 49° north because the Spaniards' longitudes were not as accurate as their latitudes; this made the likelihood of a Northwest Passage less probable. He also found a safe base in Bucareli Sound but no signs of Russian intrusion (indeed, no Russians were encountered until the fourth expedition of 1788). Of course, both the transcontinental waterway and the transoceanic intruders may have been overlooked. Then the news of Cook's third voyage prompted Madrid on 20 May 1776 to order a new voyage up the coast in an attempt to discover a Northwest Passage before Cook did so. This was delayed until 1779 by a critical shortage of personnel and shipping at San Blas, which was strained to supply both of the Californias. Only three vessels were anchored at the port, which was being shallowed by sand, and the high morbidity and the low pay hampered the recruitment of workers and sailors.[112]

So in 1777 a new ship, the 193-ton frigate *Favorita* (or *Nuestra Señora del Remedios*), was purchased and outfitted in Callao de Lima by Bodega, and another new ship, the frigate *Princesa* (or *Nuestra Señora del Rosario*), was built at San Blas. The *Favorita*, under Ignacio de Arteaga, carried 107 men, food for fifteen months, and water for seven, and the *Princesa*, under Bodega, took 98 men, food for nineteen months, and water for seven.[113] Viceroy Bucareli ordered them to reach 70° north and to explore and claim between 70° and 50°. They left San Blas on 11 February 1779 and stayed far offshore until they made the latitude of Bucareli Sound, where they rendezvoused on 3 May. The voyage had taken nearly three months; en route the two ships became separated for two weeks, and two crewmen of the *Princesa* died.[114] Six weeks were spent in Bucareli Sound making scientific observations and studying the Indians. "They are very desirous of obtaining copper and iron but they are chiefly anxious for iron," recorded the expedition's chaplain, Father John Riobó.[115] Arteaga bought several Tlingit children, hoping to train them as interpreters for future voyages. An unspecified epidemic struck the crew, including the commandant, and killed several. Two longboats explored the sound for almost a month and discovered "several arms of the sea which penetrate deeply into the land," but the Spaniards did not have time to probe them.[116] Two crewmen of the *Fa-*

vorita deserted but were returned by the Indians and were administered twenty lashes each. The expedition reached Prince William Sound (Entrada de Santiago) on 21 July and Cook Inlet (Puerto de Regla) on 2 August, but no Russians and no straits were found—"we had not found the passage we were seeking."[117] On 3 August they decided to return because of the lateness of the season, the foulness of the weather, and the debilitation of the crews; seven men had died, and several others were "dangerously ill" with scurvy.[118]

Homeward-bound, the two ships lost sight of each other for five weeks but in mid-September reached San Francisco, where nearly six weeks were spent in recuperation before returning to San Blas in late November. At San Francisco, Arteaga and Bodega learned that Bucareli had died and Spain had declared war on England. Voyages of exploration to the Northwest Coast were suspended by Madrid on 10 May 1780, since all available vessels and sailors were needed elsewhere.[119] Until the restoration of peace in 1785, the San Blas ships were preoccupied hauling soldiers, supplies, and bullion from Mexico to the Philippines and servicing the Californias; the Spaniards were not even able to reconnoiter the coast of the Santa Barbara Channel until 1782. Still, no Russian trespassers and no Northwest Passage had been located, so there was no immediate threat to the security of New Spain. And initial British reports (1780) on Cook's third voyage substantiated Viceroy Manuel Flórez's belief that the "Russian establishments were sufficiently distant from those of ours."[120] Also, the voyages were costly in piasters (silver dollars), vessels, and sailors (scurvy remained a menace), which were all sorely needed for California. Moreover, so far none of the Spanish explorers had recognized the potential of the sea otter trade, even though the Indians were keen to swap skins for iron and copper and the Spaniards already had a link with the Chinese market at Canton via Acapulco and Manila. Eventually the Spaniards did follow the British lead in the coast trade but not very successfully, thanks in large part to governmental interference.[121]

Furthermore, none of the Spanish observers were optimistic about settlement of the rainy, chilly, mountainous coast, which revealed no irresistible riches like precious metals or valuable spices; besides, the Haidas, Nootkas, Salishes, and Tlingits had certainly not proved to be meek and weak, and Spain was already overextended in Alta California. Finally, the journals of the Spanish voyages were deposited in the archives rather than published, so that Spain's claims remained unpublicized and therefore unappreciated.[122] Such secrecy was "probably the worst possible answer to the curiosity and scientific interests of modern Europe" because it served to pique rather than spike other nations' interest in the Northwest Coast.[123] An example was Cook's third voyage, which hoped at least in part to discover what the Spaniards had already learned but refused to reveal. His widely publicized venture substantiated Britain's claim in the eyes of the world and in addition shattered the isolation of the coast by exposing the potential of the sea otter trade; the British association was reinforced by the publication of several accounts of voyages to the coast by British fur traders such as George Dixon, John Meares, and Nathaniel Portlock.[124]

As a result, the Spanish did not follow up on their first three voyages. Then, however, the official account of Cook's third voyage was published in a lavish folio edition in 1784 and described a Russian settlement on Unalaska Island); and in early 1786 the French explorer La Pérouse stopped at Concepción, Chile, and displayed a map showing four Russian settlements in Alaska and supposedly another in Nootka Sound itself. And La Pérouse provided the Spaniards with empirical details about the Russian establishments when he put in to Monterey in September of the same year for repairs and supplies. Alarmed, Madrid issued orders on 25 January and again on 24 July 1787 for another expedition of two ships to verify and examine the Russian outposts. Its dispatch was delayed, however, until March 1788 by the usual shortage of vessels and officers at San Blas. The *Princesa*, with eighty-nine men, including a pilot, Estéban Mondofia, who knew some Russian, sailed under Esteban Martínez, and the *San Carlos* (nicknamed the *Filipino* because it had been built in the Philippines), with eighty-seven men under Gonzalo López de Haro, followed on 8 March, outfitted for fifteen months. Special measures were taken to combat scurvy, including the periodic airing of bedding and clothing and a thorough cleaning between decks; four barrels of diluted lime juice were carried by the flagship *Princesa*.[125] The expedition investigated two locales of suspected Russian settlement: Prince William Sound (Enseñada de Principe Guillermo) and the Kodiak archipelago. Signs of considerable foreign activity were found, including European trade goods and even English loanwords. Russians were finally encountered on Kodiak Island and Unalaska Island, and warm relations were established. The Russians ate and drank heartily and sang and danced merrily on board the Spanish ships, and one Russian became so drunk and merry that he had to be removed by force. At Three Saints Harbor on Kodiak, the Russian factor Eustrate (Yevstrat) Delarov, a Constantinople Greek who managed the operations of the Northeastern Company (and who was much amused by the similarity of

his name—"Del Haro," in Spanish]—to that of the *San Carlos*'s commander), told Haro that 462 Russians and five ships were at six settlements between Unalaska and Prince William Sound.[126] He also said that next year a
Russian expedition of two frigates would occupy Nootka Sound in order to
thwart the British maritime fur trade, not threaten the Spaniards (this was
probably a reference to the abortive Mulovsky expedition). At Captain's
Harbor on Unalaska, the pilot Potap Zaikov confirmed the projected expedition to Nootka Sound, and he also told Martínez that there were some
five hundred Russians and six galliots in Russian America, more than there
were Spaniards in both Californias.[127] Martínez was told too that a prime
sea otter skin fetched three hundred piasters in Peking.[128] On the return
voyage the two ships, whose commanders were often at odds, became
separated, with the *San Carlos* reaching San Blas on 22 October and the
Princesa arriving on 5 December.

On his return Martínez recommended to Viceroy Flórez that Spain
should garrison Trinidad Bay, the mouth of the Columbia River, Nootka
Sound, and Bucareli Sound, the land farther north being mountainous,
snowy, unforested, unarable, and sterile,[129] and he urged the viceroy to
outfit another expedition under his command in the spring of 1779 to beat
the Russians to Nootka Sound. The information on the strength and designs of the Russians and the activity of British fur traders alarmed Flórez,
as did news of the arrival on the coast of two American ships (the *Lady
Washington* and the *Columbia Rediviva*), which signified to him the U.S.
intention of becoming a transcontinental nation by settling the Pacific
coast.[130] Flórez ordered the occupation of Nootka Sound on 23 December
1788, and Madrid sanctioned this order on 14 April 1789 after the expedition's departure.[131] Flórez had to hurry to forestall foreign competition, and
this meant taking action on his own account without waiting for royal approval, which in turn explains why, in his orders to Martínez, he referred
to the "feigned settlement" of Nootka Sound and why Martínez was to
temporarily abandon it after founding it.[132] Martínez was instructed to tolerate the Russians, since Spain had an agreement with Russia on reciprocal
port visits, to challenge the British, on the grounds of priority, and to expel
the Americans; he was to defend Spanish interests and enforce the Laws of
the Indies, according to which the coast belonged to Spain and foreign
trade with the Indians was forbidden.[133]

The *Princesa* and the *San Carlos* left San Blas on 17 February for the Entrada de Nutka, the former carrying 106 crewmen and 15 soldiers and the
latter 89 crewmen and 16 soldiers, the soldiers intended for the permanent

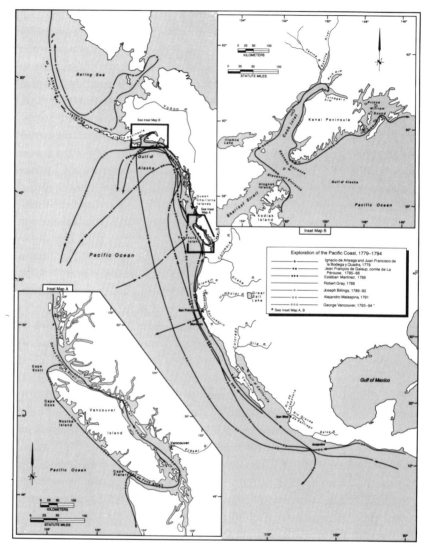

Map 14.2 Exploration of the Pacific Coast, 1779–1794.

garrison at San Lorenzo de Nutka.[134] Because of the hasty preparations, this expedition suffered not a few breakdowns, delays, and deaths. When Martínez reached Nootka Sound on 5 May he found not Russian warships but two American and one British fur-trading vessels (the *Lady Washington*, under Captain Robert Gray, the *Columbia Rediviva*, under Captain John

Kendrick, and the *Iphigenia Nubiana*, under Captain William Douglas); the British vessel was flying Portuguese colors in order to circumvent the monopolies of the East India and South Sea Companies. Martínez was hostile to the British but friendly to the Americans, especially Kendrick, since the Americans curried his favor with intelligence on the British coast trade and the Indians. Then additional British coasters arrived, and Martínez seized the *Argonaut*, under Captain James Colnett, and the *Princess Royal*, under Captain Thomas Hudson, and sent them with their crews to San Blas. He also seized the British schooner *North West America*, under Captain Robert Duffin, a ship built at Nootka Sound in 1788 by Captain John Meares; Martínez renamed it the *Santa Gertrudes* and used it to explore the Strait of Juan de Fuca. He built his own schooner as well, the *Santa Saturnine*, to reconnoiter the coast of Vancouver Island. Undoubtedly Martínez was an irascible man, and he overreacted to Colnett's insults, but he saw no alternative if Spanish sovereignty was to be upheld and British ships barred from Spanish waters, so he resorted to force; for his part Colnett was unstable and intemperate, and soon after the seizure of his ship, he lost his mind and attempted suicide. These seizures and impressments annoyed the Nootka Indians, who were benefiting from the fur trade, but during their protests, Chief Callicum was shot and killed by mistake; more important, such seizures precipitated the Nootka Sound crisis between Britain and Spain.[135] British public opinion was inflamed by a book published in 1790 by Meares, one of the backers of the ventures of the seized coasters, who claimed that when he had stopped in Nootka Sound in 1788, Chief Maquinna had granted him lands and acknowledged British sovereignty.[136] Martínez's side of the story, however, would not be published until 1964!

Meanwhile, the Spaniards felled timber, built a road, planted gardens, and erected buildings, including the fort of San Miguel on Hog Island at the entrance to Friendly Cove. But on 29 July the frigate *Aranzazú* arrived from San Blas with orders to abandon the establishment before winter, Viceroy Flórez taking this step probably in case Madrid failed to sanction the venture. So Martínez left on 30 October with another prize, the American schooner *Fair American*, under Captain Thomas Metcalfe. Then the Conde de Revillagigedo reached Mexico on 6 August to replace Flórez as viceroy, with Madrid's instructions to sustain the Californias, explore the northern coast, and thwart foreign designs. So he ordered the reoccupation of Nootka Sound in the spring of 1790 by the commandant of San Blas, Bodega, who assigned the task to Francisco de Eliza.

Although he was demoted to the rank of pilot in the new expedition,

Martínez had been one of the few Spaniards to envision the commercial possibilities of the Northwest Coast. Realizing that more than a single, small military outpost would be needed to control the coast, he proposed that a fifty-year royal monopoly be granted to a Spanish-Mexican company for the exploitation of the sea otter and fur seal trade with Canton, with the company being obliged to found at least four presidios, each manned by one hundred soldiers, and sixteen missions on the coast and to operate twelve armed vessels for supplying the settlements, preventing clandestine traffic by foreigners, and transporting furs to China; the company would also be responsible for the upkeep of the soldiers, padres, and ships. Martínez believed that the venture was bound to succeed because of the proximity and wealth of Mexico, which could provide plenty of copper, iron, abalone shells, and textiles as trade goods. The Hawaiian Islands, he proposed, should be occupied as a transpacific base and a source of provisions, having "all necessities in abundance." The furs would be exchanged at Canton for Chinese goods for Mexico, including mercury (quicksilver), which was vital to Mexican silver production and which was normally obtained from Spain but was subject to wartime disruptions. And, he suggested, Mexican industry would be stimulated by the expansion of markets to the Northwest Coast.[137]

This, then, was an archetypical mercantilistic scheme, one designed to exploit two colonies, the Northwest Coast and Hawaii, for the benefit of the motherland, Mexico. However, Spanish readers, unlike their British counterparts, were not apprised of the commercial prospects of the coast until the 1802 publication of the journal of Bodega's 1792 voyage, and by then the sea otter trade had already peaked for a second time. Meanwhile, Flórez had rejected Martínez's plan, but Revillagigedo tested it by sending a shipment of 3,356 sea otter skins to Canton. Only 2,803 of them were sold, and they did not yield much profit partly because almost all of them were lower-quality (smaller and lighter) California skins (only 208 were prime "black skins" from the Strait of Juan de Fuca) and partly because the Canton market had been overloaded by the first peak of the coast trade in 1792; however, the 35,100 pounds of mercury that were obtained proved as good as the European metal.[138]

The Eliza expedition for the reoccupation of Nootka Sound—comprising the flagship *Concepción*, the *Princesa Real* (the seized *Princess Royal*) under Manuel Quimper, and the San Blas packet boat *San Carlos*—left San Blas on 3 February 1790 with seventy-six soldiers of the First Regiment of

Catalonian Volunteers from Tepic under Lieutenant Colonel Pedro de Alberni. Eliza had received "secret instructions" from Bodega on 28 January directing him to fortify Nootka Sound and to explore "the rest of the northern coast of California" from Cook Inlet to the Strait of Juan de Fuca.[139] The flotilla arrived on 5 April. This time the Spaniards were more cautious and more diplomatic than Martínez had been. They developed close and harmonious relations with the Indians, avoiding sexual contact and trade in firearms.[140] With the willing assistance of Chief Maquinna's men, eight buildings were erected, including the new fort of San Miguel Castillo on Hog Island, New Spain's northernmost outpost. Eliza disliked the place, describing its climate as "intemperate and intolerable" and "horrible and detestable," although Alberni succeeded in developing some gardens, the first on the Northwest Coast. In the winter months many soldiers and sailors suffered from various disorders, including catarrh, rheumatism, colic, and especially scurvy and "bloody flux" (dysentery); during the first winter (1790–91), from five to nine men died, and thirty-two had to be evacuated to California in the spring to recover their health.[141] By 1792 the Spanish garrison at Nootka Sound numbered 200–250 men.[142] In the spring of the same year another fortified settlement, Puerto de Núñez Gaona, was founded at Neah Bay on the Olympic Peninsula side of the Strait of Juan de Fuca.

The early 1790s marked the apogee of Spain's presence on the Northwest Coast and the heyday of Spanish exploration there, with the possession of two bases in situ facilitating a flurry of detailed probing. The coast between Cook Inlet and Puget Sound was finally explored, more or less systematically, by Spanish navigators. Partly in response to news from St. Petersburg about the southward advance of Russian fur traders as far as the "California" coast and the dispatch of the Billings expedition, in 1790 Salvador Fidalgo in the *San Carlos* probed Cook Inlet and Prince William Sound and reconnoitered the coast southward to Nootka Sound. Again Russians were contacted in Cook Inlet and on Kodiak Island, and it was clear that there was little or no potential for Spanish activity. Captain Billings actually sent a letter in English to Lieutenant Fidalgo inviting him to meet in Prince William Sound, but the Spaniard was unable to read it and therefore missed the opportunity to gain firsthand intelligence.[143]

So the Spaniards concentrated on searching for a Northwest Passage, particularly from Juan de Fuca and Georgia Straits. Also in 1790 Quimper was assigned the task of exploring the Strait of Juan de Fuca in the *Princesa*

Real, since Colnett had not yet reached Nootka Sound to reclaim his ship. Quimper left Puerto de Nutka (or Nuca) on 31 May and spent two months exploring the northern and southern shores of the Estrecho de Juan de Fuca, finding several good harbors, including Royal Roads at present-day Victoria, and plenty of Indians and taking formal possession in four places. He also learned something of the intensity of the maritime fur trade: the Indians told him that so far that year, Clayoquot Sound had been visited by seven trading vessels and Neah Bay by five or six.[144] Quimper himself mainly traded copper sheets for numerous sea otter skins; in general, the Spaniards traded copper sheets (each measuring twenty-six inches in length and twenty-two inches in width and as thick as a coin) and Monterey shells.[145]

The explorations continued in 1791, 1792, and 1793. In 1791 Eliza was ordered to explore "the rest of the northern coast of California" from Cape Saint Elias to Trinidad Bay.[146] He sailed in the packet boat *San Carlos* and the schooner *Santa Saturnine*, or *La Orcasitas*, and examined El Gran Canal de Nuestra Señora del Rosario la Marinera (Georgia Strait) and its "indescribable archipelago of islands, keys, rocks, and big and little inlets," as well as both sides of the Estrecho de Juan de Fuca.[147] Eliza reported the probable insularity of Vancouver, or Quadra, Island and the probable existence of the Fraser River, as well as the definite existence of many spacious channels leading inland.

The primary purpose of the "Expedition of the Limits" of 1792 under Bodega was the settlement of the conflicting claims of Britain and Spain on the Northwest Coast, but the secondary purpose was the exploration and charting of the Straits of Juan de Fuca and Georgia in order to find a Northwest Passage. In 1790 the Spanish court had retreated, conceding that the British could prosecute the maritime fur trade north of Nootka Sound and establish a settlement on the sound itself. Now Bodega and Vancouver met but failed to agree on a settlement of the dispute, the latter refusing to accept the Spanish offer of a boundary through the Strait of Juan de Fuca (with the result that the Spaniards abandoned Puerto de Núñez Gaona). The failure of Bodega and Vancouver to agree was referred to their home governments for resolution, and the final convention of 1793 essentially stipulated the enforcement of the 1790 convention, entailing the payment of Spanish reparations of £20,000 and the recognition of Britain's right to navigate, traffic, and fish in the waters of the coast. The Spanish and the British commissioners finally settled the affair in March 1795 at Nootka Sound, with the Spaniards disclaiming exclusive sovereignty over the port—but not relinquishing their claims to the coast—and abandoning their fort, whose site once again became a Nootka Indian village.

Bodega had more success with exploration than negotiation. He led the ambitious "Expedition of the Limits" in an impressive array of ships: the frigates *Santa Gertrudes*, *Aranzazú*, and *Princesa*, the twin schooners *Sútil* and *Mexicana* (*Nuestra Señora de la Asuncion*), and the brig *Activa*, the last three built at San Blas. Originally Viceroy Revillagigedo had chosen Francisco Mourelle to lead the expedition, ordering him to explore the coast from 55° north to San Francisco Bay with "exactness and diligence," so that "by examining in detail all the bays, ports, rivers, capes, and inlets which enter the continent, [he] will give definitive knowledge for all time of that interesting region, today the principal object of European nations." The voyage had three purposes: (1) to provide "exact information" for "the arrangement and determination of the final convention with the officials of His Britannic Majesty . . . and the dividing line with that nation"; (2) to acquire the same "exact information" so that "in the future it will not be necessary to expend more money in such voyages of this character as up to today have been repeatedly made to those seas, and which accidents did not permit the solving of the urgent theoretical matter" that the viceroy was "confiding"; and (3) to "resolve the doubts" about "the imaginary straits which should end in Baffin Bay and Hudson's Bay" and "remove the fears which such passages, if they should be discovered in the future, may occasion at our court through the general subversion of commerce."[148] In other words, the expedition's exploratory task was to determine once and for all whether the Strait of Juan de Fuca extended completely through the continent to the Atlantic.

At the insistence of Alejandro Malaspina, who was visiting the Northwest Coast and New Spain during his grand expedition around the world, Mourelle was replaced by Bodega and two of Malaspina's best officers, Dionisio Galiano and Cayetano Valdés; they were accompanied by the naturalist José Mariano Moziño, who was to spend a productive summer at Friendly Cove. They left Acapulco on 8 March but did not reach Nootka Sound until 13 May because of the usual contrary winds; the *Mexicana* was even dismasted en route. The Spaniards were slow to learn that hugging the coast and going ashore for supplies as needed constituted an impractical way of sailing northward up the coast in the face of strong adverse winds and currents from the north and northwest; a preferable plan was to head out to sea until southerly winds were caught, steer northeastward, and strike the coast at a high latitude.[149] Also, they had yet to learn that frigates were too large and schooners too small for coastal exploration. The *Sútil* and the *Mexicana* were supposed to combine the advantages of light draft and handiness under sail or oar, but before departure both had to be enlarged and strengthened at Acapulco, where workmen and matériel were scarce.[150] Vancouver still found them too light and too small, calling them "miserable vessels" and saying that they were "the most ill calculated and unfit vessels that could possibly be imagined for such an expedition."[151] On the basis of information from the local Indians, who were generally friendly and helpful, providing fresh provisions as well as navigational directions, Galiano in the *Sútil* and Valdés in the *Mexicana* explored the most promising channels leading inland.[152] All of these, however, proved to be dead ends, except that of Rosario (Georgia Strait), which they eventually followed, rounding Vancouver Island in conjunction with Vancouver's ships (the *Discovery* and the *Chatham*) and demonstrating its insularity by returning to Nootka Sound three months after leaving it.

Off the delta of the Fraser River they conjectured, from the freshness of the seawater and the presence of floating logs, that they were in the estuary of a "considerable" river but did not enter it because they thought that it emptied into the Canal de Floridablanca (Burrard Inlet); one of the officers named the suspected river Rio Blanco.[153] Off Point Grey's Spanish Banks, the Spaniards met Vancouver, and the two expeditions agreed to explore together, although in fact they did not really collaborate, each side probing inlets on its own and declining to accept the results of the efforts of the other. Longboats were used to explore the many *estrechos* (straits), *canals* (channels), *bocas* (mouths, bays, sounds, or inlets), and *enseñadas* (passages or openings), such as Boundary Bay and Burrard Inlet, but they found that none penetrated beyond the coastal mountains into the interior. These geographical features were frustratingly deceptive:

> Most of these channels present an aspect entirely novel. Following the mainland some breaks are to be seen and on going into any of them an arm of the sea is found, usually tortuous, a half mile or 1 to 2 miles wide, formed by the sides of rocky mountains, which are very lofty and almost straight up, so that they look like a very lofty wall. In mid-channel bottom is not usually found at 80 fathoms and on sounding near the shores the lead is sometimes felt to roll down without stopping. Anyone entering to survey these channels will be surprised, and perhaps will think he has found the desired communication with the other sea [Atlantic], or an easy means of getting

many leagues into the interior of the mainland, but all his hopes will fade, when, without having seen any sign to indicate that the channel is coming to an end, he will find on turning a bend that the mountains have closed up on both sides and form an arc, leaving usually a narrow beach, on which a few steps may be taken.[154]

In addition, the two schooners were hampered by variable winds, irregular tides, eddies and whirlpools, and frequent rain. The Spaniards concluded that in the absence of a Northwest Passage, the region was worthless: "When it had once been settled, as it was as a result of this exploration, that there was no passage to the Atlantic through the Fuca Strait, the gloomy and sterile districts in the interior of this strait offered no attraction to the trader, since in them there were no products, either of sea or land, for the examination or acquisition of which it was worth while to risk the consequences of a lengthy navigation through narrow channels, full of shoals and shallows."[155]

Meanwhile, Bodega had dispatched Jacinto Caamaño to check Colnett's report of a possible waterway (the Strait of de Fonte) to Hudson Bay from the coast between 50° and 53° north.[156] Caamaño was ordered by Bodega "to sail for Puerto de Bucarely [Bucareli Sound] for the purpose of exploring its various arms, and surveying the coast lying between it and Nootka," and "to use every effort to discover and chart the principal channels, gulfs, and harbours, so far as these were yet unknown," particularly de Fonte's strait.[157] However, he had little time ("hardly more than a couple of months for the execution of a commission embracing so many objects of interest and of danger"), and his ship, the *Aranzazú*, was a slow sailer; although not very large, it drew fourteen and one-half feet of water, too much for shallow inlets, although he did have a pinnace and a cutter for working small channels.[158] In addition he noted, "Our difficulties were increased through the scanty, confused, and nonconsonant accounts of this stretch of coast given by private adventurers [maritime fur traders] (for no government expedition as yet had visited it), and by the continued fogs that are so often experienced off it."[159] Caamaño explored Clarence Strait (Canal de Nuestra Señora del Carmen) in the hope that it was the Estrecho de Fonte, but the strait did not materialize.[160]

Thus, by the end of 1792 the Spaniards knew that the Northwest Coast offered no Northwest Passage, although they had not explored as thoroughly as Vancouver, particularly to the south of the Strait of Juan de Fuca. So on 30 April 1793, Eliza in the *Activa* and Juan Martínez in the *Mexicana* were dispatched from San Blas to chart the coast from Cape Flattery to the Golden Gate, something that previous expeditions had been ordered to do but for various reasons or excuses had not.[161] In particular they were to make "a long and minute examination" of the Columbia River to its source, for if the source was found to be near or within New Mexico, the viceroy intended to establish a settlement there to support Spanish rights on the coast south of the Strait of Juan de Fuca and extend the California chain of presidios and missions northward.[162] Only the *Mexicana* reached the river, however; Eliza, in the *Activa*, blamed contrary winds and insufficient water for his premature return.[163] Martínez did enter the Columbia but ran aground fourteen miles upriver and was met by Chinook war canoes, whereupon he turned back. And in the summer of the same year Juan Matute in the *Sútil* and Salvador Valdés in the *Aranzazú* sailed to Bodega Bay to found a colony, but the latter ship drew too much water to enter the port and the former could not find suitable construction timber nearby, so the attempt was abandoned.[164]

In the meantime Spain had mounted its answer to Cook's last voyage: Malaspina's grandiose expedition around the world. It and La Pérouse's were intended to match Cook's exploits and restore some prestige to Spanish and French navigation and science.[165] Under the able and enlightened (literally and figuratively) monarchy of Carlos III (1759–88), the scientific exploration of the empire was energized: for example, the launching of the Royal Scientific Expedition of New Spain in 1786 and Malaspina's circumnavigation of 1789–94.[166] Malaspina, an Italian, left Cádiz in two corvettes, the *Descubierta* and the *Atrevida*, each nearly three hundred tons and each carrying 102 men, with orders to make scientific observations, take latitudinal and longitudinal measurements, collect curiosities, and compile economic statistics. On the Northwest Coast he was to verify Spanish claims to Vancouver Island, determine the value of extending New Spain's boundary northward to Nootka Sound, and try to find, at 60° north, the fabled Strait of Ferrer Maldonado.

The two ships reached Acapulco in early 1791 and sailed for the Northwest Coast on 1 May, taking two months to reach Lituya Bay. They spent two summers surveying, charting, and studying the coast; much cartographic, meteorologic, hydrographic, botanical, zoological, and ethnographic data were amassed, but as usual, almost none of the journals, reports, maps, and drawings were ever published—and they remain unpublished to this day. The men "did not accomplish all they desired on account of the heavy fogs on the coast," reaching as far north as 59°36′, and "only the consummate skill of the commander and the officers was able to keep them from the greatest damage."[167] In early August, off the Queen Charlotte Islands (Floridablanca), the two vessels were nearly lost in "six days of terrific storm," the worst on the entire voyage from Spain ("it seemed as if all the machinery of the universe were ready to destroy us").[168] And on the *Descubierta*, cockroaches were "such a great pest that you see some individuals with sores on their foreheads and bites on their fingers."[169] Malaspina did not enter and search Prince William Sound because his orders told him to go only as far north as 60°, and by then, mid-July, the season was advanced; at first he thought that Yakutat Bay (Port Mulgrave) opened into Maldonado Strait, but this was explored by longboats and was found to be "entirely closed on all sides by very steep high mountains."[170] Between Cross Sound and Dixon Entrance, the expedition found "an archipelago of an infinite number of islands of different sizes which covered the whole horizon"[171]—the labyrinth of the Alexander Archipelago. Malaspina himself concluded that Maldonado Strait did not exist.[172]

Once the Spaniards had established by 1793 that there was no transcontinental strait from the Pacific to the Arctic or the Atlantic Ocean, they lost interest in the Northwest Coast and retrenched. The last Spanish voyage to the Gulf of Alaska was made in 1792, when Núñez Gaona was dismantled; San Miguel de Nutka followed in 1794. Additional reasons lay behind Spain's retreat, however. The expeditions were distinguished by neither boldness nor expertness. Although the Spaniards were the first to the coast after Bering and Chirikov, they failed to press their advantage by risking the hazards of inshore navigation, being content instead to reconnoiter at a distance, just as they were content not to publicize their presence and not to occupy the coast before their imperial rivals. In the words of a French seaman, "If other navigators of these latter times had conducted their researches with the prudence and circumspection which the Spaniards employed in theirs, our knowledge would not thence have received a great increase. When a coast is to be examined, it is not by approaching *so near as not to be able to leave it, and by keeping at a proper distance, and only having a view of it from day to day*, that a navigator can hope to discover inlets, channels, bays, etc."[173] He added, "Unskilfulness, timidity, concealment: whatever may be the cause, no matter; for to us the effect is the same."[174]

The "concealment" was another negative factor. The failure of the Spaniards to publish the logbooks and journals of their voyages lessened the credibility of their claims. And their secrecy stimulated rather than dampened interest. As Vancouver acknowledged: "The profound secrecy which the Spanish nation has so strictly observed with regard to their territories and settlements in this hemisphere, naturally excites, in the strongest manner, a curiosity and a desire of being informed of the state, condition, and progress of the several establishments provided in these distant regions."[175] Moreover, for several centuries Spain had been content with the symbolic act of territorial acquisition: going ashore, erecting a cross, reciting a litany, and burying a deed of possession in a bottle under a pile of stones at the foot of the cross. But by the late eighteenth century, this ritual was no longer sufficient; it had to be augmented with surveying and mapping, publication of the results of exploration and discovery, and better yet, settlement and exploitation. Malaspina, for example, tried to have his journals and maps published after he returned, but he was not successful, for although he was promoted, he was soon exiled as a result of court intrigue. He subsequently returned from exile at the intercession of Napoleon but died in obscurity in 1809.

Substantiation of Spanish claims by occupation was unsuccessful. His Catholic Majesty's men found both the land and the people of the Northwest Coast uninviting—"useless territory" suffering from a "horrible and insufferable" climate and inhabited by "savage Indians."[176] The Spaniards did eventually establish themselves in Nootka Sound, but its economic potential was limited, especially in terms of farming and mining, and after the early 1790s it no longer even served as a rendezvous for maritime fur traders. The naturalist Moziño, who spent five months there in 1792, favored abandoning the Spanish post because it incurred "enormous expenses" and had "not produced any advantage in favor of the crown." He noted that "very few furs" were left. Also, the Spanish could not stop the fur trading by American and British coasters because there were too many harbors elsewhere for them to use; he estimated that six to eight thousand men would be needed to guard all of the harbors, and the "enormous expenses" likely would not be defrayed even if Spain was able to monopolize the coast trade.[177]

Spain's failure to ply the maritime fur trade early and fully was another weakness. The dons knew as early as 1769 that the Indians of the Santa Barbara Channel hunted sea otters for fur for capes and cloaks in the cool season,[178] and they must have known from their Manila-Canton commercial connection that there was a keen Chinese demand for furs, especially sea otter skins. Moreover, New Spain was a close source of trade goods (particularly textiles but also metals, firearms, and provisions) for the Northwest

Coast Indians, and of course, the Manila galleon afforded a readymade pipeline to the Chinese market. So the Spaniards were not lacking in prerequisites. As Cook's surgeon, David Samwell, remarked at Nootka Sound in the spring of 1778 when two silver spoons of Spanish manufacture (probably obtained from Pérez of the *Santiago* in 1774) were bought from the Indians, "The Spaniards might carry on a very profitable Trade with these People for their Furs."[179] But they did not. When Malaspina returned to Acapulco from the coast in late 1791 to winter, he recommended that Mexican entrepreneurs become involved in the sea otter trade, but his advice—unlike that of Captain James King, who completed Cook's voyage and journal—went unheeded. Perhaps the Spaniards realized that under the terms of the final Nootka Sound convention, they simply could not compete in the coast trade with the British, let alone the Americans.[180] At any rate, without an economic base, the Spanish presence on the coast could be justified only on strategic and political grounds, and those grounds evaporated with the settlement of the Nootka Sound controversy and the demonstration of the nonexistence of a strait through the continent, both of which occurred by 1793.[181]

The failure to develop the maritime fur trade meant that the Spanish base at Nootka Sound was more expendable and a Spanish retreat from the Northwest Coast more defensible. But the retrenchment was linked as closely, if not more so, to California, which was seen as more deserving of concern than the coast. In the words of Moziño, "The first object of our attentions should be California." He explained, "There our conquest has taken roots, our religion has been propagated, and our hopes are greatest for obtaining obvious advantages to benefit all the monarchy." San Francisco's harbor was "the best of any that have been seen on the entire coast." He added, "The landscape is very beautiful, the soil fertile, the mountains wooded, and the climate benign." All it needed was more colonists, since San Francisco's presidio contained only fifteen soldiers and Monterey's scarcely more than thirty.[182] Bodega realized and recommended that it was more important to buttress California than Nootka Sound.[183] Both he and Malaspina believed that maintaining Nootka from the base of Monterey was too expensive (the abortive attempt to occupy Bodega Bay in 1793 was designed in part to fortify it as a northern bastion in place of Nootka). They recommended that Nootka be abandoned in favor of the strengthening of Alta California, and that is what Viceroy Revillagigedo advised Madrid in 1792.[184] California was unquestionably underdeveloped and needed strengthening, a condition that would cost Mexico the province in the 1840s; the lifeline to San Blas, itself a poor port, was long and thin, and the intervening peninsula of Baja was largely rugged desert. In 1790 in Alta California, according to Malaspina, there were only 8,495 persons (7,530 Indians and but 965 Hispanics) with 27,000 cattle, 26,450 sheep, 6,750 horses, 550 mules, 550 pigs, 50 burros, and a harvest of 23,300 fanegas (1 fanega equals 2 1/2 English bushels of wheat) of grain, mostly wheat and corn, as well as beans and peas, at eleven missions, four presidios, three stock farms, and two pueblos.[185]

Captain Vancouver reconnoitered Alta California in 1793 and discovered what Revillagigedo himself admitted was "the deplorable state of [the Spanish] presidial defenses."[186] Vancouver observed that the Spaniards, "though possessing the very extensive and fertile tract of land lying to the northwest from San Diego," had not "turned it to any profitable advantage," mostly because of the "confined, and . . . very indolent, life" of the presidio soldiers and mission fathers, as well as "the impolicy of excluding foreign visitors," that is, the ban on foreign trade. There were no more than three hundred soldiers in Alta and one hundred in Baja California, including sixty to eighty at Monterey, sixty at each of Santa Barbara and San Diego, and thirty-six at San Francisco, all of whom were "well qualified to support themselves against any domestic insurrection" but were "totally incapable of making any resistance against a foreign invasion." Vancouver noted, "Why such a territory should have been thus subjugated, and after all the expence and labour that has been bestowed upon its colonization turned to no account whatever, is a mystery in the science of state policy not easily to be explained." He concluded that by having such scattered and unprotected frontier settlements, the Spanish, "instead of strengthening the barrier to their valuable possessions in New Spain," had "thrown irresistible temptations in the way of strangers to trespass over their boundary."[187]

The answer to Vancouver's rhetorical question was that California was opened before the appearance of a real foreign threat nearby, and once that threat materialized, Spain (like Russia) was too overextended to take much action. The year after Vancouver's visit, Viceroy Revillagigedo, whose chief concern had been Northwest Coast policy, was succeeded by the Marqués de Branciforte, who was more interested in lining his own pockets than in extending or even buttressing the *frontera del norte*.[188] And the outbreak of war between Spain and Britain in 1796 prevented any further Spanish ventures on the Northwest Coast. Spain reaped few advantages from these expeditions, thanks to the decline of its sea power in the Pacific,

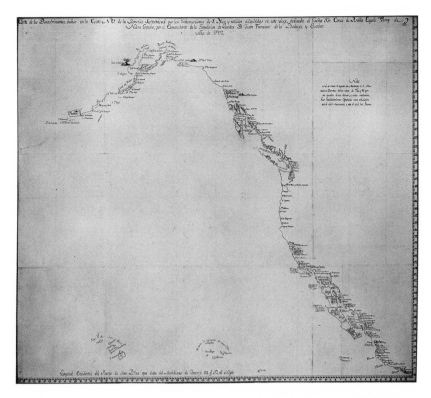

14.2 *"Carta de los Descubrimientos hechos en la Costa N.O. de la America Septentrional par las Embarcaciones de S. Blas . . ." (1793). This summary map shows the discoveries made from the Spanish naval base at the Mexican port of San Blas since 1767. The map is a good representative view of the sum of Spanish geographical knowledge of the Pacific coastal region up to the time of waning Spanish influence in the region. Courtesy and permission of the Oregon Historical Society, ORHI 74110.*

the abandonment of its long-standing claim to exclusive sovereignty in that ocean, and its increasing commitments in Europe, including involvement in the French Revolution and Napoleonic wars.[189] The decline of its empire was accelerated by the Bourbon captivity (1808–14) of the Spanish throne and, of course, by the piecemeal loss of the American colonies from the 1810s through insurrection. Meanwhile, the British Empire was growing, the loss of the Thirteen Colonies notwithstanding, and it was British, not Russian, imperial power—spearheaded by Captain Cook's third voyage—that thwarted Spain on the Northwest Coast.

British Exploration

In the seventeenth century and the first two-thirds of the eighteenth, British interest in the Pacific was motivated by commerce, plunder, and adventure (e.g., the voyages of Francis Drake, Thomas Cavendish, William Dampier, and George Anson), the South Sea being seen not as a virgin field for scientific inquiry but as the western and the eastern frontiers of a rival Spanish empire.[190] In the last third of the 1700s, trading and raiding were augmented by scientific inquiry and national strategy, the Pacific offering both an unspoiled laboratory for naval explorers and natural scientists and a potential keystone for maritime empire, with remote islands and putative continents to survey, "noble savages" to study, and exotic colonies to open as producers of cheap raw materials for the motherland and as consumers of the motherland's manufactured goods.[191] Between the ending of the Seven Years War in 1763 by the Treaty of Paris, with Britain emerging as the world's foremost colonial power at the expense of France in India and North America, where Québec and Louisburg were lost, and the outbreak of the French revolutionary wars thirty years later, both Britain and France experienced a "Pacific craze" in which naval explorers and itinerant scientists appeared as a new type of national hero.[192] Britain was spurred partly by a desire to substantiate its growing status as a global sea power and maritime empire and a nationalist desire to vie with rival empire builders and partly by a new spirit of nationally sponsored scientific inquiry, for example, the founding of the Royal Society, the activities of the naturalist Sir Joseph Banks, and the British desire to observe the transit of Venus from Tahiti in 1769.

Both the strategic and the scientific motives lay behind the search for a Northwest Passage.[193] A shorter route from the Atlantic to the Pacific offered commercial advantages for merchants and military advantages for the Royal Navy. In the first half of the nineteenth century, the search was undertaken largely by private merchants in Hudson Bay and, after their failure, by costly state expeditions in the vast and international waters of the Pacific. And once Vancouver's meticulous survey finally and thoroughly disproved the speculations of armchair geographers about a transcontinental waterway, the search would shift to the Arctic Ocean, impelled by scientific interest, national prestige, and simple curiosity and adventurousness—hence what Captain Vancouver referred to as "the several laborious undertakings projected by His Britannic Majesty, for the attainment of a true and perfect geographical knowledge of the earth."[194]

The three voyages (1768–71, 1772–75, and 1776–80) of Captain James Cook constituted the foremost of these "laborious undertakings"; indeed, they were so laborious as to have enervated Cook by the time he was killed on Hawaii in 1779 at the age of fifty-one. His first and second voyages destroyed the concept of Terra Australis, the mythical southern continent. The two strategic aims of his third voyage were to find a northwestern or northeastern passage, which would give Britain strategic command of the Pacific from the north, and on the outward passage to verify the islands of potential strategic advantage that the French had recently discovered southeast of the Cape of Good Hope (the Crozet Islands). The two scientific aims were to advance science in general and geography in particular by observing, collecting, and recording along the northern shores of the Pacific and to find a winter base in the North Pacific for such exploration and discovery.[195] Nevertheless, the primary objective remained, in the words of the Admiralty, "to find out a Northern passage by sea from the Pacific to the Atlantic Ocean."[196]

Cook was to proceed via the Cape of Good Hope to Tahiti, where he was to repatriate Omai, a passenger from his second voyage, and on to the coast of New Albion at 45° north, and "then to proceed Northward along the Coast as far as the Latitude of 65°," whereupon he was "very carefully to search for, and to explore, such Rivers or Inlets as may appear to be of a considerable extent and pointing towards Hudsons or Baffins Bays." If he found none, he was to winter at Petropavlovsk. He was instructed, "Proceed from thence to the Northward as far as, in your prudence, you may think proper, in further search of a North East, or North West Passage, from the Pacific Ocean into the Atlantic Ocean, or the North Sea."[197] Cook's flagship was the *Resolution*, 462 tons and 112 men, and his consort was the *Discovery*, 298 tons and 69 men under Captain Charles Clerke. Because of Cook's unhappy experience of quarrels and deaths with civilians on the first and second voyages, the third included fewer nonnaval men; John Webber, however, was enlisted as the requisite artist and was mainly responsible for making this the most profusely illustrated of all prephotography voyages.[198] Cook chose as officers a number of men who were to become well-known in their own rights, including James Bligh, James Burney, James Colnett, George Dixon, John Core, James King, Nathaniel Portlock, and George Vancouver.

En route to the Northwest Coast, the expedition found the Crozet Islands, landed Omai, and discovered and christened the Sandwich (Hawaiian) Islands, which with their convenient location, cheap provisions, balmy climate, and willing women would serve well as the desired North Pacific base. Reaching the New Albion coast on 7 March 1778 at Cape Foulweather in 45° north, one crewman noted, "We found it to trend North and South without the least signs of a bay or inlet; the inland parts are very mountainous but the shore is of a moderate height."[199] The prospects of finding a Northwest Passage here were further weakened by three weeks of inclement weather—"a series of the most tempestuous weather that ever blew," in the opinion of the *Discovery*'s Lieutenant John Rickman, who would publish the first surreptitious account of the voyage.[200] Another officer, surgeon's mate David Samwell, described the situation: "Squally W^r [weather], with fogs & frequent Showers of Snow, Hail and Sleet, which made it very dangerous to approach this unknown Coast too near where we knew of no Shelter, we were kept cruizing off & on the Land till the 29th, of this Month, when we luckily discovered a Harbour in Lat. 49° 28′ [Nootka Sound] into which we stood."[201] So Cook, who had planned "to range along the Coast," had to "stand off" much of the time, thereby getting only a very general outline of the shore.[202] Consequently, the mouth of the Columbia was missed, and although Cape Flattery was made and named, missed too was the Strait of Juan de Fuca. "It is in the very latitude we were now in where geographers have placed the pretended *Strait of Juan de Fuca*, but we saw nothing like it."[203] Even Nootka Sound was "luckily discovered," partly because a landfall was sorely needed to make repairs to the battered vessels and to wood, water, and brew spruce beer (as an antiscorbutic).

At King George's (Nootka) Sound, the men repaired the ships, wooded, watered, and hayed, erected a forge and observatories, and reconnoitered in longboats. The "Country was full of high Mountains whose summits were covered with snow; but the Vallies between them and the land on the sea Coast, high as well as low, was cloathed with wood,"[204] so plenty of spars and masts were available, as well as firewood and spruce for beer. The sound was as well peopled as it was timbered. The Nootka Indians were friendly and eager to barter: "We found the coast to be inhabited and the people came off to the Ships in Canoes without shewing the least mark of fear or distrust." The official journal of the voyage noted, "They . . . shewed great readiness to part with any thing they had and took whatever was offered them in exchange, but were more desireous of iron than any thing else."[205] The Indians offered mostly sea otter skins, which were readily accepted. "Nothing is so well received by us as skins, particularly those of the sea beaver or Otter, the fur of which is very soft and delicate," noted Midshipman Edward Riou.[206] The main reason for getting furs "was for clothing to secure [the men] against the cold," both now and later, farther north.[207] Another midshipman, James Trevenen, traded the rim of a broken iron bucket as an armlet for a whole sea otter skin, which he subsequently sold at Canton for $300![208] The *Discovery* alone left Nootka Sound with more than three hundred sea otter skins, plus the pelts of other furbearers.[209] When the expedition departed on 26 April, the natives "importuned [the British] much to return . . . again and by way of incouragement promised to lay in a good stock of skins for us." Cook added, "I have not the least doubt but they will."[210] Cook himself made it clear in his official account, published in 1784, not only that valuable furs, particularly sea otter skins, could be had for trifles but also that the Indians were numerous, mercantile, friendly, and honest, that the sound was roomy and deep with many sheltered anchorages, and that water, timber, and fish were abundant. The ensuing "fur rush" to the Northwest Coast by British and American shipowners is hardly surprising.

After leaving Nootka Sound, Cook intended "to keep along shore," but squalls and easterly winds forced the two ships offshore, preventing him from "keeping the Coast aboard" and checking the legendary Strait of Admiral de Fonte in 53°.[211] "It would have been highly imprudent in me to have ingaged with the land in such exceeding tempestious weather, or to have lost the advantage of a fair wind [from south-southeast to southwest] by waiting for better weather."[212] So Cook missed the Queen Charlotte Islands and the Alexander Archipelago, staying half a dozen leagues (eighteen miles) offshore. The extinct volcano of Mount Edgecumbe was named, after a promontory in Cook's birthplace of Whitby, as was the "large Inlet" of Cross Sound, but the latter was not probed. Moreover, Cook stated, "As we sail along the Coast we find it trending to the Southward & Westward according to Muller's Chart of Bering's Discoveries, which reduces our Hopes of finding a Northwest passage to a low ebb."[213]

The *Resolution* had sprung a leak during the stormy weather, and Cook resolved to put in at the first available harbor, which proved to be that which he named Sandwich (Prince William) Sound. Here one of the *Resolution*'s officers "bought as many Sea Beaver Skins for half a dozen blue Beads as sold afterwards for 40£ at Kamtschatka" and for $90–100 at Canton; another officer traded sixteen to twenty green Spanish beads from Tahiti for eight to ten sea otter pelts worth £200–300 at Kyakhta.[214] The abundance of blue and green beads among the local natives prompted speculation that the beads may have been brought by Russian traders or via a Northwest Passage.[215] Two openings in the western and northern reaches were explored uneventfully, if inconclusively, "as induced Capt Cook to conclude that there was no Passage through them, & therefore no more time to be lost at this place," which they were "now well satisfied was a Sound."[216] Rickman lamented, "It was found it [sic] be only an inlet through which there was no passage for ships to any other sea."[217] The expedition proceeded westward and on 16 May entered and ascended a "vast river" (Cook's River or Inlet) whose shores, however, became narrower and narrower and its waters fresher and fresher. "All hopes therefore of a communication with any other sea in this passage vanished."[218] Then Cook found that his river was a dead end, and he had to turn back, dubbing it the Turnagain River; for the same reason, Lieutenant John Gore's "Gulf of Good Hope" became the "Seduction River" of William Bayly, the astronomer. Thus, they were "disappointed a second time" in their "hopes of finding a Passage through the Continent" of America. "We now begin to think that our only chance will be through Bering's Straits."[219]

Cook did not delay; he was already a year behind schedule, and besides his orders directed him to seek a Northwest Passage in 65°. For this reason alone he felt that it was "very doubtfull" that either Prince William Sound (60–61° north) or Cook Inlet (59–61° north), which the Russians already knew as Chugach (Chuvash) Bay and Kenai Bay, respectively, led to "a Strait that would communicate with the Northern Seas," for he knew that in 1772 Samuel Hearne had crossed the Barren Grounds and boated down the Coppermine River to its mouth in what Hearne thought was 72° north (actually about 68° north) without bisecting a strait, so that any such strait must lie farther north.[220] "We were now upwards of 520 leagues to the Westward of any part of Baffins or Hudsons bays," wrote Cook, "and what ever passage there may be it, or some part of it must lie to the North of 72° latitude; who could expect to find a passage or strait of such extent?" He added, "We were now convinced that the Continent extended farther to the west than from the Modern Charts we had reason to expect and made a passage into Baffin or Hudson bays far less probable, or at least made it of greater extent."[221] Indeed, the extent to which Alaska projected southward as well as westward was a surprise.[222]

So Cook made for the Bering Sea and Bering Strait to seek a northwestern or northeastern passage north of 65° before the onset of winter. En route, he rounded the Alaska Peninsula and reconnoitered Bristol Bay and Norton Sound, but "the whole was a continued Coast."[223] Samwell remarked:

> Captain Cook having now run along the western Coast of America
> till he fell in with the Coast of Asia in Lat. 65° & Long. 189° 26' E, He

has proved that there is no passage through the Continent of America; for tho' we did not keep the Land in Sight all the way, yet the shoal water we had all along affords a sufficient Proof of the Continuation of the Coast, & precludes the possibility of any considerable opening in that short Space of it which we did not see which lies between. We are now in Bering's Straits which divided Asia from America as high as these two Continents are known, our only Hopes of a Passage now is round the Northern Extremity of America.[224]

However, here Cook, like Clerke a year later, was stopped by pack ice "as compact as a Wall," which proved "an impenetrable Barrier to . . . Progress beyond 70°."[225]

The two ships headed south to winter at the Hawaiian Islands, where the aging and ailing commander carelessly got himself killed. On the way they made a stopover for repairs at the Russian factory of Captain's Harbor on Unalaska Island. Here they met Gerasim Izmailov, who, according to Captain James King, said that five Russian fur-trading vessels (each of sixty to seventy tons) plied between Siberia and Alaska; their "principal object" was sea otter fur, which they sold "to the Chinese at an exorbitant profit."[226] After the British left Unalaska, Izmailov portrayed them, to the commandant of Kamchatka, as traders bent on competing with the Russians in the sea otter traffic.[227] "Such," reported Rickman, "is the jealousy the Russians entertain of the trade to the north, which they now look upon as we did formerly upon the trade to America [i.e., the Thirteen Colonies], as of right belonging to them; —founding their claim on their priority of discovery, Bhering having first traced the way to the north west continent of America."[228] Cook himself stated, "There is no doubt but a very benificial fur trade might be carried on with the Inhabitants of this vast coast." He added, "A trade with Foreigners would increase their wants by introducing new luxuries amongst them, in order to purchas which they would be the more assiduous in procuring skins, for I think it is pretty evident they are not a scarce article in the Country." He cautioned, however, that unless a Northwest Passage was found, it would be "rather too remote for Great Britain to receive any emolument from it," and the only valuable pelt was that of the sea otter; in addition, most of the skins acquired by the expedition were not prime, being lousy and already in the form of clothing.[229]

The expedition wintered in Hawaii in 1778–79 and then, with Captain Clerke having succeeded to the command at Cook's death, returned to Arctic waters via Kamchatka to try again to find a northwestern or northeastern passage. Again they were frustrated by ice, whereupon they headed home via Petropavlovsk and Canton. During the second visit to Kamchatka, Clerke died of tuberculosis and was replaced as commander by Captain King; the British sold their good sea otter skins here for 20–30 rubles (£4–6) each and their very best skins for 35 rubles (£7) each (1 ruble equalled 4s.3d.), learning that one of the former fetched 100 rubles at Kyakhta.[230] They were very well pleased with these terms of trade until they reached Canton, where they found that the skins were worth nearly twice as much as at Petropavlovsk, the Chinese setting a "great value" on them.[231] Here the crewmen sold the rest of their sea otter pelts, which had been bought for a hatchet or a saw, for $50–70 (£11 5s.–£15 15s.) apiece.[232] Not surprisingly, the eagerness of some of the men to return to the Northwest Coast to make their fortunes bordered on mutiny; in fact, several did desert in a longboat to do just that.

Thus, Cook's last voyage publicized the lucrative possibilities of the maritime fur trade, and within a year of the 1784 publication of his and King's official account, the first British trading vessel, appropriately named the *Sea Otter*, left Macao for the Northwest Coast.[233] The Russian monopoly was finally broken, and Izmailov's fears were realized. Cook had also revealed the Hawaiian Islands and their potential as a way station. But he had failed to find a Northwest Passage, at least through Prince William Sound or Cook Inlet or beyond Bering Strait. Elsewhere he had charted the coast in only a very general—even slipshod—fashion, for the charting was done by means of fixes taken aboard the ships while standing offshore. He therefore missed the mouths of the Columbia, Fraser, and Yukon Rivers, the three largest on the entire Pacific coast of North America, as well as the existence of the Strait of Juan de Fuca, the insularity of Vancouver Island, and the intricate complexity of islands and channels along the fjorded coast between Puget Sound and Cross Sound. The fact that this master mariner did so reflects the particular constraints of his orders, the difficulties of navigation of the Northwest Coast, and the physical and mental decline of Cook himself since his second voyage.[234] At any rate, there was no denying that the transcontinental strait might still exist.

Then in 1789 in London, Alexander Dalrymple, a hydrographer with the British East India Company, published a pamphlet entitled *A Plan for Promoting the Fur-Trade, and Securing It to This Country, by Uniting the Operations of the East-India and Hudson's-Bay Companys*. Dalrymple was a friend of Governor Samuel Wegg of the Hudson's Bay Company and a confidant of such maritime fur traders as George Dixon, whose Queen Charlotte Islands strongly suggested de Fonte's archipelago of Saint Lazarus and whose report of a large river near the supposed latitude of the Rio de los Reyes seemed to be confirmed by James Hanna, another maritime fur trader and the captain of the *Sea Otter*.[235] Dalrymple believed that the northwestern corner of North America was a vast archipelago and lay farther south than Hearne had indicated, so that there was a strong possibility of a navigable waterway between the coast and the interior. He therefore advocated a merger of the Hudson's Bay and the East India Companies to confer British control of both the source of, and the China market for, furs, thereby by-passing Russian middlemen, who generally took up to a quarter of Canadian beaver for resale in China, and securing half a continent for His Britannic Majesty.[236] Obviously the question of the Northwest Passage had to be settled once and for all by means of a thorough exploration of the coast. By now private fur-trading vessels were plying the coast annually, but their objective was mercantile profit, not scientific discovery, so it was left to the state to mount the requisite expedition.

The result was the five-year voyage (1791–95) of Captain George Vancouver, who spent three navigation seasons (1792–94) on the coast in the 340-ton sloop *Discovery* (with one hundred men) and the 135-ton armed tender *Chatham* (with forty-five men under William Broughton), plus the 350-ton storeship *Daedalus*.[237] The purpose was "to make an accurate survey of the coast" from 30° north to Cook Inlet (60° north) because the possibility of a transcontinental strait had been resurrected by the uncovering of a multitude of inlets and channels along the coast by the maritime fur traders, Cook not having examined the coast south of 60° north in detail. Moreover, the explorations of the Spaniards were so "defective" as to be unenlightening, thanks in part to the "extreme caution" of the Spanish.[238] Another purpose was to accept formally at Nootka Sound the "restitution" by the Spaniards of British territorial rights on the coast under the terms of the Nootka Convention of 28 October 1790.[239] The Admiralty's instructions made it clear, however, that the expedition was being undertaken primarily "for acquiring a more complete knowledge, than has yet been obtained, of the north-west coast of America" between 30° and 60° north with a view to, first, finding any transcontinental waterway and, second, gathering information on any European settlements.[240] Vancouver, incidentally, presumed "that the principal object which His Majesty had in view, by directing this expedition to be undertaken, was that of facilitating the commercial advantages of Great Britain in this part of the world."[241]

The expedition was a prolonged venture, delayed by adverse weather, frequent repairs, slow logistics, ill health, Vancouver's caution, and native opposition. It took the two ships just over a year to make the coast via the Cape of Good Hope, and it took a month to sail from the Hawaiian Islands to the Californian coast. They coasted north from Point Cabrillo (39° north) one to two leagues (three to six miles) offshore, with visibility frequently impaired by rain, fog, or haze. At sundown they usually "hauled off shore, and spent the night in the offing," returning inshore at daylight.[242] Rocky islets, sunken rocks, and sandy shallows proved troublesome. There was no sign of Aguilar's supposed river or strait between 39° and 43° north.

At the mouth of the Columbia, Vancouver spotted "the appearance of an inlet, or small river, the land behind not indicating it to be of any great extent; nor did it seem accessible for vessels of our burthen, as the breakers extended . . . two or three miles into the ocean." He even noted, "The sea had now changed from its natural, to river coloured water." But he added, "Not considering this opening worthy of more attention, I continued our pursuit to the N.W. being desirous to embrace the advantages of the prevailing breeze and pleasant weather."[243] So again the Columbia River was overlooked. Continuing northward, Vancouver met Captain Robert Gray in the *Columbia Rediviva* just north of Destruction Island and within view of Mount Olympus. Gray reported that in 1789 he had sailed fifty miles into the Strait of Juan de Fuca and that the natives had told him that it continued northward but that he had not found an "inland sea." Gray also said that he had tried in vain for nine days to enter a river (the Columbia) in 46° north but had been stymied by breakers. Vancouver, however, "continued to laugh at an Opening having been discovered by a Merchant Vessel which he said Capt. Cook could not have missed had such a one existed." Vancouver was sure of himself because between Cape Mendocino and Cape Flattery he had found that the coast "was firm and compact, without any opening into the mediterranean sea . . . or the least appearance of a safe or secure harbour." The "most fortunate and favorable circumstances of wind and weather," he wrote, had "afforded the most complete opportunity of determining its [the coast's] various turnings and windings; as also the position of all its conspicuous points," showing "the whole coast forming one compact, solid, and nearly straight barrier against the sea" and disproving "the existence of arms of the ocean, communicating with a mediterranean sea, and extensive rivers, with safe and convenient ports," contrary to the opinions of "theoretical geographers" and "closet philosophers."[244] Moreover, Vancouver had been instructed not to waste time by pursuing any inlet or river any farther than a seagoing vessel could navigate.[245] At the same time, however, he had also been instructed to determine not only the general configuration of the coast but also the direction and extent of any considerable inlet or river that might prove to be a transcontinental waterway.[246] Vancouver was too sure of himself and too uncritical of Cook. After leaving Vancouver, incidentally, Gray continued southward and found and entered the Columbia, five months before Broughton in the *Chatham* would do so.

At Cape Classet (Flattery) the geography plainly indicated an opening of considerable extent.[247] The cape was rounded and Tatoosh Island was passed, and the two ships coasted along the southern shore of the Strait of Juan de Fuca, fair weather affording a clear view of the "beautiful scenery," including the volcanic cones of Mounts St. Helens, Rainier, and Baker, all of which Vancouver named. Having missed such anchorages as Coos Bay (Oregon) and Willapa Bay (Washington), he now found a harbor in which to refit—Discovery Bay. Now too he met Indians, who occasionally gave him geographical information (between Cape Cabrillo and Cape Flattery he had met almost none). From here, Vancouver began his month-long, tedious survey of Puget Sound by pinnace, launch, and cutter in the face of frequent rains, wary natives, and scarce provisions. He soon realized that the coastline was every bit as broken as was purported by the logs and maps of the maritime fur traders and that surveying it thoroughly, in order to prove or disprove the existence of a transcontinental waterway, would be a protracted task. Vancouver wrote:

> I became thoroughly convinced, that our boats alone could enable us to acquire any correct or satisfactory information respecting this broken country; and although the execution of such service in open boats would necessarily be extremely laborious, and expose those so employed to numberless dangers and unpleasant situations, that might occasionally produce great fatigue, and protract their return to the ships; yet that mode was undoubtedly the most accurate, the most ready, and indeed the only one in our power to pursue for ascertaining the continental boundary.[248]

So the *Discovery* and the *Chatham* would anchor in a spacious and sheltered harbor where wood and water were available, spruce beer could be brewed, and an observatory and instruments could be erected. From this base, boat expeditions would survey the surrounding islands and continental shoreline, each expedition comprising two boats manned by an officer (usually Joseph Whidbey or James Johnstone), a midshipman or two, some marines, and rowers, well armed, provisioned for up to a fortnight, and carrying trade goods, gifts, instruments, and tents for the men and a marquee for the officers. Their work began at dawn and ended at dusk; brief landings were made for meals.

Vancouver was quite taken with the Puget Sound country: "The serenity of the climate, the innumerable pleasing landscapes, and the abundant fertility that unassisted nature puts forth, require only to be enriched by the industry of man with villages, mansions, cottages, and other buildings, to render it the most lovely country that can be imagined."[249] The eastern coastland of the sound from 45° to 50° north (Desolation Sound) he dubbed New Georgia; he located New Albion between 35° and 45° north, New Hanover from Desolation Sound to Point Staniforth (53° 30' north), New Cornwall from Point Staniforth to Point Rothsay (56° 30' north), and New Norfolk from Point Rothsay, or Sumner Strait, to Cross Sound (58° north). These were not, in Vancouver's opinion, breached by a transcontinental strait because he believed that the Coast Ranges, the Cascade Range, and the Coast Mountains formed "one barrier along the coast," an "insurmountable barrier to any extensive inland navigation."[250]

Leaving Puget Sound, the expedition proceeded northward into Georgia Strait. Despite noticing the sandy shallows and the different color of the water at the mouth of the Fraser River, and even surmising that there might be "a river of considerable extent" here, Vancouver missed it (as did the Spaniards).[251] Subsequently he was also to bypass the Skeena, Nass, and Stikine Rivers. He asserted that he had "with sanguine hopes and ardent exertions" sought an "inland navigation" via a "breach in the eastern range of snowy mountains," but this assertion in fact refers to the major inlets like Howe Sound and Jervis Inlet, not the major rivers.[252]

After probing Burrard Inlet, and making no comment at all on its potential as a natural harbor (today it is the port of Vancouver), Vancouver met off Point Grey the *Sútil* and the *Mexicana*, whose Spanish officers were courteous and helpful and offered to collaborate in the exploration of Georgia Strait.[253] The British commander did not really trust the Spanish surveying, however, especially of the "continental shore," the focus of his attention, so the two sides largely duplicated each other's work. Vancouver described the steeply rugged and heavily wooded shores of the strait north of 49° as "desolate and inhospitable" and "very broken and divided country."[254] Boat exploration of the broken coast was "fatiguing and hazardous service," and all along the coast stretched Vancouver's "snowy barrier," or "barrier mountains."[255] He did find that Georgia Strait afforded a channel between Vancouver Island and the mainland "which, though narrow, is fair and navigable," and on 10 July a boat expedition passed through "a communication with the ocean" (Johnstone Strait) with some help from the local Kwakiutls (earlier some Indians had assured the Spaniards that the strait did join the ocean proper to the north, thereby making Vancouver, or Quadra, Island just that).[256] At the end of the summer the two ships sailed around Cape Scott to Nootka Sound to accept the formal restitution of the latter to Great Britain from Bodega, who behaved with "politeness, hospitality, and friendship" and suggested that the Strait of Juan de Fuca form the boundary between the possessions of His Britannic Majesty and His Catholic Majesty, but Vancouver declined, citing his lack of authority to do so and agreeing to refer the matter to their home governments. At any rate, the Spanish flag was struck and the Union Jack hoisted in its place in Friendly Cove.

In October the expedition headed south to winter in Alta California. This southern trip enabled Vancouver to reconnoiter the Spanish establishments and to survey the coast south of Cape Mendocino; he sailed four to five miles from the shore, which proved compact rather than broken.[257] En route the *Chatham* entered the Columbia River, which, Vancouver concluded, was inaccessible to large vessels except in very fine weather and even then only to ships of less than four hundred tons.[258] Broughton anchored the *Chatham* in the river's mouth, and then he—unlike Captain Gray, who had confined himself to Grays Harbor at the entrance—spent a week on a boat expedition about one hundred miles upstream, naming Mount Hood and taking possession in the king's name. Turning back because his provisions were running out, he concluded that the Columbia "could hardly be considered as navigable for shipping," although Edward Bell, the ship's clerk, believed that "this River *might* communicate with some of the Lakes at the opposite side of the Continent." In leaving the river, the *Chatham* experienced the notorious bar and its "heavy breakers," which "rolled with impetuous force."[259]

In the spring of 1793 Vancouver resumed his exploration of the coast of New Cornwall—"this desolate region."[260] This season the boats were cozier and safer, each having been furnished with a canopy, a tent, more rations, and more firearms. Nevertheless, the boat work remained "tedious, arduous, and hazardous," given the tortuous channels, uncharted waters, wind and rain, and even poisonous mussels. The myriad of channels and islands formed an "intricate inhospitable labyrinth," and sometimes the boats ventured up to 150 miles from the mother ships. Vancouver

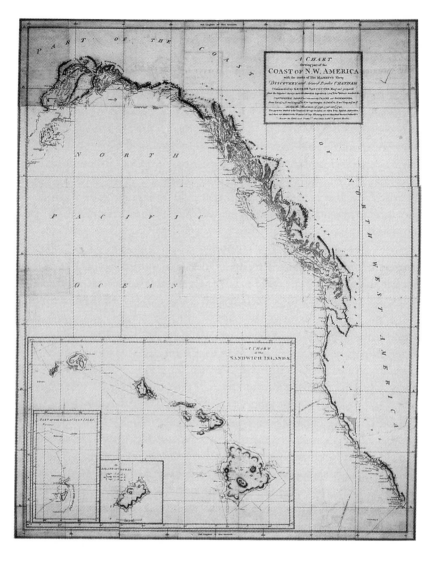

14.3 *"A Chart showing part of the Coast of N.W. America"* *(George Vancouver, 1801). Published in Vancouver,* A Voyage of Discovery *(London, 1801). Vancouver produced a number of important maps of the Pacific coastal region. The significance of this map, of course, is that it locates, for the first time on a major cartographic production, the correct location and lower course of the Columbia River. Collection of John L. Allen.*

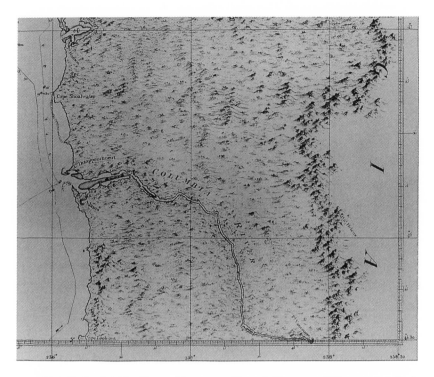

14.4 Detail of a chart by George Vancouver (from A Voyage of Discovery, *1801), showing the lower course of the Columbia River. The observations for this map were taken by Lieutenant Broughton, who entered the Columbia and penetrated approximately one hundred miles upstream. At the head of his navigation of the river, one of his officers speculated that the Columbia might "communicate" with lakes on "the opposite side of the continent." Collection of John L. Allen.*

himself chafed under "the slow and irksome process by which [the] researches were carried into execution, on account of the extremely divided state of this extraordinary inhospitable region."[261]

The survey was recommenced in Burke Channel. A series of "openings" in the continental shore in the form of fjorded inlets and arms were explored, but all proved dead ends, terminating commonly in low, marshy ground. The men could usually tell by the whiteness and freshness of the water that these firths were about to end. "All the small branches leading to the eastward either terminate at the foot of the lofty range of rugged mountains, or else form into islands parts of the shores of these inlets," wrote

Vancouver.[262] From Captain William Brown of the coaster *Butterworth* the British learned of an "extensive inland navigation" (Clarence Strait) to the north and a "large opening" (Portland Inlet) to the northeast called "Ewen Nass" by the Indians, but neither continued as a transmontane channel.[263] The work of verification was, as usual, demanding and frustrating. In one boat excursion around Revillagigedo Island the crew spent twenty-three days traveling more than 700 miles "without having advanced our primary object of tracing the continental boundary, more than 20 leagues [60 miles] from the station of the vessels." "Such," said Vancouver, "were the perplexing, tedious, and laborious means by which alone we were enabled by degrees to trace the north-western limits of the American continent."[264]

Again rivers were given short shrift. On a summer boat excursion Lieutenant Johnstone nearly overlooked the Nass River, which Vancouver described as "a little river . . . navigable only for canoes" (later Johnstone did overlook the Stikine River). The commander confidently asserted that the only two rivers that they had discovered north of the Columbia, the Skeena and the Nass, had not actually been explored but nevertheless "scarcely deserve[d] the appellation of rivulets" and disproved the "pretended discoveries" of de Fonte, that is, the Rio de los Reyes and its source, Lake Belle.[265] Lieutenant Peter Puget, however, was not so sure, declaring that he regretted that the Nass had not been explored further:

> for though it might not appear an eligible navigation for large Vessels at its entrance, which is the case with many Rivers, yet it might issue from or communicate with some interior Lake extending to a considerable distance inland & thereby afford a sufficient scope for a Voyage of two or three Moons in Canoes as reported by the Natives; in this case to ascertain the direction & extent of such an opening would not merely be an object of curiosity, but might in the end turn out of the greatest utility to the commercial interest of our Colonies on the opposite side [of the continent], by directing the adventurous & persevering views of the Canadian [North West Company] & Hudson's Bay [Company] Traders to a part of the Coast where their laudable endeavours would most likely succeed in penetrating across by an interior chain of Lakes Rivers, & by that means might be enabled to draw yearly from this Coast the greatest part of its rich & valuable Furs, for which purpose the entrance of the present opening could not be better situated, as from all accounts this is the most abundant part of the Coast for Furs of superior quality.[266]

In fact, the North West Company had done just that in the person of Alexander Mackenzie, who became the first European to cross the North American continent north of Mexico when he arrived at the mouth of the Bella Coola River at the head of the North Bentinck Arm of Burke Channel on 22 July 1793, just forty-seven days after Vancouver had been there. Mackenzie's expedition showed that the overland route from Athabaska to the Pacific was long, the cordillera was rugged, and the rivers were turbulent.[267] And in 1807 Simon Fraser found his river unsatisfactory as a route through Vancouver's mountain barrier, so that it remained for Meriwether Lewis and William Clark in 1805–6 and David Thompson in 1810–11 to demonstrate that the Columbia was the best alternative, although even it was flawed by a bar at its mouth and a gorge—the counterpart of the Fraser Canyon—in its lower course.

By September, worsening weather and shortening daytime, as well as the need for recuperation and replenishment in a milder climate, made Vancouver head south again to continue his reconnaissance of Spanish California. He explored the Californian coast from Bodega Bay south to 30° north but decided to winter in the Hawaiian Islands after the Spaniards proved less hospitable and more suspicious than in 1792. Vancouver also completed his hydrographic survey of the Hawaiian archipelago.

In the spring of 1794 the expedition returned to the Northwest Coast for its last season. The two ships sailed directly to Cook's River (Inlet), which "the theoretical navigators," who had "followed him in their closets," saw as a possible Northwest Passage. This "very extensive opening" was probed and found to terminate in an "uninterrupted barrier," so it was renamed an inlet.[268] Vancouver also found that Cook Inlet and Prince William Sound were occupied by several small posts of rival Russian fur-trading companies, to whom the local natives were tributary. The Russians at Cook Inlet told Vancouver that the water body was a dead end and that it was separated from Prince William Sound by the very narrow neck of the Kenai Peninsula, a neck frequently crossed by Russians and natives alike.[269] Vancouver stressed that because of the language barrier, he could not trust the information extracted from his Russian informants, but he did not take the time to wait and meet Alexander Baranov, who directed the operations of the Golikov-Shelikhov Company in Cook Inlet and who was to become the first governor (1799–1818) of Russian America. Nor did Vancouver bother to put in to Resurrection Bay in Prince William Sound to talk to a British shipwright, James Shields, employed by the same company. He did discover that the Russians with their enserfed native hunters were ranging as far south as Port Mulgrave (Yakutat Bay); a flotilla of seven hundred kayaks with fourteen hundred native hunters (Aleuts and Kodiaks) under ten Russians was operating from Cook Inlet as far eastward and southward as that port.[270]

In Prince William Sound the boat parties found that all of the inlets, arms, canals, and bays, like Valdez, were dead ends. Then the continental shore south to the King George the Third (Alexander) Archipelago was explored and all of its openings, like Lynn Canal and Taku Inlet, found wanting. Everywhere the "lofty snowy barrier" blocked all channels leading eastward.[271] Vancouver concluded that his "minute examination" would "remove every doubt, and set aside every opinion of a *north-west passage*, or any other water communication navigable for shipping, existing between the North Pacific, and the interior of the American continent," as well as "the existence of a *hyperborean or mediterranean ocean*" inland.[272] So contemptuous was Vancouver of the speculations of Europe's armchair geographers that he had sailed with the aim of *disproving*, not *discovering*, a transcontinental waterway for sailing ships. At the end of his meticulous and exhausting survey, he could not completely contain his glee: "In the course of the evening [of 16 August 1794 in Frederick Sound] no small portion of facetious mirth passed amongst the seamen, in consequence of our having sailed from old England on the *first of April* [April Fool's Day], for the purpose of discovering a northwest passage, by following up the discoveries of De Fuca, De Fonte, and a numerous train of hypothetical navigators."[273]

Although disdainful of a transcontinental strait, and even more so of its deskbound and landlubberly advocates, Vancouver nevertheless extolled "the very extensive, and extraordinary insular state of the region lying before the western coast of the American continent, between the 47th and 59th degrees of north latitude," particularly the "inland navigation for canoes and boats . . . from the southern extremity of Admiralty inlet, in latitude 47° 3' . . . to the northern extremity of Lynn canal, in latitude 59° 12'," that is, the one-thousand-mile long Inside Passage from Puget Sound to Cross Sound.[274] Vancouver's hydrographic mapping of this infinitely and intricately fragmented interface of land and sea was especially thorough and detailed, thanks to newer instruments than Cook had and also to the use of longboats for inshore exploration. Consequently, the possibility of a transcontinental strait was finally refuted—and Vancouver Island circumnavigated and the Columbia River entered and ascended. So accurate were Vancouver's coastal charts that they were still being used by maritime fur traders into the 1830s and by other navigators in the late 1800s. During a voyage of almost five years, Vancouver lost only five men out of a complement of one hundred on the *Discovery* (four by accident and one by disease), whereas the *Chatham* did not lose anybody.[275] The superb undertaking drained Vancouver himself, however; he returned to England a sick man, living only two and one-half more years and dying at the age of forty.

There was one more British expedition, but it was so anticlimactic as to be incidental; besides, the Asiatic rather than the American side of the North Pacific was the focus of its attention. This was the much-delayed and problem-ridden venture of Broughton in 1795–98 in the sloop of war *Providence*, which displaced four hundred tons and carried 115 men and 16 guns.[276] The original main purpose of the voyage was to explore the Pacific coast of South America, but when Broughton assumed (incorrectly) that Vancouver had already done so, the intent became the exploration of the Asiatic coast of the Sea of Japan, for as Vancouver himself had said, "The Asiatic coast, from about the latitude of 35″ to 52° North, is at present very ill defined."[277] The *Providence* was eventually lost on a reef off the Formosan coast in 1797; subsequently forty-three of the men were transferred to the *Swift* and were lost in the wreck of that vessel, and another ten men were killed by natives, accidents, and disease.[278] Nevertheless, Broughton succeeded in his mission by buying at Macao the schooner *Prince William Henry*, a former coaster, although his findings essentially confirmed those of La Pérouse. Earlier, in 1796, Broughton had visited Nootka Sound and Neah Bay, and en route from Hawaii he had searched in vain for the supposed island of Doria Maria Lajara, said to have been discovered in 28°30′ north and 202°30′ east by the Spanish ship *Hercules* in 1781. In Friendly Cove he found that the Spanish settlement had been replaced by an Indian village.[279] The *Providence*, the last Royal Navy ship to sail the Northwest Coast before the War of 1812, left Nootka Sound just before the arrival of the *Sútil*, the last Spanish vessel to visit the coast.

French Exploration

There were only two French voyages of exploration and discovery to the Pacific coast of North America before 1800, and one of them was really a fur-trading venture. French activity was undoubtedly hampered by the turmoil of the French Revolution (1789) and its aftermath, including the

French revolutionary wars (1792–1802) and the Napoleonic wars (1803–15), and was discouraged by superior British sea power (in wartime), the Seven Years War (1756–63) and its outcome, and even the failure of La Pérouse to return from his grandiose venture. In the words of one French chronicler: "France would unquestionably have continued to promote the progress of geography, if interests more important, and an expensive war carried on to support them, had not employed her entirely, and demanded all her resources for some years past. Peace [in 1783], however, recalling the attention of government in great measure to the arts and sciences, promises new expeditions for their advantage."[280]

Only one of these "new expeditions," that of La Pérouse in 1785–88, touched the Northwest Coast. It was planned as a four-year voyage, chiefly for exploration and discovery of the islands and seas of the South Pacific and the coasts and waters of the North Pacific, in two altered flutes, the frigates *Boussole* and *Astrolabe*, each carrying ninety-six men.[281] A secondary purpose of the voyage was to gather commercial and political information en route on colonies, coasts, and islands.[282] La Pérouse decided to explore the North Pacific first. His instructions ordered him to "make without delay for the north-west coast of America" and "make a strict search in the parts not yet known, to see whether there be not some river, or some narrow gulph, forming a communication, by means of the interior lakes, with some parts of Hudson's bay."[283] In the summer of 1786 the two ships searched in vain for such a transcontinental strait, although the commander realized that he did not have enough time to examine the coast thoroughly. In Lituya Bay two boats capsized in breakers, and twenty-one men drowned.[284] After leaving Botany Bay in early 1798, the two ships disappeared. Thirty years later the remains of both were found on a reef in the Santa Cruz Islands of Melanesia by the trader Peter Dillon.[285] Fortunately, materials from the expedition had been forwarded to France from Petropavlovsk and Macao in 1787 and Port Jackson in 1788.[286] At Macao in January 1787 La Pérouse had sold his one thousand sea otter skins for only ninety-five hundred Spanish silver dollars, about one-quarter the going rate that season (he contended that because of the flooding of the market by British traders, skins were worth only one-eighth to one-tenth as much as in 1780).[287] He was still optimistic about the prospects of the coast trade, however. He believed that a factory in Lituya Bay could collect ten thousand sea otter skins annually, and at Monterey a Spaniard had told him that fifty thousand could be taken yearly on the Californian coast.[288]

Nevertheless, only two French fur-trading voyages ensued, and not in heed of La Pérouse's intelligence. Homeward-bound in 1788 at Saint Helena, the British trader Nathaniel Portlock told Étienne Marchand of the possibilities of the coast trade.[289] Delayed six months by the Nootka Sound dispute, Marchand finally left France at the end of 1790 in the three-hundred-ton *La Solide* with fifty men.[290] On the coast in Sitka Sound, Marchand found skins dirtier and costlier than he had expected, at Canton he learned that their importation was prohibited, and at Marseilles he saw them impounded during the counterrevolutionary movement. And when they were eventually released, they were wormy and of little value; his backer, the firm of J. and D. Baux, lost two-thirds of its investment in the venture.[291] In 1792–93 Captain M. Magon made a coastal voyage in the six-hundred-ton *La Flavie*, seeking both La Pérouse and furs but finding only some of the latter, as well as two mutinies, so that "their expedition . . . had not answered their expectations."[292] Not surprisingly, this was the last French ship to visit the Northwest Coast until 1817. Meanwhile, the field was left to dozens of British, American, and Russian private fur-trading vessels.[293]

Corporate Exploration

Although Captain Cook did not uncover a Northwest Passage, he did expose something of equal or even greater commercial value—"black skins," the dark, lustrous pelts of the sea otter, the "soft gold" of the Russian *promyshlenniks*. Sea otter fur was prized by the upper classes of North China, mainly as fancy trim rather than as warm garb. And as Cook had shown, abundant furs could be obtained on the coast for trifles and sold at Canton for much more in silver dollars, with the Hawaiian Islands providing a convenient caravanserai. His countrymen were quick to follow his lead, and by 1792 the coast trade had already reached its first peak of some two dozen vessels; the second peak came in 1802. As one Spanish navigator described the situation in 1792:

There was hardly a single point on the coast between 37° north and 60° north which had not been visited by these ships, and so, if we have no detailed and accurate map based on the results of these voyages, it is because those who discovered a harbour or entry which had not been known before, and where they found inhabitants and were able to secure skins at a profit, availed themselves of the chance and concealed the news of their discovery, in the expectation that they would be able for a long while to carry on an exclusive trade in that district.[294]

Moreover, the fur-trading vessels had neither the personnel nor the equipment for scientific exploration and hydrographic mapping. Also, they tended to confine themselves to making the rounds of several major rendezvous or marts (like Newhitty, Skidegate, Kaigani, and Nass) rather than cruising everywhere. In addition, of course, by 1795 Vancouver had already charted the coast, and by 1798 the first edition of his account (including an atlas of sixteen charts and views) was available to shipmasters. Very few of the approximately seventy surviving logbooks and journals of the fur-trading vessels contain any maps or views, and those few are usually rough and crude; rather, they concentrate on daily sailing conditions (temperature, precipitation, winds, currents, tides, rocks, anchorage), rigging changes, and trading circumstances (marts, goods, prices), with regular observations of latitude and longitude. Few were (or have been) published; they were consulted as guides by the various shipmasters of the same shipowner.

Most of the private discovering and exploring was done by British traders, since they were the first to exploit Cook's information and ply the Northwest Coast trade. Private Russian activity was largely confined to the shores of the Gulf of Alaska and the Bering Sea. Among the British, in 1786 Captain Hanna of the *Sea Otter* named Smith Sound and Fitz Hugh Sound, and Captain John Guise of the *Experiment* named Queen Charlotte Sound;[295] in 1787 Captain William Barkley of the *Imperial Eagle* discovered the Strait of Juan de Fuca, and Captain George Dixon of the *Queen Charlotte* conjectured that the Queen Charlotte Islands, which he named, were not part of the mainland;[296] in 1788 Captain William Douglas of the *Iphigenia Nubiana* determined the insularity of the Queen Charlottes, and by that year the British recognized that there was "every Probability of the whole Country from this Strait [of Juan de Fuca] to the latitude of 60° N being an immense chain of Islands";[297] in 1790–91 Captain Colnett in the *Argonaut* "made a complete survey of the N.W. Coast from 38° to 60° N. lat."[298] On an earlier trading venture to the coast, that of the *Prince of Wales* in 1787–89, two of Colnett's shipmates were James Johnstone and Archibald Menzies, whose coastal experience served them well as officers in Vancouver's later expedition.

By 1788 American shipowners (principally out of Boston) had entered the coast trade, although they did not outnumber the British traders until the end of the century. Their presence was due in no small measure to the efforts of a Yankee member of Cook's last voyage, John Ledyard. Ledyard's own journal of that voyage, published in 1783, apprised American readers of the potential of the sea otter trade. "The light in which this country [Nootka Sound] will appear most to advantage," he wrote, "respects the variety of its animals, and the richness of their furr." Cook's expedition bought some fifteen hundred skins, mostly sea otters, he estimated, and "it afterwards happened that skins which did not cost the purchaser sixpence sterling sold in China for 100 dollars." Moreover, the men bought only a quarter of the available skins, and they would have bought all the skins if they had known the "astonishing profit" the pelts would bring at Canton. En route to China they made the mistake of selling most of the skins in Kamchatka to Russian traders for what they thought was a "great price," only to find subsequently that the pelts would have fetched twice as much at Canton.[299]

After returning from Cook's venture and publishing his account, Ledyard spent the next four years trying to find a capitalist to finance a fur-trading voyage to the Northwest Coast under his command. He was unsuccessful in the United States because of the commercial depression of the middle 1780s caused by the glut of the market, the overextension of credit, and the undersupply of specie, especially in New England, so he went to France to promote his scheme and succeeded in interesting John Paul Jones. Ledyard's plan estimated a profit of 1,000 percent on a two-ship venture with a post at Nootka Sound, but it was likely thwarted by Louis XVI, who did not want to offend his close ally, Carlos III of Spain, who regarded the entire western coast of the Americas as his exclusive domain. Ledyard then proceeded to Russia in an unsuccessful attempt to return home via Siberia. He did, however, reach Irkutsk, where in 1787 the Russian trader Shelikhov told him (hyperbolically) that there were two thousand Russians on the Aleutian archipelago and the Alaskan coast and that they procured twelve thousand skins annually.[300]

Eventually a Boston merchant, Joseph Barrell, who had read Ledyard's book, and five other entrepreneurs financed the first American fur-trading voyage in 1787. The six invested $50,000 and purchased and outfitted two vessels, the 212-ton *Columbia Rediviva* and its 90-ton tender, the sloop *Lady Washington*, under the command of John Kendrick.[301] In 1790 four of these same financers, including Barrell, and three new ones, including Captain Robert Gray, combined in 1790 to capitalize the *Columbia*'s second voyage, the total investment being $22,742 (£6,254).[302] It was this venture that made the most important American private "discovery," that of the Columbia River, which had already been discovered, of course, by Hezeta in 1775.

Gray was the first Euro-American to enter the river, and Broughton was the first Euro-American to ascend above its estuary. The *Columbia* sailed up to twenty-three miles into the estuary and spent a week there watering and trading copper, spikes, nails, and cloth "cheap" for 1,050–1,350 furs (mostly land furs) and for "excellent" salmon; Gray landed and noted that this would be a "fine place" for a factory.[303] His rediscovery of the river gave the United States a stronger claim to the Oregon Country, a claim that was to be further strengthened by Lewis and Clark when they descended the Columbia to its mouth and wintered there in 1805–6.[304]

By then, of course, the configuration of the Pacific coast of North America was well known and charted, thanks mainly to the painstaking work of Vancouver and the dissemination of his findings. Indeed the coast had been delineated so well that apart from a series of Russian round-the-world voyages begun belatedly in 1803 to match the efforts of western European science, to show the tsarist flag, to train Russian seamen, and to supply Russian America and the Russian Far East,[305] no British exploratory expedition visited the coast again until 1826–27 (Captain Frederick Beechey in the *Blossom*)[306] and 1837–39 (Captain Edward Belcher in the *Sulphur*),[307] and no American venture sailed to the coast until 1841–42 (the United States Exploring Expedition under Lieutenant Charles Wilkes).[308] The cordilleran interior now remained to be explored, and except in Alaska, that area was to be approached landward rather than seaward.

Notes

9. Spanish Penetration North of New Spain

1. David J. Weber, *The Spanish Frontier in North America* (New Haven, 1992), 55.

2. Weber, *The Spanish Frontier*, 56.

3. Paul E. Hoffman, *A New Andalucia and a Way to the Orient: The American Southeast during the Sixteenth Century* (Baton Rouge, 1990), 125.

4. Hoffman, *A New Andalucia*, 147–48.

5. Hoffman, *A New Andalucia*, 144.

6. Robert S. Weddle, *Spanish Sea: The Gulf of Mexico in North American Discovery, 1500–1685* (College Station TX, 1985), 252–59. For the Labazares expedition, see B. F. French, *Historical Collections of Louisiana and Florida, Including Translations of Original Manuscripts Relating to Their Discovery*, 2d ser., 1527–1702 (New York, 1875), 236–38.

7. Hoffman, *A New Andalucia*, 156–57.

8. Weddle, *Spanish Sea*, 255, 260–61, 265.

9. Weddle, *Spanish Sea*, 255, 260–62.

10. Cited in Weddle, *Spanish Sea*, 267.

11. Weddle, *Spanish Sea*, 267–70. For a full account of the Luna expedition, see Herbert I. Priestley, *Tristan de Luna, Conquistador of the Old South: A Study of Spanish Imperial Strategy* (1934; reprint, Philadelphia, 1980), and Herbert I. Priestley, trans. and ed., *The Luna Papers: Documents Relating to the Expedition of Don Tristan de Luna y Arellano for the Conquest of La Florida in 1559–1561*, 2 vols. (New York, 1971); also Charles Hudson, Marvin T. Smith, Chester B. DePratter, and Emilia Kelly, "The Tristán de Luna Expedition, 1559–1561," in Jerald T. Milanich and Susan Milbrath, eds., *First Encounters: Spanish Exploration in the Caribbean and the United States, 1492–1570* (Gainesville, 1989), 119–34.

12. Weddle, *Spanish Sea*, 271–74.

13. Weddle, *Spanish Sea*, 275–76.

14. Hoffman, *A New Andalucia*, 181–85.

15. Hoffman, *A New Andalucia*, 180.

16. Weddle, *Spanish Sea*, 277–79.

17. Donald W. Meinig, *The Shaping of America: A Geographical Perspective of 500 Years of History*, vol. 1, *Atlantic America, 1492–1800* (New Haven, 1986), 26–27; Weddle, *Spanish Sea*, 289–94; Joseph Judge, "Exploring Our Forgotten Century," *National Geographic Magazine* 173 (March 1988): 339, 341.

18. Meinig, *Shaping of America*, 27; Weddle, *Spanish Sea*, 251, 262, 314. For the best works on Menéndez, see Eugene Lyon, *The Enterprise of Florida: Pedro de Menéndez de Avilés and the Spanish Conquest of 1565–1568* (Gainesville, 1976), and Eugene Lyon, "Pedro Menéndez's Plan for Settling La Florida," in Milanich and Milbrath, *First Encounters*, 150–65.

19. Weddle, *Spanish Sea*, 315.

20. Hoffman, *A New Andalucia*, 224–25.

21. Hoffman, *A New Andalucia*, 227.

22. Hoffman, *A New Andalucia*, 232–36.

23. Lyon, *Enterprise of Florida*, 13–14; Edward G. Bourne, *Spain in America, 1450–1580* (New York, 1962), 177–79; Carl O. Sauer, *Sixteenth Century North America: The Land and the People as Seen by the Europeans* (Berkeley, 1971), 214; Judge, "Exploring," 335–50; Weddle, *Spanish Sea*, 315–16.

24. Hoffman, *A New Andalucia*, 239 n. 11, gives information on Urdaneta and his position as a geographical authority.

25. Weber, *The Spanish Frontier*, 70.

26. The best source on the Pardo expeditions is Charles Hudson, *The Juan Pardo Expeditions* (Washington DC, 1990); see also Charles Hudson, Chester B. DePratter, and Marvin T. Smith, "The Route of Juan Pardo's Explorations in the Interior Southeast," *Florida Historical Quarterly* 62 (October 1983): 125–58.

27. Cited in Weddle, *Spanish Sea*, 326.

28. Weddle, *Spanish Sea*, 325–27.

29. Weber, *The Spanish Frontier*, 71.

30. Weddle, *Spanish Sea*, 316–22, 329.

31. Weddle, *Spanish Sea*, 329.

32. Lyon, *Enterprise of Florida*, 185–86.

33. Sauer, *Sixteenth Century*, 222–23; Meinig, *Shaping of America*, 27; Judge, "Exploring," 357. On the Jesuit mission at Chesapeake Bay, see Clifford Lewis and Albert Loomis, *The Spanish Jesuit Mission in Virginia, 1570–1572* (Chapel Hill, 1953), and Parke Rouse Jr., "Conquistadores on the Chesapeake," *Americas* (August 1980), 28–33.

34. Weddle, *Spanish Sea*, 357–60; Judge, "Exploring," 362. For the Guale missions, see Herbert E. Bolton and Mary Ross, *The Debatable Land: A Sketch of the Anglo-Spanish Contest for the Georgia Country* (Berkeley, 1925), and John T. Lanning, *The Spanish Missions of Georgia* (Chapel Hill, 1935). For the Florida missions, see the following: Michael V. Gannon, *The Cross in the Sand: The Early Catholic Church in Florida, 1513–1870* (Gainesville, 1985); Maynard Geiger, *The Franciscan Conquest of Florida, 1573–1618* (Washington DC, 1937); and two works by Woodbury Lowery: *The Spanish*

Settlements within the Present Limits of the United States, 1513–1561 (New York, 1901) and *The Spanish Settlements within the Present Limits of Florida, 1562–1574* (New York, 1905).

35. Weddle, *Spanish Sea*, 360–61.

36. Weddle, *Spanish Sea*, 364.

37. Judge, "Exploring," 340.

38. Lynn I. Perrigo, *The American Southwest: Its People and Cultures* (New York, 1971), 63–64; John B. Brebner, *The Explorers of North America, 1492–1806* (1933; reprint, Cleveland, 1964), 208, 271–73. Brebner states that La Salle was shot at his camp on the Trinity River on 19 March 1687.

39. Weddle, *Spanish Sea*, xv, 377.

40. William S. Coker, ed., *Pedro de Rivera's Report on the Presidio of Punta de Siguenza, Alias Panzacola, 1744* (Pensacola FL, 1976), 9 n. 19.

41. Coker, *Pedro de Rivera's Report*, 9, 20 n. See also William E. Dunn, *Spanish and French Rivalry in the Gulf Region of the United States, 1698–1702* (Austin, 1917), 180–81, and Stanley Faye, "The Contest for Pensacola Bay and Other Gulf Ports, 1698–1722," *Florida Historical Quarterly* 24 (April 1946): 302–28. For the occupation of Pensacola, see Irving A. Leonard, trans., *Spanish Approach to Pensacola, 1689–1693* (Albuquerque, 1939).

42. Weddle, *Spanish Sea*, 412.

43. John F. Bannon, *The Spanish Borderlands Frontier, 1513–1821* (New York, 1970), 27.

44. Bannon, *Spanish Borderlands Frontier*, 27.

45. Meinig, *Shaping of America*, 14.

46. Weber, *The Spanish Frontier*, 78.

47. Meinig, *Shaping of America*, 407.

48. Weber, *The Spanish Frontier*, 65.

49. Carl I. Wheat, *Mapping the Trans-Mississippi West, 1540–1861*, 5 vols. (San Francisco, 1957), 1:18.

50. Oakah L. Jones Jr., *Nueva Vizcaya: Heartland of the Spanish Frontier* (Albuquerque, 1988), 18–19; Hubert H. Bancroft, *History of the North Mexican States and Texas*, Works of Hubert Howe Bancroft, 2 vols. (San Francisco, 1886), 1:54; José Ignacio Gallegos, *Historia de Durango, 1563–1910* (Torreón, Coah., México, 1982), 19–20.

51. Jones, *Nueva Vizcaya*, 19; Bancroft, *North Mexican States* 1:100; Gallegos, *Historia de Durango*, 21–22.

52. Jones, *Nueva Vizcaya*, 19–20; J. Lloyd Mecham, *Francisco de Ibarra and Nueva Vizcaya* (1927; reprint, New York, 1968), 69–71; Gallegos, *Historia de Durango*, 55.

53. Herbert E. Bolton and Thomas M. Marshall, *The Colonization of North America, 1492–1783* (New York, 1922), 53.

54. Jones, *Nueva Vizcaya*, 21; Mecham, *Francisco de Ibarra*, 75, 78, 104.

55. Jones, *Nueva Vizcaya*, 22–24; Gallegos, *Historia de Durango*, 60–61; Mecham, *Francisco de Ibarra*, 100, 113–23. Mecham (p. 123) believes that Durango was not founded until November or December 1563.

56. Jones, *Nueva Vizcaya*, 25–26; Bancroft, *North Mexican States* 1:107–10; Mecham, *Francisco de Ibarra*, 126–33, 134–86.

57. Jones, *Nueva Vizcaya*, 26; Mecham, *Francisco de Ibarra*, 230–31.

58. Bancroft, *North Mexican States* 1:116, 119; Bolton and Marshall, *Colonization*, 58.

59. Luis Navarro García, *Sonora y Sinaloa en el siglo XVII* (Sevilla, 1967), 11, 15; Oakah L. Jones Jr., *Los Paisanos: Spanish Settlers on the Northern Frontier of New Spain* (Norman, 1979), 171.

60. Navarro García, *Sonora y Sinaloa*, 18–19, 25–27, 29–30.

61. Navarro García, *Sonora y Sinaloa*, 40–41.

62. Navarro García, *Sonora y Sinaloa*, 42–43.

63. Herbert E. Bolton, *Rim of Christendom: A Biography of Eusebio Francisco Kino, Pacific Coast Pioneer* (1936; reprint, New York, 1960), 6, 16–19. For the Jesuit advance, see John F. Bannon, *The Mission Frontier in Sonora, 1620–1687* (New York, 1955).

64. Navarro García, *Sonora y Sinaloa*, 37–40.

65. Navarro García, *Sonora y Sinaloa*, 243–53.

66. Bolton and Marshall, *Colonization*, 59.

67. Bolton and Marshall, *Colonization*; Jones, *Los Paisanos*, 22–24.

68. Weddle, *Spanish Sea*, 334–40. On Carvajal, see also Timoteo L. Hernández Garza, *Breve Historia de Nuevo León* (México, D.F., 1973), 11, 25–31.

69. Weddle, *Spanish Sea*, 341–46; Jones, *Los Paisanos*, 32–33. Bolton and Marshall, *Colonization*, 60, notes that Carvajal's expedition took place in 1583.

70. Jones, *Los Paisanos*, 33–34; Bolton and Marshall, *Colonization*, 61; Hernández Garza, *Breve Historia*, 36, 51–52.

71. Jones, *Los Paisanos*, 57–67. See also Lawrence F. Hill, *José de Escandón and the Founding of Nuevo Santander: A Study in Spanish Colonization* (Columbus OH, 1926), and Florence Johnson Scott, "Spanish Colonization on the Lower Río Grande, 1747–1767," in Thomas E. Cotner and Carlos E. Castañeda, eds., *Essays in Mexican History* (Austin, 1958).

72. Bolton and Marshall, *Colonization*, 42–44, 47, 68–71. See Harry Kelsey, *Juan Rodríguez Cabrillo* (San Marino CA, 1986), for an excellent study of this expedition, and see Maurice G. Holmes, *From New Spain to the Californias, 1519–1668* (Glendale CA, 1963), for an overview of these early expeditions.

73. Weber, *The Spanish Frontier*, 287.

74. Sources on these expeditions include the following: Max L. Moorhead and Stuart R. Tompkins, "Russia's Approach to America," *British Columbia Historical*

Quarterly 13 (1949): 55–66, 231–55; Iris H. W. Engstrand, *Spanish Scientists in the New World: The Eighteenth Century Expeditions* (Seattle, 1981); Donald C. Cutter, *Malaspina in California* (San Francisco, 1960); and Warren L. Cook, *Flood Tide of Empire: Spain and the Pacific Northwest, 1543–1819* (New Haven, 1973).

75. George P. Hammond and Agapito Rey, eds., *The Rediscovery of New Mexico, 1580–1594*, Coronado Cuarto Centennial Publications, 1540–1940 (Albuquerque, 1966), 6–14; Herbert E. Bolton, ed., *Spanish Exploration in the Southwest, 1542–1706*, Original Narratives of Early American History (1908; reprint, New York, 1959), 137–39, 145–49.

76. Hammond and Rey, *Rediscovery*, 16–27, 153–242; Bolton, *Spanish Exploration*, 164–92. For important redating of the Espejo expedition, see Harry Kelsey, "The Gregorian Calendar in New Spain: A Problem in Sixteenth-Century Chronology," *New Mexico Historical Review* 58 (July 1983): 239–51.

77. Wheat, *Mapping the Trans-Mississippi West* 1:26.

78. Weber, *The Spanish Frontier*, 79.

79. Hammond and Rey, *Rediscovery*, 28–47; Albert H. Schroeder and Daniel S. Matson, *A Colony on the Move: Gaspar Castaño de Sosa's Journal, 1590–1591* (Santa Fe, 1965), 11–176.

80. Hammond and Rey, *Rediscovery*, 48–50, 323–26; Bolton, *Spanish Exploration*, 200–201.

81. Weber, *The Spanish Frontier*, 82.

82. Bolton, *Spanish Exploration*, 202–4, 220–47. For a thorough study of this expedition, see George P. Hammond and Agapito Rey, eds. and trans., *Don Juan de Oñate: Colonizer of New Mexico, 1595–1628*, 2 vols., Coronado Cuarto Centennial Publications, 1540–1940 (Albuquerque, 1953). See also Marc Simmons, *The Last Conquistador: Juan de Oñate and the Settling of the Far Southwest* (Norman, 1991), for Oñate's explorations.

83. Weber, *The Spanish Frontier*, 82.

84. Weber, *The Spanish Frontier*, 82.

85. Weber, *The Spanish Frontier*, 82.

86. Bolton, *Spanish Exploration*, 205–6, 250–63, 268–80.

87. Weber, *The Spanish Frontier*, 80.

88. Wheat, *Mapping the Trans-Mississippi West* 1:30.

89. Bolton, *Spanish Exploration*, 313–14.

90. Oakah L. Jones Jr., *Pueblo Warriors and Spanish Conquest* (Norman, 1966), 73–76, 91–94, 97–102. For descriptions of these campaigns, see Alfred B. Thomas, trans. and ed., *After Coronado: Spanish Exploration Northeast of New Mexico, 1696–1727* (Norman, 1935). One of the two hide paintings, now in the Museum of New Mexico at Santa Fe, is called "Segesser II" and depicts the scene of the Villasur encounter in

1720. It is described in Gottfried Hotz, *Indian Skin Paintings from the American Southwest* (Norman, 1970), 81–230.

91. William Goetzmann and Glyndwr Williams, *The Atlas of North American Exploration* (New York, 1992), 127–28.

92. Wheat, *Mapping the Trans-Mississippi West*, devotes all of chapter 6 (1:94–116) to the Miera map and includes an excellent reproduction of one of Miera's manuscript drawings.

93. The best sources on the Domínguez-Escalante explorations are Herbert E. Bolton, *Pageant in the Wilderness: The Story of the Escalante Expedition to the Interior Basin* (Salt Lake City, 1950), and Ted J. Warner, ed., *The Domínguez-Escalante Journal*, trans. Fray Angelico Chávez (Provo UT, 1976), xiv–xvii, 3–118, 135–96.

94. Jones, *Pueblo Warriors*, 155–56.

95. Noel M. Loomis and Abraham P. Nasatir, *Pedro Vial and the Roads to Santa Fe* (Norman, 1967), xv–xxv, 540.

96. Bernard DeVoto, *The Course of Empire* (Boston, 1952), 359–62.

97. Bolton, *Spanish Exploration*, 313–17, 320–43. For the explorations of Texas, see the excellent accounts of Donald E. Chipman, *Spanish Texas, 1519–1821* (Austin, 1992), 22–42, 67–94.

98. Bolton, *Spanish Exploration*, 284–88, 291–307; Chipman, *Spanish Texas*, 68.

99. Bolton, *Spanish Exploration*, 348, 353–67; Chipman, *Spanish Texas*, 78–81.

100. Bolton, *Spanish Exploration*, 348, 357–66, 388–404; Chipman, *Spanish Texas*, 81–83.

101. Bolton, *Spanish Exploration*, 367–85; Chipman, *Spanish Texas*, 87–91.

102. Bolton, *Spanish Exploration*, 428–30, 433–53. For Kino's explorations, see also Bolton, *Rim of Christendom*, and Herbert E. Bolton, trans. and ed., *Kino's Historical Memoir of Pimería Alta*, 2 vols. in 1 (Berkeley, 1948).

103. Wheat, *Mapping the Trans-Mississippi West* 1:74–78.

104. Charles E. Chapman, *A History of California: The Spanish Period* (New York, 1930), 240–41, 297–300, 304, 307, 316–19, 330–35, 337; Richard F. Pourade, *Anza Conquers the Desert: The Anza Expeditions from Mexico to California and the Founding of San Francisco, 1774 to 1776* (San Diego, 1971), 12–19, 196–97, 200.

105. Chapman, *History of California*, 299–300; Pourade, *Anza Conquers the Desert*, 25–64.

106. Pourade, *Anza Conquers the Desert*, 91–177.

107. Chapman, *History of California*, 229, 418–20.

108. Chapman, *History of California*, 420–34. For a thorough treatment of the explorations of Moraga, see Donald C. Cutter, "Moraga of the Military: His California Service, 1784–1810" (master's thesis, University of California, Berkeley, 1954).

109. Brebner, *Explorers of North America*, 3.

10. Early French Exploration in the Interior

1. Henry P. Biggar, *The Early Trading Companies of New France* (Toronto, 1901); Marcel Trudel, *The Beginnings of New France, 1524–1663*, trans. Patricia Claxton (Toronto, 1973).

2. Marc Lescarbot, *The History of New France*, trans. W. L. Grant, ed. H. P. Biggar, 3 vols. (Toronto, 1907, 1911, 1914), 2:196–207.

3. Henry P. Biggar, ed., *The Works of Samuel de Champlain*, 6 vols. (Toronto, 1922–36), 3:306.

4. Biggar, *Champlain* 3:308.

5. Biggar, *Champlain* 3:315.

6. Biggar, *Champlain* 1:83–189.

7. Biggar, *Champlain* 1:100.

8. Biggar, *Champlain* 1:123–24.

9. Biggar, *Champlain* 1:151–52.

10. Biggar, *Champlain* 1:153–57, 159–61, 162–64.

11. Biggar, *Champlain* 3:317–18.

12. Conrad E. Heidenreich, *Explorations and Mapping of Samuel de Champlain, 1603–1632*, Cartographica Monograph No. 17 (Toronto, 1976), 2.

13. Lescarbot, *History* 3:211–26.

14. Biggar, *Champlain* 1:321–22.

15. Biggar, *Champlain* 3:320.

16. Biggar, *Champlain* 1:205–469.

17. Biggar, *Champlain* 1:231, 4:28, 31.

18. Biggar, *Champlain* 2:5–8.

19. Biggar, *Champlain* 2:63.

20. Lescarbot, *History* 3:9.

21. Biggar, *Champlain* 2:63–64.

22. Biggar, *Champlain* 2:78.

23. Biggar, *Champlain* 2:105.

24. Biggar, *Champlain* 2:109–12, 4:33–36.

25. Biggar, *Champlain* 2:119.

26. Biggar, *Champlain* 2:121.

27. Biggar, *Champlain* 2:138.

28. Biggar, *Champlain* 2:217, 255–59.

29. Biggar, *Champlain* 4:209–16.

30. Biggar, *Champlain* 2:253–54.

31. Biggar, *Champlain* 2:217–18, 253.

32. Trudel, *Beginnings*, 104–5.

33. Conrad E. Heidenreich and Edward H. Dahl, "The Two States of Champlain's Carte Geographique," *Canadian Cartographer* 16 (June 1979): 1–16.

34. Biggar, *Champlain* 3:13–22.

35. Gabriel Sagard Theodat, *Histoire du Canada et voyages que les Freres mineurs Recollects y ont faicts pour la conversion des Infidelles* (Paris, 1636); Christian Le Clercq, *First Establishment of the Faith in New France*, ed. John G. Shea, 2 vols. (New York, 1881).

36. Biggar, *Champlain* 3:31–32.

37. Le Clercq, *First Establishment* 1:95.

38. Biggar, *Champlain* 3:42.

39. Biggar, *Champlain* 3:45.

40. Biggar, *Champlain* 3:46, 70.

41. Heidenreich, *Champlain*, 85–89.

42. Biggar, *Champlain* 3:53–58.

43. Biggar, *Champlain* 3:64.

44. Biggar, *Champlain* 3:1–176.

45. Biggar, *Champlain* 3:213–26.

46. Biggar, *Champlain* 3:216, 6:250.

47. Francis Jennings, "Susquehannock," in Bruce G. Trigger, ed., *Handbook of North American Indians*, vol. 15, *Northeast* (Washington DC, 1978), 362.

48. Biggar, *Champlain* 3:224.

49. Biggar, *Champlain* 3:226–27.

50. Biggar, *Champlain* 3:209–10.

51. Biggar, *Champlain* 2:326, 330–31, 345–47.

52. Biggar, *Champlain* 2:326.

53. Biggar, *Champlain* 5:58–73.

54. Biggar, *Champlain* 5:73.

55. Biggar, *Champlain* 5:108.

56. Theodat, *Histoire*, 658–59.

57. Theodat, *Histoire*, 222, 352, 644, 788.

58. Heidenreich, *Champlain*, 32, 94–97.

59. Theodat, *Histoire*, 880.

60. Theodat, *Histoire*, 880–92.

61. Biggar, *Champlain* 5:314–18, 6:12, 43–45, 230.

62. Biggar, *Champlain* 6:147.

63. Reuben G. Thwaites, ed., *The Jesuit Relations and Allied Documents: Travels and Explorations of the Jesuit Missionaries in New France, 1610–1791*, 73 vols. (New York, 1959) (hereafter cited as *JR*), 5:195.

64. *JR* 4:209–15.

65. François-Xavier de Charlevoix, *Histoire et description génerale de la Nouvelle*

France, avec le Journal historique d'un voyage fait par ordre du rois dans l'Amérique sep-tentrionale, 6 vols. (Paris, 1744), 1:250–57.

66. *JR* 5:203–11.

67. *JR* 5:247–55.

68. *JR* 14:15–21.

69. *JR* 6:41–89, 145–55.

70. Biggar, *Champlain* 5:58–60, 70–71.

71. Lucien Campeau, ed., *Monumenta Novae Franciae, III Fondation de la Mission Hurone, 1635–1637* (Quebec, 1987), 31.

72. Heidenreich, *Champlain*, 55–67.

73. On Champlain's map of 1632, his longitude is given as 309° east of the prime meridian through Corvo and Flores. This prime meridian was thought to be 27.5° west of Paris, making Quebec 78.5° west of Paris, an error of 5°.

74. *JR* 5:65–67. Le Jeune gives the numerical data he used and his answers but not the mathematical procedures used to derive them. The only method by which Le Jeune's answers can be replicated is spherical trigonometry (haversine formula), which also happens to be the correct method for calculating longitude over great circle routes.

75. *JR* 5:99. This eclipse occurred on 27 October 1632.

76. Peter Broughton, "Astronomy in Seventeenth-Century Canada," *Journal of the Royal Astronomical Society of Canada* 75 (August 1981): 175–208.

77. *JR* 23:179.

78. *JR* 7:67–233.

79. Marcel Trudel, "Nicollet de Belleborne, Jean," in George W. Brown, ed., *Dictionary of Canadian Biography* (Toronto, 1966), 1:516–18.

80. Conrad E. Heidenreich, "An Analysis of the 17th Century Map 'Nouvelle France,'" *Cartographica* 25 (winter 1988): 97.

81. *JR* 23:279.

82. Jean de Brébeuf left for the Huron country on 7 July 1634 (*JR* 8:75) and arrived there on 5 August (*JR* 8:89). Nicollet was with him to Alumette Island on the Ottawa River (*JR* 8:99). We know that Nicollet departed from the Huron country and returned to it the same year (*JR* 23:277–79). This means that he must have arrived among the Hurons in August, after Brébeuf, and returned before the freeze in December. In view of the distances involved, he could not have spent much time at his destination.

83. *JR* 10:83.

84. Nellis M. Crouse, *Contributions of the Canadian Jesuits to the Geographical Knowledge of New France, 1632–1675* (Ithaca NY, 1924), 79–83.

85. Lucien Campeau, *La Mission des Jésuites chez les Hurons, 1634–1650* (Montréal, 1987), 73.

86. Heidenreich, "An Analysis," 89–97.

87. *JR* 23:277.

88. *JR* 18:229.

89. Heidenreich, "An Analysis," 93.

90. *JR* 18:231.

91. *JR* 18:231.

92. *JR* 18:237.

93. *JR* 23:277–79. The passage states that Nicollet waited two days from his destination. When the Winnebagos came, they escorted him and carried his baggage.

94. *JR* 20:95, 103–5, 21:187–237.

95. *JR* 33:63.

96. *JR* 21:209–11, 23:35–37.

97. Joseph P. Donnelly, *Jean de Brébeuf* (Chicago, 1975), 186.

98. *JR* 23:205–27.

99. Campeau, *La Mission*, 22, 76.

100. Biggar, *Champlain* 5:117–19, 130–31.

101. J. Franklin Jameson, ed., *Narratives of New Netherland, 1609–1664* (New York,
1967), 139–62.

102. *JR* 6:57.

103. *JR* 21:21–35.

104. Heidenreich, "An Analysis," 75–77.

105. *JR* 23:267, 24:281, 25:43–73.

106. *JR* 28:105–15.

107. *JR* 26:29–51, 39:55–79.

108. *JR* 29:45–63.

109. *JR* 28:137; Heidenreich, "An Analysis," 77–87.

110. *JR* 29:61.

111. *JR* 30:219–21, 227–29.

112. *JR* 18:235–37.

113. *JR* 31:183–207.

114. *JR* 27:203–19, 35:275–83.

115. *JR* 32:259.

116. *JR* 31:249–55.

117. *JR* 27:47–49, 28:97, 30:109–25.

118. Joyce Marshall, ed., *Word from New France: The Selected Letters of Marie de l'Incarnation* (Toronto, 1967), 151–63.

119. *JR* 28:229.

120. Heidenreich, "An Analysis," 93.

121. Marshall, *Word*, 159–60.

122. *JR* 33:61–67, 149–55.

123. *JR* 33:61.

124. *JR* 33:149–51.

125. Arthur T. Adams, ed., *The Explorations of Pierre Esprit Radisson* (Minneapolis, 1961), 79.

126. Heidenreich, "An Analysis," 80–81.

127. *JR* 40:85.

128. *JR* 36:165, 38:169–71, 40:211.

129. Marshall, *Word*, 203, 209.

130. *JR* 40:89.

131. *JR* 40:85–89, 157.

132. *JR* 40:185.

133. *JR* 41:91–129.

134. *JR* 42:61–217.

135. *JR* 42:53, 43:127–35.

136. *JR* 42:215–17, 43:135–85.

137. *JR* 43:307, 257–73.

138. *JR* 43:149–83; Adams, *Explorations*, 45–78.

139. *JR* 40:211–15.

140. Cameron Nish, ed., *The French Régime*, Canadian Historical Documents Series, vol. 1 (Scarborough ON, 1965), 40.

141. *JR* 41:77–79.

142. *JR* 41:185.

143. Marshall, *Word*, 216. This may be the first mention of the Mississippi.

144. *JR* 42:219.

145. Grace Lee Nute, *Caesars of the Wilderness: Médart Chouart, Sieur Des Groseilliers and Pierre Esprit Radisson, 1618–1710* (1943; reprint, St. Paul, 1978), 13–26.

146. *JR* 42:219–23, 44:237–51; Adams, *Explorations*, 79–109; Nute, *Caesars*, 27–38.

147. Adams, *Explorations*, 85–86.

148. Adams, *Explorations*, 86–87.

149. Adams, *Explorations*, 88–90; *JR* 44:245–47. For the distribution of native groups in 1654, see R. Cole Harris, ed., and G. J. Matthews, cart., *Historical Atlas of Canada*, vol. 1, *From the Beginning to 1800* (Toronto, 1987), plate 37.

150. Adams, *Explorations*, 91.

151. Adams, *Explorations*, 91–93.

152. Adams, *Explorations*, 90.

153. Adams, *Explorations*, 95.

154. Adams, *Explorations*, 96–97.

155. Emma H. Blair, ed., *The Indian Tribes of the Upper Mississippi Valley and Region of the Great Lakes* (Cleveland, 1911), 306.

156. Adams, *Explorations*, 124.

157. Adams, *Explorations*, 106–7; JR 42:33, 219–23.

158. JR 42:225.

159. JR 44:249.

160. JR 44:235–51. In his letter, Father Druillettes refers to a map he made from native information and interviews with Des Groseilliers late in 1656. It is fairly certain that this map was used to contruct the northern river system on the "Tabula Novae Franciae, 1660," bound into Francisco Creuxio, *Historiae Canadensis Seu Novae-Franciae* (Paris, 1664), 1:46.

161. JR 42:33, 43:73.

162. JR 44:111, 45:105.

163. Adams, *Explorations*, 111.

164. Adams, *Explorations*, 112.

165. Adams, *Explorations*, 112.

166. JR 45:105. The Mississaugas and the Saulteurs are bands of the Ojibwa Indians.

167. Adams, *Explorations*, 112–13.

168. Adams, *Explorations*, 112. For accounts of the voyage, see also JR 45:161–63, 233–39, 46:69–71.

169. Adams, *Explorations*, 128.

170. Adams, *Explorations*, 143; JR 45:239.

171. Adams, *Explorations*, 145–47.

172. Adams, *Explorations*, 148–49.

173. Adams, *Explorations*, 104–6, 151.

174. JR 45:163, 235.

175. Adams, *Explorations*, 156.

176. JR 45:217–39.

177. JR 51:63.

178. JR 45:235.

179. JR 45:233.

180. JR 45:233.

181. JR 45:223–25.

182. JR 46:249.

183. The scattered references to Father Ménard's explorations are in JR 45:161–63, 46:75–77, 127–45, 47:115, 249–53, 307, 48:115–51, 257–77.

184. Anonymous, entitled "Mission Map," ca. 1681, Rec. 67, No. 50, Service historique de la Marine, Paris, copy in National Archives of Canada, Ph. 902, N.D.

185. *JR* 46:69, 251.

186. *JR* 46:173, 181, 249–95.

187. *JR* 46:263–65. This is probably the earliest mention of a case of the Windigo psychosis.

188. *JR* 46:255, 269.

189. *JR* 46:275.

190. Raymond Douville, "Couture, Guillaume," in David M. Hayne, ed., *Dictionary of Canadian Biography* (Toronto, 1969), 2:157–59.

191. *JR* 48:279–89, 49:17–37.

192. *JR* 48:237.

193. *JR* 49:163, 241–51, 50:249.

194. *JR* 50:213, 249–311, 51:21–71.

195. *JR* 51:53–55.

196. *JR* 51:63–69.

197. William J. Eccles, *Canada under Louis XIV, 1663–1701* (Toronto, 1964), 1–38.

198. John R. Broadhead and Edmund B. O'Callaghan, eds., *Documents Relative to the Colonial History of the State of New York*, 15 vols. (Albany, 1853–87) (hereafter cited as *NYCD*), 9:11, 25.

199. *NYCD* 9:29, 41.

200. Ralph Flenley, ed., *A History of Montreal, 1640–1672, from the French of Dollier de Casson* (Toronto, 1928), 351–71.

201. Louise Phelps Kellog, ed., *Early Narratives of the Northwest, 1634–1699* (New York, 1917), 193.

202. *JR* 54:163.

203. Pierre Margry, ed., *Découvertes et établissements des Français dans l'ouest et dans le sud de l'Amérique septentrionale, 1614–1754: mémoires et documents inédits*, 6 vols. (Paris, 1876–86), 1:81.

204. Kellog, *Early Narratives*, 191–92.

205. Kellog, *Early Narratives*, 192.

206. *JR* 54:153–65.

207. *JR* 51:71.

208. *JR* 54:197–243.

209. Kellog, *Early Narratives*, 167–209.

210. *NYCD* 9:64–67.

211. *NYCD* 9:67.

212. Margry, *Découvertes* 1:88.

213. *NYCD* 9:70.

214. *JR* 55:105–15.

215. *JR* 55:99.

216. *JR* 55:237.

217. Jean Delanglez, *Some La Salle Journeys* (Chicago, 1938).

218. *NYCD* 9:72.

219. *JR* 56:149–210.

220. Louis Jolliet, "Cette Carte montre le chemin que Louis Jolliet a fait depuis Tadoussac . . . le 8 Novembre 1679," reproduced in William P. Cumming, S. Hillier, D. B. Quinn, and G. Williams, eds., *The Exploration of North America, 1630–1776* (New York, 1974), 198.

221. *NYCD* 9:89.

222. *JR* 55:235–37, 58:93–109, 59:87–211. The best recent study of the Jolliet-Marquette expedition is Raphael N. Hamilton, *Marquette's Explorations: The Narratives Reexamined* (Madison, 1970).

223. *JR* 59:91–93.

224. *JR* 58:101–9.

225. *NYCD* 9:115.

226. *NYCD* 9:120–21.

227. *JR* 59:165–211.

228. *JR* 60:215–27.

229. Margry, *Découvertes* 1:203–16.

230. Margry, *Découvertes* 1:329.

231. Margry, *Découvertes* 1:278–80.

232. *NYCD* 9:127.

233. Margry, *Découvertes* 1:439–40.

234. *JR* 58:105.

235. Margry, *Découvertes* 1:577–78. See also Louis Hennepin, *A New Discovery of a Vast Country in America*, ed. Reuben G. Thwaites, 2 vols. (Chicago, 1903), 1:89–95.

236. Kellog, *Early Narratives*, 286–322. See also Margry, *Découvertes* 1:573–614.

237. Hennepin, *A New Discovery*, 1:122.

238. [Jean-Baptiste-Louis Franquelin], "Carte De La Louisiane Ou Des Voyages Du Sr De La Salle . . . 1684." The original is lost, but a copy made for Francis Parkman can be found in *JR* 63:end piece. Another copy was made by Bourguignon d'Anville in the eighteenth century: "Carte De La Louisianen En l'Amerique Septentrionale . . ." [1684], Cartes et Plans, Ge.D.2987, Bibliothèque nationale, Paris; National Archives of Canada, NMC-6447. These are the earliest maps depicting La Salle's discoveries.

239. Kellog, *Early Narratives*, 289–96.

240. The site for the fort was at Starved Rock on the southern bank of the Illinois River opposite the present-day town of La Salle.

241. Margry, *Découvertes* 2:55–63.

242. Margry, *Découvertes* 2:115–16.

243. Margry, *Découvertes* 2:245–58. See also Hennepin, *A New Discovery* 1:175–86, 221–313.

244. Hennepin, *A New Discovery* 1:267.

245. NYCD 9:140, 153–54.

246. NYCD 9:131–33, 141–42, 145, 153–54, 159–60; Margry, *Découvertes* 2:251, 253.

247. Kellog, *Early Narratives*, 329–34.

248. Kellog, *Early Narratives*, 333; Margry, *Découvertes*, 2:20–25.

249. Margry, *Découvertes* 2:249–54.

250. NYCD 9:145–49, 159. See also Canada (New France—1763), *Statutes: Édits, ordonnances royaux, déclarations et arrêtes du Conseil d'etat du roi concernant le Canada*, 3 vols. (Québec, 1854–56), 1:248–50.

251. Kellog, *Early Narratives*, 296–305.

252. See Margry, *Découvertes* 1:547–616, 2:163–262, for La Salle's Mississippi expedition from 1681 to 1682.

253. NYCD 9:198.

254. NYCD 9:201; Margry, *Découvertes* 2:310.

255. Margry, *Découvertes* 6:37.

256. Margry, *Découvertes* 6:38–50.

257. Margry, *Découvertes* 6:50–51.

258. Edwind E. Rich, ed., *Copy-Book of Letters Outward &c. Begins 29th May, 1680, End 5 July, 1687* (Toronto, 1948), 168, 187, 318, 322.

259. Walter A. Kenyon and J. R. Turnbull, *The Battle for James Bay, 1686* (Toronto, 1971), 94. This book contains translations of the major documents pertaining to the de Troyes expedition.

260. Jean-Baptiste-Louis Franquelin, "Amerique Septenlle Depuis environ 27 jusqu'a 62 degrez de Latit . . ." [1686], National Archives of Canada, NMC-6593.

261. NYCD 9:286.

262. Kenyon and Turnbull, *Battle*, 40–88.

263. Margry, *Découvertes* 6:495–98.

264. Guillaume De l'Isle, *Carte Du Canada ou de la Nouvelle France et des Decouvertes qui y ont éte faites . . .* (Paris, 1703), National Archives of Canada, NMC-7879. H143.

11. French Exploration in North America, 1700–1800

1. W. J. Eccles, "Sovereignty Association, 1500–1783," *Essays on New France* (Toronto, 1987).

2. W. J. Eccles, *Frontenac: The Courtier Governor* (Toronto, 1959), 24, 27, 106.

3. Greffe J-B, Adhemar, Archives Nationales du Québec à Montréal (hereafter cited as ANQM)—see for contracts in which the terms of employment are spelled out, including that the engagés be supplied with a *bagruet*, *mitasses*, *souliers sauvage*, and *grosse chemise*. Most received only a *brayet* and *mitasses*. See also James K. Smith, *Alexander MacKenzie, Explorer: The Hero Who Failed* (Toronto, 1973), 43, which describes the dress and appearance of the *hommes du nord*.

4. "Etat de ce qui est accordé annuellement aux commandants des Postes du Roy," Fonds Verreau, Carton 3, No. 205, Archives du Séminaire de Québec (hereafter cited as ASQ); Pierre Georges Roy, ed., *Inventaire des Ordonnances des Intendants de la Nouvelle France*, 3 vols. (Beauceville, Québec, 1919), 3:109; 23 aout 1748, Rations de MM.les officiers, aumoniers, et gardés magasins, *Rapport de l'Archiviste de la Province de Québec* (hereafter cited as RAPQ), 1927–28, 340–41, Memoire sur les postes du Canada adressé à M. de Surlaville, en 1741, par le Chevalier de Raymond.

5. Documents judiciares, Pièces détachées, Du 19 juin 1751, congé d'un canot accordé aux Srs Ducouquet et Langlois pour les Illinois, ANQM; RAPQ, 1947–48, 298–99, Memoire du Roi à MM de Vaudreuil et Begon, Paris, 15 juin 1716; Congé au Sr de St Pierre, Ms de Jonquière, Mtl. le 1 mai 1750, ASQ.

6. Fonds Verreau, Boite #96, Beauharnois, A Montréal le 8 juin 1743, ASQ; Collection Baby Correspondence: Fort Rouillé, 12 octobre 1751, Lefebvre Duchouquet à Monsieur . . . ?, Archives Université de Montréal.

7. ANOM Livre de comptes de La Marque Nolan, f 137 verso, 3 juillet 1728, Laronde Clignancourt & Deruisseau (Trade goods furnished); Alexander Henry, *Travels and Adventures in Canada and the Indian Territories: Between the Years 1760 and 1776*, ed. James Bain (Rutland VT, 1969), 13–15.

8. Marcel Giraud, *Le Métis canadien: Son rôle dans l'histoire des provinces de l'ouest* (Paris, 1945); J. Peterson and J. S. H. Brown, eds., *The New Peoples: Being and Becoming Métis in North America* (Winnipeg, 1985).

9. Fonds Verreau, Boite 1, No. 19, Duquesne à Contrecoeur, Mtl. 12 juin 1753, ASQ; Docs., judiciares, Pièces détachées, sans date, ANQM.

10. See George T. Hunt, *Wars of the Iroquois* (Madison, 1940); Harold A. Innis, *The Fur Trade in Canada*, rev. ed. (1956; reprint, Toronto, 1962); Bruce G. Trigger, *Natives and Newcomers: Canada's "Heroic Age" Reconsidered* (Kingston ON, 1985); and Arthur J. Ray, *Indians in the Fur Trade* (Toronto, 1974).

11. Archives Nationale, Paris (hereafter referred to as AN) C13A, vol. 1, f 236, Iberville au Ministre, Des Bayogoula, 26 fevrier 1700.

12. "Relation des aventures de M. de Boucherville a son retour des Sioux," Fonds Verreau, Boite 11, No. 36 1/2, ASQ; AN Série F3, Moreau de St. Méry, vol. 12, ff 39–40, "Memoire du Roy aux Srs Beauharnois et Hocquart, Versailles, 22 avril 1732";

Dictionary of Canadian Biography (Toronto, 1974), 3:375; AN C11A, vol. 93, f 42v, Jonquière et Bigot au Ministre, Québec, 9 octobre 1749; AN Série B, vol. 22, ff 109–23, Ministre à Chevalier Calliéres, Versailles, ff 109–23.

13. "Memoire pour servir d'instruction au Sr Le Gardeur de Saint-Pierre . . . La Jonquière," Mtl. 27 mai 1750, Fonds Verreau, Carton 5, No. 33, ASQ; Journal de Marin fils, septembre 1753, RAPQ 1963, 41:248, 253.

14. Journal de Marin fils, septembre 1753, RAPQ 1963, 41:253, 262.

15. AN Série F3, Moreau de Saint-Méry, vol. 11, ff 180–81, Arrest de la Chambre du Conseil en Canada, 18 décembre 1728.

16. AN C11A, vol 65, f 143, Beauharnois au Ministre, Québec, 17 octobre 1736.

17. See André Vachon, "L'eau de vie dans la société Indienne," *Canadian Historical Association Report, 1960*.

18. Journal de Marin fils, RAPQ 1963, 41:295.

19. Marin à son beaufrére, M. Deschambeau, 1 juin 1754, RAPQ 1963, 41:304.

20. Journal de Bougainville, 260, RAPQ 1923–24.

21. AN Série F3, Moreau de Saint-Méry, vol. 11, f 215, "Memoires touchant le Canada et l'Acadie envoyé par M. de Meulle."

22. Eric W. Morse, *Fur Trade Canoe Routes of Canada: Then and Now* (Toronto, 1969), 7–8.

23. See Eccles, *Frontenac*, 335.

24. See Marcel Giraud, *Histoire de la Louisianale le règne de Louis XIV (1698–1715)* (Paris, 1953).

25. Eccles, *Frontenac*, 335; Ernest Lavisse, *L'Histoire de France* (Paris, 1908), 8–1:79–85.

26. Ray, *Indians in the Fur Trade*, 60.

27. W. J. Eccles, "The Fur Trade and Eighteenth Century Imperialism," *Essays on New France* (Toronto, 1987).

28. Jean-François Brière, "Peche et politique à Terre-Neuve au XVIIIE siècle: La France véritable gagnante du traité d'Utrecht?" *Canadian Historical Review* 64, no. 2 (June 1983): 168–87.

29. Clive Bell, *Civilization* (London, 1928).

30. Lavisse, *L'Histoire de France* 8–2:176–79.

31. Lucie Legarde, "Le Passage du Nord-Ouest et la Mer de l'Ouest dans la Cartographie françoise du 18e Siècle, Contribution à l'Etude de l'Oeuvre des Delisle et Buache," *Imago Mundi* (London, 1989), 19–43.

32. AN Série C11A, vol. 41, f 235, Conseil de Marine, avril 1720, "Projet de la Depense necessaire pour la Decouverte de la Mer de l'Ouest"; *Nouvelle France: Documents Historiques, Correspondance échangé entre les autorités françaises et les gouverneurs*

et intendants (Québec, 1893), 1:148–89; AN Série B, vol. 61, f 521, Ministre à Beau-hanois, 20 avril 1734.

33. *Dictionary of Canadian Biography* 11: 215–16.

34. John G. Clark, *New Orleans, 1718–1812* (Baton Rouge, 1970), 27–31; *Dictionary of Canadian Biography* 3:318.

35. Geoffrey J. Walker, *Spanish Politics and Imperial Trade, 1700–1789* (London, 1979), 19–63; John F. Bannon, *The Spanish Borderlands Frontier, 1513–1821* (New York, 1970), 110.

36. John B. Brebner, *The Explorers of North America* (1933; reprint, Cleveland, 1964), 280.

37. *Dictionary of Canadian Biography* 3:317–18; Giraud, *Histoire de la Louisiane* 1:328–29; Bannon, *Spanish Borderlands Frontier*, 108–16.

38. Brebner, *Explorers of North America*, 281–83; Ralph A. Smith, "Exploration of the Arkansas River by Bernard de la Harpe, 1721–1722," *Arkansas Historical Quarterly* 10 (1951): 339–63.

39. *Dictionary of Canadian Biography* 2:215–16; Emile Lauvriére, *Histoire de la Louisiana francaise, 1673–1939* (Paris, 1940), 156, 172, 184–87, 292–95, 302–5, 381.

40. AN Série C13C, vol. 4, ff 181, "Relation du massacre des Natchez arrivé le vingt huit novembre 1729"; J. B. Dunbar, "Massacre of the Villazure Expedition by the Pawnees on the Platte in 1720," *Collections of the Kansas State Historical Society* 2 (1920?): 397–423.

41. On the significance of an "expectancy," see W. J. Eccles, "The Social, Economic, and Political Significance of the Military Establishment in New France," *Essays on New France* (Toronto, 1987), 110–24.

42. AN Série C13C, vol. 1, ff 346–56, "Exacte description de la Louisiane, de ses ports, terres et rivières, et noms des nations sauvages qui l'occupent et des commerces et avantages que l'on en peut tirer dans l'établissement d'une colonie."

43. Members of the Ordre militaire de Saint-Louis received a modest pension, eight hundred livres a year, and were barred from serving in the armed forces of a foreign power without His Christian Majesty's permission. See Marcel Marion, *Dictionnaire des institutions de la France aux XVIIe et XVIIIe siècles* (Paris, 1968), 410.

44. AN Série C13C, vol. 4, ff 130ff, "Relation du Voyage de Monsieur de Bourgmont Chevalier de l'Ordre Militaire de Saint-Louis commandant de la Rivière du Missoury."

45. *Dictionary of Canadian Biography* 11:645–47.

46. Brebner, *Explorers of North America*, 284–86; Bannon, *Spanish Borderlands Frontier*, 141–42, 197; Henry Folmer, "The Mallet Expedition of 1739 through Nebraska, Kansas, and Colorado to Santa Fe," *Colorado Magazine* 16 (1939): 163–73.

47. *Dictionary of Canadian Biography* 3:423–24.

48. Brebner, *Explorers of North America*, 287–88.

49. Henry P. Biggar, ed., *The Works of Samuel de Champlain*, 6 vols. (Toronto, 1922–36), 2:330–31.

50. See Conrad Heidenreich, "Mapping the Great Lakes: The Period of Imperial Rivalries, 1700–1760," *Cartographica* 18 (1981): 74–109.

51. AN Série C11A, vol. 51, f 24, Beauharnois et Hocquart au Ministre, Québec, 15 octobre 1729.

52. François-Xavier Charlevoix, *Histoire et description génerale de la Nouvelle France, avec le Journal historique d'un voyage fait par ordre du rois dans l'Amérique septentrionale*, 6 vols. (Paris, 1744).

53. AN Série C11A, vol. 37, f 376, Conseil de Marine, 7 décembre 1717, vol. 41, f 235, Conseil de Marine, avril 1720, "Projet de la depense necessaire pour la Decouverte de la Mer de l'Ouest." A marginal note in the above document is revealing: "SA [Son Altesse Royalle, His Royal Highness] . . . trouve cette depense trop forte faut la mettre à un autre temps [His Royal Highness find that expense too great, it must be deferred to some other day]."

54. R. P. Nau au R. P. Binin, Sault Saint-Louis, 2 octobre 1735, RAPQ 1926–27, 286; AN Série C11A, vol. 37, f 376, Conseil de Marine, 7 octobre 1717.

55. See Eccles, "The Fur Trade," 79–80.

56. Considering the high costs of transportation, the maintenance of the fur trade posts, the "presents" for the Indians, the 30 percent interest charged by merchants for goods obtained on credit (justified by the high risks involved), the vagaries of the French market for luxury furs other than beaver, and the normal three-year lease of the trade at the posts, a commandant must have counted himself fortunate to realize a profit of thirty thousand livres over the three years, yet that thirty thousand livres must have represented a small fortune, particularly since a captain's pay was a meagre ninety livres a month. Certainly the officers of the Troupes franches de la Marine sought the appointments avidly. See ASO Fonds Verreau, Carton No. 5, 38 1/2 Neul A St Pierre, Québec, 15 mai 1752, Boite 5, No. 45, Contrat de Jacques Legardeur de St-Pierre et le Sr Lechelles; AN C11A, vol. 99, ff 257–58, Ms Duquesne au Ministre, Québec, 7 octobre 1754.

57. ASO Fonds Verreau, Boite 5, No. 26, De la Jonquière à Le Gardeur de St-Pierre, Québec 17 avril 1750, Vu par Bigot, No. 37, Le Marquis de la Jonquière . . . il est ordonné au Sr Le Gardeur de St-Pierre . . . , Bibliotéque Nationale, Paris; Série Nouvelles Acquisitions françaises, vol. 2551, ff 16063, "Entreprise de M. de la Vérendrye pour la découverte de la Mer de l'Ouest . . . ," Bibliotéque Nationale, Paris; AN Série C11A, vol. 95, f 91, Jonquière et Bigot au Ministre, Québec, 20 octobre 1750; Journal de Marin fils, 16 septembre 1753, RAPQ 1963, 41:250.

58. *Dictionary of Canadian Biography* 2:581.

59. See note 51.

60. Ignace Gamelin, Déclaration sur le naufrage d'un de ses canots, ANQM Piéces judiciares, 23 aout 1737.

61. See Greffe J. David, Nos. 173 & 215, "A quittance for the succession of two Canadians killed by the Indians, one at the Lake of the Woods, the other at La Baie," Archives Nationales de Québec à Montréal; AN C11A, vol. 77, f 109v, Beauharnois au Ministre, Québec, 24 septembre 1742, 93:ff, 143–44, Galissonière au Ministre le 26 juin 1749; Fernand Grenier, ed., *Papiers Contrecoeur et autres documents concernant le conflit Anglo-Français sur l'Ohio de 1745 à 1756* (Québec, 1952), 193.

62. Morse, *Fur Trade Canoe Routes*.

63. R. P. Nau, S.J., au R. P. Richard, Provincial de la Province de Guyenne, Québec 20 octobre 1734, RAPQ 1926–27, 268–69.

64. Antoine Champagne, *Les La Vérendrye et le poste de l'ouest* (Québec, 1968), 163–77, 247–60.

65. Champagne, *Les La Vérendrye*, 181–87.

66. Roy, *Inventaire des Ordonnances*, 2:146–47, 29 mai 1733; Greffe Simonnet, No. 216, 7 septembre 1740, Greffe Guillaume Barette, No. 205, 28 novembre 1717, Archives Nationales du Québec à Montréal.

67. Lawrence J. Burpee, ed., *Journals and Letters of Pierre Gaullier de La Vérendrye and His Sons* (Toronto, 1927), 451–52.

68. Burpee, *La Vérendrye*, 421.

69. Burpee, *La Vérendrye*, 23.

70. Dale Miquelon, *New France, 1700–1744: A Supplement to Europe* (Toronto, 1987), 184.

71. Champagne, *Les La Vérendrye*, 293–96. In 1913 some schoolchildren playing on a hillock near Pierre, South Dakota, stumbled on the plaque.

72. Champagne, *Les La Vérendrye*, 385–87.

73. Eccles, *Essays on New France*, 90.

74. Série Nouvelle Acquisitions Françaises, vol. 2551, ff 160–63, "Entreprise de M. de la Veranderie . . . ," Bibliothèque Nationale, Paris; Burpee, *La Vérendrye*, 66–69; "Le Marquis de la Jonquière . . . il est ordonné au Sr Le Gardeur de St-Pierre," Fonds Verreau, Boite 5, No. 37, ASQ; AN Série C11A, vol. 95, f 91, Jonquière et Bigot au Ministre, Québec, 20 octobre 1750.

75. Journal de Marin fils, 9 novembre 1753, RAPQ 1963, 41:263ff.

76. Marin A Monsieur le Général, 1 juin 1754, "Mes ordres me porte d'aller ou d'envoyer dans le haut du Mississippi et même jusqu'a sa source . . . de m'informer s'ils y en a une . . . ," RAPQ 1963, 41:296. The cartographer Jacques Bellin was also skeptical on this score; see Lucie Lagarde, "Le Passage du Nord-Ouest et la Mer de l'Ouest dans la Cartographie française du 18e Siècle, Contribution à I'Etude de l'Ouevre des Delisle et Buache," *Imago Mundi*, 19–43.

77. "Commission au Sr Le Gardeur de St-Pierre . . . fait à Montréal le 27 mai 1750, Lajonquière," Fonds Verreau, Boite 5, No. 37, ASQ; No. 27, Congo . . . Mtl. 11 mai 1750, No. 28, Congo, Le Marq. de la Jonquière, Québec, 19 mars 1751, No. 29, Congé, Mer de l'Ouest, A Québec 20 mars 1751, La Jonquière.

78. Burpee, *La Vérendrye*, 34.

79. The draft copy of Saint-Pierre's journal is to be found in "Memoire ou Extrait Du Journal Sommaire du Voyage de Jacques Legardeur Sr de St-Pierre Chevallier de l'Ordre Royale et Militaire de St. Louis Capitaine d'une compagnie des troupes détachées de la Marine en Canada, chargé de la Découverte de la Mer de l'Ouest," Fonds Verreau, Boite 5, No. 54, ASQ.

80. See W. J. Eccles, *France in America*, rev. ed. (Toronto, 1990), 191; Grenier, *Papiers Contrecoeur*, 77–78, 84.

81. Brebner, *Explorers of North America*, 318–19, 323; Arthur S. Morton, *A History of the Canadian West to 1870–71* (1939; reprint, Toronto, 1973), 235–38.

82. *Dictionary of Canadian Biography* 3:375.

83. Murray G. Lawson, *Fur: A Study in English Mercantilism* (Toronto, 1943), 87–92, 108, 136; Innis, *Fur Trade in Canada*, 138.

84. Brebner, *Explorers of North America*, 321.

85. Walter Sheppe, ed., *First Man West: Alexander MacKenzie's Journal of His Voyage to the Pacific Coast of Canada in 1793* (Montreal, 1962).

86. Eccles, *France in America*, 229–31, 254–57; Marc de Villiers, *Du Terrage: The Last Years of French Louisiana*, ed. Carl A. Brasseaux and Glenn R. Conrad, trans. Hosea Phillips (Lafayette LA, 1982), 234–429; *Dictionary of Canadian Biography* 4:177–78.

87. Bannon, *Spanish Borderlands Frontier*, 193–95.

88. Bannon, *Spanish Borderlands Frontier*, 196–98.

89. Bernard DeVoto, *Across the Wide Missouri* (Boston, 1947).

90. Miquelon, *New France, 1700–1744*, 188. The cost of the Chickasaw campaign was calculated at 88,829 livres, 3 sols. See AN Série C11A, vol. 71, f 146, "Canada, Depense à L'occasion du Parti de Guerre Envoyé contre les Sauvages Chicachas 1739, Fait à Québec Le 4 octobre 1739, Hocquart, Veu au Controlle, Varin."

91. E. E. Rich, *The Fur Trade and the Northwest to 1857* (Toronto, 1967), 158–59.

92. Morton, *A History of the Canadian West*, 328–29.

12. British Exploration of Rupert's Land

1. This is the southern portion of James Bay, essentially from the Albany area to the Rupert River area.

2. William Schooling, *The Hudson's Bay Company, 1670–1920* (London, 1920), 5–8.

3. Schooling, *Hudson's Bay Company*, 5–8; Foxe in 1631, James in 1631–32.

4. By the Treaty of Utrecht, 1713, the control of the area of the Hudson and James Bays was conceded to Great Britain.

5. Map, 1678, Add. MS., vol. 5027A, fol. 64, British Museum, London. See Richard I. Ruggles, *A Country So Interesting: The Hudson's Bay Company and Two Centuries of Mapping, 1670–1870* (Montreal, 1990), Cat. 1B, Plate 1.

6. Hudson's Bay Record Society, *Hudson's Bay Company Letters Outwards*, 20 vols. (London, 1948), 11:42.

7. Hudson's Bay Company Archives (HBCA), A6/2, fol. 29d.

8. Henry Kelsey, *Journal of Voyage and Journey Undertaken by Henry Kelsey to Discover and Endeavour to Bring to Commerce ye Northern Indians Inhabiting to the Northward of Churchill River and Also ye Doyside Nation*, Kelsey Collection, June 17, 1689, National Archives of Canada, Ottawa.

9. E. E. Rich, *Minutes of the Hudson's Bay Company, 1679–1682* (Toronto, 1945), 35. See "Letter of Committee to John Bridgar, May 5, 1682."

10. Hudson's Bay Record Society, *Hudson's Bay*, 11:48, May 21, 1682.

11. This was very likely a tribe of the Blackfoot Indians.

12. Theodore Drage, *An Account of a Voyage for the Discovery of a North-West Passage by Hudson's Streights to the Western and Southern Ocean of America*, 2 vols. (London, 1746–47).

13. This sketch was copied, and likely improved, by James Isham, but both were lost from the company archives.

14. HBCA, B239/a/48, fol. 36.

15. HBCA, B42/a/57, "Journal of voyage."

16. See John Warkentin and Richard I. Ruggles, *Manitoba Historical Atlas: A Selection of Facsimile Maps, Plans, and Sketches from 1612 to 1969* (Winnipeg, 1970), 68, 86–91.

17. HBCA, B42/a/80, fols. 20, 21.

18. HBCA, B239/a/51, fol. 40d.

19. HBCA, B239/a/69, fols. 22–39, "Thoughts on making a Settlement Inland."

20. HBCA, B149/a/1, fols. 30–2.

21. First opened in 1743, Henley House was attacked by Indians and closed in 1759. It was reopened in 1766.

22. HBCA, B3/b/13, fol. 20.

23. HBCA, B86/a/29, fol. 23d.

24. HBCA, A5/2, fol. 23.

25. HBCA, A11/3, fol. 55. Sutherland had been sent by the factor in the spring of 1777 on foot, north from Albany as far as the Ekwan River, to accustom him to travel and to give him experience in using instruments.

26. HBCA, A11/4, fol. 73.

27. HBCA, A11/5, fol. 174d.

28. This post was named Brunswick House in 1780. In 1788 a new house was built

about two hundred miles up the Moose River at Micabanish. In 1791 this post was renamed New Brunswick House, after the old house downstream was closed.

29. Alexander Henry, "A Proper Rout, by Land, to Cross the Great Contenant of America from Quebec to the Westernmost extremity . . . ," in Stewart W. Wallace, ed., *The Pedlars from Quebec and Other Papers on the Nor'Westers* (Toronto, 1954), 575–85.

30. Wallace, *The Pedlars from Quebec*, 584.

31. Harry W. Duckworth, ed., *The English River Book: A North West Company Journal and Account Book of 1766* (Montreal, 1990), xv.

32. Apparently, while in Montreal, Pond had seen a copy of Cook's narrative of his journey along the western coast and had read of the river that Cook had ascended for some distance, noting heavy driftwood concentrations along the ocean shore.

33. This map exists in several almost similar forms, one copy of which was considered to have been given by Pond to Mackenzie to present to Empress Catherine II of Russia, in case Mackenzie succeeded in reaching the Pacific and crossing Siberia to Saint Petersburg. The map was discussed by Pond with Isaac Ogden in Quebec in the autumn of 1789; Ogden wrote a letter to his father, David Ogden, in London, outlining Pond's geographical ideas. A copy of the map eventually reached Britain.

34. Nevertheless, Mackenzie's implied goal of his expedition, as stated in the preface to his book "Voyages from Montreal," was to prove or disprove the existence of the Northwest Passage.

35. HBCA, B49/a/22, fol. 4d.

36. F. C. Swannell, "Alexander Mackenzie as Surveyor," *Beaver* (winter 1959), Outfit 290, 20–5.

37. Colonial Office, U.K., "America No. 54." Exactly when he made this map is not known. He may have sketched it at Fork Fort, in Britain before leaving in 1791–92, or even in 1794–95, when he was back in England, according to Gordon Charles Davidson, *The North West Company* (New York, 1918), 60. However, it is extremely unlikely that the map was made after his journey because of the incompleteness of the sketch, which did not show the details of his 1793 journey, particularly for the Peace River and Lake of the Plains.

13. British Exploration of the United States Interior

1. Philip Barbour, *The Three Worlds of Captain John Smith* (Boston, 1964), 127.

2. Barbour, *John Smith*, 128; John Smith, "A True Relation," in L. G. Tyler, ed., *Narratives of Early Virginia* (1925; reprint, New York, 1966), 34.

3. Barbour, *John Smith*, 132.

4. Barbour, *John Smith*, 132–33.

5. Barbour, *John Smith*, 155, 157.

6. Barbour, *John Smith*, 166.

7. Karen Ordahl Kupperman, ed., *Captain John Smith: A Select Edition of His Writings* (Chapel Hill, 1988), 87, 91; Barbour, *John Smith*, 202.

8. Kupperman, *John Smith*, 92.

9. Kupperman, *John Smith*, 93–94.

10. Kupperman, *John Smith*, 98–99.

11. Kupperman, *John Smith*, 99.

12. Kupperman, *John Smith*, 100.

13. Kupperman, *John Smith*, 106.

14. Barbour, *John Smith*, 232–38.

15. "Virginia in 1650," *Virginia Magazine of History and Biography* 17 (1909): 137.

16. William Waller Hening, comp., *Statutes at Large: Being a Collection of All the Laws of Virginia, from the First Session of the Legislature in the Year 1619*, 13 vols. (1809–23; reprint, Charlottesville, 1969), 1:262, 323–26.

17. The dates in the text are those of the old-style Julian calendar. By the present Gregorian calendar, the journey started on 6 September 1650. Edward Bland, *The Discovery of New Brittaine, 1650* (1651), in Alexander S. Salley Jr., ed., *Narratives of Early Carolina, 1650–1708* (1911; reprint, New York, 1967), 5.

18. Bland, *Discovery of New Brittaine*, 9–10.

19. Bland, *Discovery of New Brittaine*, 14.

20. Bland, *Discovery of New Brittaine*, 18.

21. Bland, *Discovery of New Brittaine*, 18.

22. William P. Cumming, ed., *The Discoveries of John Lederer* (Charlottesville, 1958), 24.

23. Robert Fallam, "A Journal from Virginia beyond the Apailachian Mountains, in Sept. 1671, Sent to the Royal Society by Mr. Clayton, and Read Aug. 1, 1688, before the said Society," in Clarence W. Alvord and Lee Bidgood, *The First Explorations of the Trans-Allegheny Region by the Virginians, 1650–1674* (Cleveland, 1912), 184.

24. William Berkeley to Lord Arlington, 27 May 1669, in Alvord and Bidgood, *First Explorations*, 175–76.

25. Alvord and Bidgood, *First Explorations*, 175.

26. Cumming, *John Lederer*, 19, 36.

27. Cumming, *John Lederer*, 32.

28. Cumming, *John Lederer*, 22.

29. Cumming, *John Lederer*, 26.

30. Cumming, *John Lederer*, 29–33. For a discussion of the dozen or so reconstruc-

tions of Lederer's journey, see Alan Vance Briceland, *Westward from Virginia: The Exploration of the Virginia-Carolina Frontier, 1650–1710* (Charlottesville, 1987), 101–23.

31. Douglas Rights, "The Trading Path to the Indians," *North Carolina Historical Review* 8 (1931): 421–26. See also Cumming, *John Lederer*, 77–86.

32. Briceland, *Westward from Virginia*, 120.

33. Cumming, *John Lederer*, 31.

34. Cumming, *John Lederer*, 5.

35. Fallam, "Journal from Virginia" (1 September), 184.

36. This was 10 September by our modern calendar. For a detailed analysis of the route, see Briceland, *Westward from Virginia*, 124–46.

37. Fallam, "Journal from Virginia" (9 September), 186–87.

38. Fallam, "Journal from Virginia" (12 September), 188.

39. Fallam, "Journal from Virginia" (13–16 September), 188–90.

40. Fallam, "Journal from Virginia" (17 September), 192.

41. Fallam, "Journal from Virginia" (17 September), 191–92.

42. Briceland, *Westward from Virginia*, 148.

43. Abraham Wood to John Richards, 22 August 1674, in Alvord and Bidgood, *First Explorations*, 210.

44. For a detailed analysis of the route, see Briceland, *Westward from Virginia*, 147–70.

45. Wood to Richards, in Alvord and Bidgood, *First Explorations*, 211–12.

46. Wood to Richards, in Alvord and Bidgood, *First Explorations*, 212–13.

47. Wood to Richards, in Alvord and Bidgood, *First Explorations*, 213–14.

48. Wood to Richards, in Alvord and Bidgood, *First Explorations*, 216–17.

49. Wood to Richards, in Alvord and Bidgood, *First Explorations*, 217–18.

50. Wood to Richards, in Alvord and Bidgood, *First Explorations*, 218–19.

51. Wood to Richards, in Alvord and Bidgood, *First Explorations*, 221–22.

52. Wood to Richards, in Alvord and Bidgood, *First Explorations*, 222–23.

53. Wood to Richards, in Alvord and Bidgood, *First Explorations*, 222–23.

54. Robert Sandford, "A Relation of a Voyage on the Coast of the Province of Carolina, 1666," in Salley, *Narratives*, 104–5.

55. William P. Cumming, S. F. Hillier, David B. Quinn, and G. Williams, *The Exploration of North America, 1630–1776* (New York, 1974), 91; Verner W. Crane, *The Southern Frontier, 1670–1732* (1929; reprint, Ann Arbor, 1958), 13.

56. Crane, *Southern Frontier*, 13.

57. Crane, *Southern Frontier*, 13; Cumming et al., *Exploration*, 91.

58. Crane, *Southern Frontier*, 12, 14, 16.

59. Henry Woodward, "A Faithful Relation of My Westoe Voiage, by Henry Woodward, 1674," a letter from Woodward to Shaftesbury, 31 December 1674, printed in Salley, *Narratives*, 130–32.

60. Woodward, "A Faithful Relation," 130–32.

61. Woodward, "A Faithful Relation," 132–34.

62. Cumming et al., *Exploration*, 92.

63. Crane, *Southern Frontier*, 35; John A. Caruso, *The Southern Frontier* (Indianapolis, 1963), 132.

64. Caruso, *The Southern Frontier*, 135; Crane, *Southern Frontier*, 40, 45–46.

65. Paul Chrisler Phillips, *The Fur Trade*, 2 vols. (Norman, 1961), 1:119; Francis X. Moloney, *The Fur Trade in New England, 1620–1676* (Cambridge MA, 1931), 20, 25–27, 41–42.

66. Moloney, *Fur Trade*, 46–48, 51–54; quotation in Cumming et al., *Exploration*, 57.

67. Moloney, *Fur Trade*, 67–69; Cumming et al., *Exploration*, 56.

68. Selection from *The Journal of John Winthrop*, "Expedition to the White Mountains, 1642," in Cumming et al., *Exploration*, 70.

69. Cumming et al., *Exploration*, 58.

70. Cumming et al., *Exploration*, 59; Charles T. Gehring and William A. Starna, eds., *A Journey into Mohawk and Oneida Country, 1634–1635*: The Journal of Harmen Mayendertsz van den Bogaert (Syracuse NY, 1988).

71. Douglas E. Branch, *Westward: The Romance of the American Frontier* (1930; reprint, New York, 1969), 15.

72. Helen Broshar, "The First Push Westward of the Albany Traders," *Mississippi Valley Historical Review* 7 (December 1920): 230–31.

73. Broshar, "The First Push Westward," 234.

74. Broshar, "The First Push Westward," 234; Cumming et al., *Exploration*, 60.

75. Broshar, "The First Push Westward," 234–35; Allen W. Trelease, *Indian Affairs in Colonial New York: The Seventeenth Century* (Ithaca NY, 1960), 269–71; Thomas Elliot Norton, *The Fur Trade in Colonial New York, 1686–1776* (Madison, 1974), 154.

76. Broshar, "The First Push Westward," 237.

77. Broshar, "The First Push Westward," 238–241.

78. Phillips, *The Fur Trade* 1:481; Cumming et al., *Exploration*, 71.

79. Phillips, *The Fur Trade* 1:501, 503, 510; John Bakeless, *The Eyes of Discovery* (New York, 1961), 303.

80. John Peter Salley, "A Brief Account of the Travels of Mr. John Peter Salley," in William M. Darlington, ed., *Christopher Gist's Journals* (Pittsburgh, 1893), 253–54.

81. Salley, "A Brief Account," 253–54.

82. Richard Batman, "The Odyssey of John Peter Salley," *Virginia Cavalcade* 31 (1981): 4–11.

83. Nicholas B. Wainwright, *George Croghan, Wilderness Diplomat* (Chapel Hill, 1959), 6, 14, 15, 30.

84. Wainwright, *George Croghan*, 37–38; "Christopher Gist's First and Second Journals, September 11, 1750–March 29, 1752," in *George Mercer Papers Relating to the Ohio Company of Virginia*, comp. and ed. Lois Mulkearn (Pittsburgh, 1954), 7–40, 461–510; Richard E. Banta, *The Ohio* (New York, 1949), 68–75.

85. Shirley S. McCord, *Travel Accounts of Indiana, 1679–1961*, Indiana Historical Collections, 47 (Bloomington, 1970), 9–12.

86. "Croghan's Journal, 1765," in Reuben Gold Thwaites, ed., *Early Western Travels, 1748–1846*, 32 vols. (Cleveland, 1904–7), 1:127–66.

87. Clarence W. Alvord and Clarence E. Carter, eds., *The New Regime*, Illinois Historical Collections, 11 (Springfield, 1916), xvii–xviii, xxi.

88. John Parker, ed., *The Journals of Jonathan Carver and Related Documents, 1766–1770* (Minneapolis, 1976), 6, 12–13.

89. Parker, *Jonathan Carver*, 14–16.

90. Parker, *Jonathan Carver*, 17–21.

91. Hennepin and Lahontan quoted in John L. Allen, *Passage through the Garden: Lewis and Clark and the Images of the American Northwest* (Urbana, 1975), 5, 8, 9.

92. Allen, *Passage through the Garden*, 27.

93. Allen, *Passage through the Garden*, 23–26, 43.

94. Abraham P. Nasatir, ed., *Before Lewis and Clark: Documents Illustrating the History of the Missouri, 1785–1804*, 2 vols. (St. Louis, 1952), 2:493, 492, 1:97, 2:494.

95. David Williams, *John Evans and the Legend of Madoc*, (Cardiff, Wales, 1963), 13–29.

96. Williams, *John Evans*, 13–29.

97. W. Raymond Wood, "The John Evans 1796–97 Map of the Missouri River," *Great Plains Quarterly* 1 (1981): 39–53.

98. Nasatir, *Before Lewis and Clark* 2:358.

99. Nasatir, *Before Lewis and Clark* 2:410–13.

100. Nasatir, *Before Lewis and Clark* 2:460–63.

101. "Extracts of Mr. Evans Journal," in Nasatir, *Before Lewis and Clark* 2:495–97.

102. Richard Glover, ed., *David Thompson's Narrative, 1784–1812* (Toronto, 1962), 172–78.

103. Nasatir, *Before Lewis and Clark* 1:106.

104. Mackay to Gayoso de Lemos, New Orleans, 8 June 1798, in Nasatir, *Before Lewis and Clark* 2:562–63.

105. Victor G. Hopwood, ed., *David Thompson: Travels in Western North America, 1784–1812* (Toronto, 1971), 147–48.

106. Hopwood, *David Thompson*, 162–69; Glover, *Thompson's Narrative*, 160–70.

107. Hopwood, *David Thompson*, 184–86; Glover, *Thompson's Narrative*, 198–201.

108. James P. Ronda, "Dreams and Discoveries: Exploring the American West, 1760–1815," *William and Mary Quarterly*, 3d ser., 46 (1989): 145–62.

14. Exploration of the Pacific Coast

1. On these, and other, problems of navigation in the Pacific, see Harry Morton, *The Wind Commands: Sailors and Sailing Ships in the Pacific* (Vancouver BC, 1975).

2. See Raymond H. Fisher, *The Voyage of Semen Dezhnev in 1648: Bering's Precursor* (London, 1981).

3. Quoted by James R. Gibson, *Feeding the Russian Fur Trade: Provisionment of the Okhotsk Seaboard and the Kamchatka Peninsula, 1639–1856* (Madison, 1969), 13.

4. Basil Dmytryshyn, E. A. P. Crownhart-Vaughan, and Thomas Vaughan, eds. and trans., *To Siberia and Russian America: Three Centuries of Russian Eastward Expansion, 1558–1867*, 3 vols. (Portland, 1988), 2:69.

5. Dmytryshyn, Crownhart-Vaughan, and Vaughan, *To Siberia and Russian America* 2:85–86.

6. F. A. Golder, *Bering's Voyages*, 2 vols. (New York, 1922–25), 1:22.

7. Golder, *Bering's Voyages* 1:23.

8. Dmytryshyn, Crownhart-Vaughan, and Vaughan, *To Siberia and Russian America* 2:90–92.

9. Dmytryshyn, Crownhart-Vaughan, and Vaughan, *To Siberia and Russian America* 2: 96–97.

10. See Raymond H. Fisher, *Bering's Voyages: Whither and Why* (Seattle, 1977); also see Gerhard Friedrich Müller, *Bering's Voyages: The Reports from Russia*, trans. Carol Urness (Fairbanks, 1986), and Carol Louise Urness, *Bering's First Expedition: A Re-examination Based on Eighteenth-Century Books, Maps, and Manuscripts* (New York, 1987).

11. Sven Waxell, *The American Expedition*, trans. M. A. Michael (Edinburgh, U.K., 1952), 44–45.

12. See Gibson, *Feeding the Russian Fur Trade*, pt. 2.

13. Golder, *Bering's Voyages* 1:33.

14. Dmytryshyn, Crownhart-Vaughan, and Vaughan, *To Siberia and Russian America* 2:98, 101.

15. Georg Wilhelm Steller, *Journal of a Voyage with Bering, 1741–1742*, ed. O. W. Frost, trans. Margritt A. Engel and O. W. Frost (Stanford, 1988), 51–52.

16. Golder, *Bering's Voyages* 1:314.

17. Dmytryshyn, Crownhart-Vaughan, and Vaughan, *To Siberia and Russian America* 2:147–148.

18. Golder, *Bering's Voyages* 1:308.

19. Golder, *Bering's Voyages* 1:317, 322, 325, 329.

20. Golder, *Bering's Voyages* 1:120.

21. Steller, *Journal of a Voyage*, 64.

22. Steller, *Journal of a Voyage*, 113; Golder, *Bering's Voyages* 1:275.

23. Golder, *Bering's Voyages* 1:209, 276.

24. Golder, *Bering's Voyages* 1:210 n. 123.

25. Waxell, *The American Expedition*, 151, 156–57, 194–95, 197.

26. Fisher, *Bering's Voyages*, 150; Gibson, *Feeding the Russian Fur Trade*, 108; Raisa V. Makarova, *Russians on the Pacific, 1743–1799*, ed. and trans. Richard A. Pierce and Alton S. Donnelly (Kingston ON, 1975), 233 n. 18.

27. Dmytryshyn, Crownhart-Vaughan, and Vaughan, *To Siberia and Russian America* 2:192–98.

28. A. Sokolov, "Ekspeditsiya k Aleutskim ostrovam kapitanov Krenitsyna i Levashova (1764–1769 gg.)" [The Expedition of Captains Krenitsyn and Levashov to the Aleutian Islands, 1764–1769], *Zapiski Gidrograficheskavo departamenta* 10 (1852).

29. Golder, *Bering's Voyages* 1:230 n. 127; Steller, *Journal of a Voyage*, 145.

30. Gibson, *Feeding the Russian Fur Trade*, 16–17; Makarova, *Russians on the Pacific*, 234 n. 22.

31. Steller, *Journal of a Voyage*, 147.

32. Makarova, *Russians on the Pacific*, 115, 139, 209–16.

33. J. C. Beaglehole, ed., *The Journals of Captain James Cook on His Voyages of Discovery*, 3 vols. (Cambridge, U.K., 1967), 3:pt. 2, 1338; W. Ellis, *An Authentic Narrative of a Voyage Performed by Captain Cook and Captain Clerke*, 2 vols. (London, 1782), 2:35–36.

34. Dmytryshyn, Crownhart-Vaughan, and Vaughan, *To Siberia and Russian America* 2:259–67. See O. M. Medushevskaya, "Cartographic Sources for the History of Russian Geographical Discoveries in the Pacific Ocean in the Second Half of the 18th Century," trans. James R. Gibson, *Canadian Cartographer* 9 (1972): 99–121, and A. V. Yefimov, ed., *Atlas geograficheskikh otkryty v Sibiri i v Severo-Zapadnoy Amerike XVII–XVIII vv.* [Atlas of geographical discoveries in Siberia and Northwestern America in the 17th–18th centuries] (Moscow, 1964), especially pt. 13.

35. Also see James R. Masterson and Helen Brower, eds. and trans., *Bering's Successors, 1745–1780: Contributions of Peter Simon Pallas to the History of Russian Exploration toward Alaska* (Seattle, 1948).

36. Martin Sauer, *An Account of a Geographical and Astronomical Expedition to the Northern Parts of Russia . . .* (London, 1802), vii.

37. Beaglehole, *Journals of Captain James Cook* 3:pt. 2, 1248.

38. Sauer, *Account of a Geographical and Astronomical Expedition*, viii-ix.

39. G. A. Sarychev, *Puteshestvie po severo-vostochnoy chasti Sibiri, Ledovitomu moryu i Vostochnomu okeanu* [A journey through the northeastern part of Siberia, the Icy Sea, and the Eastern Ocean] (Moscow, 1952), 279, 287.

40. D. A. Shirina, *Letopis ekspeditsy Akademii nauk na severo-vostok Azii v dorevolyutsionny period* [A chronicle of the expeditions of the Academy of Sciences to northeastern Asia in the prerevolutionary period] (Novosibirsk, 1983), 39.

41. See Gawrila Sarytschew, *Account of a Voyage of Discovery to the North-East of Siberia, the Frozen Ocean, and the North-East Sea* (London, 1806).

42. Sauer, *Account of a Geographical and Astronomical Expedition*, 184.

43. Sauer, *Account of a Geographical and Astronomical Expedition*, 198; Sarychev, *Puteshestvie*, 155, 158; Sarychev, *Account of a Voyage*, 22, 25.

44. Shirina, *Letopis*, 42.

45. Dmytryshyn, Crownhart-Vaughan, and Vaughan, *To Siberia and Russian America* 2:296–320, 326–33, 361–64; also see A. I. Andreyev, ed., *Russian Discoveries in the Pacific and in North America in the Eighteenth and Nineteenth Centuries*, trans. Carl Ginsburg (Ann Arbor, 1952), and Gregorii I. Shelikhov, *A Voyage to America, 1783–1786*, trans. Marina Ramsay (Kingston ON, 1981).

46. Dmytryshyn, Crownhart-Vaughan, and Vaughan, *To Siberia and Russian America*, 2:331.

47. Andreyev, *Russian Discoveries*, 71.

48. A. I. Andreyev, ed., *Russkie otkrytiva v Tikhom okeane i Severnoy Amerike v XVIII veke* [Russian discoveries in the Pacific Ocean and in North America in the 18th century] (Moscow, 1948), 282.

49. George Vancouver, *A Voyage of Discovery to the North Pacific Ocean and Round the World, 1791–1795*, ed. W. Kaye Lamb, 5 vols. (London, 1984), 4:1285 n. 1, 1308.

50. The fullest account of Spanish activities on the Pacific coast of North America is Warren L. Cook, *Flood Tide of Empire: Spain and the Pacific Northwest, 1543–1819* (New Haven, 1973). Also see Christon I. Archer's several articles, cited below, as well as his forthcoming book on the same subject. Also valuable is Mary Gormly, "Early Culture Contact on the Northwest Coast, 1774–1795: Analysis of Spanish Source Material," *Northwest Anthropological Research Notes* 11 (spring 1977): 1–80.

51. Arsenio Rey-Tejerina, "The Spanish Exploration of Alaska, 1774–1796: Manuscript Sources," *Alaska History* 3 (1988): 45.

52. Christon I. Archer, "Spanish Exploration and Settlement of the Northwest Coast in the 18th Century," *Sound Heritage* 7 (1978): 33.

53. See C. R. Boxer, "The Manila Galleon, 1565–1815: The Lure of Silk and Silver," *History Today* 8 (1958): 538–47, and William Lytle Schurz, *The Manila Galleon* (New York, 1939).

54. Archer, "Spanish Exploration and Settlement," 33.

55. Christon I. Archer, "The Transient Presence: A Re-Appraisal of Spanish Attitudes toward the Northwest Coast in the Eighteenth Century," *BC Studies*, no. 18 (summer 1973), 4.

56. See Henry R. Wagner, "Apocryphal Voyages to the Northwest Coast of America," *Proceedings of the American Antiquarian Society*, n.s., 41 (1931): 179–234.

57. Donald C. Cutter, ed., *The California Coast: A Bilingual Edition of Documents from the Sutro Collection* (Norman, 1969), 107, 109, 113, 115, 117.

58. See W. Michael Mathes, *Sebastián Vizcaíno and Spanish Expansion in the Pacific Ocean, 1580–1630* (San Francisco, 1968); also see Henry R. Wagner, *Spanish Voyages to the Northwest Coast of America in the Sixteenth Century* (1929; reprint, Amsterdam, 1966).

59. Rey-Tejerina, "Spanish Exploration of Alaska," 45.

60. Herbert Ingram Priestley, *José De Gálvez: Visitor-General of New Spain (1765–1771)* (Millwood NY, 1974), 245–46; Michael E. Thurman, *The Naval Department of San Blas: New Spain's Bastion for Alta California and Nootka, 1767 to 1798* (Glendale CA, 1967), 52.

61. Archer, "Transient Presence," 4.

62. For a full account of San Blas, see Thurman, *Naval Department of San Blas*. Also see Edward L. Inskeep, "San Blas, Nayarit: An Historical and Geographic Study," *Journal of the West* 2 (1963): 133–44.

63. Donald C. Cutter, *Malaspina in California* (San Francisco, 1960), appendix B, summary of Appendix B. Also see Charles Edward Chapman, "The Alta California Supply Ships," *Southwestern Historical Quarterly* (1915), 184–94.

64. Archer, "Spanish Exploration and Settlement," 34.

65. Adolph Van Hemert-Engert and Frederick J. Teggart, eds., *The Narrative of the Portola Expedition of 1769–1770 by Miguel Costanso* (Berkeley, 1910), 7–9; also see Douglas S. Watson, ed., *The Spanish Occupation of California . . .* (San Francisco, 1934), 24, 26.

66. Van Hemert-Engert and Teggart, *Narrative of the Portola Expedition*, 13, 15.

67. On Gálvez, see Herbert Ingram Priestly, "José de Gálvéz, Visitador-General of New Spain (1765–1771)," *University of California Publications in History* 5 (1916).

68. Watson, *Spanish Occupation of California*, 4–5.

69. Watson, *Spanish Occupation of California*, 20.

70. Watson, *Spanish Occupation of California*, 20; Van Hemert-Engert and Teggart, *Narrative of the Portola Expedition*, 17.

71. Watson, *Spanish Occupation of California*, 32.

72. Herbert Eugene Bolton, *Fray Juan Crespi: Missionary Explorer of the Pacific Coast, 1769–1774* (New York, 1971), 5–7, 15.

73. Van Hemert-Engert and Teggart, *Narrative of the Portola Expedition*, 37.

74. Van Hemert-Engert and Teggart, *Narrative of the Portola Expedition*, 27; Watson, *Spanish Occupation of California*, 36.

75. Bolton, *Fray Juan Crespi*, 2, 16; Watson, *Spanish Occupation of California*, 41.

76. Bolton, *Fray Juan Crespi*, 22, 28–30, 43–44.

77. Bolton, *Fray Juan Crespi*, 24–26, 38, 40.

78. Van Hemert-Engert and Teggart, *Narrative of the Portola Expedition*, 45.

79. Watson, *Spanish Occupation of California*, 57.

80. Watson, *Spanish Occupation of California*, 35.

81. Vancouver, *Voyage of Discovery* 3:1124–25.

82. Archer, "Transient Presence," 4; Thurman, *Naval Department of San Blas*, 118; Henry R. Wagner, *The Cartography of the Northwest Coast of America to the Year 1800*, 2 vols. (Berkeley, 1937), 1:172. On Bucareli, see Bernard E. Bobb, *The Viceregency of Antonio Maria Bucareli in New Spain, 1771–1779* (Austin, 1962).

83. Thurman, *Naval Department of San Blas*, 118.

84. Herbert Eugene Bolton, ed. and trans., *Anza's California Expeditions*, 5 vols. (New York, 1966), 5:96–97.

85. Thurman, *Naval Department of San Blas*, 126.

86. Manuel P. Servin, trans., "The Instructions of Viceroy Bucareli to Ensign Juan Perez," *California Historical Quarterly* 40 (1961): 239–43.

87. Cutter, *California Coast*, 175.

88. Cutter, *California Coast*, 161.

89. Cutter, *California Coast*, 181.

90. Cutter, *California Coast*, 193; Bolton, *Fray Juan Crespi*, 359; Thurman, *Naval Department of San Blas*, 138 n.

91. Thurman, *Naval Department of San Blas*, 138 n.

92. Christon I. Archer, "Russians, Indians, and Passages: Spanish Voyages to Alaska in the Eighteenth Century," in *Exploration in Alaska: Captain Cook Commemorative Lectures, June–November 1978*, ed. Antoinette Shalkop (Anchorage, 1980), 132; Archer, "Spanish Exploration and Settlement," 36.

93. A. J. Baker, trans., "Fray Benito de la Sierra's Account of the Hezeta Expedition to the Northwest Coast in 1775," ed. Henry R. Wagner, *California Historical Quarterly* 9 (1930): 214.

94. Baker, "Fray Benito de la Sierra's Account," 211; John Galvin, ed., *A Journal of Explorations Northward along the Coast from Monterey in the Year 1775* (San Francisco, 1964), 19.

95. Baker, "Fray Benito de la Sierra's Account," 214; Galvin, *Journal of Explorations*, 23.

96. Baker, "Fray Benito de la Sierra's Account," 218, 221; Francisco Antonio Mourelle, *Voyage of the Sonora in the Second Bucareli Exploration . . .*, trans. Daines Barrington (San Francisco, 1920), 29.

97. Baker, "Fray Benito de la Sierra's Account," 225.

98. Archer, "Transient Presence," 5.

99. Mourelle, *Voyage of the Sonora*, 35.

100. Archer, "Transient Presence," 6.

101. Baker, "Fray Benito de la Sierra's Account," 227–29; Herbert K. Beals, trans., *For Honor and Country: The Diary of Bruno de Hezeta* (Portland, 1985), 78; Mourelle, *Voyage of the Sonora*, 37, 39.

102. Baker, "Fray Benito de la Sierra's Account," 216, 225, 227–28; Beals, *For Honor and Country*, 79.

103. Baker, "Fray Benito de la Sierra's Account," 230.

104. Baker, "Fray Benito de la Sierra's Account," 231–32; Galvin, *Journal of Explorations*, 50.

105. Beals, *For Honor and Country*, 86.

106. Beals, *For Honor and Country*, 88; Baker, "Fray Benito de la Sierra's Account," 235.

107. Baker, "Fray Benito de la Sierra's Account," 238, 238 n; Beals, *For Honor and Country*, 95; Galvin, *Journal of Explorations*, 59.

108. Mourelle, *Voyage of the Sonora*, 41.

109. Baker, "Fray Benito de la Sierra's Account," 240; Mourelle, *Voyage of the Sonora*, 47–48.

110. Baker, "Fray Benito de la Sierra's Account," 240; Mourelle, *Voyage of the Sonora*, 47, 52.

111. Mourelle, *Voyage of the Sonora*, 58–59.

112. Thurman, *Naval Department of San Blas*, 166–67.

113. Walter Thornton, trans., "An Account of the Voyage Made by the Frigates 'Princesa' and 'Favorita' in the Year 1799 [*sic*, 1779] from San Blas to Northern Alaska," *Catholic Historical Review* 4 (1918): 222.

114. Thornton, "Account of the Voyage," 222–23.

115. Thornton, "Account of the Voyage," 224.

116. Thornton, "Account of the Voyage," 224–25.

117. Thornton, "Account of the Voyage," 229.

118. Thornton, "Account of the Voyage," 229.

119. Wagner, *Cartography of the Northwest Coast* 1:202.

120. Thurman, *Naval Department of San Blas*, 258 n.

121. See Adele Ogden, "The Californias in Spain's Pacific Otter Trade, 1775–1795," *Pacific Historical Review* 1 (1932): 444–69.

122. See, for example, Donald C. Cutter, "Early Spanish Artists on the Northwest Coast," *Pacific Northwest Quarterly* 54 (1963): 150–57.

123. Archer, "Russians, Indians, and Passages," 134.

124. See Archer, "Spanish Exploration and Settlement."

125. Thurman, *Naval Department of San Blas*, 263 n, 267.

126. Enriqueta Vila Vilar, *Los rusos en América* [The Russians in America] (Seville, Spain, 1966), 77.

127. Vilar, *Los rusos*, 80.

128. Vilar, *Los rusos*, 80.

129. Archer, "Russians, Indians, and Passages," 138.

130. Archer, "Spanish Exploration and Settlement," 40; Archer, "Transient Presence," 10–11.

131. Wagner, *Cartography of the Northwest Coast* 1:214.

132. Archer, "Transient Presence," 11.

133. Archer, "Spanish Exploration and Settlement," 40.

134. Thurman, *Naval Department of San Blas*, 282–83.

135. See William Ray Manning, "The Nootka Sound Controversy," *Annual Report of the American Historical Association, 1904* (1905), 279–478.

136. See John Meares, *Voyages Made in the Years 1788 and 1789, from China to the North West Coast of America* (London, 1790), appendices I–XIII.

137. Archer, "Spanish Exploration and Settlement," 45–46; Archer, "Transient Presence," 20–21; Roberto Barreiro-Meiro, ed., *Colección de diarios y relaciones para la historia de los viaies y descubrimientos: VI—Estéban José Martínez (1742–1798)* [Collection of diaries and accounts for the history of voyages and discoveries: VI—Estéban José Martínez (1742–1798)] (Madrid, Spain, 1964), 127.

138. Archer, "Transient Presence," 22–23.

139. Henry R. Wagner, *Spanish Explorations in the Strait of Juan de Fuca* (New York, 1971), 13.

140. Archer, "Transient Presence," 25–29. Because they were less widespread, as well as more transient, and did not pursue the fur trade (and perhaps too because they were under military discipline), the Spaniards had much less impact on the coastal Indians than did their imperial rivals.

141. Archer, "Spanish Exploration and Settlement"; Wagner, *Spanish Explorations*, 155.

142. Archer, "Transient Presence," 24.

143. Archer, "Russians, Indians, and Passages," 139.

144. Wagner, *Spanish Explorations*, 77, 80, 87–88, 120, 132.

145. For Quimper's journal, see Wagner, *Spanish Explorations*, 82–134.

146. Wagner, *Spanish Explorations*, 137.

147. Wagner, *Spanish Explorations*, 173–74.

148. Wagner, *Spanish Explorations*, 204, 206.

149. Cecil Jane, trans., *A Spanish Voyage to Vancouver and the North-West Coast of America . . .* (London, 1930), 6.

150. Jane, *Spanish Voyage*, 5–7.

151. Vancouver, *Voyage of Discovery* 2:593, 616.

152. Vancouver, *Voyage of Discovery* 2:32–33.

153. Vancouver, *Voyage of Discovery* 2:54, 593; Wagner, *Spanish Explorations*, 262.

154. Wagner, *Spanish Explorations*, 264–65. Also see Jane, *Spanish Voyage*, 57.

155. Jane, *Spanish Voyage*, 89.

156. Wagner, *Cartography of the Northwest Coast* 1:233.

157. Harold Grenfell, trans., "The Journal of Jacinto Caamaño," ed. Henry R. Wagner and W. A. Newcombe, *British Columbia Historical Quarterly* 2 (1938): 199.

158. Grenfell, "Journal of Jacinto Caamaño," 200, 202; Wagner, *Cartography of the Northwest Coast* 1:233.

159. Grenfell, "Journal of Jacinto Caamaño," 200.

160. Grenfell, "Journal of Jacinto Caamaño," 280.

161. Wagner, *Cartography of the Northwest Coast* 1:236.

162. Wagner, *Cartography of the Northwest Coast* 1:237.

163. Wagner, *Cartography of the Northwest Coast* 1:237.

164. Wagner, *Cartography of the Northwest Coast* 1:238.

165. See Christon I. Archer, "The Spanish Reaction to Cook's Third Voyage," in Robin Fisher and Hugh Johnston, eds., *Captain James Cook and His Times* (Vancouver BC, 1979), 99–119.

166. See Iris Higbie Wilson, "Spanish Scientists in the Pacific Northwest, 1790–1792," in John Alexander Carroll, ed., *Reflections of Western Historians* (Tucson, 1969), 31–47.

167. Wagner, *Spanish Explorations*, 199.

168. Henry R. Wagner, trans. and ed., "Journal of Tomás de Suria of his Voyage with Malaspina to the Northwest Coast of America in 1791," *Pacific Historical Review* 5 (1936): 271.

169. Wagner, "Journal of Tomás de Suria," 260.

170. Wagner, "Journal of Tomás de Suria," 246–47, 251, 262–63.

171. Wagner, "Journal of Tomás de Suria," 268.

172. Wagner, "Journal of Tomás de Suria," 267. On Malaspina's voyage to the Northwest Coast, see Thomas Vaughan, E. A. P. Crownhart-Vaughan, and Mercedes Palau de Iglesias, *Voyages of Enlightenment: Malaspina on the Northwest Coast, 1791/1792* (Portland, 1977).

173. C. P. Claret Fleurieu, *A Voyage Round the World, Performed during the Years 1790, 1791, and 1792, by Étienne Marchand . . .* , 2 vols. (London, 1801), 1:liii.

174. Fleurieu, *Voyage Round the World* 1:liii.

175. Vancouver, *Voyage of Discovery* 3:1121–22.

176. Archer, "Russians, Indians, and Passages," 141.

177. José Mariano Moziño, *Noticias de Nutka: An Account of Nootka Sound in 1792*, ed. and trans. Iris Higbie Wilson (Toronto, 1970), 91, 93.

178. Watson, *Spanish Occupation of California*, 47–48.

179. Beaglehole, *Journals of Captain James Cook* 3:pt. 2, 1103.

180. Michael E. Thurman, "Juan Bodega y Quadra and the Spanish Retreat from Nootka, 1790–1794," in Carroll, *Reflections*, 61.

181. Archer, "Transient Presence," 22.

182. Moziño, *Noticias de Nutka*, 94.

183. Thurman, "Juan Bodega y Quadra," 61.

184. Thurman, "Juan Bodega y Quadra," 62.

185. Cutter, *Malaspina in California*, summary of appendix D.

186. Thurman, "Juan Bodega y Quadra," 61.

187. Vancouver, *Voyage of Discovery* 3:1126, 1129, 1131–34.

188. Cook, *Flood Tide of Empire*, 195.

189. Donald C. Cutter, "Spanish Scientific Exploration along the Pacific Coast," in Robert G. Ferris, ed., *The American West: An Appraisal* (Santa Fe, 1963), 160.

190. P. J. Marshall and Glyndwr Williams, *The Great Map of Mankind: British Perceptions of the World in the Enlightenment* (London, 1982), 38.

191. Marshall and Williams, *Great Map of Mankind*, chapter 9.

192. Marshall and Williams, *Great Map of Mankind*, 258.

193. See Glyndwr Williams, *The British Search for the Northwest Passage in the Eighteenth Century* (London, 1962).

194. Vancouver, *Voyage of Discovery* 3:1020.

195. Basil Greenhill, *James Cook: The Opening of the Pacific* (Palo Alto CA, 1978), 25.

196. Beaglehole, *Journals of Captain James Cook* 3:pt. 1, ccxx.

197. Beaglehole, *Journals of Captain James Cook* 3:pt. 1, ccxx–ccxxii.

198. Greenhill, *James Cook*, 25. See Rüdiger Joppien and Bernard Smith, *The Art of Captain Cook's Voyages* (New Haven, 1988), vol. 3.

199. Christine Holmes, ed., *Captain Cook's Final Voyage: The Journal of Midshipman George Gilbert* (Honolulu, 1982), 68.

200. [John Rickman], *Journal of Captain Cook's Last Voyage* . . . (London, 1781), 232–33.

201. Beaglehole, *Journals of Captain James Cook* 3:pt. 2, 1088.

202. Beaglehole, *Journals of Captain James Cook* 3:pt. 1, 289.

203. Beaglehole, *Journals of Captain James Cook* 3:pt.1, 293–94.

204. Beaglehole, *Journals of Captain James Cook* 3:pt.1, 294.

205. Beaglehole, *Journals of Captain James Cook* 3:pt.1, 295–96.

206. Beaglehole, *Journals of Captain James Cook* 3:pt.1, 296, 296 n.

207. Holmes, *Captain Cook's Final Voyage*, 72.

208. Holmes, *Captain Cook's Final Voyage*, 302–3 n.

209. [Rickman], *Journal*, 246.

210. Beaglehole, *Journals of Captain James Cook* 3:pt. 1, 308.

211. Holmes, *Captain Cook's Final Voyage*, 75.

212. Beaglehole, *Journals of Captain James Cook* 3:pt. 1, 335.

213. Beaglehole, *Journals of Captain James Cook* 3:pt. 2, 1105.

214. Beaglehole, *Journals of Captain James Cook* 3:pt. 2, 1108, 1418; Ellis, *Authentic Narrative* 1:243.

215. Beaglehole, *Journals of Captain James Cook* 3:pt. 2, 1108.

216. Beaglehole, *Journals of Captain James Cook* 3:pt. 2, 1110.

217. [Rickman], *Voyage*, 250.

218. [Rickman], *Voyage*, 253.

219. Beaglehole, *Journals of Captain James Cook* 3:pt. 2, 1117–18.

220. Beaglehole, *Journals of Captain James Cook* 3:pt. 2, 353, 364.

221. Beaglehole, *Journals of Captain James Cook* 3:pt. 2, 353, 368.

222. See Glyndwr Williams, "Myth and Reality: James Cook and the Theoretical Geography of Northwest America," in Fisher and Johnston, *Captain James Cook*, 59–79.

223. Williams, "Myth and Reality," 409.

224. Beaglehole, *Journals of Captain James Cook* 3:pt. 2, 1134.

225. Beaglehole, *Journals of Captain James Cook* 3:pt. 2, 1135, 3:pt. 1, 417.

226. Beaglehole, *Journals of Captain James Cook* 3:pt. 2, 1446, 1449.

227. See James R. Gibson, "The Significance of Cook's Third Voyage to Russian Tenure in the North Pacific," *Pacific Studies* 1 (1978): 119–46.

228. [Rickman], *Journal*, 343.

229. Beaglehole, *Journals of Captain James Cook* 3:pt. 1, 371–72.

230. Beaglehole, *Journals of Captain James Cook* 3:pt. 2, 1243, 1338; Holmes, *Captain Cook's Final Voyage*, 139.

231. [Rickman], *Journal*, 385, 387.

232. Holmes, *Captain Cook's Final Voyage*, 154.

233. See James R. Gibson, *Otter Skins, Boston Ships, and China Goods: The Maritime Fur Trade of the Northwest Coast, 1785–1841* (Seattle, 1992).

234. See Sir James Watt, "Medical Aspects and Consequences of Cook's Voyages," in Fisher and Johnston, *Captain James Cook*, 129–57.

235. See Captain George Dixon, *A Voyage Round the World; But More Particularly to the North-West Coast of America: Performed in 1785, 1786, 1787, and 1788, in the King George and Queen Charlotte, Captains Portlock and Dixon* (London, 1789), 216, 223–24.

236. See Howard T. Fry, "Alexander Dalrymple and Captain Cook: The Creative Interplay of Two Careers," in Fisher and Johnston, *Captain James Cook*, 41–57.

237. Vancouver's account has recently been republished in an admirable new edition by the Hakluyt Society under the editorship of W. Kaye Lamb. What is needed now is the publication (for the first time) of the complete journals of four of

Vancouver's officers: Edward Bell, Thomas Manby, Archibald Menzies, and Peter Puget.

238. Vancouver, *Voyage of Discovery* 1:274–75, 277–78.

239. Vancouver, *Voyage of Discovery* 1:278.

240. Vancouver, *Voyage of Discovery* 1:283–84.

241. Vancouver, *Voyage of Discovery* 2:670.

242. Vancouver, *Voyage of Discovery* 2:491.

243. Vancouver, *Voyage of Discovery* 2:497–98.

244. Vancouver, *Voyage of Discovery* 2:502–3, 503 n, 510–12.

245. Vancouver, *Voyage of Discovery* 1:284.

246. Vancouver, *Voyage of Discovery* 1:284.

247. Vancouver, *Voyage of Discovery* 2:503.

248. Vancouver, *Voyage of Discovery* 2:549–50.

249. Vancouver, *Voyage of Discovery* 2:541–43.

250. Vancouver, *Voyage of Discovery* 2:572–73, 628–29.

251. Vancouver, *Voyage of Discovery* 2:580, 582.

252. Vancouver, *Voyage of Discovery* 2:588.

253. Vancouver, *Voyage of Discovery* 2:580–82, 591–93.

254. Vancouver, *Voyage of Discovery* 2:616, 628.

255. Vancouver, *Voyage of Discovery* 2:600, 652.

256. Vancouver, *Voyage of Discovery* 2:598, 606, 614–15, 628.

257. Vancouver, *Voyage of Discovery* 2:697–99.

258. Vancouver, *Voyage of Discovery* 2:693.

259. Vancouver, *Voyage of Discovery* 2:760, 760 n, 767.

260. Vancouver, *Voyage of Discovery* 3:922.

261. Vancouver, *Voyage of Discovery* 3:968, 982, 1003.

262. Vancouver, *Voyage of Discovery* 3:1008.

263. Vancouver, *Voyage of Discovery* 3:982–85.

264. Vancouver, *Voyage of Discovery* 3:1022.

265. Vancouver, *Voyage of Discovery* 3:1023–24, 1047–48.

266. Vancouver, *Voyage of Discovery* 3:1023 n.

267. See Alexander Mackenzie, *Voyages from Montreal on the River St. Laurence through the Continent of North America to the Frozen and Pacific Oceans in the Years 1789 and 1793* . . . (Edmonton AB, 1971).

268. Vancouver, *Voyage of Discovery* 4:1243.

269. Vancouver, *Voyage of Discovery* 4:1235.

270. Vancouver, *Voyage of Discovery* 4:1313, 1329.

271. Vancouver, *Voyage of Discovery* 4:1350.

272. Vancouver, *Voyage of Discovery* 4:1390–91.

273. Vancouver, *Voyage of Discovery* 4:1382.

274. Vancouver, *Voyage of Discovery* 4:1380, 1388–89.

275. Vancouver, *Voyage of Discovery* 4:1543–44.

276. William Robert Broughton, *A Voyage of Discovery to the North Pacific Ocean . . . Performed in His Majesty's Sloop Providence, and Her Tender, in the Years 1795, 1796, 1797, 1798* (London, 1804), xi.

277. Vancouver, *Voyage of Discovery* 3:489.

278. Broughton, *Voyage of Discovery*, xiii–xiv.

279. Broughton, *Voyage of Discovery*, 50.

280. L. A. Milet-Mureau, ed., *A Voyage Round the World Performed in the Years 1785, 1786, 1787, and 1788, by the Boussole and Astrolabe, under the Command of J. F. G. De La Pérouse*, 2 vols. (London, 1799), 1:xviii.

281. John Dunmore, *French Explorers in the Pacific*, 2 vols. (Oxford, U.K., 1965), 1:260–64; Milet-Mureau, *Voyage Round the World* 1:1, 4–10.

282. Milet-Mureau, *Voyage Round the World* 1:24–38.

283. Milet-Mureau, *Voyage Round the World* 1:19, 412–13.

284. Milet-Mureau, *Voyage Round the World* 1:387–88.

285. See Capt. P. Dillon, *Narrative and Successful Result of a Voyage in the South Seas . . .*, 2 vols. (London, 1829); also see J. W. Davidson, *Peter Dillon of Vanikoro*, ed. O. H. K. Spate (Melbourne, Australia, 1975).

286. See M. De Lesseps, *Travels in Kamtschatka, during the Years 1787 and 1788*, 2 vols. (London, 1790).

287. Milet-Mureau, *Voyage Round the World* 1:495.

288. Milet-Mureau, *Voyage Round the World* 1:371, 457.

289. Fleurieu, *Voyage Round the World* 1:cxviii.

290. Fleurieu, *Voyage Round the World* 1:cxix–xx.

291. Fleurieu, *Voyage Round the World* 1:192, 194–95, 221, 2:69–71, 174.

292. Vancouver, *Voyage of Discovery* 3:1072–73, 1073 n.

293. See James R. Gibson, *Otter Skins, Boston Ships, and China Goods: The Maritime Fur Trade of the Northwest Coast, 1785–1841* (Seattle, 1992).

294. Jane, *Spanish Voyage*, 90.

295. Vancouver, *Voyage of Discovery* 2:647.

296. Dixon, *Voyage Round the World*, 223–24; W. Kaye Lamb, "The Mystery of Mrs. Barkley's Diary," *British Columbia Historical Quarterly* 6 (1942): 49–50.

297. F. W. Howay, "Four Letters from Richard Cadman Etches to Sir Joseph Banks, 1788–92," *British Columbia Historical Quarterly* 6 (1942): 137 (Etches to Banks, 1788); John Meares, *Voyages Made in the Years 1788 and 1789, from China to the North West Coast of America* (London, 1790), liii–lv, 331.

298. Howay, "Four Letters," 139 (Etches to Banks, 1792).

299. James Kenneth Munford, ed., *John Ledyard's Journal of Captain Cook's Last Voyage* (Corvallis OR, 1963), 70, 166–67, 200.

300. Stephen D. Watrous, ed., *John Ledyard's Journey through Russia and Siberia 1787–1788* (Madison, 1966), 159.

301. Frederic W. Howay, ed., *Voyages of the "Columbia" to the Northwest Coast, 1787–1790 and 1790–1793* (Boston, 1941), vi.

302. Howay, *Voyages of the "Columbia,"* viii.

303. Howay, *Voyages of the "Columbia,"* 336, 396–99, 436–38.

304. See Gary E. Moulton, ed., *The Journals of the Lewis and Clark Expedition* (Lincoln, 1988–89), vols. 5–6.

305. See N. A. Ivashintsev, *Russian Voyages of Circumnavigation*, trans. G. R. V. Barratt (Kingston ON, 1980).

306. See Frederick William Beechey, *Narrative of a Voyage to the Pacific and Beering's Strait . . . in the Years 1825, 26, 27, 28*, 2 vols. (London, 1831); Barry M. Gough, ed., *To the Pacific and Arctic with Beechey: The Journal of Lieutenant George Peard of H.M.S. "Blossom," 1825–1828* (Cambridge, U.K., 1973).

307. See Captain Sir Edward Belcher, *Narrative of a Voyage Round the World . . .*, 2 vols. (London, 1843); Richard A. Pierce and John H. Winslow, eds., *H.M.S. Sulphur on the Northwest and California Coasts, 1837 and 1839: The Accounts of Captain Edward Belcher and Midshipman Francis Guillemard Simpkinson* (Kingston ON, 1979).

308. See Herman J. Viola, "The Wilkes Expedition on the Pacific Coast," *Pacific Northwest Quarterly* 80 (1989): 21–31; Charles Wilkes, *Narrative of the United States Exploring Expedition during the Years 1838, 1839, 1840, 1841, 1842*, 5 vols. (Philadelphia, 1845).

Selected Bibliography

North American Exploration, Volume 2

The second volume of *North American Exploration* encompasses the intermediate period between the thrill of first discovery in the fifteenth and sixteenth centuries and the later stages of nineteenth-century scientific inquiry. The literature for this period is voluminous, even more so than that for the first volume. Hence, the following bibliographic listing is necessarily partial and arbitrary. It is, however, a fairly comprehensive coverage of the cardinal themes of exploration during the seventeenth and eighteenth centuries. Two categories of literature will be conspicuous by their absence in the following collection: articles from periodicals and professional journals; and foreign-language publications. Both of these types of literature are contained within the notes accompanying each of the chapters in volume 2. We have tried to present in the selected bibliography materials that will be available in both medium-sized public libraries and most college and university libraries. This means that most of the materials are secondary sources. For a good selection of primary materials (also included in the bibliography), the reader will need to visit college and university libraries, along with some specialized larger private and municipal libraries (the Newberry Library in Chicago and the New York Public Library, for example).

The secondary sources offer scholars explications of the process of exploration and the stories of the people who were part of that process. They are very worthwhile reading. But even more valuable are the words of the explorers themselves and of their contemporaries. For those readers whose interest in North American exploration during the intermediate period runs deeper, those primary sources should be sought out; therefore, these too are represented in the selected bibliography. The words of the participants carry the reader up the rivers of the Atlantic seaboard and the Saint Lawrence drainage to the Great Lakes and the mountains beyond, across the barren grounds of the Far North in search of the elusive Northwest Passage. Where earlier explorers had, in their imaginations, smelled the exotic aroma of sandalwood, borne on the breeze blowing from the Spice Islands, the continental and coastal explorers of the seventeenth and eighteenth centuries sensed salt spray and river mist, heard the sound of falling water, saw the hazy uplands of the interior, and smelled the smoke of thousands of native campfires. Listen to their voices as they tell the story.

Allen, John L. *Passage Through the Garden: Lewis and Clark and the Images of the American Northwest*. Urbana, 1975.

Alvord, Clarence W., and Lee Bidgood. *The First Explorations of the Trans-Allegheny Region by the Virginians, 1650–1674*. Cleveland, 1912.

Andreev, A. I., ed. *Russian Discoveries in the Pacific and in North America in the Eighteenth and Nineteenth Centuries*. Trans. Carl Ginsburg. Ann Arbor, 1952.

Bakeless, John. *The Eyes of Discovery*. New York, 1961.

Bancroft, Hubert H. *History of the North Mexican States and Texas*. Works of Hubert Howe Bancroft. 2 vols. San Francisco, 1886.

Bannon, John F. *The Mission Frontier in Sonora, 1620–1687*. New York, 1955.

———. *The Spanish Borderlands Frontier, 1513–1821*. New York, 1970.

———, ed. *Bolton and the Spanish Borderlands*. Norman, 1964.

Barbour, Philip. *The Three Worlds of Captain John Smith*. Boston, 1964.

Beaglehole, J. C., ed. *The Journals of Captain James Cook on His Voyages of Discovery*. 3 vols. Cambridge, U.K., 1967.

Beals, Herbert K., trans. *For Honor and Country: The Diary of Bruno de Hezeta*. Portland, 1985.

Beechey, Frederick William. *Narrative of a Voyage to the Pacific and Beering's Strait . . . in the Years 1825, 26, 27, 28*. 2 vols. London, 1831.

Belcher, Captain Sir Edward. *Narrative of a Voyage Round the World . . . .* 2 vols. London, 1843.

Biggar, Henry P., ed. *The Works of Samuel de Champlain*. 6 vols. Toronto, 1922–36.

Bolton, Herbert E. *Coronado: Knight of Pueblos and Plains*. Albuquerque, 1949.

———. *Fray Juan Crespi: Missionary Explorer of the Pacific Coast, 1769–1774*. New York, 1971.

———. *Pageant in the Wilderness: The Story of the Escalante Expedition to the Interior Basin*. Salt Lake City, 1950.

———. *Rim of Christendom: A Biopraphy of Eusebio Francisco Kino, Pacific Coast Pioneer*. 1936. Reprint. New York, 1960.

———, ed. *Spanish Exploration in the Southwest, 1542–1706*. Original Narratives of Early American History. 1908. Reprint. New York, 1959.

———, ed. and trans. *Anza's California Expeditions*. 5 vols. New York, 1966.

———. *Kino's Historical Memoir of Pimería Alta*. 2 vols. Berkeley, 1948.

Bolton, Herbert E., and Thomas M. Marshall. *The Colonization of North America, 1492–1783*. New York, 1922.

Bolton, Herbert E., and Mary Ross. *The Debatable Land: A Sketch of the Anglo-Spanish Contest for the Georgia Country*. Berkeley, 1925.

Bourne, Edward G. *Spain in America, 1450–1580*. New York, 1962.

Brebner, John B. *The Explorers of North America, 1492–1806.* 1933. Reprint. Cleveland, 1964.

Briceland, Alan Vance. *Westward from Virginia: The Exploration of the Virginia-Carolina Frontier, 1650–1710.* Charlottesville, 1987.

Broughton, William Robert. *A Voyage of Discovery to the North Pacific Ocean . . . Performed in His Majesty's Sloop Providence, and Her Tender, in the Years 1795, 1796, 1797, 1798.* London, 1804.

Burpee, Lawrence J., ed. *Journals and Letters of Pierre Gaullier de La Vérendrye and His Sons.* Toronto, 1927.

Chipman, Donald E. *Nuño de Guzmán and the Province of Pánuco in New Spain, 1518–1533.* Glendale CA, 1967.

Cook, Warren L. *Flood Tide of Empire: Spain and the Pacific Northwest, 1543–1819.* New Haven, 1973.

Crane, Verner W. *The Southern Frontier, 1670–1732.* 1929. Reprint. Ann Arbor, 1958.

Cumming, William P., ed. *The Discoveries of John Lederer.* Charlottesville, 1958.

Cumming, William P., S. F. Hillier, David B. Quinn, and G. Williams, eds. *The Exploration of North America, 1630–1776.* New York, 1974.

Cutter, Donald C. *Malaspina in California.* San Francisco, 1960.

Darlington, William M., ed. *Christopher Gist's Journals.* Pittsburgh, 1893.

Davidson, Gordon Charles. *The North West Company.* New York, 1918.

De Lesseps, M. *Travels in Kamtschatka, during the Years 1787 and 1788.* 2 vols. London, 1790.

Dillon, Capt. P. *Narrative and Successful Result of a Voyage in the South Seas. . . .* 2 vols. London, 1829.

Dixon, George. *A Voyage Round the World; But More Particularly to the North-West Coast of America: Performed in 1785, 1786, 1787, and 1788, in the King George and Queen Charlotte, Captains Portlock and Dixon.* London, 1789.

Dmytryshyn, Bash, E. A. P. Crownhart-Vaughan, and Thomas Vaughan, eds. and trans. *To Siberia and Russian America: Three Centuries of Russian Eastward Expansion, 1558–1867.* 3 vols. Portland, 1988.

Dunmore, John. *French Explorers in the Pacific.* 2 vols. Oxford, U.K., 1965.

Dunn, William E. *Spanish and French Rivalry in the Gulf Region of the United States, 1698–1702.* Austin, 1917.

Eccles, W. J. *Essays on New France.* Toronto, 1987.

———. *Frontenac: The Courtier Governor.* Toronto, 1959.

Ellis, W. *An Authentic Narrative of a Voyage Performed by Captain Cook and Captain Clerke.* 3 vols. London, 1782.

Engstrand, Iris H. W. *Spanish Scientists in the New World: The Eighteenth Century Expeditions.* Seattle, 1981.

Fisher, Raymond H. *Bering's Voyages: Whither and Why*. Seattle, 1977.

———. *The Voyage of Semen Dezhnev in 1648: Bering's Precursor*. London, 1981.

Fisher, Robin, and Hugh Johnston, eds. *Captain James Cook and His Times*. Vancouver BC, 1979.

French, B. F. *Historical Collections of Louisiana and Florida, Including Translations of Original Manuscripts Relating to Their Discovery*. 2d ser., 1527–1702. New York, 1875.

Geiger, Maynard. *The Franciscan Conquest of Florida, 1573–1618*. Washington DC, 1937.

Gibson, Charles. *Spain in America*. New York, 1966.

Gibson, James R. *Otter Skins, Boston Ships, and China Goods: The Maritime Fur Trade of the Northwest Coast, 1785–1841*. Seattle, 1992.

Glover, Richard, ed. *David Thompson's Narrative, 1784–1812*. Toronto, 1962.

Goetzmann, William H., and Glyndwr Williams. *The Atlas of North American Exploration : From the Norse Voyages to the Race to the Pole*. New York, 1992.

Golder, F. A. *Bering's Voyages*. 3 vols. New York, 1922–25.

Gough, Barry M., ed. *To the Pacific and Arctic with Beechey: The Journal of Lieutenant George Peard of H.M.S. "Blossom," 1825–1828*. Cambridge, U.K., 1973.

Greenhill, Basil. *James Cook: The Opening of the Pacific*. Palo Alto CA, 1978.

Hammond, George P., and Agapito Rey, eds. and trans. *Don Juan de Oñate: Colonizer of New Mexico, 1595–1628*. 2 vols. Coronado Cuarto Centennial Publications, 1540–1940. Albuquerque, 1953.

———. *The Rediscovery of New Mexico, 1580–1594*. Coronado Cuarto Centennial Publications, 1540–1940. Albuquerque, 1966.

Hemert-Engert, Adolph Van, and Frederick J. Teggart, eds. *The Narrative of the Portola Expedition of 1769–1770 by Miguel Costanso*. Berkeley, 1910.

Henry, Alexander. *Travels and Adventures in Canada and the Indian Territories: Between the Years 1760 and 1776*. Ed. James Bain. Rutland VT, 1969.

Hodge, Frederick W., and Theodore H. Lewis, eds. *Spanish Explorers in the Southern United States, 1528–1543*. 1907. Reprint. New York, 1965.

Hoffman, Paul E. *A New Andalucia and a Way to the Orient: The American Southeast during the Sixteenth Century*. Baton Rouge, 1990.

Holmes, Christine, ed. *Captain Cook's Final Voyage: The Journal of Midshipman George Gilbert*. Honolulu, 1982.

Holmes, Maurice G. *From New Spain to the Californias, 1519–1668*. Glendale CA, 1963.

Hopwood, Victor G., ed. *David Thompson: Travels in Western North America, 1784–1812*. Toronto, 1971.

Howay, Frederic W., ed. *Voyages of the "Columbia" to the Northwest Coast, 1787–1790 and 1790–1793*. Boston, 1941.

Hudson, Charles. *The Juan Pardo Expeditions*. Washington DC, 1990.

Innis, Harold A. *The Fur Trade in Canada*. Rev. ed. Toronto, 1962.

Jane, Cecil, trans. *A Spanish Voyage to Vancouver and the North-West Coast of America. . . .* London, 1930.

Jones, Oakah L., Jr. *Los Paisanos: Spanish Settlers on the Northern Frontier of New Spain*. Norman, 1979.

———. *Nueva Vizcaya: Heartland of the Spanish Frontier*. Albuquerque, 1988.

———. *Pueblo Warriors and Spanish Conquest*. Norman 1966.

Kelsey, Harry. *Juan Rodríguez Cabrillo*. San Marino CA, 1986.

Kelsey, Henry. *Journal of Voyage and Journey Undertaken by Henry Kelsey to Discover and Endeavour to Bring to Commerce ye Northern Indians Inhabiting to the Northward of Churchill River and Also ye Doyside Nation*. Kelsey Collection, June 17, 1689, National Archives of Canada, Ottawa.

Kupperman, Karen Ordahl, ed. *Captain John Smith: A Select Edition of His Writings*. Chapel Hill, 1988.

Leonard, Irving A., trans. *Spanish Approach to Pensacola, 1689–1693*. Albuquerque, 1939.

Lewis, Clifford, and Albert Loomis. *The Spanish Jesuit Mission in Virginia, 1570–1572*. Chapel Hill, 1953.

Loomis, Noel M., and Abraham P. Nasatir. *Pedro Vial and the Roads to Santa Fe*. Norman, 1967.

Lowery, Woodbury. *The Spanish Settlements within the Present Limits of Florida, 1562–1574*. New York, 1905.

———. *The Spanish Settlements within the Present Limits of the United States, 1513–1561*. New York, 1901.

Lyon, Eugene. *The Enterprise of Florida: Pedro de Menéndez de Avilés and the Spanish Conquest of 1565–1568*. Gainesville, 1976.

Mackenzie, Alexander. *Voyages from Montreal on the River St. Laurence through the Continent of North America to the Frozen and Pacific Oceans in the Years 1789 and 1793. . . .* Edmonton, Alberta, 1971.

Makarova, Raisa V. *Russians on the Pacific, 1743–1799*. Ed. and trans. Richard A. Pierce and Alton S. Donnelly. Kingston ON, 1975.

Masterson, James R. and Helen Brower, eds. and trans. *Bering's Successors 1745–1780: Contributions of Peter Simon Pallas to the History of Russian Exploration toward Alaska*. Seattle, 1948.

Mathes, W. Michael. *Sebastian Vizcaino and Spanish Expansion in the Pacific Ocean, 1580–1630*. San Francisco, 1968.

Meares, John. *Voyages Made in the Years 1788 and 1789, from China to the North West Coast of America*. London, 1790.

Mecham, J. Lloyd. *Francisco de Ibarra and Nueva Vizcaya*. 1927. Reprint. New York, 1968.

Meinig, Donald W. *The Shaping of America. A Geographical Perspective of 500 Years of History*. Volume 1. *Atlantic America, 1492–1800*. New Haven, 1986.

Milanich, Jerald T., and Susan Milbrath, eds. *First Encounters: Spanish Exploration in the Caribbean and the United States, 1492–1570*. Gainesville, 1989.

Milet-Mureau, L. A., ed. *A Voyage Round the World Performed in the Years 1785, 1786, 1787, and 1788, by the Boussole and Astrolabe, under the Command of J. F. G. De La Pérouse*. 2 vols. London, 1799.

Moloney, Francis X. *The Fur Trade in New England, 1620–1676*. Cambridge MA, 1931.

Morse, Eric W. *Fur Trade Canoe Routes of Canada: Then and Now*. Toronto, 1969.

Morton, Arthur S. *A History of the Canadian West to 1870–71*. 1939. Reprint. Toronto, 1973.

Moulton, Gary E., ed. *The Journals of the Lewis and Clark Expedition*. 11 vols. Lincoln, 1988–96.

Mourelle, Francisco Antonio. *Voyage of the Sonora in the Second Bucareli Exploration. . . .* Trans. Daines Barrington. San Francisco, 1920.

Moziño, José Mariano. *Noticias de Nutka: An Account of Nootka Sound in 1792*. Ed. and trans. Iris Higbie Wilson. Toronto, 1970.

Mulkearn, Lois, comp. and ed. *George Mercer Papers Relating to the Ohio Company of Virginia*. Pittsburgh, 1954.

Müller, Gerhard Friedrich. *Bering's Voyages: The Reports from Russia*. Trans. Carol Louise Urness. Fairbanks, 1986.

Munford, James Kenneth, ed. *John Ledyard's Journal of Captain Cook's Last Voyage*. Corvallis OR, 1963.

Nasatir, Abraham P., ed. *Before Lewis and Clark: Documents Illustrating the History of the Missouri, 1785–1804*. 2 vols. St. Louis, 1952.

Norton, Thomas Elliot. *The Fur Trade in Colonial New York, 1686–1776*. Madison, 1974.

Parker, John, ed. *The Journals of Jonathan Carver and Related Documents, 1766–1770*. Minneapolis, 1976.

Parry, J. H. *The Age of Reconnaissance*. New York, 1963.

Phillips, Paul Chrisler. *The Fur Trade*. 2 vols. Norman, 1961.

Pierce, Richard A., and John H. Winslow, eds. *H.M.S. Sulphur on the Northwest and California Coasts, 1837 and 1839: The Accounts of Captain Edward Belcher and Midshipman Francis Guillemard Simpkinson*. Kingston ON, 1979.

Pourade, Richard F. *Anza Conquers the Desert: The Anza Expeditions from Mexico to California and the Founding of San Francisco, 1774 to 1776*. San Diego, 1971.

Priestley, Herbert Ingram. *José De Gálvez: Visitor-General of New Spain (1765–1771)*. Millwood NY, 1974.

———. *Tristan de Luna, Conquistador of the Old South: A Study of Spanish Imperial Strategy.* 1934. Reprint. Philadelphia, 1980.

———, trans. and ed. *The Luna Papers: Documents Relating to the Expedition of Don Tristan de Luna y Arellano for the Conquest of La Florida in 1559–1561.* 2 vols. New York, 1971.

Ray, Arthur J. *Indians in the Fur Trade.* Toronto, 1974.

Rich, E. E. *The Fur Trade and the Northwest to 1857.* Toronto, 1967.

———. *Minutes of the Hudson's Bay Company, 1679–1682.* Toronto, 1945.

[Rickman, John]. *Journal of Captain Cook's Last Voyage.* . . . London, 1781.

Ruggles, Richard I. *A Country So Interesting: The Hudson's Bay Company and Two Centuries of Mapping, 1670–1870.* Montreal, 1990.

Salley, Alexander S., Jr., ed. *Narratives of Early Carolina, 1650–1708.* 1911. Reprint. New York, 1967.

Sarychev, Gavrila. *Account of a Voyage of Discovery to the North-East of Siberia, the Frozen Ocean, and the North-East Sea.* London, 1806.

Sauer, Carl O. *The Early Spanish Main.* Berkeley, 1969.

———. *Sixteenth Century North America: The Land and the People as Seen by the Europeans.* Berkeley, 1971.

Sauer, Martin. *An Account of a Geographical and Astronomical Expedition to the Northern Parts of Russia.* . . . London, 1802.

Schooling, William. *The Hudson's Bay Company, 1670–1920.* London, 1920.

Schroeder, Albert H., and Daniel S. Matson. *A Colony on the Move: Gaspar Castaño de Sosa's Journal, 1590–1591.* Santa Fe, 1965.

Shelikhov, Grigorii I. *A Voyage to America, 1783–1786.* Trans. Marina Ramsay. Kingston ON, 1981.

Sheppe, Walter, ed. *First Man West: Alexander MacKenzie's Journal of His Voyage to the Pacific Coast of Canada in 1793.* Montreal, 1962.

Smith, James K. *Alexander MacKenzie, Explorer: The Hero Who Failed.* Toronto, 1973.

Steller, Georg Wilhelm. *Journal of a Voyage with Bering, 1741–1742.* Ed. O. W. Frost. Trans. Margritt A. Engel and O. W. Frost. Stanford, 1988.

Stoddard, Ellwyn R., Richard L. Nostrand, and Jonathan P. West, eds. *Borderlands Sourcebook: A Guide to the Literature on Northern Mexico and the American Southwest.* Norman, 1983.

Swanton, John R., ed. *Final Report of the United States de Soto Expedition Commission.* Washington DC, 1985.

Thomas, Alfred B., trans. and ed. *After Coronado: Spanish Exploration Northeast of New Mexico, 1696–1727.* Norman, 1935.

Thurman, Michael E. *The Naval Department of San Blas: New Spain's Bastion for Alta California and Nootka, 1767 to 1798.* Glendale, CA, 1967.

Thwaites, Reuben Gold, ed. *Early Western Travels, 1748–1846*. 32 vols. Cleveland, 1904–7.

Trelease, Allen W. *Indian Affairs in Colonial New York: The Seventeenth Century*. Ithaca, 1960.

Tyler, L. G., ed. *Narratives of Early Virginia*. 1925. Reprint. New York, 1966.

Urness, Carol Louise. *Bering's First Expedition: A Re-examination Based on Eighteenth-Century Books, Maps, and Manuscripts*. New York, 1987.

Vancouver, George. *A Voyage of Discovery to the North Pacific Ocean and Round the World, 1791–1795*. Ed. W. Kaye Lamb. 5 vols. London, 1984.

Vaughan, Thomas, E. A. P. Crownhart-Vaughan, and Mercedes Palau de Iglesias. *Voyages of Enlightenment: Malaspina on the Northwest Coast, 1791/1792*. Portland, 1977.

Wagner, Henry R. *The Cartography of the Northwest Coast of America to the Year 1800*. 2 vols. Berkeley, 1937.

Wagner, Henry R. *Spanish Explorations in the Strait of Juan de Fuca*. New York, 1971.

Wagner, Henry R. *Spanish Voyages to the North West Coast of America in the Sixteenth Century*. 1929. Reprint. Amsterdam, 1966.

Wainwright, Nicholas B. *George Croghan, Wilderness Diplomat*. Chapel Hill, 1959.

Walker, Geoffrey J. *Spanish Politics and Imperial Trade, 1700–1789*. London, 1979.

Wallace, Stewart W., ed. *The Pedlars from Quebec and Other Papers on the Nor'Westers*. Toronto, 1954.

Warkentin, John, and Richard I. Ruggles. *Manitoba Historical Atlas: A Selection of Facsimile Maps, Plans, and Sketches from 1612 to 1969*. Winnipeg, 1970.

Warner, Ted J., ed. *The Domínguez-Escalante Journal*. Trans. Fray Angelico Chávez. Provo UT, 1976.

Watson, Douglas S., ed. *The Spanish Occupation of California. . . .* San Francisco, 1934.

Weber, David J. *The Spanish Frontier in North America*. New Haven, 1992.

Weddle, Robert S. *Spanish Sea: The Gulf of Mexico in North American Discovery, 1500–1685*. College Station TX, 1985.

Wheat, Carl I. *Mapping the Trans-Mississippi West, 1540–1861*. 5 vols. San Francisco, 1957.

Wilkes, Charles. *Narrative of the United States Exploring Expedition during the Years 1838, 1839, 1840, 1841, 1842*. 5 vols. Philadelphia, 1845.

Williams, David. *John Evans and The Legend of Madoc*. Cardiff, Wales, 1963.

Williams, Glyndwr. *The British Search for the Northwest Passage in the Eighteenth Century*. London, 1962.

Contributors

Alan V. Briceland is an associate professor of history, Virginia Commonwealth University, who has also held an academic appointment at North Texas State University. He is recognized as a scholar of the exploration of eastern North America during the colonial period and is the author of several books, including *Westward from Virginia: The Exploration of the Virginia-Carolina Frontier, 1650–1710*, and has contributed over a dozen articles and book chapters to the scholarly literature. He has received several awards and was named an Outstanding Educator of America for 1974–75. Dr. Briceland was educated at the College of William and Mary (B.A.) and Duke University (M.A., 1963, Ph.D., 1965). He also has postdoctoral experience as a participant in the Military History Workshop at West Point in 1981 and at the NEH summer institute at the University of Connecticut in 1987.

W. J. Eccles is emeritus professor of history at the University of Toronto. He has held a number of academic appointments, including guest lectureships and professorships at the University of Chile, McGill University, the American University of Beirut, the Sorbonne (Paris), and McMaster University. In 1983–84 he was James Pinckney Harrison Professor of History at the College of William and Mary. He is internationally known as an expert on French exploration and settlement in North America, particularly in the eighteenth century. Dr. Eccles has authored nine books, including *The Canadian Frontier, 1534–1760*, *France in America*, and *Essays on New France*, and numerous articles in scholarly journals, and he served as general editor of the Problems in Canadian History series. He has received many prizes and awards for his scholarship, including a Senior Killam Fellowship, the Tyrrel Medal of the Royal Society of Canada, and the Best Article award from the *William and Mary Quarterly* and the *Canadian Historical Review*. He has served as a councilmember of both the Canadian Historical Association and the Humanities Association of Canada and on the editorial board of the *Historical Atlas of Canada*. Dr. Eccles received his B.A., M.A., and Ph.D. (1955) degrees from McGill University.

James R. Gibson is a professor of geography at York University, Ontario, where he has spent most of his academic career and where he served as departmental chairman from 1978 to 1981. He has also held visiting professorships at Hokkaido University in Sapporo, Japan; the University of Canterbury, New Zealand; and the University of Hawaii. Dr. Gibson, noted for his work on the exploration and settlement of the Pacific coast, has received a number of research grants, including a Guggenheim Award. He is the author of several books, including *Farming the Frontier: The Agricultural Opening of the Oregon Country, 1876–1846; Imperial Russia in Frontier America*; and *Otter Skins, Boston Goods, and China Ships*, as well as numerous scholarly articles and book chapters. He also has served as the editor of several works of scholarship, including *European Settlement and Development in North America*. Fluent in Russian, Dr. Gibson has also translated over fifty articles from the Russian professional literature. Dr. Gibson did his undergraduate work at the University of British Columbia and received master's degrees from the University of Oregon and the University of Wisconsin; his doctorate is from the University of Wisconsin–Madison (1967).

Conrad Heidenreich is a professor of geography at York University, Ontario, where he has spent virtually all his professional career. He is recognized as an authority on the early period of French exploration in North America, particularly in seventeenth-century Canada; the history of Canadian cartography; and the paleoecology of precolonial Canada. He is the author of several books, including *The Early Fur Trades: A Study in Cultural Interaction* and *Explorations and Mapping of Samuel de Champlain, 1603–1632*, and numerous book chapters and articles in scholarly journals. Dr. Heidenreich has received a number of honors and awards, including the Sainte Marie Prize in Canadian History and a Killam Research Fellowship. He was elected in 1986 to the Council of the Champlain Society, and he has served as an editor of several Canadian scholarly publications. Dr. Heidenreich received his B.A. and M.A. from the University of Toronto and his Ph.D. from McMaster University (1970).

Oakah L. Jones Jr. is professor emeritus of history at Purdue University. He is an authority on the Spanish frontier in North America (Spanish Borderlands) and on Latin American colonial and national history. Dr. Jones is the author of a number of books in the field of Spanish Borderlands history, including *Pueblo Warriors and Spanish Conquest* and *Nueva Vizcaya: Heartland of the Spanish Frontier*; in addition, he has edited several books and has contributed over a dozen articles to the scholarly literature. He has served on the editorial board for several important journals, including *The Journal of the West, Pacific Historical Review*, and *New Mexico Historical Review*, and was chairman of the editorial board of Purdue University Press in 1986–87. Dr. Jones attended the University of Tulsa and the University of Arkansas before receiving his B.S. degree from the U.S. Naval Academy at Annapolis. His graduate degrees are from the University of Oklahoma (M.A., 1960, Ph.D., 1964).

Richard I. Ruggles is emeritus professor of geography at Queen's University, Ontario, where he founded the Department of Geography in 1960 and served as its head for many years. Internationally recognized as an authority on the early exploration and cartography of Canada (particularly that involving the Hudson's Bay Company), Dr. Ruggles has authored numerous articles in the scholarly literature and several books, including *The Historical Atlas of Manitoba* (with John Warkentin) and *A Country So Interesting: The Hudson's Bay Company and Two Centuries of Mapping, 1670–1870*. He has received a number of awards for his contributions, including the National Award of Merit from the American Association for State and Local History. He has also served as president of the Canadian Association of Geographers. His academic career has included appointments to the faculties of Syracuse University, McMaster University, the University of British Columbia, and Queen's University. Dr. Ruggles received his baccalaureate from the University of Toronto, a master's from Syracuse University, and his Ph.D. from the University of London (1958). He also did postgraduate work at Columbia University and the University of Denver.

Index